FROM THE ENDS OF THE EARTH/JUDAIC TREASURES OF THE LIBRARY OF CONGRESS

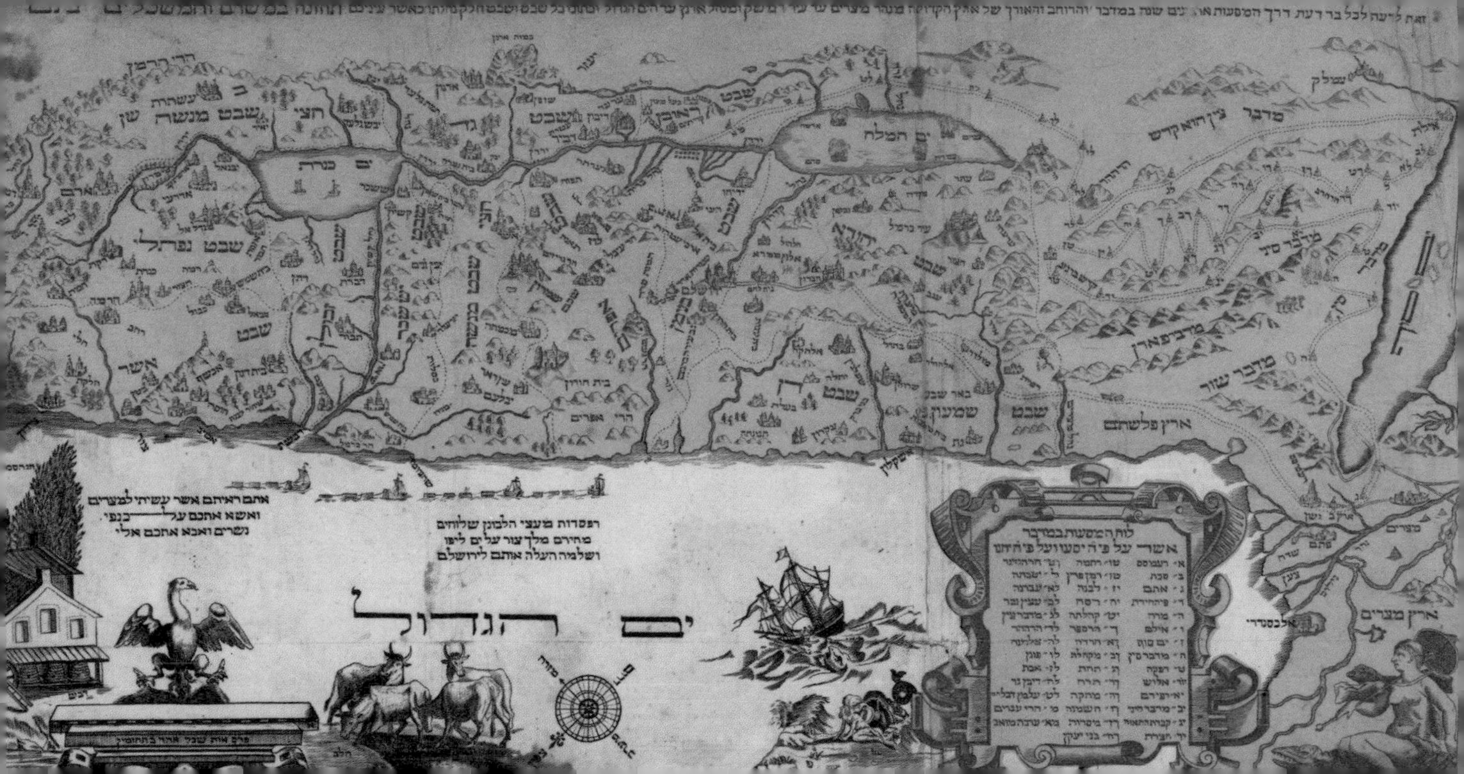

אתם ראיתם אשר עשיתי למצרים
ואשא אתכם על כנפי
נשרים ואבא אתכם אלי
רפסדות מעצי הלבנון שלוחים
מחירם מלך צור על ים ליפו
ושלמה העלה אותם לירושלם
ים הגדול
לוח המסעות במדבר
אשר על פי ה׳ יסעו ועל פי ה׳ יחנו
א׳ רעמסס
ב׳ סכת
ג׳ אתם
ד׳ פיהחירת
ה׳ מרה
ו׳ אילם
ז׳ ים סוף
ח׳ מדבר סין
ט׳ דפקה
יו״ד׳ אלוש
יא׳ רפידים
יב׳ מדבר סיני
יג׳ קברות התאוה
יד׳ חצרות
טו׳ רתמה
טז׳ רמן פרץ
יז׳ לבנה
יח׳ רסה
יט׳ קהלתה
כ׳ הר ספר
כא׳ חרדה
כב׳ מקהלת
כג׳ תחת
כד׳ תרח
כה׳ מתקה
כו׳ חשמנה
כז׳ מסרות
כח׳ בני יעקן
כט׳ חר הגדגד
ל׳ יטבתה
לא׳ עברנה
לב׳ עציון גבר
לג׳ מדבר צין
לד׳ הר ההר
לה׳ צלמנה
לו׳ פונן
לז׳ אבת
לח׳ דיבן גד
לט׳ עלמן דבלתימה
מ׳ הרי עברים
מא׳ ערבת מואב
ים כנרת
ים המלח
שבט נפתלי
שבט מנשה
אשר
ארץ פלשתים
מדבר שור
מדבר פארן
מדבר סין
ארץ מצרים

FROM THE ENDS OF THE EARTH

JUDAIC TREASURES OF THE LIBRARY OF CONGRESS

ABRAHAM J. KARP

LIBRARY OF CONGRESS
WASHINGTON 1991

∞ The paper used in this publication meets the minimum requirements of American National Standard for Information Sciences—Permanence of Paper for Printed Library Materials. ANSI Z39.48-1984.

Cover: Scenes from an eighteenth-century Italian megillah (Esther Scroll) illustrating the story of Purim that is recounted in the biblical Book of Esther. Hebraic Section. (See p. 92)

Frontispiece: Haggadah shel Pesah, Amsterdam, 1781.
Hebraic Section. Color added. (See pp. 82, 83)

Library of Congress Cataloging-in-Publication Data
Karp, Abraham J.
From the ends of the earth : Judaic treasures of the Library of Congress : [essays] / Abraham J. Karp.
p. cm.
Includes bibliographical references and index.
Supt. of Docs. no.: LC 1.2:Ju88
ISBN 0-8444-0681-3
1. Judaism—Bibliography—Exhibitions. 2. Jews—Bibliography—Exhibitions. 3. Rare books—Washington (D.C.)—Bibliography—Exhibitions. 4. Judaism—History. 5. Jews—Civilization. 6. Library of Congress—Exhibitions. I. Library of Congress. II. Title.
Z6375.L53 1991
[BM45] 90-6218
296′.074753—dc20 CIP

CONTENTS

Foreword by James H. Billington, The Librarian of Congress vii

A Message from Mark E. Talisman, President, Project Judaica Foundation ix

Project Judaica Foundation Supporters xi

The Hebraic Section by Michael Grunberger xv

Acknowledgments xvii

About the Author xx

Preface xxi

1 First Judaica and Judaic Firsts *1*

2 The Book of the People of the Book *21*

3 The Sea of the Talmud and Some Shores It Has Touched *41*

4 "From Moses to Moses, There Was None Like Moses" *55*

5 Charting the Holy Land *73*

6 Adding Beauty to Holiness *89*

7 Beauty Is in the Hands of Its Creator *119*

8 Witnesses to History *137*

9 "Let Her Works Praise Her" *167*

10 "Enthroned on Praises" *181*

11 The Starry Skies in the Heavens Above—The Still Small Voice in the Heart of Man *197*

12 In the New World *219*

13 "To Bigotry No Sanction" *231*

14 "Father Abraham" and the Children of Israel *247*

15 Four Founders: Noah, Leeser, Wise, and Lazarus *263*

16 Holy Tongue—Holy Land—Holy Words *285*

17 From Sea to Shining Sea *305*

18 From the Lands of the Czars *325*

19 "Break Forth in Melody and Song" *339*

Afterword *353*
For Further Reading *355*
Exhibition Checklist *357*
Index *369*

FOREWORD

AS A LOVER OF BOOKS WITH special responsibilities for the world's largest collection, I am especially pleased to introduce this catalog for the exhibition on the cultural and spiritual treasures of the People of the Book.

The collections of the Library of Congress, including some ninety million objects—books, films, maps, prints, photographs, and sheet music—demonstrate the exceptional hospitality of our country to the civilizations and cultures of all those who came here in search of religious or political freedom. This treasure house of America's intellectual and cultural heritage is rich in testimony to the extraordinary contributions of the Jewish community.

Some seventy-five years ago, Jacob H. Schiff, a noted New York financier and philanthropist, purchased two outstanding collections of Hebrew books for the national library. These materials form the nucleus of what is today one of the world's great collections of Judaica and Hebraica, containing letters from Presidents Washington, Madison, Jefferson, and Lincoln, among others, to prominent American Jewish leaders of their times; music composed by Leonard Bernstein, the Gershwins, Irving Berlin, and Arnold Schoenberg; papers and manuscripts of Albert Einstein and Sigmund Freud; and great Hebrew literary as well as religious treasures spanning centuries. As amply demonstrated by this exhibition, there is scarcely a corner of the great collections in the nation's library that does not attest to the remarkable ways in which Jewish Americans have contributed to the cultural history of this country.

We are deeply grateful to the Project Judaica Foundation for its staunch support of this exhibition marking the seventy-fifth anniversary of the Hebraic Section. Mr. Mark E. Talisman, President of the Foundation, has inspired us with his vision, been generous in his support, and worked tirelessly for this project since its inception in 1986. This exhibition and catalog stand as tangible proof of the Foundation's commitment "to preserve, rehabilitate, exhibit, and disseminate all forms of Judaic culture."

University of Rochester Professor Abraham J. Karp, guest curator of "From the Ends of the Earth: Judaic Treasures of the Library of Congress," has excited us with his often surprising discoveries of important Judaic treasures in almost every section of this Library. These discoveries in so many different formats and languages are evident throughout the catalog and exhibition.

This anniversary project has drawn on the talents of the Library of Congress's greatest resource: its dedicated staff of librarians, archivists, conservators, curators, managers, writers, photographers, editors, and, in particular, Dr. Michael Grunberger, the Head of the Hebraic Section. Without a doubt, it has been the creativity and dedication of this exceptional group of staff members that has enabled this ambitious exhibition and catalog to come together.

I am especially pleased that this exhibition is slated to travel to a number of North American cities. It has long been my view that the national library has an obligation to make its holdings better known—in some instances, by bringing the treasures themselves to the people. With this exhibition and catalog, we take a first step toward this goal, placing before the public a selection of Judaic treasures gathered from the very "ends" of the Library of Congress.

James H. Billington
The Librarian of Congress

A MESSAGE FROM PROJECT JUDAICA FOUNDATION

THIS BOOK RESULTS FROM a series of serendipitous conversations between representatives of the Library of Congress and Project Judaica Foundation. Dr. Daniel Boorstin, Librarian Emeritus, Dr. Michael Grunberger, Head of the Library's Hebraic Section, and I explored ways to commemorate the seventy-fifth anniversary of the Hebraic Section at the Library of Congress. This exploration has continued unabated under the leadership of Librarian of Congress James Billington.

The Hebraic Section got its start in 1912 from Jacob Schiff, who gave an initial grant of $15,000 for Judaica. This launched what has become a world-class collection devoted to the depth, breadth, and soaring height of expression of the Jewish people through all manner of print. Any commemoration would have to be true to the spirit of Schiff's gift.

One choice for the celebration was a simple one. We would publish a facsimile of the extraordinary Washington Haggadah created by Joel ben Simeon in 1478—making a true reproduction, capturing the nuances of color and illumination, reproducing each page, including signs of long family use.

However, more than a facsimile of one Haggadah would have to be published to commemorate adequately the Library to our nation and the world. The Hebraic Section represents thousands of years of the historical, intellectual, and spiritual endeavors of the Jewish people. There would have to be a world class exhibition to celebrate this collection adequately.

The Library of Congress, in partnership with Project Judaica Foundation, is planning a travelling exhibit for a selection of the Library's finest Judaic books, manuscripts, maps, photographs, letters, and much more. This book is intended to be a critical link between the selected exhibit items and the Hebraic Section of the Library of Congress, which the public will now come to appreciate.

The universal message of devotion to the written word, the unceasing attempt to adhere to a moral code, while subjected to the endless travels of a long Diaspora, will have meaning for every human being. This book and exhibit seek to convey this complicated story, thus helping the Hebraic collection of our great Library of Congress to come alive.

Of equal importance for the American Jewish Community is the special relationship which Jews have had with America from the outset of the settlement of this continent. As the new nation flourished, so did the Jewish people, along with dozens of other nationality groups seeking to be free. To Jews, America was the "Goldene Medineh." While American streets may not literally have been paved in gold, to Jewish immigrants the equivalent was realized in the opportunity granted to each person to express deeply held desires to be free to create, to build, to study, and to practice all manner of religion or none at all. This exhibit profiles how American Jews have expressed their gratitude to a nation which has not only been a physical and religious shelter but has preserved, protected, and nourished their culture.

The world represented in this vast collection is wondrously explored by Prof. Abraham Karp, guest curator. With the extraordinary guidance of the Hebraic Section's Head, Dr. Michael Grunberger; the Library's Director of Publishing, Dana Pratt; the Publishing Office's production manager, Johanna Craig, and one of its editors, Iris Newsom; Steve Kraft, the designer of this book; and Jacqueline McGlade, the project coordinator, this world has come alive and speaks to generations of all people. Through all of their efforts it is clearly possible to understand the history of an entire people, known as the "People of the Book."

Project Judaica Foundation, of which I am a part, has been pleased to participate in each aspect of this complicated project as a partner with the Library of Congress. Dr. Daniel Boorstin deserves special credit for having inspired our effort. Dr. James Billington has been unstinting in his support and encouragement.

Many staff members of the Library of Congress have been deeply engaged in ensuring success for this complicated endeavor. Special recognition is due to colleagues in the Hebraic Section, the Rare Book and Special Collections Division, the Geography and Map Division, the Manuscript Division, the Prints and Photographs Division, the Cultural Affairs Office, and the Interpretive Programs Office. Their special talent, mixed with skill and enthusiasm, produced this beautiful volume to accompany an exhibition which will inform tens of thousands of people as it reaches beyond the Library into the nation.

The Board of Project Judaica Foundation has unfailingly supported these efforts, sometimes against odds which were not easy to overcome. They deserve special recognition. They are: Sandra Weiner of Houston, Texas; Arnold C. Greenberg of West Hartford, Connecticut; Sheldon S. Cohen of Washington, D.C.; Stuart E. Eizenstat of Washington, D.C.; David Farber of Washington, D.C.; Irwin Hochberg of New York City; and Melvin Cohen of Washington, D.C., Gil J. Bonwitt, former Director of the Foundation, and Patrick McMahon, current Director of the Foundation, who devoted enormous energy and talent to ensure the success of this project.

Above all, Lewis Norry, who has served as chairman of this project, deserves special recognition. His enthusiasm was infectious. He was able to convince many people to join in this effort (as the following list of patrons clearly attests). I have taken a great deal of pride in seeing his labor clearly rewarded with such excellent contributions from so many people. Through their hundreds of hours of loving care and artistry, this creative group has realized the complicated goal of helping a large and eager public to understand the awesome sweep of history contained within the Hebraic Section.

I owe a personal word of thanks to my family. Jill, Jessica, and Raphael have sustained me during such a time-consuming undertaking and have made my effort theirs.

It is my hope that each person who contributed to this project will share the satisfaction of seeing our goals reached creatively and with dignity. In its stewardship, our national library reflects with purpose and clarity the diversity of America, only a sliver of which is represented in this effort.

After the exhibition closes, after many tens of thousands of people across America have seen the exhibition, this book will continue to represent the splendid work of the Hebraic Section of the Library of Congress in Washington, which will finally become known to so many of our citizens. Indeed, we hope a further result will be a deeper appreciation for the Library of Congress and its continuing commitment to the achievement of excellence in all which it seeks to accomplish.

Mark E. Talisman
President, Project Judaica Foundation

PROJECT JUDAICA FOUNDATION SUPPORTERS

PROJECT JUDAICA FOUNDATION and Jordan H. Goldman, Robert A. Schulman, Lewis Norry and David Lissy, Co-Chairmen of the Library of Congress Hebraica Project, gratefully acknowledge the special assistance of the following individuals:

■

Dr. and Mrs. John M. Cohen
Melvin and Ryna Cohen
The Bertha and Isadore Gudelsky Family Foundation
Mrs. Ruth N. Levinger
S. H. and Helen R. Scheuer Family Foundation
The Raymond Zimmerman Family Foundation

■

The Horace W. Goldsmith Foundation
Richard D. Levy
Regis Foundation
United Jewish Endowment Fund of the United Jewish Appeal Federation of Greater Washington

■

Mr. and Mrs. Stuart J. Frankenthal
Richard N. and Rhoda H. Goldman Philanthropic Fund
Rita and Irwin Hochberg
Jesselson Foundation
Mr. Charles Steiner
Sandra and Leon Weiner

■

Judy and Hal Abroms
Mr. and Mrs. Jordan H. Goldman
The Green Fund, Inc.
Ronne and Donald Hess
Olyn and Joseph B. Horwitz of Cleveland, Ohio
Jewish Federation of Waterbury
Carol and Gershon Kekst
H. Irwin and Jeanne Levy
The Norry Family
Ruth and Harold Roitenberg
Mr. Lowell Schulman

■

The Edmond de Rothschild Foundation
Sydney and Frances Lewis
Mrs. Louis Nathanson
Mr. and Mrs. Albert Nerken
Geraldine and Howard Polinger
Tess and Abe O. Wise

■

Stanford and Joan Alexander
Marilyn and Harry Cagin
Mr. and Mrs. Nathan David
Richard England
Mr. and Mrs. Alyn Essman
Vic and Joan Gelb
Aaron and Cecile Goldman
Mr. Leo Gross
William and Lisa Gross
Drs. Irene and Michael Karl
David E. Katz and Abe J. Levine
Mr. Simon Konover
Sue Lavien
Jack and Lilyan Mandel
Joseph and Florence Mandel
Morton and Barbara Mandel
Mr. Bernard Manekin
Mr. and Mrs. Morris F. Mintz
Mr. David Myers
Dena and Edwin Shapiro
Mr. Harry Stone
Kitty and Martin Strauss
Mr. and Mrs. Sigmund Strochlitz
Frances and Beryl Weinstein
Mr. and Mrs. George Weissman
The Abe Wouk Foundation, Inc.
Mr. Ernest Wuliger

Through their subscription to the Library's limited edition facsimile printing of the *Washington Haggadah,* an illuminated medieval manuscript from the Library's Hebraic Section, the following individuals have helped to underwrite the Library of Congress Hebraica Project.

Selma and Seymour Abensohn
Judy and Hal Abroms
Ruth and Alan Ades
Philip and Barbara Altheim
George and Frances Armour Foundation
Irma and Lionel Arond
Selma and Stanley I. Batkin
Lore and Harry Bauer
Shirley and Daniel Beaton
Mr. and Mrs. Jon D. Becker
Rosi and Saby Behar
Andrew and Froma Benerofe
Fred and Muffie Berliner
Mr. and Mrs. Mitchell Berliner
Diane and Norman Bernstein
Susan and Eliot Black
Dorothy P. Bloch (in memory of David "Bud" Bloch)
David M. Blumberg (in honor of Rena J. Blumberg)
Diane and Marvin R. Blumberg
Goldene and Herschel Blumberg
Bernard and Myrle Borine
Mr. and Mrs. Joel Boyarsky
Mr. and Mrs. David M. Brand
Brandeis University Libraries
Catherine Z. and Robert J. Brot
Mr. and Mrs. Gary Brotsky
Susan and Steven Caller
Dr. and Mrs. Joseph Carver
Dr. and Mrs. John M. Cohen
Melvin and Ryna Cohen
Murray and Joyce Arnoff Cohen
S. Robert and Joy W. Cohen
Mr. and Mrs. Sheldon Cohen
Victor J. and Ellen Cohn
Bernice and Bernie Danis
Julius Darsky
Richard, Judith, Joel, Jonathan and Ilana Darsky
Mr. and Mrs. Nathan David
Arnold and Nechami Druck
Mr. and Mrs. Stephen P. Durchslag and Family
Morris and Kathy Dweck
Ralph S. and Francis R. Dweck
Jeremy Dworkin and Barbara Denhoff
Ms. Esther Farber
Mr. Leon Farber
Mr. and Mrs. James S. Farley
Robert and Marjorie Feder
Arlene Fickler
Daniel Asher Fien-Helfman
Joshua Martin Fien-Helfman
Samantha Abigail Fien-Helfman
Jesse and Francine Fierstein
Pat and Martin Fine
Mr. Larry Fisher
The Children of Melvyn and Roberta Fisher
Victoria and Nathan Fisher
William and Lynn Foggle
Cheri Fox
Marilyn and Sam Fox
Pamela Fox
Patrice and Gary Fragin
Charlotte K. Frank
Mr. and Mrs. Stuart J. Frankenthal
Francine and Norman Freedman
Morton L. Friedkin
Gloria and Harvey Friedman
Don and Janie Friend
Charles and Nancy Ganz
R. Justin Garon
Herbert L. and Frances Gaynor
Melvin and Estelle Gelman Foundation
Gilbert Family: Stuart, Micki, Jennifer, Rachel and Marissa
Dr. Edward and Elaine Gilbert
Mr. Gary Giller
Mr. and Mrs. Lee Giller
Mr. and Mrs. Stuart Giller
Sam and Irene Gindi
Dr. Kurt A. Gitter and Alice Rae Yelen
Mr. and Mrs. Michael A. Glasser and Mr. and Mrs. Richard S. Glasser
Mr. and Mrs. Phillip Glassman
David and Victoria Glimcher
Herbert Glimcher
Robert I. Glimcher
Dr. and Mrs. Marvin Goldberg
Mr. and Mrs. Jordan H. Goldman
Mr. and Mrs. Joseph I. Goldstein
Mr. and Mrs. Robert C. Goodman, Jr.
Gene and Emily Grant
Mr. and Mrs. Alex Grass
Mr. and Mrs. Thomas R. Green
Claire Greenberg
Mr. and Mrs. Sanford D. Greenberg
Dr. and Mrs. David Greenseid
Mr. and Mrs. Harry Gross
Mr. Leo Gross
Mr. and Mrs. Manny Gross
William and Lisa Gross

Barbara and Steven Grossman
Klau Library, Hebrew Union College-Jewish Institute of Religion, Cincinnati
Joel and Francine Helfman
Mr. and Mrs. Jerry Helman
Dr. and Mrs. Gershon Hepner
Ronne and Donald Hess
The Hochberg Family Foundation
Rita and Irwin Hochberg
Philip and Ann Holzer
Francie and David Horvitz
Temple Israel, Akron, Ohio, through the
Ben Maidenburg Fund
Thomas P. Ivanyi
Fredrick L. Jaffe
Jesselson Foundation
Jewish Federation of Waterbury
The Library of the Jewish Theological Seminary of America
Dr. Abram Kanof
Jerry, Kathy, Mike and Elaine Kantor
Charlotte and Seymour Kaplan
Dr. and Mrs. Samuel C. Karlan
Isidoro Kassin
Ina and Jack Kay
Alfred D. and E. Temma Kingsley
Mrs. David Klau
George Klein
Samuel and Mildred Klein Supporting Foundation
Alan J. Kluger and Amy N. Dean
Mr. and Mrs. Robert Klutznick
Ronald M. Kramer
Dr. David Kreger
Abraham J. Kremer
Mr. and Mrs. Alan Kritz
David J. Kudish and Stratford Advisory Group
Elliott Landsman
Dr. and Mrs. David Lannick
Paul and Marjorie Lehrer
Harlan Guy Leibler
Naomi and Isi Leibler
Fred and Maxine Leventhal
Norman B. Leventhal
Mr. and Mrs. Arnold Levin
Sol and Dorothy Levites
Mr. and Mrs. Edward Levy
Richard D. Levy
Lawrence S. and Marion Ein Lewin
Sydney and Frances Lewis
Constance and Stephen Lieber
Adele and Mark Lieberman
Mr. and Mrs. Nathan R. Light
Jerome and Margaret M. Lippman and Joseph and Pamela Kanfer
Maggie and David Lissy
The Martin A. List Family
Lucy and Stanley Lopata
Lawrence and Ellen Macks, Genine and Josh Fidler, Martha Macks and Glenn Schubert (in honor of Morton J. Macks)
Mr. and Mrs. Robert A. Manekin
Marvin and Evelyne Manes
Rabbi Frederic and Trisha S. Margulies
Jerome and Helen Margulies
Miriam G. and Stanley M. Mark, M.D.
Dr. Howard M. May and Jamie Jacobs-May
Betty S. and Norton Melaver
Samuel Melton
Robert J. Meth, M.D.
Moldovan Family
Mary and Louis S. Myers Foundation
Morey and Sondra Myers
Jean and Albert Nerken
The New York Public Library
Mr. and Mrs. James Nolan
The Norry Family
Neil November
Mr. and Mrs. William Nusbaum
Ohio State Universities
Barry J. Palkovitz, Esquire
Rabbi Norman Patz
Dr. Sidney A. Peerless
Michael and Natalie Pelavin
Geri and Lester Pollack
Esther and Gary Polland
Jerry and Trudy Pollock
Morton and Barbara Rabkin
Mr. and Mrs. Randall L. Reiner
Fred and Bea Reynolds
Frank Ridge
Ira D. and Diana Riklis
M. Russ Robinson
Regina J. Rogers
Ruth and Harold Roitenberg
Belle and Jack Rosenbaum
Dulcie and Norman Rosenfeld
Elana and Jack Roth
David C. and Sarajean Ruttenberg
Melvin D. Sacks
Joseph W. and Jeanne F. Samuels
Mr. and Mrs. Leo Schachter
Carol and Philip Schatten
Albert and Judith Schmeidler
Helen and Irving Schneider
Ariel Schulman
Mr. Lowell Schulman
Robert A. Schulman
Yaniv Schulman
Rabbi Chaim and Dr. Doreen Seidler-Feller
Temple Shalom
Mr. and Mrs. Jerry Shaw

Mr. and Mrs. Nathan Shmalo
Helen and Jay Shulan
Mr. and Mrs. John D. Shulansky
Fredell and Allan N. Shulkin, M.D.
Milton and Gloria Siegel
Ruth and Jay Silberg
Ina and Jon Singer
Sol and Ruth Singer
David B. Smith
Harry B. Smith
Mr. and Mrs. Philip Spertus
Mr. Abraham Spiegel
Lee Arnold Spiegelman
Drs. Susanne and Moses A. Spira
Starkman Book Service
Alan and Karen Starr
In Loving Memory of Allen A. Stein
Bob and Joanne Stein
Lawrence Steingold
Frances and Samson B. Stern
Saul I. and Marcia Stern
Kitty and Martin Strauss
Samuel and Althea Stroum
Dr. and Mrs. Jerome O. Sugar
Mr. and Mrs. Bertram Teich
Julius, Stephanie, Sasha, Nicola and Joshua Trump
Leslie Ulanow
Mr. and Mrs. M. Viny
Beate and Henry Voremberg
Stephen Wainger
Howard N. Weiner
Sandra and Leon Weiner
Leonard and Marilyn Weinstock
Mildred and George Weissman
Mr. and Mrs. David A. Wingate
Fay and Don Wish
Yale University
Mendel Gottesman Library, Yeshiva University
Karen and Eric Zahler
Zentralbibliothek Zurich

We would also like to thank the following friends for their contribution to the Project:

Arnold and Seville Appelbaum
Dr. and Mrs. Barry B. Bercu
Nancy T. Beren and Larry Jefferson
Dr. and Mrs. Gerald Berenson
Mrs. Adolph Berger
Mr. and Mrs. Kenneth Bonwitt
Drs. Amy and Mark Brenner
Mr. Norman Buchbinder
Peggy and Joseph Carver
Phyllis and George Cohen
Mr. and Mrs. Harry Dworkin
Mr. Lawrence Epplein
Mrs. Melvin Feist
Paul and Lyn Fenton
Mr. and Mrs. James Flug
Drs. Thomas Q. and Carol Garvey
Dr. and Mrs. Marvin Goldberg
Mr. Alvin Gordon
Mr. Frank Hagelberg
Mr. and Mrs. Jerry Helman
Dr. and Mrs. Harold Horwitz
Mr. and Mrs. Lenny Kaiden
Mr. and Mrs. David Lloyd Kreeger
Dr. and Mrs. David L. Kreger
Dr. and Mrs. David E. Lannik
Rosalind and Simon Lazarus
Jim, Debbi, Alyssa and Jeffrey Nolan
Sharon and Bill Nusbaum
Mr. and Mrs. Sheldon Sadugor
Rose and Edward Sanders
Bernard J. and Helen Sheftman Foundation
Mr. and Mrs. Arnold Silvers
Jim Sokol
Dr. and Mrs. Laszlo Sokoly
Dr. Steven Solomon
Lawrence L. Steingold
Edward and Erva Wagner
Mr. and Mrs. Laurence Weiss
Mr. and Mrs. Henry Zapruder

THE HEBRAIC SECTION

THIS EXHIBITION AND CATALOG mark the seventy-fifth anniversary of the establishment of the Hebraic collections of the Library of Congress. Founded in 1914 as the Semitic Division, the Hebraic Section's beginnings can be traced to Jacob H. Schiff's gift in 1912 of nearly ten thousand books and pamphlets from the private collection of Ephraim Deinard, a well-known bibliographer and bookseller.

In the years that followed this initial gift, the Library developed and expanded its Hebraic holdings to include all materials of research value in Hebrew and related languages. Today, the section houses works in Hebrew, Yiddish, Ladino, Judeo-Persian, Judeo-Arabic, Aramaic, Syriac, Coptic, and Amharic. The section's holdings are especially strong in the areas of the Bible and rabbinics, liturgy, Hebrew language and literature, responsa, and Jewish history. Extensive collections of Israeli government publications and printed editions of the Passover Haggadah have been assembled. Unique to the section are more than one thousand original Yiddish plays—in manuscript or typescript—written between the end of the nineteenth and the middle of the twentieth centuries, that were submitted for copyright registration to the Library of Congress and were intended for the American Yiddish theater.

The Hebraic Section received its second major boost as a result of the enactment of Public Law 480 in 1958, through which twenty-five American research libraries—including the Library of Congress—were supplied with a copy of virtually every book and journal of research value published in Israel. The PL-480 program for Israeli imprints, coordinated by the Library of Congress, lasted nine years, from 1964 to 1973, and provided each of the participating institutions with an average of 65,000 items.

Since 1973, substantial efforts and resources have been expended to maintain this high level of acquisitions from Israel—efforts reflected in the overall comprehensiveness of the Library's collection of Hebrew-language materials. The collection includes an extensive range of monographs; a broad selection of Hebrew periodicals, current and retrospective, popular as well as scholarly; and a variety of Yiddish and Hebrew newspapers reflecting every shade of opinion, from the religious to the secular and from the far right to the extreme left. Of particular interest to genealogists is the Library's comprehensive collection of *yizker-bikher* (memorial volumes), documenting Jewish life in Eastern Europe before the Second World War, as well as a large collection of rabbinic bio-bibliographical works in Hebrew. Housed in an adjacent stack area, the section's 125,000 volumes are readily available for examination by researchers and scholars.

To assist readers here and across the country in locating hard-to-obtain items, the section maintains union catalogs for items in both Hebrew and Yiddish listing the holdings of scores of libraries that have contributed copies of their cataloging records over the course of the last thirty years. Containing more than six hundred thousand catalog cards and including printed cards going back as far as 1901, the Hebrew and Yiddish union catalogs are a unique national resource, citing important bibliographic data as well as locations for titles that do not appear in the Library's National Union Catalog. These special bibliographic tools contain information on variant editions, rare and out-of-print titles, and works not owned (or owned but not cataloged) by the Library of Congress.

Featured in this exhibition and catalog are Hebrew manuscripts, incunables (books printed before 1501), ketuboth (marriage contracts), micrographies, miniature books, and amulets selected from among the two thousand or so rarities housed in the special collections of the Hebraic Section. Its more than two hundred manuscripts include a Hebrew translation of the Koran, various responsa of the rabbis, an eighteenth-century Italian decorated megillah (Scroll of Esther), an early Ethiopian Psalter in Ge'ez, various commentaries on the Hebrew Scriptures, and, of course, the section's most noteworthy treasure: The Washington Haggadah, a fifteenth-century Hebrew illuminated manuscript executed by Joel ben Simeon. With twenty-four incunables housed in the section (including examples of the first books printed in Portugal, Turkey, and on the African continent) and an additional fifteen in the Rare Book and Special Collections Division, the Library of Congress ranks as one of the world's most important public collectors of Hebrew incunables.

In establishing a Semitic Division in 1914, the national library enlarged its mission to include a commitment to collect, preserve, and make available materials relating to the cultural and spiritual heritage of the Jewish people. On display here are the fruits of this abiding seventy-five-year commitment.

Michael W. Grunberger
Head, Hebraic Section

ACKNOWLEDGMENTS

THE BEGINNINGS OF THIS project can be traced to a chance tour of the Hebraic Section in 1986 by Mark E. Talisman, President of the Project Judaica Foundation. His visit that morning triggered an abiding passion: to share with others—through a major exhibition and catalog—the treasures that he had examined in the Hebraic Section's rare book enclosure. The Foundation's long-standing commitment has enabled the Library to undertake this ambitious program of events beginning with the publication of a deluxe facsimile edition of its Washington Haggadah, a fifteenth-century illuminated Hebrew manuscript, and culminating in the exhibition described in this catalog.

This project has received encouragement and unwavering support, first from Librarian of Congress Emeritus Daniel J. Boorstin and later from his successor, Librarian of Congress James H. Billington. Janet Chase, Administrative Assistant to the Librarian, arranged the early critical meetings that defined the Library's close relationship with the Foundation. Adoreen McCormick and Stephen Kelley of the Legislative Liaison Office coordinated a series of well-received tours for Members of Congress and their spouses. John Kominski, the Library's General Counsel, helped to develop the legal and fiscal instruments that were required to sustain this project. I am grateful to Ronald Morse, former director of the Library's Development Office, and staff members Marie Anderson and Norma Baker for their continuing interest and assistance.

Over the course of these last three years, I have had the pleasure of working closely with scores of colleagues, both inside and outside the Library of Congress, to help realize this project. I owe a debt of gratitude to Evelyn Cohen, Curator of Graphic Materials at the Jewish Theological Seminary, and to Grace Grossman, Curator of the Skirball Museum, who provided key advice during the early stages of the project.

Overall direction for the exhibition was provided by Irene Burnham, Interpretive Programs Officer. William Miner and Diantha Schull, former heads of the Library's Exhibits Office, helped to give the exhibition its initial shape and form. During the critical phases of this exhibition, Gene Roberts—who until April 1990 served as Acting Interpretive Programs Officer—kept the project moving forward despite acute staffing shortages in the Interpretive Programs Office, drawing up the design specifications for the show, outlining the work plans, and hiring key personnel. Jacqueline McGlade, Project Coordinator, brought abundant creativity, enthusiasm, and energy to this project. As the team member responsible for the overall coordination of the exhibit and related events, she worked with staff from the Interpretive Programs Office, Hebraic Section, Publishing Office, Project Judaica Foundation, and Conservation Office, as well as with the guest curator and exhibit designer. Andrew Cosentino, a member of the Interpretive Programs Office's curatorial staff, helped to clarify and illuminate issues connected with the exhibition. John Birmingham,

Deborah Durbeck, and Christopher O'Connor installed a well-received exhibition preview for the June 1989 meeting of the Association of Jewish Libraries and completed production work for the Washington installation. Tambra Johnson, Registrar of Exhibits, kept track of hundreds of items as they traveled through the labyrinth that is the Library of Congress. Internal communications were facilitated by Elna Adams and Gwynn Wilhelm.

From the outset, this book has been favored by the Library's Publishing Office. Dana Pratt, Director of the Publishing Office, was an early and enthusiastic supporter, helping to plan the catalog and reading through some early drafts of the manuscript. I am deeply grateful to Iris Newsom, an editor in the Publishing Office, for her diligent work on the manuscript, her valiant efforts to keep this complex publication on schedule, and her good humor and patience (both of which were sorely tried by this contributor). The catalog benefited from the talents of Johanna Craig, Production Manager, who skillfully attended to the myriad details involved in seeing this book through its production cycle and from the creativity, care, and attentiveness of Stephen Kraft who was responsible for the catalog's design. Reid Baker and James Higgins of the Library's Photoduplication Service were painstaking in their work, photographing each of the more than three hundred illustrations included in this catalog.

At an early stage, the Library's Conservation Office, under the direction of Peter Waters, became actively involved in this exhibition. Doris Hamburg, Head of the Paper Conservation Section, was central to the planning and implementation of the overall exhibition. In addition to carrying out the exacting conservation treatment of the Washington Haggadah, the centerpiece of "From the Ends of the Earth," Ms. Hamburg directed the paper conservation work that was completed for the exhibition. Thomas Albro, Head of the Book Conservation Section, surveyed the more than two hundred volumes included in the exhibit, determined the required treatments, and supervised the preservation of the book materials. Margaret Brown, Conservation Office Exhibits Liaison, worked closely with the Interpretive Programs Office and the Hebraic Section, tracking items as they made their way through the Conservation laboratory, keeping the conservation work to its own tight schedule, and helping to formulate the preservation guidelines for the traveling version of the exhibition. Selected items in the show have received preservation treatments from members of the Library's expert conservation staff, including Barbara Meier-james, Jesse Munn, Sarah Wagner, and Shirley Richardson. Most of the treatments were completed by Scott Husby and Dorothy Teringo, skilled book conservators brought on board for this exhibition.

This project has benefited from the overall direction of Ruth Ann Stewart, formerly Assistant Librarian for National Programs, and Alan Jabbour and John Cole—both of whom served as heads of the Cultural Affairs Service Unit. Roberta Stevens, Executive Officer, provided needed and effective administrative support for the project as a whole, tracking each of its component parts, and presiding over monthly meetings of the project team. John Kozar, a fund management specialist in Cultural Affairs, designed the financial reporting mechanisms, maintained a centralized fund account, and exercised strict fiscal control over the project. The dedicated staff of the Special Events Office—Nancy Mitchell, Kim Moden, James DeLorbe—orchestrated the countless meetings, tours, and receptions that were critical to the success of this project; they were ably supported by staff members Sharon Green, Walter McClughan, and Kay Wilson. The effort of the Public Affairs Office, especially of staff member Helen Dalrymple, is gratefully acknowledged as is the assistance of the Library's Gift Shop.

Curators, librarians, and archivists throughout the Library have worked with out team to make available materials from their collections. I wish to note the assistance of James Pruett, Jon Newsom, and Elizabeth Auman of the Music Division; James Hutson, David Wigdor, Mary Wolfskill, Charles Kelly, and Marvin Krantz of the Manuscript Division; Larry Sullivan, Peter Van Wingen, James Gilreath, and Robert Shields of the Rare Book and Special Collections Division, as well as Kathleen Mang, Curator of its Rosenwald Collection; Stephen Ostrow, Bernard Reilly, Cheryl Magerdigion, Phil Michel, and Carol Johnson of the Prints and Photographs Division; and Ronald Grim of the Geography and Map Division.

From the project's inception, I have worked closely with Julian Witherell, Chief of the African and Middle Eastern Division, and have appreciated his sound advice and good judgment. His steadfast support for this project as well as his skill in overcoming the many obstacles that continually arose were critical to the successful completion of this endeavor. Betty Harris, Division Secretary, was frequently called on to support the section's activities during the course of this project.

I owe a special debt to my colleagues in the Hebraic Section—at the very least, for coping with a preoccupied and often absent section head. Peggy Pearlstein, Senior Reference Librarian, kept the section functioning at its usual high level while at the same time making valuable contributions to the curatorial side of the exhibition. Sharon Horowitz, Reference Librarian, helped in tracking down elusive materials and Nahid Gerstein, Section Secretary and Bibliographic Assistant, facilitated virtually every transaction between the section and other parts of the Library. In 1989 she received a Special Achievement Award for her role in coordinating the photography of each of the items included in this catalog.

Abraham J. Karp, Guest Curator, has been the creative force behind this exhibition and a source of inspiration for those who have worked with him. His vision, enthusiasm, and mastery of Jewish history and bibliography are showcased in this exhibition and catalog no less than the items themselves. It has been a distinct privilege to collaborate with him on this exhibition.

Recognition is due my predecessors at the Library of Congress—Israel Shapiro (1914–44), Theodore Gaster (1944–47), Lawrence Marwick (1948–80), and Myron Weinstein (1981–84)—who acquired for the national library many of the Hebraic treasures displayed here. Their staunch efforts over the past seventy-five years have made this exhibition possible.

Michael W. Grunberger
Head, Hebraic Section

ABOUT THE AUTHOR

RABBI, HISTORIAN, AND AUTHOR, Abraham J. Karp is Professor of History and Religion and the Philip S. Bernstein Professor of Jewish Studies at the University of Rochester. He is also the Joseph and Rebecca Mitchell Adjunct Research Professor of American Jewish History and Bibliography at the Jewish Theological Seminary of America and a Corresponding Member of the Institute of Contemporary Jewry, the Hebrew University, Jerusalem. Over the course of a distinguished academic career, he has served as Visiting Professor at Dartmouth College, the Jewish Theological Seminary, and the Hebrew University.

One of the leading historians of the American Jewish experience, he is the author of over one hundred published works, books, monographs, articles, and reviews. Among his books are *The Golden Door to America* (1976), *To Give Life: The UJA in the Shaping of the American Community* (1980), *The Jewish Way of Life and Thought* (1981), *Haven and Home: A History of the Jews in America* (1985), *Haye Haruah shel Yahadut Amerika* [Hebrew] (1985), and *Mordecai Manuel Noah: The First American Jew* (1987).

Professor Karp served as president of the American Jewish Historical Society; is a vice-president of the Conference on Jewish Social Studies; and serves on the Editorial Board of *Midstream* and the Publications Committee of the Jewish Publication Society of America. A scholar of the book par excellence, he is often consulted by libraries and private collectors. His own collection of American Judaica was recently characterized as "the finest and most extensive in private hands." In 1976, he was the recipient of both the Lee M. Friedman Medal of the American Jewish Historical Society and the Solomon Goldman Award for Jewish Cultural Creativity.

Born in Indura, Poland, in 1921, Abraham Karp arrived in America in 1930 and was educated at Yeshiva University, Columbia University, and the Jewish Theological Seminary of America. After his ordination, he served congregations in Swampscott, Massachusetts, Kansas City, Missouri, and Rochester, New York.

Professor Karp is married to Deborah B. Karp, an author of children's books, and is the father of two sons, Hillel Judah and David Jacob.

PREFACE

AMERICA HAS BEEN HOSPITABLE to cultures as well as people. Its museums and libraries are rich repositories of the artistic and literary creations of the Old World. Its national library, the Library of Congress, is a treasure trove of the world's great civilizations. Among its treasures are books and manuscripts which record the spiritual and cultural creativity of the Jewish people.

The exhibit, From the Ends of the Earth: Judaic Treasures of the Library of Congress, presents a sumptuous sampling of these books, manuscripts, and prints for what they are: rare and important signposts on the four-thousand-year-old journey of the Jewish spirit. Through them is portrayed the civilization of the Jewish people, its ideas and ideals, its views of the world, and its interaction with it. The exhibit deals with Jewish life and thought in the Old World and the New.

The section on The Book of the People of the Book presents the greatest and most important editions of the Bible in Hebrew and other languages, and what these tell of the life of the Jews among the nations. The Sea of the Talmud and Some Shores It Has Touched deals with the central role of the legal tradition in Jewish civilization and its influence upon other cultures. Moses Maimonides, a Renaissance man three centuries before the Renaissance, is shown in "From Moses to Moses, There Was None Like Moses" as the exemplar of the Jew living creatively in two civilizations and, as a student of the law, a philosopher, and a physician, influencing both.

The exhibit is enhanced by classic maps of the Holy Land—printed, illustrated, and illuminated. Adding Beauty to Holiness presents illuminated megillah scrolls and ketuboth as well as a selection of illustrated editions of the Haggadah, crowned by the renowned Washington Haggadah, a premier example of the art of Medieval manuscript illumination.*

In Beauty Is in the Hands of Its Creators, the exhibit provides an appreciation of the book as an art form. A gathering of prayer books, rich in the variety of rites, translations, and commemorations of historic events is entitled "Enthroned on Praises." Books and manuscripts recording the long, eventful historical experience of the Jewish people are found in the section Witnesses to History. The twofold Jewish interest in The Starry Skies in the Heavens Above—The Still Small Voice in the Heart of Man is documented by illustrated Hebrew books on science and by books and manuscripts on Kabbalah, the "science of the soul." In its contemporary, secularized unfolding, this millennial dual interest is portrayed in the works and words of two of the twentieth century's most creative seminal theorists, Albert Einstein and Sigmund Freud.

In the New World introduces the Jewish experience in America. What the birth of the United States meant to the Jews of Europe, and what American Jews meant to America is shown in the section on the birth of the nation, and it includes manuscripts from the presidential papers of Washington, Jefferson,

*The Washington Haggadah has been issued in a facsimile edition by the Library of Congress. It is accompanied by a scholarly description and assessment of the manuscript.

Madison, and Lincoln. The character of the Jewish contribution to America's cultural and religious life can be glimpsed in the careers of Mordecai M. Noah, Isaac Leeser, Isaac M. Wise, and Emma Lazarus. The place of the Hebrew language, the Holy Land, and the Hebrew prayer book in the religious culture of America is depicted in Holy Tongue—Holy Land—Holy Words. The remarkable variety of Jewish life in nineteenth-century America may be reviewed and reexperienced in From Sea to Shining Sea. From the Lands of the Czars depicts through the graphic arts aspects of the life of the East European Jewish immigrant community.

The exhibit pays homage to Jewish creativity in music in Break Forth in Melody and Song, a medley of holograph manuscripts of works on Jewish themes by Jewish composers Meyerbeer, Halévy, Bloch, Milhaud, Copeland, Bernstein, and Gershwin.

A word of apology and gratitude: Apologies to the many great creative artists, writers, publishers, and printers whose works on the Library's shelves demand inclusion in a most selective exhibit of rare and important Judaica and Hebraica. Alas, space is a tyrant, and their creations remain in their places, unseen, but not unappreciated. Gratitude to the many whose encouragement and help made this work possible, and the making of it a pleasure.

At the Library of Congress: first and foremost, Michael Grunberger, Head of the Hebraic Section, his associates Peggy K. Pearlstein and Nahid D. Gerstein, and his predecessor, Myron M. Weinstein; Julian Witherell, Chief of the African and Middle Eastern Division and Dana J. Pratt, Director of Publishing, who read the manuscript and offered suggestions which were appreciated and followed; skilled editor Iris Newsom; Peter Van Wingen and his associates James Gilreath and F. Thomas Noonan in the Rare Book and Special Collections Division, as well as Kathleen Mang, able and loving Curator of the Lessing J. Rosenwald Collection; David W. Wigdor, Mary M. Wolfskill, and Charles Kelly in the Manuscript Division; Jon Newsom in the Music Division; Patrick Dempsey in Geography and Maps; Mary Ison and Maja Felaco in Prints and Photographs; William Miner, former Chief of the Exhibits Office; and Jacqueline McGlade in the Interpretative Programs Office. Hillel Norry was a Research Assistant of ability and responsibility and enthusiasm.

Special gratitude also to these outside the walls of the Library of Congress: Grace Cohen Grossman for her contribution at the launching of the project; Abraham Rothberg, gifted novelist, superb editor, and loyal friend; Wilhelm Braun, friend and colleague, whose expertise in German language and literature was frequently consulted; Perina Ostroff who transcribed written words to typed pages. To all, my appreciation and affection, and most of all to Deborah Burstein Karp, who in this, as in all matters during the past forty-five years, has been a loving coworker.

This companion volume is more than an exhibit catalog. It not only describes the chosen items but also places them in historical and bibliographical context and incorporates them into a retelling of events in Jewish history and incidents in the lives of individual Jews. Events and incidents become indicative of the role of the Jews and the influence of Judaism on the course of civilization, and illustrative of the resilience of the Jewish spirit. Special emphasis is given to the place of the Jews and their heritage in the life of the American nation.

It remains now to state and illustrate the definition of Judaica which determined the parameters of the exhibit and this volume. Webster's New International Dictionary defines Judaica as "literature relating to Jews and Judaism." We need a more precise and descriptive delineation:

Works written in the languages of the Jewish people—Hebrew first and foremost, but also Aramaic, Judeo-Arabic, Yiddish, and Ladino.

Works by Jewish authors, but only such as are representative of Jewish cultural and spiritual interests.

Works which touch upon the historic experience of the Jews and the creativity and influence of the civilization called Judaism.

All choices, by their very nature, have an element of the subjective. The curator of an exhibit, the author of a volume, is left with the responsibility of making and justifying decisions. Let me touch upon a number of such decisions.

The Hebrew Bible is Judaica par excellence, but why the Bible in translation, translated and published by non-Jews for non-Jews? Because its Jewish origin and Jewish content give it an ineradicable Jewish character that translation may diminish but cannot erase. Similarly, the Judaic character of the Holy Tongue and the Holy Land justifies the inclusion of Hebrew grammars in whatever language and maps of the Holy Land no matter by whom produced—especially the historic maps I have chosen to include, because they portray events in the history of the Jews: the exodus from Egypt, the wandering of the children of Israel through the wilderness, and the division of the Land of Israel among the twelve tribes.

In the section on science, we include seventeenth- and eighteenth-century published works in Hebrew by pious Jewish scientists, describing the world about us, seeing the cosmos as a unified, interrelated universe. But why include the two holograph manuscripts of Albert Einstein—his first work on the theory of relativity and one on the unified field theory? How are these Judaica? They are included in part because they are a twentieth-century, secular, scientific continuum of the pious theistic views of earlier Jewish scientists of an interdependent and unified universe, but more because these particular Einstein holographs remind us, in a very special way, what befell European Jewry in the thirties and forties of the twentieth century. These manuscripts were written by Einstein and sent to the Library of Congress (the relativity manuscript in aid of the War Bond effort) as an expression of gratitude to America by a Jewish refugee from Nazi terror who found here haven and home.

Sigmund Freud's manuscripts of *Moses and Monotheism* and "A Word on Antisemitism" fall well within the parameters of Judaica, but how so the first edition of his magnum opus, *The Interpretation of Dreams*? Here, too, we suggest a continuum of interest of the trimillennial Jewish obsession with dreams, already recorded in the first book of the Bible and illustrated in the exhibit by both a medieval Hebrew manuscript and a published volume. We must add that the lectures which grew into the book were delivered by Freud to appreciative audiences of the Vienna chapter of B'nai B'rith, Jews being the only ones ready to accord Freud an audience in fin de siècle anti-Semitic Vienna.

From the Library's rich store of works by Jewish composers we include only those on Jewish themes, almost all of them manuscripts in the composer's own hand. Irving Berlin's holograph of the words of "God Bless America" is included not so much because he credited the musical tradition in his cantorial father's house with influencing his music, but chiefly because it is expressive of the immigrant American Jew's love for this land, America, which had granted to the Baline family refuge when it was fleeing Czarist oppression, and to a young immigrant boy, now Berlin, freedom and opportunity.

A word about the particular personal and professional orientation of the author may be in order. His is an abiding devotion to Judaism, and a lifelong preoccupation with its cultural and spiritual creativity. His profession as a historian and his concentration on the history of the Jews in America, as well as his passionate interest in the struggles and triumphs of the human spirit, would naturally affect the content and form of both this exhibit and volume.

1

FIRST JUDAICA AND JUDAIC FIRSTS

WE BEGIN, AS ALL ACCOUNTS OF the Library of Congress must, with Thomas Jefferson, America's third president and first bibliophile. Jefferson wanted to be remembered for three achievements: first, his authorship of the Declaration of Independence; second, his creation of the Virginia Statute for Religious Freedom; and third, his founding of the University of Virginia. From the perspective afforded us by the passage of time, we may add to these achievements a fourth, his fathering of the Library of Congress. "It would be hard to overstate the importance of the Jefferson connection to the life of the Library," writes Charles A. Goodrum in *Treasures of the Library of Congress* (New York, 1980). "Jefferson gave us the *shape* of what has become the largest library in the world." He did so through the example of the personal library he built which, in a moment of national crisis, became the new nation's library.

Jefferson took a keen interest in the Library from its inception in 1800. Limited in function (it was originally intended to serve the needs of members of the Congress), the Library remained small in size and narrow in scope. On August 24, 1814, British troops set fire to the Capitol building, the flames consuming every volume which had remained there.* When news of the Library's destruction reached Jefferson, living in retirement in Monticello, he proposed his own book collection as replacement. His library, consisting of some nine to ten thousand volumes, was of such size and scope that he had decided "that it ought not continue private property" and had provided that, on his death, "Congress should have the refusal of it at their own price." Now that Congress was in need of it, he made it available for acquisition. "You know my collection," he wrote, "its condition and extent."

*Some wagon loads of books and papers had been removed in anticipation of a British invasion.

> I have been fifty years making it, and have spared no pains, opportunity or expense, to make it what it is. While residing in Paris, I devoted every afternoon I was disengaged for a summer or two in examining all the principal bookstores . . . putting by everything which related to America, and indeed whatever was rare and valuable. I had standing orders . . . [in] Amsterdam, Frankfurt, Madrid and London . . . Nearly the whole are well bound, abundance of them elegantly, and of the choicest editions existing.

Eventually, after debate, negotiations, and a close vote (81–71), Congress authorized the purchase of Jefferson's 6,487 volumes for $23,950, paid in Treasury bills. The library reflected Jefferson's interests, "architecture, philosophy, art, literature and science, as well as his political and social concerns." Goodrum reports that:

> The Congressional Library Committee . . . [and subsequent committees, as well] were fully aware that they had a national treasure in the volumes. They therefore instructed the Librarians to see that the Jefferson collection was perpetually reinforced and that whatever additions were required to keep it current, catholic and comprehensive should be secured.

The broad humanistic interests and the bibliophilic sensibilities of Jefferson served as guides to successive overseers of the Library.

The books arrived in Washington in the summer of 1815, and among the volumes that made the journey from Monticello (which, having survived another conflagration, remain part of the Jefferson collection today) are seven works of Jewish interest. These first Judaica of the Library of Congress are books on history, philosophy, and law, two of them touching upon the special situation of the Jews among the nations.

1815: FIRST JUDAICA

Works of Josephus

It is most appropriate that among the more elegant volumes in the Jefferson collection is a splendid edition of *The Genuine Works of Flavius Josephus, the Jewish Historian.* Of folio size, it contains: "Twenty Books of the Jewish Antiquities, with Appendix, or Life of Josephus, written by himself: Seven Books of the Jewish War: and Two Books against Apion." The publisher is pleased to boast that it is "Illustrated with new Plans and Descriptions of the Tabernacle of Moses; and of the Temples of Solomon, Zorababel, Herod and Ezekiel; and with correct Maps of Judea and Jerusalem." The translation into English "from the original Greek, according to Havercamp's accurate Edition," is by William Whiston, M.A., "Sometime Professor of Mathematics in the University of Cambridge." Whiston was both a mathematician and a Christian divine, a friend of Sir Isaac Newton and his successor to the professorship of mathematics. This edition is the first printing of Whiston's justly famed and widely popular translation, published in London in 1737 by W. Bowyer "for the author."

The volume was published for the translator, not the author, for the author Josephus lived more than sixteen centuries earlier in the Holy Land. Born in the year 38 CE of a noble family of priestly descent, he boasts, "By my mother I am of royal blood . . . from the children of Asmoneus." He received both a religious and classical education and was apparently gifted in diplomacy, being at age twenty-six entrusted with a mission to Rome to secure the release of a group of priests who had been imprisoned and sent to Rome by the procurator Felix—a mission Josephus successfully accomplished.

In the year 66 CE, at the outbreak of the Jewish rebellion against Rome, Josephus was appointed military commander of Galilee. Although he was among those who sought accommodation with the imperial power,

Facing page:
The author of the Declaration of Independence read the early history of the Jewish people and its struggle to rid itself of Roman domination in this copy of *The Genuine Works of Flavius Josephus, the Jewish Historian.* Translated from the Original Greek by William Whiston, London, 1737, this is the first edition of the Whiston translation which remained the standard for more than a century and a half.

William Whiston, translator, *The Genuine Works of Flavius Josephus, the Jewish Historian*, London, 1737.
Rare Book and Special Collections Division, Jefferson Library.

THE GENUINE

WORKS

OF

FLAVIUS JOSEPHUS,

THE

JEWISH HISTORIAN.

Translated from the ORIGINAL GREEK, according to *Havercamp's* accurate EDITION.

CONTAINING

Twenty Books of the *JEWISH* ANTIQUITIES,

WITH THE

APPENDIX, or LIFE of *JOSEPHUS*, written by himself:

Seven Books of the *JEWISH* WAR:

AND

Two Books against *APION*.

ILLUSTRATED

With new PLANS and DESCRIPTIONS of the TABERNACLE of *Moses*; and of the TEMPLES of *Solomon*, *Zorobabel*, *Herod*, and *Ezekiel*; and with correct MAPS of *Judea* and *Jerusalem*.

Together with

Proper Notes, Observations, Contents, Parallel Texts of Scripture, five compleat Indexes, and the true Chronology of the several Histories adjusted in the Margin.

To this BOOK are prefixed eight DISSERTATIONS, *viz.*

I. The Testimonies of *Josephus* vindicated.
II. The Copy of the Old Testament made use of by *Josephus*, proved to be that which was collected by *Nehemiah*.
III. Concerning God's Command to *Abraham*, to offer up *Isaac* his Son for a Sacrifice.
IV. A large Enquiry into the true Chronology of *Josephus*.
V. An Extract out of *Josephus*'s Exhortation to the *Greeks*, concerning *Hades*, and the Resurrection of the Dead.
VI. Proofs that this Exhortation is genuine; and was no other than a Homily of *Josephus*'s, when he was Bishop of *Jerusalem*.
VII. A Demonstration that *Tacitus*, the *Roman* Historian, took his History of the *Jews* out of *Josephus*.
VIII. A Dissertation of *Cellarius*'s against *Harduin*; in Vindication of *Josephus*'s History of the Family of *Herod* from Coins. Translated into *English*.

With an ACCOUNT of the *Jewish* Coins, Weights, and Measures.

By *WILLIAM WHISTON*, M.A.
Some time Professor of the Mathematicks in the University of *Cambridge*.

LONDON,
Printed by W. BOWYER for the AUTHOR: and are to be sold by JOHN WHISTON, Bookseller, at Mr. *Boyle's Head*: *Fleetstreet*. MDCCXXXVII.

Flavius Josephus was a leader of the rebellion against Rome (68 CE) who capitulated and became a pensioner of the Roman Emperor Vespasian. He wrote a history of the Jews and of the War of Rebellion in Greek, the scholar's language in the Roman empire. Edward Bernard (1638–1696), professor of astronomy at Oxford, prepared this scholarly Greek-Latin edition, of which only a part was published. Printed in 1686–87, it appeared with a new title page in 1700.

Flavii Josephi Antiquitatum Judaicarum, Oxford, 1700.
Rare Book and Special Collections Division, Jefferson Library.

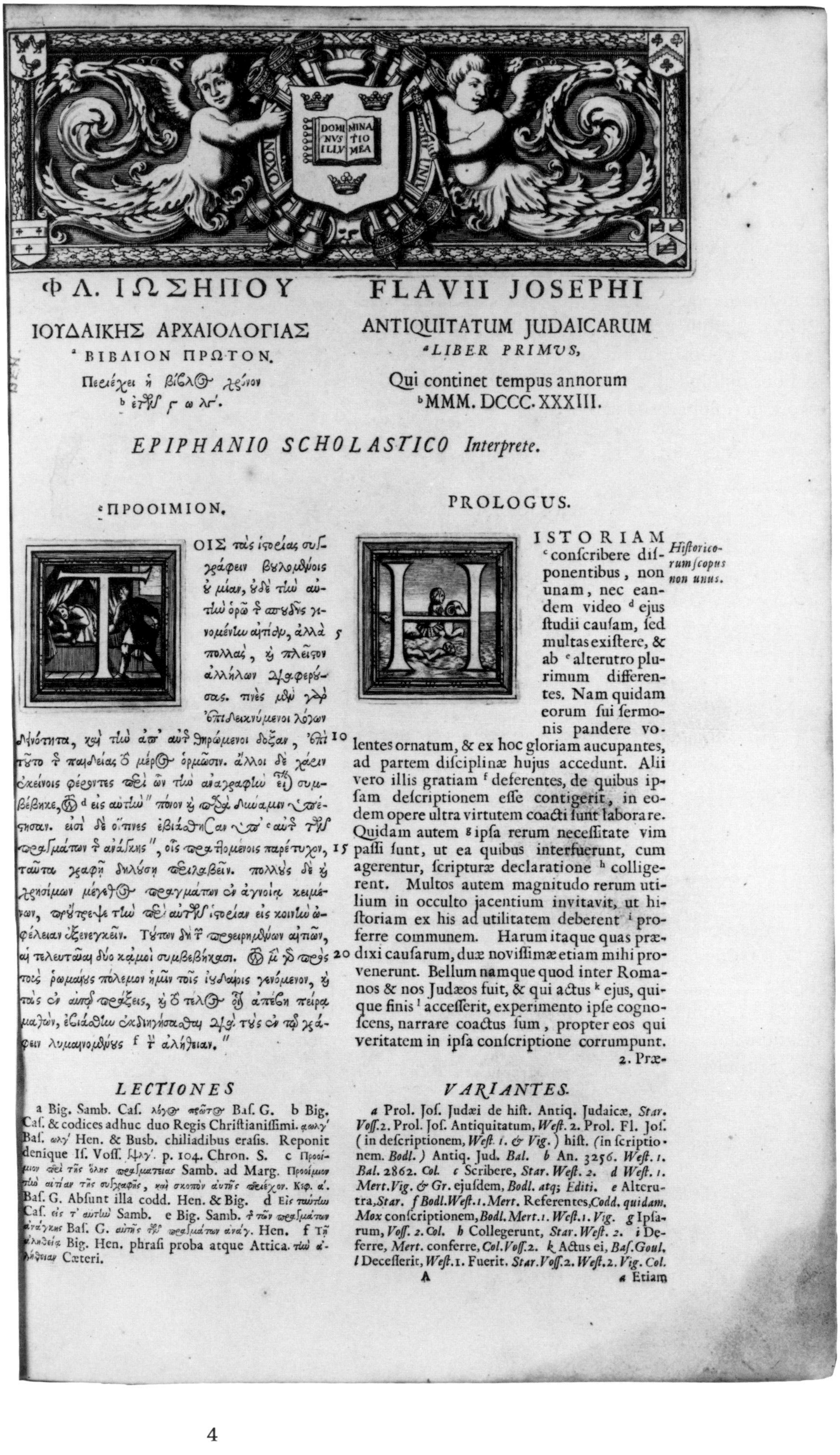
ΦΛ. ΙΩΣΗΠΟΥ

ΙΟΥΔΑΙΚΗΣ ΑΡΧΑΙΟΛΟΓΙΑΣ

[a] ΒΙΒΛΙΟΝ ΠΡΩΤΟΝ.

Περιέχει ἡ βίβλος χρόνον [b] ἐτῶν ͵γωλγʹ.

FLAVII JOSEPHI

ANTIQUITATUM JUDAICARUM

[a] *LIBER PRIMUS,*

Qui continet tempus annorum [b] MMM. DCCC. XXXIII.

EPIPHANIO SCHOLASTICO Interprete.

[c] ΠΡΟΟΙΜΙΟΝ.

Τοῖς τὰς ἱστορίας συγγράφειν βουλομένοις οὐ μίαν, οὐδὲ τὴν αὐτὴν ὁρῶ τῆς σπουδῆς γινομένην αἰτίαν, ἀλλὰ πολλάς, καὶ πλεῖστον ἀλλήλων διαφερούσας. τινὲς μὲν γὰρ ἐπιδεικνύμενοι λόγων δεινότητα, καὶ τὴν ἀπ' αὐτῆς θηρώμενοι δόξαν, ἐπὶ τοῦτο τῆς παιδείας τὸ μέρος ὁρμῶσιν. ἄλλοι δὲ χάριν ἐκείνοις φέροντες περὶ ὧν τὴν ἀναγραφὴν εἶναι συμβέβηκε, τὸν [d] εἰς αὐτὴν πόνον καὶ παρὰ δύναμιν ὑπέστησαν. εἰσὶ δὲ οἵτινες ἐβιάσθησαν ὑπ' [e] αὐτῆς τῆς τῶν πραγμάτων ἀνάγκης, οἷς πραττομένοις παρέτυχον, ταῦτα γραφῇ δηλούσῃ περιλαβεῖν. πολλοὺς δὲ καὶ χρησίμων μέγεθος πραγμάτων ἐν ἀγνοίᾳ κειμένων, προὔτρεψε τὴν περὶ αὐτῶν ἱστορίαν εἰς κοινὴν ὠφέλειαν ἐξενεγκεῖν. Τούτων δὴ τῶν προειρημένων αἰτιῶν, αἱ τελευταῖαι δύο κἀμοὶ συμβεβήκασι. τὸν μὲν γὰρ πρὸς τοὺς Ῥωμαίους πόλεμον ἡμῖν τοῖς Ἰουδαίοις γενόμενον, καὶ τὰς ἐν αὐτῷ πράξεις, καὶ τὸ τέλος ὃ ἀπέβη πείρᾳ μαθών, ἐβιάσθην ἐκδιηγήσασθαι διὰ τοὺς ἐν τῷ γράφειν λυμαινομένους [f] τὴν ἀλήθειαν.

PROLOGUS.

ISTORIAM [c] conscribere disponentibus, non unam, nec eandem video [d] ejus studii causam, sed multas existere, & ab [e] alterutro plurimum differentes. Nam quidam eorum sui sermonis pandere volentes ornatum, & ex hoc gloriam aucupantes, ad partem disciplinæ hujus accedunt. Alii vero illis gratiam [f] deferentes, de quibus ipsam descriptionem esse contigerit, in eodem opere ultra virtutem coacti sunt laborare. Quidam autem [g] ipsa rerum necessitate vim passi sunt, ut ea quibus interfuerunt, cum agerentur, scripturæ declaratione [h] colligerent. Multos autem magnitudo rerum utilium in occulto jacentium invitavit, ut historiam ex his ad utilitatem deberent [i] proferre communem. Harum itaque quas prædixi causarum, duæ novissimæ etiam mihi provenerunt. Bellum namque quod inter Romanos & nos Judæos fuit, & qui actus [k] ejus, quique finis [l] accesserit, experimento ipse cognoscens, narrare coactus sum, propter eos qui veritatem in ipsa conscriptione corrumpunt.

Historicorum scopus non unus.

2. Præ-

LECTIONES VARIANTES.

a Big. Samb. Cas. λόγος πρῶτος Bas. G. b Big. Cas. & codices adhuc duo Regis Christianissimi. ͵γωλγʹ Bas. ωλγʹ Hen. & Busb. chiliadibus erasis. Reponit denique Is. Voss. ͵δωλγʹ. p. 104. Chron. S. c Προοίμιον περὶ τῆς ὅλης πραγματείας Samb. ad Marg. Προοίμιον τὴν αἰτίαν τῆς συγγραφῆς, καὶ σκοπὸν αὐτῆς περιέχον. Κεφ. αʹ. Bas. G. Absunt illa codd. Hen. & Big. d Εἰς ταύτην Cas. εἰς τ' αὐτὴν Samb. e Big. Samb. τῆς τῶν πραγμάτων ἀνάγκης Bas. G. αὐτῆς τῆς πραγμάτων ἀνάγ. Hen. f Τῇ ἀληθείᾳ Big. Hen. phrasi proba atque Attica. τὴν ἀλήθειαν Cæteri.

a Prol. Jos. Judæi de hist. Antiq. Judaicæ, *Star. Voss.*2. Prol. Jos. Antiquitatum, *West.* 2. Prol. Fl. Jos. (in descriptionem, *West. 1. & Vig.*) hist. (in scriptionem. *Bodl.*) Antiq. Jud. *Bal.* *b* An. 3256. *West. 1. Bal.* 2862. *Col.* *c* Scribere, *Star. West.* 2. *d West. 1. Mert. Vig. & Gr.* ejusdem, *Bodl. atq; Editi.* *e* Alterutra, *Star.* *f Bodl. West. 1. Mert.* Referentes, *Codd. quidam. Mox* conscriptionem, *Bodl. Mert. 1. West. 1. Vig.* *g* Ipsarum, *Voss.* 2. *Col.* *h* Collegerunt, *Star. West.* 2. *i* Deferre, *Mert.* conferre, *Col. Voss.* 2. *k* Actus ei, *Bas. Goul.* *l* Decesserit, *West.* 1. Fuerit. *Star. Voss.* 2. *West.* 2. *Vig. Col.*

A

a Etiam

he nevertheless fought against the Roman legions. Defeated, he betrayed colleagues who had chosen group suicide over enslavement and surrendered to the enemy. His life spared, he became a pensioner of the Roman emperor, who had him brought to Rome. There in 75 CE, at age thirty-eight, he wrote *The Jewish War,* which he claims, "was the greatest of all [wars], not only that have been in our times, but, in a manner of those that ever were heard of; both of those wherein cities have fought against cities, or nations against nations." Eighteen years later, he wrote the *Antiquities of the Jews,* "to explain who the Jews originally were; what fortunes they had been subject to; and by what legislator they had been instructed in piety and the exercise of other virtues; what wars they also had made in remote ages, till they were unwillingly engaged in this last, with the Romans." Both works were classic creations, informative and absorbing. Editions of Josephus began to appear in the early years of printing, translations multiplied, and, second only to the Bible, it was the most popular work in Colonial and early republic America.

The Jewish War

The Jefferson library has an earlier edition of a section of *The Jewish War,* published in Oxford in 1700, the original Greek and a Latin translation printed in parallel columns, edited by Edward Bernard, Professor of Astronomy at Oxford. One wonders how the generation of Jefferson, having recently thrown off the yoke of domination of an imperial power, reacted to *The Jewish War,* the saga of a rebellion cruelly crushed, an uprising which brought not liberation but harsher subjugation, exile, and enslavement. For America did read of that Jewish war of liberation, editions of the *Works of Josephus* proliferating from the first American edition in the 1780s throughout the nineteenth century. Did it make the political freedom America gained in its war of liberation seem all the more precious?

Baba Kamma

A sampling of the literature of the Jewish legal tradition is provided by a fine copy of *Baba Kamma Mi'masekhet Nezikin* (Hebrew), *De Legibus Ebraeorum . . . ,* Leyden, 1637, an Elzevir publication. It contains the Hebrew text of the Mishnah of that tractate of the Talmud with its translation into Latin and an erudite commentary by Constantin L'Empereur, the "controversarium Judaicarum professor" at the University of Leyden. The purpose of this university chair of Christian polemics was the defense of the faith and promotion of conversion to it, both of which he pursued with tact and moderation. His works on the Bible, the Hebrew language, and Jewish law are valuable contributions to the Christian study of Judaism.

Philo's Opera Omnia

Harvard professor Harry A. Wolfson, a master of Jewish philosophical literature, brought to the study of Judaism the careful scrutiny of the traditional method of Talmud study and the critical freedom of the scientific method. Investigating the structure and development of philosophic systems from Plato to Spinoza, he concluded that the system of religious philosophy initiated by Philo of Alexandria in the first century dominated Western thought—Jewish, Islamic, and Christian—for the next sixteen centuries, until brought to a close by Spinoza, "the last of the medievals and the first of the moderns." These are the two Jewish thinkers whose works we find in the Jefferson collection: a four-volume edition of the works of Philo Judaeus in the original Greek with Latin translation, *Philonis Iudaei Opera Omnia Graeca et Latina* (Erlangen 1785–1788); and Benedict De Spinoza's posthumously published *B.D.S. Opera posthuma* (Amsterdam, 1677).

Born into a distinguished Jewish family in the ancient world's most cosmopolitan city, Alexandria, Philo (20 BCE–50 CE) remained a devout Jew all his life. A student of the Bible (though it is doubtful that he could read it in Hebrew) and philosophy both, he was the first to undertake conciliating the two—demonstrating harmony between faith and reason. The Islamic, Jewish, and Christian philosophers who followed all joined in the endeavor Philo initiated. Avicenna, Maimonides, Thomas Aquinas, and others did so with greater erudition, profounder insights, and more ingenious proofs, but their goal was the same: to harmonize the God-given religious tradition with the truths arrived at by the highest reaches of the human intellect (yet always accepting the primacy of faith over philosophy and revelation over reason).

Spinoza's Opera Posthuma

Baruch Spinoza (1632–1677), scion of a leading Jewish family in Europe's most cosmopolitan city in the seventeenth century, Amsterdam, provided the intellectual architecture for a philosophic structure which would level current assumptions and conclusions. For his endeavors, Spinoza was excommunicated by his own community and his name, Baruch-Benedict (which means blessed), became anathema both in the community he left and the larger community he never entered. During his lifetime, Spinoza's works were published anonymously, and even his posthumously published *Opera* contains neither place nor date of publication. His rise to a central position in the drama of humankind's search for truth came slowly but inexorably as human reason began to be more relied upon than divine dogma. Jefferson would have been one of the first Americans to have accepted Spinoza as his spiritual kin.

The fifth and final work in Spinoza's *Opera Posthuma* (with its own title page, pagination, and errata) is a Grammar of the Hebrew Language, *Compendium Grammaticus Lingua Hebraeae.* Spinoza was one of the first to subject the Bible to critical analysis but demanded that such analysis be rooted in a thorough understanding of the Hebrew language. Then, and only then, Spinoza states, may one turn to "the life, the conduct and the pursuits of the author of each book . . . [and] the fate of each book: how it was first received, into whose hands it fell, how many different versions there were of it, by whose advice it was received into the Canon, and how all the books now universally accepted as sacred, were united into a single whole."

Facing page: Did Jefferson ever study Talmud? There is evidence that he may have at least leafed through this volume of the Mishnah of Tractate Baba Kamma, with the Latin translation and commentary of Constantine L'Empereur. The evidence: Jefferson initialed this copy at signatures I(J) and T. At the bottom of page 65, he wrote a T before the I(J) and on page 145, he added a J after the T, and periods after both initials, as well.

Baba Kamma, Mi' masekhet Nezikin (Hebrew), *De Legibus Ebraeorum . . .* Latin translation and commentary by Constantine L'Empereur, Leyden, 1637.
Rare Book and Special Collections Division, Jefferson Library.

בבא קמא

CODICIS PRIMI

פרק א׳:

Cap. I.

הלכ׳ א׳ :

ארבע אבות נזיקים השור והבור והמבעה והבער לא הרי השור כהרי המבעה ולא הרי המבעה כהרי השור ולא זה וזה שיש בהם רוח חיים כהרי האש שאין בו רוח חיים ולא זה וזה שדרכן לילך ולהזיק כהרי הבור שאין דרכו לילך ולהזיק הצד השוה שבהן שדרכן להזיק ושמירתן עליך וכשהזיק חב המזיק לשלם תשלומי נזק במיטב הארץ :

§. I.

Quatuor ſunt damnorum [1] fontes: [2] bos; [3] puteus; [4] depaſcens; incendium [5]. Non ita ſe habet bos, ut depaſcens; nec depaſcens, ut [6] bos; nec hic, & ille, in quibus eſt vitalis ſpiritus, ut ignis qui ſpiritu vitali deſtituitur; nec denique hic & ille, qui ambulando ſolent nocere [7], ut puteus qui non ſolet ambulando nocere. Conditio æqualis [8] in iſtis hæc eſt, quod nocere ſoleant, iiſque attendere debeas: & quum horum aliquo damnum infertur, lædens teneatur damni pretium [9] ſolvere è præſtantiſſimo proventu.

Annotationes.

[1] Talmudiſtæ in conſtitutionibus ſuis ea quæ tractant ad ſumma capita revocare ſolent: non quod ſingula iſtis capitibus ut generibus contineantur; ſed eò ſaltem hac ratione referantur, ut quid de ſingulis judicandum ſit ex iſtis ſummis

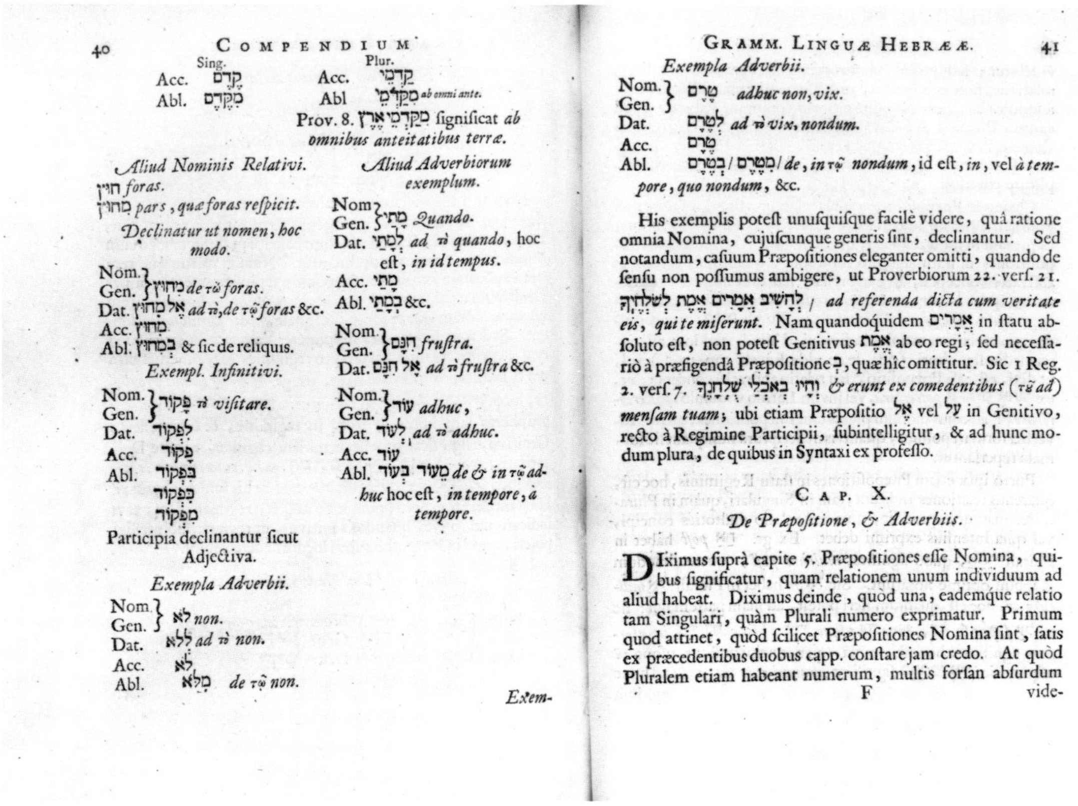

40 COMPENDIUM

	Sing.		Plur.
Acc.	קדם	Acc.	קדמי
Abl.	מקדם	Abl	מקדמי *ab omni ante.*

Prov. 8. מקדמי ארץ significat *ab omnibus anteitatibus terræ.*

Aliud Nominis Relativi.

חוץ *foras.*
מחוץ *pars, quæ foras respicit.*

Declinatur ut nomen, hoc modo.

Nom. } Gen. } מחוץ *de τῶ foras.*
Dat. אל מחוץ *ad τὸ, de τῶ foras* &c.
Acc. מחוץ
Abl. במחוץ & sic de reliquis.

Exempl. Infinitivi.

Nom. } Gen. } פקוד *τὸ visitare.*
Dat. לפקוד
Acc. פקוד
Abl. בפקוד
כפקוד
מפקוד

Participia declinantur sicut Adjectiva.

Exempla Adverbii.

Nom. } Gen. } לא *non.*
Dat. ללא *ad τὸ non.*
Acc. לא
Abl. מלא *de τῶ non.*

Aliud Adverbiorum exemplum.

Nom } Gen. } מתי *Quando.*
Dat. למתי *ad τὸ quando*, hoc est, *in id tempus.*
Acc. מתי
Abl. במתי &c.

Nom. } Gen. } חנם *frustra.*
Dat. אל חנם *ad τὸ frustra* &c.

Nom. } Gen. } עוד *adhuc,*
Dat. לעוד *ad τὸ adhuc.*
Acc. עוד
Abl. בעוד מעוד *de & in τῶ adhuc* hoc est, *in tempore, à tempore.*

Exem-

GRAMM. LINGUÆ HEBRÆÆ. 41

Exempla Adverbii.

Nom. } Gen. } טרם *adhuc non, vix.*
Dat. לטרם *ad τὸ vix, nondum.*
Acc. טרם
Abl. בטרם / מטרם / *de, in τῶ nondum*, id est, *in*, vel *à tempore, quo nondum*, &c.

His exemplis potest unusquisque facilè videre, quâ ratione omnia Nomina, cujuscunque generis sint, declinantur. Sed notandum, casuum Præpositiones eleganter omitti, quando de sensu non possumus ambigere, ut Proverbiorum 22. vers. 21. להשיב אמרים אמת לשלחיך / *ad referenda dicta cum veritate eis, qui te miserunt.* Nam quandoquidem אמרים in statu absoluto est, non potest Genitivus אמת ab eo regi; sed necessariò à præfigendâ Præpositione ב, quæ hîc omittitur. Sic 1 Reg. 2. vers. 7. והיו באכלי שלחנך *& erunt ex comedentibus (τῶ ad) mensam tuam*; ubi etiam Præpositio אל vel על in Genitivo, recto à Regimine Participii, subintelligitur, & ad hunc modum plura, de quibus in Syntaxi ex professo.

C AP. X.

De Præpositione, & Adverbiis.

DIximus suprà capite 5. Præpositiones esse Nomina, quibus significatur, quam relationem unum individuum ad aliud habeat. Diximus deinde, quòd una, eademque relatio tam Singulari, quàm Plurali numero exprimatur. Primum quod attinet, quòd scilicet Præpositiones Nomina sint, satis ex præcedentibus duobus capp. constare jam credo. At quòd Pluralem etiam habeant numerum, multis forsan absurdum

F vide-

At the request of friends, Spinoza prepared a grammar of the Hebrew language, no doubt to aid the study of the Bible in the original. The work was never completed and it appears as the fifth and final one in his *Opera Posthuma* (Posthumous Works), which was published giving only the author's initials B. D. S., and without place and date of publication, which were Amsterdam, 1677.

B. D. Spinoza, *Opera Posthuma Compendium Grammaticus Linguae Hebraeae* [Amsterdam, 1677] Rare Book and Special Collections Division, Jefferson Library.

Montefiore's Dictionary

Jefferson would have admired the adventurous spirit (and been bemused by the selective memory and autobiographical audacity) of the author of the three-volume *A Commercial Dictionary . . . First American Edition. . . ,* Philadelphia, 1804, Joshua Montefiore (London, 1762—St. Albans, Vermont, 1843). As a youth, Joshua had turned from the Montefiore business pursuits in Italy and England to begin a life of adventure on three continents: Europe, Africa, and America. Between adventures he produced a small corpus of useful commercial handbooks of which the *Dictionary* was the most notable. For the American edition he received subscriptions ranging from Halifax, Nova Scotia, to Savannah, Georgia. Since the author himself personally solicited the subscriptions, he must have done considerable traveling on the American continent as he did on others. Though his assertions are often exaggerated, they are rooted in truth. His claim to have been the first Jewish undergraduate to study at Oxford is unsupported by university records and challenged by the fact that Oxford in the eighteenth century did not officially admit Jewish undergraduates. But he apparently did receive a good education and was a fine English stylist. He also claimed to have been the first Jew to receive a commission in the British army. Though no army list contains his name, his nephew, Sir Moses Montefiore, remembered Uncle Josh with his "laced red coat and pigtail, and cocked hat and sword."

In 1784 Joshua Montefiore was admitted to practice as a solicitor in London and a year later was appointed Notary Public. But in 1787, when he applied to be admitted to the bar in Jamaica, he was turned down because a 1711 law excluded "Jew, Mulatto, Indian or Negro." Five years later, he was one of the leaders of some three hundred colonists who settled the Island of Bulama off the west coast of Africa, endeavoring to prove that tropical colonies could be cultivated successfully without slave labor. The noble experiment failed, but Montefiore subsequently published an interesting account of his adventure. He found a home in America at last, arriving possibly as early as 1803 to prepare the American edition of his *Dictionary*. He was certainly living in Philadelphia when he published the popular *The American Traders Compendium* in 1811. In 1835, at age seventy-three, he married his deceased wife's maid and moved to St. Albans, Vermont, where he farmed and relied upon the generosity of his nephew, Sir Moses, to support his growing family, which in the eight years before his death in 1843 increased by eight. Though he had little to do with Jewish life in his last years, family tradition has it that he remained an observant Jew and had his sons circumcised, though he permitted his children to be brought up as Christians. He was buried on the family farm so that he would not spend eternity in the town's Christian burial ground. Before death he prepared from memory a translation of the Jewish burial service to be read at his interment and in the family Bible he wrote out a Prayer, thoroughly Jewish in its content and language, to be recited by his children each night. It begins:

> We have sinned, O our father, pardon us O our Creator, Hear O People the Lord our God is One . . .

and concludes

> We further humbly pray and beseech you O God, to protect us, grant us health, honesty, virtue, and industry, and that we may keep and observe the Holy commandments, amen.

The life of Joshua Montefiore tells us much about Jewish life in the Old World and in the New in that fateful century, 1750–1850, when the Jews were beginning to enter the larger society—physical and spiritual uprooting and wandering, discrimination, accommodation, and assimilation.

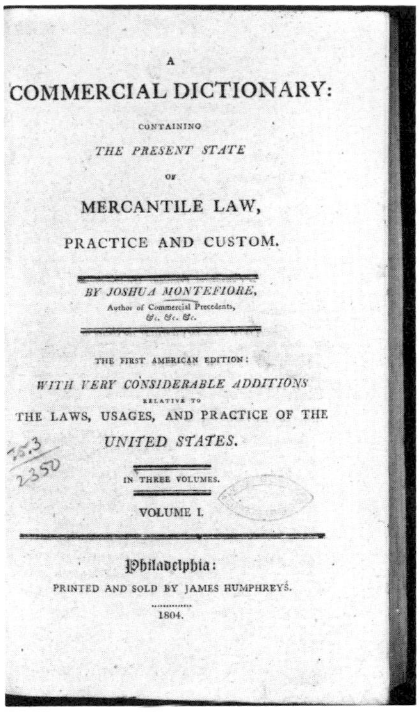

A

COMMERCIAL DICTIONARY:

CONTAINING

THE PRESENT STATE

OF

MERCANTILE LAW,

PRACTICE AND CUSTOM.

BY JOSHUA MONTEFIORE,
Author of Commercial Precedents,
&c. &c. &c.

THE FIRST AMERICAN EDITION:

WITH VERY CONSIDERABLE ADDITIONS
RELATIVE TO
THE LAWS, USAGES, AND PRACTICE OF THE
UNITED STATES.

IN THREE VOLUMES.

VOLUME I.

Philadelphia:
PRINTED AND SOLD BY JAMES HUMPHREYS.

1804.

President Thomas Jefferson purchased the three-volume "First American Edition" of Joshua Montefiore's *A Commercial Dictionary* on its publication in 1804. The English-born author, scion of a distinguished Italian-English family, after trying Africa and the West Indies, settled in the United States, and there prepared a new edition of his work, to serve the needs of the new nation where he had at last found haven. The title page announces "very considerable additions relative to the laws, usages, and practices of the United States"—200 new and interesting articles, including one on "the NATIONAL DEBT."

Joshua Montefiore, *A Commercial Dictionary,* Philadelphia, 1804.
Rare Book and Special Collections Division, Jefferson Library.

A New Discourse of Trade

A century earlier, England was engaged in a prolonged debate over whether to permit the Jews, whom she had expelled in 1290, to return and, if allowed to return, whether naturalization should be granted them. Jefferson must have read about the debate in a small volume in his library. *A New Discourse of Trade,* London, 1694. The author, Sir Josiah Child, was an English merchant, economist, and governor of the East India Company. In chapter 7 of the work (first published in 1668) he discusses whether "it be for our publick Good to permit the *Jews* to be Naturalized in common with other strangers." First he lists the objections offered by opponents:

> The Jews are a subtil People . . . a penurious people . . . they bring no estates with them . . .

To whom Sir Josiah counters:

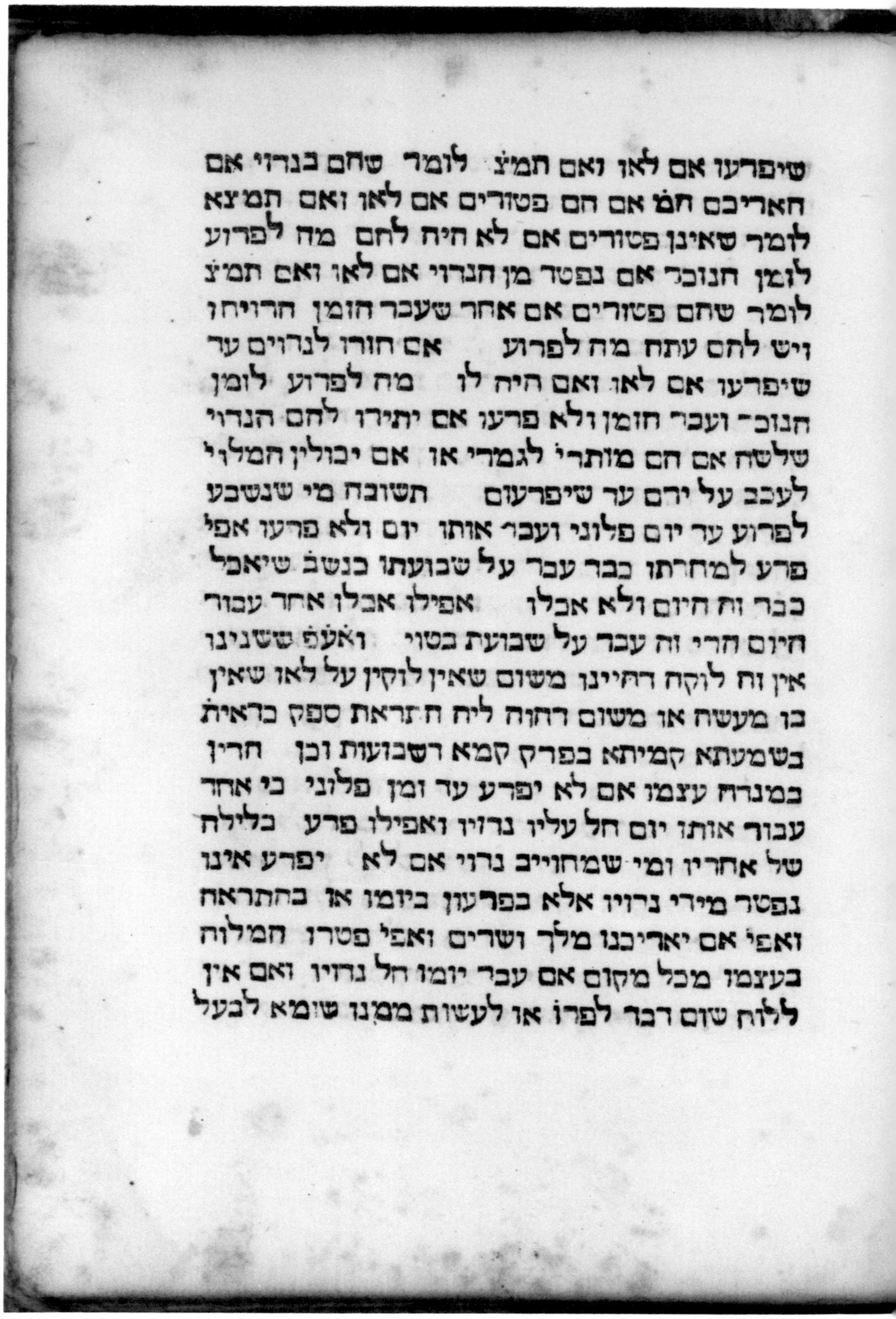

שיפרעו אם לאו ואם תמ״צ לומר שהם בנדוי אם
האריכם הה״מ אם הם פטורים אם לאו ואם תמצא
לומר שאינן פטורים אם לא היה להם מה לפרוע
לזמן הנזכר אם נפטר מן הנדוי אם לאו ואם תמ״צ
לומר שהם פטורים אם אחר שעבר הזמן הרויחו
ויש להם עתה מה לפרוע אם חוזרו לנדוים עד
שיפרעו אם לאו ואם היה לו מה לפרוע לזמן
הנזכ׳ ועבר הזמן ולא פרעו אם יתירו להם הנדוי
שלשה אם הם מותרי׳ לגמרי או אם יבולין המלו׳
לעכב על ידם עד שיפרעום תשובה מי שנשבע
לפרוע עד יום פלוני ועבר אותו יום ולא פרעו אפי׳
פרע למחרתו כבר עבר על שבועתו כנשב׳ שיאכל
כבר זה היום ולא אכלו אפילו אכלו אחר עבור
היום הרי זה עבר על שבועת בטוי ואעפ״ ששגינו
אין זה לוקה דהיינו משום שאין לוקין על לאו שאין
בו מעשה או משום דהוה ליה התראת ספק כדאית׳
בשמעתא קמיתא בפרק קמא דשבועות וכן הרין
במנדה עצמו אם לא יפרע עד זמן פלוני כי אחר
עבור אותו יום חל עליו נדויו ואפילו פרע בלילה
של אחריו ומי שמחוייב נדוי אם לא יפרע אינו
נפטר מידי נדויו אלא בפרעון בזמנו או בהתראה
ואפי׳ אם יאריכנו מלך ושרים ואפי׳ פטרו המלוה
בעצמו מכל מקום אם עבר יומו חל נדויו ואם אין
ללוה שום דבר לפרו׳ או לעשות ממנו שומא לבעל

The subtiller the Jews are . . . the more they are like to increase Trade, and the more they do that, the better it is for the Kingdom in general . . . the thriftier they live, the better Example to our people . . . Many . . . would settle here for their Lives, and their Posterities after them, if they had the same freedom and Security here as they have in Holland and Italy . . . All men by nature are alike . . . all men are in love with Liberty and security. (The Jews) Have now no country of their own . . . and therefore that is their country, and so esteemed by them, where they are best used, and have the greatest Security.

Reading these words, Jefferson must have nodded a vigorous assent.

בשבילו עזר תרע שאין אומרין בשבות זה דומה
לזה ואין לנו בהם אלא מה שהתירו בפירוש שה״י
לעתיר מתירין אותן מחמת דבר אחר שיראה קל
שמעלה וכותב בשבת בערכאות של גוים משום
קניית בית בארץ ישראל ולעתים מעמידין אותן
במקום כרת החמור כהואה ואיומ״ל
רסה עור שאלת אי זה מהם עריף
שליח צבור בשכר או
בנרבה תשובה יותר ראוי להיות שליח צבור שכור
לפי שבמקום שהוא שכור וברור מן הקהל אין פרץ
ואין צוחה שאין אחר שאינו הגון רשאי לפשוט
רגלו להתפלל ואם היה בנרבה הרשות נתונה לכל
ובפרוץ הרבר יעלה מי שאינו הגון כהגון ועל רבר
זה הוצרכנו אנו לתקן שבימים הקרושים כאשמורו׳
ראש שנה ויום הכפורים לא יהא רשות ביד ארם
לעלות לרוכן להתפלל אלא ברשות הקהל וכן
בתקיעת שופר שרבו על זה ער שתקננו וגזרנו ועור
שלרברי החולק משוי להו לכל הקהלות כטועים
שבכל מקום שוכרים שליח צבור וגם השליח צבור
נזהר בתפלתו ובתקונין למען שכור הוא
רסו שאלת ראובן ושמעון נתחייבו
לפרוע ללוי כך וכך מעות
לזמן ירוע בתנאי שאם לא יפרעם לאותו זמן שיהיו
בנרוי גמור ועבר הזמן ולא פרעו אם הם בנרוי עד

There is no agreement as to which was the first Hebrew book printed, but there is general agreement that it was one of a group printed, without place or date of publication, in Rome between 1469 and 1472. Among these is this volume of Responsa by the most prolific of respondents, the *Rashba,* i.e., Solomon ben Abraham Adret (c. 1235–c. 1310). Our volume is open to responsum 265, dealing with the question: which is to be preferred, a precentor who receives remuneration (i.e., a professional cantor), or one who volunteers his services gratis? The answer: a professional engaged by the community is to be preferred, so that one unskilled in the art will not be able "to unfurl his banner" and act the role.

Solomon ben Abraham Adret, *Teshuvot She'elot ha-Rashba* (Rome? 1469–72).
Hebraic Section.

1991: JUDAIC FIRSTS

In the one hundred and seventy years which have passed since the Jefferson collection arrived in Washington, the Library of Congress has increased ten thousand-fold. From the first Judaica, whose bibliographic distinction lies in their having been "present at creation," we can today turn to Judaic firsts, volumes of singular rarity and crowning importance in the history of the Hebrew book, culled from the Library's Hebraic treasures.

The Rome Rashba

The crown jewel of a great Hebraic collection would, of course, be the first Hebrew book printed. For that we must go to Italy, the cradle of Hebrew printing, only Spain, Portugal, and Turkey sharing its distinction of having produced Hebrew incunabula (books printed before the end of the fifteenth century). It is generally agreed by students of Hebrew typography that a group of books known as the Rome Incunabula were the first Hebrew books printed.

The Rome Incunabula, eight—perhaps nine—in number, bear no date or place of publication; however, it is widely accepted that six of these were printed between 1469 and 1472. One, the *Commentary on the Pentateuch* of Moses ben Nahman (Nachmanides) (1194–1270), has the names of the printers, three in number, "from Rome," but not *in* or *of* Rome. There is far stronger documentary evidence that another, a collection of Responsa by Solomon ben Adret, was published in Rome. This was established in 1896 by Rabbi David Simonsen, Chief Rabbi of Denmark and a noted bibliophile, who pointed out a reference (in a pamphlet published in Venice in 1566) to the responsa of Solomon ben Abraham Adret (Rashba) of Barcelona (c. 1235–c. 1310), published "in Rome," a reference that could fit only the Rome incunabulum bearing that name: *Teshuvot She'elot ha-Rashba* (The Responsa of Adret). The Library of Congress has a copy of this volume, as well as a fourteenth-century manuscript containing thirty responsa of Adret. In his definitive work on these incunabula, Moses Marx explains their "primitive" typography as an indication of their antiquity and proposes "proof" that the Commentary of Nachmanides was probably the first one printed. His point is well taken, but the type of the Adret volume looks no less primitive, being bolder and less refined. It is also slightly larger, which would argue for its earlier date, since the high cost of paper at the birth of printing would suggest that smaller type, using less paper, would be a desired later improvement. Might we then not claim that, as the only volume which is documented as being printed in Rome, the one whose typography is larger and more primitive is therefore the one that may most justifiably be called the first printed Hebrew book?

Gershom Soncino's First Book

More than one-third of the one hundred and sixty or so Hebrew incunabula which have survived were products of the Soncino family. For five generations, its members produced Hebrew books on three continents, from their very first publication (printed in 1483 in Soncino, the Italian town from which the family took its name) to their last (printed in 1562 in Cairo, Egypt)—some two hundred in all. The Soncinos' contribution to Jewish religious life and cultural creativity cannot be overstated, nor can their importance to the development of Hebrew books, the authenticity of their contents, and the quality of their typography, paper, illustrations, and embellishments.

The greatest of the Soncinos, and universally acknowledged as the towering figure in the more than five centuries of Hebrew printing, was Gershom Soncino. A wanderer's staff would have been a more appropriate printer's logo than the tower he chose. Political persecution and commercial competition caused him to be on the move constantly, setting up his printing shop successively in Soncino, Casamaggiore, Brescia, Barco,

Fano, Pesaro, Ortona, Rimini, and Cesena in Italy; then in Salonica and Constantinople in Turkey, where he died in 1534. In all, Gershom Soncino printed some one hundred Hebrew books and an equal number in Latin and Italian. His production was not only prodigious but also superb in quality.

The unique nature of the claim to fame of our second first, the *Sefer Mitzvot Gadol* of Moses of Coucy, Soncino, 1488, is as solid as it is certain: it is the first book printed by Gershom Soncino. The Library of Congress has two copies of this book and, as if that were not enough, on the end flyleaf of one copy is pasted a bill of sale unique in the annals of early Hebrew printing. It was written and signed by the seller, "Gershom, the son of Moshe Soncino (of blessed memory), Printer," and issued to one Moshe ben Shmuel Diena, stipulating that the buyer might not resell the volume for a period of two years. The bill of sale is dated "the 25th day of Tevet, (5)249 [= December 29, 1488], here in the city of Soncino" ten days after the printed date of publication. Arthur Z. Schwarz, who first brought this to the attention of the scholarly world, suggests that this volume may well be one of the first, if not the first off the press. The colophon date is the day of the "completion of the work," i.e., the printing. Some days may have passed before it was ready for distribution. Soncino's signature is his only Hebrew autograph to have survived.

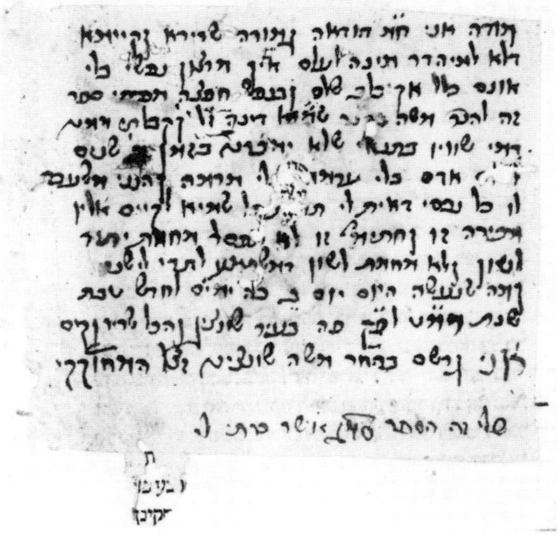

A superb copy of the first book printed by the most famous of early Hebrew printers, Gershom Soncino. A deed of sale in the hand of the printer himself is pasted in, dated only ten days after the publication date stated in the colophon. It thus may well be the first copy sold—even the first copy off the press! It is certainly one of the very first copies—and the holograph bill of sale contains the only Hebrew autograph of Soncino to survive.

Moses of Coucy, *Sefer Mitzvot Gadol,* Soncino, 1488. Rare Book and Special Collections Division.

יתרו

אשר בשעריך : כי ששת ימים עשה יהוה את השמים ואת
הארץ את הים ואת כל אשר בם וינח ביום השביעי על כן
ברך יהוה את יום השבת ויקדשהו : ס כבד
את אביך ואת אמך למען יארכון ימיך על האדמה אשר
יהוה אלהיך נתן לך : ס לא תרצח : ס
לא תנאף : ס לא תגנב : ס לא תענה ב
ברעך עד שקר : ס לא תחמד בית רעך לא תחמד
אשת רעך ועבדו ואמתו ושורו וחמרו וכל אשר לרעך :
ס וכל העם ראים את הקולת ואת הלפידם
ואת קול השפר ואת ההר עשן וירא העם וינעו ויעמדו מ
מרחק : ויאמרו אל משה דבר אתה עמנו ונשמעה ואל ת
ידבר עמנו אלהים פן נמות : ויאמר משה אל העם אל תיראו
כי לבעבור נסות אתכם בא האלהים ובעבור תהיה יראתו
על פניכם לבלתי תחטאו : ויעמד העם מרחק ומשה נגש
אל הערפל אשר שם האלהים : ס ויאמר יהוה
אל משה כה תאמר אל בני ישראל אתם ראיתם כי מן
השמים דברתי עמכם : לא תעשון אתי אלהי כסף ואלהי
זהב לא תעשו לכם : מזבח אדמה תעשה לי וזבחת עליו
את עלתיך ואת שלמיך את צאנך ואת בקרך בכל המקום

Printed entirely on vellum, this copy of the first edition of the Humash, the Five Books of Moses, once belonged to B. J. De Rossi, the noted eighteenth-century bibliographer of early Hebrew books, who calls this edition "Editio Rarissima." An Aramaic translation, the Targum Onkeles, is at the side of the Hebrew text, and the commentary of Rashi (R. Solomon b. Yitzhak) at the top and bottom of the page. The publisher was Abraham Caravita, who completed its publication in Bologna, on January 25, 1482. It is open to the Ten Commandments in the Book of Exodus.

Pentateuch with Targum Onkeles and Rashi, Bologna, 1482.
Rare Book and Special Collections Division.

The Bologna Pentateuch

To the great university city of Bologna belongs the distinction of being the place of publication of the first printed Hebrew Pentateuch, dated January 25, 1482. The text is in large, clear square letters, with the Targum (Aramaic translation) at its side and the commentary of the most favored of Bible commentators, Rashi, in cursive rabbinic type. The publisher, "who organized the entire`enterprise as well as financed it with his own silver and gold," was Joseph ben Abraham Caravita. The printer was Abraham ben Hayyim de Tintori of Pesara, "who had no rival in all the world as a master of the printer's craft." The editor was Yosef Hayyim ben Aaron of Strasbourg, from whom we derive this information about his colleagues, and who promises, "he who will purchase of these volumes will be pleased, and he who will study diligently of them will be blessed with progeny and length of days."

The Library's copy is printed on vellum and has the distinction of having once belonged to Giovanni Bernardo De Rossi (1742–1831), the Italian Christian Hebraist and bibliographer. His library of Jewish literature, of 1,432 manuscripts and 1,442 printed books (including unique incunabula) now in the Palatine library in Parma, is one of the most valuable ever assembled. De Rossi's signature appears on the last leaf.

Lisbon's First Book: A Hebrew Pentateuch Commentary

The year 1476, which saw the beginning of the final suppression of the Jews of Spain, to culminate in their expulsion from the kingdom in 1492, also saw the publication of the first Hebrew book in that country, Rashi's commentary on the Torah, printed in Guadalajara by Solomon ibn Alkabez. The Golden Age of the Jews in Spain had long since lost its glitter, but cultural creativity, now given expression through the newest of cultural tools, the printing press, continued to add to the life of the spirit. In Montalban, Toledo, Zamora and Hijar, as well as in Guadalajara, books of the Bible, volumes of the Talmud, editions of the Codes, and devotional works were published and have survived. It is presumed that as many works as survived perished without trace or memory. The Library's monument of that daring spiritual enterprise is a fine copy in handsome cursive type of a volume of the Code of Law of Jacob ben Asher (1270(?)–1340), *Tur Yoreh Deah,* published in Hijar in 1487, five years before the Expulsion.

The Library also has a copy of the Book of Judges published in Leiria, Portugal, in 1494, three years before the expulsion of all Jews from that kingdom. Printing had been introduced to Portugal in 1487 by the publication of the Pentateuch with the Onkeles Aramaic translation by Don Samuel Porteiro, in the southern Portuguese town of Faro. This was followed by an edition of the Talmud, of which only shreds of twenty-two tractates remain, the Inquisition having ordered their destruction. The first book printed in Lisbon was a Hebrew book: the *Commentary on the Pentateuch* of Moses ben Nahman (Nachmanides) (1194–1270), published by Eliezer Toledano in 1489. The Library's fine copy of this work is yet another of its distinguished Judaic firsts.

The Library also owns a copy of Lisbon's second Hebrew book, published about a half year after the first. *Abudarham,* a commentary on the prayers, was written in 1340 in Seville by David ben Yosef Abudarham because, he explains, "the customs connected to prayer vary from country to country, and most people neither know the correct ritual nor understand its meaning."

First Book in Africa

In 1497, after a harsh campaign by king and Church to convert Portuguese Jewry to Christianity, the choice offered to Jews was apostasy or exile. Among those who chose the latter were Samuel ben Isaac Nedivot and his son Isaac, who had apparently learned printing in the publishing house of Eliezer Toledano in Lisbon. After they were able at last to reestablish themselves in Fez, Morocco, where many Spanish and Portuguese Jews had found haven, they returned to their craft because by 1515 the time and circumstances seemed propitious. The Jewish community of the city had

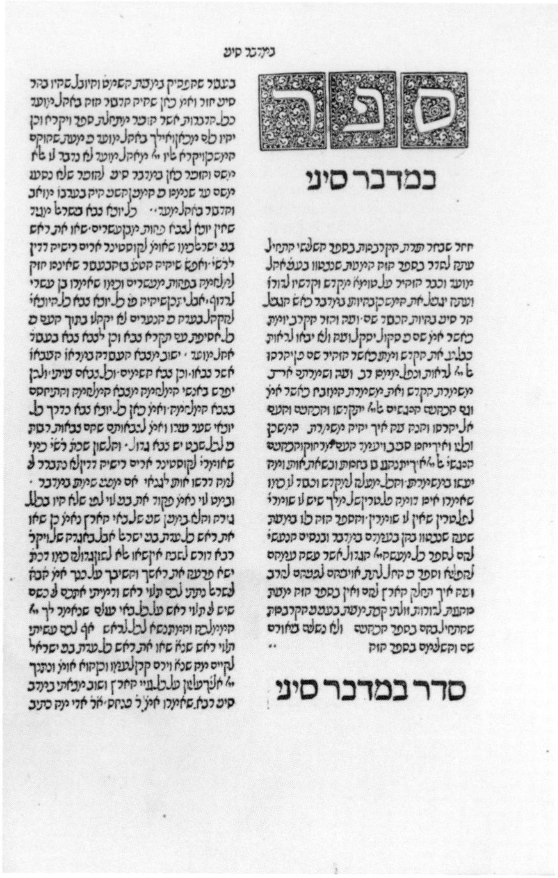

The first book printed in any language in Portugal's capital city, Lisbon, was a Hebrew book, the *Commentary on the Pentateuch* by Moses ben Nahman (Nachmanides). It was published by Eliezer Toledano in 1489, only three years before the expulsion of the Jews from Spain and only eight years before their expulsion from Portugal. The volume is open to the beginning of the commentary on *Ba-Midbar,* the *Book of Numbers.*

The Library also has a copy of Lisbon's second Hebrew book, *Abudarham,* a commentary on the Hebrew liturgy.

Moses ben Nahman, *Perush ha-Torah,* Lisbon, 1489.
Hebraic Section.

The first book printed in any language on the African continent is this volume in Hebrew dealing with Hebrew liturgy. It was printed in Fez, Morocco, in 1516, and is an almost exact copy of the *Abudarham* published in Lisbon twenty-seven years earlier. Samuel Nedivot and his son Isaac, who had learned the craft in Portugal, found haven in Fez after the expulsion of the Jews from Portugal, and established a Hebrew press there "to produce books beyond number . . ."

David ben Yosef Abudarham, *Abudarham,* Fez, 1516.
Hebraic Section.

increased to some ten thousand. The presses of the Iberian peninsula having closed down decades earlier, and those of Italy having not yet risen to eminence, the need for books was great. The father and son possessed the required skills, and in 1516 they published their first book, an exact copy of the *Abudarham* which they had initially helped to produce in Lisbon in 1489, twenty-seven years earlier. The only changes are in the colophon, which now celebrates the holy labors of "the honored and pious Samuel . . . and his learned and wise son Isaac, whose desire it is to produce books beyond number for all to study and read . . . may God reward them for their beneficence . . . and in their days may we see redemption . . . [and alluding to the contents of the published volume] then we will sing a new song in the house of God."

The printed *Abudarham* was the first book in any language printed on the African continent. In the Introduction, the publishers complain that they encountered great difficulty in obtaining paper because the Spanish government ordered that paper not be sold to them. But they persisted and in the course of a decade were able to print fifteen books. As the Library's copy bears witness, the prayerful resolve expressed in the colophon frustrated the malevolence of the "evil empire."

First Book in the Holy Land

Another wandering printer seeking asylum produced another first, the first book printed in the Holy Land. In 1573 Eliezer ben Isaac Ashkenazi of Prague, a printer of Hebrew books in Lublin, set out for the Holy Land. After three years plying his trade in Constantinople, he arrived in Safed. In the sixteenth century, Safed was one of the most spiritually creative Jewish cities in the world. The site of a great revival of mysticism through the brief but electrifying presence there of Isaac Luria (the Ari) (1534–1572), it was also the home of Joseph Caro (1488–1575), author of the authoritative code of Jewish law, the *Shulhan Aruch.* These were but two of a large group of scholars whose influence throughout the Jewish world gave Safed a place of centrality in Jewish spiritual life and culture.

A goodly number of its residents were Jewish exiles from Spain and Portugal, or the children of exiles, who brought to the community manufacturing and commercial skills as well as culture. The town seemed an ideal place for a Hebrew printing establishment and the Ashkenazi of Prague quickly found a namesake—Abraham ben Isaac Ashkenazi, whom he had met in Constantinople—to provide funds for his venture. They felt sure that Jews the world over would want holy books printed in the Holy Land, but only six books appeared, three in 1577–1580 and three more in 1587, all by Safed authors.

The first of these was *Lekah Tov* (1577), a commentary on the Book of Esther, by Yom Tov Zahalon (1559–after 1638), who later served as em-

ע״י השותפים אברהם בכר יצחק ואליעזר בכר יצחק אשכנזים

Eliezer ben Isaac Ashkenazi of Prague, an itinerant printer of Hebrew books, arrived in Safed in 1576, after plying his trade in Lublin and Constantinople, and there set up his press, which issued six books, all by Safed authors. The first, published in 1577, *Lekah Tov,* a commentary on the Book of Esther by Yom Tov Zahalon, is also the first book printed in the Land of Israel. The volume's final page bears a woodcut of the Holy Temple—a copy of the printer's mark used by Marco Giustiniani in Venice 1545–52—with the legend "Great will be the glory of this house . . . Saith the Lord of Hosts" (Haggai, 2:9). The colophon states that the volume was completed on the fourth day of Tishri 5338 (1577).

Yom Tov Zahalon, *Lekah Tov,* Safed, 1577. Hebraic Section.

issary for the community of Safed to Italy, Holland, Egypt, and Turkey. In his introduction he expresses his delight in the founding of a press in this Holy City of the Holy Land and urges authors to have their works printed there. But he urged to no avail. Even the very large type in which the name of the city was set on the title page of the second book published did not help. For two hundred and forty-five years after this valiant attempt, no Hebrew book was published in the Holy Land until 1832, when Israel Bak (1797–1874) established a Hebrew press once more in Safed. Again only six books were published there, before he reestablished his printing house in Jerusalem in 1841.

First Hasidic Book

No Jewish religious movement in modern times has had such instant success and lasting influence as Hasidism. Begun in the middle of the eighteenth century by a coterie of disciples of the charismatic figure of Israel Baal Shem Tov (1608–1760), Hasidism became a force powerful enough to seriously challenge the ways of the staid religious establishment in Eastern Europe. Within a century, its emphasis on God's immanence in the world, in the heart of man, and in every aspect of nature; its espousal of ecstatic worship of the Heavenly Loving Father; and its democratization of salvation by proclaiming sincere piety rather than learning as the more certain road to God won the allegiance of half of East Europe's Jews and evoked both admiration and hostility among the more "enlightened" Jewry of the West. Hasidism remains a religious movement of strength and influence today, a central force in the life of its adherents, and a stimulus to Jewish literary and artistic creativity.

To this day, the first published Hasidic book, *Sefer Toldot Yaakov Yosef* by Yaakov Yosef ben Zevi ha-Kohen Katz of Polonoye (Korets, 1780), has remained the single most important work in the entire hasidic literature. A volume of homilies on the Pentateuch, it is a harsh polemic against the religious leadership of its day, which he accuses of disenfranchising unlettered common folk, pious and God-loving as they might be, from fullest communion with the Heavenly Father. God, the religious teachers maintained, could be approached only by meticulously observant, gifted scholars. The book vividly espouses the vital religious way of Hasidism, with its promise of nearness to God for "all who call upon Him in truth." The significance of this volume, Samuel H. Dresner explains in his *The Zaddik,* is that it is "the main source for the teachings of the Baal Shem Tov . . . [for] we have nothing from [his] own pen (save for a few letters). What Rabbi Yaakov Yosef did was to devotedly and scrupulously record the teachings of his master and to elucidate and develop them through his own thinking in a manner so rich and fruitful that what had been the treasured property of the few was made available to all."

According to Hasidic tradition the book sold but few copies and was harshly suppressed, even put to the torch in a number of communities. The remaining copies were so sought after for study that they "were devoured by eager spirits with such appetite that they were literally worn to pieces." A complete copy in good condition, such as the one now in the Library of Congress, is a great rarity.

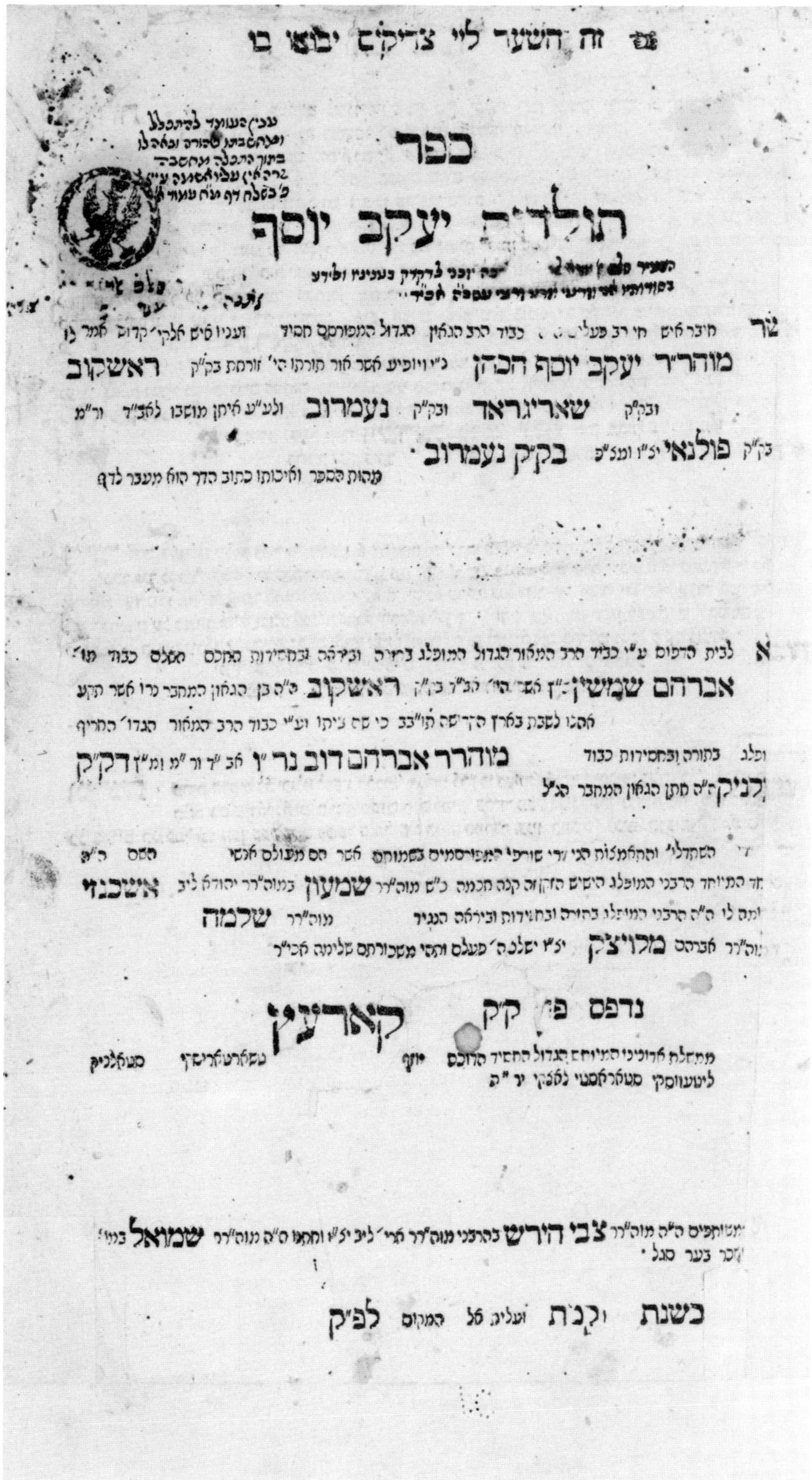
זה השער לה' צדיקים יבאו בו

ספר

תולדות יעקב יוסף

מוהר"ר יעקב יוסף הכהן

ראשקוב

שאריגראד

נעמרוב

פולנאי

בק"ק נעמרוב

אברהם שמשון

ראשקוב

מוהרר אברהם דוב

שמעון

אשכנזי

שלמה

מלוציק

נדפס פה ק"ק קארעץ

צבי הירש

שמואל

בשנת

לפ"ק

Although the main vehicle for the transmission of the doctrine and lore of the pietistic movement, Hasidism, has been the spoken word, it has nevertheless produced a distinguished literature in print. No single work has surpassed in importance its first published book, *Sefer Toldot Yaakov Yosef,* printed in Korets more than two centuries ago. Its author was Yaakov Yosef ben Zevi ha-Kohen Katz, rabbi of the community of Polonnoye, and it was brought to press by his son and son-in-law. The chief significance of the volume is that it is the most authentic source for the teachings of the movement's founder, Israel Baal Shem Tov, who left no published work.

Yaakov Yosef Katz, *Sefer Toldot Yaakov Yosef,* Korets, 1780.
Hebraic Section.

Twice seven firsts open the portals to the Judaic treasures in the Library of Congress, seven works chosen by the Library's Founding Father, and seven volumes of overarching importance and rarity in the entire realm of Judaica.

A megillah scroll (The Book of Esther) is read on the eve and morning of the Festival of Purim. The Library's scroll is unusual for its age, size, and calligraphy: late fourteenth- or early fifteenth-century; thirty-two inches high, its letters three-fourths of an inch; and its calligraphy suggests a Gothic provenance, Central or Southern Germany. One can only surmise how a scroll of such size could have been used comfortably, for it is difficult for an individual to handle. Perhaps it was meant to be read by a group of individuals or an entire small community—the reader intoning, the rest following the text.

Ashkenazi Megillah Scroll, fourteenth-fifteenth centuries. Hebraic Section.

The most sacred Jewish ritual object is the Torah Scroll, the Five Books of Moses inscribed by hand on the specially prepared skin of a kosher animal. In the Ashkenazi tradition the scribe writes with a quill on parchment; the Sefardi scribe uses a reed to write on parchment or leather. This scroll is a Sefardi scroll, its material is fine golden-hued doe skin, and it fulfills the Talmudic injunction that a Torah Scroll be "written in good ink with a fine pen by an expert sofer [scribe]." Nothing is permitted on the scroll other than the biblical text, written without the vowel points. It is therefore difficult to ascertain the date or place of its fashioning.

Sefardi Torah Scroll, eighteenth century (?). Hebraic Section.

2

THE BOOK OF THE PEOPLE OF THE BOOK

SCROLLS

BEFORE THE BOOK, THERE was the scroll. The book, in the form of a codex, where pages are bound together, is easier to handle. One can turn to desired passages without unrolling and seeking. Books are also much easier to produce and to store, whether in manuscript or in print, so, in the course of time, the book replaced the scroll, but in Jewish usage not completely. The scroll was retained for use in synagogue worship: the reading of the Pentateuch on Sabbath and holidays and the weekday services on Monday and Thursday may be done only from a Torah Scroll. The reading of the Book of Esther on the eve and morning of the Festival of Purim is done from a scroll called Megillat Esther, or just Megillah, the Hebrew for scroll.*

Every detail in the preparation of a Torah Scroll is prescribed by law. "Prepare a beautiful *Sefer Torah*" the Talmud admonishes, "written in good ink with a fine pen by an expert *sofer* [scribe]." Only the skin (parchment) of a kosher animal may be used. The ink may not contain metal, nor may the scroll be written with a metal instrument, for metal can be forged into weapons which take life while the Torah gives life. Only the words of the Torah may be inscribed on the scroll: neither instructions, nor commentary, nor illustrations, nor illuminations are permitted. The scribe must be learned and pious and must exert the greatest care in assuring correctness, copying from an examined text, not from memory. He must pronounce every word before writing it, and must make sure that his letters are well formed and that there is sufficient space between them, "so that even an ordinary school boy" can readily distinguish between even similar letters. Before writing the name of God, the scribe must state, "My intention is now to write the Holy Name"; then he must inscribe it without interruption. Should he err, he may not erase the mistake; the whole sheet must be put away, to await later reverential interment in consecrated earth. Rabbi Ishmael admonished a scribe, "be careful in thy work, as it is heavenly work, lest thou err in omitting or adding one iota, and so cause the destruction of the whole world."

*See the description of the Library's illuminated Megillah on pp. 90–92.

There is therefore remarkable uniformity in copies of the Torah scrolls, the only differences being in the size of the scrolls, the number of lines, the calligraphy, and whether the scroll is made of parchment or leather. In the Ashkenazi community (Jews living in Christian lands or their descendants), the Torah is written on parchment in letters where horizontal strokes are broad and vertical strokes thin. In Sefardi communities (Jews living in Islamic lands or their descendants), the Torah scroll is often made of leather and the letters are of uniform thickness. The scroll in the Library of Congress is a superb example of a Sefardi Torah. Its supple leather is golden in hue; the jet-black ink of the expertly fashioned letters is in an extraordinary state of preservation, which makes this a distinguished example of the North African Torah scrolls produced in the seventeenth through the nineteenth centuries.

The Library's Megillat Esther (Esther Scroll) is a Hebrew manuscript of great rarity, unique for its age, size, and calligraphy. Written in the fourteenth or possibly the fifteenth century, it is as early a Megillat Esther as is known. Particularly distinguished is its calligraphy, as majestic Ashkenazi letters as have ever been inscribed. In height of scroll (thirty-two inches) and height of letter (three-fourths of an inch) it is unsurpassed.

Its very size poses a problem. Traditionally, when the Megillah is read in the synagogue, as it is unrolled it is folded so as to look like a letter, to recall the epistle sent by Mordecai "to all the Jews in all the lands . . . near and far, to observe . . . the days which were turned from mourning to holiday . . ." (Esther IX:22). Not only does the weight of this scroll make it difficult to handle, its size makes it even harder to fold. The large Ashkenazi megillot rarely reach two feet in height, and their letters, generally one-quarter of an inch in height, make for a far shorter scroll which is much lighter and easier to handle than the Library's. Why then a megillah so grand in size?

The size of this megillah scroll, especially the size of the letters, suggests a medieval antiphonary, one of those great liturgical manuscripts of the Middle Ages, whose bold Gothic letters were made large enough for all the choir to see. The church service was pulpit centered; synagogue worship was and is congregation centered. Why not then a megillah with words large enough for all the congregation to see as it was being read, a fulfillment of the blessing which precedes its reading "on the *reading* of the *megillah.*" Thus, all the congregation, and especially those individuals who could not afford a megillah of their own, could fully carry out the injunction "to read." The pious creator of this great megillah wrought his work as an expression of gratitude to the Heavenly Father for saving His own Chosen People "in the days of old, in this season." Year after year, a congregation of Jews in the ghetto of some medieval city, or in some isolated Gothic village, found heart and new hope in the tale they read in this, their treasured Esther Scroll.

HEBREW BIBLES

The great Bibles written and printed in all the languages of Western man were cherished for their sanctity and admired for their beauty. The Torah and megillah scrolls of the synagogue were essential tools of worship. The Hebrew Bibles, most often printed with commentaries framing the text (the more the better), were the vehicles which took man to an enterprise above worship—study. Diligent study, aided and directed by spiritual giants of the past, revealed God's will to man and unfolded the blueprint of His kingdom on earth. Study of the Bible called for the engagement of the student with one or more of the classical commentators: Solomon ben Isaac (1040–1105) called Rashi, who utilized the Midrashic literature and emphasized moral instruction; Moses ben Nahman, called Ramban and Nachmanides (1194–1270), who laced his interpretations with mysticism; Levi ben Gershom, the Ralbag or Gersonides (1288–1344), whose bent was to philosophy and theology; Abraham Ibn Ezra (1089–1164), a grammarian with a critical turn of mind whose comments sowed the seeds for the critical study of the Bible; or David Kimhi (1160[?]–1235), exponent of philological analysis.

Arguably, the first Hebrew book printed was the Rome (c. 1469–73) edition of the commentary on the Torah of Nahmanides, and the first dated Hebrew book was Rashi's commentary on the Torah, printed in the small Italian town of Reggio di Calabria in 1475. Eleven of the Library's Hebrew incunabula are biblical texts or commentaries: Gersonides's commentary on the Torah, Mantua, 1476 (two copies); Kimhi's on the Psalms, Bologna(?) 1477; Gersonides's on Job, Ferrara, 1477; Rashi's on the Pentateuch, Bologna, 1482; Kimhi's on the Former Prophets, 1485, and the Latter Prophets, 1486, in Soncino (three copies of the latter), his Psalms commentary, Naples, 1487; Nahmanides on the Pentateuch, Lisbon, 1489; Nahmanides on the same, Naples, 1490; a Lisbon, 1491, edition of the Pentateuch, with the translation of Onkelos and the commentary of Rashi; and the Book of Judges with Targum Jonathan and the commentaries of Kimhi and Gersonides, Leiria, 1494.

Each of these volumes, printed in Italy or on the Iberian peninsula, has survived not only the ravages of time and use, but also the destructive hand of the Inquisition in Portugal, the burning of the Hebrew books in the Papal states in the sixteenth century, and the Church censor's scrutiny and mutilation. Their mere survival, their rescue from enemies, again and again, is an uplifting lesson on the stubborn strength of the human spirit, aided on occasion by nature itself. Thus, the copy of the 1477 Psalms, *editio princeps* in Hebrew of any portion of the Bible, has come down to us in fine physical condition but heavily censored. Because Kimhi's commentary confronts the Christian claims of Christological foreshadowing in the Biblical text, the censor's pen crossed out every passage deemed offensive to the Faith. An owner of the censored copy later wrote the censored passages in on the margin. Time, which has its own will, also entered the fray fading the censor's ink almost to extinction, but preserving in almost perfect condition the printed text beneath.

Among the above-listed volumes are a number of significant firsts. The Bologna(?) 1477 Psalms is the first Hebrew book printed in that city, as are for their cities the 1487 Psalms of Naples and the Gersonides commentary on Job, 1477, of Ferrara.

In 1516, a wealthy Venetian, Daniel Bomberg who had been born in Antwerp, was granted the privilege of publishing Hebrew books in that city. Among the first he published was a folio edition of the entire Bible

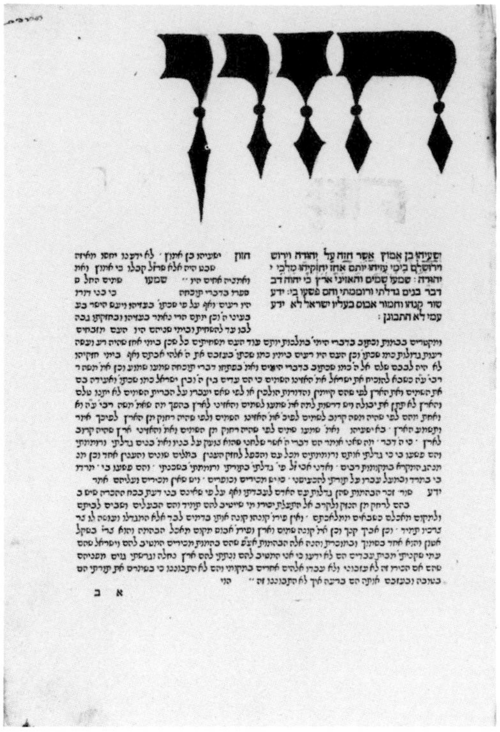

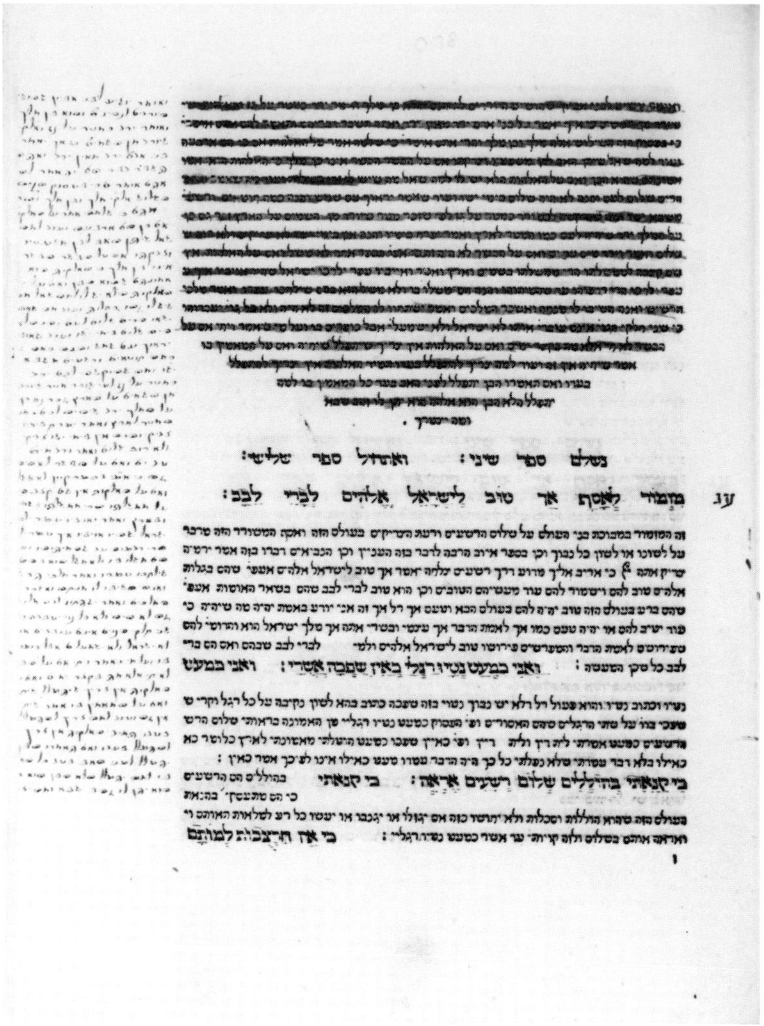

Above: No less than three censors examined this copy of *Nevi'im Ahronim* (Latter Prophets) with the commentary by David Kimhi, published by Joshua Solomon Soncino in 1486. We show the first page of the Book of Isaiah. The text is in square letters, the commentary in cursive. The large word at the top of the page, the first word of text, *Hazon* (The Vision), is in manuscript, space having been left by the printer for an artistic illumination to open the book, a provision usual in early printing. Similar space is allotted at the beginning of the other books of the Prophets included in this volume.

Nevi'im Ahronim, with Commentary by David Kimhi, Soncino, 1485–86.
Rare Book and Special Collections Division.

Above right: David Kimhi's Commentary on the Psalms put the censor on his alert and rarely escaped his heavy hand. This copy of the Bologna(?) 1477 edition of the Psalms and Commentary is heavily censored. But as we can see, what the Papal censor excised an early owner inserted in manuscript. Kimhi's comment at the end of Psalm 72 notes that Jesus could not have been the Messiah, since the mes-

with the leading commentaries, *Mikraot Gedolot* (Rabbinic Bible), which came off the press in 1516–17. Pope Leo's imprimatur was sought and granted, and Felix Pratensis, a monk born a Jew, was its editor. Bomberg published the edition because of growing interest in the Hebrew language and the Bible among learned Christians. As a good businessman, he quickly perceived that there was a substantial market for Hebrew texts among the Jews of Italy, whose numbers had been increased by an influx of Spanish and Portuguese Jewish exiles. The commentaries of Rashi, Kimhi, Nahmanides, and Gersonides attracted the Jewish clientele, but the editorship by an apostate and the blessing of the Pope made Jews avoid the edition, so Bomberg quickly published a quarto edition, without any mention of either editor or sponsor. Six years later in 1524, his second Rabbinic (i.e., with commentaries) Bible appeared. This time Bomberg emphasized that his printers were pious Jews, as was his scholarly editor. In time more than two hundred Hebrew books came off the Bomberg press, volumes of singular scholarly merit and typographical excellence.

Far larger numbers of Jewish exiles from the Iberian peninsula found haven in the Ottoman Empire than on the Italian peninsula. They brought a scholarly presence to Constantinople and established a great Jewish community in the port city of Salonica. In both cities presses were established which did much to make the Ottoman Empire a seat of Jewish

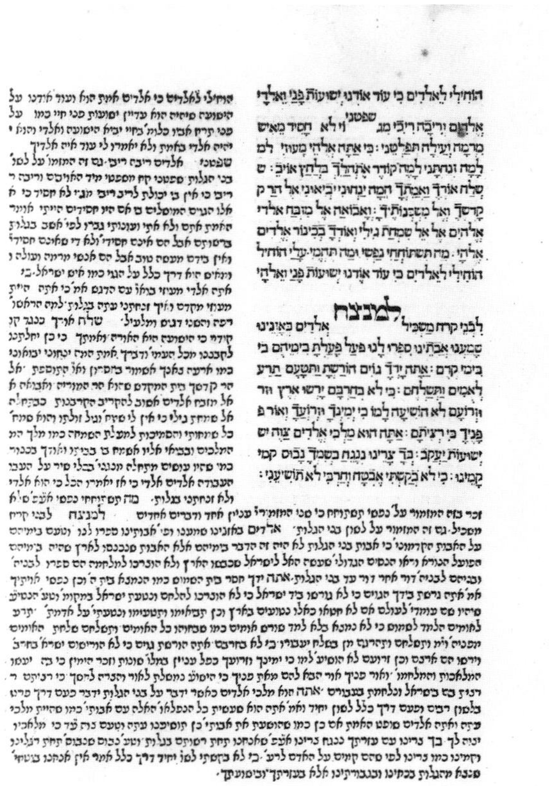

sianic prophecy that the Messiah would bring peace was not fulfilled; as Kimhi states, "there was no peace in the time of Jesus." Beginning with the sixteenth century, Jewish publishers exercised self-censorship when printing the Kimhi Commentary.

Psalms, with Commentary by David Kimhi, Bologna(?), August 29, 1477.
Hebraic Section.

Joseph ben Jacob of Gunzenhausen, a town in Southern Germany, arrived with his son Azriel in Naples in 1486 and soon set up a Hebrew printing house there. They were among a good number of Jews from other cities in Italy and the Iberian Peninsula, who were attracted to that port city by the welcome extended by King Ferdinand I. The first of the twelve volumes published by the Gunzenhausens, father, son and daughter, was the Psalms, again as in Bologna, with the Commentary of David Kimhi. In this edition, however, the text is separated from the Commentary, not only by different typography, but by the organization of the page as well. It is worthy of note that the recent arrivals felt secure enough in their new home to publish Kimhi's Commentary.

Psalms, with Commentary by David Kimhi, Naples, 4th day in Nisan, 5247 (1487).
Hebraic Section.

The first Rabbinic Bible, i.e., the biblical text accompanied by a number of commentaries, was published by the greatest of Hebrew printers in the sixteenth century, Daniel Bomberg, a Christian from Antwerp, who set up his Hebrew press in Venice in 1515 and published some 230 works. Published in 1517 and edited by the apostate Felix Pratensis who dedicated it to Pope Leo X, it apparently did not attract the anticipated Jewish audience, hence a new edition, seven years later, edited by Jacob ben Hayim, who wisely chose to print the Masoretic text. The latter edition became the standard for all future printings of the Hebrew Bible. It is opened to the end of the Book of Samuel and the first verses of the Book of Kings.

Mikraot Gedolot, 4 volumes, Venice, 1516–17.
Hebraic Section.

The greatest of Hebrew bibliographers, Moritz Steinschneider, called this edition of the Pentateuch "of highest rarity." The page before us, the opening verses of Deuteronomy, has the text in the center in large square letters. Next to it is the Aramaic translation by Onkeles. At the outer margin is the commentary of Nachmanides, and on the inner, the commentary of Rashi above, and that of Abraham Ibn Ezra below. It was published in two editions, one for the Sefardi community, the other for the Karaite. The Library's copy is for the former.

Perush ha-Torah (Commentary on the Torah), Constantinople, 1522.
Hebraic Section.

Facing page: The typographical artistry of Guillaume Le Bé and the printing skill of the Estienne family, Royal Printers in Paris, combined to fashion this work of singular typographical distinction. The twenty-four parts of the Hebrew Bible, bound in four volumes in green morocco for Charles III, Cardinal of Bourbon, have come down in pristine condition. Now a part of the Lessing J. Rosenwald Collection, they were formerly owned by Mortimer J. Schiff, son of Jacob H. Schiff, who presented two Deinard Hebraica Collections to the Library of Congress.

Torah, Nevi'im, Ketubim (Torah, Prophets, Writings), Paris, 1539–44.
Rare Book and Special Collections Division, Rosenwald Collection.

scholarship. In 1522 a fine edition of the Pentateuch, with the classic commentaries *Perush ha-Torah le-Rabi Moshe bar Nachman,* was published in Constantinople. What is of particular interest is that both the biblical text and the Onkelos Aramaic translation are not only vocalized but have cantillation notations as well. The doyen of Hebrew bibliographers, Moritz Steinschneider, accords it the accolade *summae raritatis.* The Library also has a copy of the Psalms with commentary, printed in the same year in Salonica, which is equally rare.

The most beautiful Hebrew Bible published in the sixteenth century is Robert Estienne's 1539–44 edition, printed in Paris. For five years Estienne had been the king's printer for Hebrew, and this edition is regal indeed. The Library's copy came with the Rosenwald Collection and is in pristine condition. One marvels not only at the beauty of the Le Bé type and the symmetry of the printed page, but at the whiteness of the paper and the jet-black type as well. What adds further interest to this set of volumes is that they bear the ownership plates of Mortimer Schiff, bibliophile son of philanthropist Jacob H. Schiff, who acquired two Deinard Collections of Hebraic imprints for the Library of Congress.

Of equal interest, but for quite another reason, is the Elias Hutter Hebrew Bible, Hamburg, 1587. Hutter's concern was neither for correctness of text nor beauty of typography, though he succeeded in both. His was a more practical, scholarly mission—to make the Hebrew Bible more readily accessible to the student. He therefore used two forms of type—a solid letter for the root and a hollow letter for the prefixes and suffixes, which give the page an aesthetically pleasing and subtle shading. Handsome indeed are both the engraved title page and the adorned introduction. The Library's copy is enhanced by a fine binding, as well as vellum marker tabs attached to the title pages of the individual biblical books.

It is not easy to choose among the many notable seventeenth-century editions of the Hebrew Bible, but certainly the 1667 edition of Amsterdam's famed printer, Joseph Athias, is "first among equals." The edition is justly esteemed for the correctness of its text and the distinction of its typography. For over two centuries, its text was the standard, and for almost as long, books printed in a variety of European cities carried the boast, "printed in Amsterdam type." Born into a Marrano family (Jews forced to adopt Christianity in Spain or Portugal—or their descendants—who chose to secretly cling to the ancestral faith and observe as much as possible its commandments) in Cordova in 1635, Athias fled to Hamburg as a youth so he might openly practice his religion. In 1658, now a well-to-do resident of Amsterdam, he became a publisher of books. His press soon grew into one of the leading ones in that great publishing city, printing books in Hebrew, Dutch, and Latin, and some one million English Bibles for England and Scotland. His finest production was a Hebrew Bible, painstakingly edited by the University of Leyden's Professor of Hebrew, Johannes Leusden, and produced with such care and artistry that, upon its publication in 1661, Athias was elected to the Amsterdam printer's guild—an unprecedented honor for a Jew. For its second improved edition which appeared in 1667, the Dutch government presented him with a gold medal and chain. Athias meant this Bible for both Jews and Christians. His own status as a leading member of the Jewish community and a printer of sumptuous Hebrew prayer books assured its acceptance by Jews; Leusden's

בראשית

אשר נדפס על ידי רוברטוס סטפ״נוס יצ״ו בשנת תשע ועשרים למלך האדיר
אדונינו המלך פרנציסקוס יר״ה היא שנת ש״ג לפ״ק
פה פאריש העיר הגדולה והאם בצרפת :

Liber Genesis.

PARISIIS.

Ex officina Roberti Stephani, typographi Regii.

M. D. XLIII.

עמי עשו

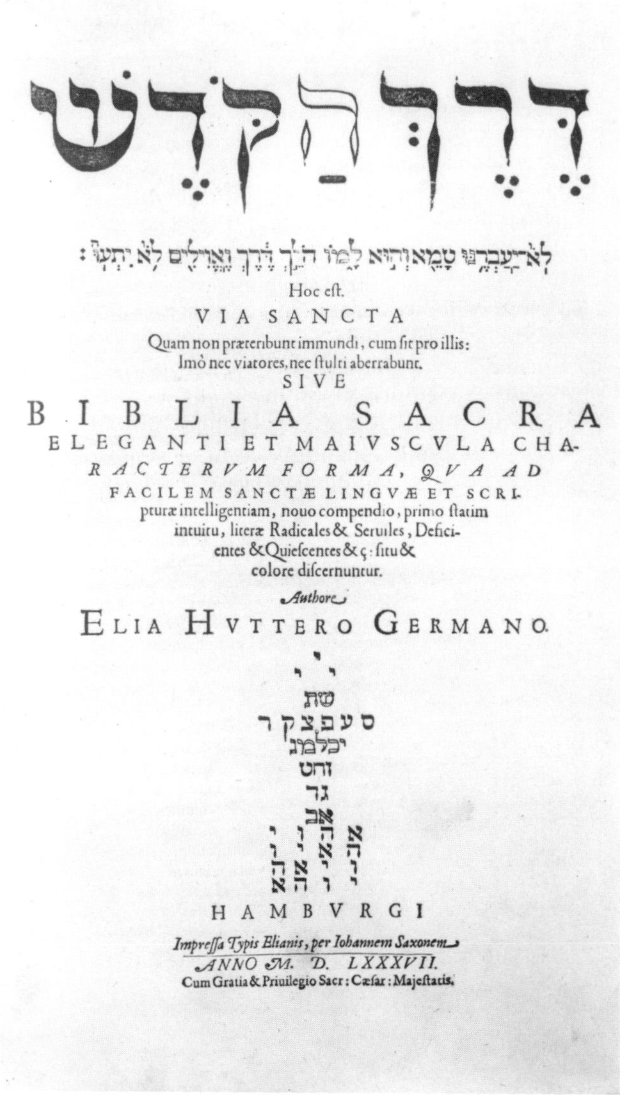

דֶּרֶךְ הַקֹּדֶשׁ

לֹא־יַעַבְרֶנּוּ טָמֵא וְהוּא לָמוֹ הֹלֵךְ דֶּרֶךְ וֶאֱוִילִים לֹא יִתְעוּ׃

Hoc est.

VIA SANCTA

Quam non prætcribunt immundi, cum sit pro illis: Imò nec viatores, nec stulti aberrabunt.

SIVE

BIBLIA SACRA

ELEGANTI ET MAIVSCVLA CHARACTERVM FORMA, QVA AD FACILEM SANCTÆ LINGVÆ ET SCRIPturæ intelligentiam, nouo compendio, primo statim intuitu, literæ Radicales & Seruiles, Deficientes & Quiescentes & c. situ & colore discernuntur.

Authore

ELIA HVTTERO GERMANO.

HAMBVRGI

Impressa Typis Elianis, per Iohannem Saxonem

ANNO M. D. LXXXVII.

Cum Gratia & Priuilegio Sacr: Cæsar: Majestatis.

The Hutter Bible was designed to serve the student of the Hebrew language as well as the student of the Bible. Shown here are the title page from the 1587 edition of Elias Hutter's Bible as well as the engraved opening page from the 1603 reissue of that work. Note the solid and hollowed-out Hebrew letters on the title page; the solid type signifies the root letters of the word, while the hollow type is used to indicate prefixes and suffixes.

Biblia Ebraea, Hamburg, Elias Hutter, 1587; reissued: Cologne, 1603.
Hebraic Section.

name, prominently featured on the engraved title page, attracted Christians. In the center of the title page stands the rampant sword-brandishing Netherland lion, and on the top and bottom of the engraving appear the biblical verses:

And this is the law which Moses set before the children of Israel. (Deut. IV:44)
Moses commanded us a law, an inheritance of the congregation of Jacob. (Deut. XXXIII:4)
And the Lord said unto Moses: "Come up to Me unto the mount, and be there; and I will give thee the tables of stone, and the law and commandment, which I have written, that thou mayest teach them." (Exodus XXIV:12)

At the top, in bold black Hebrew letters inscribed on a field of effulgent light, is the name of God.*

During the nineteenth century, two editions of the *Humash* (Pentateuch) were printed in the same part of the world at about the same time. One is a splendid edition of the Five Books of Moses in Hebrew with a Turkish Tatar translation in parallel columns, published by the Karaite community in Ortakoi, a town near Constantinople, 1832–35. The excellent condition of the Library's copy serves to emphasize the sumptuousness

*For more on Athias see pp. 71–72.

Facing page: The engraved title page of one of the most important editions of the Hebrew Bible, for which the publisher, Joseph Athias of Amsterdam, received a gold medal and chain from the Dutch government.

Hebrew Bible, Amsterdam, 1667.
Hebraic Section.

Bible O.T. Hebrew. 1667.
יהוה
Et ista lex quam posuit Moseh ad facies filiorum Israel. Deut. Cap. 4. 44.
Legem praecepit nobis Moseh haereditatem concioni Jahacob. Deut. C. 33. 4.
תורה נביאים וכתובים
BIBLIA HEBRAICA
ACCURATISSIMA,
Notis Hebraïcis
et Lemmatibus Latinis illustrata
A
JOHANNE LEUSDEN,
Philosophiæ Doctore, &
Linguæ Sanctæ in Academia
Ultrajectina Professore.
AMSTELODAMI,
Typis et sumptibus
JOSEPHI ATHIAS.
Anno. CIↃ IↃC LXVII.
CONCORDIA RES PARVÆ CRESCUNT

of the edition—the paper, crisp and strong, of the finest linen; the Hebrew letters beautifully designed and expertly cut; the page design featuring wide margins.

The Karaites, *B'nai Mikra* (Children of Scripture), are a Jewish sect which had its beginnings in the eighth century. The sect's chief characteristic is that it accepts the authority of the Bible but rejects the Talmudic rabbinic tradition. At its beginnings, Karaism constituted a serious challenge to traditional rabbinic Judaism, but as time went on its attraction receded. Its numbers remained small, concentrated in a few centers in Egypt, Turkey, Syria, the Crimea, and Lithuania. If the main body of Jews and the Karaites differed in matters of faith, they shared a common fate, until the incorporation of the Crimea and Lithuania into the Russian Empire at the end of the eighteenth century, when the situation began to change. In 1795, the Empress Catherine II permitted the Karaites to purchase land and relieved them of the double taxation imposed upon other Jews. In 1827, Karaites were exempted from the dreaded military draft, which plucked Jewish children from their families for twenty-five years and more of distant military service. It was obvious to the Karaites that it would be to their advantage to distance themselves as far as possible from other Jews. In memoranda to the Czarist government the Karaites consequently stressed their fundamental difference from other Jews, in belief

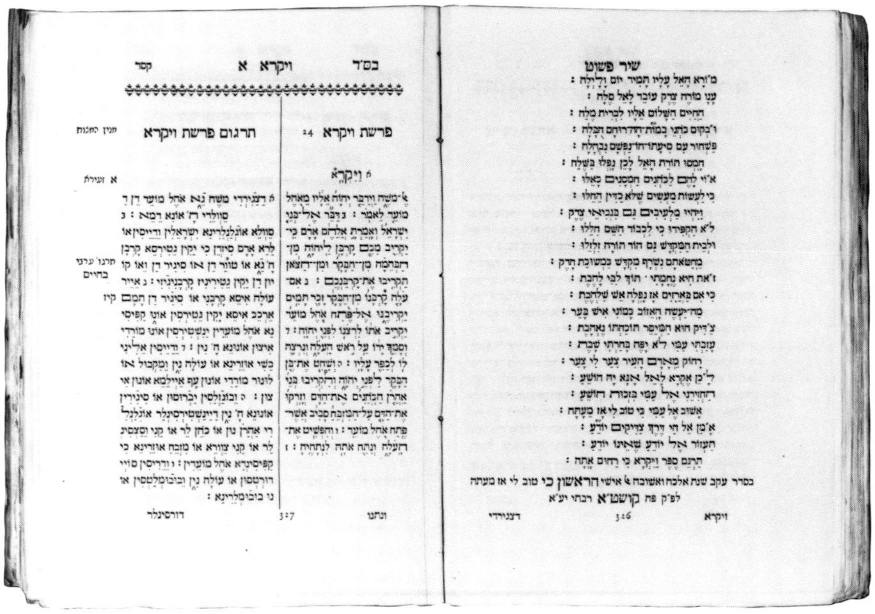

Twelve leaders of the Karaite community joined in sponsoring the publication of this *Humash* with Tartar translation, printed by Arav Oglo and sons in Ortakoi (near Constantinople), 1832–35. It appeared without a title page, and each of the Five Books of Moses is introduced by poems written by the copy editors and translators, Abraham ben Shmuel, Yitzhak ben Shmuel Kohen, and Simha ben Yosef Agiz. We see a section of the poem introducing the Book of Leviticus and the opening verses of text and translation.

Hamishah Humshe Torah (The Five Books of the Torah), Ortakoi, 1832–35.
Hebraic Section.

and in history, arguing that they were not Jews but "Russian Karaites of the Old Testament Faith," which became their official designation. In 1840 they were granted equality of status with the Moslems, and in 1863 with native Russians.

During the first decades of the nineteenth century, Russian Karaites increased in number as well as in economic well-being, status, and self esteem. What better way to mark and celebrate their ascent than to publish a splendid edition of the Torah by and for the "Children of Scripture." Appearing at the height of the Karaites' campaign to distance themselves from the Jews, the publication would serve that end as well. The Tatar translation was obviously for Karaites only. The group of Karaite scholars who edited the text and prepared the translation was headed by Abraham

Firkowitz (1786–1874), an antiquarian scholar and bibliographer who as a leader of the separation campaign wrote messages to the Czarist government and collected documents to bolster the Karaite position. On occasion he was not above doctoring the written record to support the Karaite claims. This *Humash* then is both an aesthetic creation and a political statement, declaring to the Czarist authorities: We share little with the Jews, no, not even the Bible. They have theirs, and we, like you Christians, have ours, this, our own Karaite *Humash*.

As we have noted, Hebrew printing in the Holy Land began in Safed in 1577. Six books and a few years later it came to an end. The end of the sixteenth century saw the decline of the flourishing Jewish community of that city of scholars and mystics. In the last decades of the eighteenth century and the first of the nineteenth, a small migration of some disciples of the Baal Shem Tov and some followers of the Gaon of Vilna restored to this Galilean city some of its earlier spiritual luster. Among those who arrived in their wake was one Israel Bak who came in 1831. In his native city, Berdichev in the Ukraine, he had published some thirty books; and now, in Safed, he reestablished publishing in the Holy Land.

First off the press, in 1832, was a Sefardi prayer book, the first Hebrew book printed in the Holy Land after a hiatus of 245 years. The publisher notes on the title page that the book contains some of the *Kavanot* (mystical statements of intentions of worship) of Safed's greatest luminary, Isaac Luria, and further assures that all of the workers engaged in this holy endeavour are pious Jews, and that prayers recited from a book printed in this holy city would be most efficacious. This was followed in 1833 by the *Book of Leviticus,* with the commentaries of Rashi and Hayim Joseph David Azulai, a favorite of Sefardi Jews. No traces remain of either *Genesis* or *Exodus,* if indeed they were ever published, but it is possible that they were destroyed during the peasant revolt against Muhammad Ali in 1834, in which Bak's press was destroyed and Bak himself was wounded. More likely only *Leviticus* was published, the first of a projected five-volume edition of the Pentateuch, because it was the custom to begin instruction of the *Humash* in the schools not with Genesis but with Leviticus. The school year began in the spring, when the Book of Leviticus was being read in the synagogue, and it made good sense to synchronize Bible study in the school with Bible reading in the synagogue.

Bak turned to agriculture but continued printing, even after the earthquake of 1837 devastated his shop. The Druze revolt in 1838 destroyed both his farm and press, and Bak departed for Jerusalem where, in 1841, he once again established his press, the first Hebrew press in Jerusalem.*

Among the many early Jerusalem imprints, the Library contains a fine copy of the rare *Sefer Hatakanot . . .* (The Book of Ordinances and Enactments and Customs . . . of the Holy City, Jerusalem), 1842. It was the second book printed there, but was the first in importance as the single most valuable source book for Jewish religious and communal life in that city. For thirty-three years, Bak continued to print books in Jerusalem, some 130 volumes in all, but he never completed the Pentateuch edition he had launched in Safed in 1833.

Exactly one hundred years later, in 1933 in Berlin, a society of Jewish bibliophiles, the *Soncino Gesellschaft der Freunde des jüdischen Buches,* after three years of labor, completed its *Humash.* It ranks among the most beau-

After a hiatus of 246 years, Israel Bak reestablished the Hebrew press in Eretz Yisrael, and he, like his predecessor, chose the city of Safed. His first published work, in 1832, was a Sefardi prayer book, the second, the Book of Leviticus, the first printing of a book of the Bible in the Holy Land. The title page describes the contents and the enterprise:

The Book of Leviticus, the third of the Five Books of the Torah with the commentary of Rashi, *Ba'al ha-Turim* (Jacob ben Asher), *Siftei Hahamim* (the Lips of the Wise) and . . . on the *Haftarot* and the Five Scrolls by the illustrious godly man, Hayim Yosef David Azulai . . . printed by the eminent and wise Israel Bak . . . of Berditchev. Here in Upper Galilee, in the holy city, Safed . . . under the sovereignty of the noble Mohammed Ali Basha (1833).

Book of Leviticus, Safed, 1833.
Hebraic Section.

*The St. James Press of the Armenian Patriarchate had been established in Jerusalem in 1833.

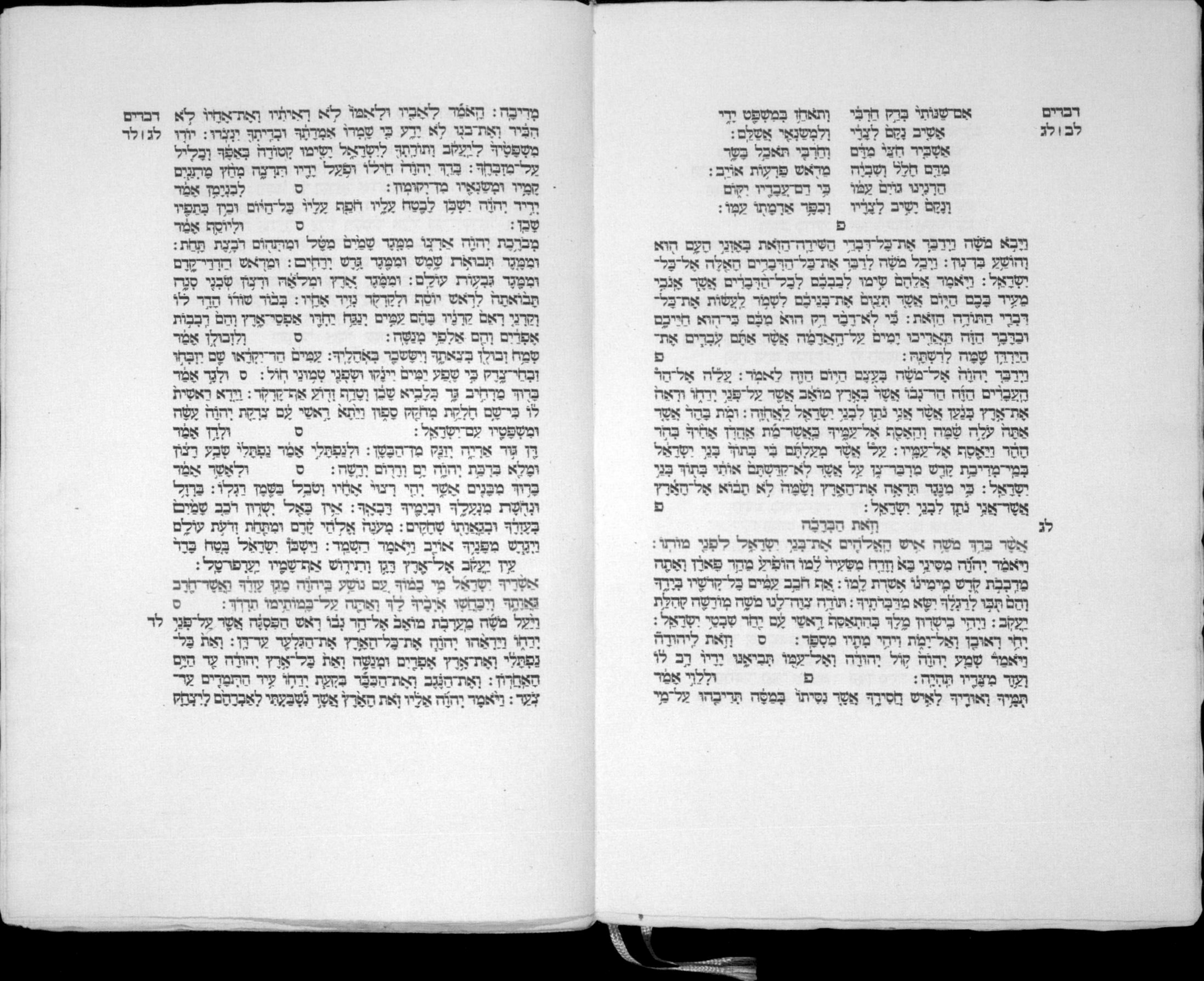

דברים לב׃לג

אם שנותי ברק חרבי ותאחז במשפט ידי
אשיב נקם לצרי ולמשנאי אשלם׃
אשכיר חצי מדם וחרבי תאכל בשר
מדם חלל ושביה מראש פרעות אויב׃
הרנינו גוים עמו כי דם עבדיו יקום
ונקם ישיב לצריו וכפר אדמתו עמו׃
פ

ויבא משה וידבר את כל דברי השירה הזאת באזני העם הוא והושע בן נון׃ ויכל משה לדבר את כל הדברים האלה אל כל ישראל׃ ויאמר אלהם שימו לבבכם לכל הדברים אשר אנכי מעיד בכם היום אשר תצום את בניכם לשמר לעשות את כל דברי התורה הזאת׃ כי לא דבר רק הוא מכם כי הוא חייכם ובדבר הזה תאריכו ימים על האדמה אשר אתם עברים את הירדן שמה לרשתה׃ פ

וידבר יהוה אל משה בעצם היום הזה לאמר׃ עלה אל הר העברים הזה הר נבו אשר בארץ מואב אשר על פני ירחו וראה את ארץ כנען אשר אני נתן לבני ישראל לאחזה׃ ומת בהר אשר אתה עלה שמה והאסף אל עמיך כאשר מת אהרן אחיך בהר ההר ויאסף אל עמיו׃ על אשר מעלתם בי בתוך בני ישראל במי מריבת קדש מדבר צן על אשר לא קדשתם אותי בתוך בני ישראל׃ כי מנגד תראה את הארץ ושמה לא תבוא אל הארץ אשר אני נתן לבני ישראל׃ פ

לג וזאת הברכה

אשר ברך משה איש האלהים את בני ישראל לפני מותו׃ ויאמר יהוה מסיני בא וזרח משעיר למו הופיע מהר פארן ואתה מרבבת קדש מימינו אשדת למו׃ אף חבב עמים כל קדשיו בידך והם תכו לרגלך ישא מדברתיך׃ תורה צוה לנו משה מורשה קהלת יעקב׃ ויהי בישרון מלך בהתאסף ראשי עם יחד שבטי ישראל׃ יחי ראובן ואל ימת ויהי מתיו מספר׃ ס וזאת ליהודה ויאמר שמע יהוה קול יהודה ואל עמו תביאנו ידיו רב לו ועזר מצריו תהיה׃ פ וללוי אמר תמיך ואוריך לאיש חסידך אשר נסיתו במסה תריבהו על מי

דברים לג׃לד

מריבה׃ האמר לאביו ולאמו לא ראיתיו ואת אחיו לא הכיר ואת בנו לא ידע כי שמרו אמרתך ובריתך ינצרו׃ יורו משפטיך ליעקב ותורתך לישראל ישימו קטורה באפך וכליל על מזבחך׃ ברך יהוה חילו ופעל ידיו תרצה מחץ מתנים קמיו ומשנאיו מן יקומון׃ ס לבנימן אמר ידיד יהוה ישכן לבטח עליו חפף עליו כל היום ובין כתפיו שכן׃ ס וליוסף אמר מברכת יהוה ארצו ממגד שמים מטל ומתהום רבצת תחת׃ וממגד תבואת שמש וממגד גרש ירחים׃ ומראש הררי קדם וממגד גבעות עולם׃ וממגד ארץ ומלאה ורצון שכני סנה תבואתה לראש יוסף ולקדקד נזיר אחיו׃ בכור שורו הדר לו וקרני ראם קרניו בהם עמים ינגח יחדו אפסי ארץ והם רבבות אפרים והם אלפי מנשה׃ ס ולזבולן אמר שמח זבולן בצאתך ויששכר באהליך׃ עמים הר יקראו שם יזבחו זבחי צדק כי שפע ימים יינקו ושפוני טמוני חול׃ ס ולגד אמר ברוך מרחיב גד כלביא שכן וטרף זרוע אף קדקד׃ וירא ראשית לו כי שם חלקת מחקק ספון ויתא ראשי עם צדקת יהוה עשה ומשפטיו עם ישראל׃ ס ולדן אמר דן גור אריה יזנק מן הבשן׃ ולנפתלי אמר נפתלי שבע רצון ומלא ברכת יהוה ים ודרום ירשה׃ ס ולאשר אמר ברוך מבנים אשר יהי רצוי אחיו וטבל בשמן רגלו׃ ברזל ונחשת מנעליך וכימיך דבאך׃ אין כאל ישרון רכב שמים בעזרך ובגאותו שחקים׃ מענה אלהי קדם ומתחת זרעת עולם ויגרש מפניך אויב ויאמר השמד׃ וישכן ישראל בטח בדד עין יעקב אל ארץ דגן ותירוש אף שמיו יערפו טל׃ אשריך ישראל מי כמוך עם נושע ביהוה מגן עזרך ואשר חרב גאותך ויכחשו איביך לך ואתה על במותימו תדרך׃ ס

לד ויעל משה מערבת מואב אל הר נבו ראש הפסגה אשר על פני ירחו ויראהו יהוה את כל הארץ את הגלעד עד דן׃ ואת כל נפתלי ואת ארץ אפרים ומנשה ואת כל ארץ יהודה עד הים האחרון׃ ואת הנגב ואת הככר בקעת ירחו עיר התמרים עד צער׃ ויאמר יהוה אליו זאת הארץ אשר נשבעתי לאברהם ליצחק

This triumph of Hebrew bookmaking—possibly the most beautiful printed Hebrew book—was projected as the first Jewish sponsored bibliophilic Hebrew Bible, by the society of Jewish bibliophiles in Germany, the *Soncinò Gesellschaft,* in 1928. In 1933, as the Pentateuch was being completed, Hitler came to power. The triumph of Nazism must have coincided with the printing of the last pages, for the printers were able to print in red the first and last verse of the Blessing of Moses, which concludes:

Your enemies shall dwindle away before you.
You shall tread upon their high place.

Hamishah Humshe Torah (The Five Books of the Torah), Berlin, 1933.

tiful Hebrew books ever printed. Founded in 1924, the Society was dedicated to typographic improvements of Jewish and Hebrew books, and it published volumes which were to serve as models of layout and typography. In 1928, the Society decided to publish "a monumental Hebrew Bible." As it proclaimed in a beautifully printed broadside issued on the 22nd of January of the following year, it was a matter of Jewish honor to undertake such an edition, as it had never been done before by Jews. The Officina Serpentis firm of E. W. Tiffenbach was to do this printing by hand. The leading type designer, Marcus Behmer, would cut a new type based on that of the 1526 Prague Haggadah. Two years later, members of the Society received as their annual memento a double-page prospectus of the first two pages of the Bible being produced for them in a limited edition of 850 copies printed on special hand-laid paper and six copies done on vellum.

Even the proof pages are of breathtaking beauty. The type is strong yet elegant. The first word is framed in the first letter, both set in an ornamented rectangle. The inner margin is doubled in size by the upper, trebled by the outer, and quadrupled by the lower to provide a classically proportioned frame for the single and doubled pages. The completed *Humash*, the second part of which was completed in 1933, surpassed the promise of the prospectus proof pages. As he slowly turned the pages, the German Jewish bibliophile must have found satisfaction in having participated in such a noble enterprise, and felt a deep sense of appreciation to the scholars and artists who had fashioned it; but when he came to its last pages, a shudder of apprehension intruded.

The apprehension was foreshadowed by the Society's memento for the year 1932: a printing in Aldus Hebrew type of the Ninety-second Psalm, the Psalm for the Sabbath Day, "It is good to give thanks to the Lord." The Psalm is printed in black, but two verses are in red: "For lo your enemies oh Lord, for lo your enemies shall perish, scattered shall be all the workers of iniquity." But the righteous "will be fruitful even in old age, blossoming in vigor." The last pages of the Soncino Gesellschaft Pentateuch are given over to the Blessing of Moses. Here again, only two verses are in red; the first and last of the Blessing.

> This is the blessing with which Moses
> the man of God blessed the children
> of Israel before his death. (Deut.33:1)
>
> Happy are you, O Israel! Who is like you
> A people saved by the Lord, who is
> The shield of your help,
> And the sword of your triumph!
> Your enemies shall dwindle away before you,
> And you shall tread upon their high places.
> (Deut. 33:29)

In 1932, the Nazis had gained their first victories at the polls; in 1933 the Nazis seized power in Germany and established the Third Reich.

The Soncino Gesellschaft Bible was never completed. The final pages of its completed *Humash* were both the cri de coeur of a dying community and the cry of faith of an Eternal People.

In 1937, the Nazi government of Prussia liquidated the Soncino Ge-

In 1947, the *Vaad Hatzala* (Rabbinical Committee of Rescue) published a Pentateuch with commentaries for the saved remnant which survived the Holocaust, then still in the Displaced Persons Camps. It was dedicated to:

His Honor, the President of the United States of America, Harry S. Truman. His courageous and kind words, his noble acts and deeds in behalf of our people have served as a ray of hope in this trying, troubled and most critical period of our people.

As the gold embossing on the leather cover indicates, this copy was presented to Gen. George C. Marshall.

Humash, Pentateuch, Munich, 1947.
Hebraic Section.

sellschaft. Ten years later, in 1947, a *Humash* was printed in Munich, dedicated by the *Vaad ha-Hatzalah,* the Rabbinical Committee of Rescue, to American President Harry S Truman. A special leather-bound copy with his name printed on its cover was sent to George C. Marshall, architect of the defeat of the Nazis. It is this copy which now rests in the Library of Congress.

In 1963, thirty years after publication of the *Humash* in Berlin, a bibliophilic printing of the whole Hebrew Bible, the Koren edition, was published in the ancient city of Jerusalem, in the new State of Israel.

THE BIBLE IN TRANSLATION

Only two books are on permanent exhibit in the Great Hall of the Library of Congress: a perfect copy of the Gutenberg Bible printed on vellum, one of only three in the world; and the last, and arguably the finest illuminated manuscript of the Bible, the Giant Bible of Mainz. Both of these bibliophilic treasures were produced in the same city, Mainz, within two years of each other. After a separation of half a millennium, they were reunited when the great collector and benefactor of the Library, Lessing J. Rosenwald, presented to the Library the Giant Bible of Mainz manuscript on the 500th anniversary of its creation.

The Gutenberg Bible is the first book produced from movable type. The earliest account of the invention of printing is in *Die Cronica van der hilliger stat van Coellen* (Cologne, 1499). It says:

> This highly valuable art was first discovered in Germany, at Mainz on the Rhine . . . in the year 1440, and from that time until the year 1450 this art and what was related to it were being investigated. In that year, 1450 . . . they began to print, the first book printed, was the Bible in Latin . . . And the first inventor of printing was a citizen of Mainz, born in Strasburg, and named Junker Johann Gutenberg.

In his chronicle of Jewish history, *Zemah David* (Prague, 1592), David Gans credits Gutenberg with the invention of printing "in the first year of the reign of virtuous Emperor Frederick," and declares:

> Blessed be He, who gives man knowledge and instructs him in wisdom . . . who favored us with this great invention, whose benefit to all mankind cannot be matched by any other from the day God placed man on earth.

Few if any inventions have had greater effect on the course of civilization. Printing, which replaced the long, laborious, and expensive production of manuscripts, made possible the wide dissemination of knowledge. Gutenberg's Bible is also a marvel of the beauty printing reached at its inception. This was possible because the volume is as much the last manuscript as the first printed book. That this new method of "writing" was first applied to fashioning a grand edition of Western civilization's supreme literary and religious creation, the Bible, is entirely appropriate. The same civilization which built and adorned cathedrals of grandeur could be expected to print magnificent Bibles.

Opened, the Library's Gutenberg would cover a card table. Its 1,282 pages in three volumes are bound in leather-covered wooden boards. Indelible ink on supple vellum and strong Gothic letters evoke the strength of the Faith. Estimates of the Gutenberg edition range from two hundred to three hundred, those printed on vellum from twenty to thirty-five. Only twenty-one complete copies survive, six in the United States; the only one on vellum is the Library's copy. The Giant Bible is, as its name claims, a volume great in its execution as well as its dimension. Its illuminations and decorations are works of art, bold in color, delicate in detail.

The Nekcsei-Lipocz Bible, of Hungarian provenance and completed about 1342, is noted for its unusually thick vellum and for embellishments "strong and filled with fantasy." More delicate and more beautiful is another Latin Bible, written in thirteenth-century England in "most minute Gothic characters on the finest uterine vellum . . . so thin as to resemble India paper, [with] many historiated initials in blue and gold, frequently spreading into the margin." Of particular beauty are tiny paintings of the baby Moses on the Nile at the beginning of the Book of Exodus, and of King David and his harp at the beginning of the Book of Psalms. This 536-page manuscript is in double columns, forty-seven lines to the page, and is less than seven inches high and five inches wide. One must marvel at the skill and eyesight of the scribe and illuminators. This lovely "pocket book" also came to the Library from Lessing Rosenwald.

One of the greatest private collections presented to the Library of Congress is the Lessing J. Rosenwald Collection of illustrated books and manuscripts. The collection is rich in its illuminated manuscripts and illustrated printed editions of the Bible. Among these is this magnificent example of early printing on vellum and manuscript illumination. The micro painting of the Garden of Eden is placed within the initial letter of this Latin Bible printed by Nicolaus Jenson.

Biblia Latina, Venice, 1476.
Rare Book and Special Collections Division, Rosenwald Collection.

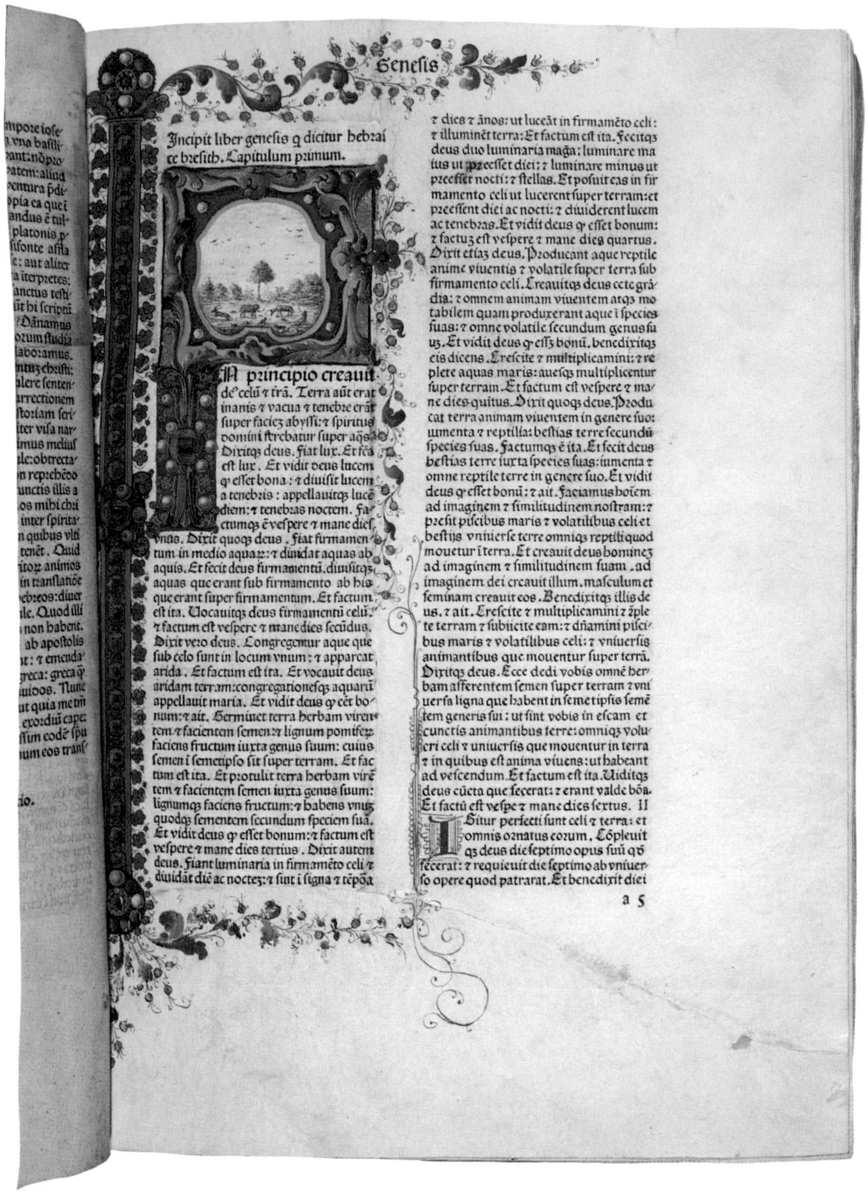

Facing page:
Of the illustrated Bibles in the Rosenwald Collection, we chose this Italian incunable for its superb woodcut illustrations, especially this panel depicting the six days of creation. God, in clerical garb, fashions heaven and earth and the seas; creates the plants that grow and calls into being the heavenly bodies that glow; and the beasts on earth and in skies above and waters below; and as the culmination of creation, man and woman—and there is satisfaction writ on the divine face, reflecting the biblical report: "and God saw that it was good."

Biblia Italiana, Venice, 1494.
Rare Book and Special Collections Division, Rosenwald Collection.

Printed illuminated and illustrated Bibles which came with the Rosenwald Collection are no less striking. The lovely Garden of Eden illumination, which opens the Book of Genesis of one, is appropriately serene in color and composition. To the unpracticed eye, it looks like yet another manuscript, but it is, in fact, a superb printing of the Bible on vellum by Nicolaus Jenson in Venice in 1476. The works of this master engraver and printer are esteemed and his *Biblia Latina,* printed on vellum, is extremely rare as well.

Another Venice edition of the Bible, in Italian translation by the monk Niccolo Malermi, *Biblia Italiana* (1494), contains some of the most charming early illustrations of Biblical narrative, done by an artist known only as "The Master of the Malermi Bible." Of particular interest are six woodcut panels of illustrations, which depict the six days of creation. God appears in human form, haloed and bearded, accomplishing his creation:

DI VNO
DI SE GVNDO
DI TERZO
DI QVARTO
DI QVINTO
DI SESTO

unfolding the light on the first day; parting the waters on the second; bringing shrubs and trees forth from the earth on the third; creating a human-faced sun, crescent moon, and satellite stars on the fourth and the birds of heaven and fish in the sea on the fifth. On the sixth and final day of labors, God is shown drawing Eve from Adam's side, a benign lion and a seemingly amused or startled rabbit looking on.

God in human form is common in Christian Bible illustrations, belief in a God who is both All God and All Man making such depiction quite natural. No such depiction would be expected in Hebrew books published under Jewish auspices or for a Jewish readership. Yet on the engraved title pages of *Minhat Shai* (Mantua, 1744), an illustration depicting Ezekiel prophesying to the dry bones shows the face and outstretched arm of God breathing life into those bones. The editor of this volume is Yedidiah Shlomo Norzi; the publisher is Raphael Hayim Italia. Similarly, in a superbly illustrated Haggadah published in 1864 in Trieste, edited by Abraham Hayyim Morpurgo and printed by Johan Cohen, God is shown in the burning bush before which Moses is kneeling. Such depictions in Jewish sacred books are unexpected, even shocking, considering how seriously the Second Commandment inhibited Jewish artistic expression, especially of aspects of the deity. It indicates how widely Jewish publishers employed Christian artists and how great was the influence of Christian art on Jewish book illustration.

More acceptable from a Jewish perspective though no less appealing to the Christian reader are the illustrations in the first printings of Martin Luther's translation of the Bible into German, *Das Alte Testament deutsch* (Wittenberg, 1524). These portray such biblical scenes as the Fall of Jericho and Solomon's Temple. The biblical experiences are made all the more immediate by illustrations which employ contemporary landscape peopled by recognizable figures clad in familiar garb of the time. Jericho, for example, is drawn as a medieval German town around which warriors in sixteenth-century military garb are marching, and each of the traditional shofars is a German horn.

To translate the Old Testament, Luther needed help. He consulted Jewish scholars, and the great Christian savant Melancthon was particularly helpful. Luther made wide use of the commentaries of Nicholas de Lyra, a French scholar who drew heavily on the commentary of Rashi, "whom he transcribes almost word for word." So frequently did Luther draw from de Lyra that a well-known couplet asserts, "Si Lyra non Lyrasset, Luther non saltasset" (Had Lyra not played, Luther could not have danced). The Luther translation of the Bible was to *Hochdeutsch* what Shakespeare was to the English language. Its immediate and lasting popularity was overwhelming; within a decade of its publication, it was reprinted some eighty times.

The most charming early Bible illustrations are the hand-tinted woodcuts in *De Bibel Int Carte* (Antwerp, 1516): Adam and Eve, Cain and Abel, Noah's Ark, the Tower of Babel, the Offering of Isaac, Joseph and His Brethren, Moses in the Nile and at the Burning Bush, David and Goliath, and Solomon and His Temple. The whole gamut of biblical heroes are portrayed in a reverent yet gently whimsical manner. There is a touching naïveté about place and persons. The colors, pale pastel, do not compete with but enhance the delineating woodcut lines. As conceptions of a pious be-

Facing page: Certainly among the most charming depictions of biblical events and characters are these hand-colored illustrations in this volume, which is a paraphrase in Dutch of portions of the Bible. The pictures display a naive piety, and the pastel colors seem appropriate to the simplicity of the conception and execution. Some of the illustrations convey continuity of activity—an early form of animation in illustration. We provide four illustrations.

De Bibel Int Carte, Antwerp, 1516.
Rare Book and Special Collections Division, Rosenwald Collection.

ghi van desen vruchtē eedt/van dien da
ghe voorts suldi sterffelijck sijn aldus be
vaelt hen god onse heere ende setter al tot
huerlieden gheboden wtgenomen vanden vruchten vanden boome die hi hem

verboden hadde Ende Adam hadde dye
heerlijch; bouen alle creatueren die god
gheschepen ende ghemaect hadde Maer
dat hi hem hueden soude te etene vandē
frupte des boōs die hi hē verbodē hadde

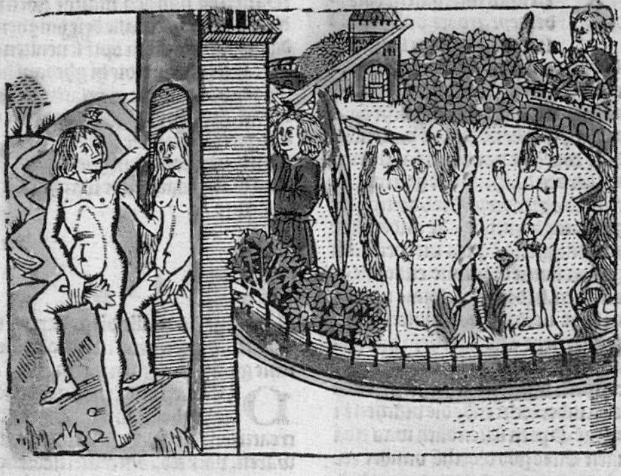

Hoe Adam eñ Eua tghebodt
gods braken doer ingheuen des
serpens Ca.iij.

T Serpent dwelcke es die alō quaet
ste beeste van allen dien god ōse he
re ghescapen hadde peysde in hem seluē
dat soude doen den mensche sulcken din-
gen op dat in sijnder macht ware dat hi
wt so grooter heerlijchept ghewerpē sou
de worden daer hem god inne gestelt had
de Maer tvoerscreuen serpent en dorste
niet spreken tegen Adam. want het wist
te wel dat die man wijs was vol sins see
re vroem ende sterck. Want Adam hadde drie de principaelste crachten Hi had-

de meer sterchepden dan noit eenich mā
hadde God onse heere gaf hem grooten
sin ende wetenhept doen hi hem inblies
die siele Hi was oock scoonder dan nopt
sterfelijck man wesen mochte want god
formeerden ghelijck een peghelijck wel
weet na sijn epgen forme of beelde. dats
na sijn ghelijcke Doen hem God ghege
uen hadde alle drie dese voerscreuē crach
ten of virtuten/te weten Cracht Sin eñ
Schoonhept. So gaf hi hem sinen vriē
wille/den welcken es ghegeuē om tgoet
te doē eñ tquait te latē Alle dit hadde Adā
Doen tvoersepde serpent sach dat A-
dam was van alsoe grooten sinnē ende

Adam and Eve

in deser arcken maken diuersce plaetsen
ende cameren. Ghi sulcse oock soe bewa
ren van buiten ende van binnen soe dat
daer gheen watre in en come ofte en can
ghecomon

Hoe Noe die arcke maecte biden beue
le van onsen lieuen heere waer inne dat
hi hem salueerde ende alle sine volck
Capittel.xiij

D Oen noe gehoort hadde ende ver
staen het gene dat hem onse lieue
heere beuolen hadde/so begōste hi te ma
ken die arcke so hem ōse here god die had
de beuolen te maken Ende doen die arcke volmaect was so sepde hem onse here
Ghi sult nemen van allen manieren vā
beesten ende vogelen die opter eerden le-
uen ende besorcht voer elcker creatueren
die daer inne sijn sal bijleuen so vele alst
noot es Ghi ende v wijf met uwe drie so

nen ende hair wiuen sult v houden inde
middel van der arcken ende besorcht oec
uwen noordorft na uwer liedē behoefte.
Want ic sal dat watere doin comen ouer
alle die werelt so hoge dat alle creatuerē
die leuende sijn opter eerden sullen ge pi
nicht worden metter doot wtghenomen
die ghene die inō arcken sijn sullen mz v
Doen nam noe vanden beesten eñ vā
den voghelen van elcker natueren so hē
god dat geboden ende beuolen hadde eñ
doen hise al in ghesēt hadde soe ghynck
hi daer in met sinen wiue ende alle dype
sine sonen met haren wiuen Ende doen
si daer al in waren soe quam onse heere
god aen die arcke ende sloot dat gat daer
noe ende die ander ingegaen waren vā
bupten Ende dwatre begonst seer ouer-
vloedelijck te comen ende de arcke begost
te heffen midts der sterchept des waters
so hoge datse nieuwers deerde en raecte

Noah's Ark

verleechden ende enige knechtkens had
den/dat si die doden souden ende datsi die
mepskens wel bewaren soudē maer die
vroede vrouwen ontsagen god ende sijn
ghebot meer dan des coninx ghebot/soe
datsi tghebot vanden coninck niet en de-
den/want si bewaerden die knechtkens
Als dpe coninck dit wiste dede hise halen

ende verspracse seer steuerlijcken/maer si
excuseerden hem ten bestē dat si mochtē
segghende dat die vrouwen vanden he-
breeuseen volcke die sciencie hadden haer
kinderen ter werelt brenghen sonder ee-
nighe ander hulpe eer si aen hem lieden
quamen so haddense ghebaert haer kit.

Hoe moyses gheboren wort eñ hoe hē
sijn moeder in een kistkē lepde ende also
inder riuieren sette Ca.lxxix.

D Je coninck dit horende gheboot si
nen volcke dz si alle die knechtkēs
die voerdane gheboren souden worden
vanden hebreeuschen volcke worpen in
der riuieren. Maer dat si wel bewaren
souden die maechdekens. Corts hier na
dat hi dit aldus gheboden hadde wasser
een man wter linaigien van leui die een
wijf nam wt sijnder linagien so die cosen

me van hemlieden was Dese ghecreech
eenen schonen sone ende doen hi geboren
was soe vercreech men dat kint ende die
moeder voedet op ontrent dype maendē
Mer doen si sach dat sijt niet langer ver
borgen en soude hebben connen so maec
tese een clein kistken in een maniere van
eenen scheepken/eñ si naghelder soe vast
datter gheen water in comen en mochte/
doen lepde si dat kint ende settet inder riuieren Die suster vā desen kinde bleef op
den cāt van deser riuieren staende om te
besien wair dit kint henen trecken soude

eñ beweent Saul die v eerlicken cleede
eñ so preciōselikē verclerde Hoe zijn nv
die stercke verslagen/ die frissche man-
nen ghebleuē inder battaliē Jonathas
in alsulckē hoogen staet ghedoot O Jo
nathas mijn beminde broedere ic hebbe
ouer groten druck vā uwer doot die soe

schone eñ minnelijc waert meer dan ee
nighe vrouwe. Ghelijck een moedere
ouer seere haer kint bemint also bemī-
den wij malcanderē. In dyen tij
de gheboot Dauid datmē den kinderē
van ysrahel soude leerē schieten met dē
hantboghe eñ met dē voetboghe.

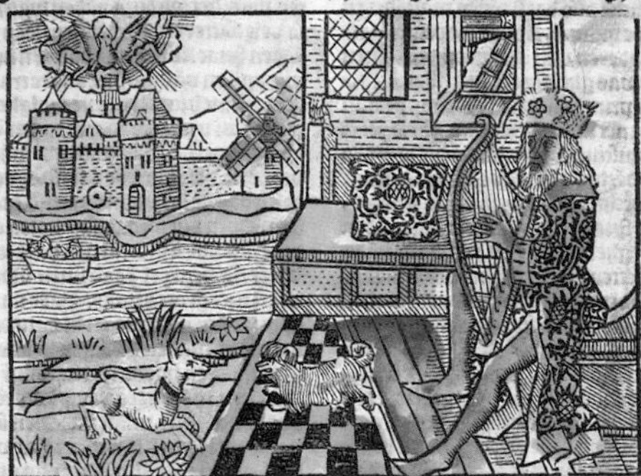

Hoe Dauid coninck ghemaect werdt
ouer die vā Juda Capittel.c.lxxv.

N A dat die clachten ghedaen warē
van dē coninck Saul eñ van Jonathas so nā Dauid raet aen onsen here wat hi doē soude Eñ onse heere dede
hē gaen in Ebron/seggende dat hi dair
eenen sekeren tijt soude bliuē woonen.
Doen ghinc Dauid in Ebron met zijn
twee wiuen Abigael eñ Achine/ eñ zijn
ghesellē dede hi wonen in die steden ontrent Ebrō. Seer corts hier na quamē
die vā den ghestachte vā Juda eñ si ma
kedē Dauid coninc in Ebron/ eñ hi reg
neerde daer. vij. iaer/ eñ. vi. iaren ouer

dat ghestachte vā Juda. Daer na quamen die tijdingen aē Dauid hoe die vā
Jabes gedaen haddē met Saul eñ Jo-
nathas/eñ hi danctese seere daer af segghende Ghebñdijt moet ghi van gode
zijn dat ghi so wel v deuoer gedaē hebt
aen uwen coninc eñ aen zijn kinderen/
mach ick v lieden eenige vrienscap doē
ic ben daer toe altijt bereet/ eñ en weest
niet ōwondert noch in gheenō sorghen
wāt die kinderen van Juda hebbē mij
coninck ghemaect ouer haer.

Hoe Joab eñ Abner elck met haren
volcke tegen malcāderen vochtē
A lo Abner hoorde (Ca.c.lxxvi.

liever fully at home with heroes of his faith—who are nonetheless familiar friends—living with them and sharing their adventures, these portraits are unsurpassed. They are as endearing to the reader as they were dear to the artist. The serpent who intruded into the lives of Adam and Eve is not so much evil as sly and slimy. The ark of Noah is everybody's overburdened boat. Abraham greeting his angelic guests is the genial host, his geniality made possible by a wife in the background busy with her chores. It is not that we enter their world but that they enter ours, which makes it so much more comfortable to be with them and to learn from them. The illustrations, aesthetically entertaining, become pedagogically powerful.

Of singular importance to the history of Christianity is Martin Luther's translation of the Bible into German. This majestic first edition followed by countless others, and inspiring further translations into virtually all the major languages of humankind, may be viewed as a monument to the influence of the Bible on the course of civilization. It is opened to the Book of Joshua, where the artistically accomplished woodcut depicts the march around Jericho by Joshua's army led by *Kohanim* (priests) sounding *Shofrot* (horns) till "the walls came tumbling down."

Das Alte Testament deutsch, M. Luther, Wittenberg, 1524. Rare Book and Special Collections Division, Rosenwald Collection.

Das Buch

Jeriho aber war verſchloſſen vñ verwaret vmb der kinder Jſrael willē das niemant aus odder eyn komē kundt. Aber der HERR ſprach zu Joſua. Sihe da/ ich hab Jeriho ſampt yhrem konige vnd kriegs leutt yn deyne hand gegebē las alle kriegs menner rings vmb die ſtad her gehē eyn mal/vnd thu ſechs tage alſzo. Am ſiebenden tage aber/las die Prieſter ſieben poſaunen des hall iars nemen fur der laden her/vnd gehet des ſelbē ſiebenden tags/ſieben mal vmb die ſtad/vnd las die Prieſter die poſaunen blaſen. Vnd wenn man das hall iars horn bleſſet vnd denet/ das yhr die poſaunen horet/ ſo ſoll das gantze volck eyn gros felltgeſchrey machen/ ſo werden der ſtad maurn zufallen/vnd das volck ſoll hyneyn fallen/eyn iglicher ſtracks fur ſich.

(Hall iars horn) Diſze poſaunen vō horner gemacht/bedeutt das Euangelion von Chriſto durch welchs geſchrey vnd predigt fellet Jeriho die wellt vnd alle yhre macht/aber die ſunderyn Rahab mit yhren freunden wirt behallten/die werck heyligen ſind alle verloren.

Da rieff Joſua der ſon Nun den Prieſtern/ vnd ſprach zu yhn/ tragt die lade des bunds/vnd ſieben Prieſter laſſt ſieben hall iars poſaunen tragen fur der lade des HERRN/ Zum volck aber ſprach er zihet hyn/vnd gehet vmb die ſtad/ vnd wer geruſt iſt/ gehe fur der laden des HERRN hyn/ Da Joſua ſolchs dem volck geſagt hatte trugen die ſieben prieſter ſieben hall iars poſaunen fur der laden des HERRN her/vnd giengen vnd blieſen die poſaunen/ vnd die lade des

3

THE SEA OF THE TALMUD AND SOME SHORES IT HAS TOUCHED

> The Talmud is a learned work, a large corpus of erudition. It contains manifold learning in all sciences. It teaches the most explicit and most complete civil and canonical laws of the Jews, so that the whole nation might live thereby in a state of happiness.
>
> It is the most luminous commentary of the Scriptural law as well as its supplement and support. It contains much excellent teaching on jurisprudence, medicine, natural philosophy, ethics, politics, astronomy and other branches of science, which make one think highly of the history of that nation and of the time in which that work was written.
>
> Johannes Buxtorf (1564–1629)
> *De Abbreviaturis Hebraicis* (1613)

THE SEA OF THE TALMUD, *Yam ha-Talmud,* is a most apt and felicitous metaphor, because the Talmud touches the shores of all human experience and its editions were printed in the widely scattered centers of Jewish habitation. Formidable indeed is the task of mastering the profundity of its contents and the intricacies of its logic; not the academic logic which constricts life into its preordained patterns, stripping it of its complexities and incongruities, but its existential logic flowing from the jagged rhythms of life.

The Library holds volumes representative of the Talmud's most important editions and translations, and among them are those that shed light on telling incidents in the Jewish historical experience.

In his classic *History of the Printing of the Talmud (Ma'amar Al Hadpasat Ha-Talmud),* Raphael Rabbinovicz writes:

> The holy Talmud, the base and source of Jewish religious and national life—how numerous were its enemies and detractors! As was the fate of those who lived by it and devoted their lives to it, so was its fate. Already in the year 1239 Pope Gregory IX ordered the burning of the Talmud, and hundreds, nay thousands of volumes were put to the torch in France and Italy.

In June 1242, twenty-four wagon loads of Talmudic tomes were publicly burned in Paris by the official executioner. Rabbi Meir of Rothenburg compared this conflagration to the burning of the Jerusalem Temple, in an elegy which has been incorporated in the *Tishah B'Av* (the holy day commemorating the destruction of the Temple) liturgy, *Sha-ali Serufah*, "Oh, inquire, thou consumed by flames . . ." Popes—Innocent IV, Alexander IV, John XXII, Alexander V—issued condemnations; monarchs—Louis IX of France and his successors Philip III and IV—ordered confiscations; and following the Council of Basle, Pope Eugenius IV issued a bull prohibiting the study of the Talmud. Fraught with danger and beset with difficulties though it was, study of the Talmud proceeded nonetheless, because without it Jews were convinced that Jewish life could not continue. But the condemnations and confiscations took their toll; very few Talmudic manuscripts have survived, and only one of the entire Talmud, the Munich manuscript of 1342.

What is the Talmud that it aroused such enmity and opposition?

The Talmud is the extraordinary compendium of law and lore of rabbinic Judaism, comprising both the Mishnah and the Gemara. Side by side with the Written Law of the Bible, over time there developed the Oral Law, which expanded upon the ordinances of the Pentateuch. This Oral Law was handed down from master to disciple, studied in Jewish academies of learning, and applied by Jewish courts of law. The period of national and spiritual crisis which followed the unsuccessful Jewish rebellions against Rome in 68 and 135 CE persuaded Judah ha Nasi, head of the Jewish community in Palestine at the turn of the third century, to compile, systematize, and reduce the Oral Law, which had come down by word of mouth, into writing. This collection of laws, legal opinions, decisions, and comments upon them is known as the Mishnah. It is less a code than a report on prevailing law and custom, and a digest of legal opinions which invite further study and discussion.

Study and discussion of the Mishnah in the centuries following were carried on in academies and applied in courts in Palestine and Babylonia. The summary and digest of this scholarly activity is called the Gemara. Not at all dry-as-dust legal argumentation, it reports on the exciting application of law to life, recording the disputations which grew out of diverse traditions and differing opinions. Here and there it is interlaced with a parable, a legend, or just a good story to make a point. The Mishnah plus the Gemara constitutes the Talmud.

The Mishnah is in Hebrew, the language of the Bible and of worship and scholarly discourse in late antiquity; the Gemara is in Aramaic, the language of common discourse of that time. There are two versions of the Talmud. The first, edited circa 325 CE, contains the discussions in Palestinian schools and courts and is called the Jerusalemite or Palestinian. The Babylonian, edited a century and half later, is the compendium of scholarly legal discussions carried on in the academies and courts of that Jewish community. Like the Mishnah, the Gemara is not a code of law (an organized body of legal decisions), but the raw material for establishing codes—the source for discussion, refinement, and application.

The spirit of the Talmudic process is expressed in a tale in tractate *Baba Meziah*. Rabbi Eliezer, a proponent of unchanging tradition—"a well-lined cistern that doesn't lose a drop," as his teacher characterized him—was engaged in a legal disputation with his colleagues. "He brought all the reasons in the world," but the majority would not accept his view. Said

Rabbi Eliezer, "If the law is as I hold it to be, let this tree prove it," and the tree uprooted itself a hundred *amma,* but they said, "Proof cannot be brought from a tree." Rabbi Eliezer persisted, saying, "Let these waters determine it," and the waters began to flow backwards, but his colleagues responded that waters cannot determine the law. Once again Rabbi Eliezer tried, asking the walls of the study house to support him. They began to totter, whereupon the spokesman for the majority, Rabbi Joshua, admonished them, "when rabbis are engaged in legal discussion what right have ye to interfere!" So the walls did not fall in respect for Rabbi Joshua, nor did they return to their upright position, in respect for Rabbi Eliezer—and "they remain thus to this day!" But Rabbi Eliezer would not surrender and cried out: "Let Heaven decide." A voice was heard from Heaven saying: "Why do ye dispute with Rabbi Eliezer; the law is always as he says it to be." Whereupon Rabbi Joshua arose and proclaimed, quoting Scripture, "It is not in Heaven!" Rabbi Jeremiah explained, "The Law was given at Sinai and we no longer give heed to heavenly voices, for in that Law it is stated: 'One follows the majority.'" God's truth, divine law, is not determined by miracles or heavenly voices, but by the collegium of rabbis, men learned in the law, committed to the law and expert in its application to the life of the pious community.

Such an attitude alone, negating the authority of the miraculous and heavenly voices, would have been sufficient to make the Talmud anathema to medieval churchmen, devoted as they were to the miraculous and to the divine reordering of the validity of the law. But there was more, of course. The Talmud is so vast a work, containing such a variety of views and assertions, that one can find statements that are extravagant, hyperbolic, even theologically outrageous, if taken literally.

The Library has not one but two incunabula editions of an anti-Talmudic work, *Thalmut. Objectiones in dicta Talmud,* Nuremberg, c. 1497, and Vienna, c. 1500. It is a polemical refutation of what the anonymous author (said to be a certain Theobaldus, a Parisian subprior) calls blasphemies, calumnies, and errors. Like other anti-Talmudic polemicists, he takes Talmudic figures of speech and rhetorical devices quite literally. Thus, the Talmudic emphasis on the importance of Talmudic study, expressed in the suggestion that God Himself should study the Talmud, is asserted by him to be a blasphemy, implying that God's knowledge and understanding is not complete—viz. His need to study. As for error, Theobaldus says, the Talmud claims that its detractors will be punished, yet the King of France caused all the books of the Talmud in his realm to be burned and suffered no punishment for it.

EDITIONS OF THE TALMUD

For the Jews, the Talmud was not a book of doctrine ("doctrina iudeorum," as Theobaldus describes it) but a compendium of laws. At the heart of Judaism is its legal tradition, the Talmud being its indispensable handbook. Compendia of laws are indispensable to a community facing religious suppression and/or exile. It is, therefore, noteworthy but not surprising to find that individual volumes of the Talmud appeared first in Spain, a community in extremis, rather than in Italy, the seat of Hebrew printing. Before Joshua Solomon Soncino printed tractate *Berakhot* in Soncino, Italy, in 1484 (the first book printed by a member of the Soncino family), more than half a dozen tractates were published in Guadalajara or Toledo in Spain. Such printing continued in Portugal. Remnants of more than twenty tractates printed on the Iberian peninsula, text with the commentary of Rashi, are extant. Joshua Solomon was joined by his nephew Gershon in publishing incunabula editions of books of the Talmud, but it has often been remarked that, in comparison to other Hebrew books (most of lesser religious importance), few books of the Talmud were published in the early days of Hebrew printing. Discretion seemed to have been the better part of valor. When in 1508 Gershom Soncino resumed printing the Talmud in Pesaro the volumes bear evidence of self-censorship. The Library has a copy of the volume which Gershom Soncino printed first, the first book of the Talmud printed in the sixteenth century, tractate *Yebamot*, Pesaro, 1508. The text is accompanied by the commentary of Rashi and of the tosaphists, as well as Maimonides's commentary on the Mishnah.

Publishing of the Talmud on a grand scale began a dozen years later in Venice at the press of Daniel Bomberg, who, having received the approval of Pope Leo X, published the complete Talmud in 1520–23. This editio princeps of the Talmud set the form which has been followed by editions of the Talmud to the present: the number and composition of the pages, a section of the Mishnah text followed by its Gemara, the commentary of Rashi on the inner margin, and that of the tosaphists on the outer. The Rashi commentary is a brief, precise explanation of the text—the text being in Aramaic and without vowel points or punctuation. The tosaphoth are longer, more involved discussions of the legal implications of the text, begun by Rashi's disciples—his two grandsons, Jacob Tam and Samuel ben Meir being among the leaders—and carried on in the schools in France and Germany in the twelfth to the fourteenth centuries. The tosaphoth, which began as commentary on the commentary of Rashi, spawned other commentaries, so that a current edition of the Talmud would contain some two dozen major and more than one hundred minor commentaries. The uniformity of the pages in all published editions was a double boon. It was of great practical usefulness to Talmud scholars, for it made for easy, standard reference citation; and it served as a symbol of the unity of the Jewish people, which Talmud studies enhanced. While the contents of the Talmud made for uniformity through law, its form made for an at homeness with every edition, be it of Venice, Constantinople, Cracow, Lublin, Amsterdam, Frankfort, Warsaw, or Vilna.

The Library has volumes from all four Venice editions and a copy of the editio princeps of the Palestinian Talmud, published by Bomberg in 1523. The Venice editions were the handiwork of a German Jewish printer who had settled in Padua, Israel Adelkind. Bomberg brought him to Venice to supervise his Hebrew press. It was he who designed the pages which became the standard. Adelkind also managed the printing establishment of Tobias Foa in Sabionetta, where he oversaw the printing of a projected edition of the Talmud begun in 1553 but never completed. What brought this project to an end was the tragic fate that befell a previously successful undertaking of Adelkind's, a truly magnificent edition of the Talmud printed in the Hebrew publishing house of Marco Antonio Giustiniani.

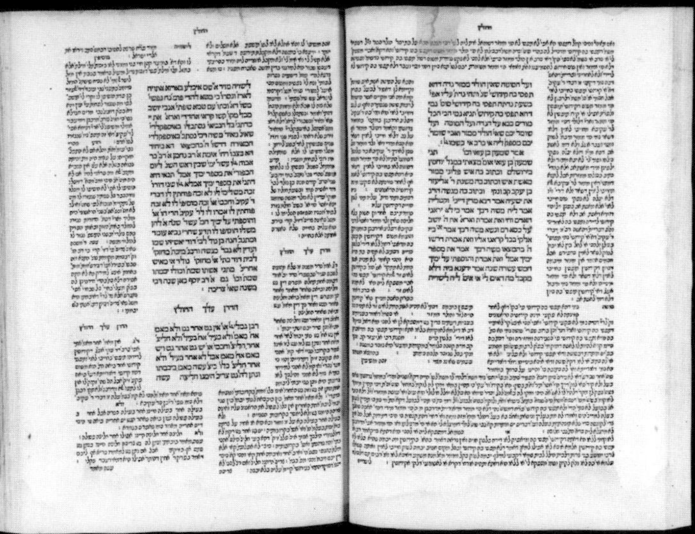

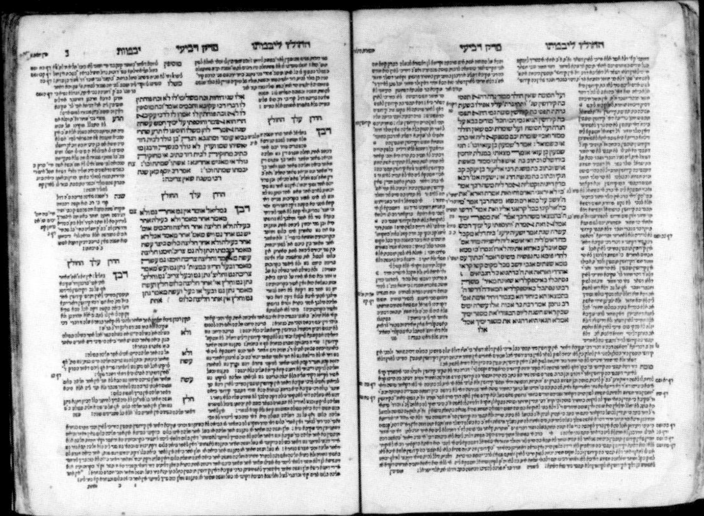

The contour of the printed page of the Talmud was fashioned by the Soncinos: the text, an island surrounded by the commentary of Rashi and that of the Tosaphists, the former on the inner margin, the latter at the outer, as can be seen on page 50A of Tractate Yebamot published by Gershom Soncino, Pesaro, 1508. The first edition of the entire Talmud, Venice 1520, adopted but slightly altered the scheme of the Soncinos. The configuration of the page and its contents became standard for all subsequent editions, as can be seen from page 50A of some early editions.

Pesaro, 1508 (*upper left*)
Venice, 1520 (*upper right*)
Cracow, 1605 (*center*)
Lublin, 1619 (*lower left*)
Amsterdam, 1644 (*lower right*)

The Talmud.
Hebraic Section.

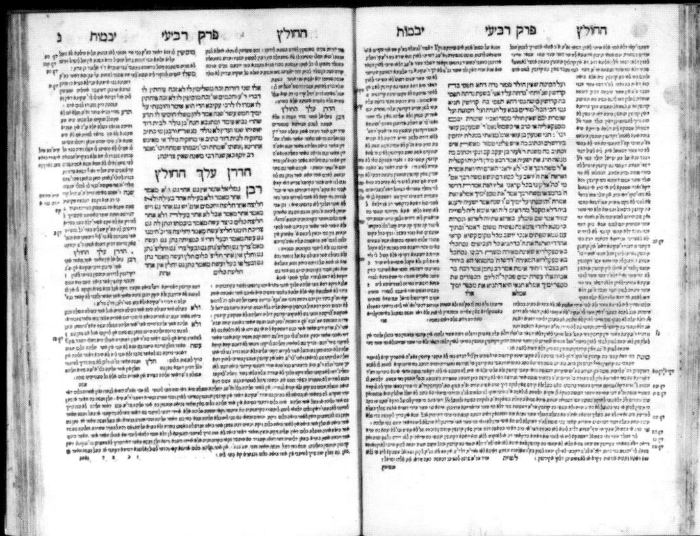

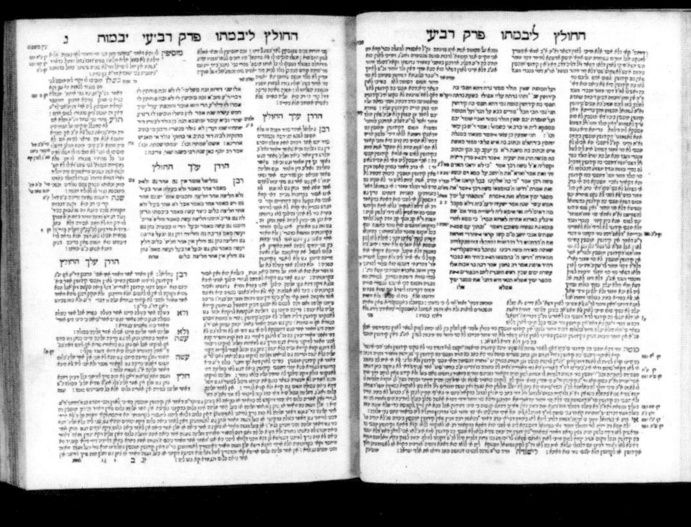

As the days of the Bomberg press were beginning to wane, two rival presses began to compete for the Hebrew book market, those of Giustiniani and of Alvise Bragadini. The Hebrew book trade must have been lucrative to have brought two such wealthy and influential citizens of Venice into such fierce competition. What exacerbated the rivalry was the publication by each of an edition of Maimonides's *Mishneh Torah*. Accusation and counteraccusation of unscrupulous practices finally led to accusations by three apostates in the employ of the battling publishers. Their presentation to a council of cardinals, headed by one who was soon to become Pope Paul IV, bore fiery fruit. The Council of Ten, with only two opposing, recommended to the Pope that the Talmud and related blasphemous works be extirpated, and the Pontiff so ordered. Homes were invaded, holy books confiscated, and on Rosh Hashanah (New Year's Day) of the year 5314 (September 9, 1553), in Rome's Campo de' Fiori, the offending books went up in flames.

The Christian Flemish diplomat and Hebraic scholar, Andreas Masius, wrote to one of the dissenting cardinals:

> Acting upon the information of two Jewish Christians, if indeed they are worthy of the name, hired by these rival booksellers, you [the Council of Cardinals] have, to the eternal shame of the Apostolic See and to the detriment of Christianity, rendered a hasty judgment. You are absolutely blind in this matter, for not one of you has ever read a single word of the books you have condemned.

But the voice of truth and reason did not quench the fire of holy zeal. Its consuming flames spread to Bologna, Ravenna, Ferrara, Mantua, Urbino, Florence, and Venice. Though Hebrew printing continued and flourished in Italy, the Talmud was never again printed there.

What came to an early end in Italy was soon taken up in Jewish communities east and north, in Salonica, Constantinople, Cracow, Lublin, Amsterdam, Frankfurt an der Oder, Frankfurt am Main, Sulzbach, Vienna, Warsaw, Vilna, Berlin, Munich, and more, as representative volumes and whole sets of the Talmud in the Library of Congress attest. Let us look at a few.

Exiles from Spain and Portugal made the port city Salonica in the Ottoman Empire a great center of Jewish life and learning, and of Hebrew printing as well. Among the early printers were the brothers Solomon and Joseph Jabez, who began to publish in 1543. All manner of calamities befell the brothers, including fires and plagues, but they pressed on with their "holy labors." For a while they sought better fortune in Adrianople, another center for Iberian exiles, and in Constantinople. Joseph resumed publishing in Salonica, announcing in 1560, "when I saw that the Talmud was burned, I resolved that it was time to do valiantly for the Lord . . . to begin publishing the Talmud again, if God would grant me life, and generous persons their aid." Only a few volumes were published, of which the Library has the tractate *Hulin* (1566). In the 1580s the brothers joined together to publish an edition of the Talmud in Constantinople. Many of the volumes which appeared have found a home in the Library.

In the sixteenth and in the first half of the seventeenth centuries, Poland was the preeminent Jewish community on the European continent. In this vibrant community—home to great scholars, flourishing schools of learning, and a busy press—no less than seven editions of the Talmud were undertaken, of which the Library has a number of volumes published in Cracow by Isaac Prosnitz, 1602–5, and in Lublin by Abraham Jaffe in 1619. An edition of the Palestinian Talmud was published in Cracow in 1609 "under the sovereignty of the great King Sigmund III, may his glory be elevated, by Isaac the son of Aaron of blessed memory of the community of Prosnitz. Out of my straits I have called upon the Lord; He answered me with abundant salvation. The Lord is my helper, I will yet see the [defeat] of my enemies." (Psalms 118:5, 7) Forty years later, the Jews of Poland called out unto the Lord, but there was neither saving nor victory. The Ukrainian rebellion against their Polish oppressor, led by Bogdan Chmielnicki, wrought havoc with Polish Jewry in 1648–49, decimating some seven hundred communities and destroying uncounted books. The books which survived are few and precious. Even in the midst of destruction, in 1648, the publisher Solomon Zalman Jaffe, his press having been previously ravaged by fire, took up the work again to publish a *Lamentation on the Dread Decrees of 1648* by the noted scholar, Yom Tov Lipmann Heller. By 1665, printing began again, on poor paper and with roughly cut type. The Library has an imperfect copy of the first book off the press, *Pelah ha-Rimon,* set in type by Sarah Jaffe, the wife of the printer.

A full set of the first Amsterdam edition of the Talmud, printed by Immanuel Benveniste, 1644–47, is the first in a run of complete editions of the Talmud in the Library's collection. Although this edition was esteemed because passages expunged by cencorship in previous editions were now restored, its relatively small size made it difficult to read—for all pages of all editions of the Talmud were uniform in text from 1520 on; the only way to fit all the text on the smaller page was to reduce the size of the type. So, soon after its publication it became necessary to reduce the price drastically, making this the first Hebrew published work to be "remaindered." Later, however, it gained popularity precisely because its smaller size made it easier to handle, store, and carry. Publishers in Amsterdam, Metz, and Offenbach subsequently solved the problem of the uniform page by dividing the page and printing it on two pages, yet retaining the standard pagination. This made it possible to have a relatively small volume with large type. The Library has a number of such half-page volumes of various tractates of the Talmud.

Half a century later, an edition published in Frankfurt an der Oder had grand size and great aesthetic distinction. The printer was a Christian, Michael Gottschalk; the publisher was Professor John Christopher Beckman, who received special permission for its publication from Duke Frederick III, Elector of Brandenburg. Publication was financed by the "court Jew," Behrend Lehmann, whose Hebrew name was Issakar Berman Segal of Halberstadt. Each of the twelve volumes has an engraved title page by M. Bernigeroth, showing Moses, Aaron, David, and Solomon, the first two flanking a tribute to the benefactor. Although each title page bears the claim that this edition is like "the one printed in Basle," a heavily censored one, many previously expurgated passages are restored, and where deletions are retained, blank spaces are left to indicate the omission to the reader and, no doubt, to permit him to fill in by pen what they dared not print. The formerly deleted tractate *Avodah Zara* (Idolatry) is now included as well, to give further integrity to the published text.

The purpose of the edition was both utilitarian and aesthetic, as is

זאת עבדת הלוים: נקיות ידים: מזלושה תמים
משה
דוד
תלמוד
גדול שהביא לידי מעשה
הקצין והנדיב פרנס
ומנהיג כה״ר בערמן סג״ל
בן הר״ר יהודה ליפמא ז״ל מעפ
תתן המנוח האלוף כמוהר״ר
יואל ז״ל מהלברשטאט
CUM DEO ET DIE

stated in approvals granted by leading rabbis for its publication. The Thirty Years War (1618–1648) devastated German Jewry, the Uprising of 1648–49 and the Swedish-Russian War which followed all but destroyed Polish Jewry. Wars over, it was time to rebuild. Scholars and schools needed the Talmud for study, and the spirit of German and Polish Jewry would be uplifted by a new edition which would surpass previous ones in grandeur. As Rabbi Moshe Yehudah, the son of Rabbi Kalonymos Cohen of Amsterdam's Ashkenazi Jewry, wrote in his approbation for the publication of this edition:

> The worthy Issakar Berman . . . resolved to produce a Talmud of equal quality and worth as the earlier editions of Cracow and Lublin, and certainly superior to the edition which appeared in Amsterdam in very small type and unclear print.

The need was attested to by Rabbi Naftali ben Yitzhak Katz of Posen in his approbation:

> Our world had turned into void and desolation. Twenty men had to use one Talmud. Each day the holy books grew fewer in number. We faced the danger that the Torah, heaven forfend, would be forgotten. There was no hope and no means to have the Talmud reprinted.

And as Rabbi Josef Shmuel of Cracow, Rabbi of Frankfurt am Main, reported in approving its publication:

> There was no more than one copy of the Talmud in a city. Many tried to reprint it but failed, until God inspired the prince and leader, Reb Berman of Halberstadt . . . for the honor of the Torah to print the Talmud on fine paper and good type, and engage good scholars to supervise the work to guard against mistakes or corruption of the text.*

A Swedish visitor to Frankfurt, Olaf Celsius, reported that he saw seven printers busily engaged in setting type, page by page, of tractate *Nazir,* and "a Jewish girl sat there too, and reached the third chapter of *Baba Kama.*" The girl was eleven-year-old Ella, who together with her brother is credited at the end of tractate *Nidah* with having set the type. In his history of the Jewish community of Halberstadt, B. H. Auerbach states that the generous patron provided 50,000 Rhenish Thaler for the 5,000-copy edition, half of which was distributed to scholars who could not afford to purchase it. It was a truly magnificent edition, in typography, adornment and integrity of text, and in the generosity of Behrend Lehmann, who used a substantial portion of his hard-earned fortune for the benefit of his faith and the uplift of his people.

On some of the shores touched by the Talmud were Christian scholars who became acquainted with portions of it through translation. Of such translations in the Library, we mention three seventeenth-century editions. The first is *Talmudis Babylonici Codex Middoth sive De Mensuris Templi,* text and translation with a commentary by the noted Christian Hebraist Constantine L'Empereur, "Professor of Theology and the Hebrew and Chaldean Languages at the University of Leyden." The volume was printed at Leyden's noted Elzivir press in 1630. The two others were published in Amsterdam: *Duo Tituli Thalmudici Sanhedrin, et Maccoth* (Hebrew text, Latin translation and commentary), 1629; and *Rosh Hashanah,* translated with commentary by Henrico Houting, published in 1695.

*Almost all Hebrew printed books inserted approbations of distinguished rabbis approving their publication. These serve as a copyright for they generally forbade the work's republication for a stated number of years.

Facing page: One of the finest editions of the Talmud was this, published in Frankfurt an der Oder in 1697. Moses and Aaron, David and Solomon frame the inscription on the engraved title page which states that it was made possible by the generosity of Berman Segal of Halberstadt. A "Court Jew," he provided 50,000 Rhenish Thaler to make possible its publication and distribution to institutions and scholars in Germany and Polish Jewish communities devastated by the seventeenth-century wars and their aftermath. The owner's inscription is that of "Isaachar, the son of the great Gaon, our rabbi and teacher, Gabriel of Cracow."

Talmud, 12 volumes, Frankfurt an der Oder, 1697. Hebraic Section.

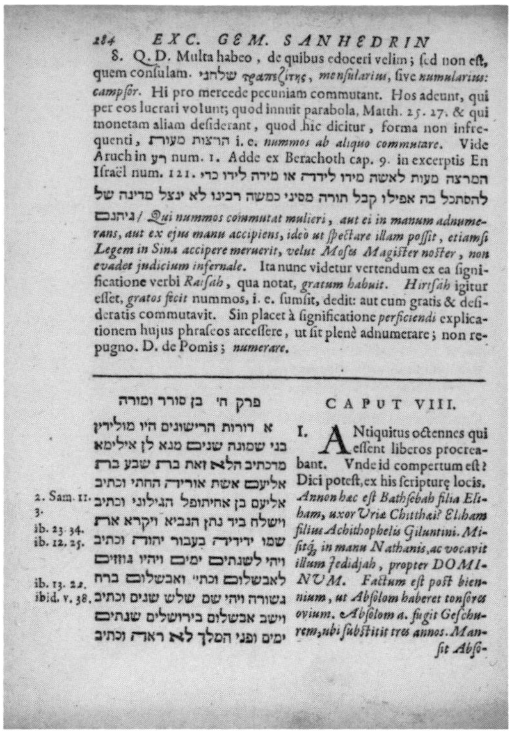

284 EXC. GEM. SANHEDRIN

8. Q. D. Multa habeo, de quibus edoceri velim; sed non est, quem consulam. שלחני τραπεζίτης, *mensularius*, sive *numularius: campsor*. Hi pro mercede pecuniam commutant. Hos adeunt, qui per eos lucrari volunt; quod innuit parabola, Matth. 25. 27. & qui monetam aliam desiderant, quod hic dicitur, forma non infrequenti, הרצות מעות i. e. *nummos ab aliquo commutare*. Vide Aruch in רץ num. 1. Adde ex Berachoth cap. 9. in excerptis En Israël num. 121. המרצה מעות לאשה מידו לידה או מידה לידו כדי להסתכל בה אפילו קבל תורה מסיני כמשה רבינו לא ינצל מדינה של גיהנם / *Qui nummos commutat mulieri, aut ei in manum adnumerans, aut ex ejus manu accipiens, ideò ut spectare illam possit, etiamsi Legem in Sina accipere meruerit, velut Moses Magister noster, non evadet judicium infernale*. Ita nunc videtur vertendum ex ea significatione verbi *Raisah*, qua notat, *gratum habuit*. *Hirtsah* igitur esset, *gratos fecit* nummos, i. e. sumsit, dedit: aut cum gratis & desideratis commutavit. Sin placet à significatione *perficiendi* explicationem hujus phraseos arcessere, ut sit plenè adnumerare; non repugno. D. de Pomis; *numerare*.

פרק ח׳ בן סורר ומורה

א דורות הראשונים היו מולידין בני שמונה שנים מנא לן אילימא מדכתיב הלא זאת בת שבע בת אליעם אשת אוריה החתי וכתיב
2. Sam. 11. 3. אליעם בן אחיתופל הגילוני וכתיב
ib. 23. 34. וישלח ביד נתן הנביא ויקרא את
ib. 12. 25. שמו ידידיה בעבור יהוה וכתיב ויהי לשנתים ימים ויהיו גוזזים
ib. 13. 23. לאבשלום וכתי׳ ואבשלום ברח
ibid. v. 38. גשורה ויהי שם שלש שנים וכתיב וישב אבשלום בירושלים שנתים ימים ופני המלך לא ראה וכתיב

CAPUT VIII.

I. ANtiquitus octennes qui essent liberos procreabant. Vnde id compertum est? Dici potest, ex his scripturę locis. *Annon hæc est Bathsebah filia Elibam, uxor Uriæ Chitthai? Elibam filius Achithophelis Giluntini. Misitq; in manu Nathanis, ac vocavit illum Jedidjah, propter DOMINUM. Factum est post biennium, ut Absolom haberet tonsores ovium. Absolom a. fugit Geschurem, ubi substitit tres annos. Mansit Abso-*

Johannes Koch (1603–1669), Dutch Christian Bible scholar and orientalist, professor of theology at Leyden, published his Latin translation for the Mishnah of tractates Sanhedrin and Maccoth with a commentary, when he was only twenty-six years old. Two poems in fine Hebrew, by John Persius of Amsterdam and a student, Henry Martinus of Bremen, extolling the translator, indicate the extent and quality of Hebrew studies among Christians in the early seventeenth century.

Johannes Coccejus, *Duo Tituli Thalmudici Sanhedrin et Maccoth*, Amsterdam, 1629.
Hebraic Section.

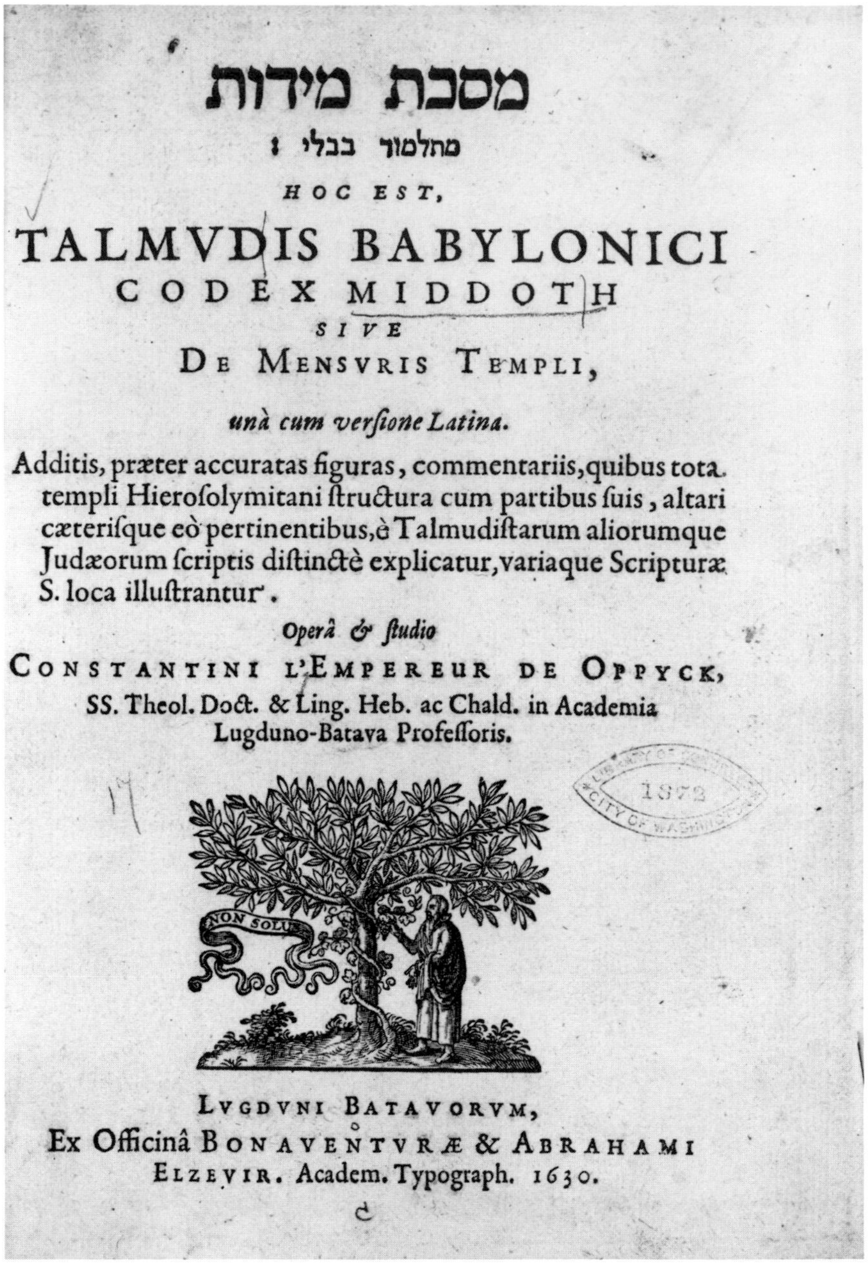

מסכת מידות

מתלמוד בבלי׃

HOC EST,

TALMUDIS BABYLONICI CODEX MIDDOTH SIVE DE MENSURIS TEMPLI,

unà cum versione Latina.

Additis, præter accuratas figuras, commentariis, quibus tota templi Hierosolymitani structura cum partibus suis, altari cæterisque eò pertinentibus, è Talmudistarum aliorumque Judæorum scriptis distinctè explicatur, variaque Scripturæ S. loca illustrantur.

Operâ & studio

CONSTANTINI L'EMPEREUR DE OPPYCK, SS. Theol. Doct. & Ling. Heb. ac Chald. in Academia Lugduno-Batava Professoris.

LUGDUNI BATAVORUM,
Ex Officinâ BONAVENTURÆ & ABRAHAMI ELZEVIR. Academ. Typograph. 1630.

Tractate Middot deals with the architecture of the Temple in Jerusalem, in which there was considerable interest in both the Jewish and Christian scholarly communities in the seventeenth century. Constantine L'Empereur's Latin translation and learned commentary is accompanied by a finely detailed floor plan map of the Temple. What gives this volume added distinction is that it was printed by the famed Elzevir Press of Leyden.

Talmudis Babylonici Codex Middoth sive De Mensuris Templi. Translation and Commentary by Constantine L'Empereur, Leyden, 1630.
Rare Book and Special Collections Division.

Among single tractates of the Talmud published, there are two in the Library's holdings which are of singular interest. In 1597–98 *Ketuboth* was published in Kuru Tschechme, a suburb of Constantinople, "in the house of the noble lady Reyna . . . the widow of the great and noble leader of Israel, the Duke Don Yosef Nasi." Why publish the tractate *Ketuboth* and no other? True, the tractate was much favored by scholars and students alike, but it also might have been published because on the death of the Lady Reyna's husband, his estate was either depleted or confiscated by the Sultan, and all she was permitted to inherit was the dowry she had brought to the marriage, as attested to in her ketubah (marriage contract). This inheritance enabled her to establish and maintain a Hebrew press. Pious woman that she was, she expressed her gratitude through publication of the Talmud tractate that deals with marriage contracts, *Ketuboth*.*

In 1842 in Berlin there appeared a truly extraordinary volume with

*For more on Doña Reyna Nasi, see pp. 167–69.

title pages in Hebrew and in German, *Talmud Babli, Babylonischer Talmud, Tractat Berachoth, Segensprüche.* "Mit deutscher Uebersetzung und den Commentaren Raschi und Tosephoth nebst den verschiedenen Verbesserungen aller früheren Ausgaben." The translator, Dr. E. M. Pinner, was also the publisher; the price was eight Reichsthaler. Even a quick perusal of the Library's fine copy vindicates the author's boast that his edition is an improvement over previous ones. A useful scholarly introduction precedes an original text punctuated as are the commentaries of Rashi and the tosaphists; the Mishnah text is vocalized as well. The classic form of the Talmudic page is retained. A fine German translation, as well as commentaries in German and Hebrew are provided. What may startle those acquainted with the history of the Jews in Russia is that the dedication is to His Majesty, Nicholas I, King of Russia, who is described as a "great monarch, rich in deeds, high-minded protector of every pure aspiration." The deeds of Czar Nicholas I caused the Jews of his empire to call him "Haman II." Nicholas's thirty-year reign represented one of the darkest eras in Russian Jewish history. Why did Pinner, a devoted Jew, dedicate the first volume of what he hoped to be a complete edition of the Talmud to such a monarch? It is easy to understand why the Czar permitted the dedication, bent as he was on "westernizing" the Jews of his realms. Thus, translations of the Talmud into European languages (he encouraged a French translation, as well) fit into his scheme of exposing his culturally insular Jews to the world about them. Pinner, fluent in German and French, would think this a benevolent attitude, as did many Jews in Russia, and he no doubt hoped that the Czar's government might subvent his projected edition. Later the Czar's government did publish books of the Bible and selections from Maimonides's *Mishneh Torah* with German translation, bearing the approbation of leading rabbis whom the government had invited to com-

Talmud: Berakot

תלמוד בבלי

מסכת

ברכות

עם

תרגום אשכנזי

ועם

פירוש רש״י ותוספות

מבוא התלמוד

אפרים משה בן רבי אלכסנדר זיסקינד ז״ל פיננער׳

כרך ראשון

בערלין

בשנת תר״ב לפק׳

Talmud Babli

Babylonischer Talmud.

Tractat

Berachoth

Segensprüche.

Mit

deutscher Uebersetzung

und

den Commentaren Raschi und Tosephoth

nebst

den verschiedenen Verbesserungen aller früheren Ausgaben.

Hinzugefügt sind:

Neue Lesarten und Parallelstellen in allen Theilen dieses Tractates und der Commentare,

Vokalisation der Mischnah,

Interpunktion der Mischnah und Gemara, Raschi und Tosephoth,

Etymologie und Uebertragung der fremden Wörter,

Erklärungen des Meharschal und Meharscha,

R. Ascher mit Erläuterung der Halachah und den abweichenden Lesarten,

R. Moscheh's, Sohnes R. Maimon's, Commentar zur Mischnah mit Berichtigungen,

Einleitung in den Talmud,

enthaltend

Grundprincipien der Methodologie und Exegetik des Talmud.

Von

Dr. E. M. Pinner,

Membre de la Société Asiatique de Paris &c. &c. &c.

Erster Band.

BERLIN 1842.

Eigenthum des Verfassers.

(Preis 8 Rthlr. Velinpapier 10 Rthlr.)

Truly an extraordinary edition of the first tractate of the Talmud, *Berachoth.* The type is large and clear; the text and commentaries are vocalized. To the traditional commentaries Dr. E. M. Pinner adds his own, contextual and etymological. The German translation and commentary are expertly done, yet no more tractates appeared. Was 1842 too early a date for the scientific study of the Talmud, or was it, perhaps, because Pinner dedicated his work to Czar Nicholas I, "high-minded protector of every pure aspiration," who in fact was so anti-Semitic a monarch that the Jews of his realm dubbed him "Haman II"?

Talmud Babli . . . Berachoth . . . , ed. Dr. E. M. Pinner, Berlin, 1842.
Hebraic Section.

ment, an invitation the rabbis could not refuse. It did not take too long for all to learn that the Czar was interested not in the integration of the Jews but in their assimilation, and in assimilation as a first step to apostasy. When Max Lilienthal (a German Jew who had served as rabbi in Riga and then as chief promoter of a Russian government program to establish a "modern" Jewish school system) came to realize the government's real intentions, he fled to America, where he served with distinction in the Reform rabbinate.

The ardor against the Talmud among reactionary religious and political spokesmen did not abate in the twentieth century. One hundred and one years after Pinner's publication one could find in Berlin and in other German cities a new edition of a small work on the Talmud, *Unmoral im Talmud* (Immorality in the Talmud, Munich, 1943), by Hitler's appointed *Kulturleiter,* Alfred Rosenberg, the most influential philosopher of Nazism. As one looks at its garish cover and leafs through its contents, one wonders why this anti-Semitic diatribe was republished at that time in the birth city of Nazism. In the year 1943, the height of the Holocaust, what need to further malign a people being brutally and efficiently put to death? Who was questioning the deed? Who was demanding justification of it? Was it directed to the perpetrators and their cohorts, or to those indifferently standing by at home and abroad?

Three years later, in summer 1946, two volumes of the Talmud, tractates *Kiddushin* and *Nedarim,* were published in Munich by "Rabbinical Representative [sic] by Central Committee of Liberated Jews in the American Occupied Zone." The "Rabbinical Representative" were Rabbis Samuel Abba Snieg, head of the Rabbinical Association of the Zone, and his young colleague, Samuel Jacob Rose. The two were survivors of both the notorious Kovno ghetto and the Dachau concentration camp. Liberated by the American Army and restored to health, they succeeded "after great exertions" in publishing these volumes by photo offset "to slake the great thirst for holy books" among Jewish survivors. This project accomplished, they embarked upon a far more ambitious one, the publication of the entire Talmud in a sixteen-volume edition.

This project they proposed to the recently arrived American Advisor on Jewish Affairs, Rabbi Philip S. Bernstein. Their argument and plea was that, true, yeshivot had been established in the American Zone, but there were no books to study from. None could be found in the makeshift synagogues serving the survivors. If one was found, a hundred hands stretched out to it. In a moving memorandum to commanding General Joseph McNarney, Rabbi Bernstein described the Talmud as one of the source springs of Jewish religion and tradition over which Jews have pored in every land and age. Hitler's hordes, the rabbi explained, had tried to destroy the Talmud by ordering Jews, upon pain of death, to carry their copies of the Talmud to the Nazi bonfires and personally consign them to the flames. Would it not be in the best tradition of American democracy, the rabbi urged, for the army which liberated the survivors to now help restore their spirits by participating in rebuilding their religious culture, which the Nazis had sought to obliterate. "A 1947 edition [of the Talmud] published in Germany under the auspices of the American Army of Occupation," Rabbi Bernstein proclaimed, "would be an historic work." General McNarney read the memorandum, heard the impassioned plea of

Facing page: The title page of the first volume of nineteen, an edition of the complete Talmud published in Munich-Heidelberg in 1948, only three years after the Holocaust, by the Rabbinic Organization in the American sector "with the aid of the American Military Command and the American Jewish Joint Distribution Committee in Germany." It is appropriately dedicated to the "United States Army," which provided the opportunity and the means for its publication. At the bottom of the page is a depiction of a Nazi slave labor camp flanked by barbed wire; above are the palm trees and the landscape of the Holy Land. The legend reads: "From bondage to freedom; from deep darkness to a great light."

Masekhet Berakhot min Talmud Bavli (Tractate Berahot of the Babylonian Talmud), Munich-Heidelberg, 1948. Hebraic Section.

משעבוד לגאולה מאפלה לאור גדול
מסכת
ברכות
מן
תלמוד בבלי
עם כל המפרשים כאשר נדפס מקדם ועם
הוספות חדשות כמבואר בשער השני.
יצא לאור ע"י ועד אגודת הרבנים
באזור האמריקאי באשכנז
בסיוע שלטון הצבא דארצות הברית והדזוינט
בגרמני'
מינכן־היידעלבערג
שנת חמשת אלפים ושבע מאות ותשע לב"ע
כמעט כלוני בארץ ואני לא עזבתי פקודיך
מחנה עבודה באשכנז בימי הנאצים

the rabbis, and was persuaded.

There followed a heroic effort on the part of all. Everything was in short supply, if available at all—paper, offset facilities, binding materials, and, not least of all, a complete set of the Talmud. A few volumes were found in a Munich cemetery, a half dozen more were obtained from France and Switzerland, but two complete sets had to be brought from New York. The number of volumes projected to complete the set was nineteen, and the number of sets the army was ready to publish was fifty. By 1950, when the edition was completed, many more volumes had come off the presses, but complete sets are a rarity. It is most appropriate that among the treasures of the Library of Congress's Hebraic Section is such a complete set.

The illustrated title pages of each volume have at the top a drawing of a Holy Land vista and the inscription, "From bondage to redemption; from deep darkness to a great light" (The Passover Haggadah). At the bottom, a depiction of a slave labor camp and a verse from Psalms (119:87): "They all but obliterated me from the earth; but I, I forsook not Thy precepts." On the reverse side, Rabbis Snieg and Rosen tell the story of its publication:

> Through the mercies of the Blessed One, we have been enabled to publish this edition of the Talmud, a work of beauty and splendor. . . . Engraved in our memories is that bitter day in the ghetto, when the decree came from the Nazis, may their memory be blotted out, to gather up all the books into one place to destroy them. The peril of death hung over those who would dare hide a book. . . . All our holy books were taken from us for abuse and set afire. Now, because of the Lord's great mercies, a remnant of His people remains, saved from the sword of their accursed destroyers, but without a book in their hands. . . . We therefore turned to the American Army Command in Germany to help us, and through the intercession of Dr. Rabbi Philip Bernstein, our desire was with God's help fulfilled. . . . During our overlong exile, our holy books were burned once and again by monarchs and governments. This is the first time in the long history of the Jewish people, that a government has helped us to publish the books of the Talmud, which are our life and length of days. Armies of the United States brought us from death to life, and they now protect us in this land. Through their aid the Talmud now appears again in Germany.

The page is in Hebrew, the Dedication, in English:

> This edition of the Talmud is dedicated to the United States Army. This Army played a major role in the rescue of the Jewish people from total annihilation, and after the defeat of Hitler bore the major burden of sustaining the DPs of the Jewish faith. This special edition of the Talmud published in the very land where, but a short time ago, everything Jewish and of Jewish inspiration was anathema, will remain a symbol of the indestructibility of the Torah. The Jewish DPs will never forget the generous impulses and the unprecedented humanitarianism of the American forces, to whom they owe so much.

The publication date is 1948, just three years after the cessation of hostilities and the liberation of *Shearit Hapleta,* the "surviving remnant."

4

"FROM MOSES TO MOSES, THERE WAS NONE LIKE MOSES"

PHILOSOPHER AND POET Jedaiah ben Abraham Bedersi concludes his prose poem *Behinat Olam* (Examination of the World), a work of philosophic rumination and religious passion, in this manner:

> To sum up: Go my heart to the left or right, but believe, believe all that our great master and teacher, Moses the son of Maimon believed. The last of the Gaonim he was in time, but first in rank, and there is none among the sages of Israel since the days of the Talmud who could compare to him.

Writing at the beginning of the fourteenth century, the pious Bedersi found an anchor for his faith in the works and views of Moses ben Maimon. Six centuries later, in 1904—in commemoration of the 700th anniversary of the death of Moses Maimonides—the Hebrew essayist, ethicist, and ideologist of cultural Zionism, Ahad ha-Am, wrote in an essay titled "Shilton HaSechel" (The Supremacy of Reason):

> In earlier centuries . . . it was almost impossible for an educated Jew (and most Jews then were educated) to pass a single day without remembering Maimonides . . . In whatever field of study the Jew might be engaged—*halachah*, ethics, religious or philosophical speculation—inevitably he found Maimonides in the place of honor . . . And not only the student, the plain Jew, who ended his morning prayers every day with the "Thirteen Articles of Faith," was not likely to forget who first formulated them.
>
> Every Jew . . . who has traveled the hard and bitter road that leads from blind faith to free reason must have come across Maimonides at the beginning of his journey, and must have found in him a source of strength and support for those first steps which are the hardest and the most dangerous.
>
> His task was so to shape the content and form of Judaism that it could become a bulwark on which the nation could depend for its continued survival. There is, however, this difference between Maimonides and his predecessors: that whereas for them the bulwark was a Judaism placed above reason, for him it was a Judaism identified with reason.
>
> (*Translation by Leon Simon*)

Bedersi, a fervent upholder of faith, and Ahad ha-Am, the advocate of reason, passionately devoted Jews both, drew sustenance and support from Maimonides, though not because Maimonides's views are imprecise or ambiguous. So clear are they and so pointed that in the past his views became the cause of religious controversies and to this day remain the focus of scholarly dispute. Maimonides was both a defender of faith and a proponent of reason. Because his presentation of each is done with such skill and erudition, because he yields neither mind nor heart to the diminution of the other, advocates of both faith and reason find support for their positions in his writings.

That the force of his intellect and the passion of his beliefs have been a continuing source of intellectual stimulation and scholarly inspiration is clear from the long tray full of catalog cards in the Library of Congress listing his works and works about him. Enter the rare books enclave of the Library's Hebraic Section and remove Maimonides's work and the commentaries they provoked, and you will have created a void on almost every shelf. The great tribute to Maimonides in Judaism's historical development is the anonymous but almost universally accepted accolade: "From Moses to Moses, there was none like Moses."

Moses ben Maimon—known to the Jewish world by his acronym, Rambam (from Rabbi Moshe ben Maimon), and to the world at large as Maimonides—was born on Passover eve, 4895 (March 30, 1135) in Cordoba, Spain. In the Golden Age of Spanish Jewry, Cordoba was Spain's leading Jewish community, but in the twelfth century both the Golden Age and the community were in decline. For more than eight generations ancestors of Moses had been leaders of the community. At the time of his birth, his father was serving as *dayyan,* chief judicial authority. But just a few months after Moses's Bar Mitzvah in 1148, the family fled Cordoba, the city having been conquered by a fanatical fundamentalist Islamic sect, the Almohads, who offered Cordoban Jews the choice of apostasy or exile.

For almost a dozen years, the family roamed the Iberian peninsula seeking refuge, until finally in 1160 they found haven in Fez, Morocco. During the years of wandering, "while my mind was troubled amid divinely ordained exiles," Maimonides continued his education, at first taught by his father, then increasingly self-taught. By the time the family settled in Fez, he had already completed his first works, *Millot ha-Higgayon,* a treatise on logic, and *Ma-amar ha-Ibbur,* a work on the Hebrew calendar. He had also begun the first of his three major works, a commentary on the Mishnah.

After five years in Fez, the family took up the wanderer's staff again. Fez too was under the Almohads, and although tolerated, the Jews there lived under constant pressure to convert, which from time to time became so insistent that many yielded and outwardly converted to Islam, while inwardly adhering to their ancestral faith. Maimon offered solace to his unfortunate brethren in his *Iggeret ha-Nehamah* (Epistle of Consolation):

> We who are in exile can be compared to a man who is drowning. The water has reached our nostrils but we still grasp hold of something . . . God's precepts and His Torah . . . whoever seizes hold of it still has hope of living . . . and surely he who holds on even only with the tips of his fingers has more hope than he who lets go completely.

Maimon, the father, offered these words of consolation and encouragement to those who had succumbed; Moses, the son, urged a plan of action to those living in a land where apostasy was demanded of them. In his *Iggeret ha-Shemad* (Epistle on Apostasy), he counseled:

> [A Jew] should on no account remain in a place of forced conversion; whoever remains in such a place desecrates the Divine Name and is nearly as bad as a willful sinner; as for those who beguile themselves, saying they will remain until the Messiah comes to lead them to Jerusalem, I do not know how he is to cleanse them of the stain of conversion.

Maimon and his children left Fez, and after a difficult storm-beset journey reached the Holy Land in 1165. The Holy Land was then under the domination of a Crusader Kingdom so, after half a year in the port city of Acre and pilgrimages to the holy cities of Jerusalem and Hebron, the family moved on to Egypt and settled in Fostat, the old city of Cairo. After the father died, Moses's brother David supported the family by dealing in precious stones, while Moses devoted himself to his studies, to his writing, and to religious communal service.

By 1168, he completed his commentary on the Mishnah. Written in Arabic, it has in its Hebrew translation been incorporated into almost all editions of the Talmud. A listing of the Principles of the Faith in his comments on the Sanhedrin, Chapter X, has, in abridged form and in poetic rendition, entered the Jewish liturgy. Thirteen in number, the Principles are found in the prayer book at the end of the weekday morning service; a poetic version, the hymn *Yigdal*, is sung at the Sabbath eve service. Transformed into liturgy they speak of Creation, Revelation and Redemption:

1. I believe with perfect faith that the Creator, blessed be His name, is the Author and Guide of everything that has been created, and that He alone has made, does make and will make all things.
7. I believe that the prophecy of Moses our teacher, was true, and that he was the chief of prophets . . .
8. I believe that the whole Torah, now in our possession, is that same that was given to Moses.
9. I believe that this Torah will not be changed, and that there will never be any other Law from the Creator.
12. I believe with perfect faith in the coming of the Messiah; and though he tarry, I will wait for him.

At long last the Maimonides family had found security in Cairo, but its serenity was shattered by the death of David, drowned when his ship went down in the Indian Ocean. The loss of his brother and the family breadwinner cast Maimonides into a deep depression. After a year he recovered and decided to study medicine, refusing to consider any vocation which would make the Torah "a spade to dig with," i.e., a source of livelihood.

THE MISHNEH TORAH AND THE GUIDE FOR THE PERPLEXED

Maimonides practiced medicine to support the family. Within a half dozen years he became the official head of the Jewish community, looked upon as "the light of the East and West, master and adornment of his generation." The decade between 1170 and 1180 he devoted chiefly to the composition of his magnum opus, the *Mishneh Torah*, the first comprehensive code of Jewish law.

The work is a marvel of erudition, organization, and Hebrew style. It is the one work Maimonides wrote in Hebrew, but excepting only the Bible and the Mishnah, which are the work of many, the *Mishneh Torah* is the greatest creation in the Hebrew language. Mishnaic Hebrew is employed with an unequaled clarity and precision. The Introduction, a concise but comprehensive essay on the Jewish legal tradition, states the purpose of the code:

> In our days, many vicissitudes prevail, and all feel the pressure of hard times. The wisdom of our wise men has disappeared; the understanding of our prudent men is hidden. Hence the commentaries of the Geonim, their compilations of laws and responsa . . . have become hard to understand. . . . Needless to add, such is the case in regard to the Talmud itself. . . . Therefore, I, Moses, the son of Maimon, the Sefardi, bestirred myself, and, relying on the help of God, blessed be He, intently studied all these works, with the view of putting together the results obtained from them . . . all in plain language and terse style, so that thus the entire Oral Law might become systematically known to all, without citing difficulties and solutions of, different views . . . but consisting of statements, clear and convincing . . . that have appeared from the time of Moses to the present, so that all rules shall be accessible to young and old.

Isadore Twersky, a foremost authority on Maimonides, calls the Mishneh Torah "a quantum jump in the development of Rabbinic literature," points to its decisive influence on the Jewish legal system, and notes its amazingly rapid distribution throughout the Jewish world—Asian, African and European—so that by 1191 Maimonides spoke of its renown in all corners of the earth. And this took place two and a half centuries before the invention of printing!

The *Mishneh Torah* was in "plain language" to make the rules "accessible to young and old." Maimonides's third and last major work, *Dalalat al-Ha'rin* (Guide for the Perplexed), a philosophic essay written in Arabic, was for a different purpose and a different audience.

As Maimonides states in his Introduction, the Guide was not meant for the common people or for beginners. It is addressed to those religious persons, well-versed in the Scriptures and loyal to the Torah, who, having studied philosophy, are embarrassed by the contradictions that seem to exist between the teachings of philosophy and the literal meaning of the Torah.

It is a work of apologetics, pure and simple; but neither pure nor simple to those whose sense of piety informed them that the need to defend is an admission of inherent weakness. During Maimonides's lifetime and thereafter, the Guide was the target of the ultrapious, who felt vindicated in their views that its greatest attractiveness was to those who had the greatest difficulty in accepting the tenets of the received tradition. But for those who are perplexed, those who are challenged by new and evolving thought, it has often been a guide to refine their commitment to the tradition, keeping it vital and viable. And, as we shall see, that was not true for Jews alone.

As Maimonides's authority as a leader of Jewry and his fame as a physician grew, individuals and communities increasingly turned to him for the healing of body and soul; communities East and West turned to him for advice. Scholars sought his decisions on matters of law, and the number of his patients increased, especially after he became a court physician to al-Fadil, Saladin's vizier. An Arabic poet and cadi wrote in his praise:

> Galen's art heals only the body,
> But Abu Imram's [Maimonides] the body and soul.
> If the moon would submit to his art,
> He would deliver her of her spots,
> Cure her of her defects . . .
> Save her from waning.

To Samuel ibn Tibbon, the translator of the Guide into Hebrew, Maimonides wrote of his weekday labors and his Sabbath "rest":

> I dwell at Fostat and the Sultan resides in Cairo. My duties with the Sultan are very heavy. I am obliged to see him every day . . . and remain in attendance if he, or his children, or any members of his harem, and any royal officers are indisposed.
>
> As a rule I depart for Cairo very early every morning, and even if nothing unusual happens, I do not return home until the afternoon . . . My antechambers are filled with people, Jews and gentiles, nobles and commoners, judges and bailiffs, friends and foes—a mixed multitude who await my return.
>
> I dismount from my animal, wash my hands, go forth to my patients, and entreat them to bear with me while I partake of some slight refreshment—my only meal of the day. Patients go in and out until nightfall, and sometimes into the night. I converse with them and prescribe for them while lying down from sheer fatigue . . . On the Sabbath, the whole congregation, or at least the majority, come to me at the end of the morning service, when I instruct them as to their proceedings during the whole week; we study a little until noon . . . Some return and read with me after the afternoon service until the evening prayers. In this manner I spend the Sabbath day.

Maimonides lived the biblical three score years and ten, being called to eternity on December 13, 1204. In Fostat three days of mourning were observed. In Jerusalem a general fast was appointed. His remains were taken to Tiberias, where his tomb has been a place of pilgrimage to the present day.

MAIMONIDEAN TREASURES

The Library is rich in Maimonidean treasures. We touch on a few to represent the many: the first edition of Maimonides's initial work; a very early commentary on his commentary to the Mishnah; a Hebrew and a Latin edition of the Guide; a Latin translation with commentary of a section of the *Mishneh Torah;* a volume of responsa and a volume of epistles; and seven of the premier editions of the *Mishneh Torah,* each of unusual bibliographic and historical interest.

Maimonides was only sixteen years old when he completed his first work, a technical treatise on logic of which the Library has the first edition, *Millot ha-Higgayon* (Terms of Logic), Venice, 1550. Written in Arabic, it was translated into Hebrew by Moses ibn Tibbon, who gave it its Hebrew name. Its theme and structure presage Maimonides's later works. The division of this first work into fourteen chapters foreshadows the fourteen-section composition of the *Mishneh Torah.* The Library has a fine copy of the first edition, printed in Venice in the publishing house of Marco Antonio Giustiniani, under the supervision of Cornelius Adelkind. By the end of the nineteenth century no less than fourteen editions had appeared, all with commentaries, the most notable of which is that of Moses Mendelssohn.

Hesed Avraham (Compassion of Abraham), Lublin, 1577, is an early commentary on the *Shemona Perakim* (Eight Chapters), Maimonides's introduction to his commentary on the tractate *Pirke Avot* (Ethics of the Fathers) of the Mishnah, by Abraham Horowitz (1550–1615). The Eight Chapters may be viewed as an independent composition on therapeutic psychology for the soul. Maimonides argues that sentiments and attitudes of mind can be shaped and if necessary reshaped through spiritual exercises. The goal is the "golden mean" between extremes. Human tendencies, when they verge on either extreme, can be moderated, indeed must be moderated, if a person is to be virtuous.

> Good deeds are such as are equibalanced, maintaining the mean between two equally bad extremes, the too much and the too little.
>
> Liberality is the mean between miserliness and extravagance; courage between recklessness and cowardice; dignity between haughtiness and loutishness; humility beween arrogance and self abasement . . . Know, that moral excellences . . . cannot be acquired or implanted in the soul except by means of the frequent repetition of acts resulting from these qualities, which, practiced during a long period of time, accustoms us to them. If these acts performed are good ones, then we shall have acquired a virtue.

Horowitz, a leading Talmudic scholar in the Golden Age of Polish Jewry, was at an early age attracted to Maimonides and became both a keen student of his works and an avid admirer of his rationalistic method. He was drawn to the Eight Chapters because it celebrates human freedom and repudiates self-denigration and spiritual self-flagellation, both of which, in his day, were deemed indications of heightened piety. What was needed was the spiritual therapy which these Chapters offered, but being grounded in philosophy, in which few are trained, they are difficult to understand. For most individuals they remain "like a dream without interpretation." At the age of twenty-six, Horowitz wrote the needed interpretation. Later in life, he turned from rationalism to mysticism and issued a new version of his commentary to "supersede the earlier one." It became the widely accepted standard commentary, appearing with the text in most editions of the Talmud.

Because of the vicissitudes of history, early Lublin imprints have become rarities, especially this edition of the work whose "authorization" was withdrawn by the author himself. The publishers, Kalonymus Jaffe and his sons, had only recently improved typography and ornamentation, so the volume is both rare and beautiful. The Library copy has the additional virtue of annotations inscribed by an early hand.

The Library also has a fine copy of the Venice, 1551 edition, the second Hebrew edition of the Guide, the first having been printed in Rome

Facing page: In his commentary on the Mishnah, written in Arabic, Maimonides wrote a lengthy treatise on ethics as the introduction to his comments on the ethical tractate *Pirke Avot* (Ethics of the Fathers). Translated into Hebrew by Samuel Ibn Tibbon, it is known as the *Shemona Perakim* (Eight Chapters) and has become a popular tract for the study of Jewish ethics. Abraham Horowitz added his own lengthy commentary, and the publication of text and commentary by the early Hebrew printer of Lublin, Kalonymus ben Mordecai Jaffe, is one of the distinguished products of early East European Hebrew printing. The Library's copy has copious marginal notes in a contemporary hand.

Abraham Horowitz, *Hesed Avraham,* Lublin, 1577. Hebraic Section.

ספר חסד אברהם

חבור וחקר ותקן הר״ר אברהם בר שבתי זצ״ל איש סורווין והוא פירש יפה על שמנה
פרקים שהקדים הרמב״ם לפירושו על מסכת אבות באמר כי דברים שהמה שבעותי בפרקי
הנ״ל הם תועלת למדות הנפש והפעם רק שלא הוסר מסוה מעל פני בחורים וילדי הזמן
לעמוד על סוף דעתו של הרמב״ם ז״ל כי עמוק עמוק הוא מי ימצאנו לכן
[illegible] אברהם הנ״ל וגילה הרבים בפירוש זה להורות להם דרך אשר
ילכון בו באופן זיסה הדרך כבושה לכל שבחורים [illegible]
ספקי׳ מבלי שיצטרכו לכלות ימים׳ ולשנות׳ [illegible]
לכן מהרו וקחו חפץ יפה אשר לא יערכנה זהב
וזכוכית ואל תתנו עיניכם [illegible]

נדפס פה ק״ק לובלין

על ידי קלונימוס בן מהר״ר מרדכי יפה זצ״ל המחוקק

מורה נבוכים

נצב פירושו בעדת אל בקרב אלדים

אלו הדיינין שדנו ואמדו דבריו ופירשו את הסתום הה

פירוש **שם טוב** ופירוש **אפודי** ומשום

דאין בית דין שקול עד השלישי באנו

והוספנו בזה על הדפסת הראשונים

פירוש האלדי ז׳ **קרשקש**

מה רב טובו והחוט

המשולש לא

במהרה

ינתק

גם כוונת כל פרק מפרקי המורה על דעת החכם החריזי

גם פירוש מלות זרות לאבן תבון בשנוי דברים מן

הראשונים :

גם כל פסוקי התורה ונביאים וכתובים אשר באו

נזכרים בספר המורה נסדרו בסדר יפה על

סדרם שכתובים בתורה אין בהם

מוקדם ומאוחר איש לא

נעדר :

נדפס **בסביוניטה** תחת ממשלת האדון **ויספסיאן גונזאגה**

והיה בראש חדש שבט שנת שי״ג לפ״ק בבית היושב והנדיב

כמ״ר טוביה פואה יצ״ו

על יד קורניליו אדיל קינד לבית הלוי

Rabi Mossei Aegyptij

Dux seu Director dubitātium aut perplexorum, in treis Libros diuisus, & summa accuratione Reuerendi patris Augustini Iustiniani ordinis Prædicatorũ Nebiensiũ Episcopi recognitus. Cuius index seu tabella ad calcem totius apponetur operis.

Moses ben Maimon

Prelũ Ascẽsianũ

Venundatur cum Gratia & Priuilegio in Triennium, ab Iodoco Badio Ascensio.

The first edition of the *Guide for the Perplexed* in Latin printed in bold black type throughout. A historiated initial opens each paragraph in this historically important and typographically distinguished edition. The translation, attributed to Jacob Mantino of Tortosa, was corrected and edited by Augustinus Justinianus. The quality of the edition is an indication of the esteem accorded the philosophy of Maimonides in the Christian world.

Maimonides, *Rabbi Mossei Aegypti, Dux seu Director Dubitatium aut Perplexorum* (Guide for the Perplexed), Paris, 1520.
Rare Book and Special Collections Division.

between 1473 and 1475. We have chosen the rarer, more beautiful, richer in commentaries and typographically more interesting 1553 Sabbioneta edition. The translation is by Samuel Ibn Tibbon. The publisher is Tobias Foa, first in a line of Foas whose presses produced Hebrew books in Sabbioneta as early as 1551, and as late as 1803 in Pisa. In the years 1551–59, Tobias Foa published twenty-six Hebrew books in Sabbioneta, years in which Hebrew books were being burned and Hebrew printing suppressed in other Italian cities. Overseeing this printing was Cornelius Adelkind, who for many years did the same for the Christian printers of Venice.

Facing page: Only two years after the publication of the Hebrew translation of Maimonides's philosophic work, *Guide for the Perplexed,* in Venice, 1551, a new edition appeared in Sabbioneta, which became a center of Hebrew printing in the dark days of the papal decree to burn all copies of the Talmud. The title page of this edition has the crest of the Foa family, printers of Hebrew books for two and a half centuries in Sabbioneta, Amsterdam, Venice, and Pisa: Lions rampant, supporting a blossoming tree on which there is a Star of David.

Moses Maimonides, *Moreh Nevukhim* (Guide for the Perplexed), Sabbioneta, 1553.
Hebraic Section.

The text of the title page is framed by architectural gates on which stand vases overflowing with fruits and vegetables, guarded by a helmeted man and a woman holding a spear. They flank a wreath enclosing the crest of the Foa family: a blossoming tree flanked by lions, a Star of David, the legend "The righteous shall flourish like a palm tree" (Psalm 92:13), and the initials T. F. The title page proudly announces that, in addition to the commentaries *Shem Tov* (by Joseph Ibn Shem-Tov) and *Efodi* (by Profiat Duran), both of which had appeared in the Venice edition, a third, that of (Asher) Ibn Crescas has been added, and "the three-fold cord is not easily sundered." (Ecclesiastes 4:12)

Rabbi Mossei Aegypti Dux seu Director Dubitatium aut Perplexorum . . . , Paris, 1520, is a beautiful copy in its original binding of the first printing of the Guide in Latin translation. The translation was not, as claimed, made by Agostino Giustiniani, Professor of Hebrew at the New College of Three Languages in Paris. Jacob Mantino, an Italian Jewish physician and translator of Hebrew texts into Latin, is thought to have done this translation which Giustiniani merely corrected and edited. In any case, the translation is poor, superseded by the far more accurate one of Johannes Buxtorf Fil., Basle, 1629.

Translations of portions of the Guide into Latin were made as early as the thirteenth century and were used by leading Christian theologians. Albertus Magnus (d. 1280) knew of "Rabbi Moyses" and accepted and used his interpretation of the book of Job as a philosophical treatise on divine providence. The greatest of Catholic theologians, Thomas Aquinas (1225–1274), was influenced by Maimonides, esteeming him for having harmonized biblical theology and Aristotelian philosophy. Duns Scotus (1266–1308) refers to Maimonides's discussion on the relation of reason and revelation, as well as his doctrine of divine attributes, and accepts his views of prophecy. It is not, therefore, surprising that the Latin translation appeared three decades before the Hebrew editions, except for the Rome edition, of which few copies were printed.

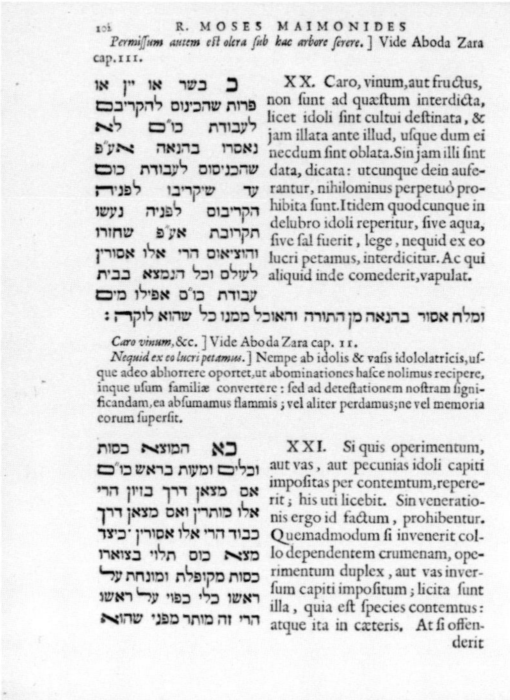
102 R. MOSES MAIMONIDES

Permiſſum autem eſt olera ſub hac arbore ſerere.] Vide Aboda Zara cap. III.

כ כשר או יין או פרות שהכינום להקריבם לעבודת כו"ם לא נאסרו בהנאה אע"פ שהכניסום לעבודת כום עד שיקריבו לפניה הקריבום לפניה נעשו תקרובת אע"פ שחזרו והוציאום הרי אלו אסורין לעולם וכל הנמצא בבית עבודת כו"ם אפילו מים ומלח אסור בהנאה מן התורה והאוכל ממנו כל שהוא לוקה:

XX. Caro, vinum, aut fructus, non ſunt ad quæſtum interdicta, licet idoli ſint cultui deſtinata, & jam illata ante illud, uſque dum ei necdum ſint oblata. Sin jam illi ſint data, dicata: utcunque dein auferantur, nihilominus perpetuò prohibita ſunt. Itidem quodcunque in delubro idoli reperitur, ſive aqua, ſive ſal fuerit, lege, nequid ex eo lucri petamus, interdicitur. Ac qui aliquid inde comederit, vapulat.

Caro vinum, &c.] Vide Aboda Zara cap. II.

Nequid ex eo lucri petamus.] Nempe ab idolis & vaſis idololatricis, uſque adeo abhorrere oportet, ut abominationes haſce nolimus recipere, inque uſum familiæ convertere: ſed ad deteſtationem noſtram ſignificandam, ea abſumamus flammis; vel aliter perdamus; ne vel memoria eorum ſuperſit.

כא המוצא כסות וכלים ומעות בראש כו"ם אם מצאן דרך בזיון הרי אלו מותרין ואם מצאן דרך כבוד הרי אלו אסורין ׳כיצד מצא כוס תלוי בצוארו כסות מקופלת ומונחת על ראשו כלי כפוי על ראשו הרי זה מותר מפני שהוא

XXI. Si quis operimentum, aut vas, aut pecunias idoli capiti impoſitas per contemtum, repererit; his uti licebit. Sin venerationis ergo id factum, prohibentur. Quemadmodum ſi invenerit collo dependentem crumenam, operimentum duplex, aut vas inverſum capiti impoſitum; licita ſunt illa, quia eſt ſpecies contemtus: atque ita in cæteris. At ſi offenderit

Christian scholars took great interest in the works of Maimonides. There are many editions of sections of his works, especially the *Mishneh Torah,* with Latin translation and commentary. One of the earliest is this edition of the section on laws pertaining to idolatry. The translator-commentator was Dionysius Voss. The publishers, the Blaeus, were of a family of noted publishers and cartographers.

Moses Maimonides, *De Idolatria* (On Idolatry), Amsterdam, 1641.
Hebraic Section.

Translations of sections of the *Mishneh Torah* into Latin and other languages are so many, that in the middle of the nineteenth century Julius Furst was able to list seventeen in Latin alone. Copies of many of these translations, as well as those in other languages, abound in the Library of Congress. We list one to represent the rest: Mosis Maimonidae, *De Idolatria,* Amsterdam, 1641, the fourth section of the first of the fourteen books of the *Mishneh Torah,* which contains laws dealing with idolatry. The translation and the accompanying commentary are by the Dutch divine, Dionysius Voss. It apparently attracted a considerable audience in each of the next two generations, for it was reprinted in 1666 and again in 1700.

Though their titles differ, these two volumes are similar in content: *T'shuvot Sh'elot V'Igrot . . .* (Responsa, Queries and Epistles . . .), Constantinople, c. 1517; and *Igrot L'Ha-maor Ha-Gadol . . . Rabeinu Moshe Hamaymoni* (Epistles to the Great Luminary Our Master Moses Maimonides), Venice, 1545.

They are the first and third editions of a collection of letters sent to Maimonides "from the East and from the West, from the North and the Sea [South], from sages in France and Spain, Yemen and Babylonia . . ." Selected passages from his replies offer us a glimpse of the man, and his passion and compassion. To Obadiah the Proselyte:

You ask if you are allowed to say in blessings and prayers "God of our fathers . . . You have chosen us . . . You have brought us out of the land of Egypt." Yes, you may say all this . . . Abraham our father, is the father of all proselytes who adopt Judaism. Do not consider your origin as inferior. While we are the descendants of Abraham, Isaac and Jacob, you derive from Him through whose word the world was created.

To another proselyte:

When your teacher called you a fool . . . he sinned grievously . . . He should have been cautious not to lose his temper with a proselyte of righteousness . . . A man who . . . forsook his birthplace, his country and its power and attached himself to this lowly and despised people because he recognized the truth and righteousness of its Law . . . He who blessed Abraham will bless you and make you worthy of beholding Israel's promised consolation.

אגרות להמאור הגדול

הנר המערבי מרנא ורבנא רבינו משה המיימוני זצ"ל
שבאו אליו · ממזרח · וממערב · מצפון · ומים ·
מחכמי צרפת · ספרד · ותימן · ובבל · ודברי
מוסר וצוואה שצוה הרב הגדול ז"ל לבנו
החכם רבי אברהם ז"ל · ושאלות
ששאלו מהרב הנזכר ז"ל
ותשובותיו עליהן ·

נדפס שנית בויניציאה העיר הגדולה המהוללה אשר
תחת ממשלת השררה יר"ה תגדל ותנשא מלכותם
אמן: בשמונה עשר יום לחדש אלול
שנת ש"ה לפ"ק:

בבית בן משק בית האדון מארקו אנטוניו יושטיניאן·

The title page of this work by Maimonides reads:

Letters to the Great Luminary, the light of the West, our teacher and rabbi Moses Maimon, that came to him from the East, from the West, from the North and from the Sea (South), from the scholars of France, Spain, the Yemen and Babylonia. And ethical admonition and the ethical will which the Great Rabbi, of blessed memory, left to his son, Rabbi Abraham, of blessed memory. And queries sent to him and his responses.

The printer's mark, the Temple in Jerusalem, is that of Marco Antonius Giustiniani. The legend above the Temple: "Great will be the glory of this house . . . Saith the Lord of Hosts," is Giustiniani's hope and boast for his press.

Maimonides, *Igrot La-maor ha-Gadol,* Venice, 1545. Hebraic Section.

הט לבי אל עדותיך ואל אל בצע ׃

ספר אחד עשר

וזהו ספר נזקים הלכותיו חמשה וזה הוא סדורן
הלכות נזקי ממון הלכות גניבה הלכות גזילה ואבידה
הלכות חובל ומזיק הלכות רוצח ושמירת נפש

הלכות נזקי ממון

יש בכללן ארבע מצות עשה וזהו פרטן ׃
א׳ דין השור ׃ ב׳ דין ההבער ׃
ג׳ דין הבור ׃ ד׳ דין הבערה ׃

הלכות גניבה

יש בכללן שבע מצות שתי מצות עשה וה׳ לא תעשה וזהו פרטן ׃
א׳ שלא לגנוב ממון ׃ ב׳ דין הגנב ׃
ג׳ לצדק המאזנים והמשקלות ׃
ד׳ שלא יעשה עול במדות ובמשקלות ׃
ה׳ שלא יהיה לאדם אבן ואבן איפה ואיפה אף על פי שאינו
לוקח ונותן בהן ׃
ו׳ שלא ישיג גבול ׃ ז׳ שלא יגנוב נפשות ׃

הלכות גזילה ואבידה

יש בכללן שבע מצות שתי מצות עשה וה׳ לא תעשה וזהו פרטן ׃
א׳ שלא לגזול ׃ ב׳ שלא לעשוק ׃
ג׳ שלא לחמוד ׃ ד׳ שלא להתאוות ׃
ה׳ להשיב את הגזילה ׃ ו׳ שלא יתעלם מן האבידה
ז׳ להשיב את האבידה ׃

הלכות חובל ומזיק

מצות עשה אחת והיא דין חובל בחבירו או מזיק ממון חבירו

הלכות רוצח ושמירת נפש

יש בכללן י״ז מצות ז׳ מצות עשה וי׳ מצות לא תעשה וזה הוא פרטן
א׳ שלא לרצוח ׃
ב׳ שלא ליקח כופר נפש הרוצח אלא יומת ׃
ג׳ להגלות הרוצח בשגגה ׃
ד׳ שלא ליקח כופר לחייב גלות ׃
ה׳ שלא ימות הרוצח כשירצח קודם עמידה בדין ׃
ו׳ להציל הנרדף בנפשו של רודף ׃
ז׳ שלא לחוס על הרודף ׃ ח׳ שלא לעמוד על דם ׃
ט׳ להפריש ערי מקלט ולהכין להם הדרך ׃
י׳ לערוף את העגלה בנחל ׃
י״א שלא יעבוד אותה קרקע ולא תזרע ׃
י״ב שלא לשים דמים ׃ י״ג לעשות מעקה ׃
י״ד שלא יכשיל תמים בדבר ׃ ט״ו לפרוק עם מי שנכשל בדרך
ט״ז לטעון עמו ׃ י״ז שלא יניחנו בדרך נבהל
במשאו נמצאו כל המצות הנכללות בספר הזה ל״ו והן
י״ח מצות עשה ועשרים מצות לא תעשה ׃

הלכות נזקי ממון

יש בכללן ארבע מצות עשה וזהו פרטן ׃
א׳ דין השור ׃ ב׳ דין ההבער ׃
ג׳ דין הבור ׃ ד׳ דין הבערה ׃
וביאור מצות אילו בפרקים אילו ׃

פרק ראשון

כל נפש

אדם שהיא ברשותו של אדם שהזיקה הבעלים חייבין לשלם שהרי ממונו הזיק שנאמר כי יגוף שור איש את שור רעהו אחד השור ואחד שאר בהמה חיה ועוף לא דבר הכתוב בשור אלא בהווה וכמה משלם אם הזיקה בדברים שדרכה לעשותם תמיד כמנהג ברייתה כגון בהמה שאכלה תבן או עמיר או שהזיקה ברגלה כדרך הילוכה חייב לשלם נזק שלם מן היפה שבנכסיו שנאמר מיטב שדהו ומיטב כרמו ישלם ואם שינתה ועשתה מעשים שאין דרכו לעשותם תמיד והזיקה בהן כגון שור שנגע או נשך חייב לשלם חצי נזק מגוף המזיק עצמו שנאמר ומכרו את השור החי וחצו את כספו וגו׳ כיצד שור שוה מנה שנגח לשור שוה עשרים והמיתו והרי הנבילה שוה ארבעה בעל השור חייב לשלם שמונה שהוא חצי הנזק ואינו חייב לשלם אלא מגוף השור שהזיק שנאמר ומכרו את השור החי לפיכך אם הבית שור שוה עשרים לשור שוה מאתים והנבילה שוה כמה אין בעל הנבילה יכול לומר לבעל החי תן לי חמשים אלא אומר לו הרי שור שהזיק לפניך קחהו ולך אפילו אינו שוה אלא דינר וכן כל כיוצא בזה העושה מעשה שדרכו לעשותו תמיד כמנהג ברייתו הוא הנקרא מועד והמשנה ועשה מעשה שאין דרך כל מינו לעשות כן תמיד כגון שור שנגח או נשך הוא הנקרא תם וזה המשנה אם הרגיל בשינויו פעמים רבות נעשה מועד לאותו דבר שהרגיל בו שנאמר או נודע כי שור נגח הוא חמשה מעשים תמים יש בבהמה ואם הועדה לאחד מהן נעשית מועדת לאותו מעשה ואלו הן הבהמה אינה מועדת מתחילתה לא ליגח ולא ליגוף ולא לישוך ולא לרבוץ על כלים גדולים ולא לבעוט ואם הועדה לאחד מהן. הרי זו מועדת לו אבל השן מועדת מתחילתה לאכול את הראוי לה והרגל מועדת מתחילתה לשבר כדרך הילוכה והבהמה מועדת מתחילתה לרבוץ על כלים קטנים וכיוצא בהם ולמעך אותן חמשה מיני בהמה מועדין בריתן להזיק ואפילו הן בני תרבות לפיכך אם הזיקו או המיתו בנגיחה או בנשיכה ודריסה וכיוצא בהן חייב נזק שלם ואלו הן הזאב והארי והדוב והנמר והברדלס וכן הנחש שנשך הרי זה מועד ואפילו היה בן תרבות כל מועד משלם נזק שלם מן היפה שבנכסיו וכל תם משלם חצי נזק מגופו בד״א כשנכנסה הבהמה לרשות הניזק והזיקתהו אבל אם נכנס הנזק לרשות המזיק והזיקתהו בהמתו שלבעל הבית הרי זה פטור על הכל שהרי הוא אומר לו אלו לא נכנסת לרשותי לא הגיעה לך הזק והרי מפורש בתורה ושלח את בעירה וביער בשדה אחר

To Hasdai ha-Levi:

As to your question about the nations, know that "the Lord desires the heart," and that the intention of the heart is the measure of all things. That is why our sages say, "The pious men among the Gentiles have a share in the world to come" (Sanhedrin 105a) . . . Every man who ennobles his soul with excellent morality and wisdom based on the faith in God, certainly belongs to the men of the world to come.

To the Rabbis of Lunel:

With regard to your request that I translate the text [of the Guide] into the holy tongue for you—I wish that I were young enough to be able to fulfill your wish concerning this and the other works which I have composed in the language of Ishmael [Arabic] . . . I have not the time even to improve my works which I wrote in the rabbinic language [Hebrew] . . . to say nothing of making translations from one language into another.

But you have in your midst the learned Rabbi Samuel ben Judah [Ibn Tibbon] on whom the Lord has bestowed the necessary insight for performing the task you have asked of me. I have already written to him about it . . . Honored friends . . . You stand alone in raising the banner of Moses . . . the study of the Torah in our communities has ceased . . . In all of Palestine there are three or four places only; in the whole of Syria only a few in Aleppo . . . In the Babylonian Diaspora only two or three groups in Yemen . . . the Jews of India know nothing of the Torah . . . what was inflicted upon the Jews of the Maghreb [North Africa] you know. Thus it remains for you alone to be the strong support of our Faith.

Be firm and courageous for the sake of our people and our God; make up your minds to be brave men. Everything depends on you.

The Venice, 1545 edition was the third; the second was published in that city only a year earlier. Almost four hundred years after they were written the words of Maimonides still spoke to the hearts of so many that a new edition was published.

THE MISHNEH TORAH

Joseph Ibn Gabir, who while knowing Arabic was able to study the *Commentary on the Mishnah,* but knowing no Hebrew was unable to read the *Mishneh Torah,* suggested to Maimonides that he produce an Arabic edition of it. Maimonides responded:

If you want to study my work you will have to learn Hebrew little by little. It is not so difficult, as the book is written in an easy style . . . I do not intend to produce an Arabic edition . . . as the work would lose its specific color. How could I do this when I would like to translate my Arabic writings into the holy tongue!

Maimonides had a profound love for the Hebrew language, a special affection for the one great work he wrote in it, and an unbounded regard for its subject, the law. The *Mishneh Torah* is his magnum opus. Except for the first printing in Rome, of which only a few copies are extant, the Library has virtually every important edition.

The *Mishneh Torah* Soncino, 1490, edition is the second production of the press of Gershom Soncino. He writes that scholars and leaders implored him to publish Maimonides's great work, offering him help and protection. "So I decided to search the great libraries for a fine manuscript

Facing page: Moses Maimonides's *Magnum Opus,* the *Mishneh Torah,* the first comprehensive code of Jewish Law, was published no less than six times in the fifteenth century, four editions on the Iberian Peninsula and two in Italy. This second Italian edition, which is also the second book printed by Gershom Soncino, was completed March 23, 1490. The Library's very fine two-volume copy is open to the eleventh of the fourteen books of the work, which deals with criminal law.

Moses Maimonides, *Mishneh Torah,* Soncino, 1490. Hebraic Section.

copy . . . May the Blessed One in his great mercies, help me complete this work." The work was completed "on the first day of Nissan, 5250, in Soncino, in Lombardy, under the sovereign, the Duke of Milan. Praise and glory to God." The Library's very fine copies preserve the beauty and excellence of the typographical artistry of the master printer.

In the fifteenth century, the *Mishneh Torah* was already viewed more as the textbook of Jewish law than a practical code. That function was being assumed by the *Arba-ah Turim* of Jacob ben Asher (1270(?)–1340), who in 1303 accompanied his father from their native Germany to Toledo, Spain. He felt that reasoning had become faulty, controversy had increased, opinions had multiplied, so that there was no halakic ruling which was free from differences of opinion, hence the need for a new code. Though he revered Maimonides and accepted his halakic authority, he found three difficulties with his classic code: it was too long, containing laws no longer applicable after the destruction of the Temple and outside of the Holy Land; it was overly theological; and it reflected the Sefardi tradition alone to the neglect of the Ashkenazi. Ben Asher based his code on Maimonides's, but its structure was existential, beginning with the laws one is to observe upon waking in the morning and presenting only laws applicable to life in the Diaspora.

The *Mishneh Torah* begins with:

The basic principle of all basic principles and the pillar of all knowledge is to realize that there is a First Being who brought every existing being into being. All existing things, whether celestial, terrestrial, or belonging to an intermediate class, exist only through this true existence.

The *Arba-ah Turim* opens with

Judah ben Tema says: be as courageous as a panther, light as an eagle, swift as a deer, strong as a lion to do the will of your Heavenly Father.

The laws in the *Turim* reflect the Sefardi tradition, as recorded by Maimonides, and the Ashkenazi usage, as presented by Jacob's father, Rabbi Asher. Both communities could look to it as an authoritative compendium of the laws of Israel. The *Mishneh Torah* concludes with a vision of Messianic days:

The Sages and Prophets did not long for the days of the Messiah that Israel might exercise dominion over the world . . . be exalted by the nations, or that it might eat, drink and rejoice. Their aspiration was that Israel be free to devote itself to the Law and its wisdom, with no one to oppress or disturb it . . . In that era there will be neither famine nor war, neither jealousy nor strife. Blessings will be abundant, comforts within the reach of all. The one preoccupation of the whole world will be to know the Lord. "For the earth shall be full of the knowledge of the Lord, as the waters cover the sea."

The *Arba-ah Turim* ends with a citation from the *Mishneh Torah:*

If one sees his fellow drowning, sees robbers attacking him and can save him, or if one learns that evil doers are conspiring against him, or if one can persuade his fellow not to harm another, and he has not done, he has transgressed the commandment, "Thou shalt not stand idly by the blood of thy neighbor." (Leviticus 19:16). But if one saves another, it is as though he has saved the whole world.

The former is an exalted vision of the "end of days," the latter, ethical

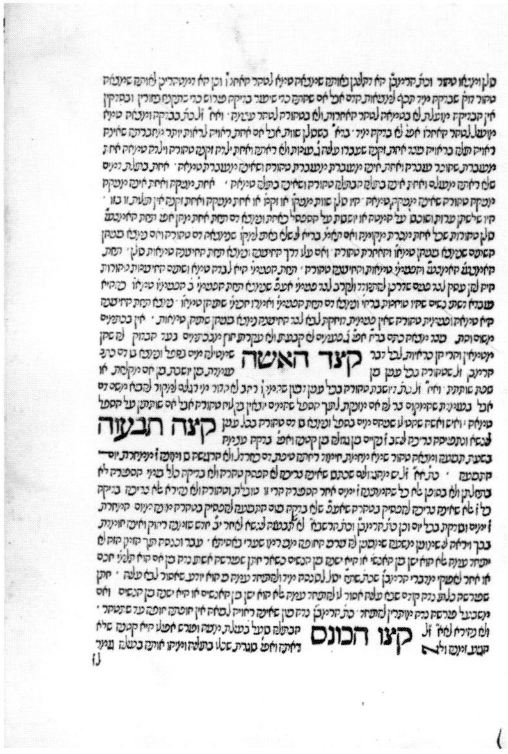

Eliezer ben Abraham Alanfansi, physician, scholar, and publisher, set up a printing press in Ixar (Hijar), a small town in Aragon (east Spain). Its first product was the *Arba-ah Turim,* Jacob ben Asher's code of Jewish law. The *Tur,* as it came to be known, was both influenced by and became a competitor to the *Mishneh Torah*—so successful a competitor that by the fifteenth century it was the more popular code. The six incunabula printings of the *Mishneh Torah* are more than doubled by the fourteen of the *Tur.*

Jacob ben Asher, *Arba-ah Turim,* Ixar (Hijar), 1485–87. Hebraic Section.

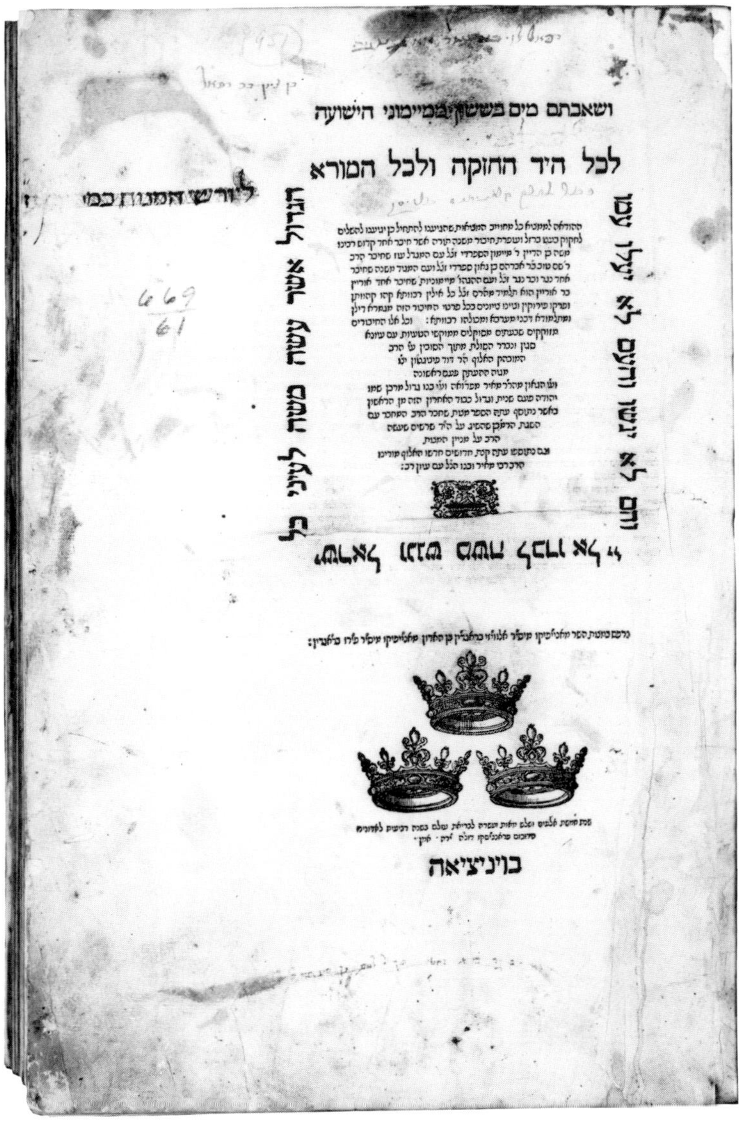
ושאבתם מים בששון ממעיני הישועה
לכל היד החזקה ולכל המורא
בוניציאה

משנה תורה
חלק שני
פה ויניציאה

instruction, more immediate and more practical. The *Mishneh Torah* was a classic, the *Turim,* a code. Both were eventually superseded as the accepted code of Jewish Law by the *Shulhan Aruch* of Joseph Caro, who prepared for the composition of his great code by writing masterly commentaries on those of Maimonides and Rabbi Jacob, but the code he wrote was an abridged, revised, and refined version of the *Turim,* not the *Mishneh Torah.*

We include Jacob ben Asher's *Tur Yoreh Deah,* Hijar, 1487, as a representative example of the works inspired by the *Mishneh Torah,* for the fruits of a tree give evidence of the tree's vitality and creativity.

Mishneh Torah, Venice, 1550–51, and *Mishneh Torah,* Venice, 1550–51, are two editions from the same place and done in the same year. And thereon hangs a tale of woe we first encountered in the chapter on the Talmud.

The first was an edition published by the newly established press of Alvise Bragadini, the second by Marco Antonio Giustiniani, who had assumed the mantle once worn by Daniel Bomberg as the premier printer of Hebrew books, declaring on his printer's mark which depicted the Temple in Jerusalem, "Great shall be the glory of this house." Recriminations,

As the sun was setting on the Daniel Bomberg Hebrew printing empire in Venice, two aspirants competed for his mantle—Marco Giustiniani and Alvise Bragadini. The former, aware of the popularity of the *Mishneh Torah,* planned a grand edition, but the latter was able to publish one earlier. The Giustiniani edition appeared in the same year, and carried an attack on the other. Attack led to counterattack, accusations, recriminations, a rabbinic ban, and soon to a papal decree ordering the burning of the Talmud—with kindred books added to the pyre.

Moses Maimonides, *Mishneh Torah,* Bragadini, Venice, 1550–51.
Moses Maimonides, *Mishneh Torah,* Giustiniani, Venice, 1550–51.

Hebraic Section.

Printing was introduced to the Near East by the brothers David and Samuel Nahmias, exiles from Spain who found haven in the Ottoman Empire. They made Constantinople the center of Hebrew printing in the first decade of the sixteenth century. Their edition of the *Mishneh Torah* was their sixth published work. Illustrated is the first page of the fourth book, dealing with family law: marriage, divorce, infidelity, etc.

Moses Maimonides, *Mishneh Torah*, Constantinople, 1509.
Hebraic Section.

accusations, a rabbinic ban, and a papal decree kindled pyres in which the Talmud and kindred Hebrew books were burned in leading Italian cities. The wanton destruction of sacred books, the hatred and fears engendered, the severe blow to Jewish cultural and spiritual life were tragic, but perhaps more tragic was the realization of the precariousness of Jewish existence. Christian printers were competing for business; apostates were currying favor with their new coreligionists by wreaking vengeance on their old; a curia eager for yet another opportunity to proclaim the "glory of God" was putting His word and His law to the flames; and Jews, fearful of frightful punishment, were offering up to the flames their most precious possessions, their sacred books.

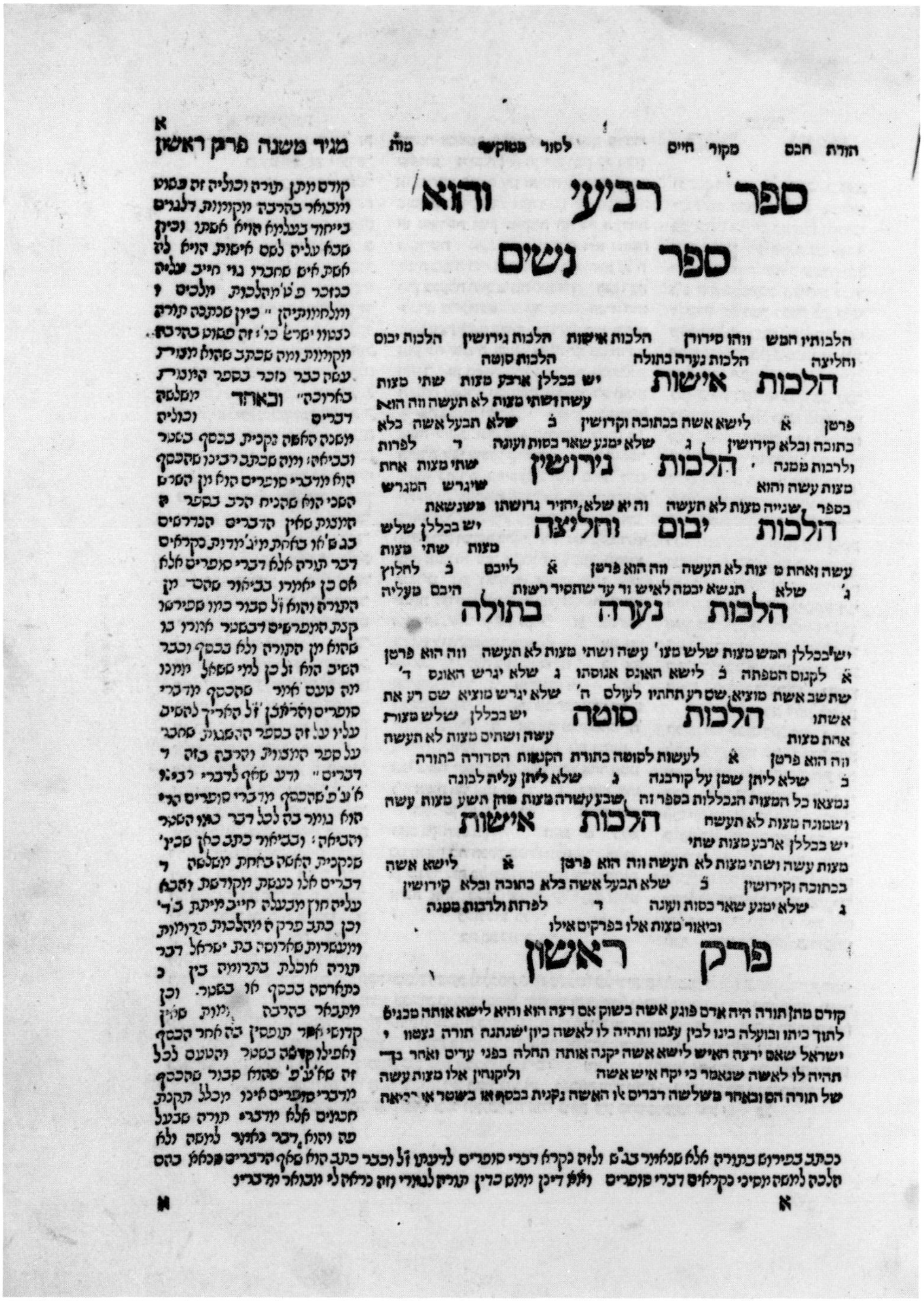

מגיד משנה פרק ראשון

ספר רביעי והוא

ספר נשים

הלכות אישות

הלכות גירושין

הלכות יבום וחליצה

הלכות נערה בתולה

הלכות סוטה

הלכות אישות

פרק ראשון

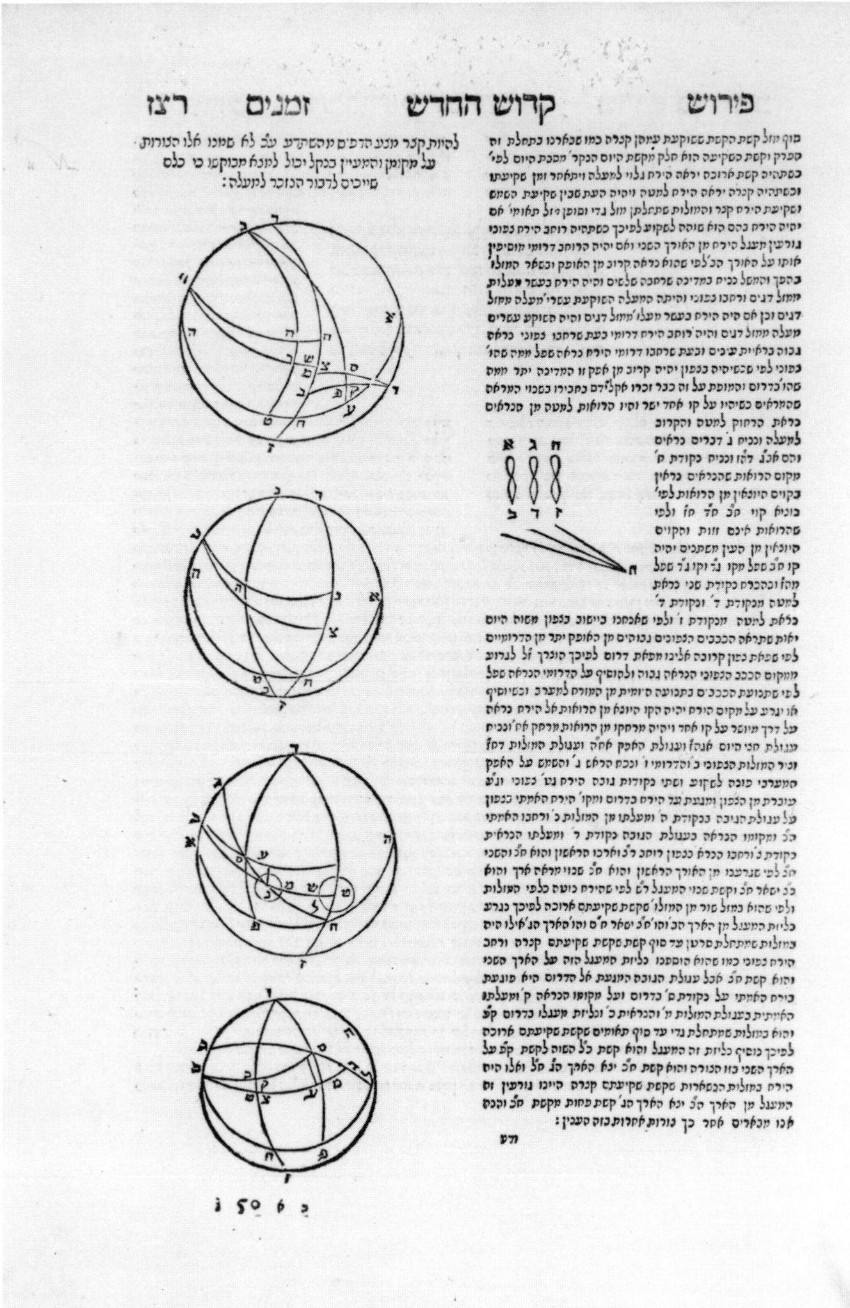

A grand edition of the *Mishneh Torah,* distinguished for its textual accuracy and aesthetic composition, was published by the Bragadini press of Venice in 1574. Its editor, Meir Parenzo, utilized a manuscript brought from Safed, and one corrected in the Egyptian academy. Its aesthetic accomplishment is represented here by a few of the many astronomical illustrations. What is most interesting, however, is the first printing of a commentary by Joseph Caro, whose code, the *Shulhan Aruch,* was destined to eclipse that of Maimonides's as the standard code of Jewish law.

Moses Maimonides, *Mishneh Torah,* Venice, 1574. Hebraic Section.

Not many copies of these historic editions remain. The Library's are made all the more precious by their rarity and by their role as witnesses to history.

The printing house of Giustiniani did not long survive, but that of Bragadini flourished. After the fires in the city squares and in the hearts of the zealots were extinguished, Bragadini published a splendid edition of the *Mishneh Torah* in 1574. It consisted of four volumes, tastefully arranged, well printed on fine paper, replete with traditional commentaries and featuring a new one, the *Kesef Mishneh* of "the wondrous scholar," Joseph Caro, published during his lifetime. This edition unites the author of the first comprehensive code of Jewish law, Maimonides, with Caro who fashioned what was to become the standard code of Jewish law, the *Shulhan Aruch.*

באמשטרדם
נשלם הספר הנכבד והנורא הזה בהוצאות ובבית הבחור הנחמד עמנואל בן הישיש הנכבד
יוסף רפאל · בן הקדוש אברהם עטיאש · אשר נשרף
על יחוד קדושת השם יתברך בעיר קורדווא · בשבעה עשר
בתמוז שנת חמשת אלפים ארבע מאות ושבעה
ועשרים לבריאת עולם:
ת ו ש ל ב ע

The most distinguished edition of the *Mishneh Torah* is the Athias edition, planned and launched by Joseph Athias in 1698 and completed by his son Immanuel in 1702. The father was born in Cordova, Spain, in 1635, just five hundred years after the birth of Maimonides there, and like him he had to flee persecution as a teenager. This edition, which set standards for devotion to accuracy and aesthetics in Hebrew bookmaking rarely equalled, has one more distinguishing characteristic—a colophon of historic significance. It records, as we can read in the illustration, that the father and grandfather of the publishers was burned at the stake in the city of Cordova, "for the sanctification of God's name," thirty-five years before the date of publication.

Moses Maimonides, *Mishneh Torah,* Amsterdam, 1702. Hebraic Section.

For a century and a quarter, no edition of the *Mishneh Torah* appeared, and but a few of the *Tur,* but editions of the *Shulhan Aruch* proliferated. It had become the widely accepted code, its predecessors of interest only to students of the Jewish legal tradition. The center of Hebrew printing had shifted from the cities of Italy, Turkey, and Poland to the cosmopolitan city of Amsterdam. At the end of the seventeenth century, Amsterdam's most distinguished printer of Hebrew books was Joseph Athias.

Athias had become a highly successful publisher of books. For his splendid editions of the Hebrew Bible, he won the approbation of his colleagues and was honored by the government. As the century waned, Athias was coming to the end of his career and, as he must have suspected, to the last years of his eventful life. What more fitting way for a devout Jew to culminate a career rich in honors and accomplishments than by crowning it with a monumental edition of the classic work of a great Jewish scholar for whom he felt a special affinity.

Joseph Athias was born in Cordoba, Spain, in 1635, exactly 500 years after Maimonides's birth there. As a young man, Athias, like Maimonides, had to flee the city because of his loyalty to his ancestral faith. After some wandering, he settled in Amsterdam where, as Maimonides had done in Cairo, he attained distinction in his chosen calling. He knew what his crowning achievement should be, an edition of the *Mishneh Torah,* which would be the finest ever produced by a Hebrew press.

In the last years of the century, Athias summoned the most skillful copyists and editors available, gathered the best manuscripts and combined them with the resources of one of the world's great presses. Printing began in 1698, but Athias did not live to see the edition's completion. He must have found some solace in the knowledge that his son and partner, Immanuel, would see it through. In 1702, a most splendid edition did appear, its size regal, its paper of the best quality, and its Hebrew type the finest anywhere. Illustrations were finely engraved. Moses Spitzer, the foremost authority on Hebrew typography, called this edition the greatest achievement of Hebrew typography. It is also a model of careful scholarship, a truly fitting monument to the greatest of medieval Jews.

The edition was not only a monument but, alas, also a memorial. On its last printed page the colophon reads:

> This great and noble edition was completed at the instance and in the printing house of the fine young man IMMANUEL, the son of the honored elder, JOSEPH RAPHAEL, the son of the martyr ABRAHAM ATHIAS, who was burned at the stake for the sanctification of God's blessed name in the city of Cordoba, on the seventeenth day of *Tammuz,* in the year of creation, five thousand, four hundred and twenty-seven [1667].*

Maimonides would have mourned the fact that in the city of his birth, more than five hundred years after his family was forced to flee from it, Abraham Athias, a Jew in his seventy-fifth year, was forced to sacrifice his life in fealty to his faith. Would Maimonides then not also have rejoiced that Abraham Athias's son Joseph took the advice Maimonides had offered half a millennium earlier, to flee the place of persecution and take up new and creative life in the service of his people and for the glory of God? This, too, is *Kiddush hashem,* sanctification of His Holy Name.

*It is remarkable that, 175 years after all Jews had been expelled from Spain, a descendant of a Jew who had been forced to convert to the dominant faith still clung to the ancestral faith with such tenacity and stubborn resolve that he chose martyrdom. And Abraham Athias was one among many, many martyrs.

5

CHARTING THE HOLY LAND

The Land of Israel is the holiest of Lands.
Numbers Rabbah

The Sages of Israel proclaimed:
The Land of Israel is the center of the world.
Jerusalem is the center of the Land of Israel.
Midrash Tanhuma

A THIRTEENTH-CENTURY CRUSADER map places Jerusalem at the center of the earth. Heinrich Bunting's world map in his *Itinerarium Sacrae Scripturae*, Helmstadt, 1581, of which the Library has a copy, depicts the earth as a three-leaf clover, each leaf being a continent: Europe, Asia, and Africa. The three are drawn together by a ring encircling a single city; that city is Jerusalem.

City and land are holy to the three great faiths of western civilization—Judaism, Christianity, and Islam. The Jew is bound to the Land by God's promise to Abraham: "Unto thy seed will I give this land" (Genesis 12:7)—this once and eternal homeland where Patriarchs trod, where Prophets preached, where ancestors began the eternal quest to know God's word and do God's will. For a millennium and more, the people Israel lived in Zion; for two millennia Zion lived in this people. Thrice daily the Jew turns in his devotions towards the Holy City. The Passover seder ritual and the Yom Kippur (Day of Atonement) liturgy conclude with the pledge and prayer, "Next year in Jerusalem."

For the Christian, the Land is the birthplace of his Lord and the site of His ministry. Jerusalem is the scene of His passion and resurrection, and when in the "end of days" He will rise again, it will be in that city, in that Land. For the present, it is a land for pilgrimage and prayer. To the Moslem, Jerusalem is holy, the city the Prophet Mohammed chose for his ascent to heaven from the sacred spot now enshrined in the Dome of the Rock.

Memory and holiness are joined in this land, where as Disraeli said in Tancred, "not a spot is visible that is not heroic or sacred"; where, as the Hebrew poet Micah Joseph Berdichevsky observed, "every stone is a book and every rock a graven tablet." Jews and Christians in every age were avid recipients of news of the Holy Land. Pilgrims made the hazardous journey there and returned to tell their tales, retold by word of mouth and often set in print. Whatever the description—holy places in ruin, a new folk and a new faith resident in sacred cities—it was the ancient land and city which continued to live in the imagination of the faithful. The best known of early Christian pilgrims was Helena, mother of Constantine the Great, the first Christian Roman emperor. Late in her life, about the year 320, she journeyed to the Holy Land to find the sacred sites. Her quest inspired the founding of churches and became the subject of legend.

Fifteen centuries later, Lady Judith Montefiore accompanied her husband Sir Moses on the second of his seven pilgrimages. In her travel journal she describes her coming to Jerusalem:

> *Thursday, 6 June 1830.* What the feelings of a traveler are, when among the mountains on which the awful power of the Almighty once visibly rested, and when approaching the city where he placed his name; where the beauty of holiness shone in its morning splendor; and to which, even in its sorrow and captivity, even in its desolation, the very Gentiles, the people of all nations of the earth, as well as its own children, look with profound awe and admiration. . . . As we drew nearer to Jerusalem . . . the Holy City itself rose full into view, with all its cupolas and minarets reflecting the splendour of the heavens. Dismounting from our horses, we sat down and poured forth sentiments which so strongly animated our hearts in devout praises to him whose mercy and providence alone had then brought us a second time, in health and safety, to the city of our fathers.

Pilgrims were few. Most experienced pilgrimages only in their imagination. Their imagination was informed, oft fired, by accounts heard or read, by pictures seen and by maps and charts which were as much history as geography. The armchair pilgrim could, in some measure, vicariously experience the emotions of St. Helena and Lady Judith by perusing maps of the Holy Land and charts of the Temple, twelve of which we briefly note.

With the Rosenwald Collection came the first travel book ever printed. Bernhard von Breydenbach's *Peregrinatio in Terram Sanctam* (Journey to the Holy Land), Mainz, 1486. In his *Treasures of the Library of Congress,* Charles A. Goodrum notes that in that volume are "the first travel pictures ever produced of a real scene drawn realistically, and were also the first known foldout inserted in any publication." One such foldout is a minutely drawn picture of Jerusalem and its "environs," which extend to Tripoli and Alexandria.

Bernhard von Breydenbach, a member of the German nobility and Dean of the Cathedral at Mainz, resolved in his later years "to undertake a pilgrimage to the Holy Land in hope of obtaining the salvation of [his] soul." Accompanied by Erhardus Revwich, a recognized woodblock artist, he set out for Jerusalem on April 25, 1483. When they returned to Mainz nine months later, the Dean and the artist collaborated on a book describing and depicting their pilgrimage. Breydenbach wrote the text while Revwich provided the illustrations, the first ever made to accompany a text. The book became an instant success. The original Latin text was translated into German four months after its publication (1486), and later into French (1488), Dutch (1488), and Spanish (1498). No less than eight editions made it the most popular travel book in Europe up to the discovery of the New World.

The plate reproduced here is a schematic "tourist map." A partially walled Jerusalem occupies half the space. Below it is the land separating it from the Mediterranean. Pilgrims are debarking from a galley and making their way towards the city. The modern tourist will immediately recognize the Dome of the Rock. In the upper left is the Sea of Galilee and Tiberias; in the lower right Alexandria, and high above, Mount Sinai. It presents a charming and, all things considered, faithful depiction of holy sites as Breydenbach's entourage found them.

"Every writer on geography," R. V. Tooley states in his *Maps and Map-Makers* (1949), "has paid tribute to the work of Ptolemy. He stands like a colossus astride the ancient world, and his influence is still felt today. Claudius Ptolemaeus (Alexandria 90–168), astronomer and geographer, achieved pre-eminence in both these branches of human knowledge . . . His *Geographia* dominated the whole of the Christian and Moslem world for 1,500 years."

None of Ptolemy's maps has survived the classical period. They were, however, reconstructed in manuscript and engraved on copper or carved in wood for editions of the Ptolemy atlas. In 1482, the first woodcut edition, containing the first map of the world to include contemporary discoveries, was published in Ulm, Germany. It contains a brightly hand-colored map of the Holy Land, which can be seen in a beautifully preserved copy in the vault of the Library's Geography and Map Division.

Kenneth Nebenzahl, in his *Maps of the Holy Land* (1986), informs us that the Ulm edition was based on a manuscript version of a Ptolemaic atlas by a German Benedictine Donnus Nicholaus Germanus, working in Florence, Italy. He, in turn, "copied directly" from "the first modern map of Palestine," that of Marino Sanuto and Petrus Vesconte, who produced it in Venice, c. 1320, a map whose influence, Nebenzahi asserts "extended through three hundred years."

Claudius Ptolemy, second-century Alexandrian astronomer and geographer, was the first great cartographer of lasting influence. His maps did not survive, but were reconstructed and published in the atlases which bear his name. From the first woodcut edition we show the hand-colored map of the Holy Land.

Claudius Ptolemy, *Cosmographica*, Ulm, 1482. Geography and Map Division.

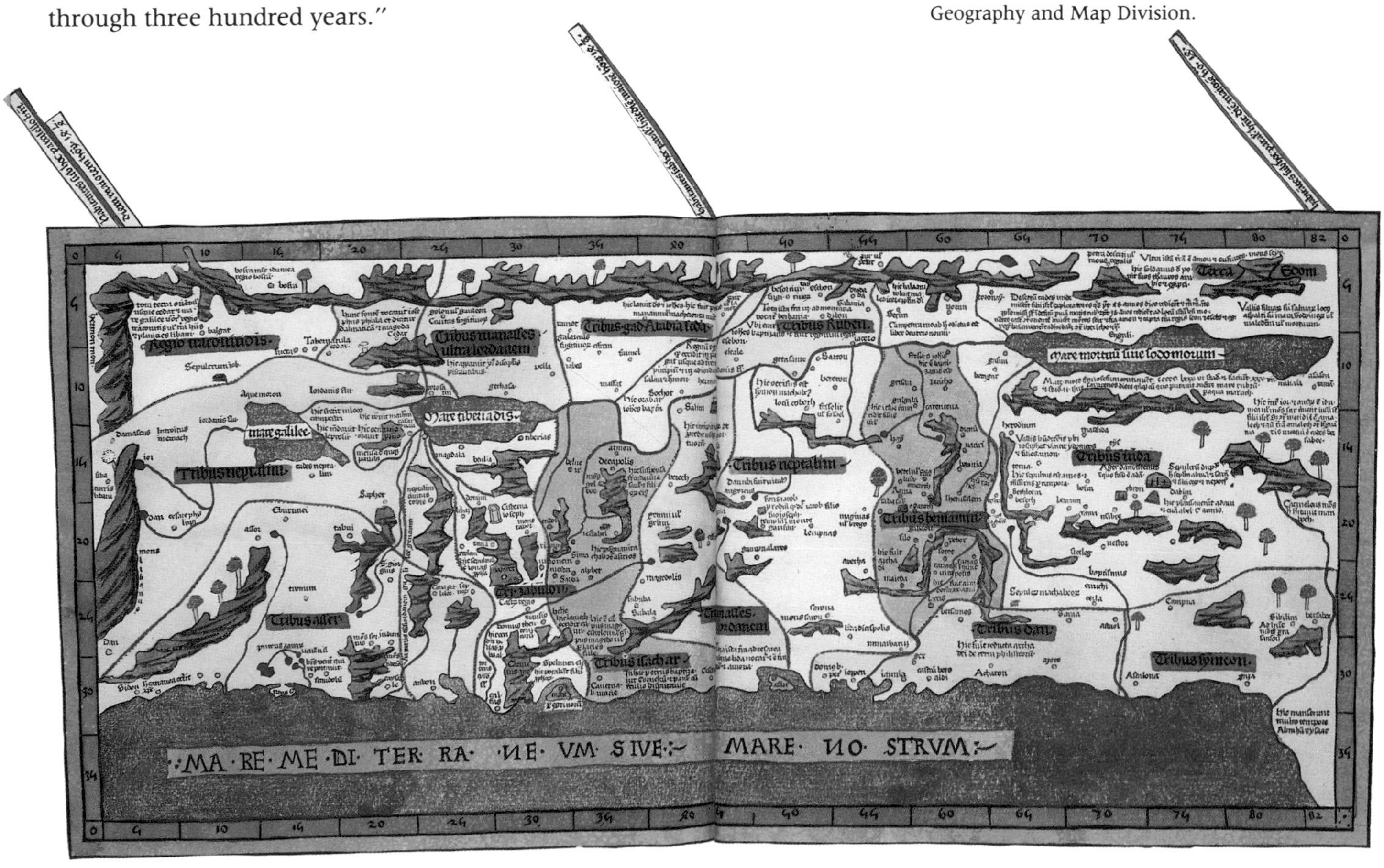

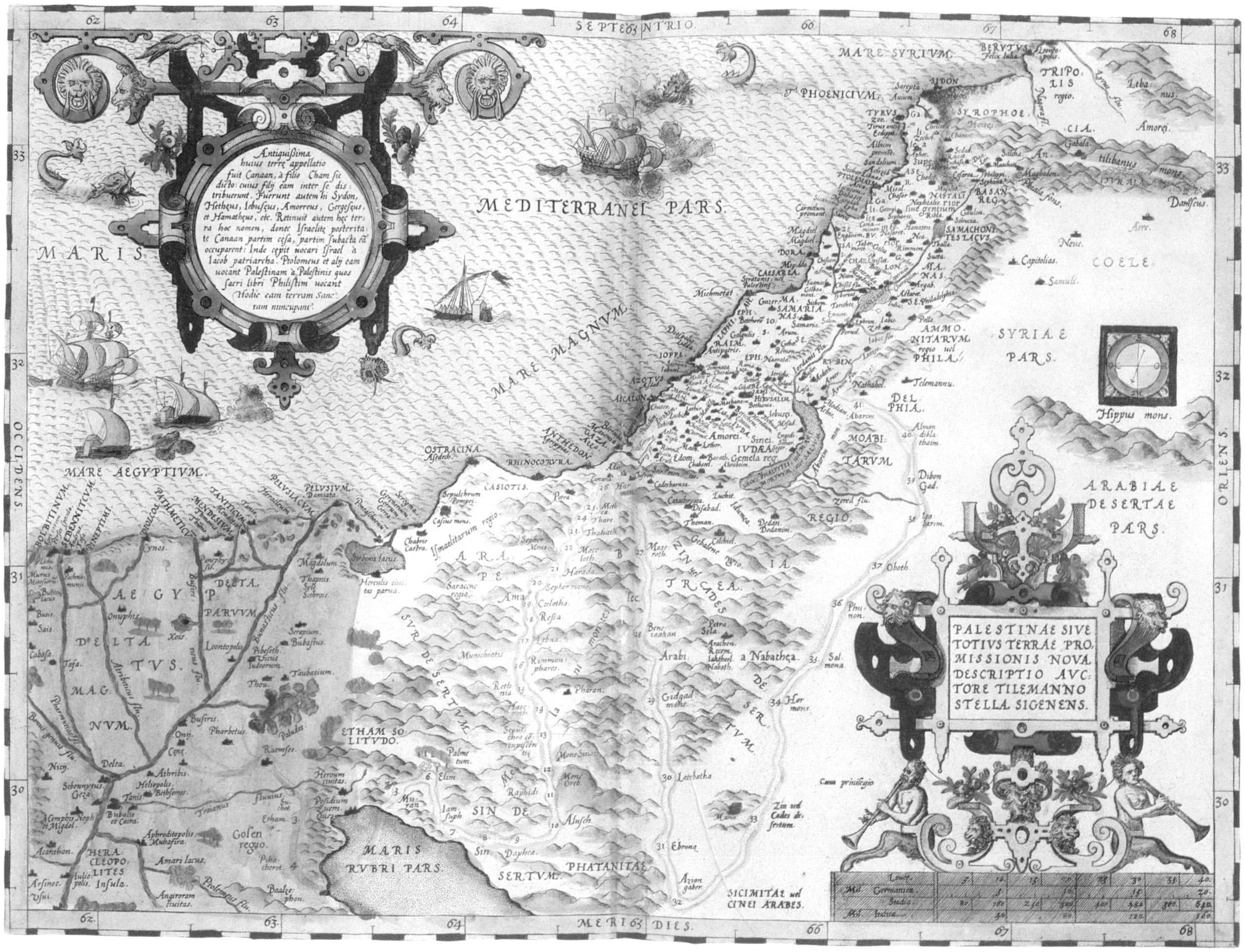

From the 1575 Antwerp edition of Abraham Ortelius's atlas *Theatrum Orbis Terrarum,* one of the four maps of the Holy Land. The one shown depicts the path traversed by the Children of Israel as they wandered through the Sinai wilderness to the Promised Land. Note that each year of travel is indicated by number.

Abraham Ortelius, *Theatrum Orbis Terrarum,* Antwerp, 1575.
Geography and Map Division.

The Holy Land is oriented with east at the top . . . Mountains and rivers are carefully located . . . Cities are placed close to their correct positions.

From the mountains of Lebanon, the Jor and the Dan descend to form the Jordan . . . Old Testament iconography is emphasized and includes the location of the Ten Tribes, a depiction of the Tomb of Job, and inscriptions marking where Lot's wife was turned into a pillar of salt.

The above features, as we shall see, presage those contained in the maps which followed.

The "first modern atlas," *Theatrum Orbis Terrarum,* was published by Abraham Ortelius (1527–1598) in his hometown, that great center of printing, Antwerp. He started out as a map engraver, then turned to business but, apparently influenced by Mercator, the greatest cartographer of the age, he returned to mapmaking. First published in 1570, the *Theatrum* immediately won wide popularity with no fewer than twenty-five editions appearing during Ortelius's lifetime, and editions continued to appear till 1612. Among the fifty-three maps included, four are of the Holy Land. To the publisher's credit, he freely acknowledged the sources of his maps, a practice rarely followed by fellow cartographers. A map that became a prototype for the modern cartography of the Holy Land, "Palestinae sine Totius Terrae Promissionis Nova Descriptio" is credited to Tilemanno Stella in bold letters in the colorful cartouche which gives its title. Stella drew it in 1557, influenced in his delineation of the coastline and Dead Sea by the maps of Jacob Ziegler, whose atlas of Palestine and environs acknowledges indebtedness to Ptolemy.

The map of the Holy Land that we take from the Library's 1575 Antwerp edition of the Ortelius Atlas has as its historical theme the Exodus from Egypt. The wanderings of the children of Israel in the desert are sharply delineated, each year of travel indicated from departure from Rameses to arrival at the Jordan. More central than the departure and arrival is the wandering, for the center of the map and its largest portion is the Sinai Desert.

The "Terra Sancta quae in Sacris Terra Promissionis olim Palestina" map of Willem Blaeu affords the armchair pilgrim an opportunity to accompany the Children of Israel in their journey across the Sinai wilderness, to reexperience their adventures there. Delicately engraved tiny vignettes which demand a sharp eye or a magnifying glass abound, the route marked out in events, not in numbers as in the map of Ortelius. The de-

Seventeenth-century Dutch cartographer Willem Blaeu, in his "Terra Sancta quae in Sacris Terra Promissionis olim Palestina" hand-colored map, takes the Children of Israel across the Sinai wilderness on the way to the Promised Land. Significant events of the journey are depicted in tiny vignettes, which afford us a vicarious experience of their wandering.

Willem Blaeu, *Atlas Maior,* Amsterdam, 1662–65. Geography and Map Division.

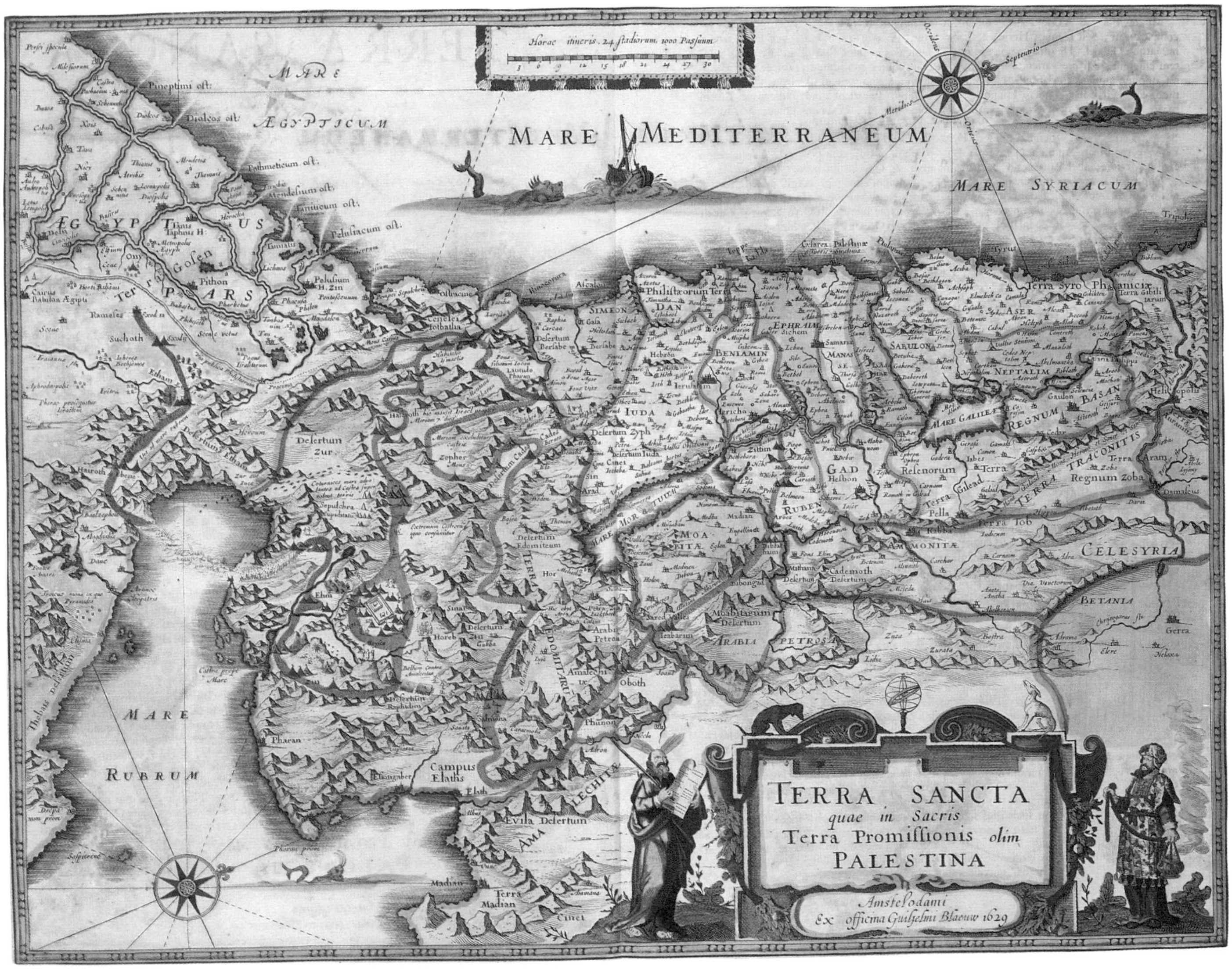

parture is from Rameses, and the cartographer recommends that we consult Exodus 12. A bit further on, we camp at Succoth, then at Etham, which is where the Lord began to go before the wanderers, "by day in a pillar of cloud . . . and by night in a pillar of fire." Cloud and fire are made more vivid still by the illuminator whose colors remain as bright today as three hundred years ago when he first applied them. We march across the Red Sea and see the pursuing Egyptian army sinking under the waves, only their spears visible above the waters. In the wilderness of Zin, we gather manna with the Children of Israel and welcome the soaring quail "who came up and covered the camp." We see Moses standing on a rocky promontory, his arms held aloft by Aaron and Hur. Below, as the map states, are armies arrayed for, *Bellum contra Amelecitas,* the war against the Amalekites.

We are at Sinai. Above us, on the mountain's summit, haloed in a cloud of glory, is Moses, holding aloft the Tablets of the Law. On the plain below, the Children of Israel prance around a golden calf. We near the borders of the Promised Land. Two men are returning from spying out that land, carrying a huge vine heavy laden with its grapes. We remember the ten spies who warned against entering the land. The journey turns once more to the wilderness, for forty years, till a new, more courageous generation arises.

At long last we are at Mt. Nebo. *Hic Mortuus Moyses* we read, "Here Moses died." The tiny dots which mark the route of the journey take us to the River Jordan which we cross to inherit the land Moses could see only from afar, a land which, on this map, stretches all the way to Tripoli. Here, the delineation of historic events comes to an end. Buildings denoting Jerusalem, Hebron, Samaria, and other cities can be seen, but no historic incidents, no people; as its title indicates, it is a map of the *Terra Promissionis,* the Promised Land. The Children of Israel having entered, it is no longer that, the promise having been fulfilled.

The orientation is to the west. At the top is the Mediterranean. A ship is caught in a storm. Near it is a "great fish" but quite benign. Jonah is nowhere to be seen. The cartouche has the classical depictions of Moses and Aaron. The Lawgiver, rod in hand, holds the Tablets of the Law; the High Priest, in full regalia, head turbaned, the Urim and Tumin breastplate on his chest, holds a censer billowing fragrant smoke.

This charming map was drawn in 1629 and incorporated into Blaeu's *Atlas Maior,* Amsterdam, 1662–65. The Library has a superb copy, whose paper remains crisp and whose colors have retained their freshness, with glinting gold highlights.

A map published in Amsterdam sixty-five years later also features the Children of Israel wandering in the wilderness. But while we can only conjecture why Ortelius and Blaeu chose to emphasize the wandering in their maps, it is obvious why Abraham bar Jacob did so. He intended his map to be inserted in an edition of the Passover Haggadah for which he had prepared a new set of illustrations. His map was to illustrate an aspect of the Exodus which the Haggadah celebrates, the journey from Egypt to the Promised Land. The course of the wandering is laid out in dotted parallel lines, each year of the journey marked by a Hebrew number, the resting places listed by identifying numbers in the cartouche.

The orientation is to the southeast. At bottom right is a female figure

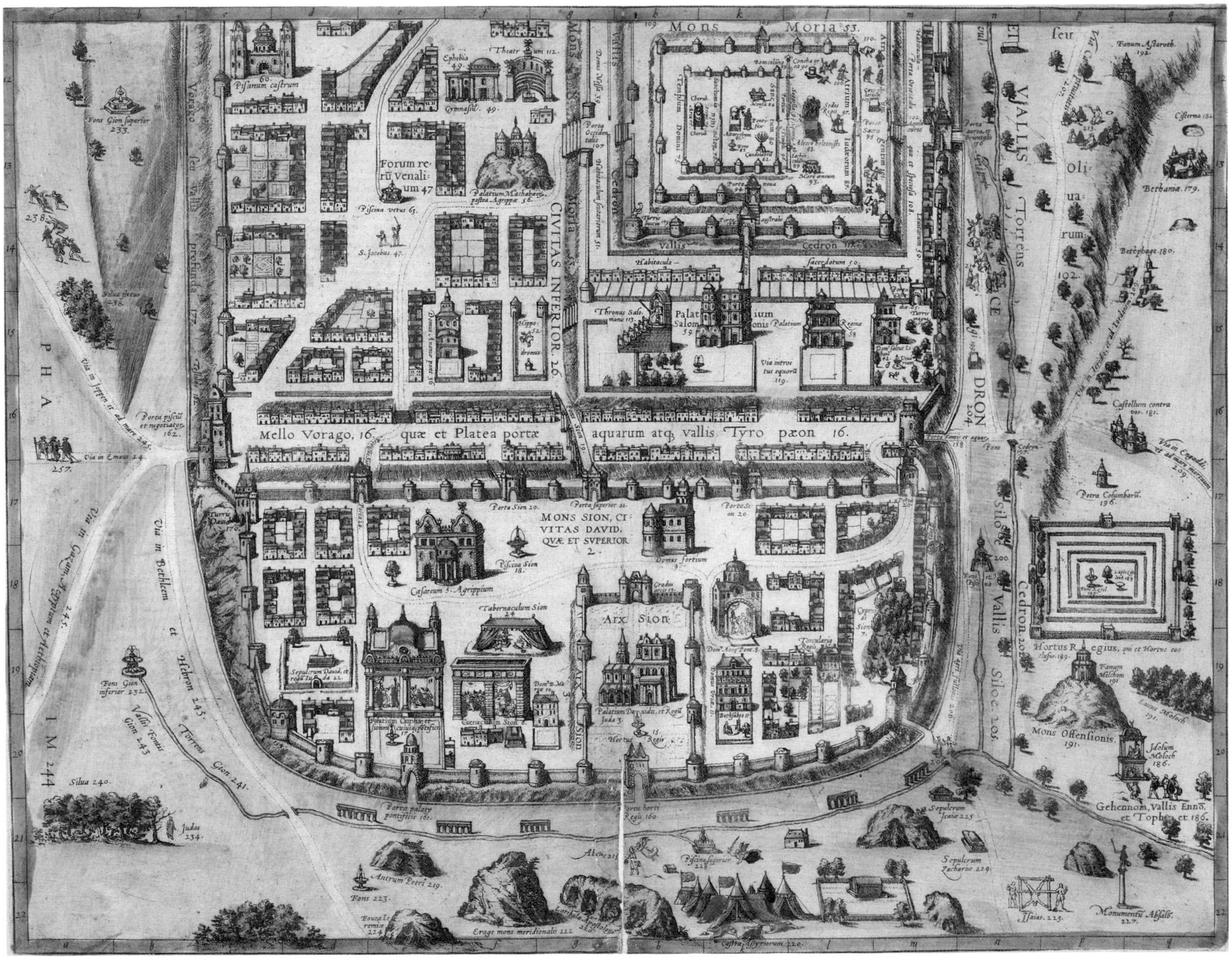

on the back of a crocodile, protecting herself from the sun with an open parasol. The inscription above her indicates both the geographic location and what the figure represents, "The Land of Egypt." In the center of the sea is a large fish, mouth open ready to swallow a man being cast from a ship, but a further depiction shows Jonah spewed out of the fish's mouth, safe on dry land—saved! At bottom left are illustrations touching upon the dual theme of this map as stated by an inscription at its top: "This [map] is to inform every knowing person of the route of the forty-year journey in the desert, and the breadth and length of the Holy Land from the River of Egypt to the City of Damascus and from the Valley of Arnon to the Great Sea, and within the land, the territory of each tribe as your eyes will see, and the wise will understand." An eagle with wings outstretched under a verse stating, "Ye have seen what I have done to the Egyptians, and how I bore you on the wings of eagles, and brought you unto myself" (Exodus 19:4), and leafy trees, marked "The Festival of Sukkoth," touch upon the Exodus theme. Four cows with the inscription "milk," and three honeycombs with the word "honey" refer to the Land of Israel, a "Land of milk

The finest early artistic map of Jerusalem architecturally depicted is Christian von Andrichom's double-page plate in Braun and Hogenberg's atlas of the great cities of the world, *Civitates Orbis Terrarum*. Shown is the lower plate which depicts the Temple of Solomon, the City of David, Mt. Zion, all in contemporary sixteenth-century architecture.

George Braun and Franciscus Hogenberg, *Civitates Orbis Terrarum*, vol. 4, Cologne, 1612.
Geography and Map Division.

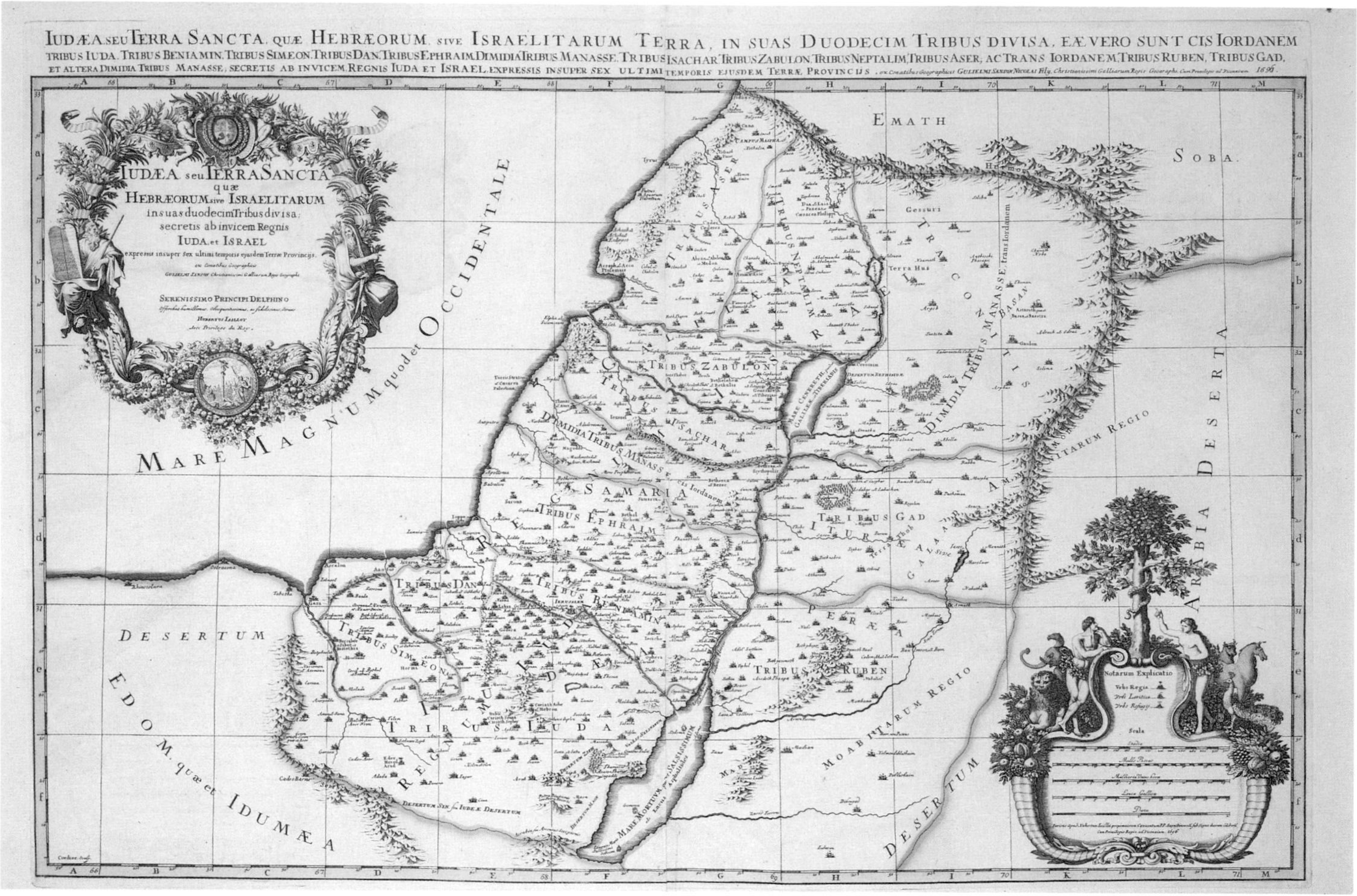

When the forty-year journey from Egypt to the Holy Land was over, the land was divided among the Twelve Tribes, as this hand-colored map by French cartographer Nicholas Sanson depicts. Each tribe's territory is marked in bold letters; cities and towns are noted by picture and name.

Nicholas Sanson, *Judaea Seu Terra Sancta,* Amsterdam, 1696.
Geography and Map Division.

and honey." The theme of the land dominates the map, an emphasis fortified by a vignette not found in other maps, sailing ships towing barges. An inscription describes them as "Rafts of cedars of Lebanon, sent by Hiram, King of Tyre, on the sea to Jaffa, from whence Solomon brought them up to Jerusalem." We have thus the introduction of a later period of Jewish history and a foreshadowing of later Jewish cartographers' interest in the city of Jerusalem and the Temple of Solomon.

The cartographer's name at the bottom is Abraham bar Jacob. A Christian pastor in the Rhineland who had converted to Judaism and become a copper engraver in Amsterdam, he provided the illustrations for the Haggadah of 1695, which have appeared in many Haggadot up to the present day. The map is in Hebrew. A special feature of this map, that seems heretofore not to have been noticed, is bar Jacob's treatment of the Exodus not as leaving but as returning. He depicts the traditional Goshen to the Jordan route, but adds another one beginning in Hebron and ending in Goshen, the route the family of Jacob took to Egypt. The route is marked by the only historical vignette on the map, a wagon representing those which Joseph sent to bring his family to Egypt. The Library has a fine copy of the 1695 Haggadah with a map; the map displayed here is from its 1781 edition.

The shift of emphasis from the Exodus to life upon the land itself can be seen in Nicholas Sanson's Holy Land map, published in 1696. No delineation of the Exodus route appears. The map's interest is, as it states, in depicting the Holy Land as it was divided among the Twelve Tribes, "duodecim Tribus divisa." Nine and a half tribes live between the Jordan and the *Mare Magnum,* the Great Sea; two and a half remain east of the river. Tribal division maps became popular, particularly because they lent themselves to the Biblical illustration and instruction which flourished during the eighteenth and nineteenth centuries. Different coloring divides the tribal holdings, and two decorative cartouches give it balance. The upper left features Moses and Aaron, both seated; the lower right depicts Adam and Eve in the Garden of Eden, with docile animals—camel, elephant, lion, ox, horse, and ostrich—and lush greenery. Eve is pointing to the Tree of Knowledge entwined by the serpent. Chin on hand in contemplation, Adam looks at the tempting fruit, torn between fear and desire.

A dozen years before Sanson, the greatest of early French cartographers, published an edition of *Geographia sacra* that contained the prototype for the above map, the English divine and historian Thomas Fuller issued *A Pisgah-Sight of Palestine,* London, 1650. Here, the "tribal division" depiction of the Holy Land finds its fullest expression. A pullout map of

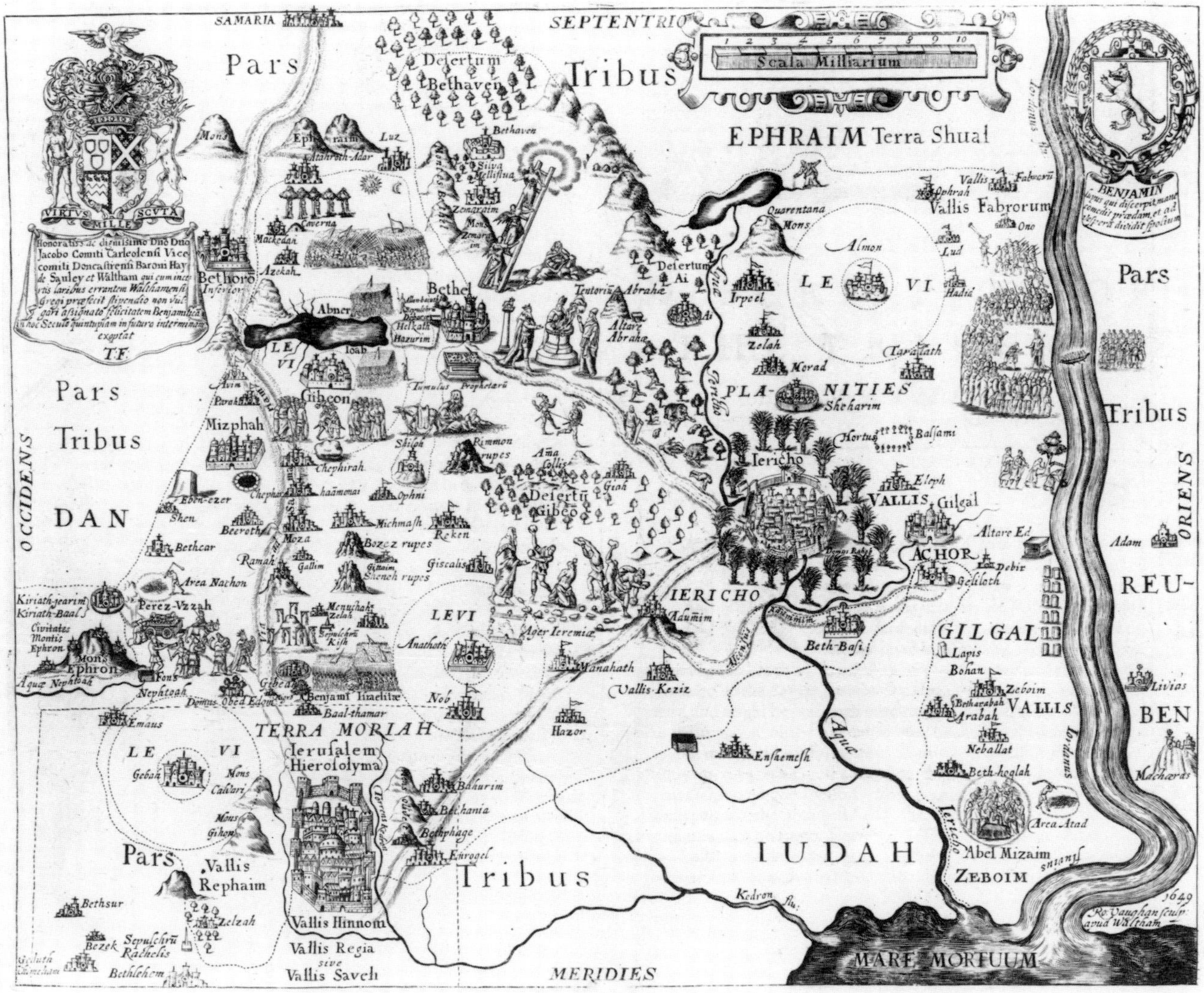

The maps in Thomas Fuller's *A Pisgah-Sight of Palestine,* are as much biblical history as geography. Long descriptions accompany the depiction of events. We see Jerusalem and Jericho, the Children of Israel crossing the Jordan, and the Patriarch Jacob's dream of angels on the ladder ascending to heaven in this map of the land of the Tribe of Benjamin.

Thomas Fuller, *A Pisgah-Sight of Palestine,* London, 1650. Rare Book and Special Collections Division.

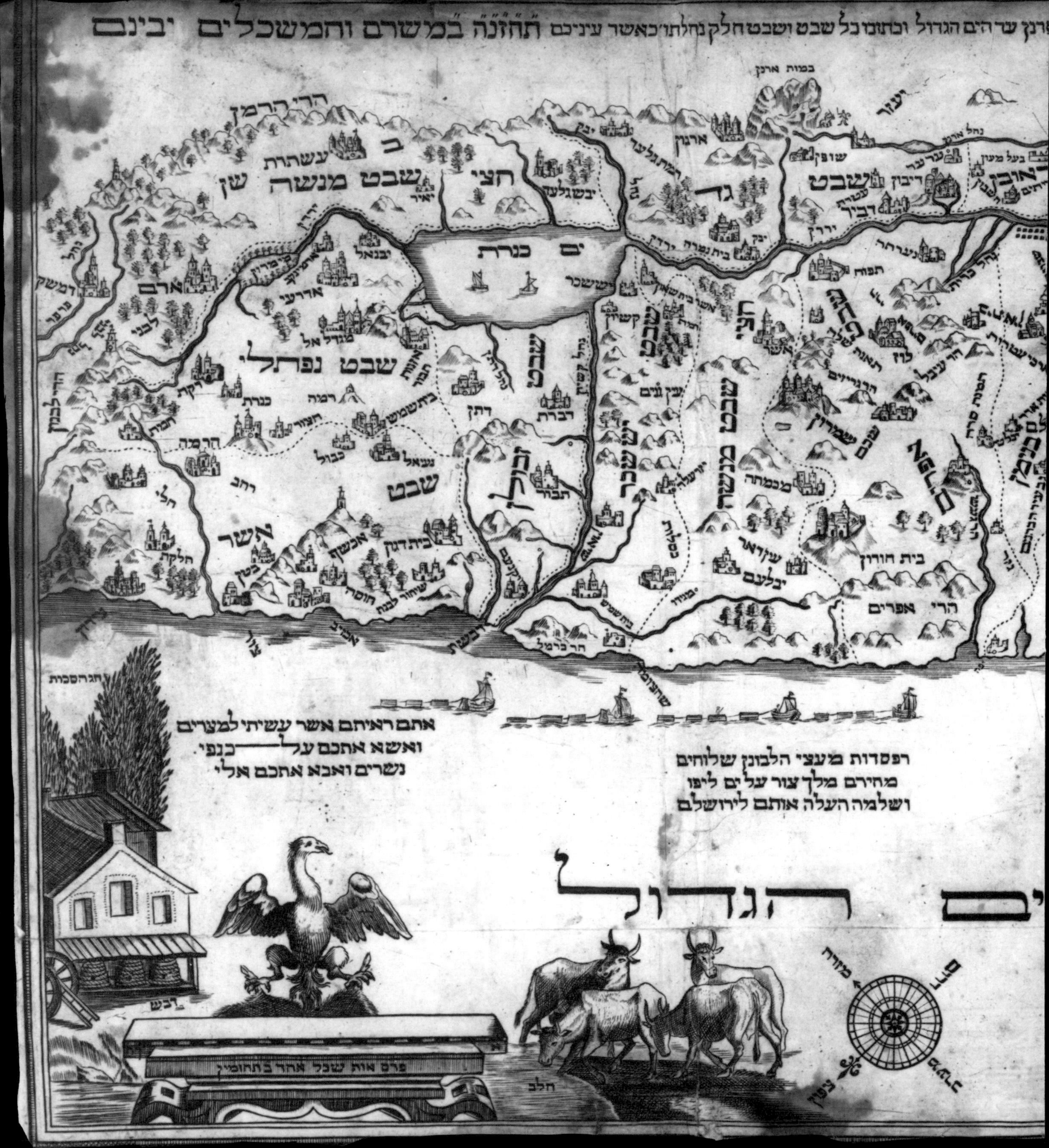

רדן עד הים הגדול ותחומו כל שבט ושבט חלק נחלתו כאשר עיניכם תחזינה במשרים והמשכלים יבינם
הרי הרמון
שבט מנשה
גד
ים כנרת
שבט נפתלי
שבט אשר
הרי אפרים
אתם ראיתם אשר עשיתי למצרים
ואשא אתכם על כנפי
נשרים ואבא אתכם אלי
רפסדות מעצי הלבנון שלוחים
מחירם מלך צור על ים ליפו
ושלמה העלה אותם לירושלם
ים הגדול
מזרח

זאת לדעת לכל בר דעת דרך המסעות א... ים שנה במדבר והרוחב והאורך של א״הק הקדושה מנהר מצרים עד עיר דמ
ים המלח
מדבר צין הוא קדש
מדבר סיני
מדבר פארן
מדבר שור
ארץ פלשתים
ארץ מצרים
עמלק
אילת
יהודא
שבט
שבט שמעון
שבט דן
עיר כרמל
באר שבע
אשקלון
חברון
גשן
פתום
מצרים
אלכסנדרי
לוח המסעות במדבר
אשר על פי ה׳ יסעו ועל פי ה׳ יחנו
א׳ רעמסס טו׳ רתמה כט׳ חרהגדגד
ב׳ סכת טז׳ רמן פרץ ל׳ יטבתה
ג׳ אתם יז׳ לבנה לא׳ עברנה
ד׳ פיהחירת יח׳ רסה לב׳ עציון גבר
ה׳ מרה יט׳ קהלתה לג׳ מדבר צין
ו׳ אילם כ׳ הרספר לד׳ הרההר
ז׳ ים סוף כא׳ חרדה לה׳ צלמנה
ח׳ מדבר סין כב׳ מקהלת לו׳ פונן
ט׳ דפקה כג׳ תחת לז׳ אבת
יוד׳ אלוש כד׳ תרח לח׳ דיבן גד
יא׳ רפידם כה׳ מתקה לט׳ עלמן דבלתים
יב׳ מדבר סיני כו׳ חשמנה מ׳ הרי עברים
יג׳ קברות התאוה כז׳ מסרות מא׳ ערבת מואב
יד׳ חצרת כח׳ בני יעקן
אברהם בר יעקב

the land opens the volume. Each tribe is accorded a delightfully illustrated two-page map and a sprightly account of the geographic and historical illustrations. R. V. Tooley rightly describes these as "the most quaint and decorative series of maps." Let us look at one, that of the Tribe of Benjamin.

The Jordan River emptying into the Dead Sea captures our attention. A mighty river, at its western bank are "the twelve great stones set up by *Joshua* in memorial that there they passed over the river Jordan on foot." In an aside, Fuller calls them "The *Jewish* Stonehenge." Above stands Saul, first king of Israel, crown on head. Bowing before him is the prophet Samuel, who has just anointed him. They are surrounded by crowds of people and troops of soldiers, one of which follows a trumpet-sounding leader off to battle. We skip across a Levitical City of Refuge, picturesque towns, and countryside, to arrive at Beth El where Jacob sleeps on his rocky pillow and dreams of a ladder ascending to heaven, on which we see three angels. We also observe King Jeroboam, joined by the High Priest in idol worship, to whom a prophet has come to protest and denounce. Fuller describes it in his rich seventeenth-century prose:

> Here *Jeroboam* set up one of his golden calves: and how busie was he about sacrificing unto it, when a Prophet sent from God denounced the destruction of his Altar, which presently clave asunder . . . An Altar, which (were it of brass or stone) was softer then the miracle-proof heart of Jeroboam, which neither was broken, nor bruised thereat . . . Indeed he conceived, that his kingdome must have idolatry for the pillars, which had Rebellion for the foundation thereof.

We travel southward. To our left is Jericho, surrounded by palm trees, its walls in the process of falling. Further south, we see the armies of Benjamin and of the Israelites engaged in battle. To the west, King David, crown on head, harp in hand, accompanied by musicians with horns and drum, escorts a wagon bearing the Ark of the Lord to Jerusalem. The Great City is depicted as domed and turreted stone buildings surrounded by a wall. Fuller reserves description of Jerusalem and subsequently devotes to it a detailed map and a full chapter.

The greatest early cartographic-artistic representational map of Jerusalem is that of Christian von Andrichom (1533–1585). George Braun and Franciscus Hogenberg adapted it for inclusion in their monumental *Civitates Orbis Terrarum* published in six volumes between 1572 and 1617. It has rightly been called the most impressive and elaborate collection of city views ever produced. Jerusalem is accorded two consecutive sheets, which show the city as it was conceived to be in the time of Jesus. A wall encloses a well laid out metropolis with imposing buildings, wide avenues, and spacious plazas and verdant surroundings; in short, a model medieval European city whose anachronistic character gave to the viewer a sense of immediacy and comfortable familiarity. The seventeenth- and eighteenth-century viewer could "walk its streets" and vicariously experience those momentous events which took place there and so radically altered human history.

Jerusalem was and remains the holiest of cities in the Holy Land, but Jews also gave a measure of holiness to three other cities there: Hebron, Safed, and Tiberias. The holiness of Jerusalem arises in part from what remains there, but more from what took place there. So it is with its sister

Preceding pages:
By far the most popular Hebrew map of the Holy Land is the one drawn by the proselyte Abraham bar Jacob for the Amsterdam 1695 edition of the Passover Haggadah, for which he also prepared the pictorial engravings. We show the one reproduced in a 1781 edition of the Haggadah published by the widow and orphans of the late Jacob Proops, printers in Amsterdam. An ownership inscription reads: "Samuel Hart, Passover Book, January 28th 1784." A resident of Halifax, Nova Scotia, at the end of the eighteenth century, Hart was a member of the Nova Scotia House of Assembly from 1793 to 1799, the first Jew to be a member of a legislative body in Canada.

Haggadah shel Pesah, Amsterdam, 1781.
Hebraic Section.

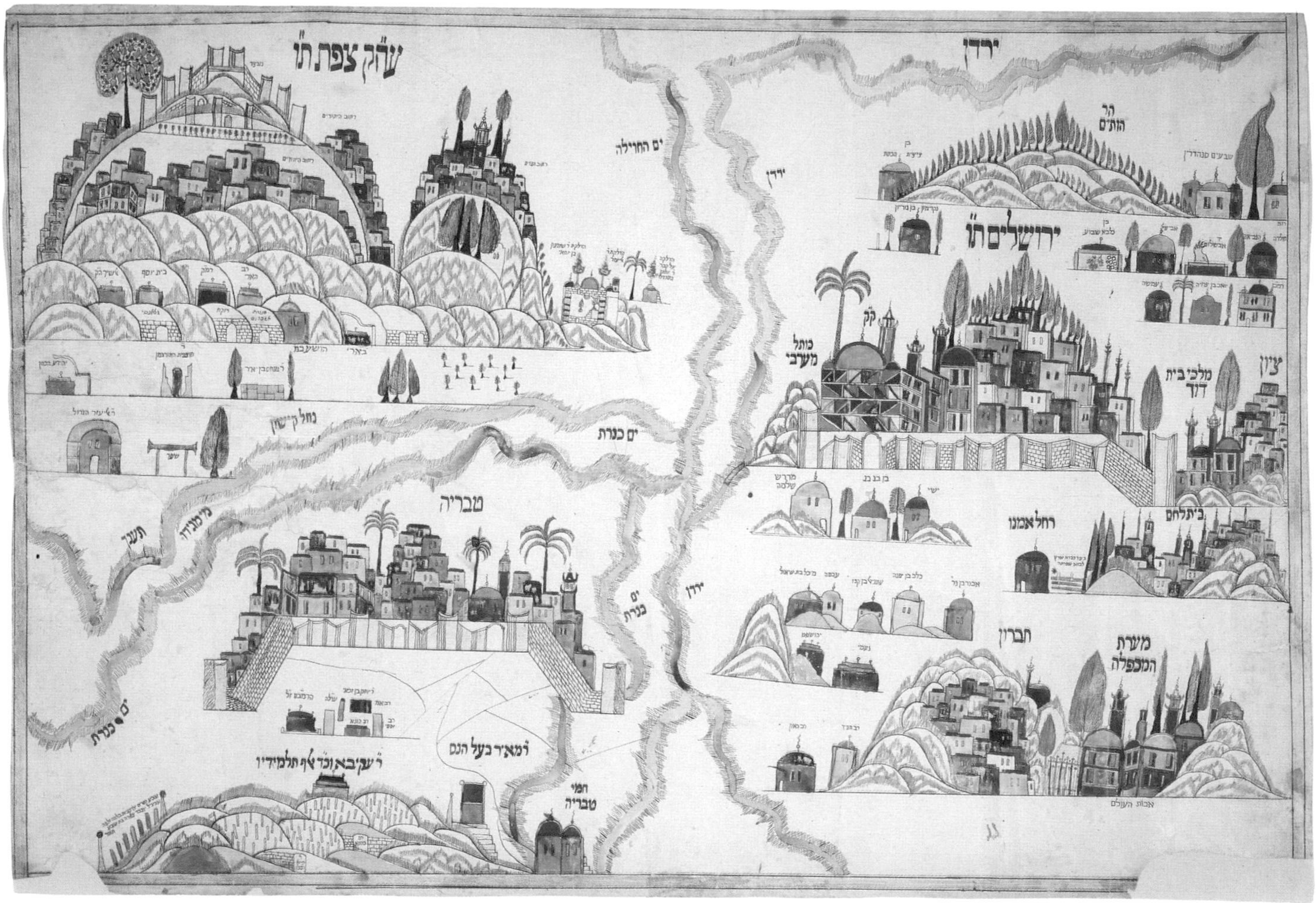

cities. Hebron is where the patriarchs and matriarchs lived and are buried, and it was the first capital of King David. Tiberias, on the shore of the Sea of Galilee, was chosen by the patriarch of the Jews in the second century as his seat. The Palestinian Talmud was largely composed in its great rabbinical academy. In the environs of Safed, high in the Galilean hills, are the graves of the leading rabbis of late antiquity. Its stature as a holy city was enhanced in the sixteenth century, when it was the greatest center of Jewish mysticism and seat of Jewish legal scholarship. To gain entree into the company of the three more ancient holy cities, it called itself Beth-El, suggesting identity with the biblical site which Jacob called "The Gate of Heaven."

A striking pastel-colored manuscript "holy site map" links these four holy cities together. Drawn and painted in Palestine in the second half of the nineteenth century, it depicts those venues which indicate their holiness. There is a suggestion of their geographic positioning, but the "map" is far more a statement of the place these cities hold in Jewish veneration, than of the geographical site they occupy. To pious Jewish families, such wall plaques were more meaningful depictions of the Holy Land than the most aesthetically beautiful and topographically exact representations.

A small illustrated guide book to the burial places of biblical figures and saintly rabbis in the Holy Land, *Zikaron Birushalayim,* appeared in

This charming pastel watercolor wall plaque depicting the holy cities of the Holy Land—Jerusalem, Hebron, Tiberias, and Safed—was painted in Palestine in the second half of the nineteenth century. The depiction is neither geographic nor topographic but religio-historical, presenting this holy venue not as it existed on earth but as envisioned by a pious resident or pilgrim who was a gifted primitive artist.

"Holy Cities" Wall Plaque, Pastel Watercolor, Jerusalem (?), c. 1870.
Hebraic Section.

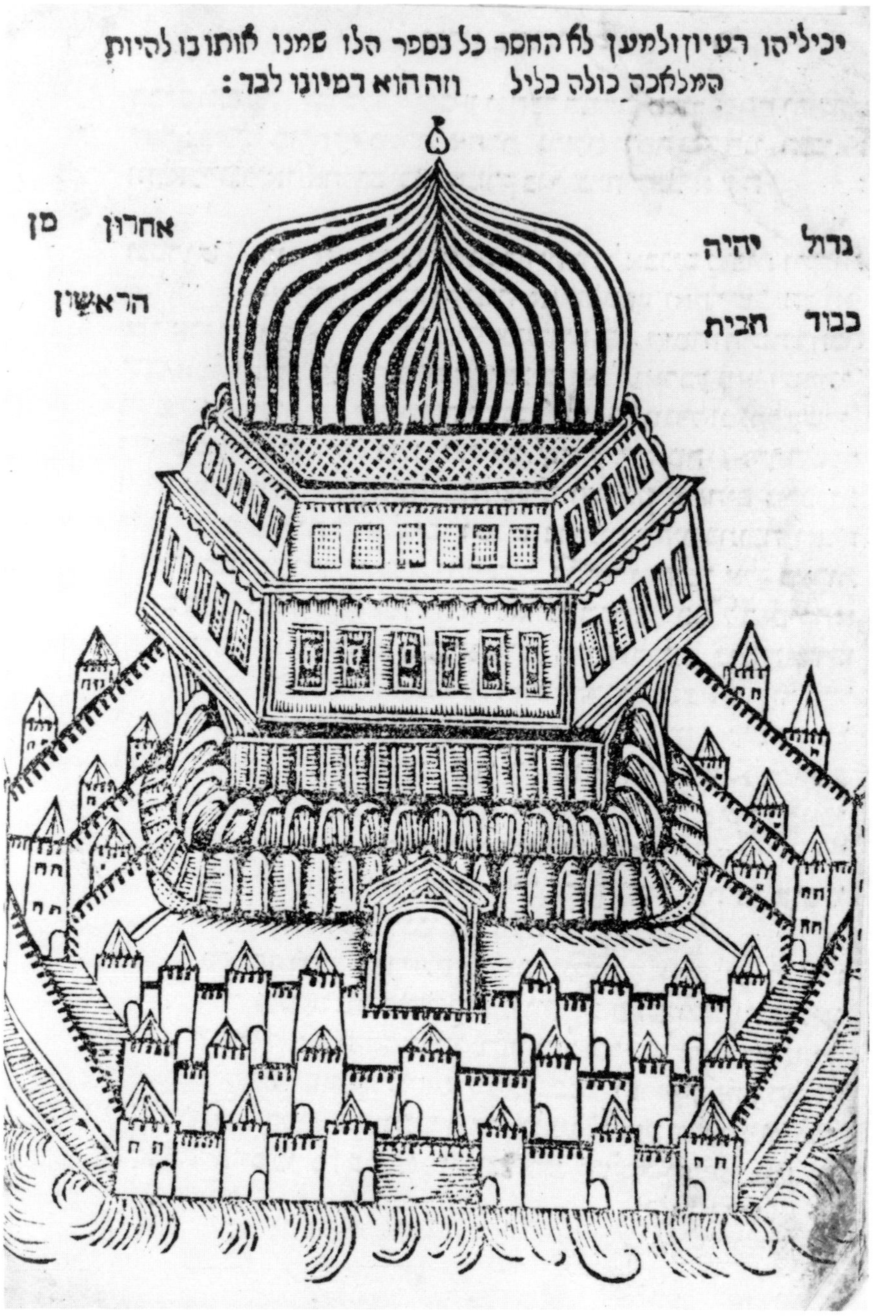

Two woodcut depictions of Holy Land sites: the first of the Temple in Jerusalem, and the second of Jericho, with Joshua and the Children of Israel positioned outside the city walls.

Zikaron Birushalayim (Remembrance of Jerusalem), Constantinople, 1743.
Hebraic Section.

Constantinople in 1743. It tells the pious pilgrim where graves may be found and what prayers are to be said. Prefaced by a panegyric to the land, it cites a midrashic statement that, in time to come, when Jerusalem shall be rebuilt, three walls—one of silver, one of gold, and the innermost of multicolored precious stones—will encompass the dazzling city.

In Hebron the pilgrim is not only directed to the holy grave sites, but also regaled with wondrous tales. One tells of a sexton of the community sent down to search for a ring which had fallen to the depths of the patriarchs' burial cave, finding at the floor of the cave three ancient men seated on chairs, engaged in study. He greets them; they return his greetings, give him the ring, and instruct him not to disclose what he had learned. When he ascended and was asked what he had seen, he replied: "Three elders sitting on chairs. As for the rest, I am not permitted to tell."

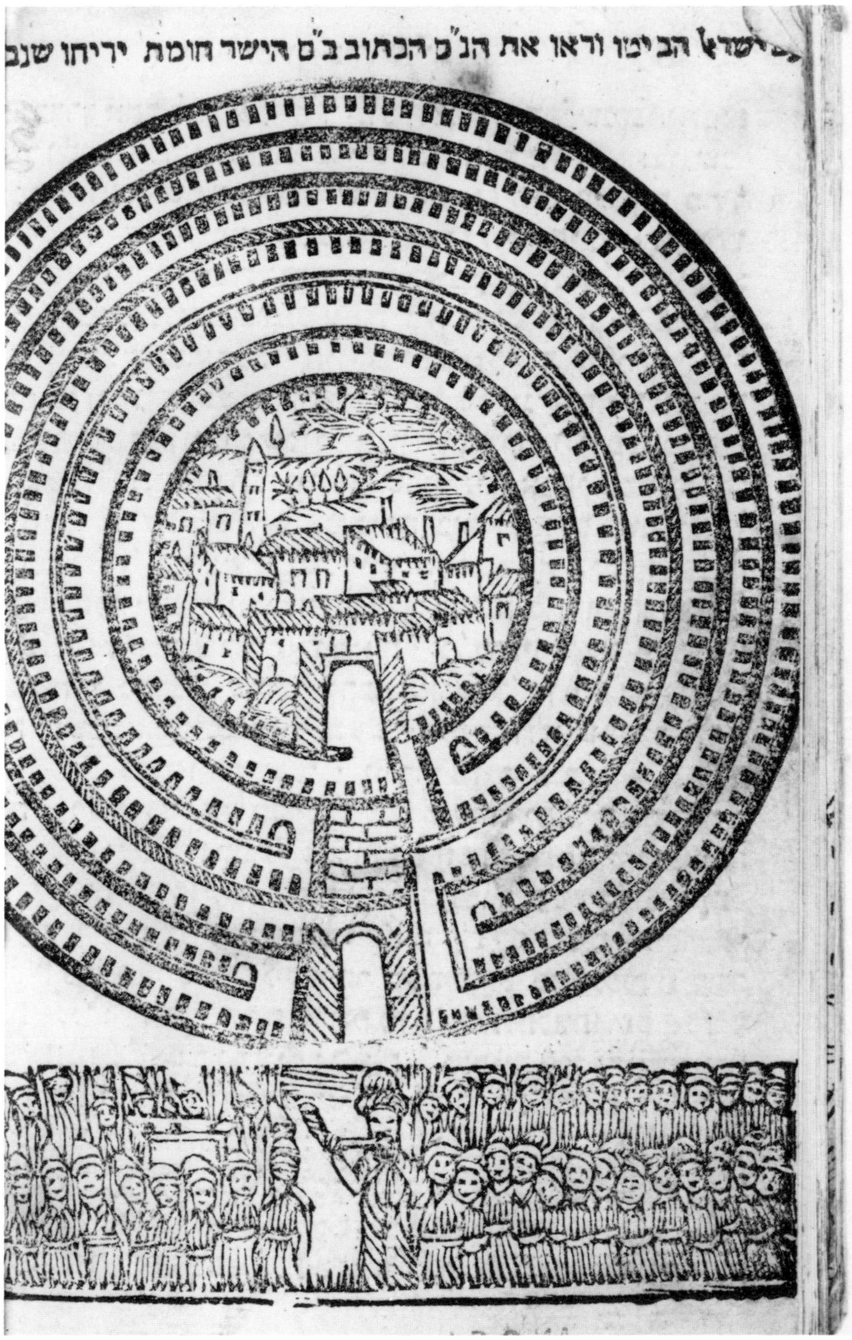

For actual pilgrims, the little volume provided factual information. For pilgrims in their own imagination, it offered edification through tales and quaint illustrations. The last page has a woodcut of Jericho, a seven-walled city, below which a man surrounded by a multitude is sounding a shofar. The most striking woodcut is of an imposing building, representing the Temple in Jerusalem.

In the concentric circles of holiness cited in the *Tanhuma*, Jerusalem is at the center of the Holy Land; the Holy Temple at the center of Jerusalem; and the Holy of Holies at the center of the Holy Temple. The Temple is prominently featured in illustrated books about the Holy Land. In *A Pisgah-Sight of Palestine*, three chapters describe and three engravings portray the Temple. Early Hebrew books are quite poor in illustrations, because relatively few deal with subjects that demand visual presentation.

Below left: In the gradations of holiness of space, the Holy Land is the holiest of lands, Jerusalem the holiest of cities, and its holiest place is the Temple Mount, whose holiest spot is the Holy of Holies in the Temple itself. Among the architectural engravings in this work on the Temple is a pullout map of the Temple, identifying its component parts. The Holy of Holies is the uppermost square room.

Moses Gentili, *Sefer Hanukat ha-Bayit*, Venice, 1696. Hebraic Section.

Below right: Yom Tov Lipmann Heller's description of the Temple, "the future Temple as envisioned by the prophet Ezekiel," *Zurat Beit ha-Mikdash*, was first published in Prague, 1702. For this Grodno, 1789 edition, Moses Ivier added illustrations, notably this architectural map of the "once and future Temple." It is similar to, yet different from the depiction by Gentili.

Yom Tov Lipmann Heller, *Zurat Beit ha-Mikdash* (The Form of the Temple), Grodno, 1789. Hebraic Section.

Among these are books dealing with laws concerning the Temple, and since its architecture and vessels are pertinent to the laws, they invite illustration. A case in point is *Sefer Hanukat Ha-Bayit* by Moses (Hefez) Gentili (1663–1711), published in Venice in 1696. A treatise on the building of the Second Temple, it abounds in engraved architectural illustrations, including a menorah, the seven-branched candlestick; most notable is a large pull-out map of the Temple, identifying fifty-eight components of the Temple's structure. The engravings were added after the printing, as was the map, and a copy containing both is rare.

Moses Gentili, born in Trieste, lived in Venice where he taught Talmud and Midrash, and perhaps philosophy and science as well. His best-known work, *Melekhet Mahashevet*, Venice, 1710, a commentary on the Pentateuch, contains a picture of the author, a clean-shaven, ministerial-looking gentleman.

There are many published descriptions and illustrations of the Temple's appearance in many languages. Some are based on careful study of the available sources, others are creations of the imagination, generally inspired by the grandest building the artist knew. A plan of the Temple to be is found at the end of the 1789 Grodno edition of *Zurat Beit Ha-Mikdash* (The Form of the Holy Temple) by Yom Tov Lipmann Heller (1579–1654), one of the major figures in Jewish scholarship in the first half of the seventeenth century. The book is one of Heller's earliest works and is a projection of the plan of the Temple as envisaged in the prophecy of Ezekiel.

We have thus traversed the Holy Land and glimpsed its holy places, past, present, and future.

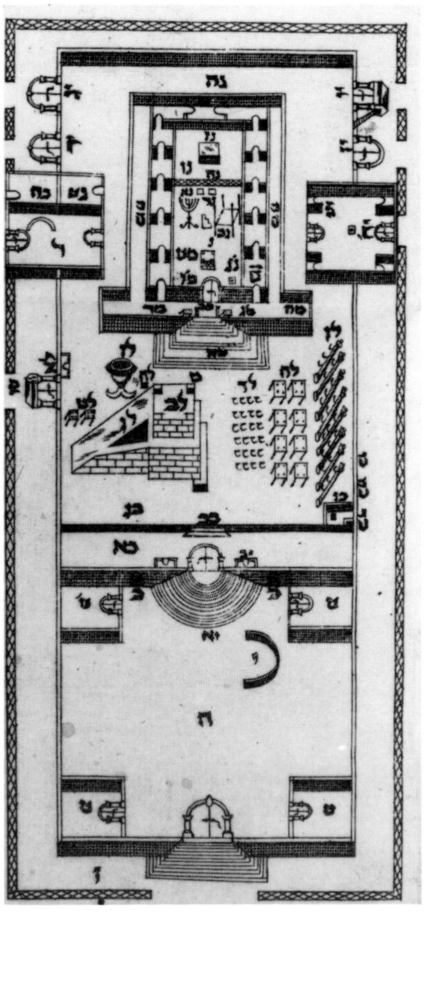

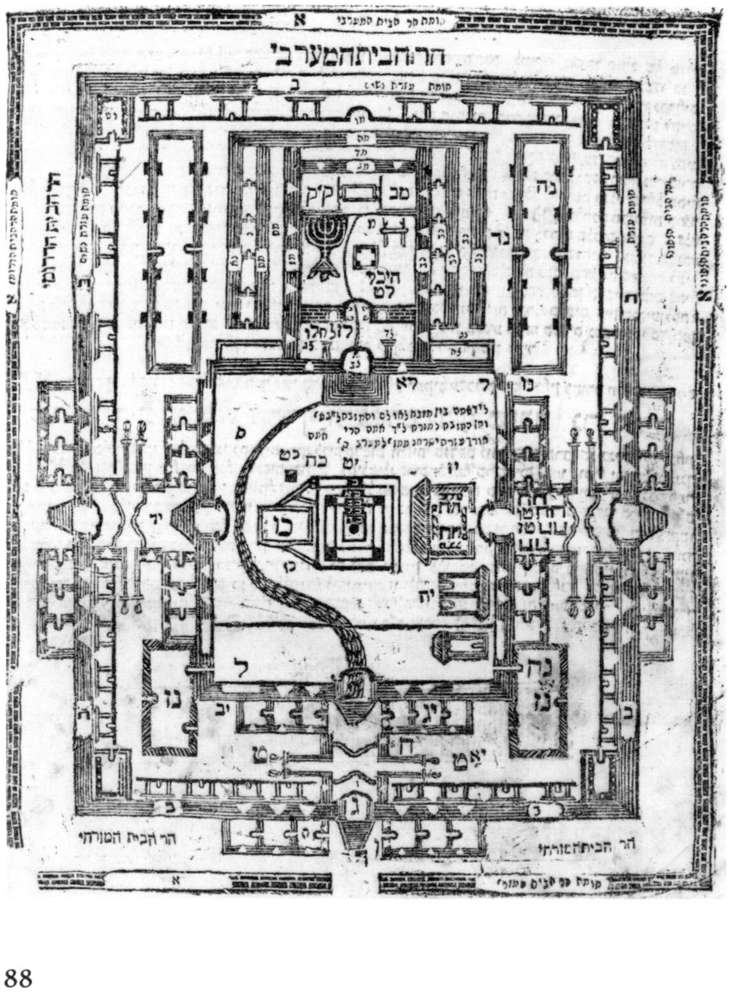

6

ADDING BEAUTY TO HOLINESS

THE JEWISH ATTITUDE TO visual art is well described by art historian Bezalel Narkiss in his introduction to *Hebrew Illuminated Manuscripts*, Jerusalem, 1969:

> It is generally assumed that Jews have an aversion to figurative art. This assumption is, in a way, true, since Jewish life in accordance with the halakah, has been directed toward belief and righteous behavior, with a verbal rather than visual expression of its tenets.
>
> However, artistic expression, far from being prohibited, was actually encouraged, either for educational purposes or for what is known as *hiddur mitzvah*, that is, adornment of the implements involved in performing rituals. Once these reasons were established, a place for artistic expression was found in Judaism. Gradually, the art gathered momentum. Embellishing biblical, ritual, legal, or even Hebrew secular books and manuscripts was one of the most important ways in which a Jew could express his devotion to the written word.

The special adornment of objects employed in ritual observance is most pronounced in the illustration and illumination of the Purim megillah, the Passover Haggadah, and the marriage ketubah. From the Hebraic Section of the Library, we draw notable examples of these as well as a most interesting illuminated *Shivviti* tablet, and a representation of the most Jewish of art forms, micrography.

The most joyous of Jewish holidays is the Festival of Purim. It is a day for merriment—eating and drinking, "until one can no longer discern between blessed Mordecai and accursed Haman"—a day of exchanging gifts and giving charity to the poor. It commemorates the events in ancient Persia described in the Biblical Book of Esther: The great monarch King Ahasuerus, whose kingdom extends from "India unto Ethiopia," in a moment of rage, deposes his queen Vashti, then sets about choosing another in her stead, the queenly post being won by the fair young maiden Esther, who, unbeknown to the king, is a Jew. Ahasuerus then raises a certain Haman to be his chief minister. Mordecai, cousin of the new queen, refuses to bow to the imperious Haman, who determines to punish not only Mordecai but his whole people with him. Through the intercession of Queen Esther—as well as the fortuitous saving of the king's life by Mordecai—Haman's wicked plan, the destruction of all the Jews in the realm, is thwarted, and turned against him. By royal decree, the Jews are permitted to defend themselves, and Haman and his sons are hanged. Mordecai is raised to highest station, and sends letters

> unto all Jews that were in the provinces of the King . . . enjoining them that they should keep . . . the days wherein the Jews had rest from their enemies . . . days turned from sorrow to gladness, from mourning to rejoicing . . . that they should make them days of feasting and gladness, of sending portions one to another, and gifts to the poor.
>
> Esther 9:20–22

The fourteenth day of the month of Adar, the day which Haman had chosen by lots (Hebrew: *purim*) for the destruction of the Jews, became a day to celebrate their being rescued. In time Purim became a holiday celebrating salvation from evil decrees and threats of annihilation wherever and whenever they occurred in the long history of persecution of the Jewish people, for, as the Haggadah reminds Jews each Passover, "In every generation, they rise up to destroy us, but the Holy One, Blessed be He, saves us from them."

The festival is not only celebrated in the home through feasting and merrymaking but commemorated in the synagogue as well through special additions to the liturgy and most importantly through the evening and morning reading of the Book of Esther from a megillah scroll. The scroll read in the synagogue contains the text alone, without illustration or decoration, but individual Jews began to commission such scrolls with ornamentation and illumination from the seventeenth century on in middle and southern Europe, and later in the Near East. Some of these were accompanied by a special sheet containing the blessings recited before and after the reading, and most incorporated hymns.

AN ILLUMINATED MEGILLAH

Among the dozen scrolls of the Book of Esther in the Library is one which is both illustrated and illuminated on fine vellum, accompanied by a sheet of blessings.

The blessings are the traditional ones, to which the scribe appends a listing of those to be cursed and blessed. And in tiny letters he offers this plea: "As thou hast taken retribution against our ancient [enemies], do so against the evil doers now and in the future, Amen!"

The scribe also adds an acrostic poem, whose verses begin with the letter ABRM, by the biblical commentator, grammarian, and poet Abraham Ibn Ezra, which is included in some Sefardi liturgies to be recited before the reading of the megillah, or on the Sabbath of Remembrance before Purim, *Shabbat Zakhor.* It is found in no less than seven manuscripts of comprehensive prayer books from Algiers and the Yemen, and its refrain reads: "Those who read the megillah, sing joyous songs to God, for it was a time of exultation for Israel." From Babylonian exile to Messianic redemption is its theme; at the center of the drama is the confrontation between Haman and Mordecai.

Above the blessing, in pleasing colors, is a scene of seven men and two women seated around a table at which a man is apparently reading to them from one of several open books. Doors are open on either side of the room. Above the poem is a scene of two men and two women dancing in a garden; on either side is a musician playing a horn. One man has doffed his hat. Below the blessings is a picture showing a man reading from a book to a boy and a girl. In the center are a crowned king and queen in royal dress. Under the poem, which ends with "May the Redeemer arrive," is a depiction of the walled city of Jerusalem. On the way to the city is a man on a donkey, before whom a herald sounds his shofar. It is the Messiah about to enter the Holy City.

Both the scene at the table and the Messiah at Jerusalem are copied from the Venice Haggadah of 1609, 1629, 1695, or 1740, though there is one more person and books have replaced food on the table. Musicians and mixed dancing also point to the Italian provenance of the megillah and its sheet of blessings. Cecil Roth describes northern Italian "Jews and the . . . theater, music and dance" in his *The Jews and the Renaissance.* Later Italian rabbis often inveighed against their flock for having surrendered to "the ways of the environment."

The megillah is illustrated with scenes from the biblical narrative.

Some megillah scrolls are accompanied by the blessings said before and after the reading of the Book of Esther in the synagogue. A few have the blessings inscribed on the scroll itself, before the text; more often they are on a small parchment of their own. The blessing broadside which accompanies the Washington Megillah contains not only the blessings and a liturgical poem by Abraham Ibn Ezra, but illuminations appropriate to the Festival of Purim, some of which are copied from the illustrated Italian Haggadot published between 1609 and 1740.

Megillah Benedictions and Illuminations, Painting on Parchment, Italy, eighteenth century (?).
Hebraic Section.

Illustrations in color accompany the text throughout, depicting every major scene in the Esther-Mordecai-Ahasuerus-Haman drama. The illuminations, drawn with a naive charm, are appropriate to the biblical narrative which at its heart is history recounted in the form of a folk tale. The costumes worn by the actors in the drama, and the illustrations depicting celebrants indicate an early eighteenth-century Italian provenance for this charming manuscript on vellum.

The Washington Megillah (*Megillat Esther,* The Book of Esther), Scroll on Parchment, Illuminated, Italy (?), eighteenth century (?).
Hebraic Section.

Vashti, the queen, as commentators suggest, was to have appeared without clothes. She refused, but our artist complies. The illustrations unfold before us scenes at the court, Esther before Ahasuerus, battles being waged, and musicians playing. The full drama of the narrative is brought to life by the eighteenth-century north Italian landscape, its recognizable buildings, dress, furnishings, and martial and musical instruments—lance and viol. Ahasuerus and Vashti, Haman and Zeresh, Mordecai and Esther become contemporaries. The illustrations do not intrude upon the text; they give it life. Alas, we know nothing of the illustrator-scribe, not even his name.

THE WASHINGTON HAGGADAH

Even more than the megillah of Esther, the Haggadah which is read in Jewish homes at the Passover seder, and which tells of the Exodus from Egypt, has been reproduced in many and varied forms of artistic decoration. An illuminated manuscript Haggadah, also fashioned in northern Italy, is the Library's justly famed Washington Haggadah. The anonymous artisan who produced the megillah was a pedestrian calligrapher and illustrator and, perhaps precisely because of that, his megillah has a folk vitality and naive charm often lacking in the work of more sophisticated and gifted artists. It is a fine example of what a moderately skilled scribe aspiring at *hiddur mitzvah* can accomplish. As such it is a valuable contribution to Jewish folk art. The Washington Haggadah is of another order. Its creator, Joel ben Simeon, was the most prolific Hebrew artist-scribe of the fifteenth century. No less than eleven manuscripts bearing his name, written in his native Rhineland and in Northern Italy, are now the treasured possessions of libraries in Europe, Israel, and America. "Most of Joel's illuminations," Bezalel Narkiss writes, "consist of colored pen drawings. . . . The best . . . is the expressively drawn Washington Haggadah of 1478." Narkiss includes it among the sixty beautiful and important works which comprise his *Hebrew Illuminated Manuscripts,* first published in Jerusalem in 1969, and more recently in 1984, in a revised and improved Hebrew edition. He describes it:

> It is illuminated entirely in Italian style, with no trace of German motifs other than the iconography. All of the illustrations are placed in the margins, and are mainly ritual or literal . . . Beside the four sons, other illustrations typical of German iconography are the cooking and the roasting of the Passover lamb and a man pointing to his wife while saying *maror zeh.*
>
> Joel ben Simeon, called Feibush Ashkenazi of Bonn, calls himself the humblest of scribes, stating that "the work was completed on the 25th of *Shevat,* 5238" [January 29, 1478].*

*The Washington Haggadah has been issued in a facsimile edition by the Library of Congress. It is accompanied by a scholarly description and assessment of the manuscript.

What appeals most to this observer about the Washington Haggadah is its economy of decoration and its use of the illustrations, even their place upon the page, to express a point of view. Illustrations are only in the margins, preserving the centrality of the text; decorations are there to adorn and may not intrude upon the text. The wise and wicked sons are and should be farther apart from one another than the simple sons. Why should the wise one not seem to be shoving the wicked one downward? More than half of the figure of the wicked son is below the text, removed from it, as the wicked son "removed himself from the congregation [of Israel]." The artist becomes the subtle commentator, in the tradition of Jewish religious works: text and commentary.

Speaking of the sons: the wise one sits on a chair, book in hands on lap, as if in the process of teaching. The simple son is not a simpleton; he too has a book before him, but he sits on the floor as an inquiring student. He does ask, "What is this?" and in a question is the beginning of wisdom. The artist-scribe does not fall into the error of so many illustrators of the Haggadah who depict the *tam* as a simpleton, a tradition brought to a head by Jakob Steinhardt who places a dunce cap on the *tam* in his Berlin, 1923, Haggadah. *Tam* means innocent and simple, honest, and harmless. A faith tradition which extols the question—the Talmud begins with a question, the Haggadah itself flows from the Four Questions—would never view a questioner as a simpleton. A simpleton is one who "lacks the capacity to ask a question," and he is so portrayed in the manuscript, as a fool or jester. Our artist-scribe knows he is a scribe first, copying a sacred text, then adorning it and illuminating it with subtle visual commentary, but the text must dominate.

There are a considerable number of illuminated Haggadot, larger in format and richer in illustrations. They are finer artistic creations than the Washington Haggadah, but very few, if any, are grander Haggadot, i.e., sacred liturgical texts whose purpose is to help the celebrant reexperience history and renew his appreciation for the gift of freedom. Its modest size,

P. 94, 95, 96, 97

Among the greatest of medieval Hebrew illuminated manuscripts is the Washington Haggadah fashioned by Joel ben Simeon, the most productive scribe and illuminator of Hebrew manuscripts in the fifteenth century. Though not elaborately illustrated as many other illuminated Haggadot, the beauty of its calligraphy, which is never subordinated to the illustrations, the proportions of the page, and the vividness of the illumination, which has come down in unusually fine condition, make this one of the most admired of Hebrew manuscripts. We display four pages.

The Washington Haggadah, Illuminated, Central Europe, 1478. Hebraic Section.

Ho Lahma "This bread of affliction"

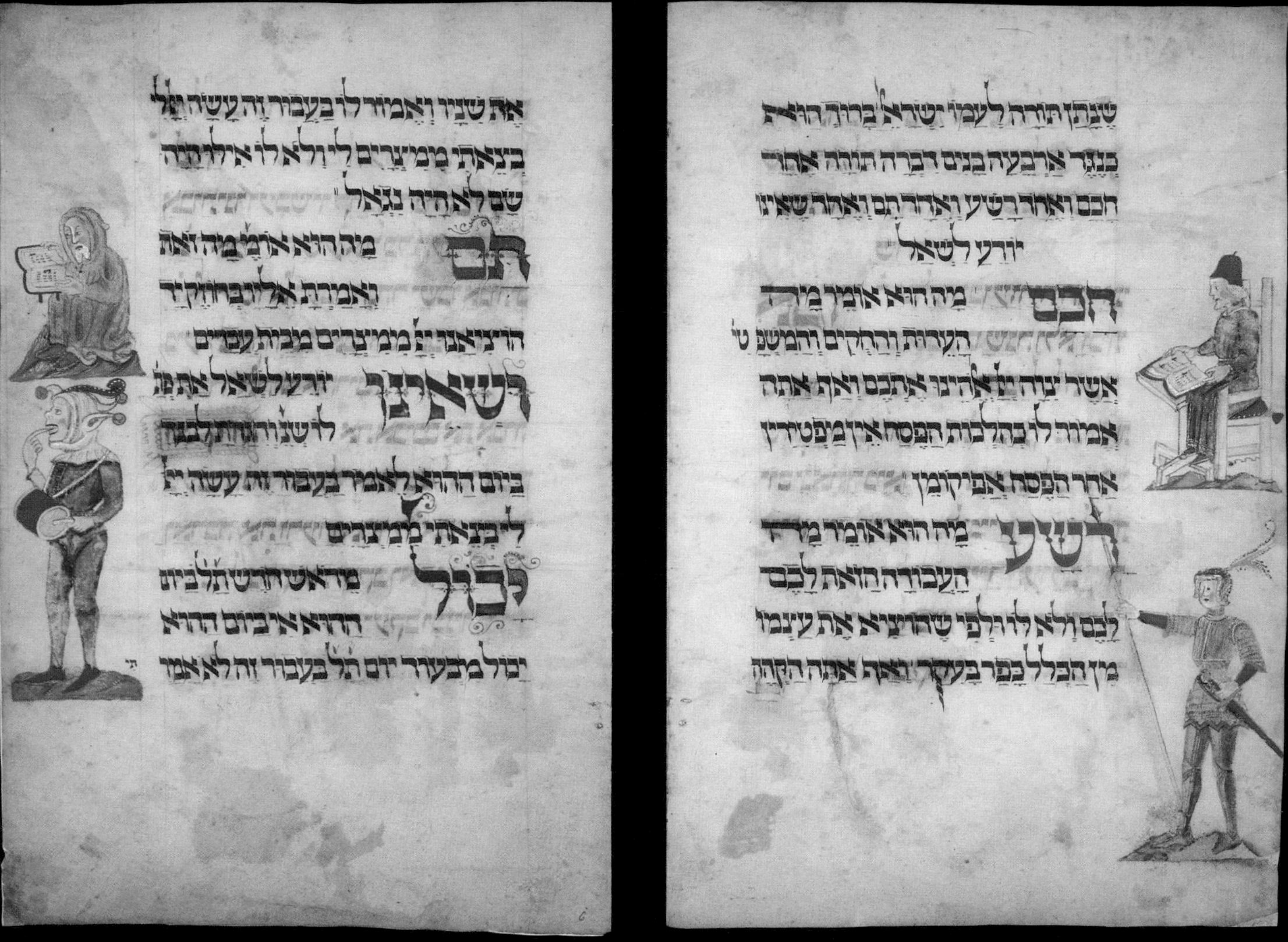
שנתן תורה לעמו ישראל ברוך הוא
כנגד ארבעה בנים דברה תורה אחד
חכם ואחד רשע ואחד תם ואחד שאינו
יודע לשאל
חכם מה הוא אומר מה
העדות והחקים והמשפטים
אשר צוה יי אלהינו אתכם ואף אתה
אמור לו כהלכות הפסח אין מפטירין
אחר הפסח אפיקומן
רשע מה הוא אומר מה
העבודה הזאת לכם
לכם ולא לו ולפי שהוציא את עצמו
מן הכלל כפר בעקר ואף אתה הקהה

את שניו ואמור לו בעבור זה עשה יי לי
בצאתי ממצרים לי ולא לו אילו היה
שם לא היה נגאל
תם מה הוא אומר מה זאת
ואמרת אליו בחוזק יד
הוציאנו יי ממצרים מבית עבדים
ושאינו יודע לשאל את פתח
לו שנאמר והגדת לבנך
ביום ההוא לאמר בעבור זה עשה יי
לי בצאתי ממצרים
יכול מראש חדש ת״ל ביום
ההוא אי ביום ההוא
יכול מבעוד יום ת״ל בעבור זה לא אמרתי

The Four Sons

שפך

חמתך על הגוים אשר לא ידעוך
ועל הממלכות אשר בשמך לא
קראו

כתוב [illegible] ולכתוב סדר של פסח ✡ כבודך יי׳

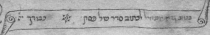

וצריך לבדוק בכל פנה
ופינה מחדר לחדר׳
כל חמירא דאיכא
בביתא הדין דלא חזיתיה ודלא ביערתיה
יהא בטל ותיהוי [illegible]
כעפרא׳

וצריך לשמור [illegible]
[illegible]
[illegible]
[illegible]
[illegible]
[illegible]
[illegible]
[illegible]
ושורפין [illegible]

וכשורפין [illegible]
כל חמירא דאיכא
בביתא הדין [illegible]
ודלא חזיתיה [illegible]
ודלא ביערתיה יהא
בטל ותיהוי כעפרא׳

[illegible]
[illegible]
[illegible]
[illegible]
[illegible]

לארבעה עשר בודקין את החמץ לאור
הנר כל מקום שאין מכניסין בו חמץ
אין צריך בדיקה׳ [illegible]

ברוך אתה יי׳ אלהינו מלך העולם אשר קדשנו
במצותיו וצונו על ביעור חמץ

חמירא
דאיכא
ברשותי דחזיתי ודלא חזיתי דחמיתי ודלא חמיתי דביערתי
ודלא ביערתי יהי בטל ויהוי כעפרא דארעא׳

סדר אחר לפסח

קדש ורחץ כרפס יחץ מגיד רחצה מוציא
מצה מרור כורך שלחן עורך צפון
ברך הלל נרצה

א

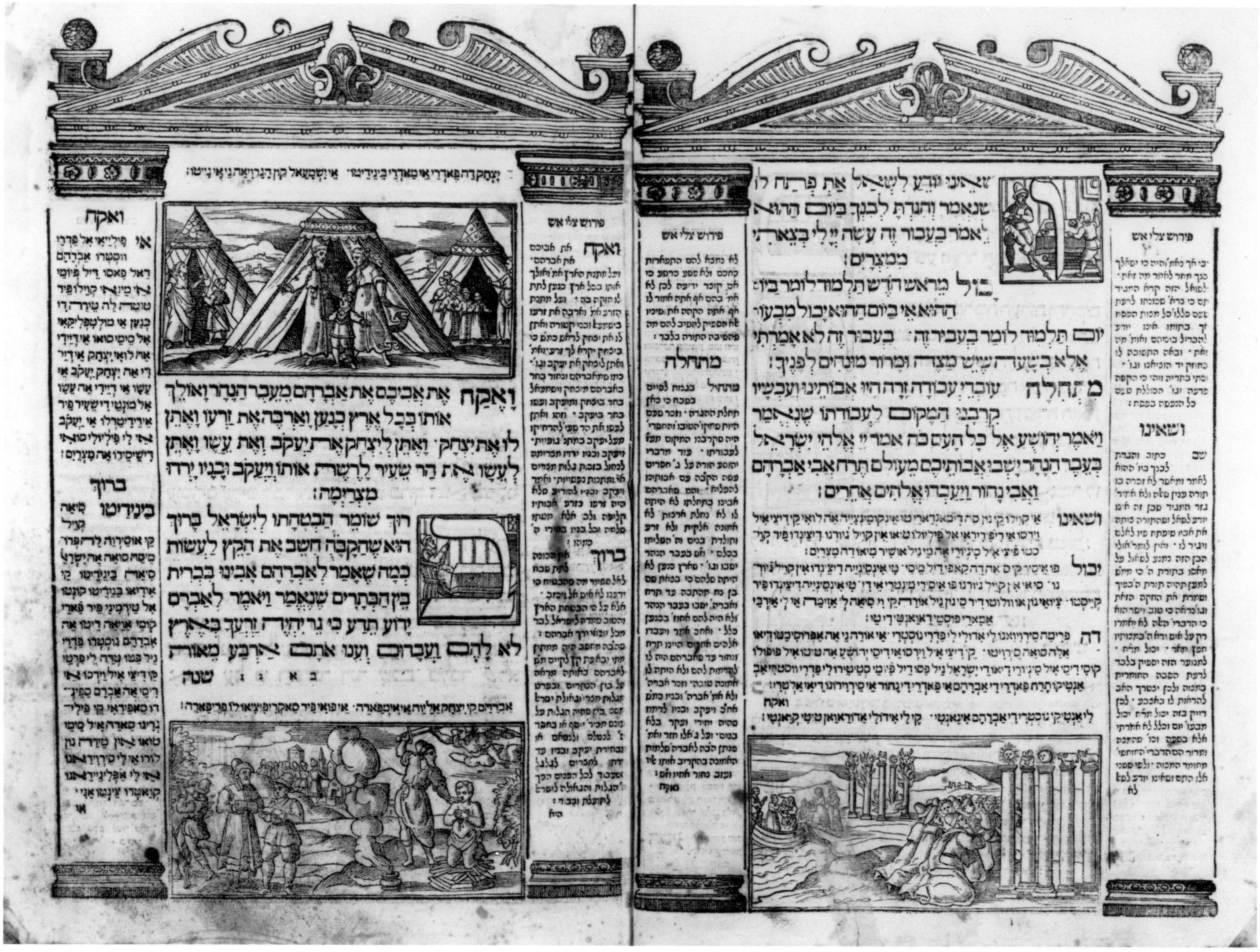

This profusely illustrated Haggadah was edited by the noted seventeenth-century Venetian rabbi and author, Leone da Modena, who provided a Judeo-Italian translation and a new commentary *Tseli Esh* (Roasted in Fire), an abridgement of the commentary of Isaac Abravanel, *Zevah Pesah* (Passover Sacrificial Offering). The illustrations shown depict incidents in the life of the patriarch Abraham. At the top: Abraham's choice of his younger son Isaac and rejection of the older, Ishmael, is indicated by the placement of Abraham, Sarah, and Isaac at the center tent, while Hagar and Ishmael stand alone at theirs. At the bottom: the sacrifice of Isaac.

Seder Haggadah shel Pesah (Passover Haggadah), Venice, 1629.
Hebraic Section.

six inches by nine, indicates that it was meant to be used at the seder table, and the pale wine stains on its vellum bear witness that it was.

ILLUSTRATED HAGGADOT

The illuminated Haggadah manuscripts paved the way for unending editions of illustrated Haggadot which continue to the present day. From the Library's impressive collection of Haggadot, we choose seven. Four illustrate the ongoing influence of early and late seventeenth-century editions; three are pictorial departures which appeared once and were never copied.

In 1609, a Haggadah of singular beauty was published in Venice by Israel ben David Zifroni, a veteran printer and copy editor of Hebrew books in Italy and Switzerland. Each page is framed by an artistically wrought border. Woodcut illustrations of the Passover ritual and the contents of the Haggadah abound, as well as depictions of Moses, Aaron, Kings David and Solomon, and miniature vignettes framed by the large initial letters. What is most rewarding to the student of history are illustrations of contemporary preparations for the holiday, including the baking of matzoh. This Haggadah appeared in three versions, with translations and instructions in Judeo-German (Yiddish), Judeo-Italian, and Judeo-Spanish (Ladino), all printed in Hebrew letters. A second printing appeared in 1629, with a new title page extolling the beauty of the illustrations and announcing the inclusion of a commentary *Tseli Esh* (Roasted in Fire), an abridgement by Leone da Modena of Isaac Abrabanel's *Zebah Pesah* (Passover Sacrifice), because

> It already includes illustrations to delight the eye, how much better it now is to add explanations which will delight the "spiritual eye" [the soul].

The edition was commissioned by Moses ben Gershon Parenzo, the last of three generations of Hebrew printers, and issued by the Bragadini press. The Library's crisp copies of this edition and one published in 1740 display the durability and popularity of those illustrations by an artist whose name is unknown but whose creations continued to beautify Haggadot published in the nineteenth and the twentieth centuries, as for example, in a 1904 Livorno edition with an Arabic translation for Tunisian Jews.

The illustrations most widely copied in illuminated manuscripts (e.g., the exact copy by the artist-scribe Ya'akov ben Yehudah Leib, written in Hamburg in 1728) and in hundreds of printed editions are those which first appeared in a lavishly illustrated and beautifully printed Haggadah published in Amsterdam in 1695. For the first time in any edition of a Haggadah, the illustrator is identified, Abraham bar Jacob "of the family of Abraham our Father," i.e., a proselyte to Judaism. For the first time, too, the illustrations are copper engravings rather than the woodcuts of earlier editions. Engraving made possible more richly detailed delineations, and these were copies or adaptations of biblical engravings by the Swiss artist Mattaeus Merian, which were first published in 1625–30. The simple son is copied from Merian's depiction of Saul as he was being anointed by the Prophet Samuel. The shepherd's crook held by Saul is changed into a staff, and the person portrayed is "Judaized" by placing a hat on what was, in Merian's depiction, a bald head. The look of the simple country bumpkin is retained. The most dramatic depictions are of the Children of Israel leaving Egypt and standing at Mt. Sinai, Moses descending from the mountain, a Tablet of the Law in each hand, and Aaron waiting below, surrounded by tents and people in Oriental and medieval garb.

The Library's fine copy contains the inserted map, previously described, which is missing in many copies, no doubt removed for framing by devotees of cartography. It is perhaps ironic that illustrations which for over two centuries have been the most widely reproduced (e.g., the crude copies in the Furth, 1755 edition; or the perfected engravings in the Vienna, 1823 printing)—which for almost three centuries have been viewed as the most authentic Haggadah depictions—stem from biblical scenes drawn by a Christian.

The first edition of the Haggadah with an English translation, done by "A. Alexander and Assistants" and printed for him, was published by the translator in London, 1770. Having published a bilingual edition of "our Tephilloth, or Common-Prayer-Book," Alexander now undertook a "second Attempt, in Publishing this small Book of the Haggadah or the Cere-

The title page of this Haggadah extols this edition's virtues:

a fine commentary and beautiful illustrations of the miracles wrought by God for our ancestors. Added to that, all the journey through the wilderness until the division of the land among the tribes, and a depiction of the Temple, may it be rebuilt and renewed, soon, in our day, Amen, and so may it be Thy will. Engraved on Copper plates by the young man Abram bar Jacob, of the family of Abraham our Father [i.e., a proselyte to Judaism].

The illustrations were reproduced in many subsequent editions until the present day. We see Moses and Aaron before the Pharaoh; the enslaved Children of Israel at labor are in the background.

Seder Haggadah shel Pesah (Passover Haggadah), Amsterdam, 1695.
Hebraic Section.

הגדה ט פירש אברבנאל

ובאותות זה המטה כמו שנאמר ואת המטה הזה תקח בידך אשר תעשה בו האותות: ובמופתים זה הדם כמו שנאמר ונתתי מופתים בשמים ובארץ דם ואש ותמרות עשן: דבר אחר ביד חזקה שתים ובזרוע נטויה שתים ובמורא גדול שתים ובאותות שתים ובמופתים שתים: אלו

Facing page:
The Venice 1740 Haggadah edition also has a Judeo-Italian translation, but it is meant to appeal to Yiddish-speaking German Jews as well, for the hymn *Adir Hu* (Exalted Be He) appears with a translation in Judeo-German. The Hebrew alphabetical acrostic is matched by one in Yiddish extolling God's virtues.

Seder Haggadah shel Pesah (Passover Haggadah), Venice, 1740.
Hebraic Section.

monies of the Passover" accompanied by an explanatory introduction and notes. Facing the title page is a frontispiece whose engraved Hebrew legend declares, "And they built for Pharaoh store-cities Pithom and Raameses." Depicted are medieval towers being built, slaves laboring, and an overseer cruelly beating a slave, mouth wide open in a scream of pain—again a copy of an illustration in the Amsterdam Haggadah.

In the nineteenth century, illustrators departed from the slavish copying of the early Venice editions by Italian publishers, and of the early Amsterdam by central and eastern European printers. A most attractive edition, both for its Hebrew typography and its elegantly executed woodcut illustrations, was published in Basel in 1816, by Solomon Coschelberg at the press of Wilhelm Haas. It is, as stated, "a simple edition without com-

חסל סדור פסח כהלכתו · ככל משפטו וחקתו · כאשר זכינו לסדר אותו כן נזכה לעשותו · זך שוכן מעונה · קומם קהל מי מנה · קרב נהל נטעי כנה · פדוים לציון ברנה ׃

פירוש צלי אש

אדיר הוא יבנה ביתו בקרוב במהרה במהרה בימינו בקרוב · אל בנה אל בנה בנה ביתו בקרוב ׃

בחור · גדול · דגול · הדור · ותיק · זך · חסיד · טהור · יחיד · כביר · למוד · מלך · נאור · סגיב · עזוז · פודה · צדיק · קדוש · רחום · שדי · תקיף הוא יבנה ביתו בקרוב · במהרה במהרה בימינו בקרוב · אל בנה אל בנה בנה ביתו בקרוב ׃

בליל שני של פסח מתחילין העומר

ברוך אתה יי אלהינו מלך העולם אשר קדשנו במצותיו וצונו על ספירת העומר · שהיום יום אחד בעומר ׃

יהי רצון מלפניך יי אלהינו ואלהי אבותינו שיבנה בית המקדש במהרה בימינו ותן חלקנו בתורתך ׃

4784
THE
הגדה של פסח
CONTAINING THE
CEREMONIES and PRAYERS
Which are uſed and read
By all FAMILIES, in all HOUSES
OF THE
ISRAELITES,
THE
Two firſt Nights of PASSOVER:
Faithfully TRANSLATED from the
ORIGINAL HEBREW.
TO WHICH IS ADDED,
The EXPLANATIONS thereon.
TRANSLATED by A. ALEXANDER,
And ASSISTANTS.
LONDON:
Printed for the TRANSLATOR, by W. GILBERT.
A. M. 5530.
Engraved for the Hebrew & English Hawgoda.
ויבן ערי מסכנות לפרעה
את פתם ואת רעמסס

Alexander Alexander, having published the prayer book in Hebrew with an English translation in London, 1770, undertook "a second attempt," publishing in the same year "this small Book of the Haggadah, or the ceremonies of Passover, together with a Notation thereon." His English is poor in both translation and "Notation," nor did it improve in the Festival and Holy Days prayer books and the Pentateuch which he subsequently published, and which his son Levy Alexander republished. The frontispiece, Moses slaying the Egyptian, "Engraved for the Hebrew Hawgoda," is a copy of bar Jacob's illustration in the Amsterdam Haggadah, which itself is a copy of a biblical engraving by Matthaeus Merian.

Haggadah shel Pesah (Passover Haggadah), London, 1770. Hebraic Section.

mentary . . . but a correct text, printed in large letters and with many appropriate illustrations." The illustrations, twenty-four in number, are copied from Friedrich Battier's, which appeared in a 1710 edition of a Basel German Bible. The spare woodcuts and the square Basel type blend harmoniously. One note which may raise an eyebrow is the depiction of a seder scene with twelve men surrounding a long-haired central figure seated at a set table, the classic portrayal of the Last Supper. A seder scene, to be sure, and one fraught with memory. It must have escaped the scrutiny of the Jewish publisher, because it was hardly an appropriate replacement for the historic seder scene of the Amsterdam edition in which "Rabbis seated in Bnei Brak are discussing the exodus from Egypt," or the contemporary seder shown in the Venice editions.

The beautifully illustrated Trieste, 1864 Haggadah was published by

Colombo Coen (Joshua Cohen) and edited by Abraham Hayyim Morpurgo, the editor of *Corriere Israelitico* and scion of a noted scholarly Italian Jewish family. The illustrations are by a young artist, K. Kirchmayer whose name is inscribed at the bottom of the title page, on which appear David and Solomon crowned, Aaron mitred, and Moses bareheaded, rays of light shining from his brow. Most of the illustrations are updated redrawings of those found in the Venice editions. Thus, father and son still search for leaven, mother is still doing her pre-Passover cleaning, but they are now dressed in modern clothing, and the house furnishings are those of a mid-nineteenth-century middle-class Italian home. This edition, too, has a jarring note. Moses is depicted kneeling before the burning bush, and clearly visible in the bush is the bearded face of God. The figure and face of God can be seen in many Christian biblical illustrations, but this is the only one in a Jewish publication, except the barely noticeable face of the divine in the "Ezekiel and the dry bones" panel on the engraved title page of the *Minhat Shai* edition of the Hebrew Bible, published by Raphael Hayim, Italia, Mantua, 1744. Did both Cohen and Morpurgo overlook it or, seeing it, did they deem it appropriate?

בָּם חֲרוֹן אַפּוֹ · עֶבְרָה וָזַעַם וְצָרָה · מִשְׁלַחַת מַלְאֲכֵי רָעִים · עֶבְרָה אַחַת · וָזַעַם שְׁתַּיִם · וְצָרָה שָׁלֹשׁ · מִשְׁלַחַת מַלְאֲכֵי רָעִים אַרְבַּע · אֱמוֹר מֵעַתָּה בְּמִצְרַיִם לָקוּ אַרְבָּעִים מַכּוֹת · וְעַל הַיָּם לָקוּ מָאתַיִם מַכּוֹת :

רַבִּי עֲקִיבָא אוֹמֵר מִנַּיִן שֶׁכָּל מַכָּה וּמַכָּה שֶׁהֵבִיא הַקָּדוֹשׁ בָּרוּךְ הוּא עַל הַמִּצְרִים בְּמִצְרַיִם הָיְתָה שֶׁל חָמֵשׁ מַכּוֹת · שֶׁנֶּאֱמַר יְשַׁלַּח בָּם חֲרוֹן אַפּוֹ · עֶבְרָה וָזַעַם וְצָרָה · מִשְׁלַחַת מַלְאֲכֵי רָעִים · חֲרוֹן אַפּוֹ אַחַת · עֶבְרָה שְׁתַּיִם · וָזַעַם שָׁלֹשׁ · וְצָרָה אַרְבַּע · מִשְׁלַחַת מַלְאֲכֵי רָעִים חָמֵשׁ · אֱמוֹר מֵעַתָּה בְּמִצְרַיִם לָקוּ חֲמִשִּׁים מַכּוֹת · וְעַל הַיָּם לָקוּ חֲמִשִּׁים וּמָאתַיִם מַכּוֹת :

This Haggadah's type is pleasing to the eye and easy to read; the German translation in Hebrew characters by Joel Brill is in fine literary language; and the woodcut illustrations are copied from a Bible printed in Basel in 1710. Editor Solomon Coschelberg put them together to form this charming Haggadah. The illustration on the right depicts the Children of Israel crossing the Red Sea in safety while the Egyptians go under; the one on the left shows the Children of Israel gathering food and drawing water in the wilderness.

Haggadah shel Pesah (Passover Haggadah), Basel, 1816.
Hebraic Section.

The Viennese publisher Anton Schmidt issued a number of printings of the Haggadah utilizing the delicately engraved popular illustrations of Abraham bar Jacob. They are especially expertly executed in this 1823 issue. Two popular commentaries by Moses Alscheich and Ephraim Lenczycz added to the popular illustrations made for many editions. The Haggadah is opened to the illustrations depicting the order of the seder.

Ma'ale Bet Horin, Vienna, 1823.
Hebraic Section.

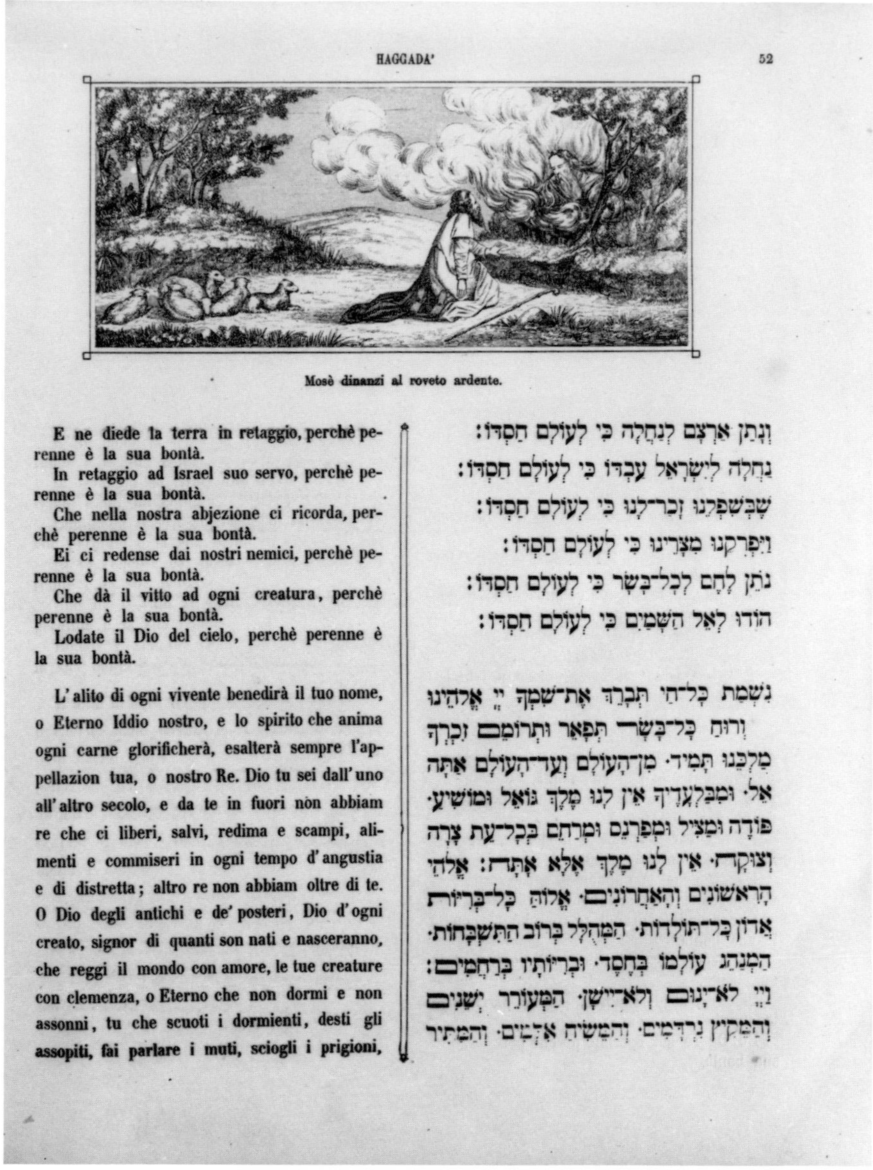

Mosè dinanzi al roveto ardente.

E ne diede la terra in retaggio, perchè perenne è la sua bontà.

In retaggio ad Israel suo servo, perchè perenne è la sua bontà.

Che nella nostra abjezione ci ricorda, perchè perenne è la sua bontà.

Ei ci redense dai nostri nemici, perchè perenne è la sua bontà.

Che dà il vitto ad ogni creatura, perchè perenne è la sua bontà.

Lodate il Dio del cielo, perchè perenne è la sua bontà.

L' alito di ogni vivente benedirà il tuo nome, o Eterno Iddio nostro, e lo spirito che anima ogni carne glorificherà, esalterà sempre l'appellazion tua, o nostro Re. Dio tu sei dall' uno all' altro secolo, e da te in fuori nòn abbiam re che ci liberi, salvi, redima e scampi, alimenti e commiseri in ogni tempo d' angustia e di distretta; altro re non abbiam oltre di te. O Dio degli antichi e de' posteri, Dio d' ogni creato, signor di quanti son nati e nasceranno, che reggi il mondo con amore, le tue creature con clemenza, o Eterno che non dormi e non assonni, tu che scuoti i dormienti, desti gli assopiti, fai parlare i muti, sciogli i prigioni,

וְנָתַן אַרְצָם לְנַחֲלָה כִּי לְעוֹלָם חַסְדּוֹ:

נַחֲלָה לְיִשְׂרָאֵל עַבְדּוֹ כִּי לְעוֹלָם חַסְדּוֹ:

שֶׁבְּשִׁפְלֵנוּ זָכַר-לָנוּ כִּי לְעוֹלָם חַסְדּוֹ:

וַיִּפְרְקֵנוּ מִצָּרֵינוּ כִּי לְעוֹלָם חַסְדּוֹ:

נֹתֵן לֶחֶם לְכָל-בָּשָׂר כִּי לְעוֹלָם חַסְדּוֹ:

הוֹדוּ לְאֵל הַשָּׁמַיִם כִּי לְעוֹלָם חַסְדּוֹ:

נִשְׁמַת כָּל-חַי תְּבָרֵךְ אֶת-שִׁמְךָ יְיָ אֱלֹהֵינוּ וְרוּחַ כָּל-בָּשָׂר תְּפָאֵר וּתְרוֹמֵם זִכְרְךָ מַלְכֵּנוּ תָּמִיד· מִן-הָעוֹלָם וְעַד-הָעוֹלָם אַתָּה אֵל· וּמִבַּלְעָדֶיךָ אֵין לָנוּ מֶלֶךְ גּוֹאֵל וּמוֹשִׁיעַ· פּוֹדֶה וּמַצִּיל וּמְפַרְנֵס וּמְרַחֵם בְּכָל-עֵת צָרָה וְצוּקָה· אֵין לָנוּ מֶלֶךְ אֶלָּא אָתָּה· אֱלֹהֵי הָרִאשׁוֹנִים וְהָאַחֲרוֹנִים· אֱלוֹהַּ כָּל-בְּרִיּוֹת· אֲדוֹן כָּל-תּוֹלָדוֹת· הַמְהֻלָּל בְּרוֹב הַתִּשְׁבָּחוֹת· הַמְנַהֵג עוֹלָמוֹ בְּחֶסֶד· וּבְרִיּוֹתָיו בְּרַחֲמִים: יְיָ לֹא-יָנוּם וְלֹא-יִישָׁן· הַמְעוֹרֵר יְשֵׁנִים וְהַמֵּקִיץ נִרְדָּמִים· וְהַמֵּשִׂיחַ אִלְּמִים· וְהַמַּתִּיר

The vivid, expertly executed illustrations by K. Kirchmayer on almost every page have made this Haggadah a favorite of connoisseurs and collectors. Edited by Abraham Hayyim Morpurgo, it was published in variant issues—all Hebrew or Hebrew with an Italian translation. Illustrated is Moses at the burning bush; and almost unique in Jewish iconograpy, God's face is depicted!

Seder ha-Haggadah shel Pesah (The Order of the Passover Haggadah), Trieste, 1864.
Hebraic Section.

KETUBOTH

In his compendium of the 613 biblical commandments, *Sefer Ha-Mitzvot*, Maimonides lists first, "Be fruitful and multiply and fill the earth" (Genesis 1:28). A number of verses later the Bible explains, "It is not good that the man should be alone: I will make him a helpmeet for him . . . therefore shall a man leave his father and his mother and shall cleave unto his wife, and they shall be one flesh" (Genesis 2:18, 24). Love and marriage are lauded in the Bible, and the prophets Hosea, Isaiah, and Ezekiel use them as a metaphor for the relationship of God and his people Israel.

It is not surprising, therefore, that the celebration of a marriage became the most joyous of communal events. The Talmud records that it was common practice, even for rabbis, to "dance before the bride." Rabbi Judah danced before the bride, myrtle branch in hand; to the astonishment or consternation of his colleagues, Rav Aha danced with the bride on his shoulders; and Samuel ben Rav was sternly criticized for doing a juggling dance. What may have been unseemly for rabbis was nonetheless encouraged in others in order to "bring joy to the bridegroom and bride" at their nuptials.

"To dance before the bride" was not sufficient for joy which also requires peace of mind. To provide that, the rabbis enacted the ketubah, a legal document recording the obligations of a husband to his wife during their marriage: "I will work for thee, honor, support, and maintain thee as Jewish husbands are accustomed to do"; and in case of divorce or death, there is a stipulation for monetary payment to the wife. At the wedding ceremony the ketubah is presented by the groom to the bride, and the bride is required by law to keep it during her lifetime.

Because the ketubah was preserved, it became the lasting memento of the wedding ceremony, and the custom arose to make it a beautiful memento, a sentiment fortified by the precept of *hiddur mitzvah.* A fragment of a tenth-century decorated and colored ketubah on parchment was found in the Cairo Geniza (a storage space in a Cairo synagogue for worn, unusable Hebrew books and discarded Hebrew documents). In Vienna's National Library, are preserved four parchment fragments of a ketubah written in Krems, Austria, in 1392. Their finely wrought calligraphic text is framed by decorated borders. At either end of the top corners are the figures of the bride and groom, he extending his left hand towards her, holding an enlarged ring, she stretching forth her right hand to accept it. The custom of illuminated ketuboth disappeared among Ashkenazi Jewry, but was retained and developed among Sefardi communities from Italy to Persia. In Italy, influenced by the blooming of art in the Renaissance, it was raised to an art form in the sixteenth to nineteenth centuries.

"The influences of the Renaissance can be found in those of the sixteenth to seventeenth centuries, of the Baroque in the ketuboth of the eighteenth," David Davidovitch writes in his *The Ketubah* (Tel Aviv, 1968), "while those of the nineteenth century bear the stamp of the Empire, neoclassicism, etc." He also remarks on the Ancona and Corfu schools of ketubah illumination. To these and the "etc." we turn, for the Library of Congress has notable examples of them.

So great was the desire for a splendidly illuminated ketubah in the Ancona Jewish community in the latter part of the eighteenth century, that Jewish communal authorities found it necessary to forbid spending more than forty paoli for ketubah ornamentation. (Limitations on expenditure for wedding celebrations are found in the regulations of a number of Jewish communities.) But artistic ketuboth persisted nonetheless in that Adriatic port. Ancona was one of the oldest of Italian-Jewish communities, with memories both of times of relative security and well-being, and times of oppression and persecution. In this papal city in the fifteenth and the first half of the sixteenth centuries, the Jews were made welcome by the papal authorities and they flourished; in the second half of that century Jews were terrorized by Pope Paul IV's policies and representatives. Right up to the twentieth century the Jews of Ancona remembered twenty-four martyrs who were hanged and whose bodies were burned at the stake in 1555, an act so brutally outrageous that the rabbis of Turkey decreed a boycott against the Ancona seaport. Confined to a ghetto, restricted and humiliated by papal decrees as late as 1775, the Ancona Jews remained determined to beautify their inner life against the ugliness outside.

The Ancona ketubah of the Library of Congress was fashioned in a happier time. From 1797 to 1814, the city was under Napoleon's domination. The ghetto gates were removed, repressive decrees were abrogated, and three Jews were appointed to the municipal council. In those "good days," on June 12, 1805, Aaron ben Hayim Cesana of Corfu was married to Sarah Rivka bat Mordecai d'Ovadia. The Cesanas were a leading Corfu family who numbered among their members Samson Cesana, who was granted a coat of arms (on its escutcheon, Samson is tearing open the mouth of a lion), and two noted physicians. The Ovadias seem no less distinguished a family, as indicated by the artistic quality of the ketubah. On parchment, it is similar in contour, style and artistry to other distinguished Ancona ketuboth, like the 1772 ketubah now in the Jewish National and University Library of Jerusalem, and another of 1804 now in the British Library. In all of them biblical figures or scenes are incorporated which touch upon the names of the celebrants.

In the 1772 ketubah are two cutouts of events in the life of the biblical Isaac. In the 1804 wedding, where the groom is also named Isaac, at the top cartouche we find a depiction of *Akedat Yitzhak,* the Binding of Isaac. In the Library's ketubah, the dominant cartouche is given to Moses receiving the Ten Commandments—probably because the wedding date was the fifteenth of *Sivan,* a week after the Festival of Shavuot, the "Season of the Giving of the Law." In cartouches in the side panels are portraits of a lady, identified as the biblical Sarah (the name of the bride), and one of the biblical Aaron labeled, not "the Priest," but "Aaron the Prophet." Although, according to rabbinic tradition, Aaron was indeed also a prophet, he is never called that. Very likely this designation was used to indicate that the groom named Aaron was not a *Kohen,* a descendant of the priestly clan. At the bottom there are two rampant lions, and under the text of the ketubah there is an addendum, listing further stipulations. Among these is one stating that a civil contract is to be drawn up by the parties involved.

An Italian ketubah in the Library's collection, written more than two decades later in the small town of Maddalena on the Po, in northwest Italy near the French border, shows the economy and simplicity of both illustration and illumination. It is tastefully adorned with colored flowers and birds, but though the names of the groom, his father, and the bride's father—David, Moses, and Judah—would have easily lent themselves to biblical illustration, that period is over, as is that of the baroque illumination and adornment. That era had yielded to a style of illustration more suited to nineteenth-century life, more classically direct and simple, and more integrated into the general community.

Three nineteenth-century Corfu ketuboth illustrate form following life. The second largest of the Greek isles, Corfu, both island and city, was the home of an old, cosmopolitan Jewish community. The twelfth-century Jewish traveler, Benjamin of Tudela, found only one Jew there in 1147, but not long thereafter when the island came under the sovereignty of the Angevin kings of Naples, a large number of Jews settled there. Over the course of time three Jewish communities were established on Corfu: Greek, Spanish, and Italian. For a time each retained a separate identity with their own synagogues, burial places, customs, and liturgies; but grad-

Facing page: This colorful, well-executed ketubah bears witness that on June 12, 1805, Aaron ben Hayim Cesana of Corfu and Sarah Rivka bat Mordecai d'Ovadia were wed in Ancona. The names of the bride and groom are artistically incorporated into the ketubah, through the depictions of the biblical Sarah and Aaron.

Ketubah, Ancona, 1805.
Hebraic Section.

בסימנא טבא ובמזלא מעליא
לחתנא ולכלתא ולכל ישראל
אמן:
ברביעי
אהרן הנביא
שרה

The ornate ornamentation of the Ancona ketubah is replaced by a tasteful decoration of birds and flowers in this ketubah written and illuminated for a wedding in a small Italian town near the French border. Nor are biblical figures used, though the groom, his father, and the bride's father bore names from the Bible, David, Moses, and Judah.

Ketubah, Maddalena on the Po, 1839.
Hebraic Section.

Corfu ketuboth are distinguished for using double dating, the year since creation and the year since the destruction of the Temple. The two dates on this ketubah read at the wedding of Yani, the son of Raphael De Osmo, and Esther, daughter of David De Mordo, are 5573 and 1745. The decoration is calligraphic, inscribing verses from the Books of Isaiah and Ruth which speak of bridegroom, bride, rejoicing, and blessings.

Ketubah, Corfu, 3 Heshvan, 5573 (1812).
Hebraic Section.

ual, then more rapid integration took place, especially in the nineteenth century. That century also saw great discrimination against and oppression of the Jews. Under French rule (1805–1815), as the *Jewish Encyclopedia* states, "the Jews enjoyed all the rights of citizenship, and their rabbi ranked with the Catholic bishop and the Orthodox archbishop. But when, together with other Ionian islands [Corfu] formed a republic under the protectorate of England (1815–1863), the Jews were not only forbidden to practice in the courts, but lost all their rights." The rights were regained when Greece annexed Corfu in 1863, but the following year Jews suffered from anti-Semitic riots which caused many Jews to leave. In 1891 a "blood libel" accusation led to an even greater exodus.

Three Corfu ketuboth are among the treasures of the Hebraic Section. The first begins:

> On the third day of the week, the third day of the month *Mar-Heshvan,* in the year of creation 5573 [1812] and 1745 years since the destruction of the Second Temple, may it be rebuilt soon in our time, and in the time of the whole House of Israel, Amen! as we are accustomed to count time here in the isle and city of Corfu, may the Lord protect it . . . we the undersigned bear witness that . . . the young man Yani Osmo, the son of the honored Raphael De Osmo, said to the virgin . . . Esther, daughter of the honored David De Mordo . . . be thou my wife.

This ketubah follows the unique tradition of Corfu ketuboth in dual reckoning of time, from the creation of the world and the destruction of the Temple, but it departs from the Italianate rococo style of ketubah illumination in use in Corfu at that time, as may be seen in the 1804 and 1819 ketuboth in the Israel Museum. What makes this departure more striking is that both the De Osmos and the De Mordos were old and well-known families in Corfu's Italian Jewish community.

The decoration on this Corfu ketubah is solely calligraphic. Framed biblical verses enclose the text:

> I will greatly rejoice in the Lord,
> My soul shall be joyful in my God;
> For He hath clothed me with the garments of salvation,
> He hath covered me with the robe of victory,
> As a bridegroom putteth on a priestly diadem,
> And as a bride adorneth herself with her jewels.
> (Isaiah, 61:10)

Right below: In 1835 another De Osmo-De Mordo wedding was celebrated, Raphael to Rembizia. Calligraphy gave way to decoration; flowers and geometric designs in color were used to frame this ketubah.

Ketubah, Corfu, 1835.
Hebraic Section.

Left below: This 1874 Corfu ketubah's decoration is rich looking, symmetrically folded drapes, done by a professional hand. The artist seems to wish for the bridegroom, Joshua Raphael Eliasoff, and his bride, Hannah Belleli, a well-ordered, richly endowed, harmonious life together.

Ketubah, Corfu, 1874.
Hebraic Section.

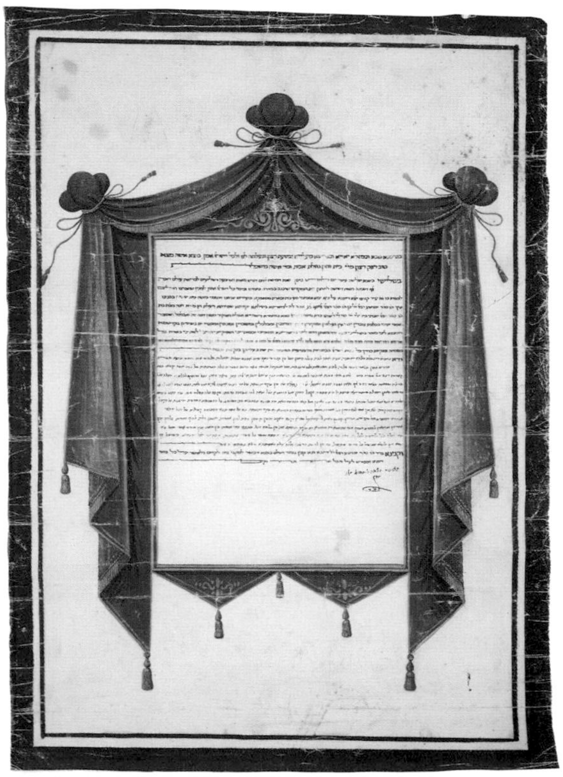

For as a young man espouseth a virgin,
So shall thy sons espouse thee;
And as the bridegroom rejoiceth over the bride,
So shall thy God rejoice over thee.

(Isaiah, 62:5)

So God give thee of the dew of heaven,
And of the fat places of the earth,
And plenty of corn and wine

(Genesis, 27:28)

The blessing with which Isaac blessed his son Jacob is followed by the blessing with which his neighbors blessed Boaz, when he took Ruth as his wife.

The Lord make the woman that is come unto thy house like Rachel and like Leah, which two did build the house of Israel . . . and let thy house be like the house of Perez, whom Tamar bore unto Judah, of the seed which the Lord shall give thee of this young woman.

(Ruth, 4:11–12)

The "seed" that came of the 1812 wedding was the bridegroom at another De Osmo-De Mordo wedding, this one in 1835, when Raphael De Osmo married Rembizia De Mordo. In content, these are twin ketuboth, though twenty-three years apart. But styles had changed, as life changed; life was quieter in 1835 than it had been in the war year 1812. A renewed exuberance of spirit and artistic style produced a colorful ketubah, framed by a yellow and orange decorative border, adorned by flowered cornucopia and flowers and geometric designs.

The third Corfu ketubah, written in 1874 for the wedding of Joshua Raphael Eliasoff and Hannah Belleli, is framed by full wine-colored drapes. The Bellelis were among the early Greek families on the Isle. Under the Greek constitution the Jews were then enjoying equal rights. The carefully arranged, symmetrical lush drapes exude bourgeois well-being. They would perfectly fit in the room of the family celebrating the seder, depicted in the rare Haggadah published in Corfu in 1877, of which the Library has a fine copy. Sixty years separate the three ketuboth. Yet the texts remain the same, except for the names of the celebrants and the dowries brought. Through their ornamentation, however, the ketuboth provide indications of the changes wrought by political, social, and cultural developments in the life of the Corfu Jewish community in the nineteenth century.

Galata was a section of Constantinople inhabited by Jews in the nineteenth century. There on 17 Tevet, 5601 (January 10, 1841), the wedding of Shamma ben Yisrael Ashkenazi and Mirele bat Ya'akov Kopel was solemnized. The ketubah reflects the Islamic environment and is indicative of the artistic sensibilities and skills of the Jewish calligraphers. It is not representational; flowers and trees are suggested, but not depicted. The colors are strong—black, green, and metallic gold—so that the bold primitive nature of the illustrations makes them look modernistic. The serviceable calligraphy makes no attempt at beauty. The ornamentation is typical of that time and place, as may be seen from a ketubah written in Constantinople a decade earlier, which is now in the British Library. The Islamic venue would, of course, preclude depictions of man or nature; its strong primitive harshness may well indicate the quality of life in that place at that time.

Facing page:
Galata, a Jewish neighborhood in Constantinople, celebrated the wedding of Shamma ben Yisrael Ashkenazi to Mirele bat Ya'akov Kopel. The whole community, Ashkenazi as well as Sefardi, must have joined in the festivities, for the groom named Ashkenazi was a Sefardi and the bride, Mirele, an Ashkenazi. The ketubah decoration reflects the Islamic environment. The decoration is nonrepresentational—trees and flowers are suggested not depicted—as was the Islamic custom.

Ketubah, Galata, 1841.
Hebraic Section.

באחד

בסימנא טבא

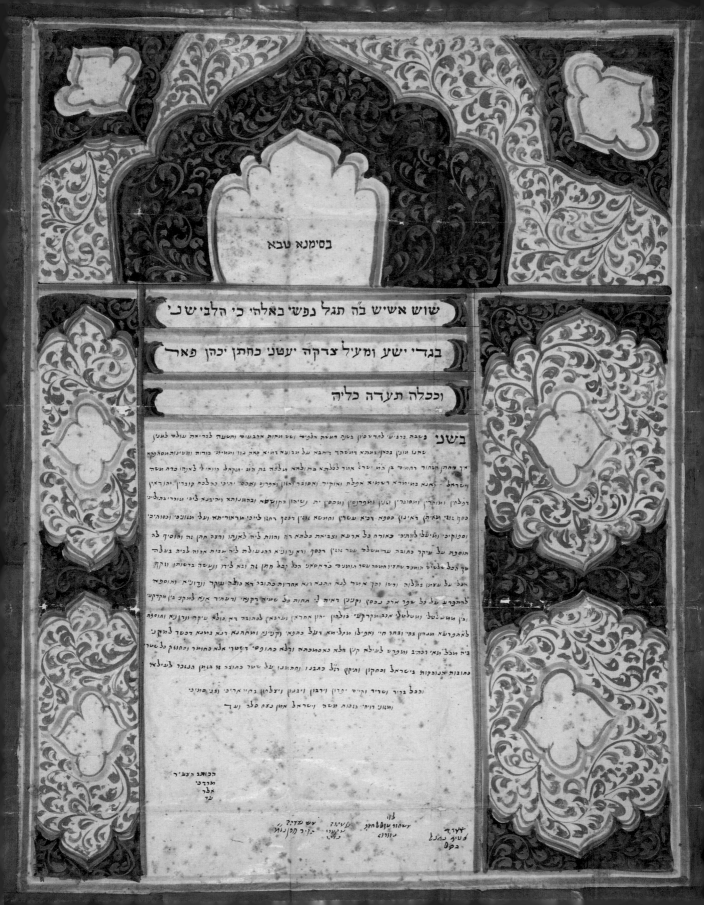

שוש אשיש בה׳ תגל נפשי באלהי כי הלבישני

בגדי ישע ומעיל צדקה יעטני כחתן יכהן פאר

וככלה תעדה כליה

בשני בשבת ברביעי לחדש סיון בשנת חמשת אלפים ושש מאות ארבעים ותשעה לבריאת עולם למנין
שאנו מונין בכאן במתא דמשהד דיתבא על מבועא דמיא כאה גון ומואיי בורות ומעינות מספקא
איך מחתן הבחור רחמים בן המ׳ ישראל אמר לכלתא בתולתא מלכה בת המ׳ יחזקאל הוואי לי לאנתו כדת משה
וישראל ואנא במימרא דשמיא אפלח ואוקיר ואסובר ואזון ואפרנס ואכסי יתיכי כהלכת קוברין יהודאין
דפלחין ומוקרין ומסוברין וזנין ומפרנסין ומכסין ית נשיהון בקושטא ובהמנותא ויהיבנא ליכי מוהרי בתוליכי
כסף זוזי מאתן דאינון כספא דכיא עשרין וחמשא זוזין דכסף דחזון ליכי מדאוריתא ועלי מזוני וכסותיכי
וספוקיכי ומיעל לותיכי כאורח כל ארעא וצביאת כלתא דא והוות ליה לאנתו ורצה חתן זה והוסיף לה
תוספת על עיקר כתובה עד משלם עשר זוזין דכסף ודא נדוניא דהנעילת ליה מבית אבוה לבית בעלה
סך הכל שלשים חומש שחזין חמשה עשר תומנים כרואסאני הכל קבל חתן זה ובא לידו ונעשה ברשותו וזקף
הכל על עצמו במלוה ורשו וכן אמר לנא חתנא דנא אחריות כתובה דא כולה עיקר ונדוניא ותוספא
להתפרע על כל שפר ארג נכסין וקנינין דאית לי תחות כל שמיא דקנאי ודעתיד אנא למקני בין מקרקעי
ובין מטלטלי ומטלטלי אגב מקרקעי כולהון יהון אחראין וערבאין לכתובה דא כולה עיקר ונדוניא ותוספת
לאתפרעא מנהון בחיי ובתר חיי ואפילו מגלימא דעל כתפאי וקנינא ומחתנא דנא גמנא דכשר למקני
ביה מכל מאי דכתיב ומפרש לעילא קנין דלא כאסמכתא ודלא כטופסי דשטרי אלא כחומר וכחוזק כל שטרי
כתובות הנוהגות בישראל וכתקון ותיקן רז״ל כתבנו וחתמנו על שטר כתובה זו בזמן הנזכר לעילא

והכל גריר ושריר וקיים יפרון וירבון ויבנון ויצלחון בחיי אריכי וגני סומכי
ומזוני רויחי בזכות משה וישראל אמן נצח סלה ועד

הכותב הצעיר
מרדכי
אלבר
עד

דוד
בעיף נהנל
בכמ

לוי
עשהור עזפטחנג
גוורון

עזיוז
עזעוו
כהן

עש עזיז
הגיר חסן גזאל

Meshed, in the northeastern section of Persia near the Afghan border, is, in the Shiite Moslem tradition, "a place of martyrdom," the site of the tomb of Imam Riza, who is supposed to have been poisoned by the Caliph Mamun. In Jewish historical memory it is also a place of martyrdom. In March 1839, a mob broke into the Jewish quarter, burned the synagogue, and was intent upon murdering all the Jews. Only mass conversion to Islam prevented the complete annihilation of the Jewish community. The new Muslims continued, however, to practice Judaism, remaining Muslims in name only. Many left the city in order to live openly as Jews, while others remained, living as best they could as crypto-Jews.

When getting married they conducted a Jewish ceremony in secret, then proceeded to the mosque for the public one. "For the marriage ceremony it was their custom to write two ketuboth, simultaneously," David Davidovitch reports in *The Ketubah*. "One was an Islamic marriage contract . . . written in . . . Arabic script in the Arabic and Persian languages . . . the other was an 'illegal' ketubah in Hebrew and Aramaic," the traditional ketubah. The Library's Meshed ketubah is in Hebrew and Aramaic on paper, as Meshed ketuboth are, and colorfully illuminated with floral and geometric designs, and a red border which frames and rises to an angular dome shape at the top. Within the frame are decorative adornments in bright blue and gold. The groom is Rahamin ben Yisrael; the bride, Malka bat Yehezkel. The wedding took place in 1889, fifty years after the Jewish community there was forced to convert to Islam.

Of greatest interest and rarity is a decorative Samaritan ketubah, inscribed in the Samaritan language, for the wedding of the groom, Tamim ben Yisrael ben Yishmael Danafi, and his bride, Pu'ah bat Abraham ben Marhib Safari, which was solemnized in Shechem (Nablus) March–April 1901. The Samaritans, an ancient Jewish sect, go back to biblical days. Their scriptures are the Five Books of Moses, and their religion centers on the meticulous observance of Pentateuchal law and worship at Mt. Gerizim, especially the offering up of the Paschal sacrifice there. They observe kashrut (dietary laws), laws of purity, circumcision, and seven holidays—among them Passover, Shavuot, Sukkot, the Day of Atonement, Sh'mini Atzeret and a festival of the seventh month celebrated on the same day as the first day of Rosh Hashanah.

On the fourth day of a week of rejoicing which celebrates a wedding, the groom takes a piece of parchment to a priest and asks him to write the ketubah. In the evening, the bride arrives accompanied by singing and instrumental music. The groom hands the ketubah to the high priest, who reads it aloud slowly, expounding upon the status of the families and the virtues of the bride and the groom, and detailing the marital stipulations and agreements. The ketubah is then presented to a representative of the bride, her father or a relative, for safekeeping.

In late antiquity, the Samaritans constituted a significant segment of the population of the Holy Land, but in cruelly crushed uprisings against the Byzantines in the fifth and sixth centuries, their numbers began to dwindle. Widescale massacres accompanying the Arab conquest in the seventh century further diminished their number, so that in 1163 Benjamin of Tudela found only about one thousand in Shechem and vicinity. The number of Samaritans at the time of the writing of the ketubah was, according to a British consulate census, about 190. They were recognized

Facing page: This Meshed ketubah reflects its provenance, for its form, colors, and decorative patterns suggest a Persian prayer rug. The ketubah, however, represents mute evidence of the power of the Jewish spirit to resist environmental pressure when it threatens Jewish survival. In 1839, the Jewish community was forced to convert to Islam, but it did so only formally, retaining Jewish loyalties and living as Jews secretly. Now fifty years later, there is a Jewish wedding, expressing a passion for Jewish survival, and a richly illuminated ketubah celebrating commitment to Jewish continuity.

Ketubah, Meshed, Persia, 1889.
Hebraic Section.

as Jews by the State of Israel, and in 1954 those in Israel formed one community in Holon, a suburb of Tel Aviv. The Six Day War in 1967 united these with those Samaritans who had remained in Shechem, marking also a reunification with the Jewish people after some twenty-five centuries of separation.

A MENORAH AND MICROGRAPHY

Two singularly Jewish art forms are the *shivviti* plaques for synagogue or home and micrographic illustrations. The name for the former is taken from the opening word in Hebrew of the verse, "I have set the Lord always before me" (Psalms, 16:8). Most often these were set before the precentor's stand in the synagogue. Generally profusely decorated and illuminated with verses forming a menorah, the seven-branched temple candelabrum, they frequently contained artfully formed verses pertaining to prayer. For home use, they were hung as amulets on a wall near the entrance of the house. These contained biblical verses, liturgical formulas, mystical incantations, and kabbalistic symbols. Especially esteemed were *shivviti* plaques made in the Holy Land, featuring drawings of sacred sites.

A gaudily colored *shivviti* for the home is called a menorah by its artist-scribe, since it features three menorot (candelabra) and is intended for the home, as indicated by the inscription, "Blessed be you when you come in, and blessed be you in your going out." At the four corners are six-pointed Stars of David, enclosing six-petalled flowers. On the top border is the inscription, "Know before whom you stand, before the King of Kings, the Holy Blessed One." Below, flanking a cartouche containing the name of the Lord, is the inscription, "I have set the Master of All, Single and Solitary [God], before me always." Beneath are three menorot, one large and knopped—the temple candelabrum—flanked by two smaller ones standing on double-cupped beakers. In the menorah stems are verses from the Psalms and the liturgy. Below is the inscription, "It is a tree of life to those who hold it, and all who uphold it are rendered happy." At the bottom are depictions of three holy sites: in the center, the Western Wall; on one side, the Cave of Machpelah, and on the other, the Place of the Holy Temple. In the side panels are blessings for peace made up of citations from the Psalms.

In the bottom border panel is the artist's dedication: "This Menorah rises before my honored and cherished friend, a man full of wisdom, fearing the Lord, Solomon [a tear in paper . . .] from me, Shneur Zalman, from the Holy City of Hebron, may she be restored and rebuilt, soon in our time." Shneur Zalman Mendelowitz was a member of the Habad hassidic community in Hebron, in the nineteenth century. He spent most of his life traveling as far west as England and as far east as India, as an emissary of his community to gather funds for the support of its members and its institutions. These were long, often dangerous journeys in small ships on stormy seas to lands infested by brigands. Once, after three and a half years away from home, his community and his own family urged him to continue on, for the sums he had sent them were not sufficient. At home, he published a number of books, the most valuable of which is *Zichron Yerush-*

Facing page: A Samaritan ketubah is an oddity and rarity in a display of ketuboth. Unlike the other ketuboth whose language is Hebrew and Aramaic, this is in the Samaritan language, the language of an ancient Jewish sect, now all but extinct. Let us record the name of the bride and groom whose 1901 marriage was their commitment to Samaritan survival when they numbered but one hundred and ninety: Tamim ben Yisrael ben Yishmael Danafi and his bride, Pu'ah bat Abraham ben Marhib Safari.

Samaritan Ketubah, Shechem, (Nablus), 1901. Hebraic Section.

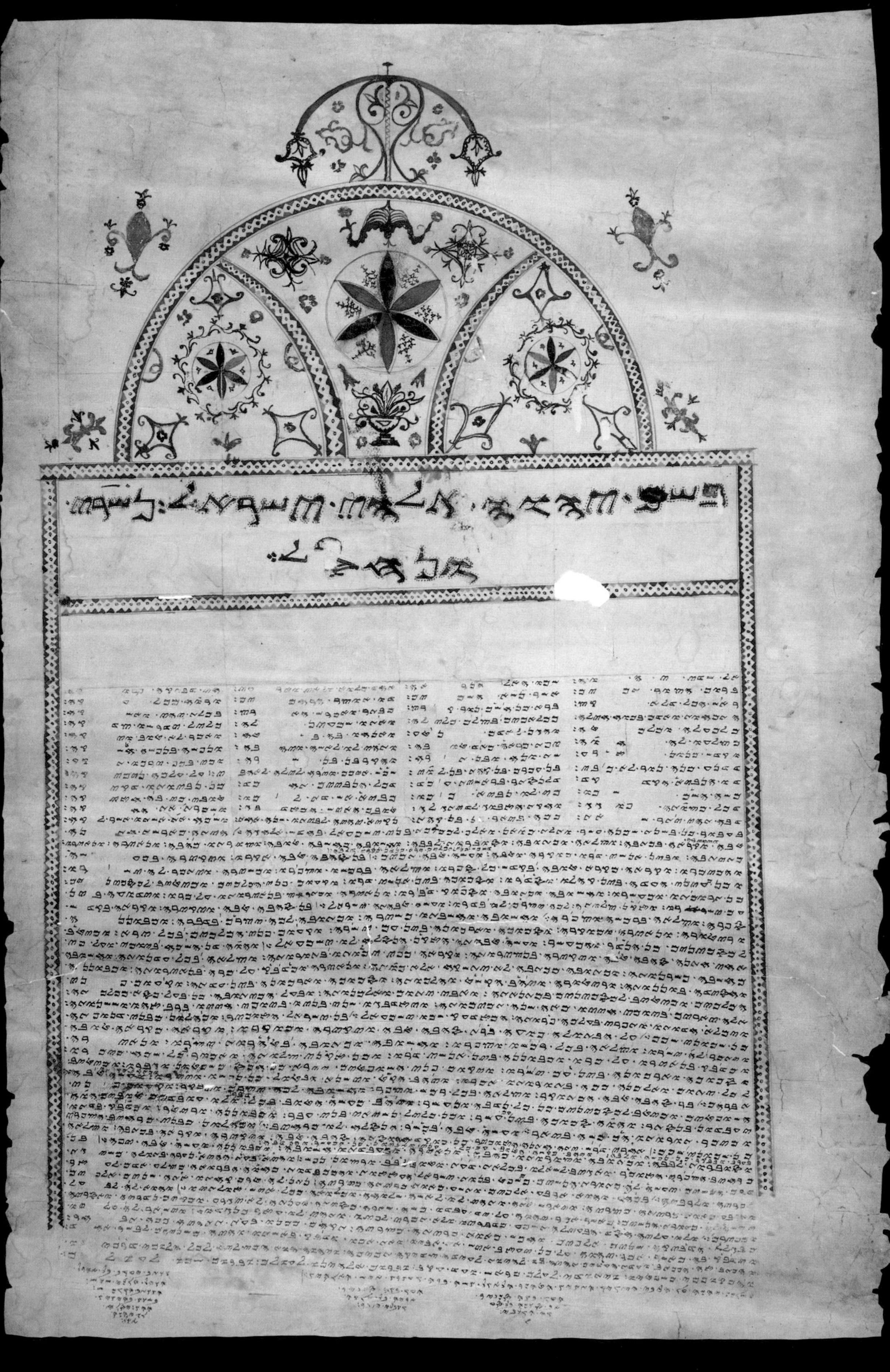

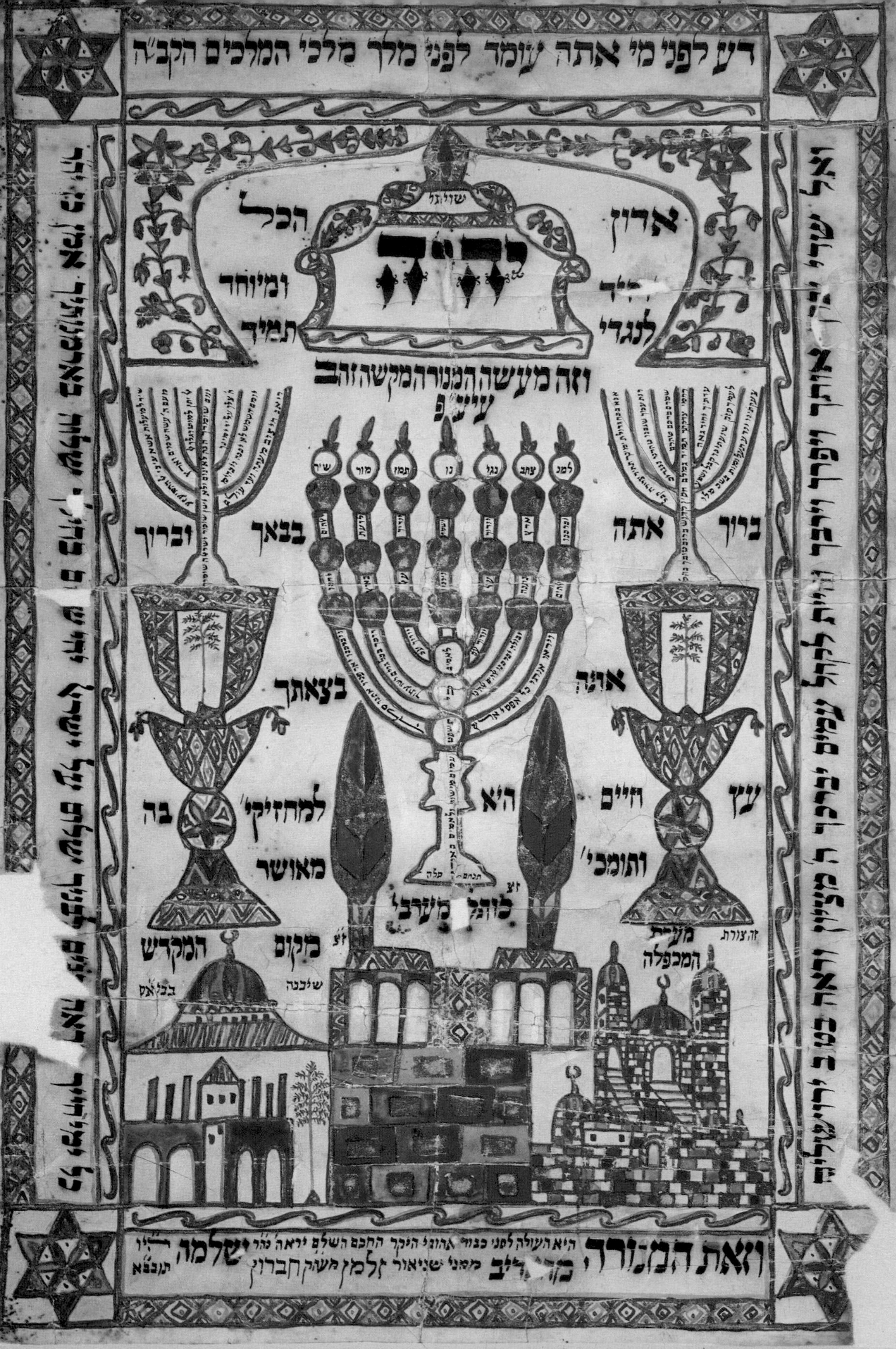

דע לפני מי אתה עומד לפני מלך מלכי המלכים הקב״ה
ארון
הכל
יחיד
ומיוחד
לנגדי
תמיד
וזה מעשה המנורה מקשה זהב
ברוך
אתה
בבאך
וברוך
אותה
בצאתך
עץ
חיים
היא
למחזיקים
בה
ותומכי׳
מאושר
כותל מערבי
מערת
המכפלה
מקום
המקדש
וזאת המנורה

alayim (Jerusalem, 1876), descriptive of the Holy Land at that time. In it are detailed reports of synagogues, academies of learning, charitable institutions and various social organizations, as well as legends. In the second part Mendelowitz writes about the cities he visited during his travels, among them Damascus, Aleppo, Baghdad, Basra, Bombay, Calcutta, Cairo, Alexandria, Izmir, Adrianople, Constantinople, Kremenchug (Russia), London, Paris, Amsterdam, Frankfurt am Main, Hamburg, Berlin, and Halberstadt. He mentions the names of those who helped him in his charitable mission and those who extended him hospitality.

His chief benefactors were members of the Sassoon family in the Near East and in Europe, who provided the funds for building two Habad synagogues in Hebron. In appreciation Mendelowitz presented to Solomon Sassoon an illustrated menorah tablet similar to the one in the Library of Congress. We know of no other of his artistic works which have survived.

This peripatetic emissary, author, and artistic scribe used his talents to promote his mission, distributing his published works and rewarding philanthropists with the fruits of his scribal artistry. The Library's *shivviti* menorah tablet is just such a gift presented to a Solomon, whose last name is lost.

Lovely micrographic drawings of "The Ship of Jonah" by Moses Elijah Goldstein, and Hillel Braverman's "Portrait of Moise" represent the Library's holdings in this art form. Micrography draws a design, portrait, or scene associated with the subject by using words composed of tiny letters, whose forms are barely legible to the naked eye. Widely used in medieval Hebrew manuscripts, micrography experienced a revival at the end of the

Facing page: Shivviti plaques, generally decorated with biblical verses forming a menorah (seven-branch candelabrum), were used in the synagogue and home; in the former, hung before the precentor's stand, in the latter, as a religious wall hanging denoting that one is always aware of the Lord's presence. This colorful artistically executed one was made by the itinerant charity emissary from Hebron, Shneur Zalman Mendelowitz, and presented to Solomon ———, a tear in the paper obliterates the rest of the name.

Shivviti Plaque, late nineteenth century.
Hebraic Section.

Micrography is the forming of pictures of persons or objects with the words in tiny letters of verses appropriate to the subject. Thus the story of Jonah, the reluctant prophet, the boat, the fish, the ocean are all formed from the words of the biblical book bearing his name. It was fashioned by Moses Elijah Goldstein in 1897 and presented to Herr Gustave May.

"The Ship of Jonah," Micrography, 1897.
Hebraic Section.

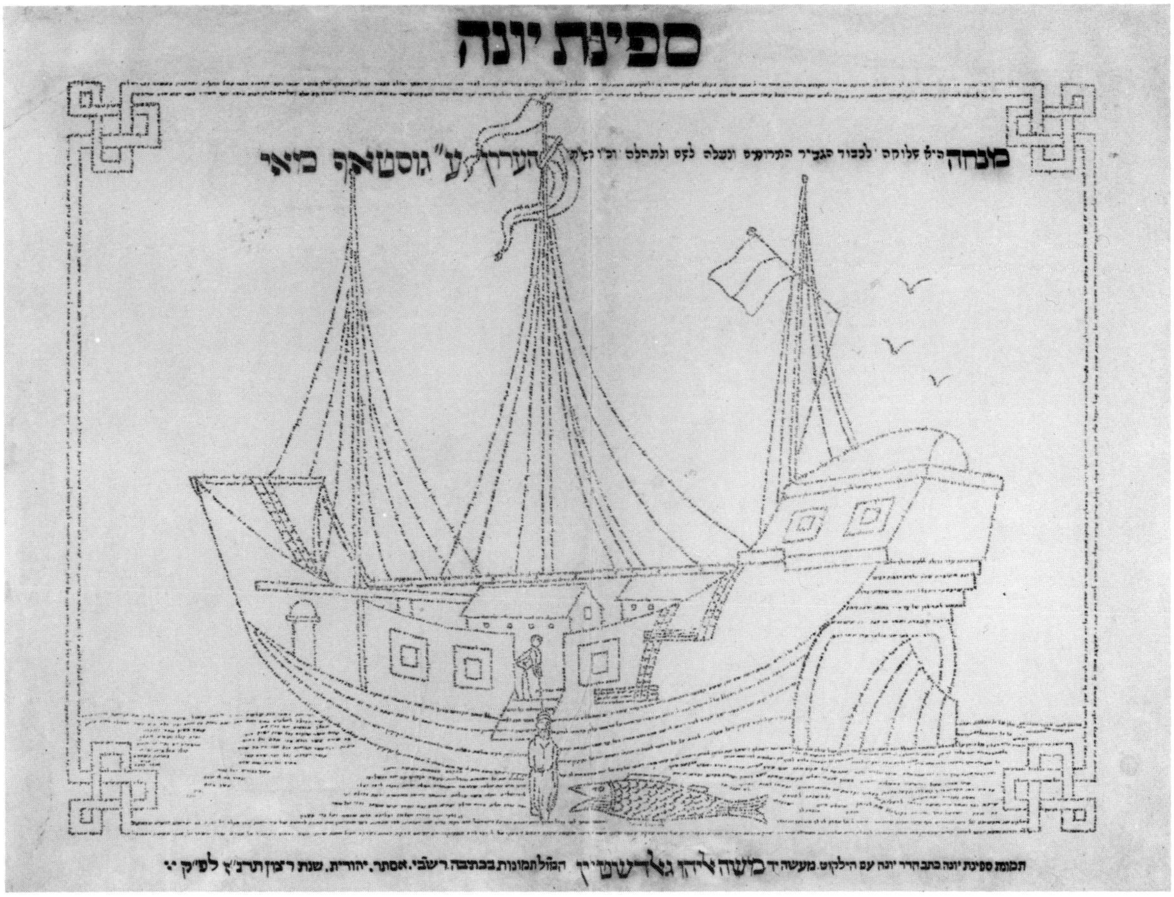

The Book of Deuteronomy written in tiny letters forms this portrait of Moses. The artist's own translation in English of the Hebrew and French descriptive statement reads:

PORTRAIT OF MOISE
Laws giver of the Israelites and
the greatest of the Prophetes . . .
(Containing the fifth Book) Written
in small letters by Hilel Braverman

"Portrait of Moise," Micrography, late nineteenth century.
Hebraic Section.

nineteenth and the beginning of the twentieth century. It has been esteemed by Jews, because it makes it possible to draw a picture of a sacred event without "casting away" the sacred words which describe it in a classical religious text; thus, micrography permits the welding together of the visage of a saint or sage with the very words he uttered or which were written in praise of him.

"The Ship of Jonah," completed in 1881, was presented to "the exalted and notable philanthropist, Herr Gustave May," in 1897 by the artist, who had already published micrographic portraits of Simeon bar Yohai, Esther, and Judith. The ship depicted is a galleon, Jonah has just been cast from it, and a fish no larger than he swims toward him, mouth open to swallow him. The reader, magnifying glass in hand, can follow the story of the prophet who was reluctant to heed God's injunction to preach repentance to the feared and hated city of Nineveh; and having been taught by God that He is the father of all, Jonah accedes and thereby becomes Nineveh's savior. This message of God's loving concern for all humankind has been incorporated into the Day of Atonement liturgy when the entire book of Jonah is read at the afternoon service.

7

BEAUTY IS IN THE HANDS OF ITS CREATORS

■ MORE EVEN THAN IN THE EYE of the beholder, beauty lies in the hands of its creators. From the inception of printing creative artists labored to enhance the visual beauty of the book. Few if any subsequent printed books have surpassed the beauty of the first, the Gutenberg Bible. For Hebrew books the process began later and developed more slowly. For sacred books in the sacred tongue, excepting only the Haggadah, the beauty favored was the beauty of the word, and almost all Hebrew books in the first three centuries of printing remained in that category. Nevertheless, there was a continuing impulse towards beauty in typography, decoration, and even illustration. Most often, such embellishments were limited to the title page, but not always.

Artistic bindings adorn many Hebrew books, and we choose one for its artistry as well as for its historic interest. In 1907, Israel Fine of Baltimore published *Nginash Ben-Jehudah*, a Selection of Poems and Memorials in Hebrew with partial translation into English. A poem in honor of President Theodore Roosevelt's birthday opens the volume. In the Library's Hebraic Section is a presentation volume bound in leather; inside, in fine cloth and appropriate colors, the flag of the United States appears on one cover, and an American seal and shield on the other. Someone has cut out the name of the recipient which was printed on the cover, but there is little doubt that it must have been President Roosevelt, for the author states that three years earlier, on October 24, 1904, he headed a delegation of prominent Baltimoreans, who called on the president and presented him with a poem "in the Hebrew language . . . composed by Mr. Israel Fine and translated into English by his son, Mr. Louis Fine, hand-written on parchment in scroll shape and covered with a silk American flag."

A number of early Hebrew books were printed entirely on vellum to better preserve them and make them more attractive. Among these is *Siddur Tefillah* (Order of Prayer) *According to the Rite of Rome,* published in 1557 by Jacob ben Naphtali Ha-Kohen and "edited and arranged as a set table with all beauty by the scribe Meir ben Ephraim Sofer of Padua."

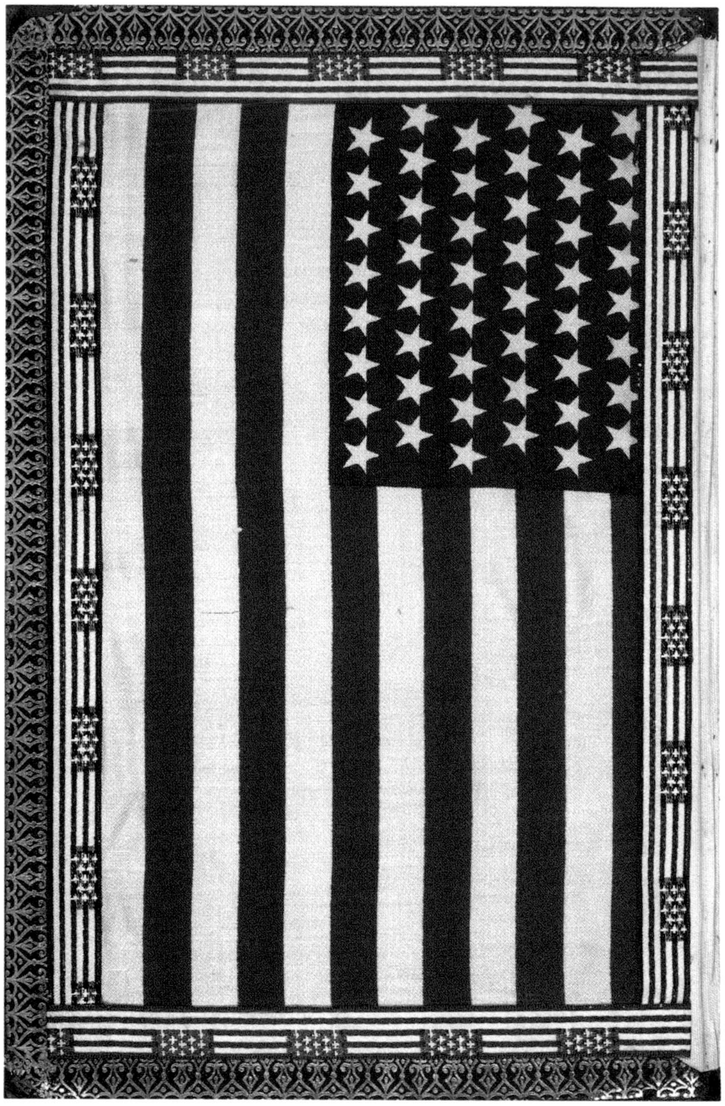

A presentation copy by the author, Israel Fine of Baltimore, of his volume in Hebrew and English, *Nginash* [sic] *Ben-Jehudah,* which contains poems and memorials in memory of his parents, his sons, and "celebrated men, well-known institutions, houses of worship, etc." Among these is a poem in honor of President Theodore Roosevelt, to whom this copy was no doubt presented. The volume is bound in leather. On the inside of one cover is the flag of the United States; of the other, an American seal and shield, both of fine cloth and in appropriate colors.

Israel Fine, *Nginash* [Heb. Negînoth] *Ben-Jehudah,* Baltimore, 1907.
Hebraic Section.

For aesthetic reasons books were printed on colored paper. A volume of the Mantua edition of the *Zohar* was printed on blue paper, quite common in early nineteenth-century Russia, but very rare in sixteenth-century Italy. More unusual still is a miniature $6\frac{1}{2}$ by 5 cm. ($2\frac{1}{2}$ by 2 inch) *Tefilat ha-Derekh* (Prayers for a Journey) published on the Isle of Djerba in 1917 on rose-red paper. Books were also printed in colored type. An unusual example is *Talpiot,* a book of prayers by Elijah Gutmacher, published in 1882 in Jerusalem by Hayyim Hirschenson. The title page is indited in two shades of gold, and the text of the prayer is in gold throughout.

Many Hebrew books, especially prayer books and psalters, were in miniature editions so they could easily be carried in a pocket for daily devotions and for reciting the psalms while on a journey. The Library's Hebraic Section has a fine collection of such miniatures, among them, in a contemporary leather binding with matching box, a *Seder Tefilot L'Moadim Tovim* (Order of Prayer for the Holidays), Amsterdam, 1739, 4 by 6 cm. ($1\frac{5}{8}$ by $2\frac{2}{8}$ inches).

A gifted craftsman will often produce an artistic creation without conscious intention. Thus, a scribe in eighteenth-century Italy writing a *Tikkun*

ולרצון ביום ראש החדש הזה זכרנו יי אלהינו
בו לטובה ופקדנו בו לברכה והושיענו בו לחיים
טובים בדבר ישועה ורחמים וחוס וחננו ורחם
עלינו והושיענו כי אליך עינינו כי אל מלך חנון
ורחום אתה: ותחזינה וכו׳
ברוך אתה יי אלהינו מלך העולם אשר קדשנו
במצותיו וצונו לקרא את ההלל:
הללויה
הללו עבדי יי הללו את שם יי: יהי שם יי
מברך מעתה ועד עולם: ממזרח שמש עד
מבואו מהלל שם יי: רם על כל גוים יי על
השמים כבודו: מי כיי אלהינו המגביהי לשבת:
המשפילי לראות בשמים ובארץ: מקימי
מעפר דל מאשפת ירים אביון: להושיבי עם
נדיבים עם נדיבי עמו: מושיבי עקרת הבית

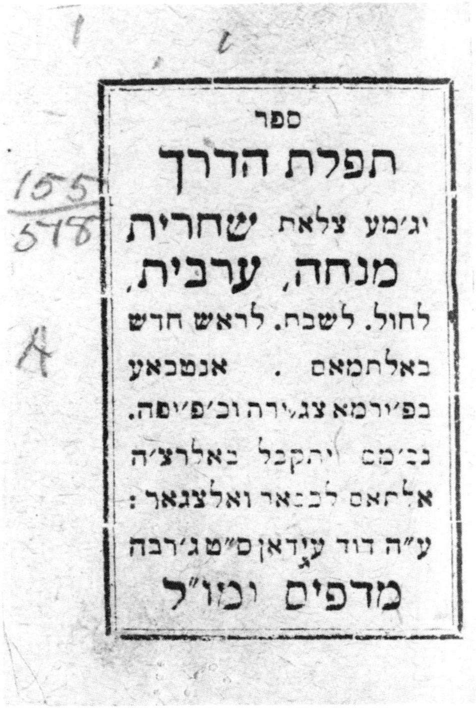
ספר
תפלת הדרך
יג׳מע צלאת שחרית
מנחה, ערבית,
לחול. לשבת. לראש חדש
באלתמאם . אנטבאע
בפ׳ירמא צג׳ירה וכ׳פ׳יפה.
נב׳מם יתקבל באלרצ׳ה
אלנאס לבנאר ואלצגאר:
ע״ה דוד עידאן ס״ט ג׳רבה
מדפים ימו״ל

Its printing on rose-red paper makes this miniature prayer book all the more attractive and desirable. Its Djerba provenance adds to its desirability, for this ancient Tunisian Jewish community, which developed its own ritual and liturgical customs, has long fascinated scholars, even as its publications, though recent, have attracted collectors. The title of this 6½ by 5 centimeter book advertises its practicality, for it is called *Tefilat ha-Derekh* (Prayers or Prayer Book for a Journey).

Tefilat ha-Derekh, Isle of Djerba, 1917.
Hebraic Section.

Books were printed on vellum for wealthy subscribers. Among those is this Roman Rite prayer book, printed entirely on vellum, published in Mantua, 1557, by Jacob ben Naphtali Ha-Kohen, edited by Meir ben Ephraim of Padua. It is opened to *Hallel,* the Psalms of Praise.

Siddur Tefillah (Order of Prayer), Roman Rite, Vellum, Mantua, 1557.
Hebraic Section.

Hazot (Order of Service for Midnight Devotions), by Moses Zacut, produced pages of remarkable calligraphic and compositional artistry. A more conscious attempt to add beauty to the printed book comes in the artistic frame of lion, ox head, angels, and decorative branches which fills the margins of the first page of *Sefer Shorashim, Book of Roots,* published in 1491 by Joshua Soncino in Naples. The Soncino family worked consciously at quality book production. The title page of the 1526 Rimini edition of *Sefer Kol Bo,* printed by Gershom Soncino, not only has a stylized border, but features a very large representation of the Soncino logo—a tower, surrounded by the biblical verses: "The name of the Lord is a tower of

Miniature prayer books were published for aesthetic and utilitarian reasons. Being so small they have jewellike attractiveness and are easily portable. The publication of this tiny holiday prayer book, 4 by 6 centimeters, printed by Naftali Harz Levi, was sponsored by three brothers "who would not be separated, the comely students Zemach, Jacob, David, sons of the Hon. Meir Cresques." The chronogram uses the verse in Ecclesiastes "And the Threefold Cord will not be easily sundered." The book is in a contemporary companion case.

Seder Tefilot L'Moadim Tovim (Order of Prayer for the Holidays), Amsterdam, 1739.
Hebraic Section.

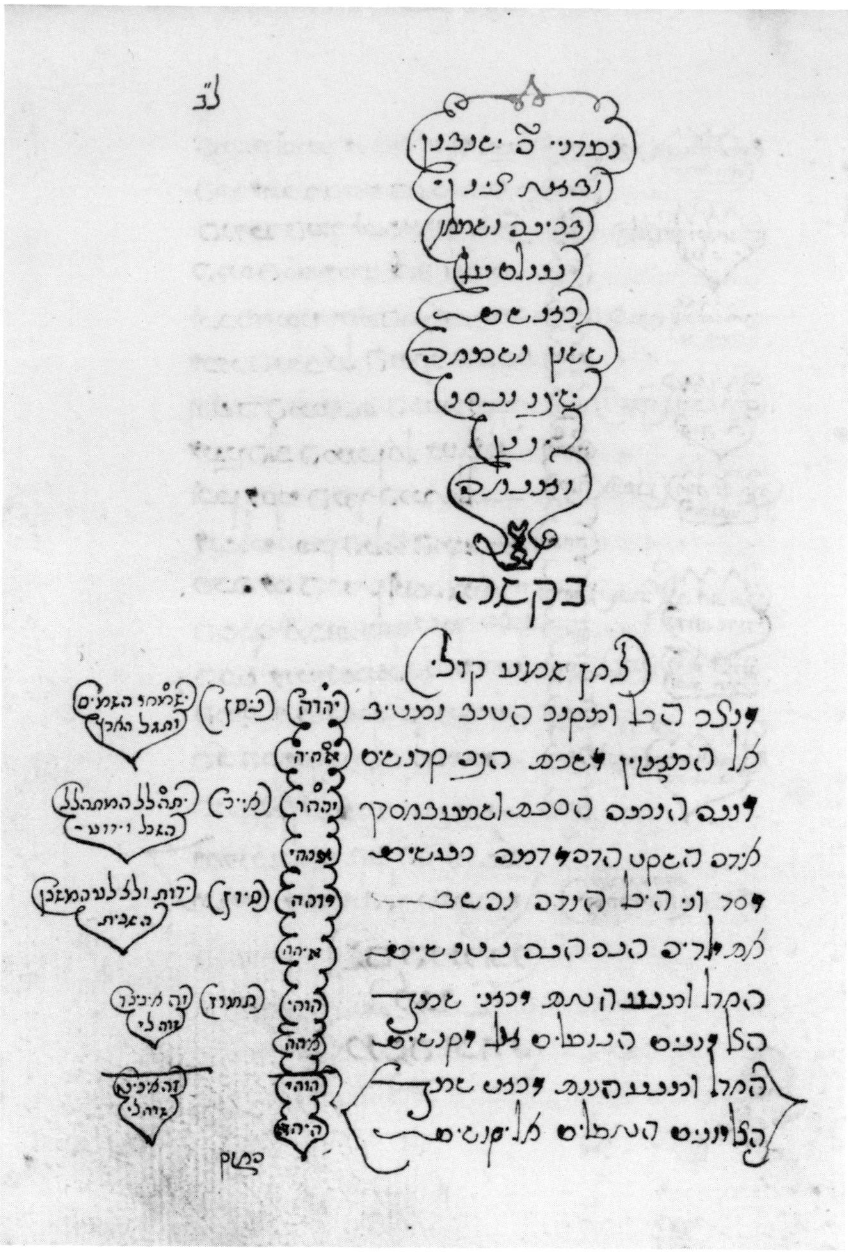

The gifted eighteenth-century scribe who wrote this manuscript of the Order of Midnight Devotions by Moses Zacut must have sensed that the power of mystic devotional prayers would be enhanced if they would touch the eye as well as the other senses. The page before us, a petition to "hear my voice," in its artistic composition conjures up an altar, with clouds of devotional prayers, the "sacrifice of the heart" rising heavenward. The pious scribe did not just inscribe words, the artist in him derived and inspired devotion.

Moses Zacut, *Tikkun Hazot* (Order of Service for Midnight Devotions), Decorated Manuscript, eighteenth century.
Hebraic Section.

Facing page:
Printers' marks (we would call them logos today) were common in early printed books. The well-known twentieth-century Hebrew bibliographer, Abraham Yaari, notes in his *Hebrew Printers' Marks* that "in the fifteenth century the printer's mark was placed in the colophon at the end of the book, but later was transferred to the title page." Gershom Soncino did so in spectacular fashion, for as we see, his mark, a tower, dominates the title page of *Sefer Kol Bo*, printed in Rimini in 1526. The placement of the tower in the center of the page centralizes the focus of attention, which otherwise would have been drawn to the powerful decorations framing the page. It also focuses attention on the publisher, already famed for the quality of his products.

Sefer Kol Bo, Rimini, 1526.
Hebraic Section.

strength, the righteous man runs into it and is safe" (Proverbs, 18:10); and "In him my heart trusts and I am helped; And my heart exults and with song I will give thanks to him" (Psalms, 28:7).

A very beautiful title page was produced by the French artist and engraver Bernard Picart for the *Tikkun Soferim* Pentateuch, Amsterdam, 1726. At its top is the crown of Torah sustained by two putti angels; two other angels beneath hold an unfurled Torah scroll. Three cartouches surround the Hebrew title and the names of the three publishers—Samuel Rodriges Mendes, Moses Zarfati De Gerona, and David Gomez Da Silva. Each cartouche has an engraved biblical scene depicting an event in the lives of the biblical namesakes of the publishers. Under a royal crown, David meets Jonathan with the descriptive biblical verse: "The life of my lord shall be bound up in the bonds of life" (Samuel I, 25:29). Under the crown of priesthood are Hannah and her infant son, Samuel, "And she called his name Samuel, for 'I asked him of the Lord'" (Samuel I, 1:20). In the third

ספר כל בו

דרא ביה כולא ביה

זה הספר של מנחם פירארי יצ״ו

בו בטח לבי ונעזרתי ויעלוז לבי ומשירי אהודנו

מגדל עז שם יי

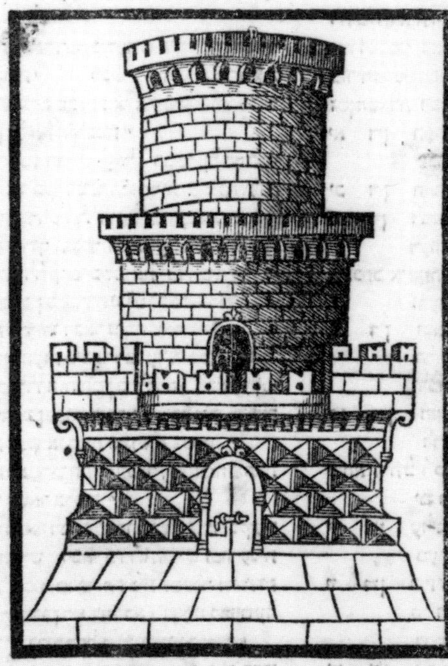

בו ירוץ צדיק ונשגב

תקון סופרים

הוגה בעיון נמרץ ומזוקק
שבעתים ומנוקה כסולת נקיה
מכל טעיות ושגיה ואלה מוסיף
על הראשונים בהגהות אור תה״
באמשטירדם
במצות הגבירים
הזן שמואל רודריגיז מינדיז
משה צרפתי דיגירונא
דוד גומיש דא סילוא

בשנת
שמואל הלך יגדל יטוב
לפ״ק

ותקרא את שמו שמואל
כי מיי שאלתיו :

והיתה נפש [illegible] צרורה
בצרור החיים:

ותקרא שמו משה ותאמר כי מן
המים משיתהו:

יעקב טיליש דה קוסטה זצ״ל

R. Decare del. 1745

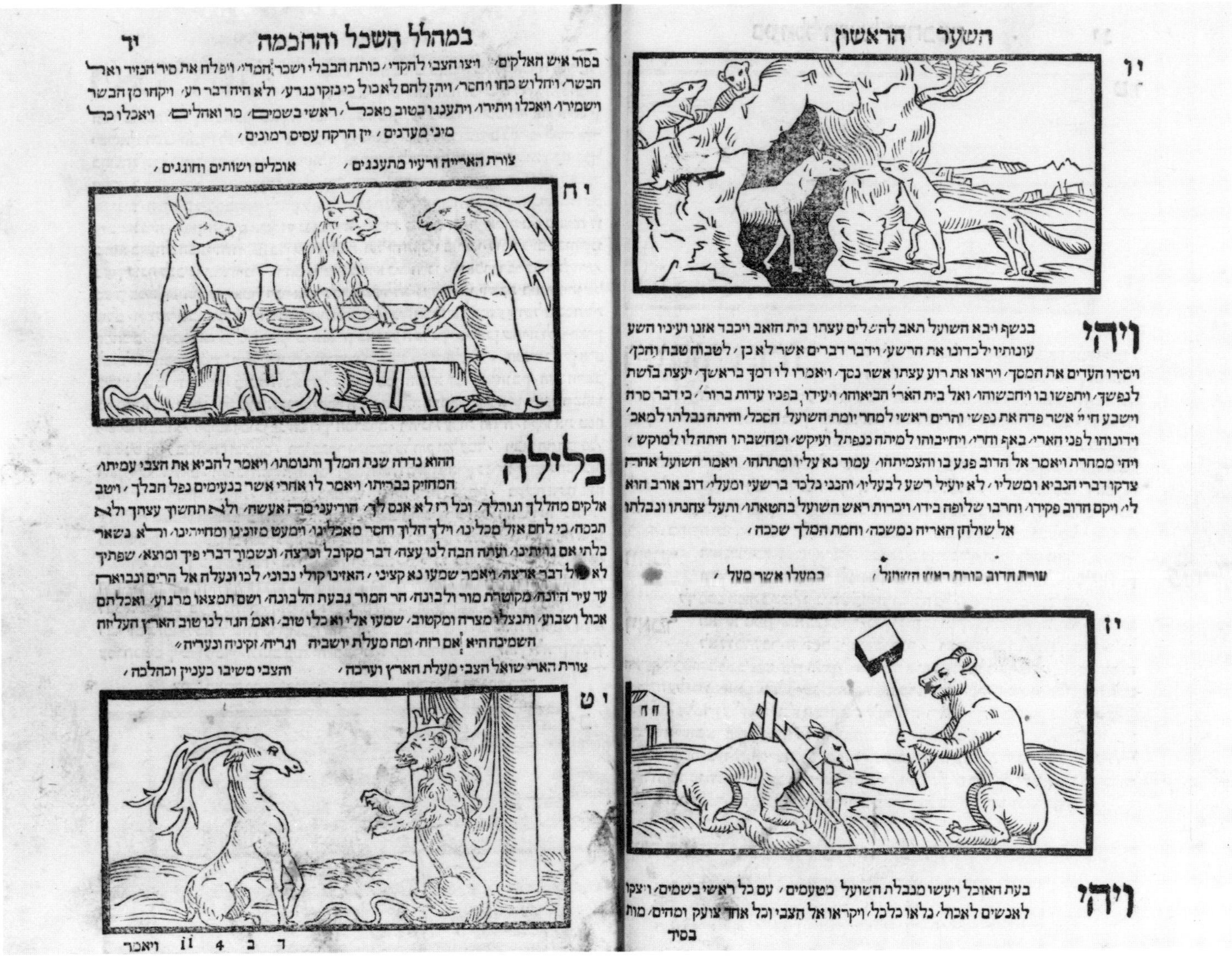

cartouche, the baby Moses is brought before the Pharoah's daughter, "And she called his name Moses, because I have drawn him out of the waters" (Exodus, 2:10).

The most profusely illustrated early Hebrew printed book was *Mashal ha-Kadmoni* (The Fable of the Ancient). This 1546 Venice edition is influenced by its Italian provenance. The animals are drawn in the flowing fine lines of Italian fine cursive printing.

Isaac ben Salomon Abi Sahula, *Mashal ha-Kadmoni*, Venice, 1546.
Hebraic Section.

THE ILLUSTRATED BOOK

The illustrated Hebrew book par excellence is *Mashal ha-Kadmoni* (The Fable of the Ancient), written in 1281 by Isaac ben Salomon Abi Sahula, a Castilian poet and student of Kabbalah. From its first printing in Brescia (1491) by Gershom Soncino, through six Hebrew and nine Yiddish editions, it has contained woodcut illustrations. This book of fables whose characters are animals is described by Galit Hasan-Rock:

> Its sources were in the Talmud and Midrash. . . . their moral lessons are Jewish, and the animals, well versed in Jewish learning: the deer is an expert in Talmud, the rooster, a Bible scholar, and the hare knows the *posekim* [legal authorities]. They are also knowledgeable in such fields as logic, grammar, and biology.

Facing page:
French artist and engraver Bernard Picart, who drew the finest engravings of eighteenth-century Jewish religious life, engraved this title page for the Amsterdam, 1726 bibliophilic edition of the *Humash* (Pentateuch). The finely drawn cartouches are scenes in the lives of the biblical namesakes of the sponsors of the publication, Samuel Rodriges Mendes, Moses Zarfati De Gerona, and David Gomez Da Silva. The original binding is in gold-tooled leather.

Tikkun Soferim (Pentateuch), Amsterdam, 1726.
Hebraic Section.

משל הקדמוני

צורת המקשה והמחבר
זה אל זה ידבר

The heavy, dark, angular illustrations of the Frankfurt an der Oder, 1693 edition of *Mashal ha-Kadmoni* (The Fable of the Ancient) reflects the gothic influence on Hebrew printing and illustration.

Isaac ben Salomon Abi Sahula, *Mashal ha-Kadmoni*, Frankfurt an der Oder, 1693.
Hebraic Section.

Illustrations differ in the various editions. Thus, in the 1546 Venice printing, the animals are charmingly drawn in fine line illustrations. On pages fourteen and fifteen a crowned lion dines with his friends, the deer and fox; the lion and deer consulting; the fox calling on the wolf; and a bear beheading the fox. The illustrations in the Frankfurt an der Oder 1693 edition are heavier and darker, and so is the type. Book illustration has moved from the lighter, graceful Romanesque to the angular, heavier Gothic. One illustration shows a seated scholar, a book on a stand before him, discussing with a standing disputant, since the work is a dialogue.

In post-World War I Germany there was a sudden efflorescence of bibliophilic illustrated books. The finest creations were by such graphic artists as Jakob Steinhardt and Joseph Budko. Two works by Steinhardt, in editions limited to one hundred copies, and one by Budko serve as good examples: *Gleichnisse* by Jizchak-Leib Perez (Isaac Leib Peretz), the great master of Yiddish literature, in German translation by Alexander Eliasberg, with eight lithographs by Jakob Steinhardt, published by the Verlag für Jüdische Kunst und Kultur, Berlin, 1920; and by the same author, translator, artist and publisher in the same year, *Musikalische Novellen;* Joseph Budko and Arno Nadel produced *Das Jahre des Juden* (The Jewish Year) for the same publisher, also in 1920. A series of twelve short poems by Nadel on the Jewish holidays, *Das Jahre . . .* has each poem illustrated by a Budko etching, reproduced in heliogravure and tipped-in. The frontispiece is a Budko woodcut.

The words of Isaac Leib Peretz of Warsaw, in German translation, and the artistry of Jakob Steinhardt of Berlin (later of Jerusalem) meet in this bibliophilic edition. The post-World War I years saw a flourishing of Jewish graphic art in Germany in which Steinhardt played a major role, and of which this volume, published in 1920 by Verlag für Jüdische Kunst und Kultur (Jewish Art and Culture Publishing House), is a fine example. This copy is number 33 of an edition of 100 and is open to the illustration, "The Days of the Messiah." The elder is telling the young lad of a Jerusalem rebuilt and restored to its former glory.

Isaac Leib Peretz, *Gleichnisse,* Lithographs by Jakob Steinhardt, Berlin, 1920.
Rare Book and Special Collections Division.

Published in 1923 in Berlin for children, this most beautiful of Hebrew alphabet books has become a favorite of collectors of Jewish graphic art. A collaboration of Jerusalemites associated with the Bezalel School of Art—Levin Kipnis, words, and Zev Raban, art—it was published in Germany, since in 1923 Palestine did not yet have the facilities to produce so fine an illuminated book. Published by Hasefer (The Book) publishing house.

Alef-Bet (Alphabet), illustrations by Z. Raban, verses by L. Kipnis, Bezalel—Jerusalem, Berlin, 1923. Hebraic Section.

An artistic collaboration in Jerusalem of Levin Kipnis, who provided the verses, and Zev Raban, a teacher at the Bezalel School of Art, produced the most beautiful of Hebrew alphabet books. Printed in Berlin in 1923, in brilliant colors, it is especially notable for the gold of the alphabet letters. Each letter is illustrated with an object whose name in Hebrew begins with that letter, as, for example: the *het* by a stork, *hasida;* and *tet* by a peacock, *tavas.*

An almost unknown masterpiece of the genre is a hand-colored book of woodcuts in a limited edition of 200, *Oif Waitkajten Krajzende Fal Ich* (In Circular Distances I Fall), Lodz, 1921. The Yiddish words are by David Zitman, the illustrations by Ida Brauner. In the bibliophilic books printed in Germany, there is a remarkable control, symmetry, balance, and calm—these were, after all, the heady days of the Weimar Republic. In this small Zytman volume, printed in post-World War I Poland, neither letters nor words are uniform or in alignment, and the impressionistic illustrations are jarring in color and composition. The new Poland had risen only a year earlier, and Polish Jews viewed their future with trepidation. Their world was not at all in order.

At first glance, the most chilling bibliophilic book of that time seems the most benign, *Had Gadyah,* Berlin, 1920. Illustrated in color by Menachem Birnbaum, its words in lovely Hebrew and German type, it contains the song, beloved by children, which closes the Passover seder service:

> A kid, an only kid
> My father bought for two *zuzim.*
> Came a cat and ate the kid,
> Came a dog and ate the cat,
> Came a stick and hit the dog,
> Came a fire and burned the stick,
> Came water and extinguished the fire,
> Came an ox and drank the water,
> Came a slaughterer and slew the ox,
> Came the angel of death and slew the slaughterer,
> Came the Holy One, blessed be He,
> And slew the angel of death.

Violent, to be sure, but with such a wonderful ending, the promise of life eternal!

The illustrations begin idyllically. The father holds a pure white kid in his arms; the child clings to the father. The lamb is meek, the cat is big and black. The dog biting the cat fills the page with his menacing presence; a minuscule cat now, the victim has shrunk in the presence of its attacker. It is not a stick which hits the dog, but a mammoth bludgeon. The slaughterer revels in his slaughter, and blood-red is the dominant color of that illustration. The angel of death is white-winged darkness with talon claws gouging out the eyes of its bloodied victim. In the final frame, God appears—a shaft of light cleaving the darkness. But somehow the darkness of death and its white wings and talons dominate the scene, its dark presence hemming in the narrow ray of light.

The Jewish artistic flourishing in the early years of the Weimar Republic, Germany, extended to Poland. The poet David Zitman and the artist Ida Brauner collaborated on this powerfully evocative little volume, *In Circular Distances I Fall.* The words are of mystical yearning, the illustrations, arresting in their color and strength. Few, very few, copies of this little volume, published in an edition of 200, have survived the Holocaust. The Library's copy is number 67.

Oif Waitkajten Krajzende Fal Ich (In Circular Distances I Fall), words composed by David Zitman, hand-colored woodcuts by Ida Brauner, Lodz, 1921.
Hebraic Section.

פאַלן פלאַמען
גיסן זיך זונען אין מײַנע אויגן
גרויס
ווי גאט

A kid, an only kid.

Came a cat and ate the kid.

Came a dog and ate the cat.

Came a slaughterer and slew the ox.

Came the Angel of Death and slew the slaughterer.

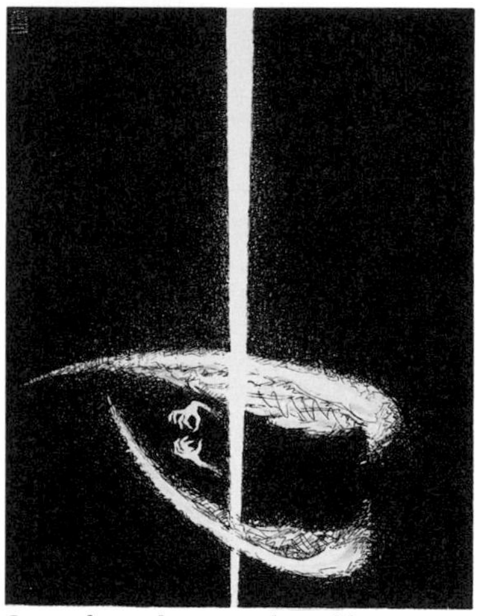
Came the Holy One, Blessed be He, and slew the Angel of Death.

Menachem Birnbaum's *Had Gadyo,* Berlin, 1920, is a tour de force of prescience. The illustrations he drew for the simple children's song which concludes the Passover Seder are fraught with foreboding, warning of the power of persistence of violence—the violence he saw unloosed in World War I and which culminated in Auschwitz, where the artist breathed his last. The first illustration is serenity itself: a little Jewish child clings to his father who is holding a pure white kid in his arms; the tenth and last: the shaft of light representing God's mercy narrows as it descends; dominating the scene are the wings and talons of the Angel of Death.

Had Gadyo, illustrated by Menachem Birnbaum, Berlin, 1920.
Hebraic Section.

Facing page:
Marc Chagall put all other work aside when invited by Abraham Sutzkever, hero-survivor of the Holocaust, to illustrate his poem, *Sibir,* which was published in Yiddish, English, and Hebrew editions. Here we show Chagall's illustration which accompanies the poet's description of his father in Siberia.

Abraham Sutzkever, *Sibir* (Siberia), Illustrations by Marc Chagall, Jerusalem, 1958.
Hebraic Section.

The artist is crying out his warning; the pictures become the text. Happy endings are only in children's songs. Reality is what I have just seen in four long years of bloody war. Each devours another. In this world of ours, only violence persists.

Menachem Birnbaum (1893–1944), son of the Nathan Birnbaum who coined the term Zionism, was born in Vienna. A portraitist and graphic artist, he worked as an art editor for Jewish journals, and after World War I became the art director of two Jewish publishing houses. He fled the Nazis to Holland, but in 1943 he was seized in Amsterdam and sent to Auschwitz, where the Angel of Death—slain only in *Had Gadyo*—reigned supreme. His *Had Gadyo* illustrations warn of the enduring ominous presence of violence and evil on the European continent and in the heart of man, a first book prophetically foreshadowing the Holocaust two decades before it began.

The Yiddish poet Abraham Sutzkever survived the Holocaust in the Vilna ghetto and, as a partisan in his native Lithuania, received an award for heroism from the Soviet Union. In 1947, he went to Palestine, where he has remained an honored citizen of the State of Israel, editing the country's leading Yiddish literary journal, *Die Goldene Kayt* (The Golden Chain).

chagall

Ben Shahn
ברוך אתה " אלהינו מלך העולם
שהחינו וקימנו והגיענו לזמן הזה

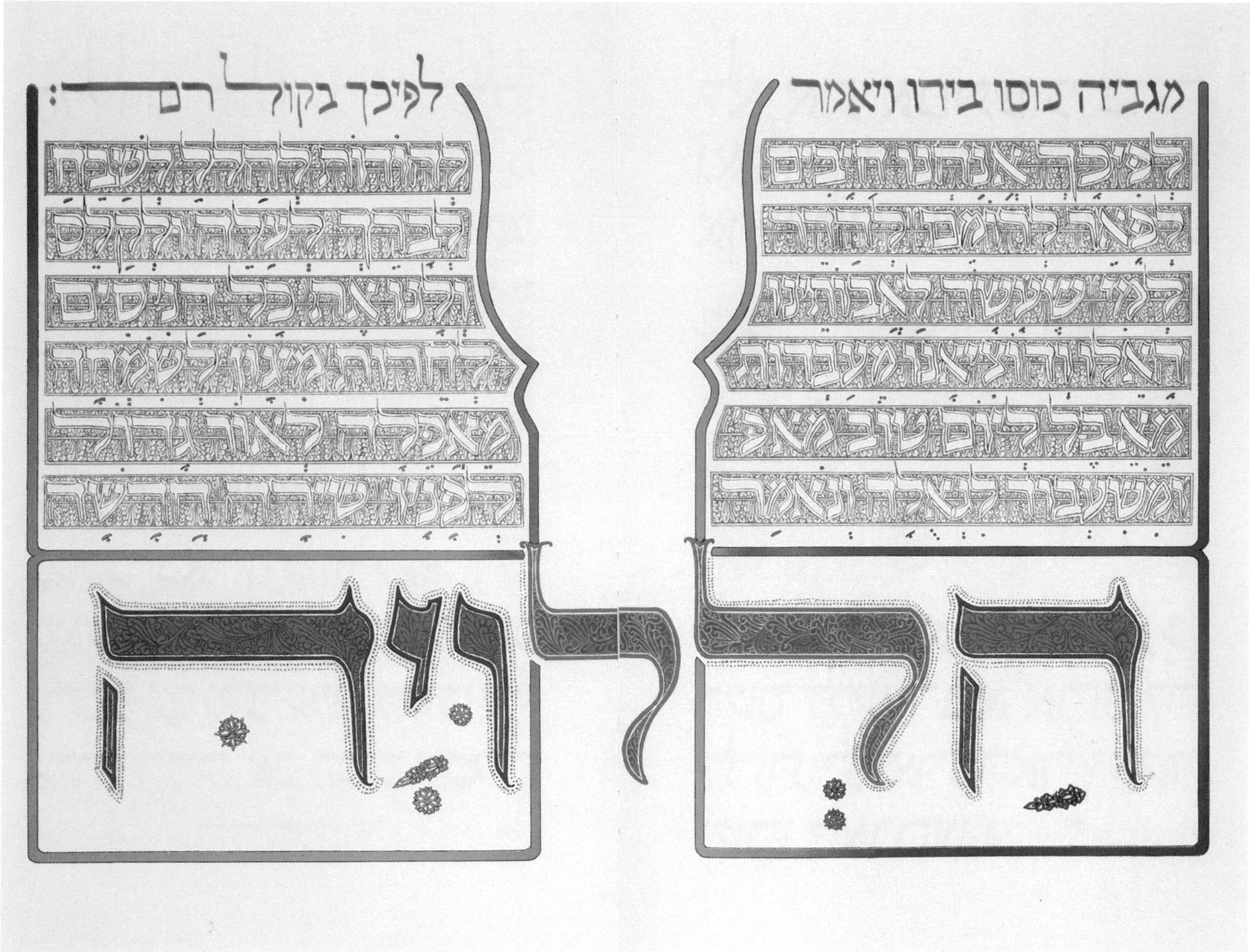

A marvelously inventive illustrated and illuminated Haggadah by the American-Israeli artist-calligrapher David Moss, published in an edition of 550. The artist adapted the variety of artistic forms used in earlier illuminated manuscript Haggadot. It is open to the Cup of Redemption section. Note that the gold extensions flowing from the two central letters, the *lameds,* form the outline of a wine goblet. The letters before and after these letters are in a different color, for they spell the name of God.

David Moss, *Song of David,* 2 volumes, Bet Alpha Editions, Rochester, N.Y., 1987.
Hebraic Section.

Facing page: The American artist Ben Shahn dedicated this Haggadah which he calligraphed and illustrated in color to his father, for "it reflects my memories of the Passover in my father's house." The Library's Rosenwald Collection copy is one of the first off the press of the special signed and numbered edition issued by the Trianon Press. The box it comes in contains proof sheets in various stages, stencils, and pages on the various papers on which copies were printed.
Open to the frontispiece, a menorah in the impressionistic idiom, resplendent in gold, purple, and blue—colors regal and Jewish. Below, the artist has written the benediction: "Blessed art thou, O Lord our God, who has kept us in life, sustained us, and enabled us to reach this day."

Haggadah for Passover, copied and illustrated by Ben Shahn, with a Translation, Introduction, and Historical Notes by Cecil Roth, Trianon Press, Boston, 1965.
Rare Book and Special Collections Division, Rosenwald Collection.

His poem *Sibir,* describing his family's experience in Siberia during World War I, was published in Israel in Hebrew (1952) and in Yiddish (1953), and in English in London (1961). All the editions are similar, with eight magnificent Marc Chagall drawings. A Chagall preface appears in the English section only, in which the artist writes:

> We had not yet met personally when he [Sutzkever] approached me with the request to illustrate his poem, *Siberia.* Of course, I put all my other work aside at once, and set myself to tackle his world of Russian Siberia. . . . I wanted to show him and his friends . . . the men of the Resistance . . . my love and respect for what they had done: they have raised high our Jewish banner and our Jewish honor. . . .
>
> Considering such Jews as Sutzkever, I would wish us all to find within ourselves, now and in the future, our inner Jewish strength to preserve and cultivate our purity of soul, which alone can and must lead us toward genuine human ideals. It alone has been in the past, and must be in the future, the basis of art, of social life and of culture, and only for its sake is our life worth living and our art worth creating.

Particularly poignant is Sutzkever's written memory of his father in Siberia, and Chagall's visual depiction of it:

> White as the moon is my father's face.
> The silence of snow rests on his hands.
> He cuts the black loaf
> with his white blade of mercy
> and his face grows blue.
> Sharp images cut through my mind
> as I dip in salt a slice of my father's bread.
> (Translation by Jacob Sonntag)

THREE HAGGADOT

In 1939, the year World War II broke out, Arthur Szyk, after seven years of labor, completed his illuminated Haggadah. It was published a year later in an edition of 250 copies on vellum, half to be distributed in the United Kingdom, half in the United States. Cecil Roth, who edited the publication, writes in his Introduction:

> In the general deterioration of the art of book-production in the nineteenth century, the Hebrew Book considered as an aesthetic object sank to its lowest depths. . . . The art of the scribe, the calligrapher and the illuminator . . . waned with the eighteenth century. . . . It has been left to a contemporary, Arthur Szyk, to rediscover the secret and revive the art. . . . To call him the greatest illuminator since the sixteenth century is no flattery. It is the simple truth. . . . He does not illuminate a page. . . . He thinks of each page in its relation to the text and to the volume, integrating calligraphy, illumination, illustration and narrative into one harmonious whole.

The Szyk Haggadah is more than a work of simple beauty; it is also, as all great works of illustration must be, a commentary. In Szyk's portrayal of the Four Sons, Roth notes:

> The Wicked son . . . according to a very ancient tradition . . . is always shewn as a soldier . . . —an eloquent expression of the peace-loving nature of the Jew. . . . Yet

Facing page:
Arthur Szyk, who revived the art of medieval manuscript illumination, lavished his great artistic gifts on the fashioning of this Haggadah, completed on the eve of World War II after seven years of labor. Dedicated to King George V of England, it was published in an edition of 250 signed and numbered copies on French-fold vellum, half for distribution in England, half for the United States. The Library's is copy number 35. It is opened to the illumination of the "Four Questions," the young inquiring of their elders, they in turn responding—an expression of the essence of Jewish survival, continuity and creativity, for in the question is the beginning of knowledge and wisdom.

The Haggadah, executed by Arthur Szyk, edited by Cecil Roth, London, 1940.
Rare Book and Special Collections Division.

נִשְׁתַּנָּה
הַלַּיְלָה
הַזֶּה מִכָּל
הַלֵּילוֹת:
שֶׁבְּכָל
הַלֵּילוֹת
אָנוּ אוֹכְלִין
חָמֵץ וּמַצָּה
הַלַּיְלָה
הַזֶּה כֻּלּוֹ
מַצָּה:
שֶׁבְּכָל
הַלֵּילוֹת
אָנוּ אוֹכְלִין
שְׁאָר יְרָקוֹת
הַלַּיְלָה

הַזֶּה מָרוֹר. שֶׁבְּכָל הַלֵּילוֹת אֵין אָנוּ מַטְבִּילִין אֲפִילוּ פַּעַם
אֶחָת, הַלַּיְלָה הַזֶּה שְׁתֵּי פְעָמִים. שֶׁבְּכָל הַלֵּילוֹת אָנוּ
אוֹכְלִין בֵּין יוֹשְׁבִין וּבֵין מְסֻבִּין, הַלַּיְלָה הַזֶּה כֻּלָּנוּ מְסֻבִּין:

recent events have indicated that, in these days of organized brutality, non-resistance may sometimes be equivalent to suicide. . . . The real betrayer of his people to-day is the full-blooded assimilator, who will do his best . . . to out-Junker the Junkers: and it is thus that Szyk shows him. It is not a pleasant type: nor is it intended to be.

Where Szyk turned to the medieval scribe for his artistic inspiration, Ben Shahn absorbed it from contemporary America. Of his *Haggadah for Passover,* Boston, 1965, Shahn writes:

The making of this book has proceeded much more in the manner of a painting perhaps, than of a proper book. It reflects my memories of the Passover in my father's house. . . . If the work is less than accurate from the purely pedantic point of view, let us say that it more than compensates for such lapses by being full of the glory and mystery that form the essential meaning of the Passover, that kind of meaning which is so woefully lacking in the customary Haggadas.

The Hebrew title page and facing menorah frontispiece are an aesthetic delight. The blessing beneath the menorah, "Blessed art thou, O, Lord, our God, King of the Universe, who hast kept us in life, and enabled us to reach this time and season," is appropriate to a Jew in the post-Holocaust world.

For Shahn, the celebration of Passover is memory. For the American-Israeli calligrapher-artist David Moss, Passover is a spiritual experience. For him "Next year in Jerusalem" is a religious mandate, as is his creation of a bibliographic Haggadah. As Szyk's Haggadah is in the tradition of its illuminated medieval predecessors, as Shahn drew on contemporary artistic idiom, so Moss's *Haggadah* is most authentically Jewish in its eclectic nature. The classical Hebrew book is more an anthology to which the author adds his mite, than a work of original creativity. Though Moss is marvelously inventive in his illuminated pages, he has consciously striven to have them reflect the variety of artistic expressions of those before him who had made Hebrew manuscripts and books things of beauty, as he accomplished in his own creative effort. His Haggadah is a splendid addition to the bibliophilic Hebrew book, the most authentically Jewish art form.

8

WITNESSES TO HISTORY

In every generation it is the duty of a Jew to regard himself as if he personally went forth from Egypt.

The Passover Haggadah

HISTORY IS REMEMBERING AND reexperiencing: of the two, the latter is the more rewarding. For the student of Jewish history, the Library of Congress offers a sumptuous feast; solid fare and occasional delicacies making for a rich, variegated menu. Classic works in Hebrew, Yiddish, Latin, English, German, French, Spanish, and Russian abound. Multivolume works of the great historians, from first century Josephus writing in Greek to twentieth-century Salo Baron writing in English, share the shelves with communal and topical histories, anthologies, periodicals, and monographs, from classic pioneering studies to sophisticated contemporary works on the cutting edge of the discipline.

For both researcher and reader the most exciting finds are those works—book, broadside, and manuscript—which witnessed and recorded history in the making or which themselves partook in the unfolding of the Jewish historical experience. We can offer only a small sampling of the rich lode of primary source materials, printed and written, which enable us, fortified with knowledge and imagination, to reexperience historic events.

"AND MAY THE MESSIAH COME SOON, IN OUR TIME"

The grandest of prophetic visions is of the "end of days," the days of the Messiah, as envisaged by the prophet Isaiah:

> A scion of the house of Jesse . . .
> Filled with the spirit of the Lord . . .
> Who with righteousness shall judge the poor . . .
> And with the breath of his lips slay the wicked . . .
> And the wolf shall dwell with the lamb . . .
>
> Nation shall not lift up sword against nation
> Neither shall they learn war anymore . . .
> They shall not hurt nor destroy . . .
> For the earth shall be filled with the presence of the Lord.
>
> Isaiah (Ch. 11 and 2)

Among the saddest chapters in Jewish history are those which tell the tales of messiahs.

In February 1524, there arrived in Rome an exotically dressed figure riding on a white horse, who announced himself to be David Reuveni, brother to Joseph, King of a Jewish kingdom in the heart of the Arabian peninsula. At an audience granted him by Pope Clement VII, Reuveni stated his mission, which was to effect an alliance between that kingdom and the Christian world against the Moslems. Intrigued by the prospect, the Pope gave him a letter to the King of Portugal, who received him warmly. He received an even greater welcome from the Portugese Marranos, Christians in name only, who still adhered to their ancestral faith despite having formally surrendered it. These Marranos saw Reuveni as a herald of the Messiah.

None was more taken than a brilliant young man, Diogo Pires, born in Lisbon of Marrano parents, who at age twenty-one was appointed secretary to the king's council and recorder at the court of appeals. His meteoric rise did not assuage young Diogo's spiritual malaise. Obsessed by a yearning for the faith of his father, Pires met Reuveni in 1525 and hearing Reuveni's tale of Jewish dominion and aspirations, decided to return to the ancestral faith and asked to be circumcised. Reuveni warned him against it, pointing to the peril to his life from the Inquisition, so Pires circumcised himself, almost bleeding to death in the process. He took the Hebrew name Shlomo Molcho and fled Portugal to wander in the Near East—Damascus, Safed, and Jerusalem—studying and to a remarkable degree absorbing the teachings and mysteries of his reacquired faith.

He went to Salonica to study Kabbalah, Jewish mysticism, and soon student became teacher. During the fifteenth and into the sixteenth century Salonica was a haven for Jewish exiles fleeing the Iberian peninsula and Italy. Of Salonica, the haven, Portuguese Marrano chronicler Samuel Usque writes in his *Consolacam as tribulacoems des Israel* (Consolation for the Tribulations of Israel) Ferrara, 1553 (English edition, translated and edited by Martin A. Cohen, Philadelphia, 1965): "the largest number of the persecuted and banished sons from Europe and other places have met therein and have been received with loving welcome, as though it were our venerable mother Jerusalem." It was a community of communities living with historic memories and messianic expectations. In 1527, the year Molcho arrived in Salonica, Catalan Jews who had fled from that Spanish province and its major city Barcelona, in order to retain their historic identity, published a *Mahzor L'Nusach Barcelona Minhag Catalonia* (Festival Prayer Book, According to the Custom of Barcelona of the Catalonian Rite) whose colophon records: "The work was completed before the Great Fast, here in the city of Salonica, under the sovereignty of our great king, Sultan Suleiman, by the young Moses Soncino in the printing establishment of the noble Don Abraham Seneor, at the behest of the survivors of the expulsion from Catalonia, especially the sage Eliezer Shimoni, the light of whose Torah shines upon them, may he see progeny and length of days." The Library of Congress copy of this exceedingly rare volume bears the ownership inscription of Moshe bar Shmuel Falcone.

A coterie of disciples gathered about Molcho, before whom he preached eloquent sermons announcing the certainty of an imminent messianic redemption. His disciples prevailed upon Molcho to permit publi-

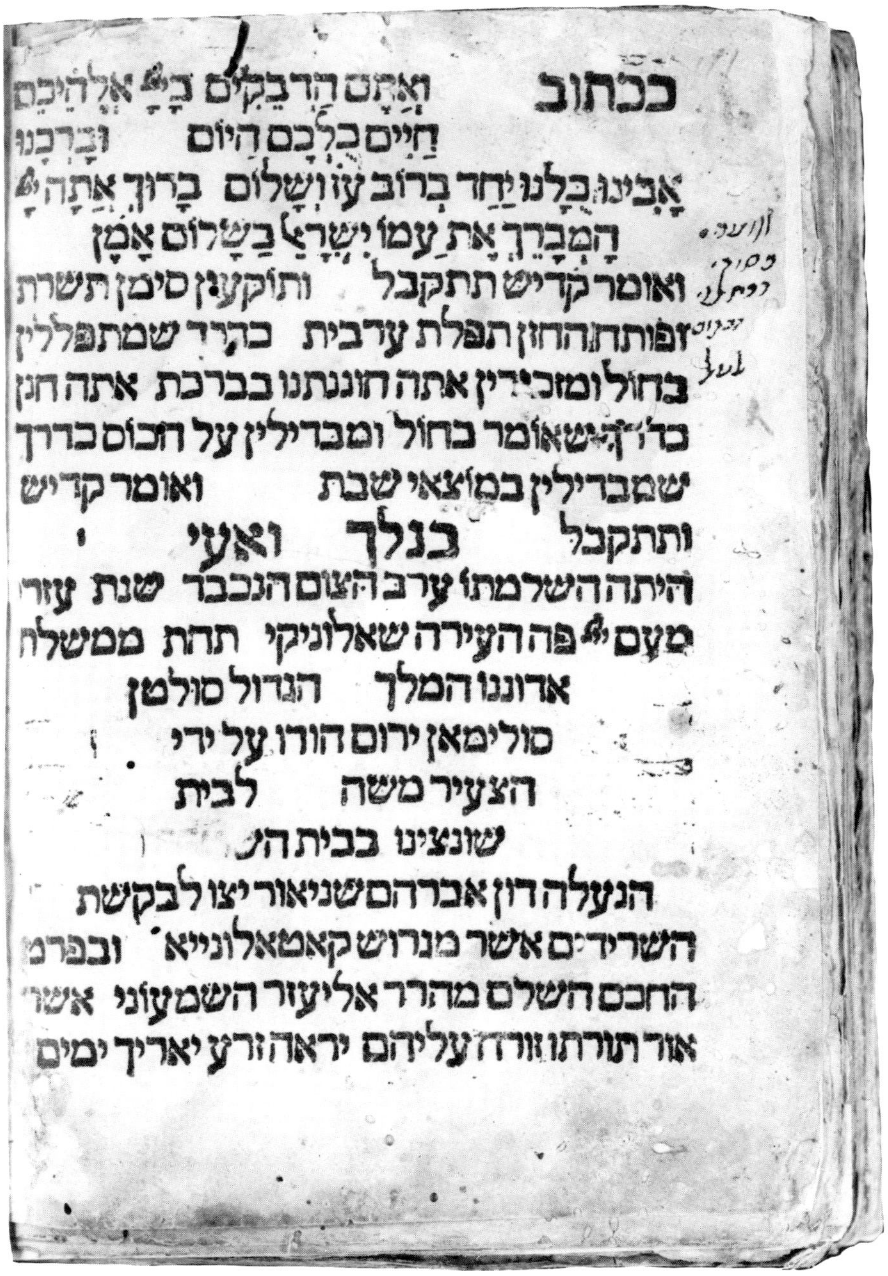
ככתוב ואתם הדבקים ב״ה אלהיכם
חיים כלכם היום וברכנו
אבינו כלנו יחד ברוב עוז ושלום ברוך אתה ה׳
המברך את עמו ישראל בשלום אמן
ואומר קדיש תתקבל ותוקעין סימן תשרת
ופותחין החזן תפלת ערבית כדרך שמתפללין
בחול ומזכירין אתה חוננתנו בברכת אתה חונן
כד׳׳ן שאומר בחול ומבדילין על הכוס כדרך
שמבדילין במוצאי שבת ואומר קדיש
ותתקבל בנלך ואעי
היתה השלמתו ערב הצום הנכבד שנת עזרי
מעם ה׳ פה העירה שאלוניקי תחת ממשלת
אדוננו המלך הגדול סולטן
סולימאן ירום הודו על ידי
הצעיר משה לבית
שונצינו בבית הנ׳
הנעלה דון אברהם שניאור יצו לבקשת
השרידים אשר מגרוש קאטאלונייא ובפרט
החכם השלם מהרר אליעזר השמעוני אשר
אור תורתו זורח עליהם יראה זרע יאריך ימים

cation of some of those sermons, as Molcho states in the Introduction: "For my dear brothers and friends living in Salonica, who ask of me to send them some expositions and explanations of biblical verses and rabbinic sayings. To fulfill their request I write this work, though I lack the requisite knowledge and understanding, for my sins cast me out of the inheritance of the Lord [i.e., the Jewish people], yet I trust that His divine mercy will lead me along the correct path." Molcho sees the history of the world as a struggle between Esau and Israel. "The evil decrees which befall the Jewish people," he proclaims, "are sent to try them, not to destroy them." The war of Gog and Magog, prelude to the coming of the Messiah, had already begun in 1527, in the sacking of Rome by German and Spanish soldiers; in 1529 when *Derashot*, later called *Sefer Ha-Mefo'ar*, appeared, Molcho was certain the Messiah would soon appear, probably in 1540; and he began to entertain the idea that he had been chosen for that role.

The Ottoman Empire extended welcome to Jews exiled from Spain in 1492 and Portugal in 1497. Salonica became a major Jewish center through the new immigrants. The colophon of this prayer book printed in Salonica, 1527, is a document in the saga of their immigration and settlement.

Completed on the eve of the Great Fast in the year 'My help is from the Lord' [i.e., 1527], here in the City of Salonica under the sovereignty of the great King, Sultan Suliman . . . by Moses Soncino, in the printing house of the noble Abraham Senior, for the exiles of Catalonia, especially Eliezer Shimoni, the light of whose Torah illumines them.

Mahzor L'Nusach Barcelona Minhag Catalonia (Festival Prayer Book . . .Custom of Barcelona of the Catalonian Rite), Salonica, 1527.
Hebraic Section.

In a letter to his disciples in Salonica, Molcho wrote: "Seir [the Christian world] will fall into the hands of its enemies. The people of Israel will reveal its power. God will have mercy upon His servants . . . I will take vengeance and pay to each his deserts."

Molcho saw visions, announced prophecies—at least two of which, a flood in Rome and an earthquake in Portugal, came to pass—and, in fulfillment of a Talmudic depiction of the Messiah, sat fasting and praying for thirty days with the beggars and the afflicted at the gates of Rome. As he began to act the Messiah, adherents multiplied, and the Pope offered his protection. Together with David Reuveni, Molcho approached the Emperor Charles V, who decided to put an end to this messianic adventure. The emperor took Molcho to Mantua, where he was tried as a heretic, convicted and, after refusing to recant and return to the Christian faith, was burned at the stake. At his martyrdom, Molcho was only thirty-two years old. Many of his disciples were certain that he had survived the flames and awaited his advent as the Messiah in 1540, the promised year of redemption. We look at Molcho's only monument, his *Derashot* (*Sefer Ha-Mefo'ar*), a small, worn volume of consolation and hope, a work which bolstered the spirits of a generation painfully recovering from the trauma of apostasy and expulsion, and we shudder at the martyr's death imposed on this well-born, gifted, and favored young man, who gave up all for the love of God and His people Israel.

If the martyr's death of Molcho in 1532 was a personal tragedy, the apostasy of the messianic-pretender, Shabbetai Zvi in 1666, was a national calamity. Born in Smyrna in 1626, he showed early promise as a Talmudic scholar, and even more as a student and devotee of Kabbalah. More pronounced than his scholarship were his strange mystical speculations and religious ecstasies. He traveled to various cities, his strong personality and his alternately ascetic and self-indulgent behavior attracting and repelling rabbis and populace alike. He was expelled from Salonica by its rabbis for having staged a wedding service with himself as bridegroom and the Torah as bride. His erratic behavior continued. For long periods, he was a respected student and teacher of Kabbalah; at other times, he was given to messianic fantasies and bizarre acts. At one point, living in Jerusalem seeking "peace for his soul," he sought out a self-proclaimed "man of God," Nathan of Gaza, who declared Shabbetai Zvi to be the Messiah. Then Shabbetai Zvi began to act the part, as Gershom Scholem describes:

> Riding around on horseback in majestic state [he] summoned a group of his followers, appointing them as apostles or representatives of the Twelve Tribes of Israel. The messianic news spread like wildfire to other communities in Palestine . . . First reports about Shabbetai Zvi reached Europe early in October 1665 . . . detailed accounts, deeply involved with legendary material, arrived in Italy, Holland, Germany and Poland.
>
> Messianic fervor took hold of communities that had no immediate experience of persecution and bloodshed as well as those which had. . . . Repentance alternating with public manifestations of joy and enthusiasm was the order of the day.
>
> From many places delegations left bearing parchments signed by the leaders of the community which acknowledged him as the Messiah and king of Israel.

Not only did Shabbetai Zvi gain militant adherents in his native Turkey and in the Near East, but even in such cosmopolitan European cities

אמר החכם המקובל החסיד שלמה מלכו

שש אנכי על אמרתך כמוצא שלל רב
לעולם לא אשכח פקודיך כי בם חייתני
מה אהבתי תורתך כל היום היא שיחתי
הבינני ואצרה תורתך ואשמרנה בכל לב
מה נמלצו לחכי אמרתך מדבש לפי
לולי תורתך שעשעי אז אבדתי בעניי
כלתה לתשועתך נפשי לדברך יחלתי
ואדברה בעדתיך נגד מלכים ולא אבוש

The engraved title page of this collection of prayers to be said for the "King Messiah," Shabbetai Zvi, depicts him sitting on a throne, a crown on his head, holding a scepter, guarded by twelve lions and eight disciples. Four putti angels support the crown of dominion above his head, the "Crown of Zvi." Below, he is seated at a table with his twelve disciples; in the background is the multitude of his followers. The chronogram on the printed title page uses a biblical verse of messianic promise.

Tikkun K'riah (Penitential Prayers for Night and Day), Amsterdam, 1666.
Hebraic Section.

Left: Derashot (titled *Sefer ha-Mefo'ar* in later editions), published in Salonica, 1529, is a collection of the sermons of the returned to Judaism, Christian-born Marrano Shlomo Molcho preached in that city, in which he pronounced his faith in imminent messianic redemption. He may also have declared himself a messianic candidate to his disciples. After a brief meteoric career, the would-be Messiah was burned at the stake for heresy.

Shlomo Molcho, *Derashot,* Salonica, 1529.
Hebraic Section.

as Venice, Livorno, and Amsterdam leading rabbis and sophisticated men of affairs were caught up in the messianic frenzy.

Mute witnesses to all this are two books in the Library's collections, published in Amsterdam in 1666. The first is a small prayer book of daily readings, called a *Tikkun,* whose title page is framed by the prayer:

> Do thou, oh Lord our God, raise up the horn of David thy servant
> And the radiance of the son of Jesse, thy Messiah.
> May his majesty be exalted
> And his dominion established over all the earth.

On the engraved frontispiece Shabbetai Zvi, seated on a throne, holds a scepter. Four cherubs hold aloft a large crown marked "the crown of Zvi," and the throne is guarded by twelve lions, surrounded by eight worshipful disciples. On the steps which elevate the throne is inscribed:

> In those days and at this time,
> I will cause a shoot of righteousness to grow up unto David;
> And he shall execute justice and righteousness in the land.
> Jeremiah, 33:15

The chronogram on the title page of this compendium of Jewish legal documents, *Nahalat Shiv'ah*, which proclaims, "Messiah, the son of David has come," dated 5426, i.e. 1666, the year of its publication in Amsterdam. The reference is to the pseudo-Messiah, Shabbetai Zvi, who was heralded to assume dominion in that year—the year in which he became a convert to Islam.

Nahalat Shiv'ah, Amsterdam, 1666.
Hebraic Section.

Below is a panel depicting a larger than life Shabbetai Zvi seated at a round table with twelve apostles, books in hand, against a background of a crowd of people. In the same year an edition of *Nahalat Shiv'ah*, a collection of legal documents, was published in Amsterdam. Its chronogram reads, "Messiah the son of David has come."

On September 15, 1666, Shabbetai Zvi, brought before the Sultan and given the choice of death or apostasy, prudently chose the latter, setting a turban on his head to signify his conversion to Islam, for which he was rewarded with the honorary title "Keeper of the Palace Gates" and a pension of 150 piasters a day.

The apostasy shocked the Jewish world. Leaders and followers alike refused to believe it. Many continued to anticipate a second coming, and faith in false messiahs continued through the eighteenth century. In the vast majority of believers revulsion and remorse set in and there was an active endeavor to erase all evidence, even mention of the pseudo messiah. Pages were removed from communal registers, and documents were destroyed. Few copies of the books that celebrated Shabbetai Zvi survived, and those that did have become rarities much sought after by libraries and collectors.

Two centuries later another pseudomessiah emerged in the Yemen, the southwestern corner of the Arabian peninsula which harbored an ancient Jewish community not often in contact with other Jewish communities. Over the centuries the Yemenite Jews produced an indigenous culture, with a distinctive liturgy rich in religious poetry. For almost all its existence this community lived in great poverty and even greater piety. Consequently, and because its neighbors were Zaydi Muslims who awaited the imminent appearance of an imam-redeemer, the Jews of Yemen experienced more messianic claimants than any other Jewish community. In the 1860s, it was one Judah ben Sholom, known as Shukr Kuhayl, who appeared in San'a, the site of Yemen's largest Jewish community, and declared that the prophet Elijah had appeared to him in a vision, and proclaimed him Messiah. In 1862–64, Shukr Kuhayl traveled about Yemen, performing "signs and miracles," which won him many adherents in the Jewish community, and some in the Muslim as well. His success with the latter led to his assassination, but he had earlier promised his followers that he would rise again.

Three years after his death, one claiming to be the risen Shukr appeared and sent letters to the Jewish communities of Yemen and neighboring countries announcing his return. When this came to the attention of Jacob Saphir, the scribe of the Ashkenazi community in Jerusalem, he alerted the rabbinate of that city, both Sefardi and Ashkenazi, to the danger such a pseudomessiah represented. On their behalf he sent an epistle to the Jews of Yemen, warning them of the threatening calamity. Saphir had earlier traveled in the Oriental countries to collect funds for the construction of a great synagogue in Jerusalem. He was the first emissary, indeed the first Jew in modern times, to visit the Yemenite Jews for a protracted period of time. He described their life and culture in his two-volume *Even Sapir.* During his stay, he became acquainted with Yemenite rabbis and communal leaders and he now addressed his epistle to them. In the printed copy, preserved among the rare books in the Library's Hebraic Section, we read his measured, reasoned appeal. Saphir reminds them of the debacles caused by the Molcho and Zvi messianic movements, outlines the guidance tradition offers for testing messianic claimants, and warns of the dangers inherent in the anger which messianic movements evoke in governmental authorities and among religious leaders of Islam, the dominant faith. Saphir also pleads with them that the exposure of yet another false Messiah would cause Jews in other lands, already wavering in their piety, to lose all faith in the coming of the true Messiah. On the last page of the epistle, the leading rabbis of Jerusalem confirm the truth of Saphir's argument and the cogency of his cautions.

CONSECRATION . . . CONGREGATION . . . COMMUNITY

Six documents bring into focus various aspects of the social, communal, and cultural life of eighteenth- and nineteenth-century European Jewry.

קונדמאכונג

די פארשטעהר דער לעמבערגר איזראעליטישן גמיינדע מאכן בקאנט לכל בני ישראל אין גאליציען קראקא אונד דר בוקאווינא דאס די פריפונג ביי דעם קרייזאמט וועגן דער הייראטס בוויליגונג הערט שון אויף :

ביז העהר איזט געוועזן איין קייזערליך געזעץ פאן דעם יאהר 1805 , דאס יעדע חתן כלה מוזן פר דר חתונה זיך אב פריווען ביי דעם קרייזאמט דאס זיא קענן דייטש לעזן אונד שרייבן אונד רעכנן אונד די צעהן געבאט אונד נאך אנדרע זאכן אויס דעם ביכל בני ציון . האבן זיא אבר די פריפונג ניכט גמאכט איזט נאר קיינע מעגליכקייט געוועזן אויף דר הייראטס בוויליגונג איינצורייכן . האט עס זיך איינמאל געטראפן דאס איינר האט אויף קיינן פאל ניכט געקאנט די פריפונג מאכן , האט ער גמוזט דאריבר צו דער האהן ק׳ ק׳ שטאטהאלטריא איינרייכן . — יעצט אבר איזט דאס האהע מיניסטעריום זא גנעדיג געוועזן אונד האט אם 20 טען יענער 1858 צום געזעץ גמאכט , דאס דיזע פריפונג ביי דעם קרייזאמט הערט גאנץ אויף . נאר ווער עס וויל הייראטן בדארף ניכט מעהר נאר איין צייגניס פאן דער שולע דאס ער האט אין דר שולע גלערנט אדר דאס ער האט אין דר היים דייטש גלערנט אונד האט זיך אב גפריווט אין דער שולע , אונד איין צייגניס פאן דעם רב אדר פאן דעם רעליגיאנסווייזר דאס ער האן די רעליגיאן , מיט די ביידע צייגניסע רייכט ער איין צו דעם פארשטאנד פאן זיין שטאדט , דער פארשטאנד איבערשיקט עס צו דעם קרייזאמט , אונד ער בקומט די בוויליגונג צו הייראטן . ער ווירד איין ארדענטליכר פאמיליאנט לכבוד ולתפארת , איין בעל הבית אין דר גמיינדע וויא עס זיך געהערט . —

אלזא דאס אליין איזט אויך שון איין זעהר גרוסע גנאדע , אבר דאס האהע מיניסטעריום איזט נאך מעהר גנעדיג געגן אונז , דען וייל עס זינד אין גאליציען נאך זעהר פיהל שטעדט דא וואס האבן נאר קיינע שולן אין זיך , דרום איזט די פעראָרדנונג גגאנגן צו דער האהען ק׳ ק׳ שטאטהאלטריא . דאס יעדעס קרייזאמט האט די מאכט די חתן כלה פאן דעם שול צייגניס צו בפרייאן ווען עס זעהט אין דאס זיא האבן ניכט געקאנט דייטש לערנן . נעמליך :

א) ווען אין דעם ארט וואו דר חתן אדר די כלה וואונט אונד אויך ביז איין האלבע שטונד ווייט אדר איין פירטל מיילע ווייט אין דר געגנד ארום . איזט קיין יודישע הויפטשולע דאס הייסט איין שולע מיט פיר קלאסן וויא אין לעמבערג אונד אין בראדי אונד אויך קיין קריסטליכע הויפטשולע דא . דען וואו האבן זיא געקאנט לערנן ווען עס איזט דארט קיין שולע דא .

ב) ווען דארט וואו דר חתן אדר די כלה וואונט אונד אויך ביז איין האלבע שטונד אדר איין פירטל מיילע אין דער אומגעגנד איזט קיין הויפטשולע אונד קיין יודישע טריוויאל שולע (דאס הייסט איין שולע מיט דריא קלאסן וויא אין באלחוב) אונד אויך קיין קריסטליכע טריוויאל שולע דא . דען ווען עס איזט דארט דא איין טריוויאל שולע מוזן די חתן כלה האבן איין צייגניס פאן דיזר שולע . דאס זיא האבן דארט דייטש גלערנט אדר דאס זיא האבן צו הויז גלערנט אונד אין דר שולע די פריפונג גמאכט .

A proclamation, on March 22, 1858, by the representative body of the Jewish community of Lemberg, informing the Jews of Galicia, Cracow and Bukovina that the special test for grooms and brides before their marriage, imposed by royal decree in 1805, has been rescinded by the government.

Kundmachung, Lemberg, 1858.
Hebraic Section.

Lemberg, 1858. A three-page broadside in Yiddish, issued by the representatives of the Lemberg Jewish Community, informs the Jews of Galicia (of which Lemberg was the capitol), Cracow, and Bukovina of a change in the Austrian Imperial government's marriage requirements law. A royal decree issued in 1805 made it mandatory for a Jewish bride and groom to pass a test in reading and writing in German, arithmetic, and Jewish knowledge in order to receive Imperial permission to marry. A new law, announced on

January 20, 1858, rescinded the test, substituting in its stead proof that bride and groom had studied German at school or at home, and an authentication by a rabbi or a religious teacher that they had sufficient Jewish religious knowledge. The law further provided that a bride and groom would be released from such requirements on submission of proof that economic hardship made it impossible to study, e.g., if they were orphans, common laborers, servants, etc.

The broadside discloses that many Orthodox couples resisted the government decree to study German and Judaism from a governmentally approved textbook, *B'nai Zion,* which they considered not only religious coercion but forced assimilation which might lead to apostasy. They married secretly, "according to the Laws of Moses and Israel," without registering their marriages with the government. Legally, they remained unmarried, which the broadside reminds, led to all sorts of problems and scandals. Now, the broadside announces, the new legal provision makes it possible for all Jews to disclose their marital status without fear of punishment, and it urges all Jewish brides and grooms to conform to these governmental requirements.

This broadside brings into sharp focus the conflict between segments of the Jewish community in the Austro-Hungarian Empire, which promoted emancipation, and welcomed "enlightenment," even if governmentally inspired or promoted, and the majority of Jews who resisted such religious and cultural coercion, however well-meaning and benign it might be.

Mantua, 1791.

The Rules and Regulations of the Society, *Baale B'rith Abraham* (Members of the Covenant of Abraham). The Society was founded in 1716 on the proposition that birth may be a personal, family matter, but circumcision, entering the "Covenant of Abraham," was an event of communal import and a cause for public celebration. To make it possible for even the poorest families to welcome the newborn with the traditional celebration, sixty individuals joined together to pledge their interest and support. In addition to dues, each member contributed four lire for each circumcision. From among the members, one was chosen by lot to act as *sandek* (godfather) at the ceremony. He in turn was responsible for careful use of the monies collected for the celebration and for the needs of the newborn child. When all sixty had served, a new group would come into being. In 1791, the fifth cycle was inaugurated, four other editions of the Rules having been published in 1744, 1771, 1779, and 1784. Besides the rules and regulations these pamphlets also listed the names of the sixty members.

The *Baale B'rith Abraham* was one of some twenty such charitable, cultural, and religious societies in Mantua at the end of the eighteenth century. Among them were those obliged to dower the brides, heal the sick, visit the confined, bury the dead, console the mourners, clothe the needy, redeem captives, educate the young, and offer hospitality to the stranger, free loans to the hard-pressed, and midnight prayers for the coming of the Messiah. Such a network of voluntary societies could be found in every Jewish community of size, and the most basic ones existed in every hamlet.

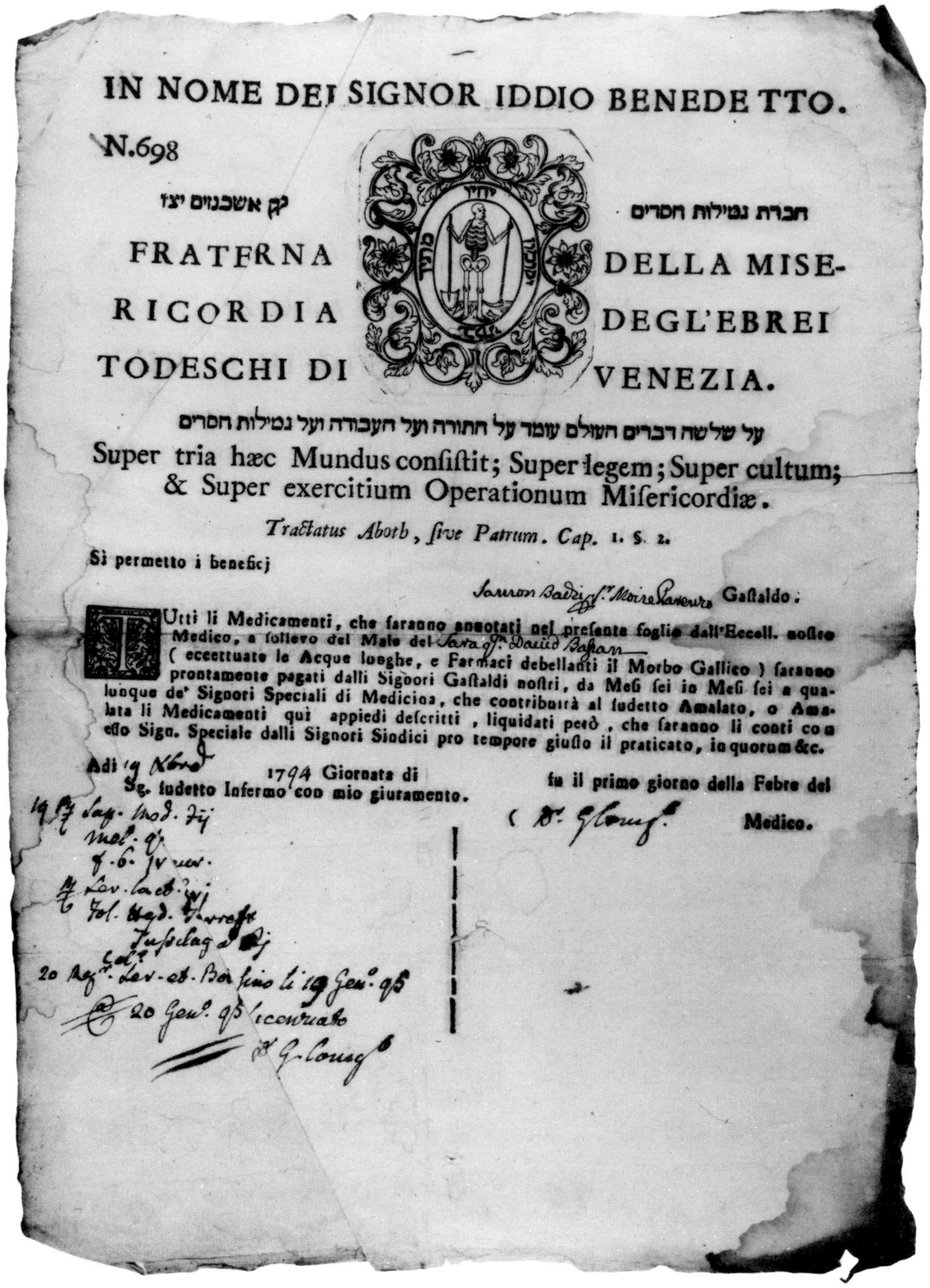
IN NOME DEI SIGNOR IDDIO BENEDETTO.

N.698

ק"ק אשכנזים יצ"ו

חברת גמילות חסדים

FRATERNA DELLA MISERICORDIA DEGL'EBREI TODESCHI DI VENEZIA.

על שלשה דברים העולם עומד על התורה ועל העבודה ועל גמילות חסדים

Super tria hæc Mundus consistit; Super legem; Super cultum; & Super exercitium Operationum Misericordiæ.

Tractatus Aboth, sive Patrum. Cap. 1. S. 2.

Si permetto i benefici

Gastaldo.

Tutti li Medicamenti, che saranno annotati nel presente foglio dall'Eccell. nostro Medico, a sollievo del Male del … (eccettuate le Acque lunghe, e Farmaci debellanti il Morbo Gallico) saranno prontamente pagati dalli Signori Gastaldi nostri, da Mesi sei in Mesi sei a qualunque de' Signori Speciali di Medicina, che contribuirà al sudetto Amalato, o Amalata li Medicamenti qui appiedi descritti, liquidati però, che saranno li conti con esso Sign. Speciale dalli Signori Sindici pro tempore giusto il praticato, in quorum &c.

Adì 19 Xbre 1794 Giornata di … fu il primo giorno della Febre del Sg. sudetto Infermo con mio giuramento.

Medico.

An authorization for the payment of the medicine listed in the left-hand column by the physician whose signature is in the column on the right, by the Brotherhood of Charity of the Ashkenazi Jewish Community of Venice, dated 1794. The document states that all medicine prescribed will be paid for, except for "the French disease."

Hebrat G'milut Hasadim, Fraterna Della Misericordia Degl'Ebrei Todeschi di Venezia (Brotherhood of Charity of the Ashkenazi Jewish Community of Venice), 1794.
Hebraic Section.

Venice, 1794. A broadside in Italian and Hebrew of the *Hebrat G'milut Hasadim* of the Ashkenazi Jewish Community, *Fraterna Della Misericordia Degl'Ebrei Todeschi de Venezia* (Brotherhood of Charity of the Ashkenazi Jewish Community of Venice). Its logo shows a skeleton holding a scythe in one hand and a shovel in the other, surrounded by the inscribed promise, "Your dead will rise and live." The document, in print and manuscript, is a promise by the Brotherhood to pay for all medicines prescribed by the physician (except those for the "French disease"). The prescription names the patient and the medicines and is signed by a doctor.

אלה דברי הברית אשר כרתו והסכימו
בני החברה הקדושה והם
בעלי ברית אברהם
כאשר נועדו יחד אחרי תום ההקף הרביעי
יזכר אלהינו לטובה לנפשות חסידיו אשר הורונו בישר פעלם ברחלם
להוציא לאור משפטי החברה הנ"ל למען יהיה לזכרון לכל אחד
מהחברים על שלשים ועל רבעים הקמים תחתם דור אחר דור ·
והיתה זאת ראשונה בשנת הת"קד על ידי מעלות הממונים כמ"הר עמנואל ציוויטה
וכמ"הר דוד חיים לומברוזו ז"ל וכמ"הר עזריאל באסאני יצ"ו ·
שנית בשנת אשר"יך על ידי מעלות הממונים כמ"הר פינחס הכהן וכמ"הר רפאל
שבתי יונה ס"ט וכמ"הר אברהם חיים נורצי ז"ל ·
שלישית בשנת התק"לט על ידי מעלות הממונים כמ"הר דוד באסאני ז"ל וכמ"הר
יהודה שמואל מלוואולטה וכמ"הר אהרן שמואל חי הכהן ס"ט ·
רביעית בשנת התק"מח על ידי מעלות הממונים כמ"הר אליעזר חיים בירלה
וכמ"הר יהושע אליעזר נורצי וכמ"הר אברהם חי טראבוטי ס"ט ·
ועתה חמישית ראו אור על מטיבי לכת מעלות הממונים
כמה"חר הרופא יעקב קזיס וכמ"הר עזריאל חיים הכהן
וכמ"הר דוד חיים אריאני אתה ה' תשמרם אב"יר

מנטובה
בדפוס מעלת הרופא המובהק תמים דעים
כמה"ר אליעזר שלמה מאיטאליה יצ"ו
בשנת קנאת ה' צבאות תעשה זאת לפ"ק
1791
CON LICENZA DE' SUPERIORI.

The rules and regulations of the Society of the Covenant of Abraham in Mantua, which provided the wherewithal that enabled each family, no matter how impecunious, to have a joyous celebration at a son's *brit milah* (circumcision).

Baale B'rith Abraham (Society of the Covenant of Abraham), Mantua, 1791.
Hebraic Section.

Mantua, 1818–1870.

Seven vellum memorial plaques list the departed to be memorialized with the dates of their death. These plaques, in candle stub or cartouche form, were placed on the memorial wall under the *Ner Neshama* (Lamp of the Soul) in the Scudo Cases Synagogue founded in Mantua in 1590. Among those memorialized are four members of the old and honored Finzi family and the equally aristocratic Levi, Bassani, and Viterbo families. Descendants of the family would offer their personal prayers of remembrance on the day of *Yahrzeit* (anniversary of death). Hanging before the entire congregation, the plaques became a congregational memorial as well.

These memorial plaques on parchment recording the name of the deceased and the day of death, were hung on the day of *Yahrzeit* (anniversary of death) in the Scudo Cases Synagogue in Mantua. Represented are the Finzi, Levi, Bassani, and Viterbo families.

Memorial Plaques, Mantua, 1818–70.
Hebraic Section.

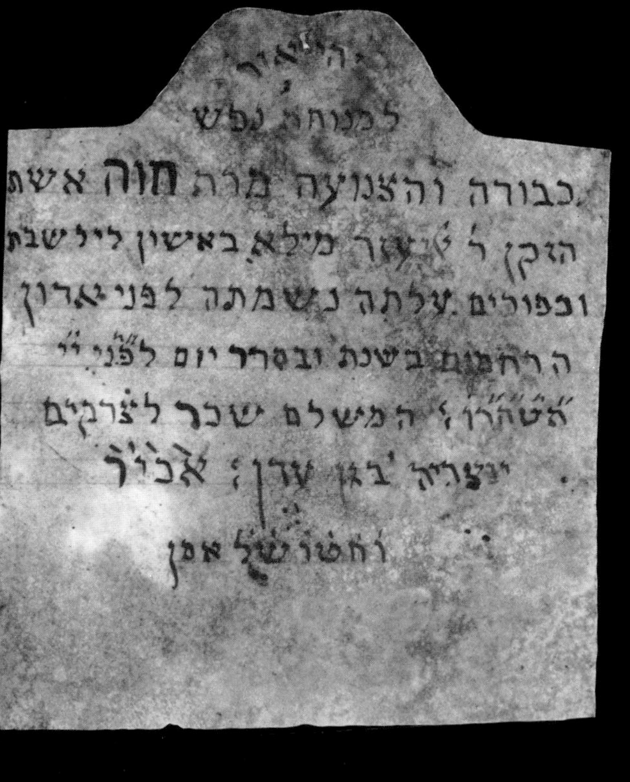

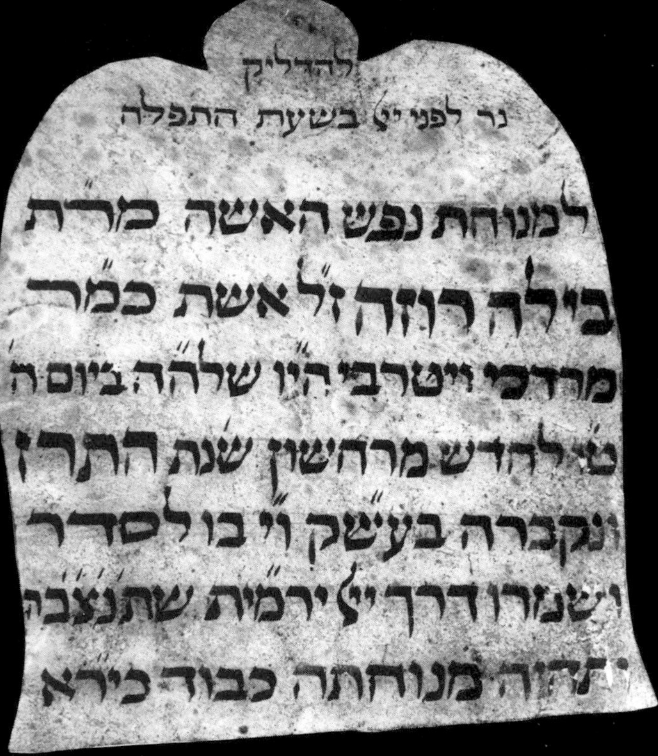
להדליק
נר לפני יי' בשעת התפלה
למנוחת נפש האשה מרת
בילה רוזה ז"ל אשת כמ"ר
מרדכי וייטרבי הי"ו שלה"ה ביום ה'
ט' לחדש מרחשון שנת התרז
ונקברה בע"שק ו' בו לסדר
ושמרו דרך יי' ירמית שתנצב"ה

למנוחת נפש הזקן הנכבד כמ"ר
יצחק חיים פנצי ז"ל
שנקרא לחיי העולם הבא ליל ש"ש
בשבת תשא י"ז לחדש אדר
ראשון שנת התרל ונקבר

London, 1827. Printed volume with pages of manuscript addenda of the *Laws of the Congregation of the Great Synagogue, Duke Place, London, Revised and Enacted 5587, London, 1827.* Printed on the leather binding of this volume is: "Synagogue Chambers Duke Place," which makes this volume the congregation's copy of its laws. The Great Synagogue is the "cathedral synagogue" of London's Ashkenazi community, and manuscript pages bound into the book contain the laws enacted by the congregation after 1827. As such, it is an indispensable source for the history of English Jewry in the middle decades of the nineteenth century. There we find enactments reflecting the union of Ashkenazi Jewry through agreements reached by the Great, Hambro, and New Synagogues to collaborate in communal and charitable endeavors, the Great Synagogue assuming obligations for half the funding. These agreements laid the foundation for the emergence of the United Synagogue, British Jewry's central religious organization, of which the Great Synagogue was the mother institution. These new laws also reflect the ascendancy of Ashkenazi Jewry to leadership of the community, especially in the Board of Deputies of British Jews, made possible by the emergence of the Rothschild and Goldsmith families as leading powers in the British financial world. Enactment 346, inscribed by hand provides: "That the body of Deputies of British Jews be the only official medium of communication with the Government of the country."

Two companion volumes indicate the rapid acculturation of English Jewry and the freedom they felt to express irreverent views of persons in high places. The 1827 edition of the *Laws* is in elegant English, while the 1791 edition is in an archaic Yiddish peppered with Hebrew phrases. Another copy of the 1827 edition contains factual notations in manuscript, as well as such critical remarks as: the "highly gifted and worthy" printed evaluation of Dr. Solomon Hirschel, the Chief Rabbi, is underlined in pen and accompanied by a marginal note, "highly gifted—*fudge.*"

Padua, 1858. *Regolamento per L'Instituto Convitto Rabbinico* (Regulations of the Rabbinical Institute), Padua, 1858. The rabbinical seminary established in Padua in 1829 by I. S. Reggio was the first modern institution for training rabbis. That this took place in Italy, one of the smaller European Jewish communities, attests to the high degree of integration into modernity of the Italian Jewish community. What gives the Library's copy particular value is its inclusion of a large folio insertion (nine pages in size) of the "Internal Regulations" for students and faculty, among them:

Books or papers not related to the lesson may not be brought into the classroom.

Students are to give serious attention to the instruction of the professor, and will behave towards him, inside the school and out, with the respect and filial affection due him.

Students must attend services at the major Ashkenazi synagogue.

All students are required to eat together in the refectory at the designated times. They may not gather the fruit growing in the college orchard.

Students may not bring any visitors into the College, especially to their rooms, without written permission.

N. 378

ISTITUTO CONVITTO RABBINICO DEL REGNO LOMBARDO-VENETO

REGOLAMENTO

DISCIPLINARE INTERNO DELL'ISTITUTO

Visto il Regolamento dell'Istituto;
Viste le Normali disciplinari interne fin qui in corso;
Avuto riguardo alle osservazioni emerse sulle medesime negli anni precedenti, e che dimostrarono il bisogno di farvi modificazioni ed aggiunte;
La Direzione stabilisce quanto segue:

CAPITOLO I.

DEGLI ALUNNI.

1. Gli alunni devono trovarsi nella Scuola prima dell'ora fissata nell'*Orario* per la Lezione.
2. Nella Scuola non si portano nè libri, nè carte che non siano relativi alla Lezione.
3. Nessun alunno può assentarsi dalla Lezione durante la medesima senza preventivo permesso del Professore.
4. Gli alunni prestano seria attenzione all'insegnamento del rispettivo Professore, e si comportano verso i loro maestri, entro e fuori della Scuola, con modi rispettosi e con affetto figliale.
5. Gli alunni devono scrupolosamente osservare tutte le pratiche religiose.
6. Devono intervenire agli Uffiej Divini nel Tempio Maggiore di rito tedesco, prendendo posto nèi banchi ad essi destinati; in tutti i giorni alle orazioni pomeridiane (תפילת מנחה וערבית); ed al Servizio della mattina (תפילת שחרית) almeno in tutti i giorni di ספר. Il solo caso di malattia, riconosciuto dal Sig. Prefetto, può esimerli da tale pio obbligo.
7. Nei casi eccezionali di non intervento degli alunni alla pubblica Ufficiatura mattutina e pomeridiana, dovranno riunirsi in apposito locale del Collegio per la recita delle consuete orazioni, ed uno di essi farà le funzioni di Cappellano a scelta del Sig. Prefetto.
8. Soltanto in caso di assoluto impedimento per motivo di salute di sortire dalla propria cella, l'alunno potrà recitare in privato le obbligatorie preghiere.
9. Durante il Servizio Divino, gli alunni dovranno contenersi in modo esemplare di silenzioso raccoglimento e di divozione.
10. Devono gli alunni pranzare tutti uniti nel refettorio dell'Istituto nell'ora destinata al Capitolo III, rimanendo assolutamente proibito di dare il pranzo agli alunni, nè in ora diversa, nè fuori del Collegio.
11. Gli alunni devono rispetto ed obbedienza ai Signori Segretario e Prefetto, col mezzo dei quali ricevono gli ordini della Direzione; e debono trattare con modi urbani e dolci il Bidello, la sua famiglia, ed ogni altra persona.
12. Nelle ore in cui gli alunni devono rimanere nel Collegio secondo l'*Orario*, non potranno sortire per qualsiasi motivo senza averne esposta la domanda, ed averne ottenuto il permesso dal Sig. Prefetto, il quale lo concederà soltanto in casi urgentissimi e comprovati, e di cui renderà conto alla Direzione nel Rapporto settimanale.
13. Gli alunni non potranno por mano nell'orto del Collegio senza permesso del Sig. Prefetto, e rimane poi loro proibito d'asportare fuori dell'Istituto alcun frutto derivante dall'orto medesimo.
14. Rimane severamente inibito agli alunni d'introdurre qualsivoglia persona in Collegio, e molto meno nelle loro celle, senza permesso in iscritto del Sig. Direttore.
15. Gli alunni anche fuori del Collegio dimostrano la coscienza della onorevole, grave, e sacra carriera che intraprendono, col loro contegno, colla buona scelta delle relazioni, colla decenza, serietà, e dolcezza dei modi.
16. Sarà cosa grata alla Direzione se gli alunni vestiranno di nero.

CAPITOLO II.

ORARIO DELLE LEZIONI.

1. Tutti i giorni della settimana, tranne le vacanze, sono giorni di scuola.
2. Sono giorni di vacanza, oltre il Sabbato, tutte le altre feste solenni degli Israeliti, la vigilia ed il giorno di Purim, i digiuni di precetto, ed in fine le ferie pasquali ed autunnali stabilite dal § 47 del Regolamento.
3. Gli studj devono incominciare col giorno 2 Novembre precisamente.
4. Le ore di scuola sono:

Nel primo Semestre.

dalle 9 antim. alle 12 merid. per la cattedra del sig. Prof. Luzzatto.
dalle 1 pom. alle 4 pom. per la cattedra del sig. Prof. Della Torre.

Nel Secondo Semestre.

dalle 8 antim. alle 11 antim. per la cattedra del sig. Prof. Luzzatto.
dalle 12 merid. alle 3 pom. per la cattedra del sig. Prof. Della Torre.

5. I sig. Professori devono trovarsi nel Collegio prima dell'ora fissata per incominciare la respettiva loro Lezione, e devono porgere l'insegnamento con zelo, durante le tre ore fissate per cadauna Lezione.
6. Nel giorno di Martedì vi sarà soltanto la Lezione della mattina del sig. Professore Luzzatto, e nel Venerdì soltanto quella del pomeriggio del sig. Professore Della Torre.
7. Qualora uno dei sig. Professori nel corso della settimana avesse, per motivi indipendenti dalla sua volontà, dovuto mancare di dare una Lezione, dovrà supplirla dandone una rispettivamente nelle mezze vacanze del Martedì o Venerdì.

CAPITOLO III.

DISTRIBUZIONE DELLA GIORNATA PER GLI ALUNNI.

1. Dopo l'Ufficio Divino del mattino sino all'ora della Lezione, e nell'ora d'intervallo tra l'una e l'altra delle Lezioni, gli alunni hanno riposo in ogni stagione.
2. L'*Orario* delle lezioni è fissato nell'antecedente Capitolo II.
3. Nei mesi di Novembre, Decembre, Gennajo, e nella prima metà di Febbrajo gli alunni sono in libertà dopo il termine delle Lezioni sino alla preghiera del vespero. Dopo questo Servigio Divino si riuniscono per il pranzo collegiale. Poscia sono in libertà sino alle ore 8 pom., nella qual ora devono ritrovarsi tutti riuniti nell'interno del Collegio, con proibizione di sortire fino al giorno susseguente.
4. Dalla seconda metà di Febbrajo fino al termine dell'anno scolastico, il pranzo collegiale precede l'orazione del vespero, ed ha luogo precisamente alle ore 4 pom. — Il pranzo finisce in modo di potersi ritrovare nel Tempio all'incominciamento del vespero, dopo il quale sono in libertà fino alle ore 9 pom., salvo il loro dovere di assistere alla תפילת ערבית ove venisse celebrata in ora posteriore al vespero.
5. Rientrati in Collegio nelle fissate ore 8, o 9 pom., gli alunni si pongono a studiare, e nell'inverno in una stanza comune riscaldata, rimanendo vietato che alcuno possa recare disturbo agli altri in qualsivoglia maniera.

CAPITOLO IV.

DEL PREFETTO.

1. Il Prefetto sopraintende alla disciplina, ed al buon contegno religioso e morale degli alunni, tanto nell'interno del Collegio, che fuori dello stesso; alla polizia interna dello Stabilimento ed alla stretta osservanza delle presenti Normali disciplinari.
2. Ha diritto d'introdursi nelle celle degli alunni ogniqualvolta per importanti motivi giudicasse necessaria la di lui presenza, ed in qualunque ora.
3. Soltanto in urgentissimi e comprovati casi permette agli alunni di assentarsi momentaneamente dal Collegio nelle ore in cui vi devono permanere, e ciò nei modi fissati nel Capitolo I. Art. 12.
4. Concede agli alunni soltanto nelle sere di Venerdì e Sabbato di rientrare nel Collegio, nell'inverno alle ore 10 pom., e di estate alle ore 11 pom.; e tale permesso egli lo accorda, o lo niega, secondo la subordinazione, più o meno dimostrata dall'alunno nel corso della settimana.
5. Invigilerà sul contegno degli alunni nel Tempio, e nei previsti casi che non v'intervenissero, sorveglierà perchè adempiano con eguale esattezza e devozione i religiosi loro doveri; e ciò in relazione al disposto dal Cap. I. Art. 5. 6. 7. 8.
6. Deve trovarsi in Collegio in tutte le ore in cui gli alunni sono tenuti a rimanervi, eccettuate le ore di Lezione, ed invigilare il contegno dei medesimi durante il pranzo, anche per l'adempimento dei relativi doveri religiosi.
7. Darà nota ai Sig. Professori di quegli alunni che approfitteranno delle ore di libertà per dedicarsi allo studio, perchè ne facciano onorevole ricordanza.
8. Al termine d'ogni settimana darà rapporto al sig. Direttore Onorario di ogni emergenza in Collegio, della condotta religiosa e morale d'ogni alunno; ed anche fuori di tal epoca, qualora lo credesse urgente per qualsiasi motivo.
9. Avrà dovere di pernottare nel Collegio durante l'anno scolastico per tutto il tempo che vi saranno gli alunni.
10. Il Prefetto nell'esercizio delle funzioni di Bibliotecario osserva le apposite Normali che gli furono comunicate.
11. Il Prefetto sorveglia tutto l'andamento dello Stabilimento, e fa note alla Direzione le eventuali emergenze.

CAPITOLO V.

DELLE CENSURE.

1. Esiste presso la Direzione un *Libro* intitolato *delle Censure*, nel quale sono notate le censure che la Direzione infligge agli alunni in causa di trasgressioni alle presenti *Normali disciplinari interne del Collegio*.
2. Negli Attestati semestrali degli studj, oltre alla classificazione sulla condotta religioso-morale dell'alunno, si pose un'apposita rubrica dinotante se l'alunno incorse, o meno, in censure nel corso del semestre, in relazione al precedente Art. 1.
3. L'alunno che nel corso d'un semestre sia incorso in una censura, ne ottiene la radiazione, quando nel semestre immediatamente successivo, la sua condotta rimanga scevra da ogni censura.
4. Se le censure in un semestre fossero state due, tre, o più, abbisognerebbero altrettanti semestri successivi incensurati, per avere altrettante radiazioni.
5. L'alunno che ottenne la radiazione di tutte le censure incorse in un semestre precedente, ha diritto di produrre alla Direzione il Certificato semestrale avente marca di censura, affinchè vi si annoti la radiazione, ovvero gli si rinnovi il Certificato, secondo meglio sembrerà alla Direzione.
6. Saranno modificate le formule dell'*Attestato finale d'idoneità* per modo che sia distinto l'alunno che compì il suo corso triennale senza alcuna censura, dall'alunno che avesse avuto la sciagura d'incorrervi, senza aver potuto ottenerne la radiazione.
7. La Direzione si riserva, a perfezionamento di questo gravissimo argomento, di fissare le conseguenze ulteriori che dovranno derivare dalle reiterate censure.

CAPITOLO VI.

DEL BIDELLO.

Il Bidello-Custode ha cura della nettezza dell'edifizio, della salubrità delle celle, refettorio e scuole; sopravveglia a chi entra e sorte dal Collegio, attenendosi alle disposizioni di questo interno Regolamento; eseguisce gli ordini della Direzione, Amministrazione, del Segretario, e Prefetto; presta assistenza agli alunni e specialmente in caso di malattia; nelle sedute dell'Amministrazione e della Direzione rimane nell'anticamera pel servigio, e presta ogni altro occorrente ufficio nelle pubbliche cerimonie.

Dalla Direzione dell'Istituto Convitto Rabbinico del Regno Lombardo-Veneto.

Padova, li 22 Ottobre 1854.

IL CAV. DELL'ORDINE IMPERIALE DI **FRANCESCO GIUSEPPE I.**, DIRETTORE ONORARIO

CONSOLO.

IL SEGRETARIO
Ab. SALOM.

Tip. [illegible]

The duties of the professors, Lelio Della Torre and Samuel David Luzzato, are minutely spelled out. Six hours of teaching each day of the week, and if a lesson is missed, it must be made up. The prefect may enter a student's room at any time and must "keep vigil" over the behavior of the students in the dormitory, in the classroom, and at services. He is to keep a record of student conduct noting punishments and censures but, in a nod to the traditional concept of *t'shuva* (repentance), if conduct improves, the notations of censure will be erased from the record.

This pullout broadside is tipped in the Regulations of the Rabbinical Institute at Padua, the first modern rabbinical seminary, established by I. S. Reggio in 1829. It deals with the internal regulations for the faculty and students and spells out, in detail, the obligations and restrictions placed on both.

Regolamento per L'Istituto Convitto Rabbinico, Padua, 1858.
Hebraic Section.

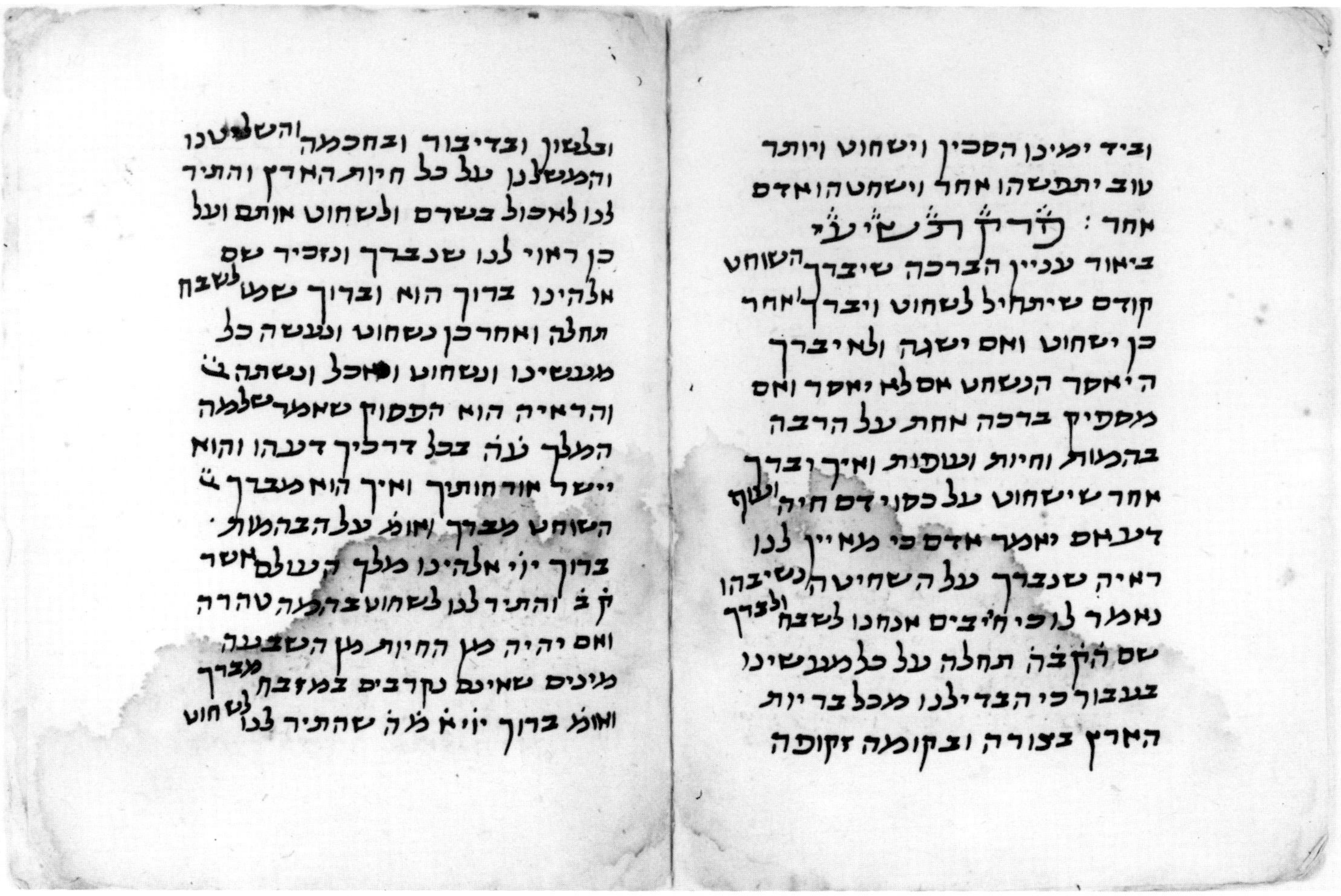

Written in 1397 by Joseph ben Abraham ben Joseph, this manuscript of the Karaite laws of *Shehita* (ritual slaughtering), by Israel Ma'arabi, is the oldest manuscript in the Hebraic Section. It is open to the beginning of Chapter Nine, which deals with the blessings to be recited at the ritual slaughter of the fowl or animal.

Israel Ma'arabi, *Hilhot Shehita.*
Scribe: Joseph ben Abraham ben Joseph, n.p., 1397.
Hebraic Section.

THE WRITTEN WORD

Three manuscripts in the Hebraic Section permit us to witness the extent of Karaite sectarianism in the fourteenth century; a visit to an Egyptian synagogue in the nineteenth; and a glimpse at Jewish life in the Islamic Middle East in the eighteenth.

The oldest dated Hebrew manuscript at the Library is a thirteen-page *Hilhot Shehita* (Laws of Ritual Slaughtering) by the Karaite scholar Israel Ma'arabi, written in 1397 by the scribe Joseph ben Abraham ben Joseph. The Karaite sect, as noted, had its origins at the beginning of the eighth century and rejected Talmudic-rabbinic tradition, so it is not surprising to find in this manuscript that a Karaite shohet (ritual slaughterer) is required to deny the Rabbanites' "Mishnah and Talmud."

A manuscript wall calendar for the year 5575 (1815), which apparently hung in an Egyptian synagogue, is of interest to students of the Jewish calendar, the synagogue, and Egyptian Jewry. Twenty-four by eighteen inches in size, it contains the reckonings of *Mar* Samuel and *Rav* Adda. The former, head of the Nehardea Academy in Babylon in the second century, reckoned the year to consist of fifty-two weeks and one and one-quarter days. Over the course of twenty-eight years he made the adjustments necessary to bring the solar and lunar calendars into harmony. A more exact

Facing page: A wall calendar in manuscript, hung in an Egyptian synagogue, to be available to all members of the community. It contains all pertinent calendrical information for Jewish observance and lists the Islamic months as well.

Wall Calendar, Egypt, 1815.
Hebraic Section.

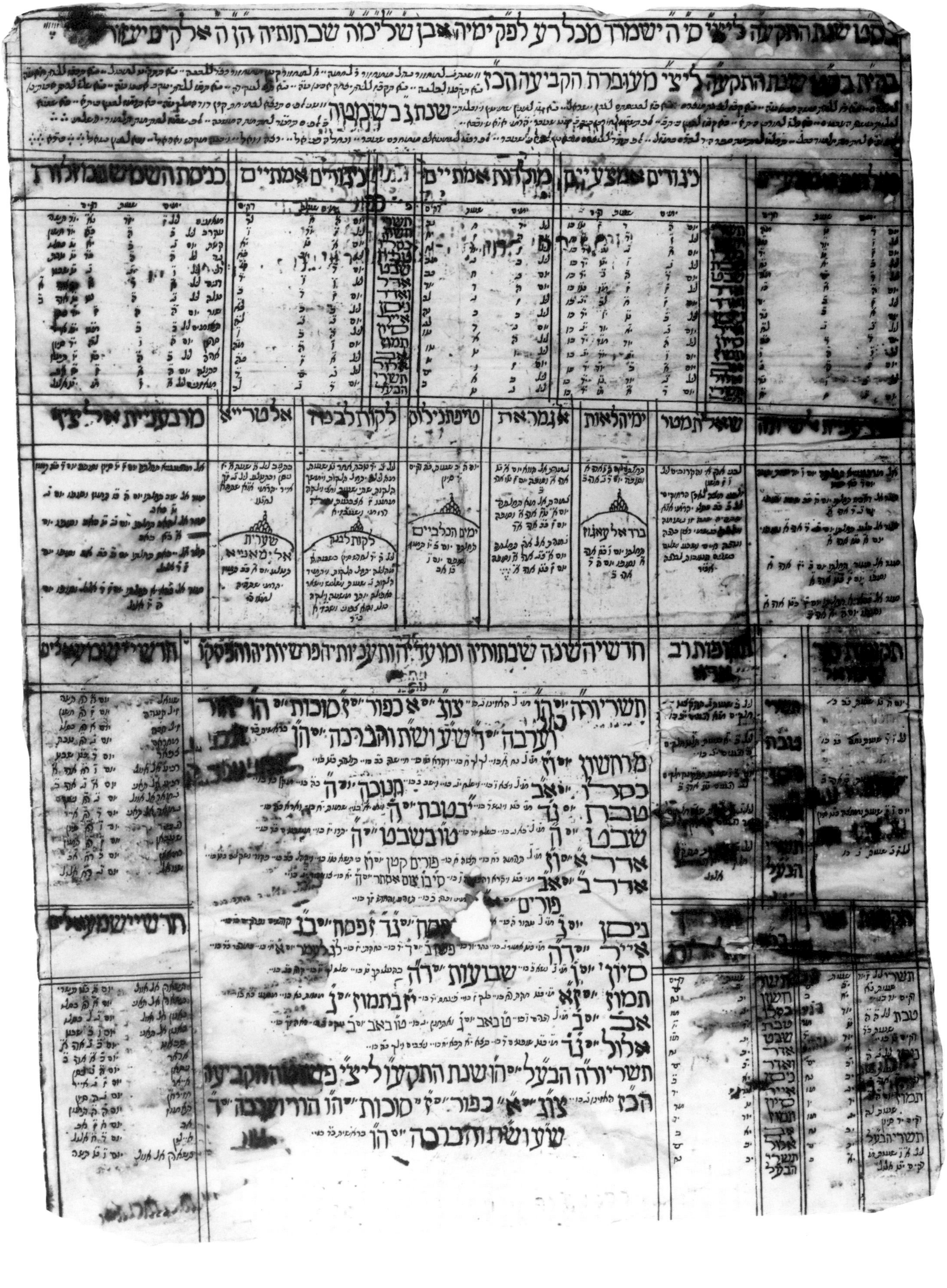
מולדות אמתיים
כניסת השמש במזלות
לקות לבנה
שאל המטר
חדשי השנה שבתותיה ומועדיה ותעניותיה ופרשיותיה והפסקו
תשרי
מרחשון
כסלו
טבת
שבט
אדר א
אדר ב
פורים
ניסן
אייר
סיון
שבועות
תמוז
אב
אלול

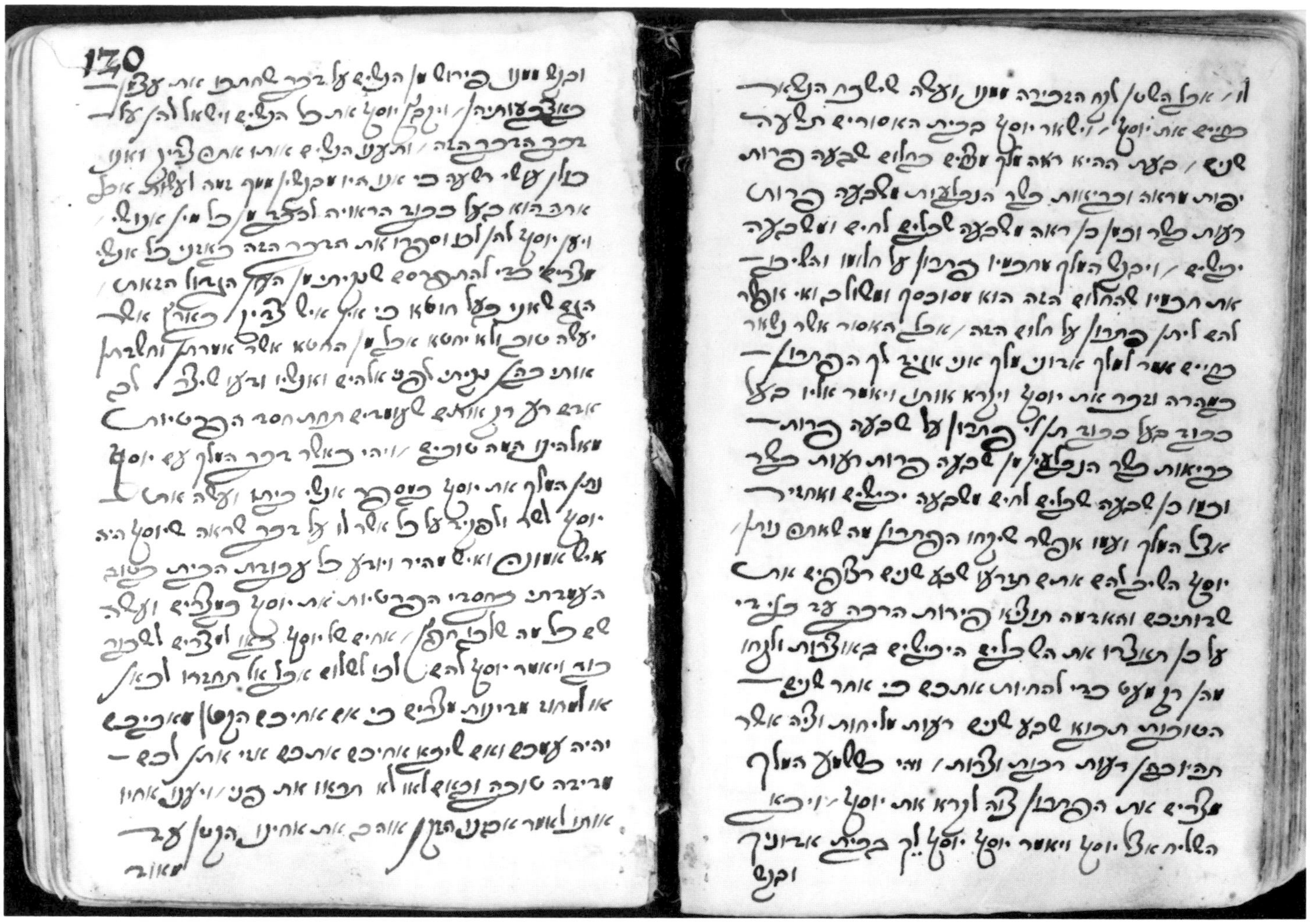

One of the three recorded manuscripts of a Hebrew translation of the Koran, written in Cochin in the middle of the eighteenth century, it opens with: "The customs of Ishmaelites," i.e., Moslems: "The Moslems believe in God who is One; One Essence, One Form, Creator of Heaven and Earth, He rewards those who do His will, and punishes those who transgress His ordinances . . . and Mohammed was His great prophet, who was sent by God to teach mankind the way to eternal life."

Koran, Hebrew Translation [Cochin], 1757.
Hebraic Section.

calculation of the length of the year is attributed to a *Rav* Adda (probably, *Rav* Addah ben Ahavah), a third-century Babylonian scholar. Both ancient calculations persist in this nineteenth-century Jewish calendar, which also notes the "Islamic months."

The most interesting manuscript is a Hebrew translation of the Koran, one of only three such extant Hebrew manuscripts, the others being in the Bodleian Library at Oxford, and the British Library in London. The Library of Congress Hebrew Koran is a manuscript of 259 leaves, without a title page, and it contains no indication as to translator, scribe, or place and date of composition.

In a tour de force of bibliographical sleuthing, Myron M. Weinstein, former Head of the Hebraic Section, using both painstaking scholarship and creative imagination, offers the missing date and even a nineteenth-century provenance. In his "A Hebrew Qur'an Manuscript" in *Jews in India,* edited by Thomas A. Timberg, Weinstein, in elegant narrative style, leads the reader along a thoroughly documented road, at whose end we are convinced that this Hebrew version is a translation from a Dutch copy which is itself a translation from the French translation of the original Arabic. Weinstein also persuades us that the translator is Leopold Immanuel Jacob van Dort, a Jewish convert to Christianity who was professor of theology in Colombo, Ceylon, and that the scribe was David Cohen, a native of Berlin then residing in Cochin, a city on the southwest coast of India. Weinstein is equally persuasive about the manuscript being written in Cochin in the 1750s or 1760s, probably in 1757, when van Dort was visiting that city, and that is the volume the missionary Joseph Wolff saw in Meshed, Persia, in 1831, when he encountered a group of Jewish Sufis. Wolff writes:

> I met here in the house of Mullah Meshiakh with an Hebrew translation of the Koran, with the following title: "The Law of the Ishmaelites, called the Koran, translated from the Arabic into French by Durier, and from the French into Dutch by Glosenmachor, and I, Immanuel Jacob Medart, have now translated it into the holy language, written here at Kogen, by David, the son of Isaac Cohen of Berlin."

From Cochin to Meshed to Washington, and who knows where in-between, a hegira from the ends of the earth indeed!

FOR STUDENTS OF KABBALAH

Books and manuscripts in the Library's Hebraic Section bear witness to the role of Kabbalah, Jewish mysticism, in Jewish religious and cultural history. Consider an intriguing set of the first edition of Kabbalah's foremost classic, the *Zohar,* Mantua, 1558–60. Of this work, Hayim Joseph David Azulai remarked, "Reading the *Zohar* is good for the soul, even if wrong and full of mistakes." Volume 1 of the Library's set belonged at one time to Abraham Joseph Graziano (d. 1684), rabbi of Modena, a halakic scholar criticized for his leniency, a popular poet, and a noted bibliophile. Graziano signed himself *"Ish Ger"* (stranger), the signature found on the title page. Of far greater importance are the many marginal notations in his hand throughout the volume. Graziano wrote a known commentary on the *Shulhan Aruch;* his comments on the *Zohar* now await scholarly attention. Volume 2, cut smaller in size, is printed on the blue paper often found in nineteenth-century books printed in Russia; to find it in a sixteenth-century book printed in Italy is very rare. Volume 3 has very wide unmarked margins which await the notations for which they were intended.

Kabbalistic symbols and illustrations await further study and interpretation of a visiting scholar. Two works rich in both are *Shefa Tal,* Hanau, 1612, by the "renowned skilled physician" of Prague, Shabbetai Sheftel Horowitz (c. 1561–1619). The Library's copy is in pristine condition, quite unusual for this much admired first edition of a popular Kabbalistic work. The Library's first edition, Amsterdam, 1701, of the oft-reprinted *Sefer Raziel*—attributed by tradition to Adam!—is filled with marginal annotations of an as yet unidentified commentator.

A one-hundred-page manuscript written in Vilna, 1817–18, is the commentary of Reb Elijah, the Gaon of Vilna, on a section of the *Zohar, Sifra di-Zeni'uta* (Book of Concealment). It antedates the first printing of this commentary in Vilna, 1820. Of interest to students of Kabbalah or of the Gaon of Vilna are paste-in insertions in the manuscript copy. For the bibliophile interested in provenance, the manuscript's first owner is known, Jacob ben Arye Katz, and those drawn to the unusual will note the presence in a manuscript copy of a censor's seal, that of Moshko Zeligovitch, 1837.

The owner's signature on the title page of this first edition of the *Zohar,* Mantua, 1558, is of Modena's seventeenth-century rabbi, Abraham Joseph Graziano, who signs himself *Ish Ger* (A stranger I was in the land). What makes this copy of unusual importance is that this noted scholar and bibliophile made copious notes on the wide margins of his copy.

Sefer ha-Zohar, 3 volumes, Mantua, 1558–60. Hebraic Section.

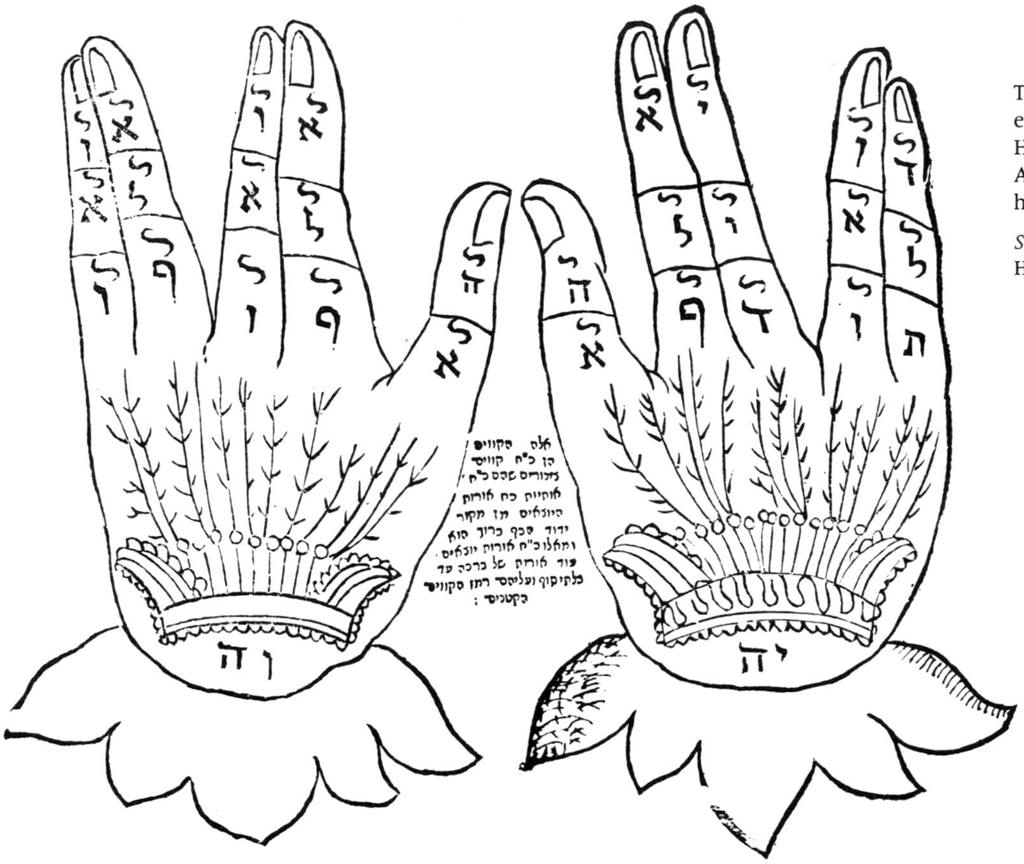

These hands are divided into twenty-eight sections, each containing a Hebrew letter. Twenty-eight, in Hebrew numbers, spells the word *Koach* = strength. At the bottom of the hand, the two letters on each hand combine to form YHWH, the name of God.

Shefa Tal, Hanau, 1612.
Hebraic Section.

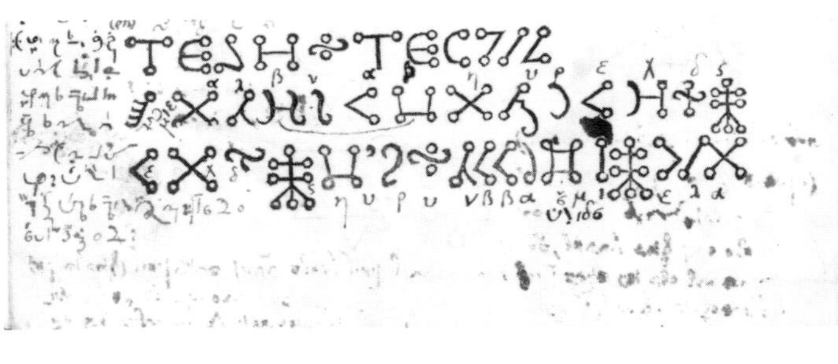

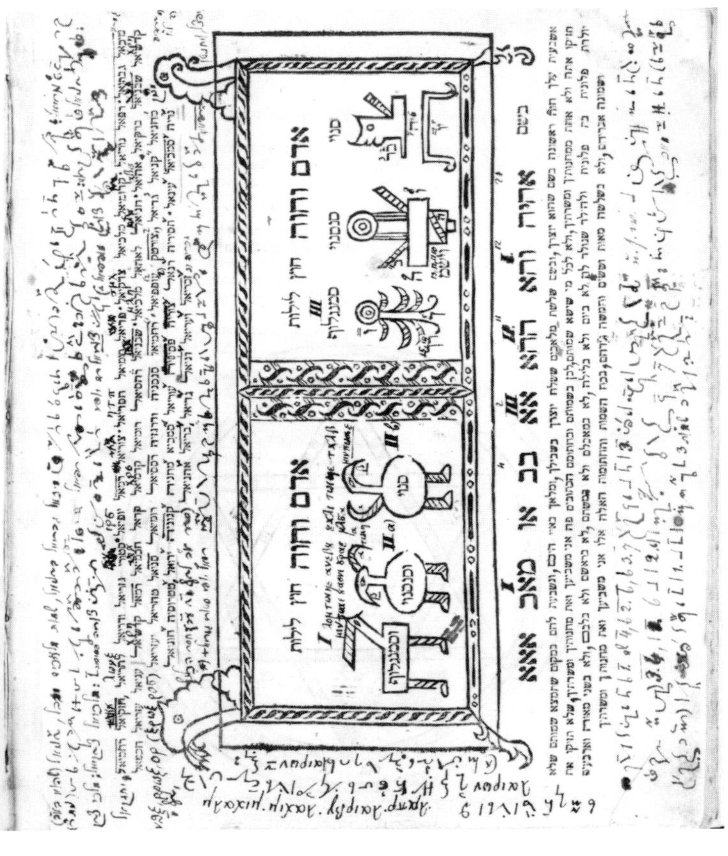

We see on one page a kabbalistic alphabet, on the other, kabbalistic figures to ward off evil, and a catalog of the names of angels. On both pages, kabbalistic marginal notes have been handwritten.

Sefer Raziel, Amsterdam, 1701 (First Edition).
Hebraic Section.

A GLIMPSE AT JEWISH RELIGIOUS LIFE IN THE SEVENTEENTH CENTURY

Title Page

What better way to catch a glimpse of Jewish religious life in the late Middle Ages in central Europe than through the illustrations of a book on Jewish customs. Those in the 1707 Amsterdam edition of *Minhagim,* published by Solomon ben Joseph Proops, have become the standard. The woodcut illustrations are authentic and comprehensive, covering Sabbath and holiday observance, and home and synagogue rituals. Among them are a mother blessing the Sabbath lights of a Sabbath oil lamp; a father chanting the Habdalah (service of "separation" at the conclusion of the Sabbath), while he holds a cup of wine by the light of a candle held by a child whose sibling holds a spice box; four men blessing the new moon; a rabbi preaching on the Great Sabbath (preceding Passover); grinding flour for and baking matzoh; searching for hametz (leaven); and scouring pots and pans. Also shown are a man having his hair cut on *Lag B'Omer*—the thirty-third day of the fifty between Passover and Shavuot, when restrictions obtaining during that period of semimourning are relaxed; Moses on Sinai receiving the Ten Commandments; worshippers seated on the floor on *Tisha B'Av,* mourning the destruction of the Temple; the sounding of the shofar on Rosh Hashanah, the New Year; a man building his tabernacle for the Feast of Tabernacles; the gathering of palms, willows, and myrtle to join the citron in its celebration; children receiving sweets to celebrate the Joy of the Law, Simhat Torah; the kindling of a Hanukkah lamp; and Purim jesters sounding their musical instruments. The life cycle is also marked: bride and groom under the huppah (canopy); an infant boy entering the Covenant of Abraham; and finally, a body borne in a coffin to its eternal resting place.

The woodcut illustrations of Jewish holiday and ritual observance in *Minhagim* (Customs), published by Solomon Proops, Amsterdam, 1707, with descriptions and instructions in Yiddish, offer us a glimpse of Jewish life at the end of the seventeenth and the beginning of the eighteenth centuries.

Minhagim (Customs), Amsterdam, 1707.
Hebraic Section.

Blessing the Sabbath Candles

The *Habdalah* Service

Sounding the Shofar on Rosh Hashanah

The *Lulav:* Palm Branch, Myrtle, and Willow

Hanukkah, Festival of Lights

Removing Leaven from the Home

The Merry Festival of Purim

Under the Huppah, the Wedding Service

A CHOICE SAMPLING

Witnesses to history, too, are some exotic morsels of special interest to bibliophiles, historians, and collectors. Only Venice might justifiably dispute the claim that Amsterdam was the greatest center of Hebrew printing. The first book printed in Amsterdam would then be of singular interest to bibliophiles. The colophon to *Sefer Shvilei Emunah* (Paths of Faith), by Meir Ibn Aldabi, printed by Daniel da Fonseca, states: "Praised be the Lord who gives strength to the weary . . . who helped me complete this heavenly work, first product of (Hebrew) printing in this city." Authorities on Hebrew typography nonetheless award primacy to *Seder T'filoth K'Minhag K.K. Sefarad,* a Sefardi prayer book published by Menasseh ben Israel, which came off the press on January 1, 1627, a few months before the Fonseca publication. It may well be that work on Fonseca's book began first, but took a longer time to produce because of the inefficiency of its printer. Its editor Abraham da Fonseca, found no less than one hundred printer's errors! Daniel da Fonseca published only one more book, while Menasseh ben Israel's press flourished for a quarter of a century.

Some three dozen Hebrew books have appeared with the notation that space was being left in each copy for the signature of the author, editor, or publisher. One such volume, *Sefer Amudei Bet Yehudah* (The Pillars of the House of Judah) Amsterdam, 1766, calls for the signatures of both author and publisher. Both author and printer clearly ask purchasers to buy only copies which have both signatures, yet most extant copies lack the author's. The Library's copy has both that of author Judah ben Mordecai ha-Levi Hurwitz, and of the publisher-printer Yehudah Leib Susmans. This work also has the distinction of bearing the approbation of Moses Mendelssohn, the only Hebrew book so honored.

Two books published 120 years apart, one in Amsterdam in 1687, the other in Mexico in 1807, are joined together by language. The former, *Seder B'rachot* (Order of Benedictions), in Hebrew with a Spanish translation, is a compendium of benedictions and liturgical selections as well as some laws generally not found in the prayer book. Its brief Hebrew introduction is a dedication to Isaac Aboab, a wealthy East India merchant and a patron of rabbinical works, who was himself a scholar and writer. Aboab's father fled from the Inquisition in Mexico and reverted to Judaism in Amsterdam, taking the name Mattathias. Benjamin Senior Godines, publisher of the compendium, found the house of Isaac Aboab "filled with books; rare printed volumes, as well as manuscripts," among them this work, which he calls in Spanish, *Orden de Benedictiones.* The Spanish was intended for former Marranos or their descendants, who were still not at home in the Hebrew language. The last two benedictions are forms of memorial prayers, with places for the insertion of a name and with proper pronouns for a man and for a woman "who was burned at the stake for the sanctification of the Holy Name . . . may the Lord seek recompense for his/her blood, and visit retribution on the enemy."

In Mexico, in 1807 the editor of *La Gazeta,* Don Juan Lopez Cancelada, published a volume with some curious illustrations, *Decreto de Napoleon . . . Sobre Los Judios.* One illustration accompanies an account of divorce in Poland "en tiempo de Casimiro," i.e., King Casimir the Great (1310–1370) the legendary protector and benefactor of the Jews. The Jewish woman wears a headdress which seems to be a version of a large phylactery. The four other illustrations are of Jews being tortured by the Inquisition.

From the manuscript collection in the Library's Hebraic Section, we call attention to two thick volumes of the classic of Lurianic Kabbalah, the *Sefer Etz Hayim* of Hayim Vital; to a ledger of the Jewish community of Mantua for the years 1784–96, which lists the distribution of honors and contributions to charity; and to a collection of prayers for Simhat Torah, Shavuot, and the ceremony of Brith Milah (circumcision). Also included is a contingent decree of separation and support payments issued in 1880 by the rabbinic court of Constantinople and endorsed and countersigned

עמודי
בית יהודא
לתורה ולתעודה

אמר המחבר והמדפים

באנו מן המודיעים ולפנ"ים בישראל · להציל את נפש עם
האל · מחרב החרמות והגזירות שגזרו גאוני רבני
הארץ · על מסיגי גבולי · ולבל יגזול איש לבבי ועמלי ·
אבקש מאחינו בני ישראל · שלא לקנות חיבור זה בלתי עדותינו ·
המדפיס והמחבר שנינו · כי אנחנו נחתום
ונכתוב את שמינו · על כל הספרים בחתימת ידינו · ועל
השומע יבוא ברכת אלקינו :

To protect their investment, the author and publisher of this work exhorted purchasers only to buy copies that contained both of their signatures. Shown here is one of the copies bearing both signatures.

Judah Hurwitz, *Sefer Amudei Bet Yehudah* (The Pillars of the House of Judah), Amsterdam, 1766. Hebraic Section.

In this illustration a Jewish woman wears a headdress resembling a large phylactery, a Jewish ritual object which usually is composed of two small square leather boxes containing slips inscribed with spiritual passages and traditionally worn on the left arm and on the head during morning weekday prayers.

Cancelada, Don Juan Lopez, *Decreto de Napoleon . . . Sobre Los Judios,* Mexico, 1807.
Rare Book and Special Collections Division.

by the *Hakham Bashi* (Chief Rabbi). Here the husband is accused of cursing and abusing his wife, reviling her parents, and raising his hand to do her harm. Intermediaries attest that the husband has promised to mend his ways but, in the meantime, he is obligated to support her, even while they are separated. We find a report of the injury suffered in 1809 by Rachel Cavalieri, who went up to the attic to watch a balloon flight and fell off a chair. And, to end on a happy note, there is a doily with a dedication to Rabbi Adolf Jellinek (of Vienna) on his seventieth birthday, June 24, 1891, inscribed by his student Zeev Wolf Sbrieser.

The company of collectors of Haggadot is large and enthusiastic, and the Library houses a collection worthy of their patronage. We cite a few of uncommon historic interest and a few which are not what they seem. The first Haggadah with a French translation was published in 1818 in Metz. Its translator is David Drach, rabbi, doctor of law, a graduate of the Faculty of Letters of the Academy of Paris. He was also the son-in-law of Rabbi Emanuel Deutz, the Grand Rabbi of France. Four years later, Drach converted to Roman Catholicism and persuaded his brother-in-law, the Chief Rabbi's son, to do likewise. In his later years the latter returned to the Jewish faith but Drach remained loyal to and active in his new faith—translating, editing, and writing. Among his works are conversionary tracts and Hebrew poems in honor of the Pope and Cardinals. For obvious reasons not many copies of his translation of the Haggadah have survived.

In Vilna, in 1852 and again in 1860, editions of the Haggadah were published with the commentaries of Zvi Hirsch of Grodno and Jacob of Dubno "arranged according to the custom of Rabbi Elijah Gaon," but severely self-censored. The portion of "This is the bread of affliction" that reads "this year we are slaves, next year we shall be free," is altered to read, "this year we are slaves in many places, next year we shall be free as we are in this our land." The section, "Pour out thy wrath upon the nations which have not known thee, and upon the kingdoms which have not called upon thy Name; for they have devoured Jacob and laid waste his dwelling place" is completely eliminated.

A Haggadah called *Gufo shel Pesah, etc.* (The Essence of Passover or a Haggadah for Jewish Tots), Berlin, 1830, in Hebrew and Yiddish, is not what it purports to be, but is instead a missionary tract "published . . . to rouse the hearts of Jewish children to seek the path of salvation." Nor is the *Hagodeh far Gloiber un Apikorsim*, published in Moscow, 1927, for "Be-

A takeoff on the traditional Passover Haggadah was published in Moscow in 1927. Written by M. Altshuler, it attacked both Judaism and Zionism, advancing the cause of international communism instead. The cover shows a group of Jews partaking of the seder meal, while hovering about them are ghosts, demons, and assorted inhabitants of the spirit world.

M. Altshuler, *Hagodeh far Gloiber un Apikorsim* (A Haggadah for Believers and Atheists), Moscow, 1927. Hebraic Section.

lievers and Atheists," the Passover Haggadah. It, too is a missionary tract, but of a different order. It proclaims, "May all the aristocrats, bourgeois . . . Bundists, Zionists . . . Poale Zion . . . be consumed in the fire of revolution. . . . May annihilation overcome all the outdated rabbinic laws and customs." An anarchist Haggadah published in New York in the 1890s is of a similar nature.

The *Haggadah Shel Pesah,* printed in Munich, 1947, is what it proclaims to be, a photo-offset edition of the traditional Haggadah with an English translation. It was published and distributed in Germany by the American Jewish Joint Distribution Committee for the survivors of the Holocaust, who could now proclaim, "This year we are free . . . Next year, in Jerusalem."

9

"LET HER WORKS PRAISE HER"

■ IN THE MAKING OF THE Jewish book, women have played a role as publishers, printers, patrons, and writers.

The first woman involved in printing Hebrew books was Estellina, the wife of the physician Abraham Conat, who introduced Hebrew printing in Mantua and published six Hebrew books there in 1474–77. A printing press had been established in that cultured city in 1471 and others followed. As David W. Amram writes in his *The Makers of Hebrew Books in Italy:*

> At one of these presses Conat caught the inspiration to print Hebrew books, and communicated it to his worthy helpmeet, Estellina. She printed on her own account . . . "Investigation of the World" by Jedaiah Bedersi and in the colophon she writes, "I, Estellina, wife of my master my husband, the honored Rabbi Abraham Conat, may he be blessed with children and may his days be prolonged, Amen! wrote this book, 'Investigation of the World'" . . . She "wrote" the book, as her husband said, "with many pens without the aid of a miracle," for the art had not yet invented the word "printing" by which to define itself.

It seems clear that she had a hand in the printing and proofreading, both of which the word "wrote" connotes. It is most fitting that the Mantua of the Gonzagas, rulers who were patrons of the arts, be the place where a Jewish woman entered into Hebrew bookmaking. The Jews of that city were the most integrated into the general culture of any contemporary Jewish community, women as well as men. "The libraries of the women of Mantua," Shlomo Simonsohn writes in his *History of the Jews in the Duchy of Mantua,* "testify to their enlightenment and their literary interests." The Library of Congress has a fine copy of one of the volumes produced by the Conats, the Commentary of Rabbi Levi Ben Gershon on the Pentateuch.

Estellina had a hand in the actual production of books. Doña Reyna Nasi, a century and more later, was purely the patron publisher. Her mother was one of the most remarkable women of her time, Doña Grazia Mendes, whose wealth and diplomatic acuity had enabled her to transfer both family and fortune from Christian countries in Europe, where a Marrano past threatened their security, to the relatively safe Ottoman Empire.

Among the earliest of Hebrew books is this commentary on the Pentateuch by Levi ben Gerson (Gersonides), printed by Abraham Conat in Mantua, c. 1476. Abraham's wife, Estellina, apparently participated in the publication of the books issued by her husband and thus becomes the first of a notable list of women involved in the printing and publication of Hebrew books. We see here the end of Genesis.

Peirush ha-Ralbag 'al ha-Torah (Commentary of Gersonides on the Pentateuch), Mantua, c. 1476.
Rare Book and Special Collections Division.

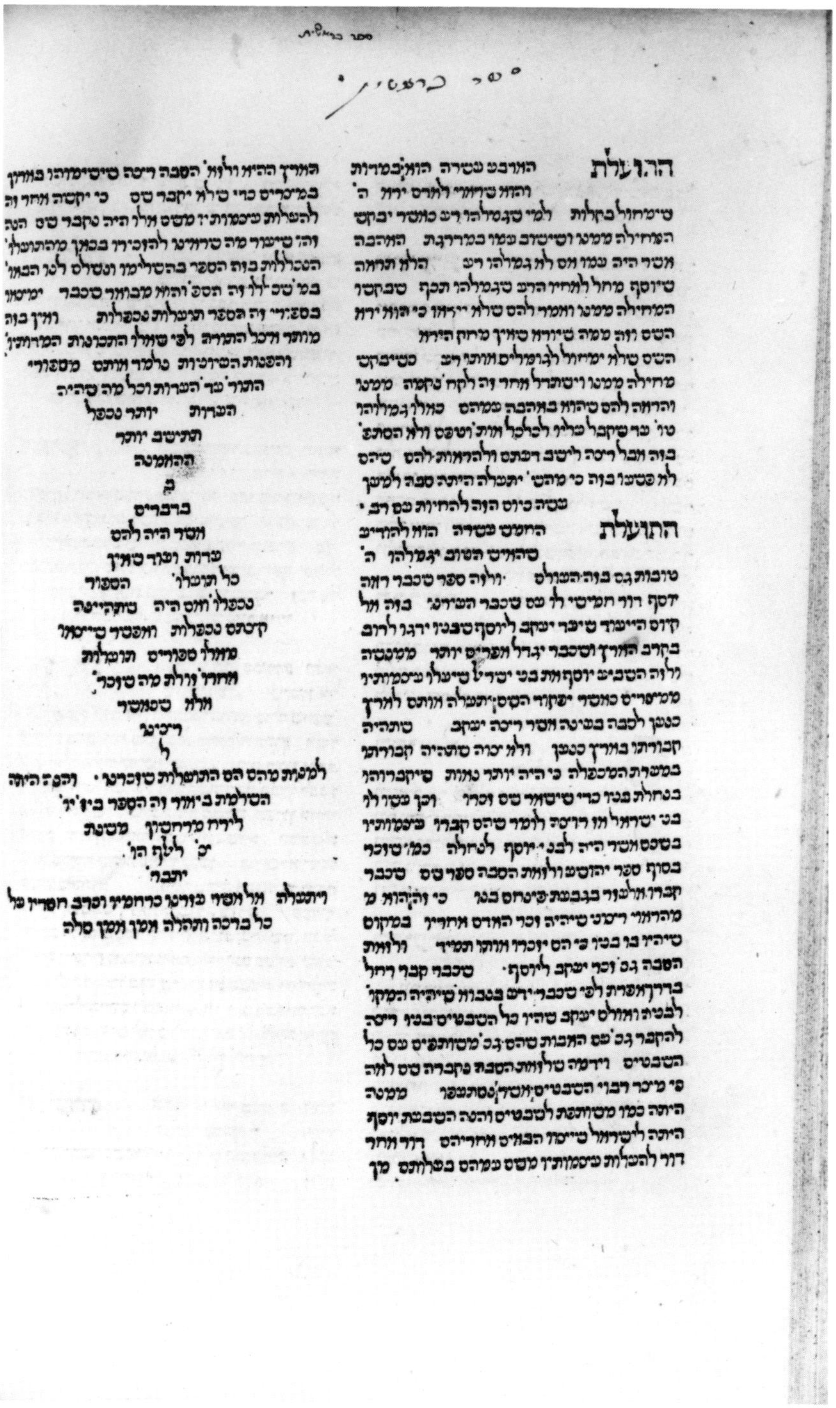

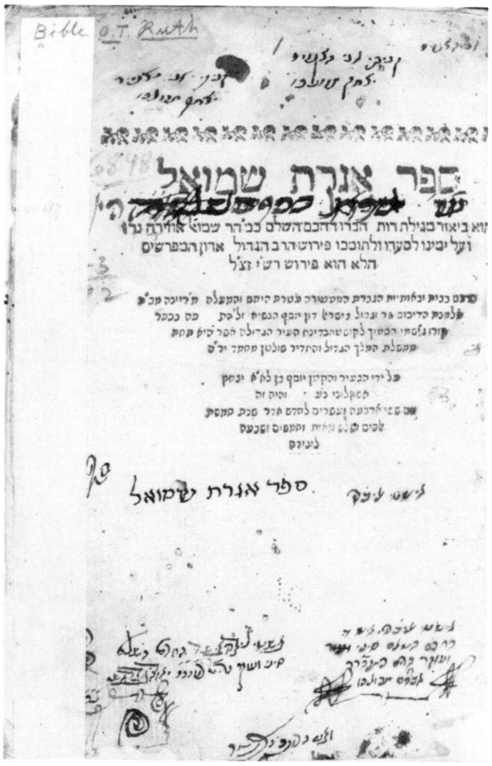
ספר אגרת שמואל

After the death of her husband, Don Joseph Nasi, Duke of Naxos, the widow Doña Reyna established a Hebrew press in her home in Belvedere which she continued in Kuru Tschechme, a suburb of Constantinople. Shown is the title page of *Iggeret Shmuel*, a commentary on the Book of Ruth by Samuel di Uzeda, which states: "Printed in the publishing house and with the type font of the noble lady of noble lineage, Reyna, widow of the Duke and Prince in Israel Don Yosef Nasi by Joseph ben Isaac Ascaloni."

Samuel di Uzeda, *Iggeret Shmuel*, Kuru Tschechme, 1597.
Hebraic Section.

Doña Reyna was wife to her cousin, Don Joseph Nasi, who rose in that empire to become Duke of Naxos. Nevertheless, upon Joseph's death in 1579, the sultan expropriated much of the widow's wealth except for the 90,000 dinars stipulated in her ketubah (marriage contract). With this inheritance, Doña Reyna established a Hebrew press, first in her palatial residence in Belvedere, then in Kuru Tschechme, a suburb of Constantinople. Of the books printed in the first press, the Library has a copy of *Torat Moshe* (c. 1593–1595), the commentary on the Pentateuch by Moses Alsheikh, "a resident of Upper Galilee."

A commentary on the Book of Ruth by Samuel di Uzeda, *Iggeret Shmuel,* the first book published by Doña Reyna's relocated press in Kuro Tschechme in 1597, is in the Library's Hebraic Section. It is fitting that a book about the biblical Ruth, a woman convert to Judaism, is published by Reyna, a woman who returned to Judaism from an apostasy imposed on her by her ancestors. The title page acclaims the patron-publisher: "Printed in the house and with the type of the Crowned Lady, crown of descent and excellency, Reyna (may she be blessed of women!), widow of the Duke, Prince and Noble in Israel, Don Joseph Nasi of Blessed Memory."

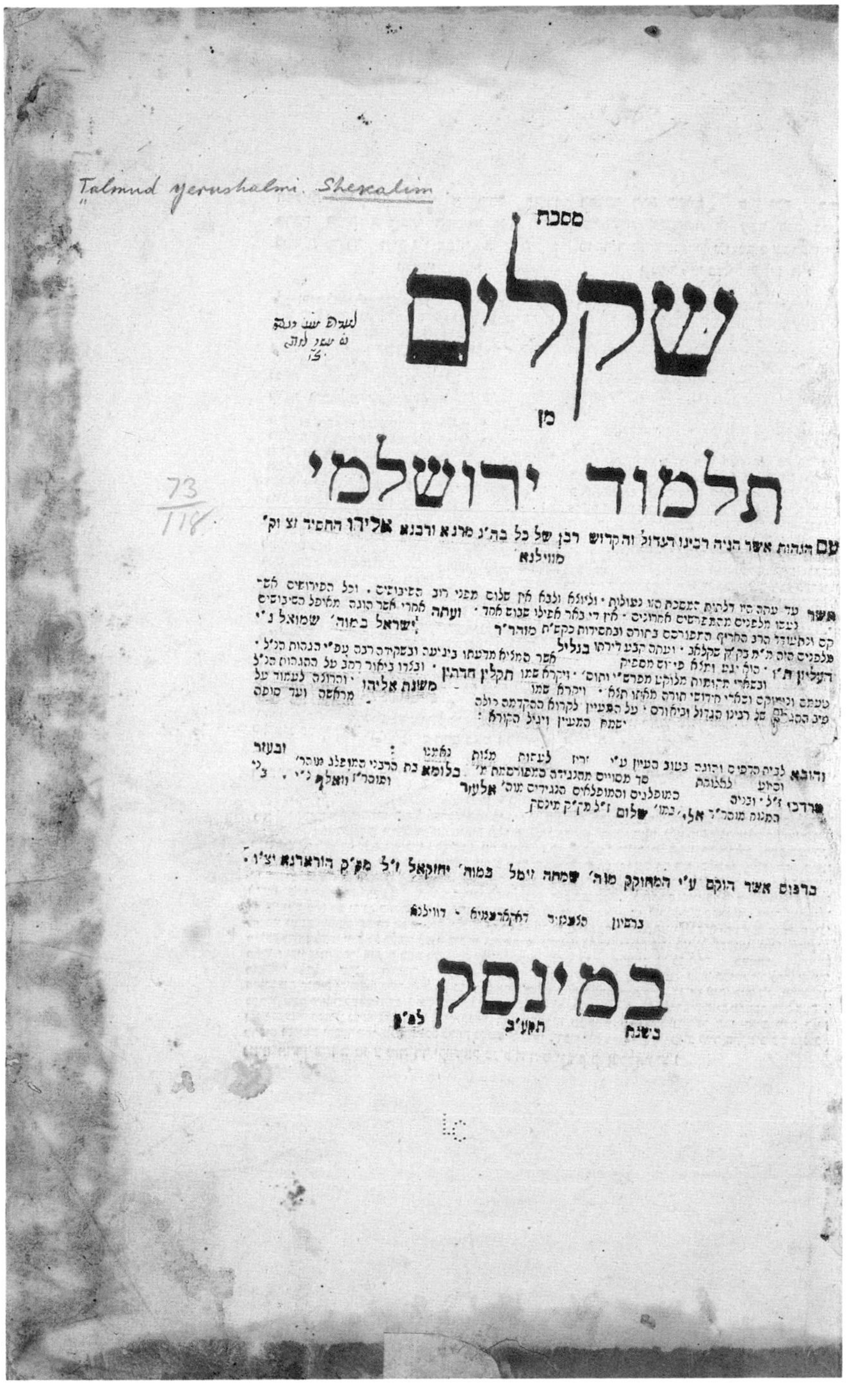
Talmud yerushalmi Shekalim

מסכת

שקלים

מן

תלמוד ירושלמי

במינסק

The tractate *Shekalim* of the Palestinian Talmud, with the commentary of Elijah, the Gaon of Vilna, prepared for the press by his student and disciple Israel ben Shmuel of Shklov, "now a resident of Upper Galilee [Safed]," and published with the "generous monetary aid of the noted philanthropist Bluma, daughter of Mordecai, and her sons."

Masekhet Shekalim, Minsk, 1812.
Hebraic Section.

More than two centuries later another woman patron, also a widow, Bluma daughter of Mordecai, widow of Eli ben Shalom, published a book in Minsk, Russia, in 1812. It is a commentary on the tractate *Shekalim* of the Palestinian Talmud, whose editor, Israel ben Shmuel of Shklov, is a resident of the Palestinian "Upper Galilee," i.e., the city of Safed. Like Doña Reyna, Bluma used a portion of her inheritance to become a patron of the Hebrew book, but unlike Doña Reyna, Bluma was a humble woman, unknown to history, except for this one act of pious philanthropy, which gained her some small measure of immortality.

WOMEN PRINTERS

Rachel, daughter of printer Isaac ben Judah Leib Katz, called Jeiteles, was a typesetter. She learned her craft in her father's house and, in 1691, set type for Moses Bloch, the printer in Sulzbach. The colophon of his edition of the *Hovot Ha-Levavot* (Duties of the Heart) by Bahya ben Joseph ibn Pakuda bears the colophon notation that she was one of two typesetters for the volume.

נעשה ונגמר על ידי הפועל במלאבת הקודש הזעצר אברהם בר אליעזר כ״ץ זצ״ל במדינת אשכנזי יצ״ו

נעשה ונגמר על ידי הפועלת הזעצרן רייכל בת כמר יצחק כ״ץ זצ״ל מהוקק ממשפחת הגרשוני מק״ק פירדא

Shown is the final line of the final page of *Hovot ha-Levavot* which records:

Done and completed by the typesetter Rachel, daughter of the late Isaac Katz, the printer, of the Gershuni family of Fürth.

Bahya ben Joseph ibn Pakuda, *Hovot ha-Levavot* (Duties of the Heart), Sulzbach, 1691.
Hebraic Section.

A contemporary younger colleague was Ella, daughter of the convert Moses the son of Abraham Our Father. Moses, native of Moravia, lived first in Prague, then in Amsterdam, where he converted to Judaism and worked there in Hebrew printing houses. In time he set up his own printing house in Amsterdam, then later in Berlin, Frankfort an der Oder, and Halle. Most of his ten sons and two daughters followed his trade. The elder of his daughters, Ella, set type with her brother for tractates of the great Frankfort an der Oder 1697–1700 edition of the Talmud, and it is so noted at the end of the tractate *Nidah*. The Library has a fine set of that edition. Ella began her work while yet a child, and a most touching colophon comes at the end of a prayer book published with a Yiddish translation in Dessau in 1696. In Yiddish rhyme, it reads:

> The type of the translations I set with my own hand, Ella, daughter of Moses from Holland. My years are no more than nine; of six children I am the only daughter. If you find an error in type, please remember, that it was set by a child.

She was still a child when she was typesetter for the Talmud two years later.

The above were chosen from the two hundred or so women, from the cradle days of the Hebrew book to the present, whose names appear on title pages as publishers or patrons, or in colophons as printers. Books were printed by women, and books were printed for women. We briefly note but few of the many in the Library's collections.

BOOKS FOR WOMEN

Professor Salo Baron has suggested that the best measure of the degree of a Jewish community's assimilation in its host culture is the extent of its use of the vernacular for sacred purposes. The publication of *Mitzvot Nashim* (Laws for Women) with an Italian translation in Padua in 1625, points to the high degree of Italian Jewry's cultural integration and linguistic assimilation at the beginning of the seventeenth century. The Library's volume would not only be of interest to the cultural historian, but

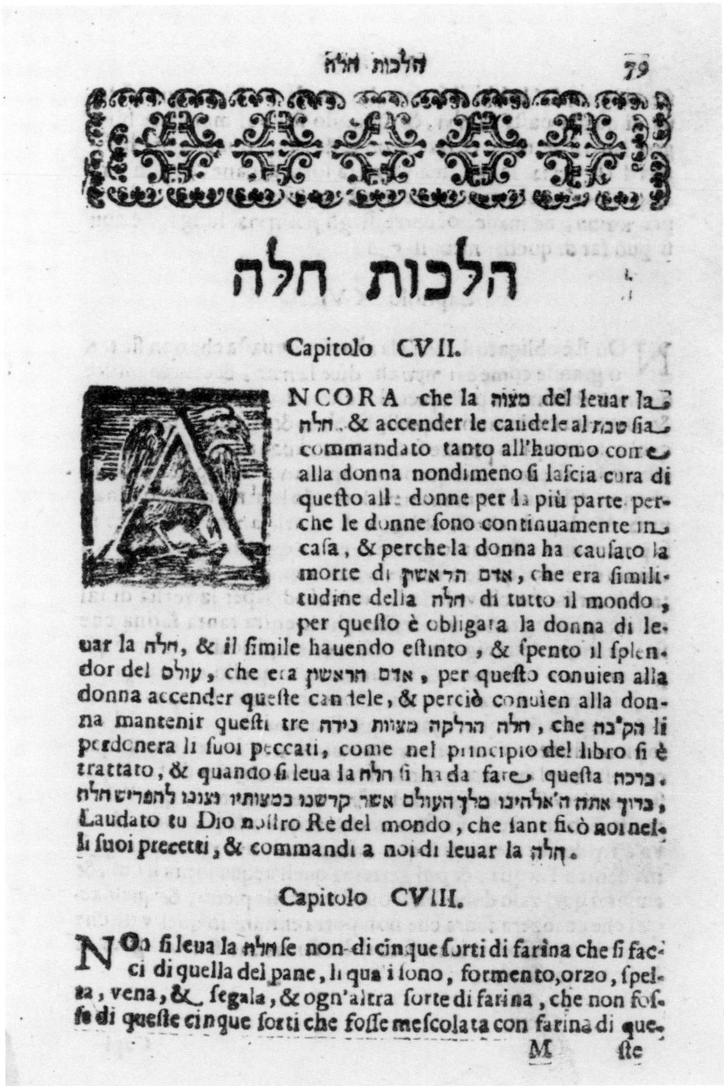

הלכות חלה 79

הלכות חלה

Capitolo CVII.

ANCORA che la מצוה del leuar la חלה, & accender le candele al שבת sia commandato tanto all'huomo come alla donna nondimeno si lascia cura di questo alle donne per la più parte perche le donne sono continuamente in casa, & perche la donna ha causato la morte di אדם הראשון, che era similitudine della חלה di tutto il mondo, per questo è obligata la donna di leuar la חלה, & il simile hauendo estinto, & spento il splendor del עולם, che era אדם הראשון, per questo conuien alla donna accender queste candele, & perciò conuien alla donna mantenir questi tre חלה הדלקה מצות נדה, che הק"בה li perdonera li suoi peccati, come nel principio del libro si è trattato, & quando si leua la חלה si ha da fare questa ברכה. ברוך אתה ה' אלהינו מלך העולם אשר קדשנו במצותיו וצונו להפריש חלה, Laudato tu Dio nostro Rè del mondo, che sant ficò noi nelli suoi precetti, & commandi a noi di leuar la חלה.

Capitolo CVIII.

NOn si leua la חלה se non di cinque sorti di farina che si facci di quella del pane, li quali sono, formento, orzo, spelta, vena, & segala, & ogn'altra sorte di farina, che non fosse di queste cinque sorti che fosse mescolata con farina di que-

M ste

An edition of an oft-printed handbook for Jewish women on the laws pertaining to the menstrual cycle, to Sabbath hallah (bread) preparation and candle lighting, and "becoming conduct," translated into Italian. This Padua, 1625 edition is dedicated to Signora Miriam of Montagnana. It is opened to the laws pertaining to the baking of Sabbath hallah.

Mitzvot Nashim (Laws for Women), Padua, 1625. Hebraic Section.

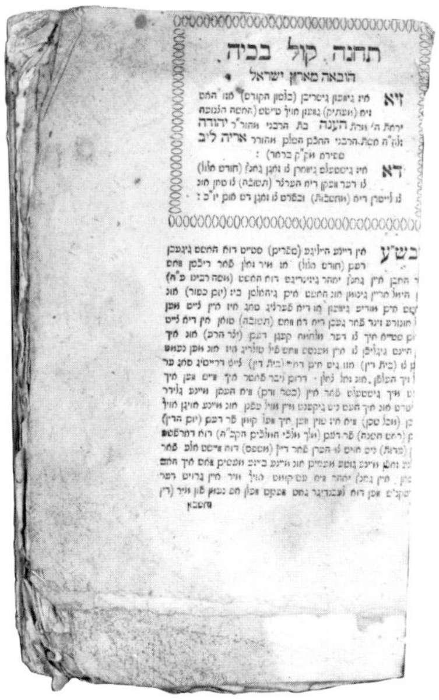

תחנה . קול בכיה .
הובאה מארץ ישראל

The Sound of Weeping is the name of this penitential prayer for women, originally composed in Hebrew and translated into Yiddish by Henna, daughter of Rabbi Judah and wife of Aryeh Leib Shapiro. Note that it was brought from the Land of Israel, the Holy Land, to be said in preparation for the High Holy Days, the Days of Awe.

Tehina Kol Bekhiya (A Penitential Prayer: The Sound of Weeping) n.p., n.d.
Hebraic Section.

מַחְזוֹר נָשִׁים
oder
Frauen-Machsor.

Cyklus der Festgebete
der Israeliten
in deutscher Sprache
mit hebräischem Texte für die Haupt- und Pflichtgebete.

Neu übersetzt und herausgegeben
von
Moritz Fränkel und Dr. G. Kleefeld,
bevorwortet
von
der wohllöbl. Rabbinats-Verwaltung zu Berlin.

Erster Theil:
Gebete für das Neujahr- und Versöhnungsfest,
מַחְזוֹר רֹאשׁ הַשָּׁנָה וְיוֹם כִּפּוּר.

Berlin, 1841.
Liebmann & Comp.

Title page of volume 1, "Prayers for the New Year and the Day of Atonement" of a *Frauen Machzor* (Holiday Prayer Book for Women) specially prepared for women, translated and published by Moritz Frankel and Dr. G. Kleefeld, with the approval of the Rabbinical Association of Berlin.

Frauen Machzor (Holiday Prayer Book for Women), Berlin, 1841.
General Collection.

would also be an important source for the historian of religion for a consideration of which laws are stressed and how the subtleties of translation might suggest the nature of the assimilation. It might also serve the student well to compare this collection with another published in Italy a century and a half later, also with an Italian translation, *Sefer Eshet Hayil* (Book for the Woman of Valor), Livorno, 1782.

A collection of tehinnot (penitential prayers) published in several places at various times, sewn together by a pious Jewish woman for her personal use, is an anthology of liturgical works written by women. Consider one, *Tehina Kol Bekhiya* (A Penitential Prayer: Sound of Weeping), "brought from the Land of Israel." The prayer is in Yiddish. "Written in the Holy Tongue, it was translated by the God-fearing and virtuous Henna, daughter of Rabbi Judah, of blessed memory, wife of the rabbi and sage, Aryeh Leib Shapiro of the city Brod." It is to be said the whole month of Elul (the month preceding the High Holy Days) "to arouse the hearts to repentance and to purify the thoughts, and should be recited especially on the Day of Atonement":

> Lord of the Universe. In your holy books it is written that you have given us the month of Elul, so that we may repair what we have destroyed by sinning during the year. You took Moses, our teacher, peace be unto him, into heaven and kept him till the Day of Atonement, and informed him that the forty days [between the first day of Elul and the Day of Atonement] is a time when the sins of those who repent are forgiven. In these days I rise as one ready to do battle with the evil inclination, and I see myself as one who owes money and is brought to court, and the court grants him thirty days to help himself by paying the debt. Dear Father, if I would stand before an earthly tribunal, how my body would shiver, how my mouth would remain shut, how I would not be able to lift up my eyes. How much more so, when I stand on the Day of Atonement, on Yom Kippur, before the King of Kings, the Holy One, Blessed be He!

A simple, direct statement to a stern judge who is yet an intimate friend.

A liturgical publication of a different order is a *Frauen-Machzor* (Holiday Prayer Book for Women), published in Berlin, 1841. "Newly translated into German" and bearing the approbation of the Berlin Rabbinical Organization, it is in the proper, if staid language of public worship. Each of the above is appropriate to its audience: *The Sound of Weeping* for the unsophisticated pious Yiddish-speaking women of Eastern Europe, *Frauen-Machzor* for the wordly, linguistically assimilated ladies of the West.

The women's book par excellence, a retelling of the Pentateuchal narrative in Yiddish, made vivid by the use of midrashic tales and medieval commentaries, is the *Ze'enah U-re'enah* (Go Out and See). Written by Jacob ben Isaac Ashkenazi at the end of the sixteenth century, it has since gone through well over two hundred editions. (The second edition was published in Cracow in 1620; the place and date of the first edition are unknown.) It became standard reading for Jewish women in Central and Eastern Europe, who became acquainted with biblical tales and persons not through the Bible text but from this exegetical retelling of it. It was one of the very few religious books to have illustrated editions, and its woodcuts, especially those of the Sulzbach printings—the Library has both 1798 and 1836 illustrated editions—conveyed directly to generations of Jewish women who saw them, and children to whom they were shown, how people of the Bible looked and acted.

This illustrated Sulzbach edition of the *Ze'enah U-re'enah* (Go Out and See) is one of the very many printings of the retelling of the Humash narrative in Yiddish for women. The Bible text is simplified and enlivened by tales from the Midrash and medieval commentaries. Open to an illustration of Isaac blessing Jacob, with Rebecca, the wife and mother who manipulated both, looking on. In the far distance is the rejected son, Esau the hunter.

Ze'enah U-re'enah (Go Out and See), Sulzbach, 1836. Hebraic Section.

IN NINETEENTH-CENTURY AMERICA: WOMEN POETS

From women publishers, women patrons, and women printers we turn to women authors, and limit ourselves to one place, one time, and one genre of literature. In nineteenth-century America we may seek in vain for one Jewish male we might call a poet, but we do meet four women who gained distinction as poets: Penina Moise (1797–1880), Rebekah Hyneman (1812–1875), Minna Kleeberg (1841–1878), and Emma Lazarus (1849–1887).

Penina Moise

Born in 1797 in Charleston, S.C., then the largest Jewish community in America, Penina Moise lived there the rest of her life. After her father died when she was twelve, she had no further formal education; nevertheless, she persisted in study and reading and soon turned to writing. Self-taught, she became a widely published writer, her poems and sketches appearing in the Washington *Union,* New York's *The Home Journal,* Boston's *Daily*

Facing page: *Fancy's Sketch Book* is the name the Charleston poet, Penina Moise, chose for her little book of poems. Five are of Jewish interest, "The Hero of Gilead," "Cain," "Joseph's Dream" on biblical themes, and two on the contemporary American Jewish scene, "On the Death of My Preceptor Isaac Harby, Esq.," and "To Persecuted Foreigners." Charleston newspaper editor Isaac Harby was the founder of the Reformed Society of American Israelites. The persecuted foreigners are her own people in the old world, whom she urges to come to the new, promising:

Oh, not as strangers shall your welcome be,
Come to the homes and bosoms of the free.

Penina Moise, *Fancy's Sketch Book,* Charleston, South Carolina, 1833.
Rare Book and Special Collections Division.

Times, the New Orleans *Commercial Times,* Isaac Leeser's *The Occident, Godey's Lady's Book,* and her hometown newspapers. Members of her large family intermarried and strayed from the faith, but for Penina her religion was the center of her life. For some time she was superintendent of Beth Elohim's Sunday School in Charleston, and after the Civil War, she joined her sister and niece in running a private school. By that time she had gone blind, but she continued her literary activity by dictating poems and essays to her niece.

Two books remain to bear witness to her gifts. A collection of her early poetry, *Fancy's Sketch Book,* was published in Charleston in 1833. Few copies have survived. Looking through the Library's copy, we find verses of general interest and a few of Jewish content, such as "The Hero of Gilead" and "On the Death of My Preceptor Isaac Harby Esq." A poem inviting those who seek freedom to come to these shores, "To Persecuted Foreigners," has a verse which speaks to her Jewish brethren:

If thou art one of that oppressed race,
Whose pilgrimage from Palestine we trace,
Brave the Atlantic—Hope's broad anchor weigh,
A Western Sun will gild your future days.

Her poems were soon forgotten, but her hymns continued to be sung. Of the 210 hymns in *Hymns Written for the Use of Hebrew Congregations,* Charleston, which, in the two years 1856 and 1857, went through four editions, 180 are by Penina Moise. A hymn "For the Sick" closes with:

Lengthen out the little span
    Of Thy worshipper, O Lord!
Nor, till I reform my plan,
    Cleave fore'er the vital cord.

As the dial's shadow turned
    At the pray'r of Judah's king;
Let not my appeal be spurned,
    Save me still Thy praise to sing.

In the eighty-third year of her life the vital cord was cloven fore'er. A stanza in one of Miss Moise's hymns might serve as her epitaph:

Lord! To Thee will I adhere
    Though condemned in grief to languish
Though the whole of my career
    May be spent in tears and anguish.
See I not a better land?
    Hold I not a Father's hand?

Rebekah Hyneman

Born in Philadelphia to a Jewish father and Christian mother, Rebekah Gumpert, raised in her father's faith, remained a devout Jew all her life. Following a business failure, her father had to take the family to Bucks County, where there were no facilities for formal education. Like Penina Moise, Rebekah acquired her literary background by individual study, mastering French and German, and later in life, Hebrew. She married Ben-

FANCY'S SKETCH BOOK.

BY

MISS PENINA MOISE.

> " 'Tis but to fill
> A certain portion of uncertain paper:
> Some liken it to climbing up a hill,
> Whose summit, like all hills, is lost in vapour."
>
> BYRON.

Charleston, S. C.
PUBLISHED AND PRINTED BY J. S. BURGES.
1833.

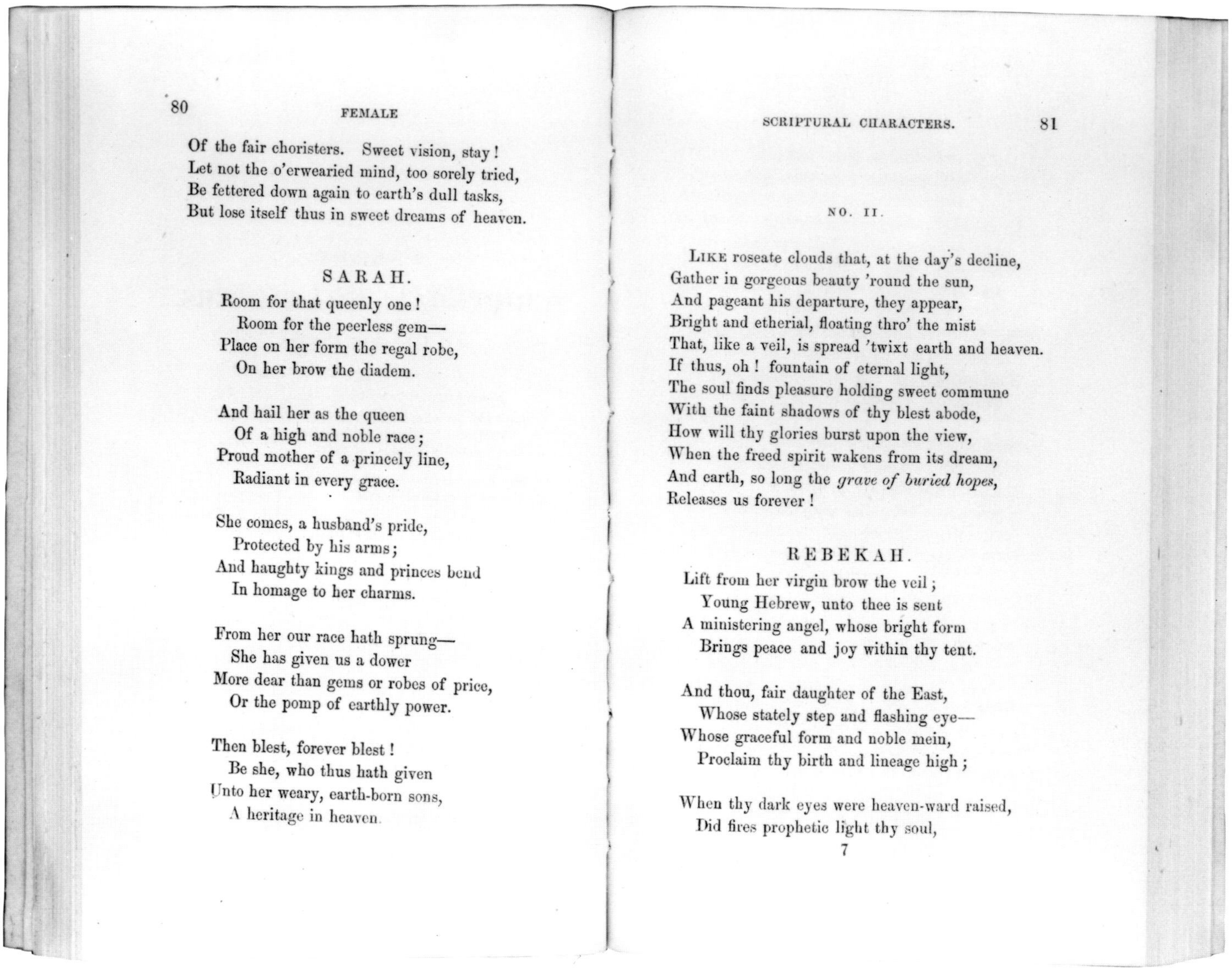

80 FEMALE

Of the fair choristers. Sweet vision, stay!
Let not the o'erwearied mind, too sorely tried,
Be fettered down again to earth's dull tasks,
But lose itself thus in sweet dreams of heaven.

SARAH.

Room for that queenly one!
Room for the peerless gem—
Place on her form the regal robe,
On her brow the diadem.

And hail her as the queen
Of a high and noble race;
Proud mother of a princely line,
Radiant in every grace.

She comes, a husband's pride,
Protected by his arms;
And haughty kings and princes bend
In homage to her charms.

From her our race hath sprung—
She has given us a dower
More dear than gems or robes of price,
Or the pomp of earthly power.

Then blest, forever blest!
Be she, who thus hath given
Unto her weary, earth-born sons,
A heritage in heaven.

SCRIPTURAL CHARACTERS. 81

NO. II.

LIKE roseate clouds that, at the day's decline,
Gather in gorgeous beauty 'round the sun,
And pageant his departure, they appear,
Bright and etherial, floating thro' the mist
That, like a veil, is spread 'twixt earth and heaven.
If thus, oh! fountain of eternal light,
The soul finds pleasure holding sweet commune
With the faint shadows of thy blest abode,
How will thy glories burst upon the view,
When the freed spirit wakens from its dream,
And earth, so long the *grave of buried hopes*,
Releases us forever!

REBEKAH.

Lift from her virgin brow the veil;
Young Hebrew, unto thee is sent
A ministering angel, whose bright form
Brings peace and joy within thy tent.

And thou, fair daughter of the East,
Whose stately step and flashing eye—
Whose graceful form and noble mein,
Proclaim thy birth and lineage high;

When thy dark eyes were heaven-ward raised,
Did fires prophetic light thy soul,
7

The first book of poems on Jewish themes was Rebekah Hyneman's *The Leper and Other Poems,* issued by the Jewish publisher and communal leader of Philadelphia, Abraham Hart. In her preface, the author proclaims "the very sincere love I bear for the faith of my adoption" (she having been born of a Jewish father but a Christian mother). That love is found on almost every page, especially in her series of twelve poems on "Female Scriptural Characters." The first two are on Sarah and Rebecca, of which our illustration offers a sampling.

Rebekah Hyneman, *The Leper and Other Poems,* Philadelphia, 1853.
General Collection.

jamin Hyneman, took his name and reaffirmed his faith as her faith; but when she was five years wed, mother of a son and expecting another child, her married life came to an end. Benjamin never returned from a business trip to the West. It was believed that he was murdered for the valuable jewelry he carried to sell. Rebekah never remarried and took to writing stories, a novelette entitled *Woman's Strength,* but most of all poems, many published in *The Occident.* In 1853 a collection of them, *The Leper and Other Poems,* was published in Philadelphia.

The love for her faith, its people, its holy days and holy places shines through her words. She writes of her biblical namesake:

When thy dark eyes were heaven-ward raised,
Did fires prophetic light thy soul,
And point to thee the weary path,
Thy children tread to win their goal?

Deep in each earnest Jewish heart
Are shrined those memories of the past,
Memories that time can ne'er efface,
Nor sorrow's blighting wing o'ercast.

Of "Israel's Trust," she writes:

Borne down beneath insulting foes,
Defamed, dishonored, and oppressed,
Our country fallen and desolate,
Our name a by-word and a jest—

Still are we Thine—as wholly Thine
As when Judea's trumpets' tone
Breathed proud defiance to her foes,
And nations knelt before her throne.

We are Thine own; we cling to thee
As clings the tendril to the vine;
Oh! 'mid the world's bewildering maze,
Still keep us Thine, forever Thine!

Again and again, her life was scarred by tragedy. Early widowed, she also lost her two sons. Barton suffered long from a fatal disease; Elias Leon, who at twenty-eight volunteered for service in the Civil War, was captured and imprisoned in the dread Andersonville prison. In half a year, cruel treatment and starvation took its toll. These lines she wrote are a fitting epitaph:

Now let me die!
The bloom of earth has passed away—
Its pleasures pall, its flowers decay—
The hopes that lured with dazzling ray,
Low, withered lie.

Oh! placid sleep,
I sink at last in thy embrace;
My task is done—a weary race
Was mine on earth; let my resting-place
Be lone and deep.

Minna Kleeberg

When Minna Kleeberg arrived in the United States from her native Germany in 1866, she brought with her a reputation as a well-regarded poet. A year earlier she had gained wide recognition for her poem, "Ein Lied vom Salz," a powerful plea for the removal of the Prussian tax on salt. Her poetry expressed devotion to her faith and a passion for social justice.

Daughter of a physician, she received as fine an education as a girl could obtain in mid-nineteenth-century Germany. After her marriage to Rabbi L. Kleeberg, her poetry turned to liturgical creations, while continuing to serve as a vehicle for social expression. Her poetry appeared in a variety of German-language periodicals in Germany and in the United States. Most of her poems were lyrical, some topical—urging the emancipation of women, calling for the broadening of democracy—and some liturgical. A gathering of her poems, *Gedichte*, was published in 1877 in Louisville, where her husband was serving as rabbi.

Minna Kleeberg was best known to the American Jewish community for her hymns which appeared in the most widely used Jewish hymnal in nineteenth-century America, Isaac M. Wise's *Hymns, Psalms and Prayers, In*

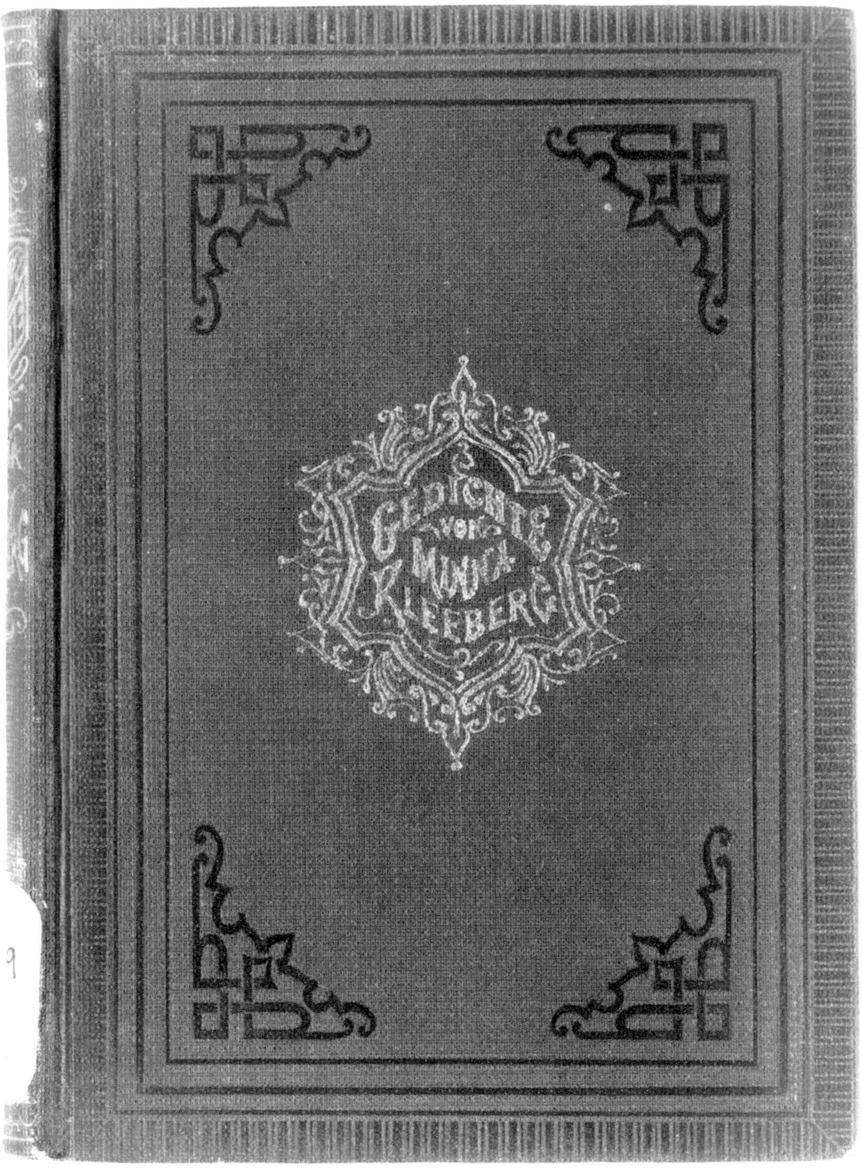

A poet on two continents was Minna Kleeberg, who gained some renown in her native Germany, and again in America where she relocated with her husband, Rabbi Louis Kleeberg. Her book of poems, *Gedichte*, was published in Louisville, 1877, where her husband was serving as rabbi. She was better known in her adopted country for her liturgical poems. Ten hymns in German, the largest number by any poet, appear in Isaac M. Wise's *Hymns, Psalms and Prayers*, Cincinnati, 1868.

Minna Kleeberg, *Gedichte*, Louisville, 1877.
General Collection.

Facing page:
Almost the entire second volume of *The Poems of Emma Lazarus* is devoted to Jewish poems. Among these are evocations of deeply felt Jewish sentiments, passionate cries for the renewal of the Jewish national spirit and translations from medieval Jewish poets Solomon Ibn Gabirol, Judah ha-Levi, and Moses Ibn Ezra. Certainly the most gifted and best known American Jewish literary figure of the nineteenth century, her essays on Jewish themes are no less important than her poetry.

(Emma Lazarus) *The Poems of Emma Lazarus*, 2 volumes, New York (1889).
Rare Book and Special Collections Division.

English and German (Cincinnati, 1868). Ten German hymns by Minna Kleeberg form the largest number by any poet. They celebrate the Torah, man, faith, and the holidays.

Less than two years after settling in New Haven, to which her husband had been called, she breathed her last on the last day of 1878. In his eulogy for his dear departed wife, Rabbi Kleeberg recalled:

> Almost from her childhood she complained of the subordinate position which tradition and custom assigned to woman. Upon her thirteenth birthday and the following Sabbath she shed bitter tears that she was not, like Jewish boys of her own age, entitled to take part in the public reading of the law, and by this rite be solemnly consecrated to the cause of Israel . . . The vindictive accusations of Richard Wagner . . . she met in a widely circulated paper, with a few bristling articles. Her poetical effusions, as well as her bold and vigorous defence of her co-religionists, were acknowledged by many letters of appreciation from all quarters, even from the other side of the ocean. The Crown Prince of Prussia, the Chancellor Bismarck, Edward Lasker . . . The departed was a poet by the grace of God.

Emma Lazarus

The leading Jewish literary figure by far in nineteenth-century America was the poet Emma Lazarus. Her sonnet, "The New Colossus," engraved on the base of the Statue of Liberty, has assured her a measure of immortality. More will be said of her later.* For now, let the stanza of one of her

*See p. 277 ff.

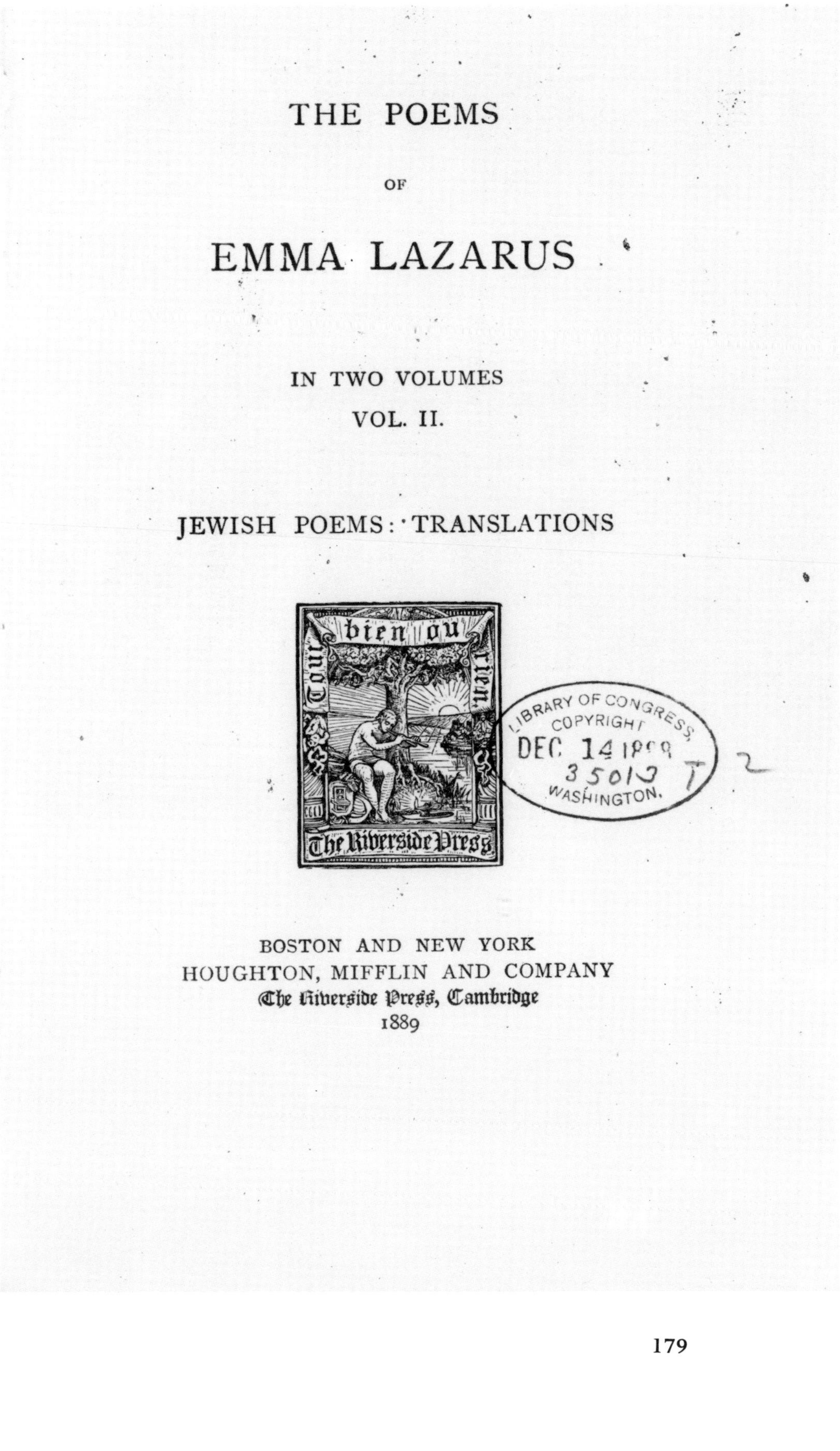

THE POEMS

OF

EMMA LAZARUS

IN TWO VOLUMES

VOL. II.

JEWISH POEMS: TRANSLATIONS

BOSTON AND NEW YORK
HOUGHTON, MIFFLIN AND COMPANY
The Riverside Press, Cambridge
1889

poems suffice, a poem for the New Year 5643 (1882–83), which saw the onset of Jewish immigration from Eastern Europe to Palestine and to America:

> In two divided streams the exiles part,
> One rolling homeward to its ancient source,
> One rushing sunward with fresh will, new heart.
> By each the truth is spread, the law unfurled,
> Each separate soul contains the nation's force,
> And both embrace the world.

10

"ENTHRONED ON PRAISES"

THE POWER OF PRAYER IS expressed in the metaphor of God "enthroned on the praises of Israel." Prayers of petition invoke His presence; paeans of praise establish it. Both forms of prayer are found in the Bible. At the Red Sea, the Children of Israel proclaimed God's saving power:

> I will sing unto the Lord for He has
> triumphed gloriously;
> Horse and rider has He hurled into the
> sea.
> The Lord is my strength and my song;
> He has become my salvation.
> This is my God, and I will praise Him,
> My father's God, and I will exalt Him.
> Exodus, 15:1–2

Hannah, longing for a child, "prayed to the Lord, and wept bitterly":

> Oh Lord of Hosts, if thou wilt take
> notice of my troubles and remember me,
> if thou wilt not forget me and grant
> me a son, I will give him to the Lord
> for all the days of his life.
> Samuel, 1:11

Granted a child, who was to become the Prophet Samuel, the mother offered this prayer:

> My heart rejoices in the Lord,
> Through Him, I hold my head high
> There is none except thee,
> None so holy as the Lord
> No rock like our God . . .
>
> He will guard the footsteps of his
> faithful
> But the wicked will sink into silence
> For not by might shall a man prevail . . .
> The Lord is judge to the ends of earth.
> Samuel, 2:1,2,9,10

The Psalms contain prayers of both public praise and private petition, exalting a just yet merciful God, calling upon His justice, pleading for His mercy. Prayers accompanied the sacrificial rites in the Temple, and prayers and scripture readings became the form of worship in the synagogue. The rubric of the synagogue liturgy, blessings, prayers, and scripture was ordained by the rabbis in late antiquity. Rav Amram (d. c. 875) laid out the order of prayer for the entire year in his prayer book *Seder Rav Amram*, as did also Maimonides in his *Mishneh Torah*.

Though the prayer book was unitary and always in the Holy Tongue, its versions were various. At the heart were the rabbinically ordained Eighteen Benedictions (seven on the Sabbath) and the Shema, "Hear O Israel," verses of the Bible. Local custom added benedictions, psalms, piyyutim (prayer poems), and special prayers. Unlike the Bible which, viewed as the word of God, was a text admitting of no alteration, the prayer book, as the creation of the Jewish people, was open to variation and particularly to addition.

The rubric of prayer has remained constant, a few changes taking place in the order of prayers and the text. The most pronounced changes which took place over centuries were in augmenting the liturgy to reflect local religious usage and communal interests. History and geography played their role in creating variety in prayer books. This variety has an overarching unity, a basic unified text and order, but there is as well a division of rite: Ashkenazi and Sefardi; Romaniot (Byzantine) and Roman; and such localized versions as those of Avignon, Carpentras, Catalonia, Aragon, Yemen, Aleppo, and Cochin. Communities favored liturgical works by native sons, partly out of communal pride, but also because such liturgy often commemorated historic events in the life of the particular community—from martyrdom to miraculous saving. Prayers for specific monarchs appear in a number of prayer books, and in the case of the Avignon rite, special prayers for the Pope! In recent centuries, translations of the Hebrew prayers into the vernacular have added to the variety.

The many siddurim (daily and Sabbath prayer books), mahzorim (holiday prayer books), Selihot (penitential prayers), tikkunim (prayers and texts for study for special occasions) on the shelves of the Library of Congress illustrate the richness of Jewish liturgical creativity. Three groups are especially worthy of note: some early printed prayer books; the liturgy in translations; and liturgical works commemorating special historical events.

SOME EARLY PRINTED PRAYER BOOKS

As in so many beginnings in Hebrew printing, the Soncinos were first again. The Soncino family printed the first complete Hebrew Bible and the first tractates of the Talmud, and in the first month of the year 5246 AM (September 10–October 9, 1485), *B'nai Soncino* (the Sons of Soncino) began the printing of the first Hebrew prayer book, *Mahzor Minhag Roma* (A Prayer Book of the Roman Rite), in the city of Soncino. In the Ashkenazi tradition, a mahzor contains only holiday prayers; the Sefardim use the term mahzor to mean a prayer book containing the entire liturgy—daily,

This Roman rite prayer book, printed by Joshua Solomon Soncino in 1486, is one of the earliest published. Volume 2, containing the prayer for the High Holy Days, Rosh Hashanah (the New Year) and Yom Kippur (the Day of Atonement), is open to a penitential prayer in the fifth and final service of the Day of Atonement, *Ne'ilah* (the closing of the gates). It begins: "Thou stretcheth forth thy hand to the sinner, and thy right hand is open to receive the repentant." It is the only prayer printed in large type throughout. Could this have been done with Marranos in mind, those who had been forcibly converted but retained loyalty to the ancestral faith?

Mahzor Minhag Roma (A Prayer Book of the Roman Rite), Casalmaggiore, 1486.
Rare Book and Special Collections Division.

Sabbath, and holiday. The Soncino mahzor is such a comprehensive one and took almost a year to complete. Part of the reason it took so long was that in the process the press had to be moved—a sudden, forced move—to the town of Cassalmaggiore, where the mahzor was completed on "the second day of the week [i.e., Monday], the twentieth day of the month of Elul, in the year 5246 AM [August 21, 1486]." Of this edition David W. Amram wrote in his *The Makers of Hebrew Books in Italy:*

> A bulky volume is this first Soncino edition; found entire only when pieced together from stray fragments and pages by the care and knowledge of the booklover. It seems especially to have aroused the ire of the Inquisitors, for its destruction is almost complete; of the copies extant all bear traces of the hand of its foes, and torn pages still further defaced by the ink scrawl of the censors are eloquent in their silence.

The Library has a fine copy of Volume 2, the first Hebrew book printed in Cassalmaggiore. The censor's blotting out of words and phrases throughout the volume does not deface it; it adds a silent majesty to it, particularly so because the censor's ink has faded, while the printed letters he sought to erase endure in all their clarity.

The last of the five services of worship on the Day of Atonement, *Ne'i-lah,* a supplication, is printed in letters twice the normal size. One assumes this was done because this service is at twilight, and the editor-printer wanted to be sure it could be read—and because it is a message of hope. The prayer begins with:

> Thou stretchest forth thy hand to the wicked, and thy right hand is extended to receive those who repent . . .

and concludes with:

> Thou desirest the repentance of the wicked and not their death, as it is written: "Have I any desire, says the Lord, for the death of the wicked man? Would I not rather that he should mend his ways and live?"
>
> Ezekiel, 18:23

Thirty-five years later, Gershom Soncino printed a new edition of this mahzor, to which he added "penitential prayers, supplications and readings sweeter than honey." In it he reprints the colophon of the first edition written by his grandfather, Israel Nathan, "the father of all the Soncinos," who likened the mahzor he had published to a "ladder set up on earth whose top reaches unto heaven upon which we may ascend to supplicate our Maker, blessed be He." Gershom writes a colophon of his own, which concludes with:

> Praise be to God who has not withheld his Mercy from us. His left hand casts us off, but His right brings us nearer to him. So may He, in His mercies, sustain our souls and grant us life among those who do His will. This book was completed in the city of Rimini, which is under the dominion of Pope Leo X, may his glory be exalted, this 21st of March, corresponding to Nisan 13. Praise to the Lord, to whom blessing is due, and glory to His great Name.

Leo X was the most benevolent of pontiffs, whose reign was a happy one for the Jews. He permitted Elijah Levita to establish a Hebrew press in Rome, and Daniel Bomberg to print the Talmud. His benevolent attitude influenced the Ecclesiastical Council of Rimini to permit Gershom Soncino to establish a Hebrew press in that city, and Soncino is grateful for it.

Among the liturgical oddities in the Library is a pamphlet published in Venice, 1792, *A Prayer . . . in Ferrara . . . for the life of our sovereign king, the Pope.* The prayer, to be recited at every daily minha (afternoon service), except on the eve of the Sabbath or a holiday, is for Pope Pius VI. Of him Cecil Roth, in his article on popes in the *Encyclopaedia Judaica,* writes:

> Pius codified, reinforced, and intensified the whole of former, degrading anti-Jewish legislation, however barbarous it was, and went so far as to forbid Jews from passing the night outside the ghetto, under the pain of death.

A large pulpit-sized edition of the Roman rite mahzor was published in Bologna in 1540, accompanied by what was meant to be a popular commentary, as its author Johanan Treves explains:

> [I] did not invent anything, but gathered from existing authors . . . as the gleaner

איכה

Gershom Soncino, greatest of early Hebrew printers, issued a comprehensive prayer book marked by excellence of typography, page design and ornamentation, as was his wont. In his colophon, he notes that the city of Rimini, where he had set up his press, "is under the dominion of Pope Leo X," the benevolent Pope who permitted Elijah Levita to set up a press in Rome. Open to the service for *Tisha B'Av* (Ninth Day of Ab), the Fast Day commentary on the destruction of the Temple. Note the ornamentation surrounding the first word of the Book of Lamentations read that day.

Mahzor, Rimini, 1521.
Hebraic Section.

follows the harvester . . . I did not seek to produce fine flour, but flour made from roasted ears [in Aramaic *Kimha de-Avishuna,* the title of the work].

The Library of Congress copy was formerly in the Great Synagogue of Ferrara, as is indicated in manuscript on the ornate title page, and also noted on the first page.

An even larger, grander edition of the Ashkenazi mahzor, containing the liturgy for "the Sabbath, the Holidays, the New Month as well as for Purim, *Tisha B'Av* . . . the wedding ceremony and circumcision," was published in three large volumes in Venice in 1711. Its title page is ornate, in the grand Italian style. Its publishers, Joseph and Jacob Hai Cohen, announce that their prayer book is published for the congregations in Venice: the Ashkenazi, the Sefardi and the Italian; as well as for those of Padua, Rovigo, Verona, Mantua and Casale Monferrato, Gorizia, and their environs. The special authorizations are printed in very large letters on the first two pages; that of the Padua authorities stipulates that as many copies as were published in 1600 may now be published, and the other grants a copyright for twelve years. Approbation by leading rabbis affirms the

Volume 1 of the Bologna, 1540 edition of the Roman Rite Mahzor (Festival Prayer Book) contains the commentaries of Maimonides and Ovadiah Sforno. On the title page, the letters *bet, heh,* and *kof* written in the blank square at the top, are the initials of *B*et *Ha-K*enesset (the Synagogue); on the square below, "Ferrara." At the bottom of the printed words, the manuscript notation in large letters, "B'kehilla Kedosha Ferrara" (in the Holy Community Ferrara). On the page following, it states that this volume was bought by the Great Synagogue of Ferrara.

Mahzor Romi (Roman Rite Festival Prayer Book), Bologna, 1540.
Hebraic Section.

בעזרת ה' נורא ואדיר
שער בת רבים
מחזור חלק ראשון עם פירוש
הדרת קדש כמנהג קהל קדוש
אשכנזים ישמרם האל:
ובו שני המאורות המאור הגדול לממשלת
שבתות וימים טובים וראשי חדשים:
והמאור הקטן לממשלת זום ביומו ופורים· ותשעה באב· קנות· ציונים·
סליחות· נשואין· ומילה·
נדפס לתשוקת קהלות קדושות יצ"ו
שבמדינות איטלייאה· ואלו הן· ק"ק ויניציאה
אשכנזים· וק"ק ספרדים· וק"ק איטאלייאני·
וק"ק פאדובו'· וק"ק רווינו· וק"ק וירונה· וק"ק
מאנטובה'· וק"ק קסאל' מונפיראט·
וק"ק גוריציאה'· וכל גלילותיהם:
Nella Stamparia Bragadina:
Con Licenza de' Superiori.
Appresso Gioanni de' Paoli.
פה
ויניציאה
הבירה

This majestic pulpit prayer book containing all the prayers for all the services of the entire year was published in three volumes in Venice, to fulfill the needs of all the Italian Jewish communities and all the variety of rites. The publishers, having received the approbation of the Venice rabbinate, traveled from city to city seeking subscriptions and soliciting the financial aid of the wealthy "for the expenditure is great." To protect the rights of the publishers, the rabbinate forbade the publication of any other edition for twelve years.

Mahzor, Sha'ar Bat Rabim, Venice, 1711.
Hebraic Section.

twelve-year period during which no other editions may be published. The publishers had spent a huge sum of money for so grand a publication and wanted to protect their investment. The Library's copy, bound in parchment, is in such pristine condition that either it was handled with the greatest reverence or was little used.

A MINYAN IN THE VERNACULAR

Saadiah Gaon (882–942), the greatest of Babylonian scholars in the Geonic period, was a halakist, a philosopher, a grammarian, a Bible scholar, and a liturgist as well. Author of many highly praised piyyutim, some of which translated into Arabic were circulated throughout the Arabic-speaking Jewish world, he also compiled a comprehensive siddur containing prayers for the whole year. His *Kitāb Jamī al-Salawōt wa al-Tasebīh* (Collection of All Prayers and Praises) was written in Arabic, the first translation of the Hebrew prayer book into the vernacular. Since that tenth-century work, translations of "prayers and praises" into the vernacular have abounded. A brief sampling of ten of those in the Library's Hebraic Section follows:

1. *Orden de las Oraciones de Ros-Ashanah y Kipur,* London, 1740. The translation of the High Holy Days prayer book into Spanish is the work of Isaac Nieto (1687–1773), haham (rabbi) of the Sefardi community in London. Son of Haham David Nieto, he was in 1732 appointed to his late father's position. The translation is highly regarded for its literary style, as is that of the daily prayers, published in 1771.

A new translation of the prayer book for the High Holy Days in Spanish, for the Sefardi congregation in London, by its *Haham* (rabbi), Isaac Nieto.

Orden de Las Oraciones de Ros-Ashanah y Kipur, London, 1740.

General Collection.

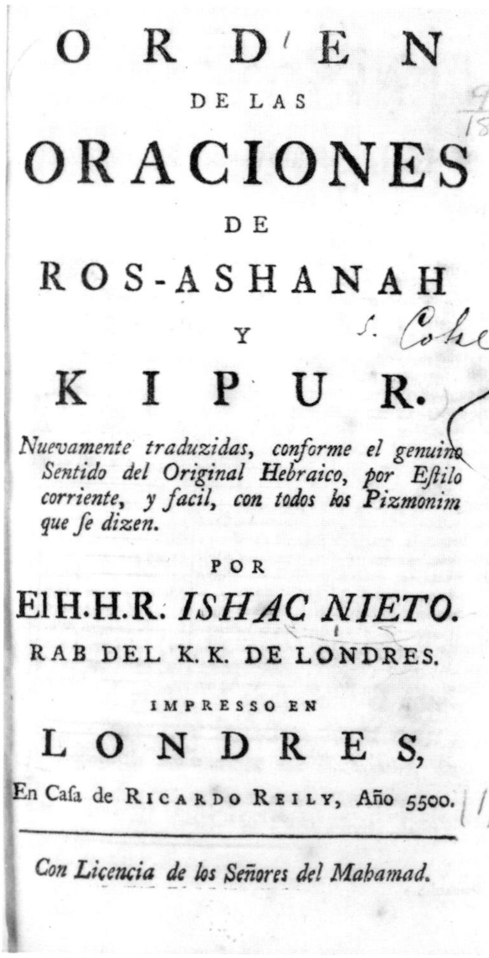

ORDEN
DE LAS
ORACIONES
DE
ROS-ASHANAH
Y
KIPUR.

Nuevamente traduzidas, conforme el genuino Sentido del Original Hebraico, por Eſtilo corriente, y facil, con todos los Pizmonim que ſe dizen.

POR

El H.H.R. *ISHAC NIETO.*

RAB DEL K.K. DE LONDRES.

IMPRESSO EN

LONDRES,

En Caſa de RICARDO REILY, Año 5500.

Con Licencia de los Señores del Mahamad.

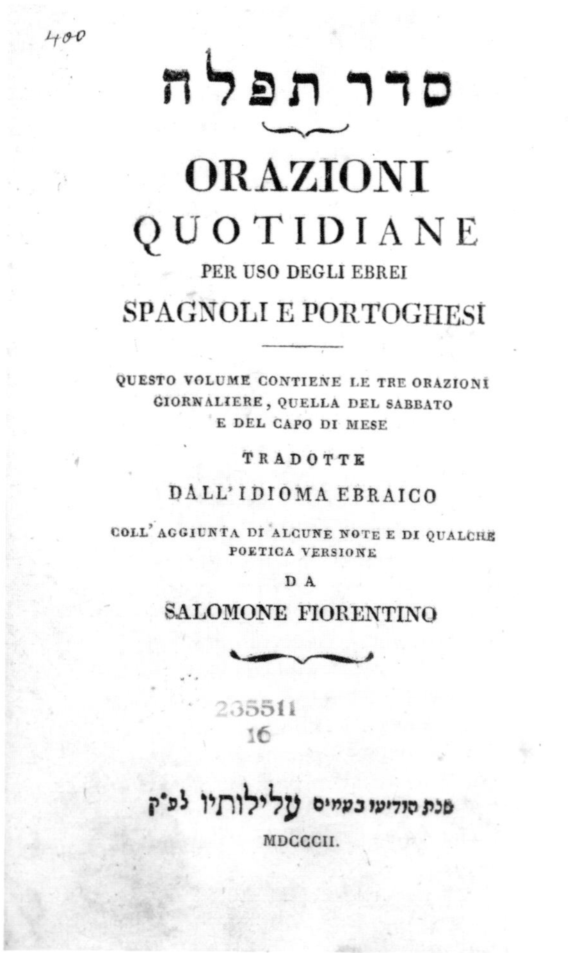

סדר תפלה

ORAZIONI
QUOTIDIANE
PER USO DEGLI EBREI
SPAGNOLI E PORTOGHESI

QUESTO VOLUME CONTIENE LE TRE ORAZIONI GIORNALIERE, QUELLA DEL SABBATO E DEL CAPO DI MESE

TRADOTTE
DALL' IDIOMA EBRAICO

COLL' AGGIUNTA DI ALCUNE NOTE E DI QUALCHE POETICA VERSIONE

DA
SALOMONE FIORENTINO

שנת הודיעו בעמים עלילותיו לפ״ק

MDCCCII.

Hebrew text and Italian translation by Solomone Fiorentino, of the Daily and Sabbath prayer book, "for use by the Spanish and Portuguese Jews," i.e., the Sefardi rite. Though by 1802, the date of publication of this prayer book, there had been no Jews in Spain and Portugal for more than three centuries, the descendants of those exiled from those countries still retained their "place of origin" identities.

Orazioni Quotidiane, Basel, 1802.

Hebraic Section.

2. The first translation of the prayer book into English was as part of a work on Jewish ceremonies, the *Book of the Religion, Ceremonies and Prayers of the Jews,* London, 1738, by the apostate Abraham Mears, who used the pseudonym Gamliel ben Pedahzur. It was not intended for liturgical use, so it is not in effect a prayer book. That distinction belongs to an American edition, of which the first part, *Evening Service of Roshashanah and Kippur,* appeared in New York, in 1761, followed five years later by *Prayers for Shabbath, Rosh-Hashanah and Kippur.* The translator was Isaac Pinto, who published the translation only. The Hebrew text with translation by B. Meyers and A. Alexander was published in London in 1770, soon followed by Alexander's translations of the entire Ashkenazi and Sefardi liturgies in a stilted, pedestrian English. The Library displays *Seder Tefilot Sukkot* (The Tabernacles Service), London, 1775.

3. Solomone Fiorentino (1743–1815), an Italian poet of sufficient merit to be appointed court poet by Grand Duke Ferdinand III, taught Italian literature at the Jewish Academy in Leghorn and published, in 1802, *Seder Tefillah* (Order of Prayer), a Hebrew text with an Italian translation of the Sefardi daily and Sabbath prayer book which he called *Orazioni Quotidiane per uso degli Ebrei Spagnoli e Portoghesi.* In the same year there appeared an Italian translation by Samuel Romanelli of the prayers for the Sabbath according to the Sefardi rite, but without the Hebrew text.

4. For a German translation, we have chosen the first edition of the first Reform prayer book for public worship, *Seder ha-Avodah . . . Minhag Kehal Bayit Hadash* (Order of Service . . . According to the Rite of the New Temple Congregation), titled in German *Ordnung der Oeffentlichen Andacht . . . nach dem Gebrauche des Neuen Tempel-Vereins,* Hamburg, 1819. Edited by S. I.

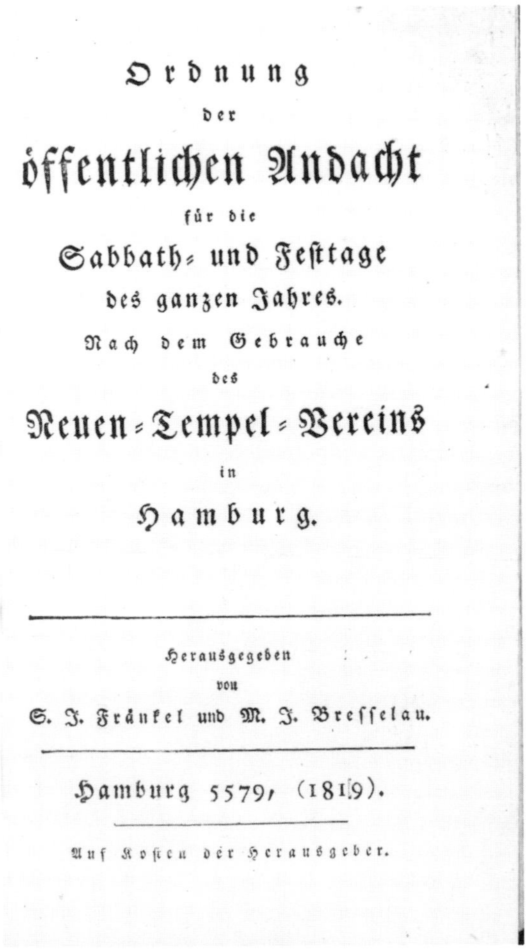
Ordnung
der
öffentlichen Andacht
für die
Sabbath- und Festtage
des ganzen Jahres.
Nach dem Gebrauche
des
Neuen-Tempel-Vereins
in
Hamburg.

Herausgegeben
von
S. J. Fränkel und M. J. Bresselau.

Hamburg 5579, (1819).

Auf Kosten der Herausgeber.

Edited by S. I. Frankel and I. M. Bresslau for the newly established reform congregation in Hamburg. Unlike all the other prayer books we show, this was not a translation but a reordering of the liturgy, and unlike the others, it is paginated from left to right, indicating that its basic language was German, not Hebrew.

Ordnung der Oeffentlichen Andacht . . . (Order of Service . . .), Hamburg, 1819.
Hebraic Section.

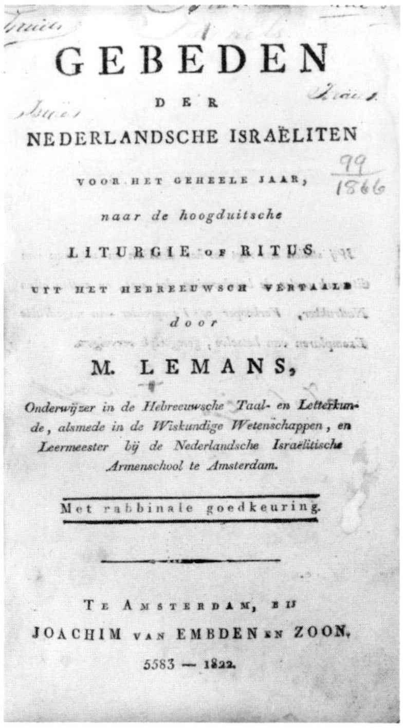
GEBEDEN
DER
NEDERLANDSCHE ISRAËLITEN
VOOR HET GEHEELE JAAR,
naar de hoogduitsche
LITURGIE OF RITUS
UIT HET HEBREEUWSCH VERTAALD
door
M. LEMANS,
Onderwijzer in de Hebreeuwsche Taal- en Letterkunde, alsmede in de Wiskundige Wetenschappen, en Leermeester bij de Nederlandsche Israëlitische Armenschool te Amsterdam.
Met rabbinale goedkeuring.
TE AMSTERDAM, BIJ
JOACHIM VAN EMBDEN EN ZOON.
5583 — 1822.

Prayer book translated into Dutch by Moses Lemans, educator, author, translator, and mathematician. He served as headmaster of the school for the children of needy Jews in Amsterdam, compiled a Hebrew-Dutch dictionary, and translated the Bible into Dutch.

Gebeden der Nederlandsche Israeliten (Prayer Book for the Israelites of the Netherlands), Amsterdam, 1822. Hebraic Section.

Frankel and I. M. Bresslau, this prayer book was paginated from left to right, the Hebrew text was abridged and changed, and all references to a return to Zion and a restoration of Temple worship were altered or eliminated. The prayer book was severely criticized by the Hamburg rabbinate and publicly denounced in its synagogues.

5. The Dutch translation of Moses Lemans (1785–1832)—a Hebraist, mathematician, and long-time headmaster of Amsterdam's first school for boys of indigent parents—*Gebeden der Nederlandsche Israeliten* (Prayer Book for the Israelites of the Netherlands) was published in Amsterdam in 1822 with "rabbinic approval." The traditional Ashkenazi prayer book, it has a Hebrew text and vernacular translation.

6. The first printing of the Hebrew prayer book with a French translation appeared in Metz in 1827. Previous translations of the Sefardi liturgy by Marduchee Venture and of the Ashkenazi daily prayers by D. Drach were published without the Hebrew text. The Metz edition, *Rituel Des Prières Journaliènes,* has the Hebrew text with a translation by Joel Anspach, the only brother of Philippe Anspach, who, as deputy attorney general, counselor at the Court of Appeals and the Court of Cassation in Paris, was the first Jew to serve in the supreme magistracy of France.

7. *Atirot Yeshurun* or *Israel Fomaszai* (Prayers of Israel), the Hebrew text with Hungarian translation by Herman Fekete, was edited by Moricz Rosenthal and published in Posony (Bratislava or Pressburg) in 1846. The midnineteenth century saw the confrontation between the Orthodox and liberal religious forces in Hungary. This translation was a product of those who advocated modernity in language, culture, and way of life, yet it was published in Posony, the center of Orthodoxy in Hungary and the seat of Rabbi Moses Sofer, leader of the traditionalist forces.

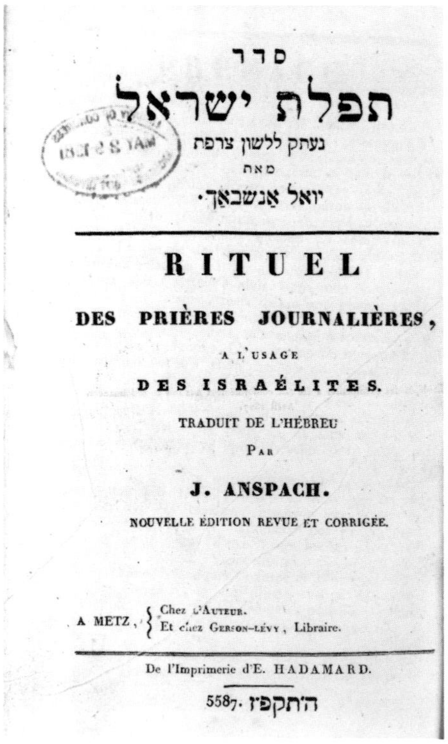
סדר
תפלת ישראל
נעתק ללשון צרפת
מאת
יואל אנשבאך.
RITUEL
DES PRIÈRES JOURNALIÈRES,
A L'USAGE
DES ISRAÉLITES.
TRADUIT DE L'HÉBREU
PAR
J. ANSPACH.
NOUVELLE ÉDITION REVUE ET CORRIGÉE.
A METZ, Chez l'Auteur. Et chez Gerson-Lévy, Libraire.
De l'Imprimerie d'E. HADAMARD.
5587. התקפ״ז

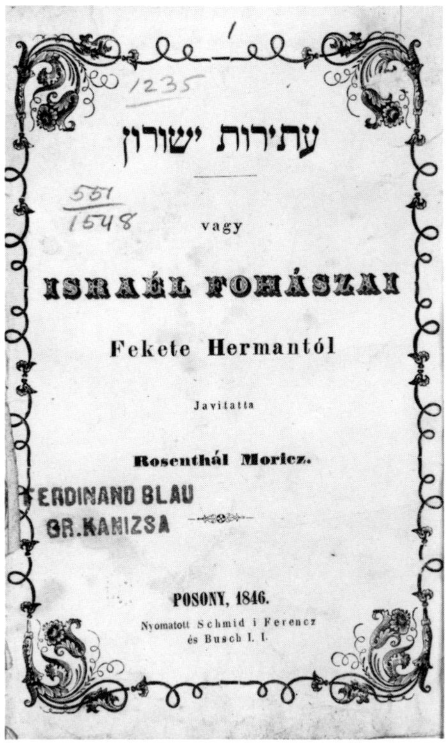
עתירות ישורון
vagy
ISRAÉL FOHÁSZAI
Fekete Hermantól
Javitatta
Rosenthál Moricz.
FERDINAND BLAU
GR.KANIZSA
POSONY, 1846.
Nyomatott Schmid i Ferencz és Busch I. I.

Left: The translation of this "new edition, reviewed and corrected," is by Joel Anspach. The prayer for the government is not the usual one, "Thou who givest dominion to kings," but an invocation for the monarch, Charles X, King of France and Navarre, followed by six special blessings to which the congregation responds "Amen!"

Rituel Des Prières Journalières (Ritual for Daily Worship), Metz, 1827. Hebraic Section.

Right: The translation of this prayer book into Hungarian by Herman Fekete was edited by Moricz Rosenthal and published in 1846 in Pressburg, a center of orthodoxy in Hungary.

Atirot Yeshurun, Israel Fomaszai (Prayer of Israel), Posony (Pressburg, Bratislava), 1846. Hebraic Section.

8. *Tefilot Yisrael* (Prayers of Israel), "Translated for the First Time into the Russian Language," as its subtitle proclaimed, appeared in Warsaw in 1869. Its translator was Joseph Hurwitz, a well-regarded poet who was then serving as the *Kazyonny Ravvin* (Official Rabbi) of the city of Grodno. Though this office was imposed upon the Jews by the Czarist government from 1857 to 1917, its occupants were never accepted as spiritual leaders by the Jewish community. A variety of individuals, some admired and respected, but most no more than tolerated, held the office, among them a foremost authority on the history of the Jewish legal tradition, Chaim Tchernowitz in Odessa, the Zionist leader Shemaryahu Levin in Grodno, and famed Yiddish author Shalom Aleichem in Lubny.

Though the government defined their function, "to supervise public prayers and religious ceremonies," most were no more than keepers of vital statistics; but others made significant contributions to communal well-being and cultural creativity. Joseph Hurwitz no doubt felt that he was serving both through his translation of the prayer book into the vernacular.

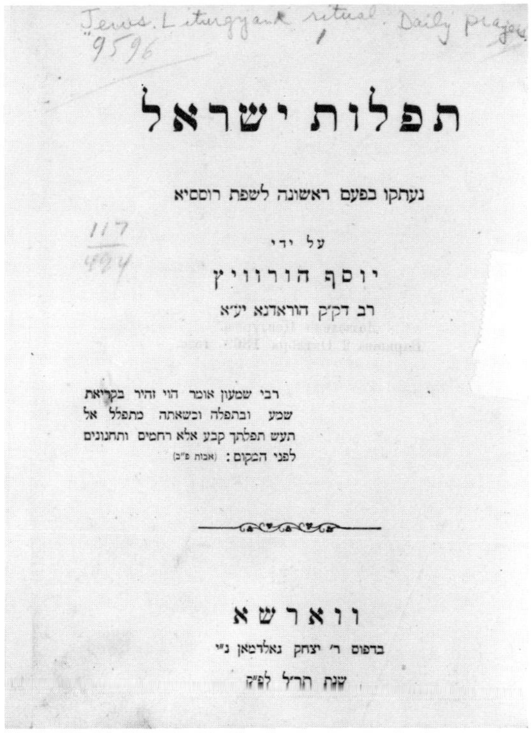
תפלות ישראל

נעתקו בפעם ראשונה לשפת רוססיא

על ידי

יוסף הורוויץ

רב דק"ק הוראדנא יע"א

רבי שמעון אומר הוי זהיר בקריאת שמע ובתפלה וכשאתה מתפלל אל תעש תפלתך קבע אלא רחמים ותחנונים לפני המקום: (אבות פ"ב)

ווארשא

בדפוס ר' יצחק גאלדמאן נ"י

שנת תר"ל לפ"ק

Not till 1869 was the prayer book translated into Russian, because Russian Jewry, which was by far the largest Jewish community in the world, was also the most traditional. The translation which it found useful was the Yiddish and that, as is often stated in Yiddish translations of sacred texts, was for "women and the young." The translation was published in Warsaw, the capital of the Polish provinces of the Russian Empire, which was the place of residence of the majority of its Jews. The translator was Joseph Hurwitz, the *Kazyonny Ravvin*, the governmentally appointed rabbi of Grodno.

Tefilot Yisrael (Prayers of Israel), Warsaw, 1869. General Collection.

9. *The Jewish Propitiatory Prayers. Or A Prayer for the Forgiveness of Sins.* It was translated from Hebrew into Marathi by Joseph Ezekiel Rajpurker, teacher in David Sassoon's Benevolent Institution; published by the Bene-Israel Improvement Society, Bombay, and printed at Gunput Krushnajee's Press, 5619 (=1859).

This is the first of the more than twenty Rajpurker translations of Hebrew liturgical works into Marathi. At the time of publication, he was a teacher at the school which the Iraqui-Indian merchant and philanthropist David Sassoon had established for the Bene-Israel. The origins of this ancient community of Jews is clouded in legend. By the time it came to the attention of world Jewry at the end of the eighteenth century, its cultural assimilation in dress, language, and way of life was almost complete. The community, however, retained its distinctive religious identity and, with the help of Near-Eastern Jews who settled in Bombay in the nineteenth century, became reunited with world Jewry. During that century, Joseph Ezekiel Rajpurker (1834–1905) was its leading scholar and teacher. For forty years he served as the principal of the Sassoon School, and in 1871 he was appointed Hebrew examiner at the University of Bombay.

The Library's copy once belonged to Rabbi Henry Cohen of Galveston, Texas.

10. An even more exotic community of Jews were the Falashas of Ethiopia. Like the Bene-Israel, they traced their origins to biblical days, and their assimilation was even more complete. Yet here, too, a distinct religious identity persisted in observances of Sabbath, holidays, dietary and purity laws, and the use of liturgy. In 1868 French orientalist and Hebrew writer Joseph Halévy (1827–1917) was sent to Ethiopia by the Alliance Israélite Universelle to study the Falashas. He affirmed their Jewishness and translated their liturgy from Ge'ez into Hebrew, publishing *Seder tefilot ha-Falashim* (Order of Prayers of the Falashas) in Paris in 1876. Like their neighbors, the Falashas spoke Amharic but their sacred texts are in the ancient Ge'ez.

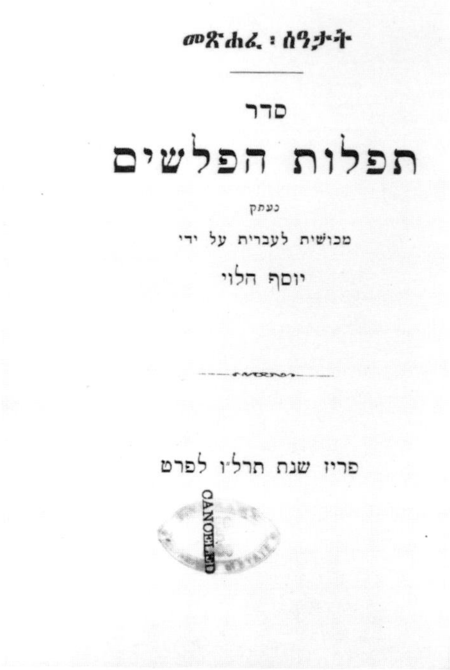
መጽሐፈ ፡ ሰዓታት

סדר

תפלות הפלשים

נעתק

מכושית לעברית על ידי

יוסף הלוי

פריז שנת תרל"ו לפרט

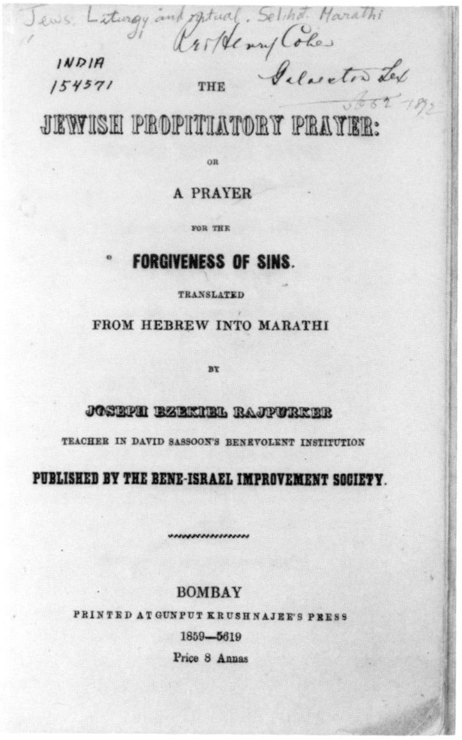
INDIA
154571

THE

JEWISH PROPITIATORY PRAYER:

OR

A PRAYER

FOR THE

FORGIVENESS OF SINS.

TRANSLATED

FROM HEBREW INTO MARATHI

BY

JOSEPH EZEKIEL RAJPURKER

TEACHER IN DAVID SASSOON'S BENEVOLENT INSTITUTION

PUBLISHED BY THE BENE-ISRAEL IMPROVEMENT SOCIETY.

BOMBAY

PRINTED AT GUNPUT KRUSHNAJEE'S PRESS

1859—5619

Price 8 Annas

Left: Unlike the other prayer books which were translated from Hebrew into the vernacular, this prayer book was translated by the French scholar Joseph Halévy into Hebrew from its original Ge'ez, the sacred language of the Falasha Jews of Ethiopia.

Seder Tefilot ha-Falashim (Order of Prayers of the Falashas), Paris, 1876.
Hebraic Section.

Right: Joseph Ezekiel Rajpurker, a teacher in David Sassoon's Benevolent Institution in Bombay, India, translated more than twenty liturgical works into Marathi, of which this was the first. The ownership inscription is that of Henry Cohen, Galveston's famed rabbi.

The Jewish Propitiatory Prayer, Bombay, 1859.
Hebraic Section.

IN CELEBRATION AND COMMEMORATION

Throughout its long history, the synagogue commemorated historical events at regular and special services, and persons of note were honored with liturgical odes. The liturgy collection of the Library's Hebraic Section is rich in such special commemoration and celebration publications.

An aesthetically pleasing order of service, *Simhat Mitzvah* (Joy of the Commandment), celebrating the dedication of its new synagogue, was issued by the Italian congregation (the other was the Spanish and Portuguese) of Florence in 1793. On page four of the publication we note the presence of a choir and musicians, and special directions to their leader. This is a representative publication of the many others which celebrated dedications of synagogues, schools, orphanages, homes for the aged, and other communal institutions.

Of greater historical significance are the many special services, poems, and prayers published in praise or memory of non-Jewish persons of power—some, like Pope Leo X, deserving of Jewish praise; some, like Pope Pius VI, not. Maria-Theresa, honored by one of the most beautiful of liturgical publications, was surely unworthy of the praise showered upon her; while her son, Joseph II, Holy Roman Emperor and ruler of Austria and the north Italian provinces, was. In 1781 he abolished the Jew's badge, rescinded the poll tax, and issued his *Toleranzpatent*, providing for gradual elimination of restrictions against Jews and allowing them to enter the broader political and cultural life of his domains. "Toleration" was not granted but imposed, for in return it demanded a too rapid assimilation on the part of the Jews in the life of the society at large. Joseph II's attitude towards the Jews was that of a benevolent despot; to him they were human beings, consumers, and tax payers, useful, if kept in check. Jews were still confined to ghettoes, restricted in marriage rights, and forbidden to hold office; but the most humiliating edicts were removed, and opportunities for participation in educational and economic life were expanded.

In 1789 the Jewish community of Mantua seized the opportunity to express its gratitude to Joseph II by celebrating his army's success in the siege of Belgrade. It took the form of an elegant publication, *L'Elohei M'uzim Roni Todot* (To the Lord of Might Sing Gratitude), prayers and poems in Hebrew with Italian translation by Azriel Isaac Levi, rabbi and scribe of the Mantuan community, Rabbi Solomon Norsa, scion of one of the city's leading families, and Rabbi Abraham Cologna, who later gained fame as vice-president of the Sanhedrin convened by Napoleon in 1807.

Napoleon's benevolence to the Jews was far greater. Ghetto walls fell, and he permitted the participation of Jews in political, social, and economic life. On August 15, 1808, the Jews of Livorno celebrated the emperor's birthday with special prayers in their Great Synagogue, and issued *Hod Malchut* (Glory of Sovereignty), an order of service in Hebrew with Italian translation, which culminated in a benediction for "His Imperial Majesty, Napoleon I, Emperor of France, King of Italy and Protector of the Confederation of the Rhine."

May the King of Kings place compassion in the heart of the Emperor and his counsellors and officers, to deal kindly with us, and with Israel our brethren. In his days and ours, may Judah be saved, and Israel dwell securely, and may the Redeemer come to Zion.

A special *Order of Service and Prayer* "for the Day of Assembly, devoted to mourning by the Jewish Congregations, throughout England" was published in London, for use on the 24th of Tamuz, AM 5590 (July 15, 1830), that "being the day of burial of His late, Most Gracious Majesty, King George IV." By all accounts George IV was a profligate, immoral, contentious king but, together with all other English subjects, the Jews gathered in their houses of worship to join in public mourning and announced their participation by issuing a two-page broadside containing the prayers recited.

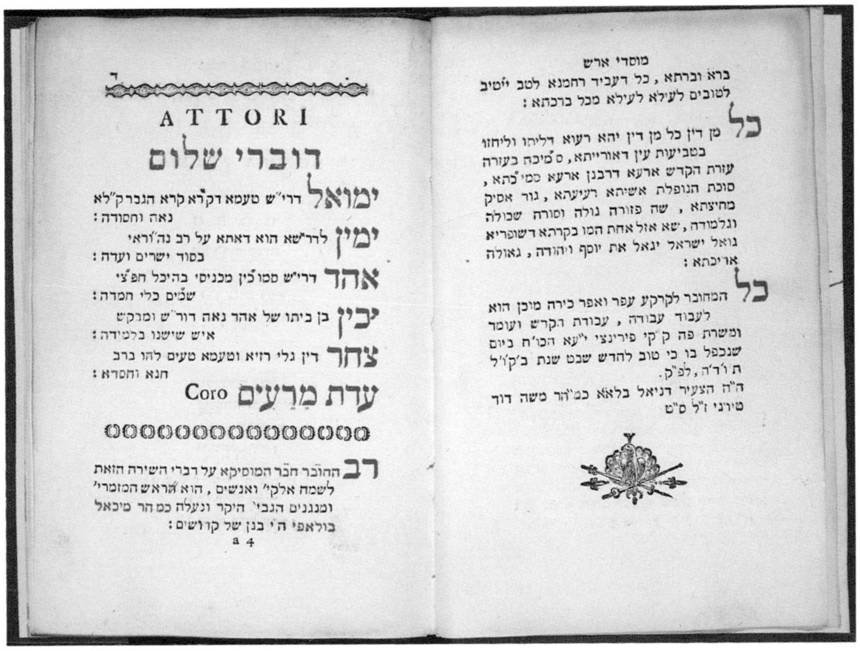
ד

ATTORI

דוברי שלום

ימואל דרי״ש טעמא דקרא קרא הגברק״לא
נאה וחסודה :

ימין לדר״שא הוא דאתא על רב נה׳וראי
בסוד ישרים ועדה :

אהד דרי״ש סמוכין מכניסי בהיכל חפצי
שכים כלי חמדה :

יכין בן ביתו של אהד נאה דור״ש ומבק״ש
איש שישנו בלמידה :

צחר דין גלי רזיא וטעמא טעים להו ברב
חנא וחסדא :

עדת מרעים Coro

רב ההובר חבר המוסיקא על דברי השירה הזאת
לשמח אלקי׳ ואנשים, הוא הראש המזמרי׳
ומנגנים הגבי׳ היקר ונעלה כמהר מיכאל
בולאפי ה״י בנן של קדושים :

a 4

מוסדי ארש

ברא וברתא, כל דעביד רחמנא לטב ייטיב
לטובים לעילא לעילא מכל ברכתא :

כל מן דין כל מן דין יהא רעוא דליהו וליחזו
בטביעות עין דאורייתא, סמיכה בעזרה
עזרת הקדש ארעא דרבנן ארעא סמיכתא,
סוכת הנופלת אשיהא רעיעהא, גור אסיק
מחיצתא, שה פזורה גולה וסורה שכולה
ונלמודה, שא אזל אחת המו בקרתא דשופריא
גואל ישראל יגאל את יוסף ויהודה, גאולה
אריכתא :

כל המחובר לקרקע עפר ואפר כירה מוכן הוא
לעבוד עבודה, עבודת הקדש ועומד
ומשרת פה ק״ק פירינצי יע״א הכו״ח ביום
שנכפל בו כי טוב לחדש שבט שנת ב׳ק׳ו׳ל
ת׳ו׳ד׳ה, לפ״ק.
ה״ה הצעיר דניאל בלאא כמ״הר משה דוד
טירני ז״ל ס״ט

The Italian rite congregation in Florence dedicated its new synagogue in 1793. The dedication service, published in black and red type that year, indicates the presence of a choir and musicians, and records the special instructions given to their director.

Simhat Mitzvah (Joy of the Commandment), Florence, 1793.
Hebraic Section.

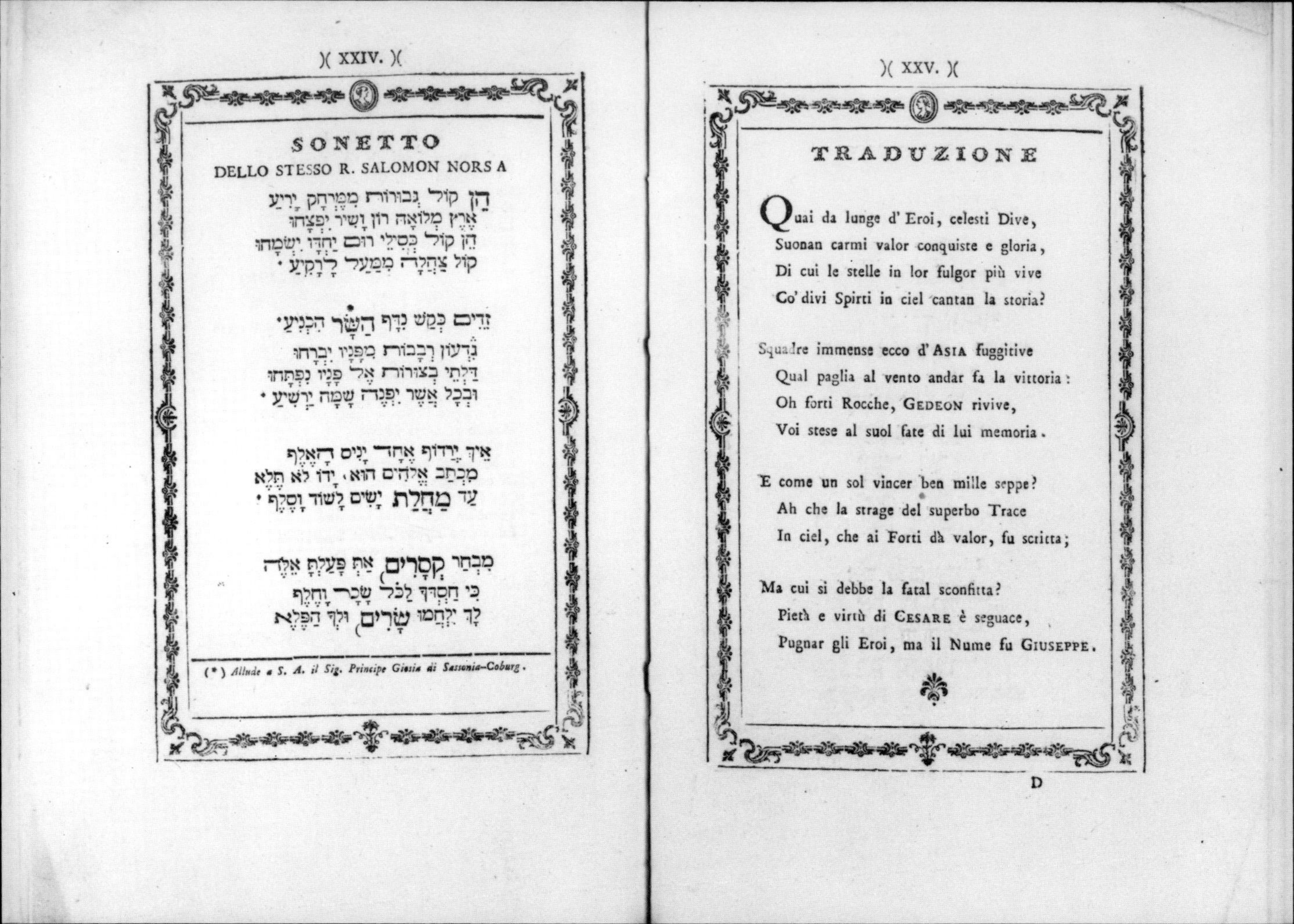

)(XXIV.)(

SONETTO

DELLO STESSO R. SALOMON NORSA

הן קול גבורות ממרחק יריע
ארץ מלואה רון ושיר יפצחו
הן קול כסילי רום יחדו ישמחו
קול צהלה ממעל לרקיע ·

זדים כקש נדף השר הכניע*
גדעון רבבות מפניו יברחו
דלתי בצורות אל פניו נפתחו
ובכל אשר יפנה שמה ירשיע ·

איך ירדוף אחד ינים האלף
מכתב אלהים הוא, ידו לא תלא
עד מחלת ישים לשוד וסלף ·

מבחר קסרים את פעלת אלה
כי חסדך לכל שכר וחלף
לך יתחמו שרים ולך הפלא

(*) Allude a S. A. il Sig. Principe Giosia di Sassonia-Coburg.

)(XXV.)(

TRADUZIONE

Quai da lunge d' Eroi, celesti Dive,
Suonan carmi valor conquiste e gloria,
Di cui le stelle in lor fulgor più vive
Co' divi Spirti in ciel cantan la storia?

Squadre immense ecco d' Asia fuggitive
Qual paglia al vento andar fa la vittoria:
Oh forti Rocche, Gedeon rivive,
Voi stese al suol fate di lui memoria.

E come un sol vincer ben mille seppe?
Ah che la strage del superbo Trace
In ciel, che ai Forti dà valor, fu scritta;

Ma cui si debbe la fatal sconfitta?
Pietà e virtù di Cesare è seguace,
Pugnar gli Eroi, ma il Nume fu Giuseppe.

D

The Jewish community of Mantua, then under the sovereignty of the Austrian Emperor Joseph II, held a special service to celebrate the victory of the emperor's force in its battle for the conquest of the city of Belgrade. A collection of prayers and poems specially prepared for the celebration was published by the community in 1789. We see here Rabbi Solomon Norsa's sonnet in Hebrew and Italian.

L'Elohei M'uzim Roni Todot (To the Lord of Might Sing Gratitude), Mantua, 1789.
Hebraic Section.

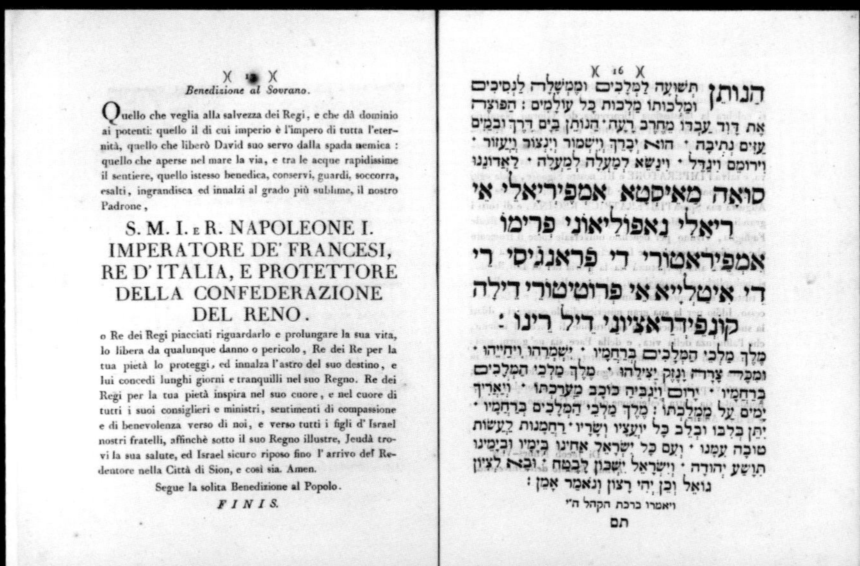

)(15)(

Benedizione al Sovrano.

Quello che veglia alla salvezza dei Regi, e che dà dominio ai potenti: quello il di cui imperio è l'impero di tutta l'eternità, quello che liberò David suo servo dalla spada nemica: quello che aperse nel mare la via, e tra le acque rapidissime il sentiere, quello istesso benedica, conservi, guardi, soccorra, esalti, ingrandisca ed innalzi al grado più sublime, il nostro Padrone,

S. M. I. e R. NAPOLEONE I.
IMPERATORE DE' FRANCESI,
RE D'ITALIA, E PROTETTORE
DELLA CONFEDERAZIONE
DEL RENO.

o Re dei Regi piacciati riguardarlo e prolungare la sua vita, lo libera da qualunque danno o pericolo, Re dei Re per la tua pietà lo proteggi, ed innalza l'astro del suo destino, e lui concedi lunghi giorni e tranquilli nel suo Regno. Re dei Regi per la tua pietà inspira nel suo cuore, e nel cuore di tutti i suoi consiglieri e ministri, sentimenti di compassione e di benevolenza verso di noi, e verso tutti i figli d' Israel nostri fratelli, affinchè sotto il suo Regno illustre, Jeudà trovi la sua salute, ed Israel sicuro riposo fino l' arrivo del Redentore nella Città di Sion, e così sia. Amen.

Segue la solita Benedizione al Popolo.

FINIS.

)(16)(

הנותן תשועה למלכים וממשלה לנסיכים ומלכותו מלכות כל עולמים: הפוצה את דוד עבדו מחרב רעה· הנותן בים דרך ובמים עזים נתיבה· הוא יברך וישמור וינצור ויעזור וירומם ויגדל· וינשא למעלה למעלה· לאדוננו

סואה מאיסטא אמפיריאלי אי
ריאלי נאפוליאוני פרימו
אמפיראטורי די פראנגיסי רי
די איטלייא אי פרוטיטורי דילה
קונפידראציוני דיל רינו:

מלך מלכי המלכים ברחמיו· ישמרהו ויחייהו· ומכל צרה ונזק יצילהו· מלך מלכי המלכים ברחמיו· ירום ויגביה כוכב מערכתו· ויאריך ימים על ממלכתו: מלך מלכי המלכים ברחמיו· יתן בלבו ובלב כל יועציו ושריו· רחמנות לעשות טובה עמנו· ועם כל ישראל אחינו בימיו ובימינו תושע יהודה· וישראל ישכון לבטח: ובא לציון גואל וכן יהי רצון ונאמר אמן:

ויאמרו ברכת הקהל ה"י

תם

The Jews of Livorno (Leghorn) celebrated the thirty-eighth birthday of Emperor Napoleon I with a service of worship, for which a special liturgy was prepared and published in Hebrew and Italian. Here we see the prayer for:

His Imperial Majesty, Napoleon I, Emperor of France, King of Italy and Protector of the Confederation of the Rhine.

Hod Malchut (Glory of Sovereignty), Livorno, 1808.
Hebraic Section.

ويعظم سيدنا المشير محمد الصادق باشا باي
نصره الله امين
سلطان في الاعلام وساكنا في القدس برحمته يحفظه
ويحييه ومن كل حزن واذي يحجبه ويمدد الايام
بدوام ذكره اياما على ايامه يزيد الملوك
سلطان الرؤف الرحيم الكثير الرحمة يرفع نجم قدره
يمكث زمانا طويلا على مملكته تاج الملك فوق
راسه وخزاينه فضة وذهبا يكون في قصور الملوك
سلطان المنتخب يوصي ملايكته يحفظوه في ساير
طريقه لبلا يعثر بين فرسانه وساير جيشه
وغلمانه واولاد بيته بكثرة الشعب شرف الملوك
سلطان القوي يبني لجنوده من السماء يحاربه فيكون مع
جيشه جميع حيثما يتوجه لم يتعطل خطواته
منسوب دايما الملوك
سلطان الصالح يقوم خطواته يكون مجده كالزيتون
تمتد اغصانه الحق يلبس والصدق ينزل على جيب
قميصه الصدقه والصدق حافظا للملوك
למעלה למעלה לאדוננו
המלך אלמושיר מחמד
אצאדק באשא באיי
ירום הודו ומלכותו
מלך מרום וקדוש ברחמיו ישמרהו
ויחייהו : ומכל צרה ונזק יצילהו:
אורך ימים ישביעהו: ימים על ימי מלך
מלך רחום בחסדיו יגביה כוכב מערכתו:
ויאריך ימים על ממלכתו : צנוף
מלוכה על ראשו וכל
בית נכתה : והיא בהכלי מלך
מלך דגול יצוה מלאכיו: על כפים ינשא
לשמרו מכל דרכיו : ופרשיו וחילו
וירק את חניכיו : ברב עם הדרת מלך
מלך כביר יחוה לגדודיו : מן שמים נלחמו
וחילו יחדו : בכל אשר יפנה
לא יצרו צעדיו : ותצעידהו למלך
מלך ישר יישר ארחותיו : יהי כזית הודו
וילכו יונקותיו : צדק ילבש וחסד
יורד על פי מדותיו: חסד ואמת יצרו מלך
מלך

Special prayers for life and peace for the new Bey of Tunis, Muhammad al-Sadiq, were intoned and published in Hebrew and Arabic in 1860, by the Jews of Tunis.

Bakashat ha-Hayim V'ha-Shalom L'Adoneno ha-Melech (Entreaty for Life and Peace of Our Master, the King), Tunis, 1860.
Hebraic Section.

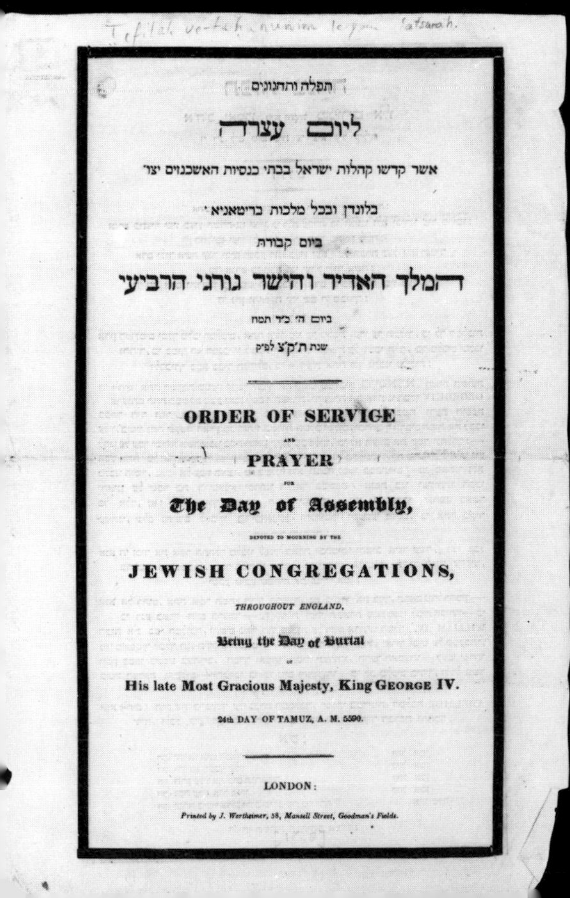

The illustration says it all, that Jewish congregations throughout England held special services in memory of their departed monarch George IV, on the day of his burial, July 15, 1830, using this published uniform liturgy, in Hebrew with English translation.

Order of Service and Prayer, London, 1830.
Hebraic Section.

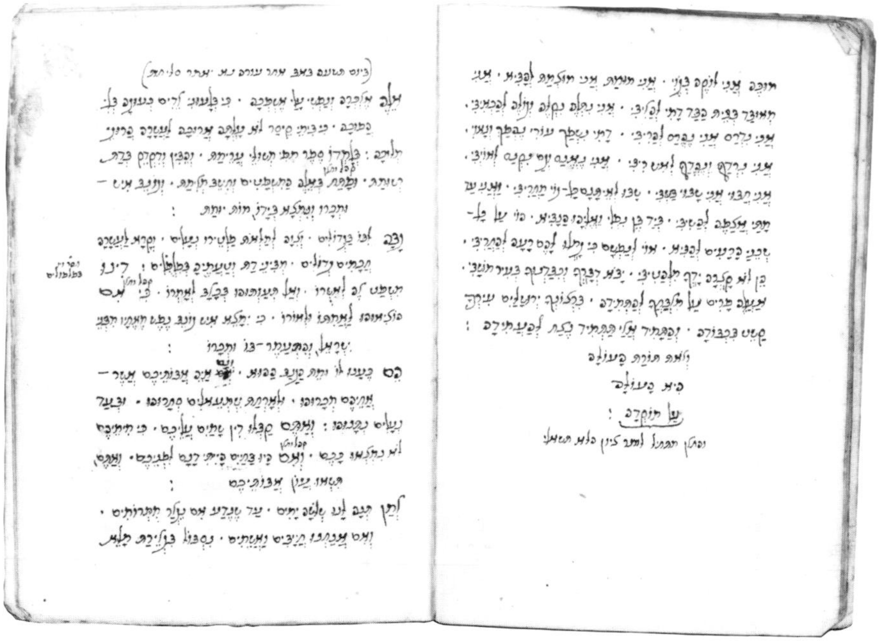

Among the many liturgical manuscripts in the Hebraic Section of the Library of Congress is this compendium of various prayers and petitions for special occasions and special needs. Open to a dirge to be said on *Tisha B'Av*, the Fast Day commemorating the destruction of the Temple, *Ele Ezkara* (These Things Do I Remember).

Tefilot U-Vakashot (Prayers and Petitions), Casale Monferrato, 1817–18.
Hebraic Section.

The supplications "for life and peace" for the newly crowned Bey of Tunis, Muhammad al-Sadiq—expressed by "the Jews dwelling under his sovereignty, here, in the city of Tunis," and published there in 1860 in Hebrew and Arabic—were genuine. His predecessors, Ahmad and Muhammad, treated their Jewish subjects with a benevolence unmatched in the Islamic world, the former so much so that he was called the "bey of the Jews"; the latter, under French pressure to be sure, issued a constitution which provided that duress may not be used to force Jews to change their faith, nor may they be hindered in the free observance of their religion. Jews had every reason to expect the new bey would continue these policies, hence, the prayers for his well-being, but a revolution in 1864 brought about abrogation of the constitution, and the Jews suffered both from revolution and abrogation. Only in 1881, when Tunis became a dependency of France, were its Jews accorded equal rights.

A collection of occasional prayers, written in Casale Monferrato in 1817, is one of a number of such collections in the manuscripts collection of the Hebraic Section. Under French occupation from 1799 to 1814, the Jews of that area were granted equal civil rights, which with the end of French rule were revoked. The ghetto, established in 1724, was reinstituted, and rights granted were rescinded. In 1817 the scribe, remembering fifteen years of freedom and equality now gone, inscribed the most mournful dirge in all the liturgy, *Ele Ezkara,* recounted on the Day of Atonement, with a full heart.

These things do I remember and my heart is grieved. How the arrogant have devoured my people! . . . With humble and mournful hearts we pray to Thee, O merciful God, look down from heaven on the blood of Thy righteous. Oh make an end of bloodshed by man and wash away the stain, O thou King, who sittest on the throne of mercy.

It was not until 1848 that Jews were granted full emancipation.

11

THE STARRY SKIES IN THE HEAVENS ABOVE— THE STILL SMALL VOICE IN THE HEART OF MAN

THE BIBLE OPENS WITH TWO creation narratives. The first speaks of the world: "In the beginning God created the heaven and the earth" (Genesis, 1:1); the second, of humankind: "The Lord God formed man from the dust of the earth, and breathed into him the breath of life, and man became a living being" (Genesis, 2:7). From its beginning, Judaism was preoccupied with man and with the world about him, seeing God in the heavens above and in the heart of man. Four illustrated Hebrew books on science attest to this continuing interest in the world without, and four kabbalistic manuscripts speak of the world within.

THE WORLD WITHOUT

Religious needs mandated interest in astronomy. Because the Jewish calendar is lunisolar, the months being reckoned by the moon and the year by the sun, astronomical expertise is required to make the necessary adjustments. Indeed, there is a long tradition of religious authorities, including the Babylonian Amora, Samuel and Maimonides, being well-versed in astronomy. Of his astronomical knowledge Samuel said, "The paths of the heavens are as clear to me, as the paths of [his native city] Nehardea" (Berakhot 58b). Maimonides devotes a section of his *Mishneh Torah* to what he lists as a positive commandment: "to know how to determine which is the first day of each month of the year."

To help an individual fulfill the commandments, "the young servant of the Exalted Heavenly Father, Eliezer the son of Jacob Belin Ashkenazi," prepared a handbook in 1722, *Sefer Ebronot* (Book of Intercalations), which proved useful and popular and of which many manuscript copies

This edition (the fifth) of Eliezer ben Jacob Belin's *Sefer Ebronot*, published in Offenbach in 1722, is noted for its astronomical-mathematical charts and illustrations. Notable among these are the circular chart and the multilayered paper volvelles.

Eliezer ben Jacob Belin, *Sefer Ebronot*, Offenbach, 1722. Hebraic Section.

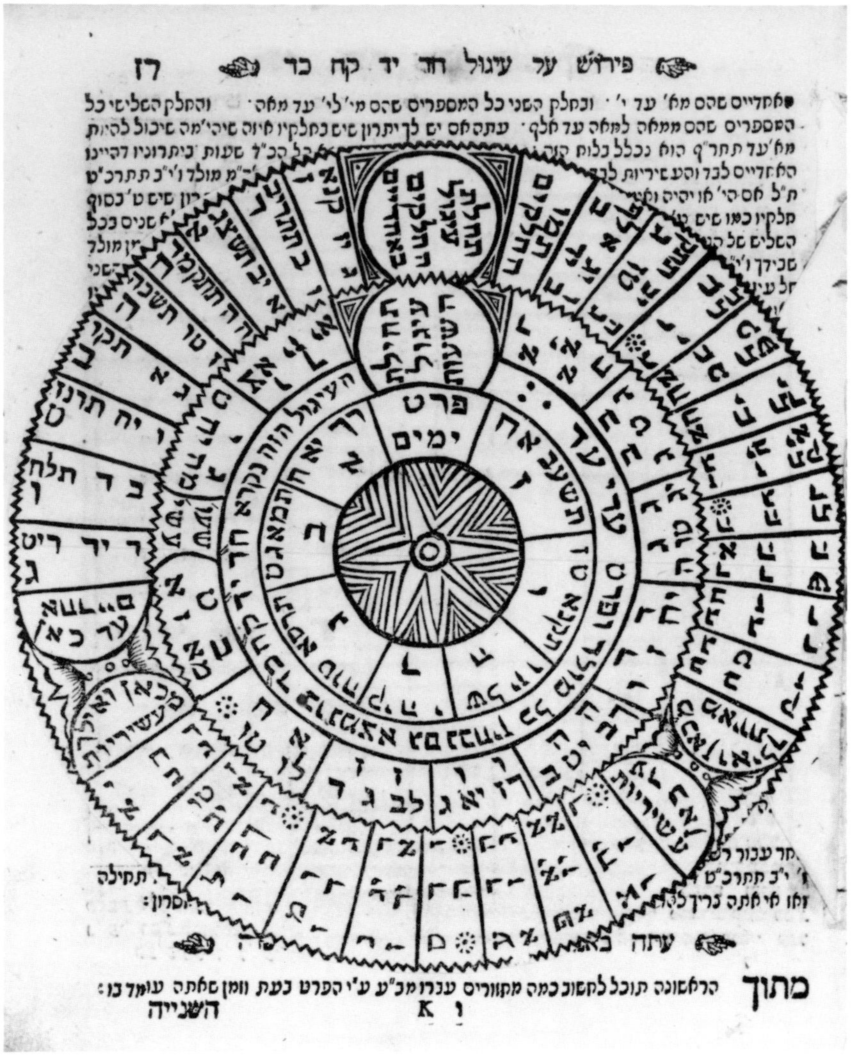

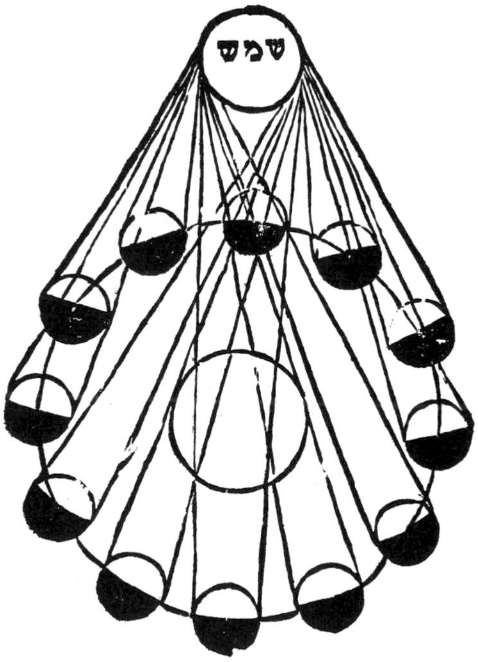

From astronomer and chronicler David Gans's book on astronomy.

David Gans, *Nehmad Ve-Naim* (Delightful and Pleasant), Jessnitz, 1743. Hebraic Section.

were made. In print it went through four editions from 1614 to 1720. The fifth, published in Offenbach, is a particularly beautiful edition with fine illustrations and volvelles for calculations.

Sefer Ebronot was a brief handbook for one small area of astronomical calculation. *Nehmad ve-Naim* (Delightful and Pleasant), Jessnitz, 1743, by David Gans (1541–1613) was an astronomical and mathematical work aimed at a comprehensive presentation of the subject. Gans had studied rabbinics with two of the foremost Jewish scholars of the sixteenth century, Rabbis Moses Isserles of Cracow and Judah Loew of Prague. In Prague, in pursuit of his scientific studies, he met two of the leading astronomers of that age, Tycho Brahe and Johannes Kepler.

Gans was the author of *Zemah David* (Offspring of David), a chronicle of Jewish and general history, first published in Prague in 1592, which was republished a number of times in its original Hebrew as well as in Yiddish, Latin, and German. The purpose of Gans's work was, in part, to provide his coreligionists with a history of their people in the context of world history and also, apparently, to impress the world that Jewish history did not end with the destruction of the Temple or the birth of Christianity.

Similar reasons evidently motivated him to write his work on astronomy, in part to provide the latest scientific knowledge to his people but also as an expression of Jewish pride. In his Introduction, Gans argues that astronomy was already known to Abraham, who transmitted it to his son Isaac, and he, in turn, to his son Jacob. Jacob and his sons taught it to the Egyptians, from whom the Greeks derived their knowledge of astronomy and mathematics. "The essense of this wisdom," Gans asserted, "first emerged among the sons of the Jewish People." If Christians in the Renaissance were unearthing their cultural heritage why should not Jews proclaim that Israel too was the source not only of religious knowledge but of scientific knowledge as well. Why else were a Latin translation of the Introduction and a synopsis of the volume's contents in that language appended to the volume?

Joseph Delmedigo (1591–1655), physically and spiritually restless, was born in Candia, Crete, and studied medicine at the University of Padua and astronomy under Galileo. In his pursuit of knowledge he traveled to Cairo and Constantinople; and in pursuit of a livelihood to Poland, Am-

Philosopher, scientist, physician, Joseph Delmedigo's book of science, *Sefer Elim,* is replete with astronomical and mathematical illustrations. Of special interest and importance is the portrait of the author, a native of Crete, engraved in 1628 in Amsterdam when he was thirty-seven years old. The engraving by W. Delff is from a portrait by W. C. Duyster.

Joseph Delmedigo, *Sefer Elim* (The Book of Elim), Amsterdam, 1629.
Hebraic Section.

דף מח

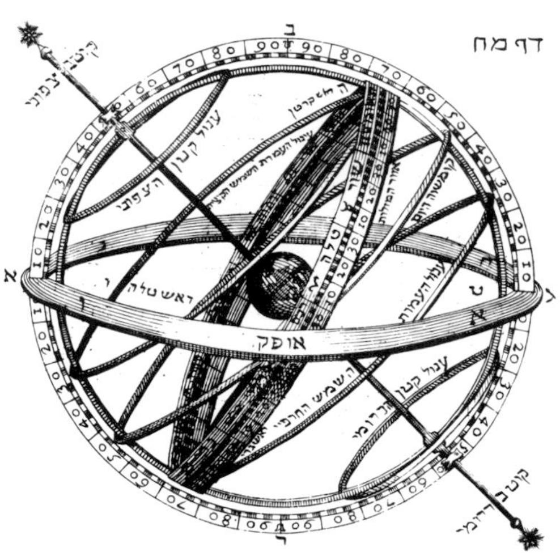

דף נג

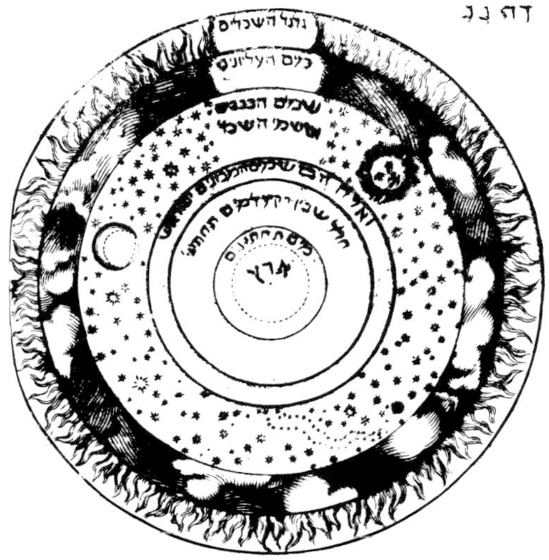

דף צ

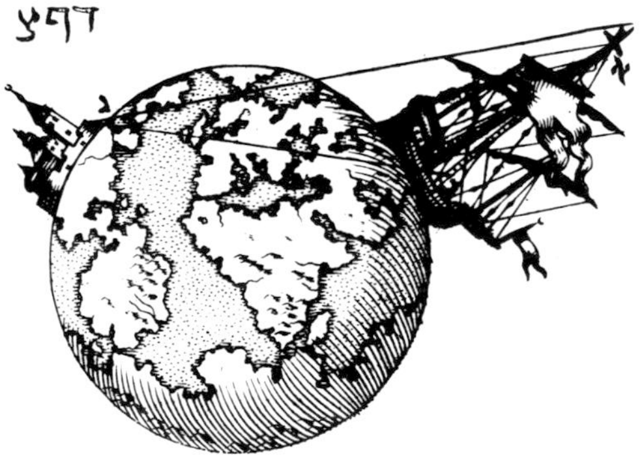

Ma'aseh Tuviyyah, a popular book on science by the much traveled physician Tobias Cohen, contains sections on astronomy, geography, physiology, pharmacology, and medicine. Of the many fine illustrations which fill the volume, none is more striking than this full-page engraving (*facing page*) of the human body compared to a house in the function of its parts and organs. "The eyes are the windows, the nose the aperture to the attic," etc.

Tobias Cohn, *Ma'aseh Tuviyyah* (The Work of Tobias), Venice, 1707.
Hebraic Section.

sterdam, Frankfort, and Prague, engaging in the study not only of science but also of Kabbalah. A prolific writer, though most of his works are known only through his own lists of his writings, Delmedigo, in response to requests by Karaites, to whose faith he seems to have been attracted, wrote a book on mechanics. His magnum opus, *Sefer Elim* (The Book of Elim), was published in a richly illustrated edition by Menasseh ben Israel, Amsterdam, 1629, where Delmedigo was then serving as a rabbi. Elim was the oasis where during the Exodus the Children of Israel camped after encountering the bitter waters of Marah, an oasis of twelve springs and seventy palm trees. The book *Elim* contains twelve scientific expositions and seventy mathematical paradoxes.

Restless spirit that he was, Delmedigo was critical of the Kabbalah, of the restrictive nature of Jewish learning, and of the scant attention paid to science in Jewish studies; but he grudgingly acknowledged that there were Jewish giants of the spirit, men like Saadiah Gaon, Abraham bar Hiyyah, Abraham Ibn Ezra, Isaac Israeli, Moses Almosino, and David Gans, among others, who through their scientific endeavors "made a great contribution to the house of Israel." Delmedigo's impressive tombstone can still be seen in Prague's historic Jewish cemetery, not far from the more modest stone of David Gans. The book *Elim* provides a finer monument, its frontispiece an artistic engraving of its author, face weary with wisdom but curious eyes still in quest of more knowledge.

Tobias Cohn (1652–1729) was, like Delmedigo, a graduate of the Faculty of Medicine at the University of Padua, and like him, a wanderer who traveled in Germany, Poland, Italy, Adrianople, Constantinople, and Jerusalem, and also a student of science. Echoing Gans, he maintained:

> It is already well known that our sages, blessed be their memory, exerted themselves more than did the scholars of other nations to know and understand the science of astronomy . . . In the days of King David, this science spread among Israel . . . and so it was during the days of the first and second Temples, when the spirit moved the Babylonians, Persians, Greeks and Romans to learn from (the sages of Israel) and discuss with them the science of the heavenly bodies and other sciences, as Aristotle attests . . .

Written in Adrianople, where Cohen was physician to five successive sultans, his *Ma'aseh Tuviyyah* (The Work of Tobias), Venice, 1707, is a miniencyclopedia on astronomy, medicine, hygiene, botany, and cosmography and theology. There are sections on Shabbetai Zvi, an essay on the four elements, and a Hebrew-Latin-Turkish medical dictionary.

Notable for its splendid illustrations, it has an engraved portrait of the author on the verso of the title page, charts of the heavens and the internal organs, and an astrolabe. Most striking is the full-page engraving comparing the human body to a house: the head is a superstructure on the roof; the eyes are windows; the mouth, an open lattice; the shoulders, a lower roof; the lungs, a ventilated balcony; the heart, a pump; the stomach, a boiling cauldron.

Cohn's volume ties man to the world about him. It also fortifies claims to the antiquity of Jewish scientific interest and knowledge. His works and those of Gans and Delmedigo reflect the accepted division of the sciences into their various major components, but one also finds in them a unity imposed by the Creator and sustained by His continuing interest in His creation.

בית חדש
קו
דף קו

THE WORLD WITHIN

Medieval Jewish men of science had a mechanistic view of the world and of man; they saw both as marvelous, divinely contrived machines. Not so the teachers of Jewish mysticism, the Kabbalah. Kabbalah had its own cosmogony, with creation as emanation from the One; and its own theosophy, the special relationship between an immanent Creator and the world, and most especially, man. "What exists in God," Gershom Scholem wrote in his *Kabbalah* (New York, 1987), "unfolds and develops in man."

> Man is the perfecting agent in the structure of the cosmos . . . the process of creation involves the departure of all from the One and its return to the One, and the crucial turning-point of this cycle takes place within man, at the moment he begins to develop an awareness of his true essence and yearns to retrace the path from the multiplicity of his nature to the Oneness from which he originated.

Kabbalah's mission is to help man develop this awareness and turn him onto the path. Four manuscripts in the Hebraic Section touch upon this quest, dealing with dreams and their interpretation; transmigration of souls; healing the soul; and remedies and recipes for such healing. In the Bible, dreams were understood as vehicles for God's communication to man. Only the chosen could understand such communication as, for example, Joseph and Daniel, who were the biblical interpreters of dreams par excellence. In Talmudic days, dreams were also interpreted psychologically as windows to the soul through which one might glimpse the dreamer's innermost thoughts and feelings. Said Rabbi Jonathan, "a man is shown in a dream only what is suggested by his own thoughts" (Berakhot 55b).

Maimonides, ever the rationalist, saw dreams as products of the imagination, but the *Zohar,* the classic text of Jewish mysticism, gives dreams both reality and potency. Among the kabbalists, and particularly in the mystical teachings of Isaac Luria (1534–1572), dreams and their interpretation are of central concern. Thus, Hayim Vital (1543–1620), Luria's chief disciple, fills his spiritual autobiography, *Sefer ha-Hezyonot,* with dreams and visions.

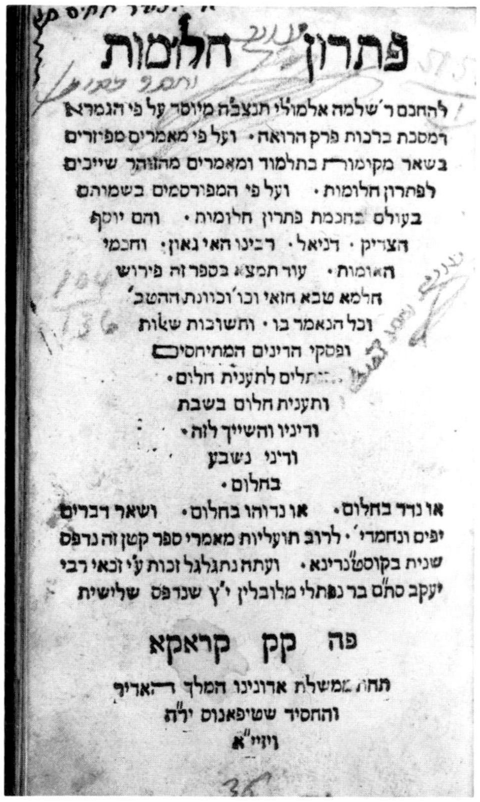
פתרון חלומות
להחכם ר׳ שלמה אלמולי תנצב״ה מיוסד על פי הגמרא
דמסכת ברכות פרק הרואה · ועל פי מאמרים מפוזרים
בשאר מקומות בתלמוד ומאמרים מהזוהר שייכים
לפתרון חלומות · ועל פי המפורסמים בשמותם
בעולם בחכמת פתרון חלומות · והם יוסף
הצדיק · דניאל · רבינו האי גאון · וחכמי
האומות · עוד תמצא בספר זה פירוש
חלמא טבא חזאי וכו׳ וכוונת ההטב׳
וכל הנאמר בו · ותשובות שאלות
ופסקי הדינים המתיחסים
...תלים לתענית חלום ·
ותענית חלום בשבת
ודיניו והשייך לזה ·
ודיני נשבע
בחלום ·
או נדר בחלום · או נדוהו בחלום · ושאר דברים
יפים ונחמדי׳ · לרוב תועליות מאמרי ספר קטן זה נדפס
שנית בקושטנדינא · ועתה נתגלגל זכות ע״י זכאי רבי
יעקב סת״ם בר נפתלי מלובלין י״ץ שנדפס שלישית
פה קק קראקא
תחת ממשלת אדונינו המלך האדיר
והחסיד שטיפאנוס יר״ה
ויזי״א

Title page of the third edition of Solomon Almoli's popular treatise on the interpretation of dreams, *Pitron Halomot*. The author states that the work is:

based on the chapter on dreams in Tractate Berakhot and on statements scattered throughout the Talmud, on passages in the Zohar, as especially on those noted for their skill in interpreting dreams, Joseph, Daniel, Hai Gaon, and the scholars of the nations of the world.

Solomon Almoli, *Pitron Halomot* (The Interpretation of Dreams), Cracow, 1580.
Hebraic Section.

The most popular of the works on dreams was Solomon Almoli's *Pitron Halomot* (Interpretation of Dreams), first published in Salonica, 1515, as *Mefasher Halmin.* In full or abridged form it has since been republished at least a dozen times in Hebrew, twice in Yiddish, and twice in Persian translations. Almoli, born in Spain before 1485, lived in Constantinople, where he served as a rabbi and physician. His work is a dissertation on the history of the role of dreams in the Jewish religious tradition, views on the subject drawn from the classical texts of non-Jewish authors, and a handbook for the interpretation of dreams. The Library owns a manuscript version of the work, apparently from the eighteenth century, as well as the rare Cracow edition of 1580.

The doctrine of the transmigration of souls, alternately accepted and refuted by Jewish religious leaders and scholars, was raised to a dogma by Kabbalah. Those who upheld it claimed that it was an expression of God's justice and mercy—otherwise how could one explain the suffering of the righteous, the prosperity of the wicked, the suffering of children? Only punishment for sins committed and rewards for righteousness performed in earlier manifestations, in other bodies, could explain such inequities.

Isaac Abrabanel (1437–1508) argued that God in His mercy grants a grievous sinner yet another opportunity for repentance and redemption by affording his soul another life in another body. Even the great suffering inflicted upon the righteous may be an expression of God's mercy, Abrabanel maintains, for it may be a lesser punishment here on earth for sins committed in an earlier manifestation, instead of the justly deserved harsher punishment which would have to be meted out in the next world. To which Leone Modena (1571–1648) countered: Why send the soul into another body for punishment, why could the punishment not have been inflicted on the soul while still in the body which abetted the sin? And would it not be more in keeping with God's mercy to recognize the weakness of the body and to forgive, rather than to punish?

Luria's disciples raised the dogma of transmigration of souls to a science and an art. The concept of "impregnation of souls" permitted a soul that had attained purity in a former life to enter the body of another individual to help his resident soul in its quest for purity. Souls which missed attaining full purity could try for the required "elevation" in a new body, in the process "elevating" another soul. The process took on material and cosmic proportions. The purified souls of Israelites unite with the impure souls of other peoples to free them of their taint and uplift them so that the whole world may come closer to redemption. Hence, the dispersal of Israel is not intended as punishment but as the salvation of humankind.

The classic work on transmigration of souls according to Lurianic doctrine is *Sefer ha-Gilgulim* (Book of Transmigration) by Hayyim Vital of Safed, the recorder—some would say the author—of the teachings of Isaac Luria. This material comprises the fourth section of his magnum opus, *Etz*

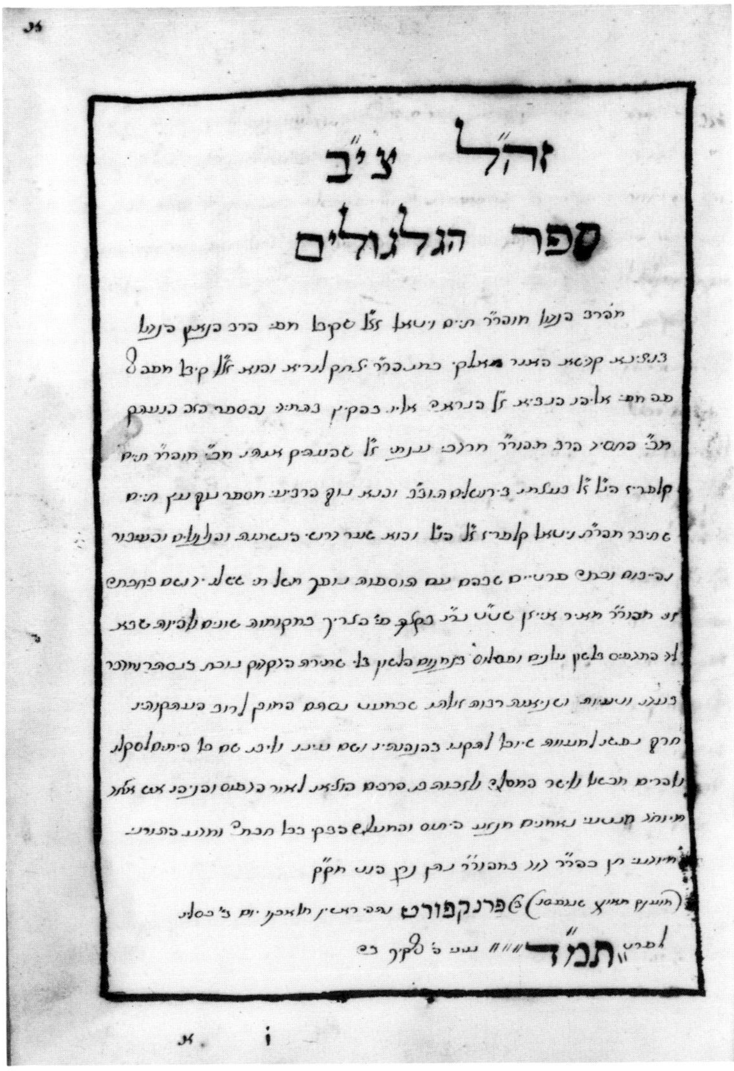

The opening page of a manuscript copy of the Frankfurt-am-Main 1684 edition of a work on the transmigration of souls, so central to Lurianic Kabbalah, by the chief disciple of Isaac Luria, Hayyim Vital, whose writing presented and popularized the Kabbalistic teaching of his master.

Hayyim Vital, *Sefer ha-Gilgulim* (Book of Transmigration), Italy, eighteenth century.
Hebraic Section.

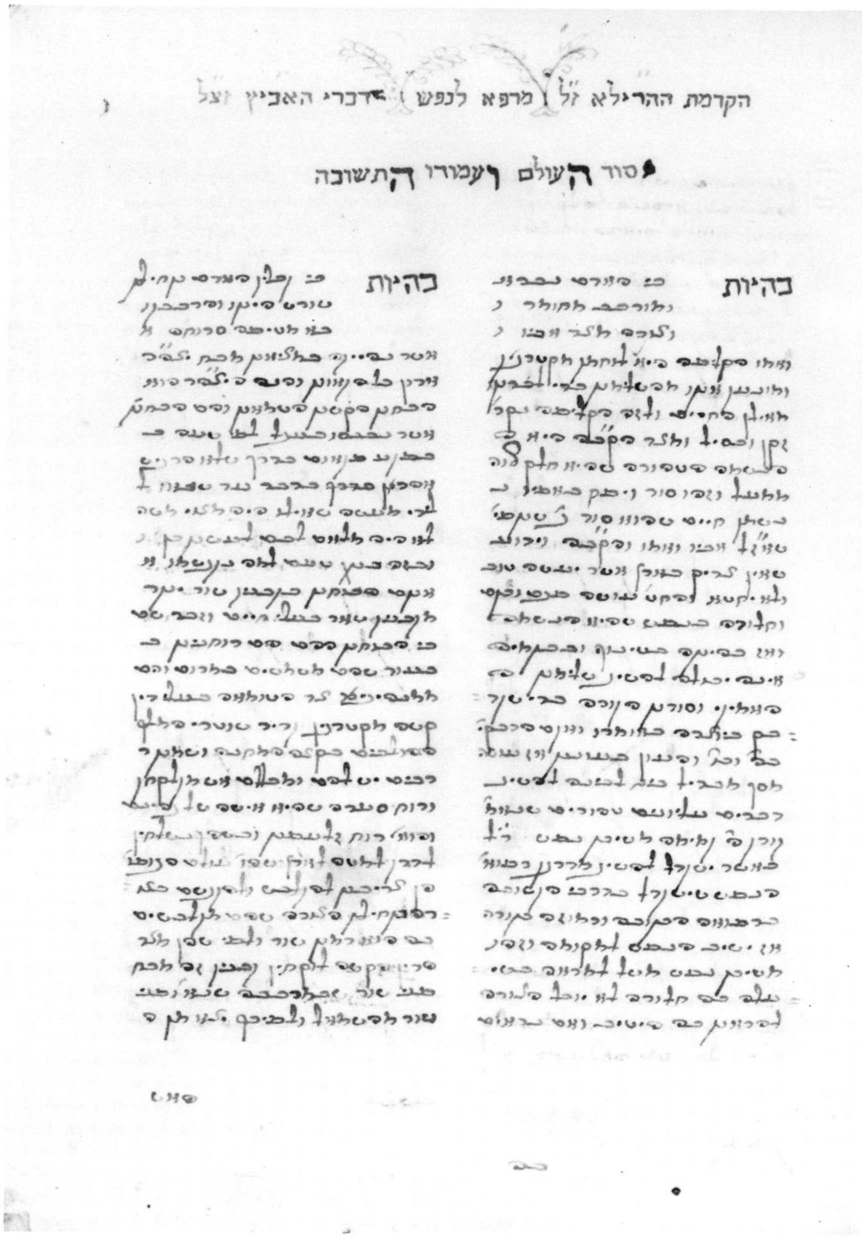

הקדמת ההרי"לא ז"ל מרפא לנפש דברי האביץ יצ"ל
סוד העולם ועמודי התשובה
בהיות
בהיות

A treatise on the cures for the healing of the way-ward or afflicted soul. The text in the right column is attributed to Isaac Luria, the greatest of kabbalists; the left column is the commentary of Abraham ben Isaac Zahalon.

Open to the introduction which deals with the foundation of the physical world, whose undergirding is spiritual repentance. The scribe Abraham ben Mattathias Treves wrote the manuscript in 1609.

Marpe La-Nefesh (Healing for the Soul), 1609.
Hebraic Section.

Hayyim (Tree of Life). The Library's manuscript is a copy of the first edition of that oft-reprinted work, published in Frankfort-am-Main in 1684. Vital lists a number of contemporaries and the sparks of which souls were united with theirs. The soul of the biblical commentator Moses Alsheikh, he said, was united with that of the Amora Samuel ben Nahman, from which he derived his great talent as a preacher; sixteenth-century Safed kabbalists Moses Cordovera and Elijah de Vidas were such great friends because both shared the soul of the good King Zechariah. The soul of Moses which had once been in the body of Simeon ben Yohai, the "father of Kabbalah," was now in the body of Isaac Luria, who assured his disciple Vital that this soul was one which remained untainted by Adam's sin.

Tainted souls, sinful souls can be cured and uplifted, and the kabbalists provided the means of doing so: the study of sacred texts at propitious times. Thus, *Marpe La-Nefesh* (Healing for the Soul), compiled by Abraham ben Isaac Zahalon from the teachings of Isaac Luria on ethical behavior and penitence, is "medicine for the soul." Completed in Baghdad in 1593, it was published in Venice in 1595. The Library's manuscript of the work contains Luria's and Zahalon's words in parallel columns.

If the soul needed uplifting and healing, so too did the body. For that, there is a manuscript of *Sefer Sodot U'Segulot, U'Refuot V'Ta-alot* (A Collection of Secret Formulas, Incantations, Medicines, and Cures) written in Genoa in 1711, which contains 386 "magic formulas for everything from toothache and insomnia to growing hair and improving the memory, from destroying one's enemies to currying favor with the mighty. And there are, of course, many love potions."

Dreams and their interpretation, a prelife of the soul and its psychic consequences, the need and the formulas for the healing of the soul-psyche attest to the centrality of interest in man—not man as a mechanism or as the noblest of all creatures, but man as so unique and complex a being that his essence is different from that of the rest of creation.

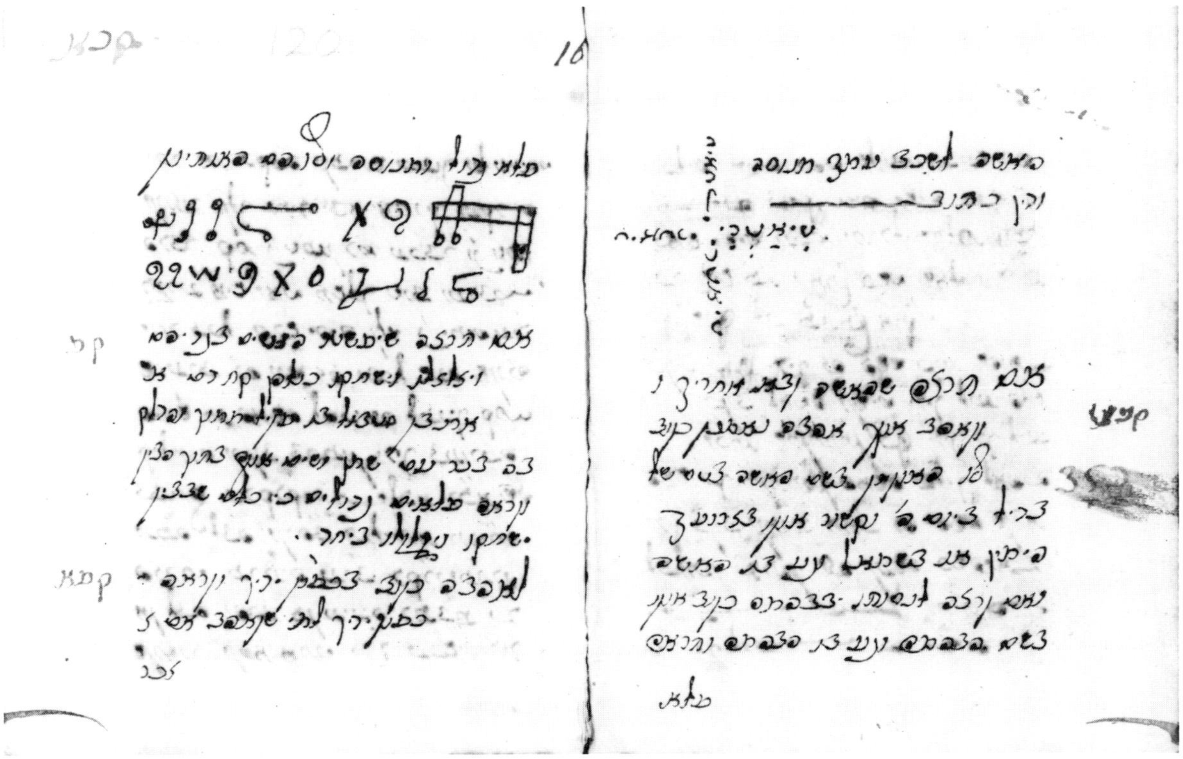

The letters to be used in preparing a love philter, as the text instructs us, "if you wish for the woman you desire to respond to you, go after you and love you truly." The manuscript contains 386 magic formulas, spells, and incantations for healing a toothache, curing insomnia, growing hair, and improving memory, as well as making love philters.

Sefer Sodot U'Segulot . . . (A Collection of Secret Formulas . . .), Genoa, 1711.
Hebraic Section.

THE WORLD AND MAN IN THE TWENTIETH CENTURY

The dual Jewish interest in the world about and the world within us was expressed in the twentieth century in secular, scientific terms in so radically revolutionary a fashion that the world and man will never again seem the same. Einstein and Freud wrought the revolutions in perception, and the intellectual battles they fought are fully recorded in books, pamphlets, and periodicals on the Library's shelves and in its manuscript collections. We shall pause briefly to consider one printed work of each and some manuscript material, of which the first thing to be noted is that Einstein's handwriting reflects calm lucidity, Freud's iconoclastic rage.

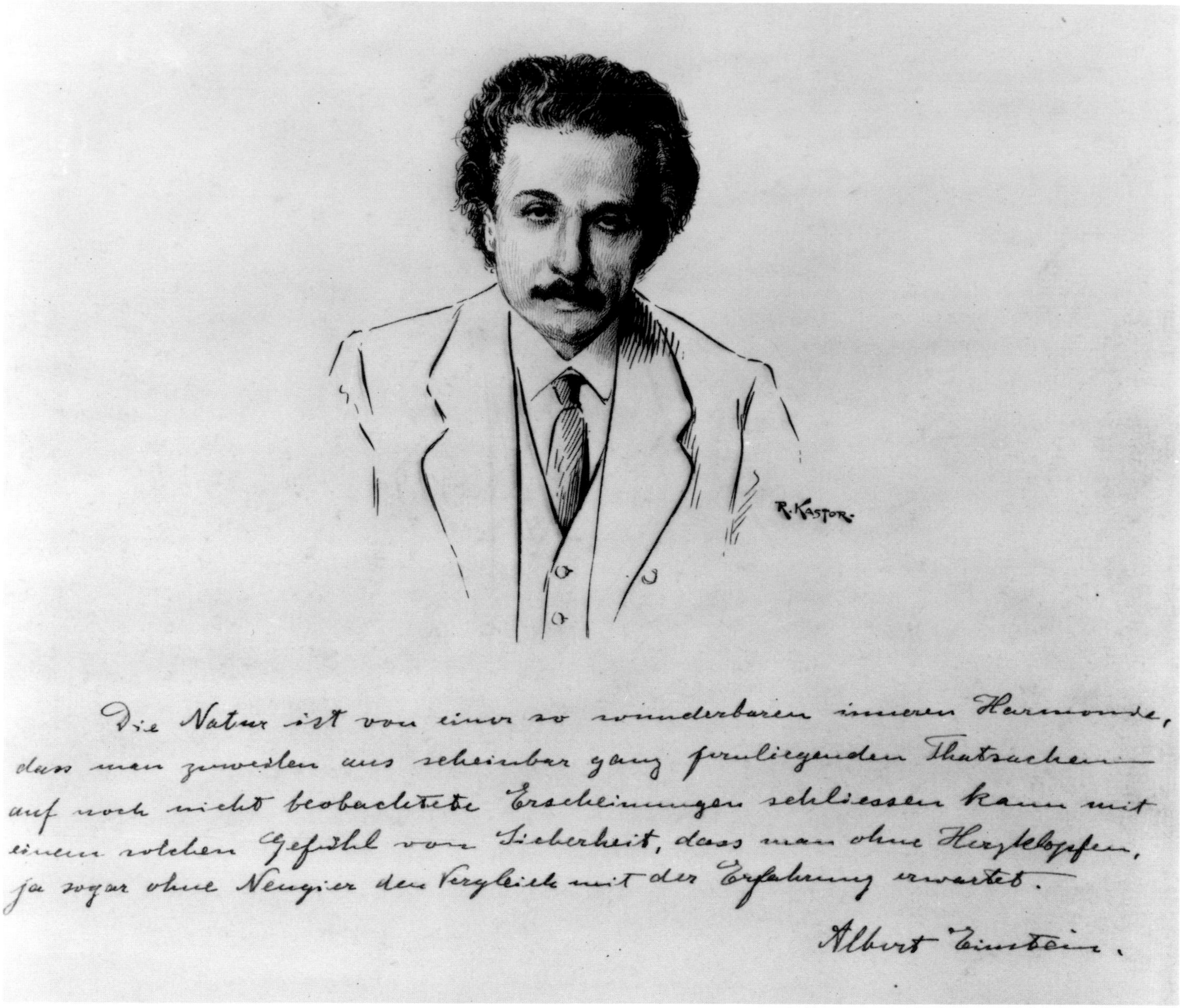

R. KASTOR.
Die Natur ist von einer so wunderbaren inneren Harmonie,
dass man zuweilen aus scheinbar ganz fernliegenden Thatsachen
auf noch nicht beobachtete Erscheinungen schliessen kann mit
einem solchen Gefühl von Sicherheit, dass man ohne Herzklopfen,
ja sogar ohne Neugier den Vergleich mit der Erfahrung erwartet.
Albert Einstein.

Albert Einstein (1879–1955)

Born in Ulm, Germany, Einstein grew up in Munich. As a boy, he already showed great interest in and talent for mathematics and physics. His family moved to Italy, and young Albert, unhappy with the authoritarian discipline of the German schools, went on to study at the Swiss Federal Institute of Technology in Zurich. Of the four graduates in 1900, he was the only one who was not given a position at the Institute; instead, he became a Swiss citizen and took a job at the Swiss patent office in Berne.

In 1905, Einstein was granted a doctorate by the University of Zurich. His thesis, *Eine neue Bestimmung der Molekuldimensionen* (A New Determination of Molecular Dimensions), Berne, 1905, was his first independently published work (five papers had previously been published in *Annalen der Physik*). The Library's copy of Einstein's twenty-one-page doctoral dissertation was received on January 18, 1907, as a "Smithsonian Deposit." In

"Subtle is the Lord . . . " The Science and Life of Albert Einstein (New York, 1982), Abraham Pais, of Rockefeller University, writes:

It is not sufficiently realized that Einstein's thesis is one of his most fundamental papers . . . It had more widespread application than any other paper Einstein ever wrote. Of the eleven scientific articles published by any author before 1912, and cited most frequently between 1961 and 1975, four are by Einstein. Among these four, the thesis . . . ranks first.

In 1921, Einstein accompanied Chaim Weizmann on a tour of the United States to raise funds for the proposed Hebrew University in Jerusalem. Among other honors, Einstein was received at the White House by President Harding. The Library has a photograph taken at the Farewell Dinner of the American Palestine Campaign. On it are Professor and Mrs. Einstein, financier Felix Warburg, Zionist leaders Robert Szold, Morris Rothenberg, and Rabbi Stephen S. Wise, as well as Jefferson Seligman of the banking family. The Prints and Photographs Division also contains a print of a pen and ink drawing of Einstein by Robert Kastor on which is inscribed in Einstein's own hand in German:

Nature has so wonderful a harmony that at times, one can draw conclusions from distant facts about not yet observed phenomena, and do so with such certainty, that he can look forward without fear to comparing these conclusions with observed reality.

When Hitler came to power in 1933, Einstein resigned his position in the Royal Prussian Academy of Sciences. On October 17 of that year the Einsteins arrived in the United States and settled in Princeton, where Einstein had accepted a professorship at the Institute for Advanced Studies. Five years later, July 13, 1938, he wrote to Dr. Herbert Putnam, Librarian of Congress:

My good friend, Professor E. Lowe, informs me that you would like to have one of my manuscripts for the Library of Congress. I am sending you herewith a specially prepared copy of my newest theory which I consider particularly worthy.

Einstein, a Jew fleeing Nazi terror, finding refuge in the United States, expresses his gratitude to this haven which became his home through a gift to the Library of Congress. The enclosed manuscript was "Einheitliche Feldtheorie" (Unified Field Theory), inscribed and dated in Einstein's hand 6 VII (July 6), 1938. Einstein began his pursuit of a unified field theory in 1919 and continued it to the last years of his life.

Five years later, in 1943, his new country now at war with the one he fled, Einstein aided the War Bond campaign by presenting through it another manuscript to the Library of Congress. (A Kansas City life insurance company was awarded the honor of being the official donor for its $6.5 million purchase of bonds.) He described his manuscript in an accompanying note:

The following pages are a copy of my first paper concerning the theory of relativity. I made this copy in November 1943. The original manuscript no longer exists having been discarded by me after its publication. The publication bore the title Zur Electrodynamic Bewegter Körper.

A. Einstein, 21 XI, 1943

Facing page:
Portrait of Albert Einstein in pen and ink by Robert Kastor, 1925, for inclusion in a volume on the world's greats. Einstein writes in German:

Nature has so wonderful a harmony, that at times one can draw a conclusion from distinct facts on not as yet observed phenomena, and do so with such certainty, that one can without fear look forward to comparing it with the facts of life, i.e., reality.

Robert Kastor, "Albert Einstein," 1925.
Prints and Photographs Division.

Einheitliche Feldtheorie.

In den letzten Monaten habe ich zusammen mit meinem Assistenten P. Bergmann eine einheitliche Feldtheorie entwickelt, welche durch Verallgemeinerung von Kaluza's Theorie des elektrischen Feldes entstanden ist. Im Folgenden soll diese Theorie unabhängig von ihren historischen Wurzeln dargestellt werden, damit ihre logische Struktur möglichst deutlich hervortrete.

§1. Die Raumstruktur

1. Es wird ein fünfdimensionaler Raum mit einer regulären Riemann-Metrik

$$d\sigma^2 = g_{\mu\nu}\, dx_\mu\, dx_\nu \quad \ldots (1)$$

zugrunde gelegt. Diese sei von solcher Art, dass für die infinitesimale Umgebung eines Punktes bei passender Wahl eines lokalen Koordinatensystems $d\sigma^2$ in die Form gebracht werden kann

$$d\sigma^2 = dx_1^2 + dx_2^2 + dx_3^2 - dx_4^2 + dx_0^2 \ldots (2)$$

2. Bezüglich der durch die Koordinate x_0 charakterisierten Dimension sei der Raum in sich geschlossen. Dem entspricht die Möglichkeit einer Koordinatendarstellung, in welcher die $g_{\mu\nu}$ in x_0 periodische Funktionen sind, derart dass

$$g_{\mu\nu}(x_1, x_2, x_3, x_4, x_0 + n\lambda) = g_{\mu\nu}(x_1, x_2\, x_3, x_4, x_0) \ldots (3)$$

wobei λ unabhängig von x_1, x_2, x_3, x_4, x_0 und n eine beliebige ganze Zahl ist. Einem Punkt P des Kontinuums entsprechen in dieser Darstellung unendlich viele Punkte $\ldots P^{-1}, P, P^{1}, \ldots$, welche zu den ganz-zahligen n gehören. Wir sprechen in diesem Sinne von homologen Punkten und speziell von benachbarten homologen Punkten.

3. Durch jeden Punkt unseres Raumes soll es eine und nur eine in sich singularitätsfrei geschlossene „raumartige" geodätische Linie geben. In der periodischen Darstellung des Raumes heisst dies: Zwischen den benachbarten homologen Punkten P und P^1 gibt es eine und nur eine geodätische Linie, welche durch alle P zugeordneten homologen Punkte hindurchgeht.

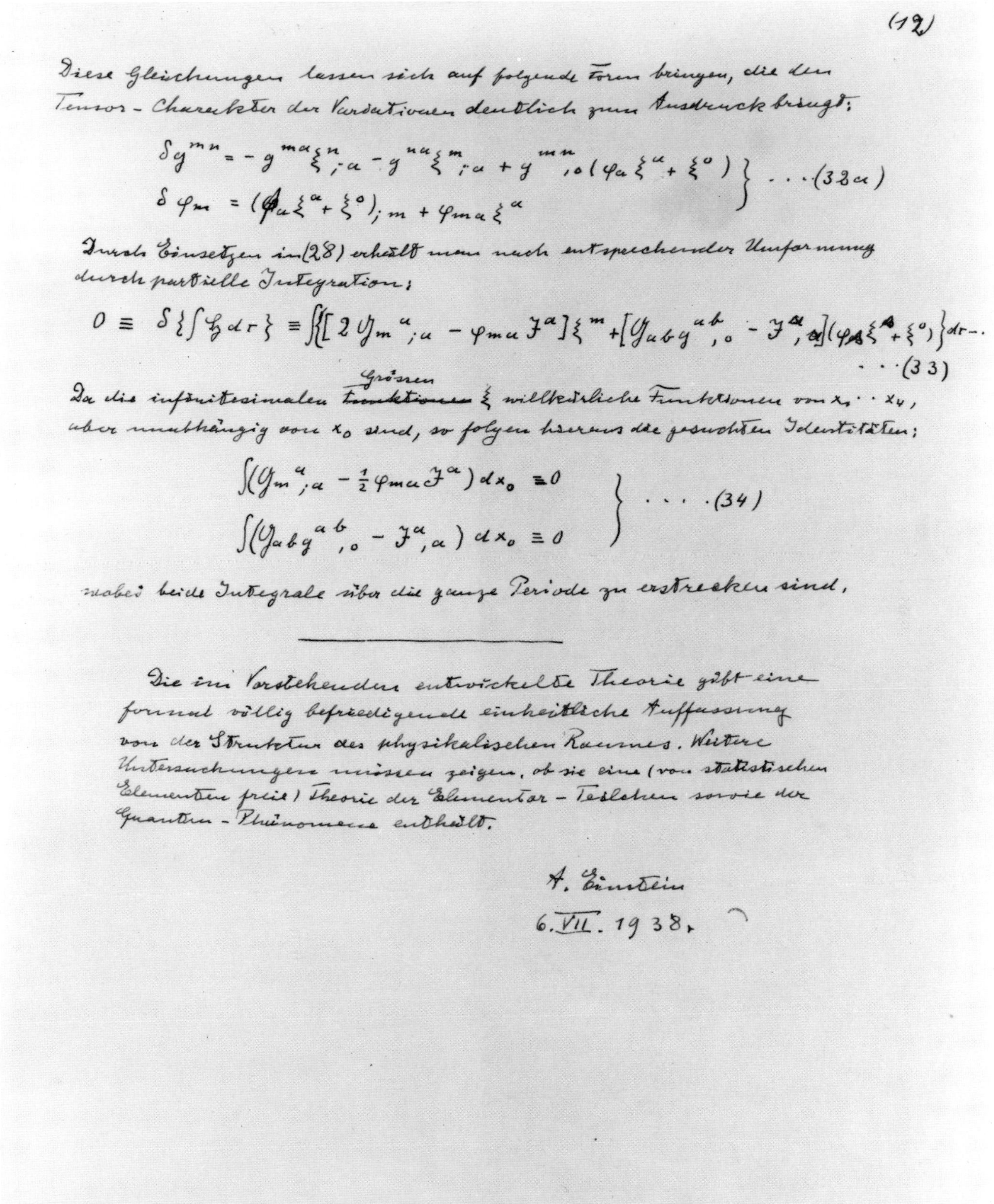

(12)

Diese Gleichungen lassen sich auf folgende Form bringen, die den Tensor-Charakter der Variationen deutlich zum Ausdruck bringt:

$$\left.\begin{aligned} \delta g^{mn} &= -g^{ma}\xi^{n}{}_{;a} - g^{na}\xi^{m}{}_{;a} + g^{mn}{}_{,0}(\varphi_a \xi^a + \xi^0) \\ \delta \varphi_m &= (\varphi_a \xi^a + \xi^0)_{;m} + \varphi_{ma}\xi^a \end{aligned}\right\} \quad \ldots (32a)$$

Durch Einsetzen in (28) erhält man nach entsprechender Umformung durch partielle Integration:

$$0 \equiv \delta\left\{\int \mathfrak{H}\, d\tau\right\} \equiv \int\left\{\left[2\mathfrak{G}_m{}^{a}{}_{;a} - \varphi_{ma}\mathfrak{F}^a\right]\xi^m + \left[\mathfrak{G}_{ab}\, g^{ab}{}_{,0} - \mathfrak{F}^a{}_{,a}\right](\varphi_a \xi^a + \xi^0)\right\} d\tau \quad \ldots (33)$$

Da die infinitesimalen ~~Funktionen~~ Grössen ξ willkürliche Funktionen von $x_1 \cdots x_4$, aber unabhängig von x_0 sind, so folgen hieraus die gesuchten Identitäten:

$$\left.\begin{aligned} \int\left(\mathfrak{G}_m{}^{a}{}_{;a} - \tfrac{1}{2}\varphi_{ma}\mathfrak{F}^a\right) dx_0 &\equiv 0 \\ \int\left(\mathfrak{G}_{ab}\, g^{ab}{}_{,0} - \mathfrak{F}^a{}_{,a}\right) dx_0 &\equiv 0 \end{aligned}\right\} \quad \ldots (34)$$

wobei beide Integrale über die ganze Periode zu erstrecken sind.

Die im Vorstehenden entwickelte Theorie gibt eine formal völlig befriedigende einheitliche Auffassung von der Struktur des physikalischen Raumes. Weitere Untersuchungen müssen zeigen, ob sie eine (von statistischen Elementen freie) Theorie der Elementar-Teilchen sowie der Quanten-Phänomene enthält.

A. Einstein

6. VII. 1938.

On July 6, 1938, Albert Einstein sent to the Library of Congress a twelve-page manuscript in his own hand of his "Einheitliche Feldtheorie" (Unified Field Theory), "my newest theory which I consider particularly worthy." It is one of three Einstein holograph manuscripts on scientific subjects in the Library's Manuscript Division.

Albert Einstein, "Einheitliche Feldtheorie," July 6, 1938.
Manuscript Division, Albert Einstein Collection.

Einleitung.

Dass die Elektrodynamik Maxwells – wie dieselbe gegenwärtig aufgefasst zu werden pflegt – in ihrer Anwendung auf bewegte Körper zu Asymmetrien führt, welche den Phänomenen nicht anzuhaften scheinen, ist bekannt. Man denke z. B. an die elektrodynamische Wechselwirkung zwischen einem Magneten und einem Leiter. Das beobachtbare Phänomen hängt hier nur ab von der Relativbewegung von Leiter und Magnet, während nach der üblichen Auffassung die beiden Fälle, dass der eine oder der andere dieser Körper der bewegte sei, streng voneinander zu trennen sind. Bewegt sich nämlich der Magnet und ruht der Leiter, so entsteht in der Umgebung des Magneten ein elektrisches Feld von gewissem Energiewerte, welches an den Orten, wo sich Teile des Leiters befinden, einen Strom erzeugt. Ruht aber der Magnet und bewegt sich der Leiter, so entsteht in der Umgebung des Magneten kein elektrisches Feld, dagegen im Leiter eine elektromotorische Kraft, welcher an sich keine Energie entspricht, die aber – Gleichheit der Relativbewegung bei den beiden ins Auge gefassten Fällen vorausgesetzt – zu elektrischen Strömen von derselben Grösse und demselben Verlaufe Veranlassung gibt, wie im ersten Falle die elektrischen Kräfte.

Beispiele ähnlicher Art, sowie die misslungenen Versuche, eine Bewegung der Erde relativ zum „Lichtmedium" zu konstatieren, führen zu der Vermutung, dass dem Begriffe der absoluten Ruhe nicht nur in der Mechanik, sondern auch in der Elektrodynamik keine Eigenschaften der Erscheinungen entsprechen, sondern dass vielmehr für alle Koordinatensysteme, für welche die mechanischen Gleichungen gelten, auch die gleichen elektrodynamischen und optischen Gesetze gelten, wie dies für die Grössen erster Ordnung bereits erwiesen ist. Wir wollen diese Vermutung (deren Inhalt im Folgenden „Prinzip der Relativität" genannt werden wird) zur Voraussetzung erheben und ausserdem die mit ihm nur scheinbar unverträgliche Voraussetzung einführen, dass sich das Licht im leeren Raume stets mit einer bestimmten, vom Bewegungszustande des emittierenden Körpers unabhängigen Geschwindigkeit V fortpflanze. Diese beiden Voraussetzungen genügen,

The Library proudly exhibits its new treasure, noting that it was first published in the *Annalen der Physic*, Leipzig, 1905, and that it was:

> Written by Einstein at the age of twenty-six, while he was living at Berne, Switzerland, the theory, though not immediately recognized as such, represents the first step toward one of the greatest intellectual triumphs of modern times.

In March 1955, a month before he died, Einstein wrote to Kurt Blumenfeld, "I thank you belatedly for having made me conscious of my Jewish soul." This consciousness had come forty-five years earlier when Blumenfeld directed him to Zionism. Although never a member of a Zionist organization, in 1924 Einstein did become a member of a Berlin synagogue to declare his Jewish identity and he served the cause of Zionism throughout his adult life. He visited Palestine, served on the Board of the Hebrew University, and willed his papers to it. In 1946, Einstein appeared before the Anglo-American Committee of Inquiry on Palestine and made a strong plea for a Jewish homeland.

When Israel's first president, Chaim Weizmann, died, Israeli Prime Minister David Ben Gurion invited Einstein to stand as a candidate for the office, but Einstein declined because, he said, though he was deeply touched by the offer, he was not suited for the position. During his final illness, Einstein took with him to the hospital the draft of a statement he was preparing for a television appearance celebrating the State of Israel's seventh anniversary, but he did not live either to complete or deliver it.

Facing page: The first page of a holograph copy of "Zur Electrodynamic Bewegter Körper," which Einstein describes as "my first paper concerning the theory of relativity." He had discarded the original manuscript after it had been published in *Annalen der Physic*, volume 17, Leipzig, 1905. In November 1943, Einstein rewrote this paper so that it might be presented to the Library of Congress to help promote the sale of U.S. War Bonds.

Albert Einstein, "Zur Electrodynamic Bewegter Körper," November 1943.
Manuscript Division, Albert Einstein Collection.

Sigmund Freud (1856–1939)

Among the manuscripts in the Library's collections is a letter written by Albert Einstein to Sigmund Freud on April 29, 1931, on the occasion of Freud's 75th birthday.

> 29 IV 31
>
> Honored Sir,
>
> I am very happy that your 75th birthday provides me the opportunity to thank you. You see, every Tuesday I read from your works with a lady who is a friend of mine, and cannot admire enough the beauty and truth of your presentation. Excepting only Schopenhauer, there is no one can write or could have written in such a manner.
>
> The psychological insights are accessible to a thick-skinned person like me only by way of reason but not in direct fashion. So that I react alternately with faith or a lack thereof, but cannot really judge.
>
> From my very heart I wish you the full measure of pleasure you provide the cultivated individual, and cordially greet you.
>
> Yours,
> A. E.

The letter is in the Library's Freud Collection.

Einstein's two manuscripts would be an adornment for any library. The sixty thousand or so items in the Freud archives make the Library of Congress the greatest repository of Freudiana, a veritable treasure house for scholars and students alike; and among those treasures are items of Jewish interest.

In the Library's Rare Book and Special Collections Division is an excellent copy of the first edition of Freud's greatest work, *Die Traumdeutung*

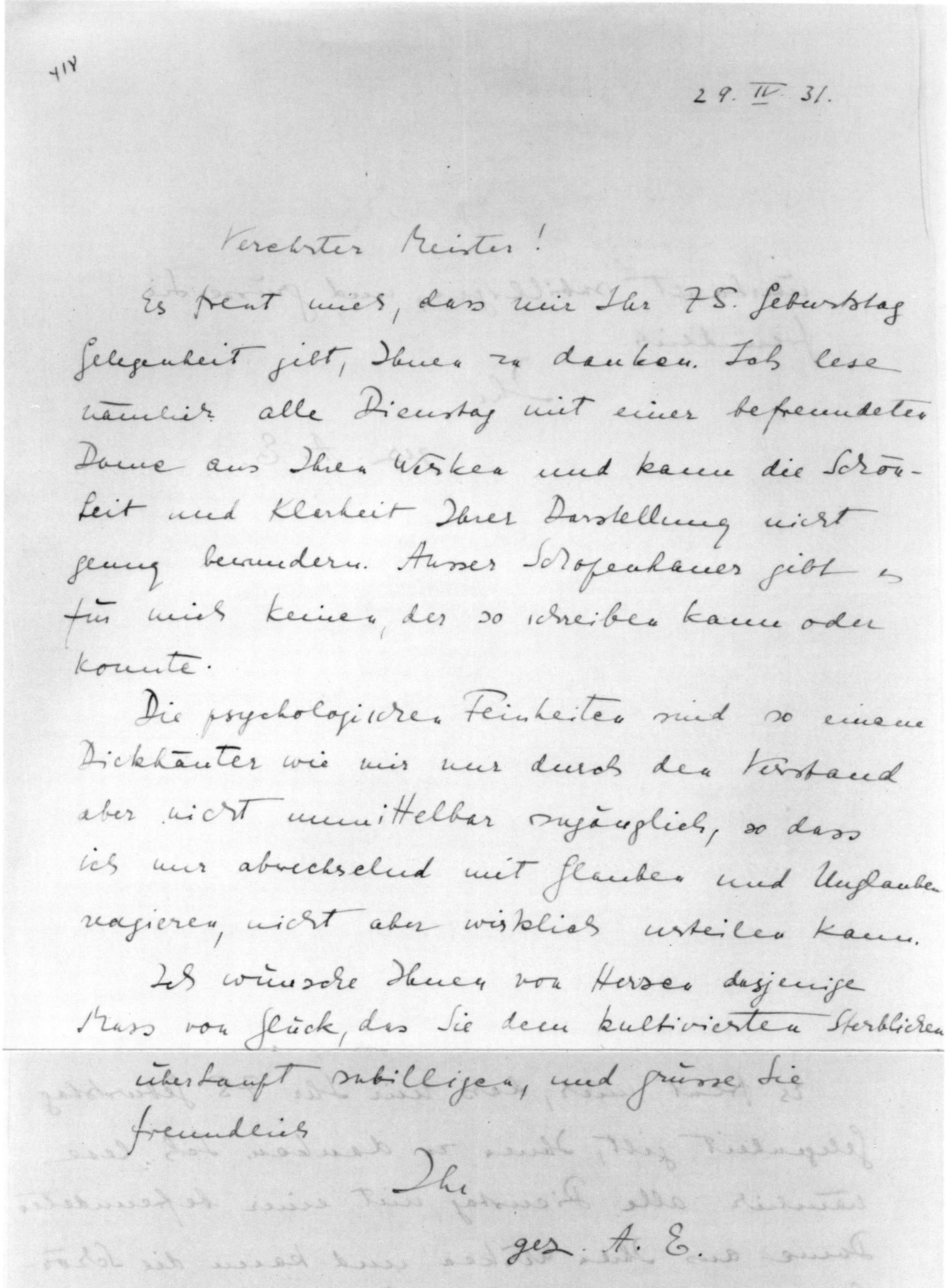
29. IV. 31.

Verehrter Meister!

Es freut mich, dass mir Ihr 75. Geburtstag Gelegenheit gibt, Ihnen zu danken. Ich lese nämlich alle Dienstag mit einer befreundeten Dame aus Ihren Werken und kann die Schönheit und Klarheit Ihrer Darstellung nicht genug bewundern. Ausser Schopenhauer gibt es für mich keinen, der so schreiben kann oder konnte.

Die psychologischen Feinheiten sind so einem Dickhäuter wie mir nur durch den Verstand aber nicht unmittelbar zugänglich, so dass ich nur abwechselnd mit Glauben und Unglauben reagieren, nicht aber wirklich urteilen kann.

Ich wünsche Ihnen von Herzen dasjenige Mass von Glück, das Sie dem kultivierten Sterblichen überhaupt zubilligen, und grüsse Sie freundlich

Ihr

gez. A. E.

A letter from Einstein to Freud on the occasion of Freud's seventy-fifth birthday, April 29, 1931. The letter, though informal in tone, is rather reserved in sentiment, for though Einstein and Freud each recognized the eminence of the other, their relationship never developed into friendship.

Albert Einstein, Letter to Sigmund Freud, April 29, 1931. Manuscript Division, Sigmund Freud Collection.

(Interpretation of Dreams), Leipzig and Vienna, 1900 (really 1899), which was once the property of "Med. Dr. Fritz Magyar, Wien I, Hegelgasse 4." Freud presented his earliest views on dream interpretation at the *Jüdische akademische Lesehalle,* first in 1896 and again a year later. On December 7 and 14, 1897, he delivered papers on "Traumdeutung" to the Vienna lodge of B'nai B'rith, of which he had become a member in September. These were the first of twenty-seven lectures before B'nai B'rith between 1897 and 1917. The society's journal reports on the first two:

Two lectures by Brother Dozent Dr. Freud about interpretation of dreams. The lecturer beginning with the familiar physiological causes of dreams, discussed the psychology of dream life and established the principles of a self-contained theory. In the conclusion of his ingenious interpretation, he said:
"whoever is occupied with the dreams of man and understands their true meaning peers into the secrets of the human soul as into a crater imbedded within the earth's dark interior."

Under his portrait drawn in pen and ink by Robert Kastor, 1925, for inclusion in a book on the greats of the world, Sigmund Freud wrote:

There is no medicine against death, and against error no rule has been found.

Robert Kastor, "Sigmund Freud," 1925.
Prints and Photographs Division.

Dennis B. Klein, whose *Jewish Origins of the Psychoanalytic Movement*, New York, 1981, informs us about this phase of Freud's life and activities, records the reaction of the audience. One reported: "From beginning to end, everyone present listened with rapt attention to Freud's words"; another, "The audience expressed their gratitude and approval with unrestrained applause."

Why did Freud seek out a Jewish audience for his scientific lectures? The answer is, alas, that no other group would provide him a platform, or a sympathetic hearing. In the spring of 1897, Emperor Franz Josef, after four refusals, finally accepted the outspoken anti-Semite Karl Lueger as Mayor of Vienna. Anti-Semitism was rife in Vienna, and Freud had felt its sting, being denied professional promotion once and again. Only fellow Jews provided the audience and the appreciation the father of psychoanalysis needed so desperately at that stage in his life and work, as he was moving from his career as a physician to becoming the "Founding Father" of the movement.

In 1926, when Freud's lodge brothers celebrated his seventieth birthday, illness kept him from attending the celebration, but he wrote to them:

> What bound me to Judaism was, I must confess, not belief and not national pride . . . Other considerations . . . made the attractiveness of Judaism and Jews irresistible . . . Because I was a Jew I found myself free from many prejudices which limited others in the use of their intellect, and being a Jew, I was prepared to enter opposition and to renounce agreement with the "compact majority."

Like Einstein, Freud served on the Board of the Hebrew University, but unlike him, Jewish interests and Jewish identity were not major concerns. The Library has the manuscript copy of his "Ein Wort Zum Antisemitismus" (A Word on Anti-Semitism), which appeared in *Die Zukunft: ein neues Deutschland ein neues Europa*, November 25, 1938, a German émigré weekly edited by Arthur Koestler, published in Paris. In it Freud includes the précis of an essay ostensibly by a non-Jew which defends the Jews. Critical of the nature of Christian protest against anti-Semitism, which the author contends was scanty and came too late, he writes:

> We profess a religion of love. We ought to love even our enemies as ourselves. We know that the Son of God gave his life on earth to redeem *all* men from the burden of sin. He is our model and it is therefore sinning against His intention and against the command of the Christian religion if we consent to Jews being insulted, ill-treated, robbed and plunged into misery. We ought to protest against this, irrespective of how much or how little Jews deserve such treatment.
>
> For long centuries we have treated the Jewish people unjustly and we are continuing to do so . . . Jews are no worse than we are . . . Nor can we call them in any sense inferior. Since we allowed them to co-operate in our cultural tasks, they have acquired merit by valuable contributions in all spheres of science, art and technology, and they have richly repaid our tolerance. So let us cease at last to hand them out favors when they have a claim to justice.

Ernest Jones suggests that these words were written by Freud himself, and he may well be right. They were written soon after Freud completed his one major work of Jewish interest, which was published in 1939 in Amsterdam as *Der Mann Moses und die Monotheistische Religion*, and that same year as *Moses and Monotheism* in New York, a work which raised a storm of protest in the Jewish world. To maintain that monotheism was

Facing page:
The November 25, 1938, issue of the German emigré weekly *Die Zukunft* (The Future), edited by Arthur Koestler, published Freud's "Ein Wort Zum Antisemitismus" (A Word on Anti-Semitism), Freud's most significant statement on the subject. The three-page signed holograph manuscript is in the Library's Freud Collection.

Sigmund Freud, "Ein Wort Zum Antisemitismus," 1938. Manuscript Division, Sigmund Freud Collection.

Ein Wort zum Antisemitismus.

Während ich die Äußerungen in Presse und Literatur ~~[illegible]~~ studierte, zu denen die letzten Judenverfolgungen Anlass gegeben haben, fiel mir ein Aufsatz in die Hand, der mir so außergewöhnlich schien, dass ich ihn zu meinem Gebrauch exzerpierte. Der Verfasser sagte darin ungefähr folgendes: „Ich stelle voran, dass ich Nichtjude bin, es ist also nicht [illegible]

[illegible]

12

an Egyptian invention and Moses an Egyptian who was murdered by the Jews because of his message, was to rob the Jewish people of its greatest contribution and its greatest leader. To do this at a time when Judaism was being viciously maligned and Jews were being brutally treated gave all Jews pause.

In the Freud Collection we find the manuscript of the work in its three parts, "Moses Ein Ägypter" (Moses an Egyptian); "Wenn Moses Ein Ägypter War . . ." (If Moses were an Egyptian . . .); and "Moses, Sein Volk, und die Monotheistische Religion" (Moses, His People, and Monotheistic Religion). The manuscript also bore an earlier title, *Der Mann Moses, Ein Historischer Roman* (The Man Moses, A Historical Novel). The first two parts appeared in 1937 in the Viennese journal *Imago;* the third part was first published as the third section of the completed book.

Interpretation and critique of *Moses and Monotheism* are wide and varied. Professor Yosef Hayim Yerushalmi in the Lionel Trilling Lecture he delivered at Columbia University on November 14, 1986, noted that none of the scholars and critics had mentioned a manuscript of the work. He expressed delight that his inquiry to the Freud archives at the Library of Congress had brought him a Xerox copy of the original draft "different in significant ways from the published version." He found an original unpublished introduction, which Freud concluded with:

> My immediate purpose was to gain knowledge of the person Moses, my more distant goal to contribute thereby to the solution of a problem, still current today.

Yerushalmi also found that the manuscript draft and printed work differ substantially in their opening sentence. The original read: "One will not easily decide to deny a nation its greatest son because of the meaning of a name" (Moses is an Egyptian name). In its final form it reads: "To deprive a people of the man whom they take pride in as the greatest of their sons is not a thing to be gladly or carelessly undertaken—*especially when one himself belongs to that people*" (emphasis added). Yerushalmi argues, elegantly and forcefully, that *Moses and Monotheism* is a work neither of negation nor degradation but of affirmation and pride in belonging to a people from whom, Freud writes:

> there rose again and again men who lent new color to the fading tradition, renewed the admonishments and demands of Moses, and did not rest until the lost cause was once more regained . . . And it is proof of a special psychical fitness in the mass which became the Jewish people that it could bring forth so many persons who were ready to take upon themselves the burden of the Mosaic religion . . . It is honor enough for the Jewish people that it has kept alive such a tradition and produced men who lent it their voice, even if the stimulus had first come from the outside, from a great stranger.

In 1920, Freud began to be obsessed by death. This has been attributed to the death of his beloved daughter, Sophie, about which he wrote to Sandor Ferenczi, "Since I am profoundly irreligious . . . there is no one I can accuse." Yet among his family papers, this profoundly irreligious man retained a small book of special Jewish prayers dealing with death. In box B3 we find a black-covered Yahrzeit booklet issued by a Berlin undertaker, which contains prayers in Hebrew and German to be said on the anniversary of the death of a loved one and at memorial services. Inscribed on the

Facing page:
Retained in the Freud family papers is this *Yahrzeit und Trauer-Andachtsbuch*, presented to the bereaved family of Freud's brother-in-law and distant relative, Maurice Freud, who died in Berlin on September 7, 1920. Freud cancelled an important trip to England to hasten to Berlin to be with the bereaved family at that time. Both Freuds, Maurice and Sigmund, had been born the same year, 1856.

Yahrzeit und Trauer-Andachtsbuch, Berlin, 1920. Manuscript Division, Sigmund Freud Collection.

Dem Andenken
meines unvergeßlichen Vaters
Maurice Freud
gewidmet.

Sterbetag:
am 7. Septemb. 1920
24. Elul 5680
im 64 Lebensjahre.

Ehre deinem Andenken!

 Herausgegeben vom Verlag für Trauerbücher, Berlin W 50, Ansbacherstr. 35

first page is the name of the one to be memorialized and the date of his death: "Maurice Freud, 24 Elul, 5680 (September 7, 1920)." Maurice or Moritz Freud was a cousin once-removed who was married to Sigmund's sister Marie. He died suddenly of a heart attack in Berlin, and Sigmund cancelled a professionally important trip to England "to go back to Berlin to see Marie and the orphan." Why did Freud retain the Yahrzeit booklet? It might help to point out that Sigmund was well aware that Moritz had been born in 1856, the year of his own birth. I leave it to Freudians to ponder.

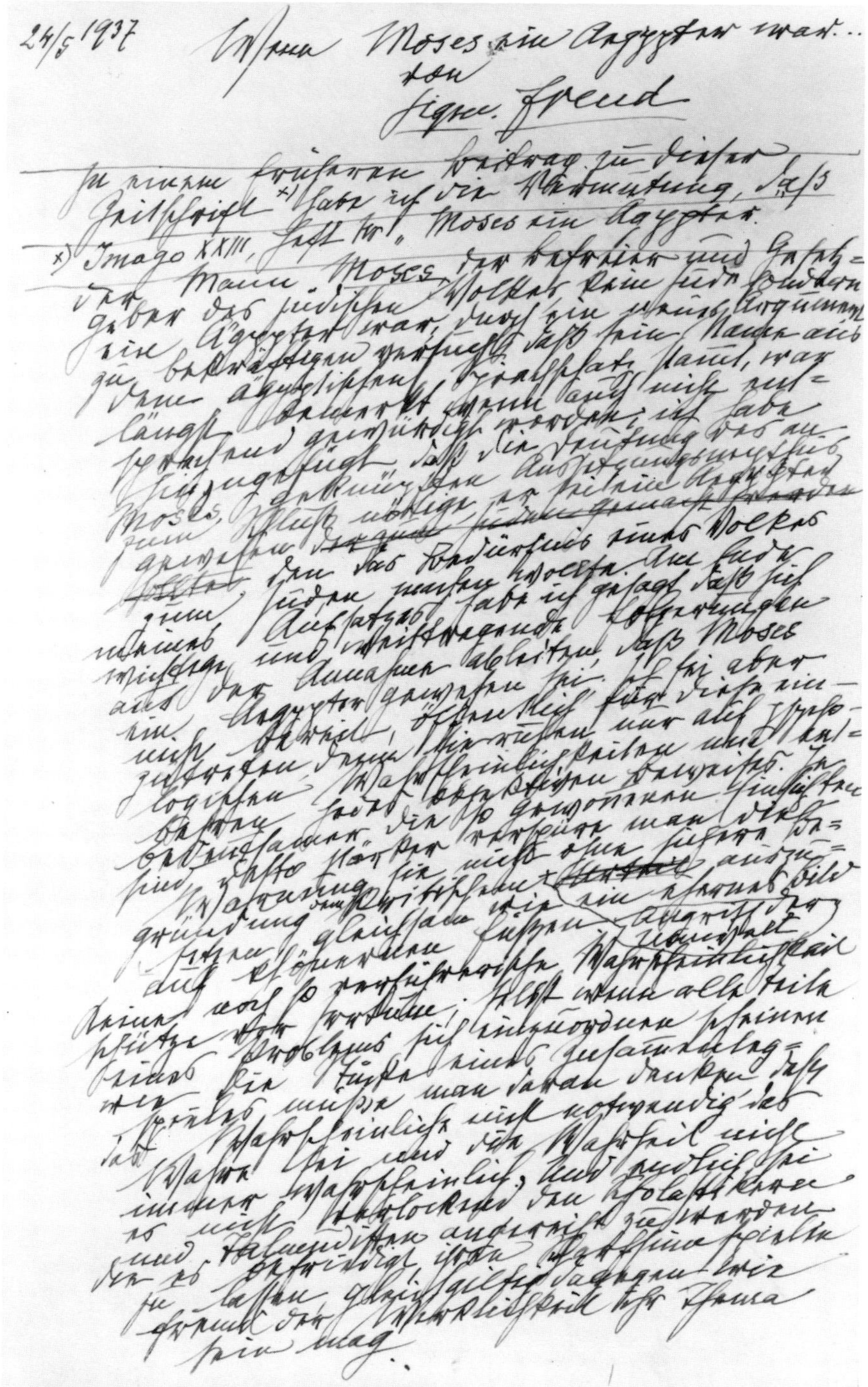
24/5 1937 Wenn Moses ein Ägypter war...
von
Sigm. Freud

The complete holograph manuscript of the three parts of Freud's *Der Mann Moses und die Monotheistische Religion* (Moses and Monotheism), as well as the corrected galleys, are in the Library's Freud Collection. The first page shown of "Wenn Moses Ein Ägypter War . . ." (If Moses Were an Egyptian) is dated 24/5/1937.

Sigmund Freud, *Der Mann Moses und die Monotheistische Religion*, 1937.
Manuscript Division, Sigmund Freud Collection.

12

IN THE NEW WORLD

THE EXODUS (AUGUST 3, 1492)

The Spanish noon is a blaze of azure fire, and the dusty pilgrims crawl like an endless serpent along treeless plains and bleached highroads, through rocksplit ravines and castellated, cathedral-shadowed towns.

Noble and abject, learned and simple, illustrious and obscure, plod side by side, all brothers now, all merged in one routed army of misfortune.

Whither shall they turn? for the West hath cast them out, and the East refuseth to receive.

O bird of the air, whisper to the despairing exiles, that to-day, to-day, from the many-masted, gayly-bannered port of Pallos, sails the world-unveiling Genoese, to unlock the golden gates of sunset and bequeath a Continent to Freedom!

Emma Lazarus

IT WAS CHRISTOPHER COLUMBUS, the "world-unveiling Genoese" himself, who first linked the Jews and the New World. In his letter to the king and queen of Spain which opens the *Journal of the First Voyage,* Columbus writes:

So after having expelled the Jews from your dominions, Your Highnesses, in the same month of January, ordered me to proceed with sufficient armament to the said region of India.

Actually, Columbus set sail on August 3, 1492, a day after the expulsion of the Jews from Spain began. Much has been written of Columbus's purported Jewish origins and of Jews who accompanied him on his first voyage. It is certain only that the expedition's interpreter, Luis de Torres, was born a Jew but had converted shortly before the expedition set sail; that two "New Christians," Luis de Santangel and Gabriel Sanchez, had a hand in the financing; and that two Jews, Abraham Zacuto and Joseph Vecinho, provided technical expertise that helped Columbus navigate the "Ocean Sea."

Abraham Zacuto (c. 1452–1515), a historian and astronomer, who wrote his major astronomical work, *Ha-Hibur ha-Gadol,* in Hebrew under the patronage of the bishop of Salamanca, served as court astronomer to kings John II and Manuel I of Portugal, where he took refuge after the expulsion from Spain. Zacuto prepared the charts used by Vasco da Gama on his successful journey to India, but his high position and contribution

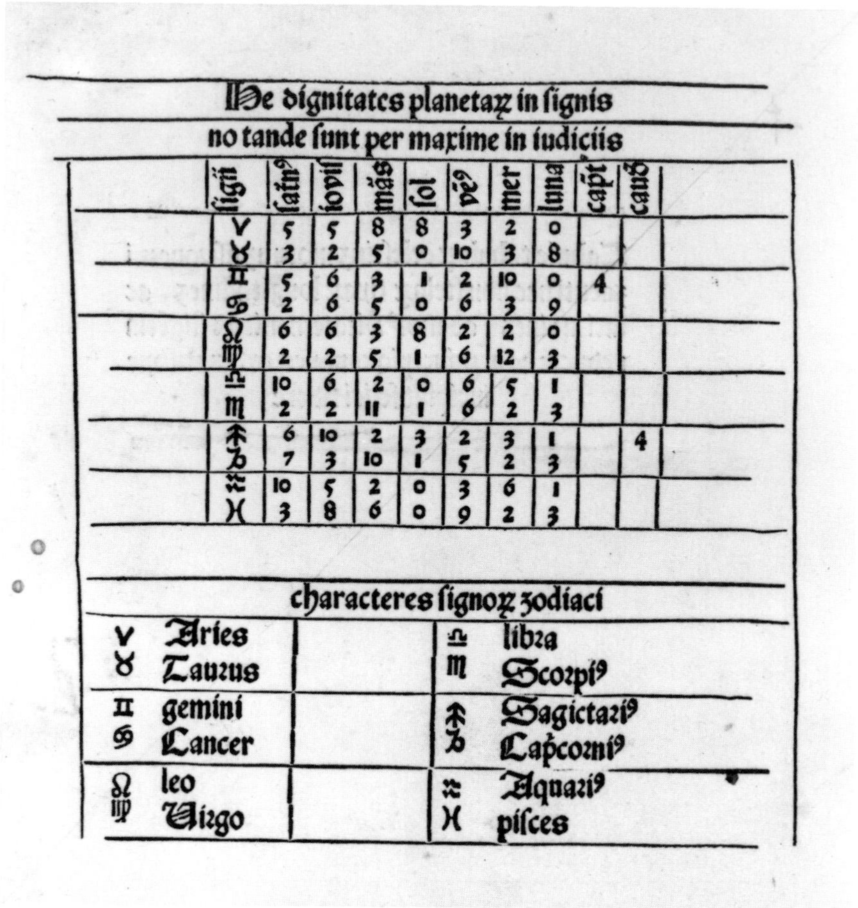

De dignitates planetaꝝ in signis
no tande sunt per maxime in iudiciis

signi	satn⁹	iovis	mãs	sol	ve⁹	mer	luna	capt	caud
♈	5	5	8	8	3	2	0		
♉	3	2	5	0	10	3	8		
♊	5	6	3	1	2	10	0	4	
♋	2	6	5	0	6	3	9		
♌	6	6	3	8	2	2	0		
♍	2	2	5	1	6	12	3		
♎	10	6	2	0	6	5	1		
♏	2	2	11	1	6	2	3		
♐	6	10	2	3	2	3	1		4
♑	7	3	10	1	5	2	3		
♒	10	5	2	0	3	6	1		
♓	3	8	6	0	9	2	3		

characteres signoꝝ zodiaci

♈	Aries	♎	libra
♉	Taurus	♏	Scorpi⁹
♊	gemini	♐	Sagictari⁹
♋	Cancer	♑	Capcorni⁹
♌	leo	♒	Aquari⁹
♍	Uirgo	♓	pisces

The astronomical tables of the astronomer and rabbi, Abraham Zacuto, published by the last of the Jewish printers in Portugal, Abraham Orta, one year before the Jews were expelled. What makes this book of particular historical importance is that Christopher Columbus used the Zacuto astronomical tables in his journeys of discovery.

Abraham Zacuto, *Tabulae astronomicae*, Leiria, 1496. Rare Book and Special Collections Division.

to Portuguese imperial expansion availed him little when, in 1497, the Jews in Portugal were forced to convert, and he was forced once again to flee. In Tunis, in 1504, Zacuto completed his historical narrative, *Sefer ha-Yuhasin,* in which he claimed: "My astronomical charts circulate throughout all the Christian and even Muslim lands."

Among those who made use of Zacuto's astronomical tables was Christopher Columbus. A copy of those tables with Columbus's notes is preserved in Seville. What made the tables accessible to Columbus was their having been translated into Spanish by a pupil of Zacuto, Joseph Vecinho, physician to King John II. According to tradition Vecinho gave his translated work to Columbus for his journey, which he had heretofore recommended against. In 1496, the tables were published in both Latin and Spanish editions in Leiria, Portugal, by Samuel D'Ortas. The D'Ortas family, Samuel and his three sons, had previously printed two Hebrew books in that city, *Proverbs* with commentary in 1492, and the *Former Prophets* with commentary in 1495. The contents of *Tabulae astronomicae* of Abraham Zacuthus, Leiria, 1496, are described by the full title: *Tabula tabulay celestius motuuz astronomi zacuti necnon stelay firay longitudinez ac latitudinez.*

In the Library's fine copy of the Polyglot Psalter in the Hebrew, Latin, Greek, Arabic, and Chaldean (Aramaic), published in Genoa, 1516, is Christopher Columbus's first printed biography. In a Latin note on the phrase "the ends of the earth" from Psalm 19, the commentator, Agostino Giustiniani, states that the ends of the earth were discovered in his time

Facing page: The lower part of the Latin commentary on the right-hand side of this page of the Genoa, 1516 Polyglot Psalter provides the first description of Christopher Columbus and his discoveries in a Hebrew book. What occasioned this digressive comment are the words "the end of the earth" in verse 4 of chapter 19 of the Psalms. The learned commentator was eager to inform the reader of the intrepid Genoese who discovered "the ends of the earth."

Psalter, Genoa, 1516. Hebraic Section.

ودنو الغربا عتقو
وداروا عرجا
في طرقهم حي
هو الله تبارك
الله
خلاصي
تعالى الرب الذي انقذني
الله الذي وهب لي الانتقام
اخضع الشعوب تحتي
ونجاني من يد اعدائي
المبغضين ورفعني من الذين
قاموا علي ومن
الرجال الاثمة
نجاني لذلك
اشكرك يارب بين الشعوب
وارتل اسمك
يا معظم خلاص
الملك وصانع الرحمة
لمسيحه داود
وزرعه الى الابد
المزمور الثامن عشر
السموات تنطق
بمجد الله والفلك
يخبر بعمل يديه
يوم يبدي كلامه
ليوم وليل يبدي
علما لليل
ليس بقول ولا
بكلمات الذين لا تسمع
اصواتهم خرجت
اصواتهم في الارض كلها
وبلغ كلامهم اقطار
المسكونة جعل مسكنه في
الشمس وهو مثل العريس
اذا خرج من خدره
يفرح
مثل الجبار
الذي يسرع
في سبله من اطراف
السما خروجها

קדמי בני עממיא יסופון
ויטלטל מברניתהון קיים
הוא יי ובריך תקיפא
דמן קדמוי מתיהב לי
תקוף ופורקן ומרומם
אלהא תקוף פורקני :
אלהא דעבד פורענות לי
ומתבר עממיא דקיימין
לאבאשא לי תחותי :
משיזב יתי מבעלי דבבי
דקיימין לאבאשא לי
תגברינני מן גוג ומשר׳
עממין חטופין דעמיה
ישיזבינני : מטול היכנא
אודה קדמך ביני עממיא
יי ולשמך אימר תושבחן :
מסגי למעבד פורקן
עם מלכיה ועביד טיבו
למשיחיה לדוד :
ולזרעיה עד עלמא :
לשבחא
תושבחא לדוד
דמסתכלין בשמיא משתעי׳
יקרא דיי עובדי אידוי
מחוון דמדיקין באוירא :
יומא ליומא מוסיף ומועי
מימרא ולילייא ללילייא
פחות ומחוי מנדעא :
לית מימר דתורעמא ולית
מילי דשגושא ולית
משתמע קלהון : בכולא
ארעא מתח עגייניהון
ובסייפי תבל מליהון
לשמשא שוי משרוי
ויהורא בהון והוא כצפרא
כחתנא נפק מגנוניה
ברירובא ובפלגות יומא
יחדי היך גיברא ומטר
למירהט בתקוף באורח
מעלני בפניא : מסייפי
שמיא מפקניה

ī pſētia mea. Filii populoꝝ cōſumētur
& migrabunt de pretoriis ſuis. Viuit
DEVS ipſe, & benedictus fortis,
quoniam ante eum dabitur mihi
fortitudo & redemptio, & exaltetur
DEVS fortis redemptio mea.
DEVS qui vltus eſt me,
& proſtrauit populos, qui exurgunt
ad offenſionem meam ſub me.
Eripuit me de p̄onis inimicitie mee,
īſup pluſq̄ illos q exur. vt noceāt mihi
valētiorē me efficies, ab gog āt & ab(
pplóꝝ rapaciū, q ſt cū illo (exercitibꝯ
eripies me. Propterea
laudabo te in populis
DEVS & nomini tuo laudes dicam.
Magnifico vt faciat redemptionem
cum rege ſuo, & facienti bonum
MESSIE ſuo Dauidi,
& ſemini eius vſq; in eternum.

XIX. In laudem.

Laudatoria Dauidis.
Qui ſuſpiciunt celos enarrant
gloriam DEI, & opera manuum eius
annunciant qui ſuſpiciunt in aera.
Dies diei apponit, & manifeſtat
verbum & nox nocti
diminuit & nunciat ſcientiam.
Nō eſt verbū lamentationis, & nō ſunt
ſermones tumultus & non
audiuntur voces eorum. In omnem
terram extenſi ſunt effectus eorum,
& in fines orbis omnia verba eorum,
ſoli poſuit tabernaculum,
illumiationē aūt ī illos. Et ipſe ī mane
tanq̄ ſponſus procedēs de thalamo ſuo
pulcherrime, & dum diuiditur dies
letatur vt gigas, & obſeruat
ad currendam in fortitudine viam
occaſus veſptini. Ab extremitatibus
celorum egreſſus eius,

F. Libro midras tehilim in calce huius pſalmi ומהו מגדול שנעשה לדם פון המשיח נמגדול שנ׳ מגדול ישועות ובתי׳ מגדול עז שם יי בו ירוץ צדיק ונשגב .i. Et quod eſt caſtrum, uel que eſt turris, que facta eſt eis ∴ Rex MESSIAS, queādmodum dictū eſt turris ſalutis, & ſcriptū eſt turris fortitudinis nomen DEI in ipſum currit iuſtus & ſuſtolletur.

A. Secundum ex ſeptem nominibus quibus hebrei celum ſignificant, impoſitū uerius ab extendendo quam a firmando.

B. Non auditur uox eorū, Iuxta illud. Nō enim uos eſtis qui loquimini, ſed ſpiritus patris ueſtri qui loquitur in uobis. Et hic literalis ille ſenſus, qui cum ſpiritali coincidit, uti ſcripſit Faber principio comentariorum ſuarum.

C. In omnem terram exiuit filum ſiue linea eorū. eo intellectu quo linea p̄prie ſignificat filum illud, quo materiarii utūtur fabri ad ſignandam materiam, perinde ac ſi dixiſſet propheta. exiuit ſtructura ſine edificiū eorum,

D. Et in fines mundi uerba eorum, Saltem tēporibus noſtris q̄bꝯ mirabili auſu Chriſtophori columbi genuenſis, alter pene orbis repertus eſt chriſtianorumq; cetui aggregatus. At uero quoniam Columbus frequēter p̄dicabat ſe a Deo electum ut per ipſum adimpleretur hec prophetia. non alienū exiſtimaui uitam ipſius hoc loco inſerere. Igitur Chriſtophorus cognomento columbus patria genuenſis, uilibus ortus parentibus, noſtra etate fuit qui ſua induſtria, plus terrarum & pellagi explorauerit paucis mēſibus, quam pene reliqui omnes mortales uniuerſis retro actis ſeculis. Mira res, ſ; ta

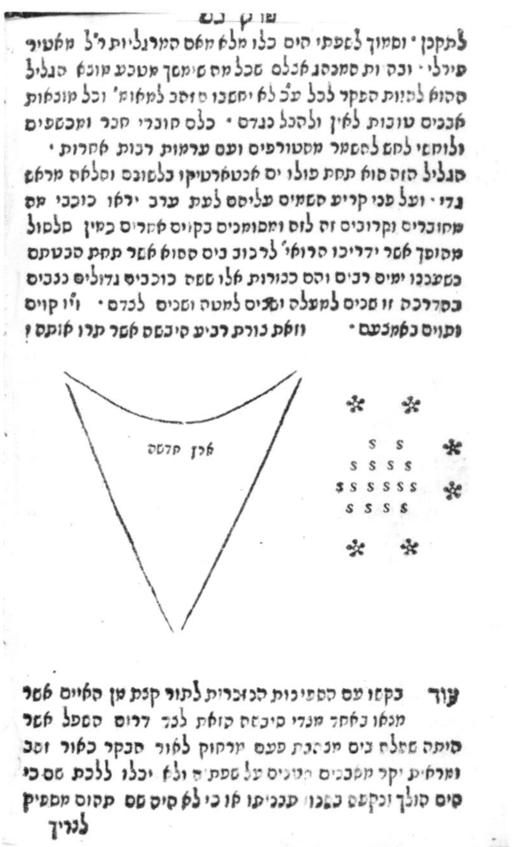

The shieldlike figure is labeled "New Land" in Hebrew, in this pioneer work in Hebrew on geography. The author, Abraham Farissol, informs the reader of "the three areas of habitation, Asia, Africa and Europe . . . also of the far-off islands recently discovered by the Portuguese . . . of the River Sambatyon, and of unknown places where Jews reside, the borders of the Land of Israel and Paradise on earth" and of the discovery of a New World, a fourth area of habitation.

Abraham Farissol, *Iggeret Orhot Olam*, Venice, 1586. Hebraic Section.

Facing page:
The title of *Jewes in America* continues: "Probabilities that the Americans are Jewes." One of the earliest of the many books asserting that the American Indians are descended from the Ten Lost Tribes of Israel. The author documents his assertion with the account of "Aaron Levi, alias Antonie Monterinos," who returned to Amsterdam from Brazil with a tale that he had met representatives of the descendants of the Ten Lost Tribes, now resident in South America.

Thomas Thorowgood, *Jewes in America*, London, 1650. Rare Book and Special Collections Division.

through the daring deeds of Christopher Columbus of Genoa, claiming also that this native son of Genoa has explored more lands and seas than anyone else in all the world. Because of him, then, the words of the Psalmist that the glory of God would be proclaimed "to the ends of the earth" were now fulfilled.

The first mention of the discovery of the New World and the first description of it in Hebrew literature is in *Iggeret Orhot Olam* (A Tract on the Paths of the World), Venice, 1586. It was written in 1524 by Abraham Farissol (1451–1525), a contemporary of Columbus. Bible scholar and polemicist, he served as a cantor in the Ferrara synagogue and was also a copyist of manuscripts. Aware of the world about him and much taken by the great voyages of discovery, Farissol turned his attention to geography and cosmography. His small volume is divided into thirty chapters which deal with "the distant islands recently discovered by the Portuguese; on the River Sambatyon and the Jews who lived beyond it (i.e., the Ten Lost Tribes); the boundaries of the Land of Israel . . . and the earthly Garden of Eden." In Chapter 29 he reports on Columbus's discovery of the New World in 1492:

It is now an established fact that the Spanish ships which were sent on an expedition by the King of Spain . . . almost gave up hope of ever returning. . . . But divine providence had decreed for them a kinder fate than death amid sea. . . . Those at the topmost mast discerned a strip of land . . . When they had sailed along its shores . . . and saw its exceeding large size, they called it because of its great length and breadth, "The New World." The land is rich in natural resources. They have an abundance of fish . . . large forests . . . teeming with large and small beasts of prey, and serpents as large as beams. The sand along the shores of the rivers, contain pure gold . . . precious stones . . . and mother of pearl.

Farissol attempts a crude "map" of the New World, no more than lines forming a shieldlike figure and some typographical markings. *Orhot Olam* was translated into Latin, published in Oxford, in 1691, as *Tractus Itinerum Mundi,* and was republished many times in Hebrew. The most notable edition is that of Prague, 1793, which contains interesting illustrations.

In the Rare Book and Special Collections Division are two books bearing the same title, *Jewes in America,* by the same author, but published in London ten years apart, in 1650 and 1660. The author, Thomas Thorowgood, a British divine, has as the subtitle of the first edition: "Probabilities that the Americans are Jewes." These are the first of many books and articles identifying the American Indians as the descendants of the Ten Tribes of Israel, who were exiled by the Assyrian monarch Sennacherib in 722 BCE and "lost."

Thorowgood argues that, "The Indians do themselves relate things of their Ancestors suteable to what we read in the Bible . . . They constantly and strictly separate their women in a little wigwam by themselves in their feminine seasons . . . they hold that Nanawitnawit (a God overhead) made the Heavens and the Earth." He further proposes that, "The rites, fashions, ceremonies, and opinions of the Americans are in many things agreeable to the custom of the Jewes, not only prophane and common usages, but such as he called solemn and sacred." His final and crowning proof, "The Relation of Master Antonie Monterinos, translated out of the French Copie sent by Manasseh Ben Israel," begins:

The eighteenth day of Elul, in the yeere five thousand foure hundred and foure

Iewes in America,

OR,

PROBABILITIES

That the AMERICANS are of that Race.

With the removall of ſome contrary reaſonings, and earneſt deſires for effectuall endeavours to make them Chriſtian.

Propoſed by THO: THOROVVGOOD, B. D. one of the Aſſembly of Divines.

CANT. 8. 8. *We have a little ſiſter, and ſhe hath no breaſts, what ſhall we doe for our ſiſter in the day when ſhe ſhall be ſpoken for?*
MAT. 8. 11. *Many ſhall come from the Eaſt, and from the Weſt, and ſhall ſit downe with* Abraham, *and* Iſaac, *and* Jacob *in the Kingdome of Heaven.*

Æthiopes vertuntur in filios Dei, ſi egerint pœnitentiam, & filii Dei tranſeunt in Æthiopes ſi in profundum venerint peccatorum: Hieronym. in Eſai.

London, Printed by *W. H.* for *Tho. Slater*, and are be to ſold at his ſhop at the ſigne of the Angel in Duck lane, 1650.

from the creation of the World (1644), came into this city of *Amsterdam* Mr. *Aron Levi, alias, Antonie Monterinos,* and declared before me *Manassah Ben Israell,* and divers other chiefe men of the Portugall Nation, neer to the said city that which followeth.

What follows is a fanciful tale by Montezinos (his correct name) of meeting in Brazil representatives of a mysterious mighty nation of Indians who claimed descent from Abraham, Isaac, Jacob, and Israel, and from the Tribes of Reuben and Joseph. They announced their readiness now to rise up and drive the Spanish and Portuguese invaders from their continent.

Two years later, in 1652, Roger L'Estrange countered with his *Americans No Jewes* (London, 1652). In answer, the 1660 edition reaffirmed, "that those Indians are Judaical, made more probable by some Additional . . . learned conjectures of Reverend Mr. John Eliot." Eliot, the "Apostle to the Indians," was more interested in promoting his missionary endeavors among the Indians than in proving their Jewishness, so his lengthy epistle is not so much a defense of the Thorowgood thesis, as of the New England Colonists and a call for aid from the mother country for their New World emissaries who are bringing the word of the Lord to the natives.

To bring the "good news" to the natives of the New World, Eliot translated the Bible into the Massachusetts dialect of the Algonquian language. It was published in Cambridge in1663 under the title *The Holy Bible Containing the Old Testament and the New. Translated into the Indian Language and Ordered to be Printed by the Commissioners of the United Colonies in New*

If Thorowgood was right (see exhibit item 215), then the first Bible printed in America was for the descendants of that people which gave the Bible to the world. Be that as it may, before us is the title page of an edition published in Cambridge in New England in 1663, *Translated into the Indian Language and Ordered to be Printed by the Commissioners of the United Colonies in New England* . . . The translator was John Eliot, "Apostle to the Indians," and his and its purpose was the conversion of the Indians to Christianity. The first English Bible in America was not published for 120 years, and the first Hebrew for 150.

The Holy Bible . . . Translated into the Indian Language . . . , Cambridge (New England), 1663.
Rare Book and Special Collections Division.

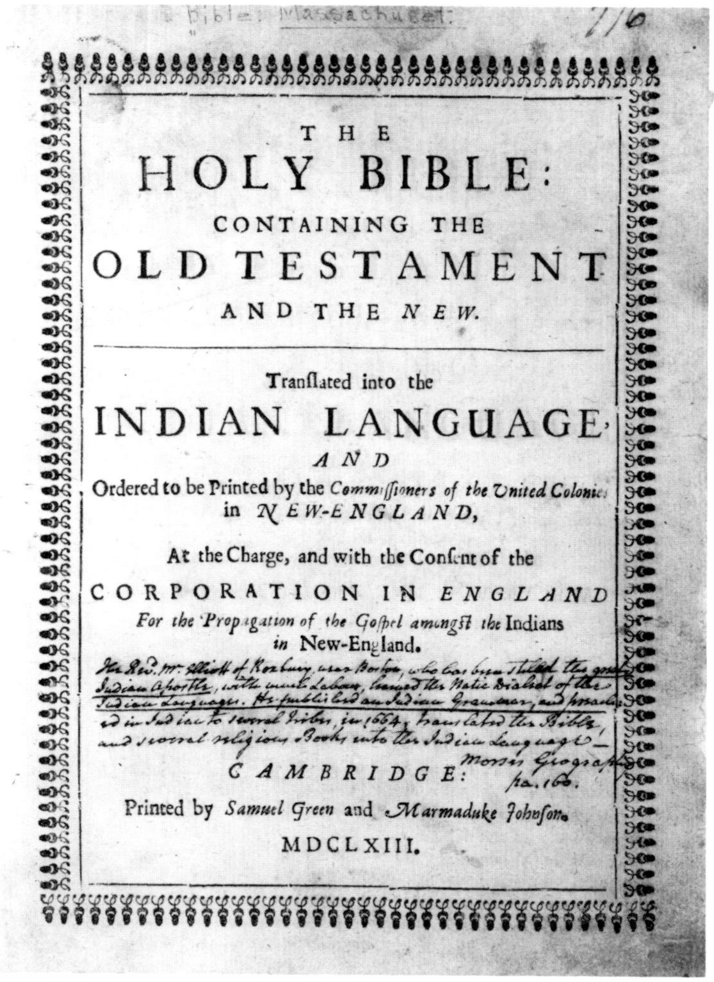

THE

HOLY BIBLE:

CONTAINING THE

OLD TESTAMENT

AND THE *NEW.*

Tranflated into the

INDIAN LANGUAGE,

AND

Ordered to be Printed by the *Commiffioners of the United Coloni[e]s* in *NEW-ENGLAND,*

At the Charge, and with the Confent of the

CORPORATION IN *ENGLAND*

For the Propagation of the Gofpel amongft the Indians *in* New-England.

The Rev. Mr. Eliott of Roxbury, near Boston, who has been stiled the great Indian Apostle, with much labour, learned the Natic dialect of the Indian Language. He published an Indian Grammar, and preached in Indian to several tribes, in 1664, translated the Bible, and several religious Books into the Indian Language — Morse's Geography pa. 160.

CAMBRIDGE:

Printed by *Samuel Green* and *Marmaduke Johnfon.*

MDCLXIII.

England . . . , Cambridge, 1663. The first Bible printed in America, it appeared 120 years before the first English edition. A second edition appeared two years later. If, indeed, Eliot believed the Indians to be the descendants of the Ten Lost Tribes, his was a work of restoring the Book to the People of the Book. In full, or in part, in either edition, the Eliot Bible is a book of great rarity, and the Library's copy is in uncommonly fine condition.

Twenty-three years earlier, a translation of the Psalms into English, the so-called Bay Psalm Book, was published in Cambridge, New England. Printed by Stephen Daye in 1640, it is the very first book published in the English settlements of America. Its title reads: *The Whole Book of Psalmes Faithfully Translated into English Metre.* The Preface by Richard Mather contains five Hebrew words, the first appearance of Hebrew in any work printed in the New World. The Library of Congress has one of the eleven extant copies of this work, which, if not the rarest of American imprints, is surely the most important.

AT THE BIRTH OF THE NATION

Raphael Mahler begins his monumental *History of the Jews in Modern Times* with the birth of the United States of America, which, he argues, marked for the Jews a revolutionary change from bestowed tolerance to equal rights. A map celebrating the birth of this nation, *The United States of America laid down From the best Authorities Agreeable to the Peace of 1783,* might then be considered a document of Jewish history. Published in London by John Wallis on April 3, 1783, five months before the final signing of the Treaty by the American delegation headed by Benjamin Franklin, it is particularly noteworthy for its cartouche. At the top is a heralding angel, sounding a trumpet, laurel wreath in one hand, a flag of thirteen bars and thirteen stars in the other. On one side is George Washington ushering in Lady Columbia with a freedom cap on her staff. On the other is Benjamin Franklin, quill in hand, writing. Above him stand owl-helmeted Wisdom and blindfolded Justice, sword and scales in hand, against a background of Northern pine and Southern pineapple. This map, heralding the peace and freedom which came to America, was published in London.

In 1795, there appeared in London a curious little volume in Hebrew, *Ma-amar Binah L'Itim* (An Essay on the Understanding of the Times), by one who called himself Elyakim ben Avraham. It was a rather rambling work on Messianic speculation, and particularly on when the Messiah will appear. Basing his prediction on an interpretation by Raphael Levi of Hanover (whom our author does not credit), Elyakim concludes that 1783 is the year, but that was already a dozen years past, so he informs the reader that the drama of Messianic redemption had begun in 1783 and would have its culmination in 1840. To document his conclusions, he points to an event of Messianic import which occurred in the year 1783:

Know then, that the year 1783 was indeed the End of Days. In that year peace and freedom was declared for the inhabitants of America. From there that light of freedom spread and reached France. It continues to light up the world, urging the world to rid itself of its abominations.

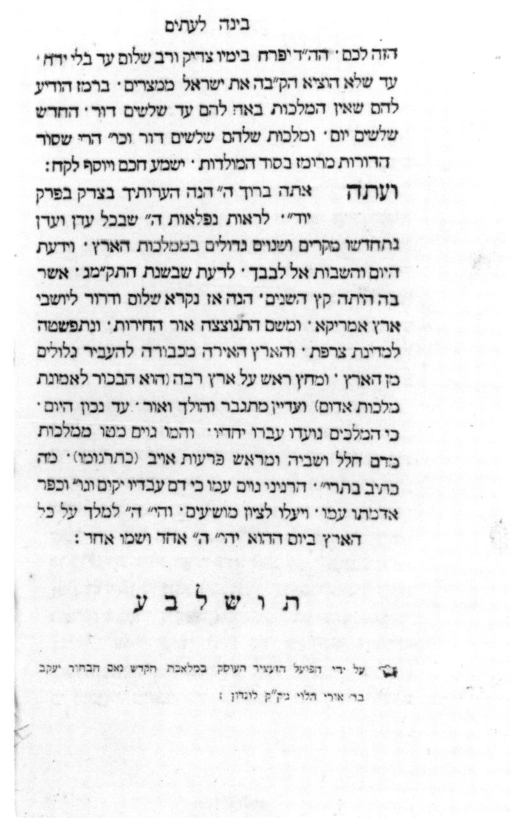
בינה לעתים

הזה לכם · הה"ד יפרח בימיו צדיק ורב שלום עד בלי ירח · עד שלא הוציא הקב"ה את ישראל ממצרים · ברמז הודיע להם שאין המלכות באה להם עד שלשים דור · החדש שלשים יום · ומלכות שלהם שלשים דור וכו' הרי שסוד הדורות מרומז בסוד המולדות · ישמע חכם ויוסף לקח :

ועתה אתה ברוך ה' הנה הערותיך בצדק בפרק יוד"· לראות נפלאות ה' שבכל עדן ועדן נתחדשו מקרים ושנוים גדולים בממלכות הארץ · וידעת היום והשבות אל לבבך · לדעת שבשנת התק"מג · אשר בה היתה קץ השנים · הנה אז נקרא שלום ודרור ליושבי ארץ אמריקא · ומשם התנוצצה אור החירות · ונתפשטה למדינת צרפת · והארץ האירה מכבודה להעביר גלולים מן הארץ · ומחץ ראש על ארץ רבה (הוא הבכור לאמונת מלכות אדום) ועדיין מתגבר והולך ואור · עד נכון היום · כי המלכים נועדו עברו יחדיו · והמו גוים כמו ממלכות כדם חלל ושביה ומראש פרעות אויב (כתרגומו) · כמה כתיב בתרי"· הרנינו גוים עמו כי דם עבדיו יקום וגו' וכפר אדמתו עמו · ויעלו לציון מושיעים · והי" ה' למלך על כל הארץ ביום ההוא יהי" ה' אחד ושמו אחד :

ת ו ש ל ב ע

על ידי הפועל הצעיר העוסק במלאכת הקדש נאם הבחור יעקב בר' אורי הלוי בק"ק לונדון :

London-born Jacob Hart took the pen name Elyakim ben Avraham to publish five small Hebrew volumes. Among them was *Ma'amar Binah L'Itim,* an essay on messianic speculation, in which he argues that the year 1783 was the prophesied "End of Days." He documents his assertion on the final page of his essay, the page before us:

Know then, that the year 1783 was indeed the End of Days.
In that year peace and freedom was declared
for the inhabitants of America [the reference
is to the Treaty of Paris]. From there that
light of freedom spread and reached France.
It continues to light up the world.

Elyakim ben Avraham (Jacob Hart), *Ma'amar Binah L'Itim,* London, 1795.
Hebraic Section.

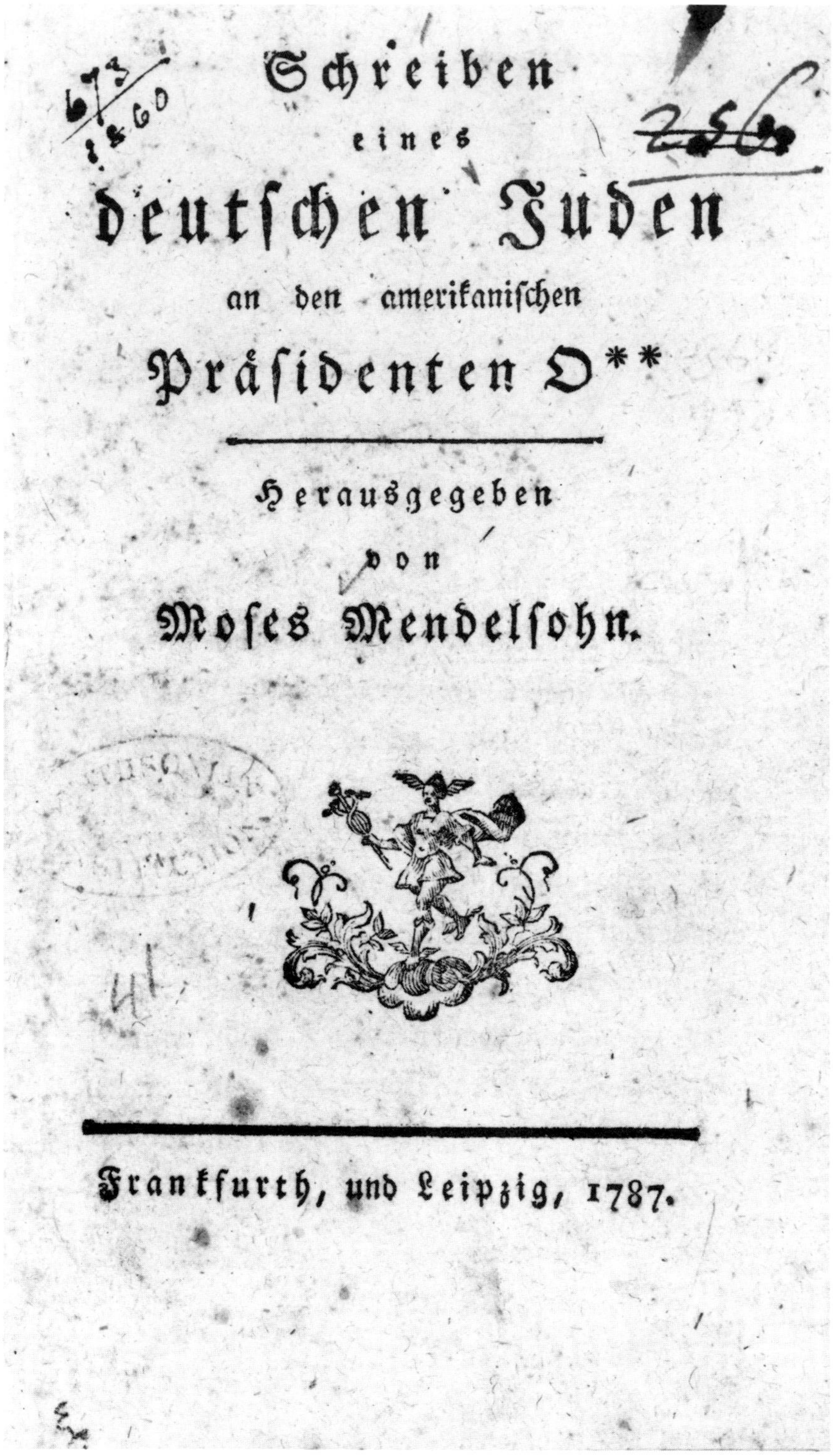
Schreiben
eines
deutschen Juden
an den amerikanischen
Präsidenten O**

Herausgegeben
von
Moses Mendelsohn.

Frankfurth, und Leipzig, 1787.

The title page of this small pamphlet states that Moses Mendelsohn [sic] published this *Letter of a German Jew to the American President*. Neither is correct: no letter was sent, Mendelssohn did not write one, and it is unlikely that it was written by a Jew. What is significant is that the freedom enjoyed by the Jews of America was invoked in this plea for Jewish emancipation in Germany, which was first published in a German periodical in 1783.

*Schreiben eines Deutschen Juden an den amerikanischen Präsidenten O,*** Frankfurt und Leipzig, 1787.
Rare Book and Special Collections Division.

Elyakim ben Avraham was, in fact, the pen name of Jacob Hart, a London-born Jew, a jeweler by trade, who became the finest Jewish scholar of his generation in England. His five published works, all written in excellent literary Hebrew, show him to be a man of broad culture, acquainted with the classical philosophers Socrates and Plato and such contemporary scientists as Newton and Descartes. A proud Englishman, he writes, "Descartes did not reach to Newton's ankles"; as a perceptive Jew, he saw the birth of a new nation under freedom as an event of cosmic significance.

In June 1783, there appeared an anonymous article, "Letter of a German Jew to the President of the Congress of the United States of America" in *Deutsches Museum,* a Leipzig periodical. It reads, in part:

> Many of us have learned with much satisfaction, from the peace made by the mighty American states with England, that wide tracts of land have been ceded to them which are as yet almost uninhabited. More than a century may elapse before the inhabitants of the thirteen united provinces will so increase as to populate . . . the land which is possessed. . . . Your religion cannot prohibit you from leaving these deserts to us for cultivation; besides you have for a long time been tolerating Jews among you . . . You have the legislative power in your hands, and we ask no more than to be permitted to become subjects of these thirteen states, and would gladly contribute two-fold taxes if we can obtain permission to establish colonies at our own cost to engage in agriculture, commerce and the arts . . . Supposing that two thousand families would settle in the desert of America and convert it into a fertile land, will the old inhabitants of the provinces suffer thereby? Let the conditions be stated to us, gracious President, under which you will admit us.

The bulk of the "Letter" is given to describing the intolerable social, political, and economic conditions under which German Jews lived.

Four years later, the "Letter" was republished as a small pamphlet, *Schreiben eines Deutschen Juden an den nordamerkanischen Präsidenten O*** (A Letter of a German Jew to the American President O..), Frankfurt and Leipzig, 1787. The title page states that it was published by Moses Mendelsohn (sic) and contains a purported letter from him to an Isaac Tr——n.:

> You have probably read Mr. D——'s excellent work on the civic improvement of the Jews; if not, then read this brief essay in form of a letter by a German Jew to the President of the Congress of the United States of America, in which he sums up all one may find in his abovementioned work.

There is general agreement that both article and pamphlet were written and issued in support of German Jewry's campaign for political emancipation. The Library's copy of the pamphlet points to the perception of America as a prospective haven and home for the oppressed Jews of Europe and the understanding by European Jews that the freedoms extended to Jews in this New World of the new nation can be used in the struggle for freedom and equality by Jews of the Old. As indeed it was!

Through its Declaration of Independence, America proclaimed equality and promised full freedom, but promise and reality were not identical. Moses Mendelssohn (1729–1786), the "Father of Jewish Enlightenment," in a footnote appended after he had completed his magisterial plea for freedom of religion and conscience and the separation of church and state, *Jerusalem* (Berlin, 1783), notes sadly, "Alas, we hear also that the Congress in America is singing the old tune, and speaking of an *established religion*." Could he have been alarmed by the publication of the Aitken Bible a year earlier, which stated:

> That the United States in Congress assembled approve the pious and laudable undertaking of Mr. Aitken, as subservient to the interest of religion, as well as an instance of the progress of arts in the country . . . they recommend this edition of the Bible to the inhabitants of the United States, and hereby authorize him to publish this recommendation in the manner he shall think proper.

The "edition of the Bible" recommended by Congress was Protestant and contained the New Testament, which the Jewish Bible does not, and

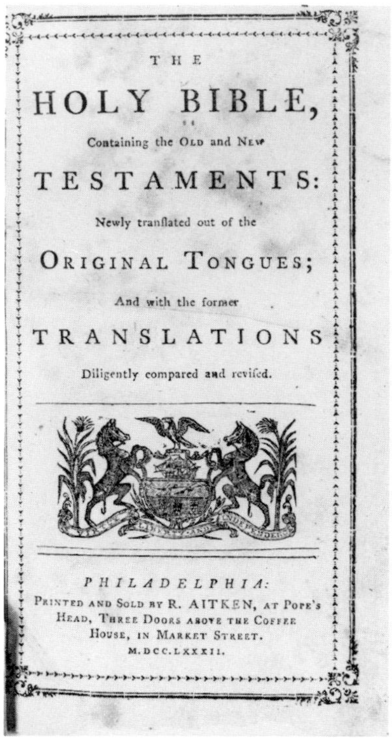

THE

HOLY BIBLE,

Containing the OLD and NEW

TESTAMENTS:

Newly tranflated out of the

ORIGINAL TONGUES;

And with the former

TRANSLATIONS

Diligently compared and revifed.

PHILADELPHIA:

PRINTED AND SOLD BY R. AITKEN, AT POPE'S HEAD, THREE DOORS ABOVE THE COFFEE HOUSE, IN MARKET STREET.

M.DCC.LXXXII.

The first printing of an English Bible on American soil (editions in "the Indian language" and in German had preceded it) and the only edition of the Bible ever to be recommended by the Congress of the United States. It has been called "The Bible of the Revolution" because of its publication at the birth of the American nation. Furthermore, because publication of the Bible in English was forbidden by the mother country in her colonies, its very publication before the signing of the Treaty of Paris was a revolutionary act, a declaration of independence by its publisher Robert Aitken.

The Holy Bible . . . Newly Translated out of the Original Tongues . . ., Philadelphia, 1782.
Rare Book and Special Collections Division.

Facing page:
Gershom Mendes Seixas, the "patriot rabbi" of the Shearith Israel Congregation, New York, left the city because of the British occupation during the Revolutionary War and did not return till after its liberation. Through this *Discourse* delivered at the synagogue on a national Day of Humiliation, he integrates the synagogue into the new nation's religious landscape. On that day and through this service which was held in response to the "Recommendation of the President of the United States of America," Shearith Israel became an *American* house of worship as well as a Jewish one.

Rev. G. Seixas, *A Discourse . . .*, New York, 1798.
Rare Book and Special Collections Division.

did not include the Apocrypha, which the Catholic Bible does.

The Library of Congress copy contains the preliminary two pages recording the authorization proceedings of this edition. The first was a petition by the publisher, Robert Aitken, January 21, 1781. The petition was then referred to the chaplains of "the United States in Congress assembled," who stated that "being ourselves witnesses to the demand for this invaluable book, we rejoice in the present prospect of supply." Two days later, on September 10, 1782, the Congress approved. These actions took place a dozen years before the Bill of Rights. The publication of a Bible in America was yet another expression of the new nation's independence from the mother country, which heretofore had maintained a monopoly on Bible publications in English.

Far more ominous to the Jews of the new nation was the publication of *Cursory Remarks on Men and Measures in Georgia*, n. p., 1784, an anonymous pamphlet by one who signed himself "A Citizen." It contains a forceful legal argument that in 1784 the Jews in the state of Georgia shared the same legal status as the Jews of England in 1732, when Georgia was granted its charter. By extension, the author implied that such legal status would apply to Jews in other states as well. His basic assertion was that, in the various states, Jews had no inherent rights, only such rights as the legislatures of the various states had granted them. Reasoned argument soon descends into unbridled bigotry, reviving the vilest anti-Semitic canard, the blood libel accusation. The pamphlet was a reminder that bigotry dies hard, even in the nation founded on the principle that "all men are created equal . . . and endowed with inalienable rights."

The anonymous pamphleteer declares:

> After having said so much against the Jews, it may probably be suspected that I am not only an enemy, but that I wish to stir up intolerance against that dispersed and unhappy people. Let me tell the reader, I am as far removed from being a votary or friend to persecution as any man upon the earth. Had the Jews of this state but conducted themselves with common modesty and decorum . . . But we see these people eternally obtruding themselves . . . one day assuming the lead in an election, the next taking upon them to direct the police of the town, and the third daring to pass as jurors upon the life and death of a free man, what are we to expect but to have Christianity enacted into a capital heresy, the synagogue to become the established church, and the mildness of the New Testament compelled to give place to the rigour and severity of the old?

The irrational bias of such accusation must have been self-defeating, for we find no record of rejoinder; but to be reminded that leaving the Old World did not mean leaving its hatred behind alerted the Jews as to how much had yet to be done to match reality to promise.

Only four years later, on July 9, 1788, the *Pennsylvania Packet* reported on the July 4 celebration of the "establishment of the Constitution":

> The clergy of almost every denomination united . . . the clergy of the different Christian denominations, with the Rabbi of the Jews, walking arm in arm.

A decade later, in 1798, the Reverend Gershom Mendes Seixas, Hazzan-Minister of the Shearith Israel Congregation of New York, in a *Discourse Delivered in the Synagogue in New York on the Ninth of May, 1798, Observed As a Day of Humiliation, etc., etc. Conformably to a Recommendation of the President of the United States of America*, was pleased to state:

A

DISCOURSE,

DELIVERED

In the Synagogue

IN

NEW-YORK,

ON

THE NINTH OF MAY, 1798,

OBSERVED AS A DAY

OF

HUMILIATION, &c. &c.

Conformably to a Recommendation

OF

THE PRESIDENT OF THE UNITED STATES OF AMERICA.

BY REV. G. SEIXAS.

New-York:
Printed by WILLIAM A. DAVIS & Co.
For NAPHTALI JUDAH, Bookseller and Stationer,
No. 47 Water street.

1798.

It hath pleased God to establish us in this country where we possess every advantage that other citizens of these states enjoy, which is as much as we could in reason expect in this captivity.

The reservation expressed in the last clause is in part due to Seixas's pious faith in messianic redemption, and in part to his candid perception that Jews might possess "every advantage," but were not yet accorded full acceptance. He no doubt agreed with what, twenty years later, Jefferson would say to Mordecai M. Noah: "But more remains to be done; for although we are free by law, we are not so in practice."

Much had already been done. The life and career of Gershom Mendes Seixas (1746–1816) is a point in case. Born in New York of a Sefardi father and an Ashkenazi mother, he was both a product of the American milieu and a participant in the young nation's developing society and culture. At age twenty-two, he was appointed hazzan of the New York congregation and in the course of time came to be called "the reverend" and "rabbi" by Jew and Gentile alike. Together with members of his congregation he left New York when it was occupied by the British during the War of Independence and served Congregation Mikveh Israel in Philadelphia. After the Colonists' victory, Seixas returned to his New York congregation, which he continued to serve with increasing distinction to the end of his life. In 1784, Seixas was made a regent of Columbia College, and served in that capacity until 1815. In grateful tribute, the college struck a medal with his likeness, bearing the legend, "Gershom M. Seixas Congregationis Hebraeae Sacerdos Novi Eboraci" (Priest of the Hebrew Congregation of New York). As an *American* clergyman, he preached the *Discourse* at a special service, as did all other American clergymen in response to the call of the president.

In the endeavor to establish an atmosphere conducive to the fullest acceptance of the Jews into the legal and social fabric of the new republic, much had been accomplished by 1798, and much more was to be accomplished in the decades that followed by the nation's first presidents, as documents in the Library's Manuscript Division demonstrate.

13

"TO BIGOTRY NO SANCTION"

■ A SPECIAL PRAYER IN HEBREW and English for the United States and "His Excellency George Washington, Captain, General and Commander in Chief of the Federal Army of these States," was read by the Reverend Gershom Mendes Seixas at the Consecration Service of the new synagogue of Congregation Mikveh Israel, in Philadelphia on April 3, 1782. Seven years later, Washington, now the newly elected president of the United States, was again the recipient of expressions of adulation and felicitations from American Jewish congregations. In the Washington Papers at the Library of Congress are the original addresses to him from the Hebrew Congregation in Newport, Rhode Island, and the Hebrew Congregations in Philadelphia, New York, Charleston, and Richmond. Also present are the retained copies of the president's replies to them and to the Hebrew Congregation of the City of Savannah. These are but the first of a large number of letters from Jewish organizations and from individual Jews to and from American presidents in the Library of Congress, which is the depository of the papers of all the presidents from George Washington to Calvin Coolidge, with the exception only of John Adams. Some such letters in the papers of Washington, Jefferson, Madison, and Lincoln should be allowed to speak for themselves.

THE FATHER OF HIS COUNTRY

The first Jewish community to address the newly elected George Washington was the Hebrew Congregation of Savannah, Georgia, on May 6, 1789. "Our eccentric situation," Levi Sheftal writes in behalf of the congregation, "added to a diffidence founded on the most profound respect has thus long prevented our address." The congregation declares itself beholden to Washington for his "unexampled liberality and extensive philanthropy [which] have expelled that cloud of bigotry and superstition which has long, as a veil, shaded religion—unrivetted the fetters of enthusiasm—

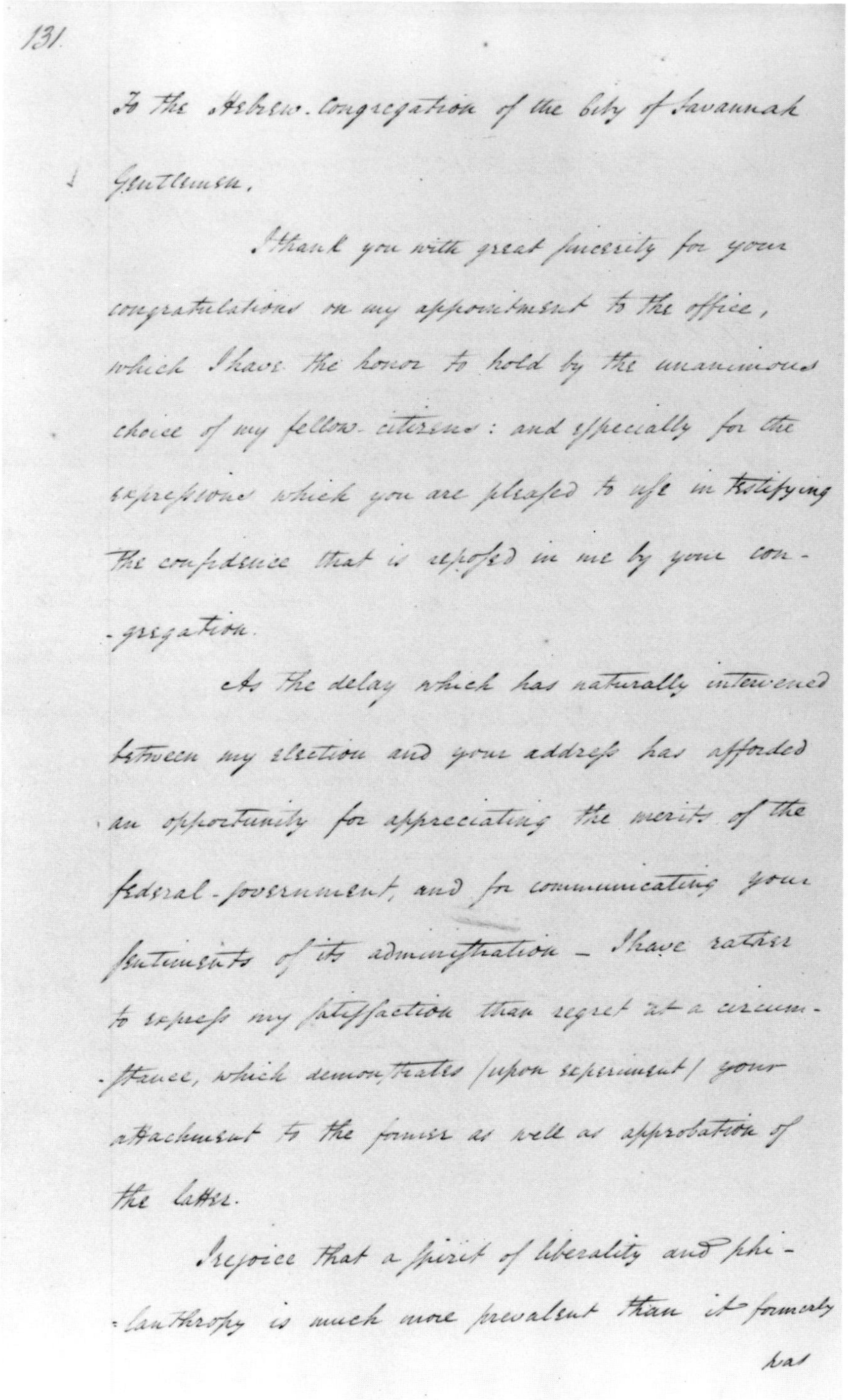

131.

To the Hebrew Congregation of the City of Savannah

Gentlemen,

I thank you with great sincerity for your congratulations on my appointment to the office, which I have the honor to hold by the unanimous choice of my fellow-citizens: and especially for the expressions which you are pleased to use in testifying the confidence that is reposed in me by your congregation.

As the delay which has naturally intervened between my election and your address has afforded an opportunity for appreciating the merits of the federal-government, and for communicating your sentiments of its administration — I have rather to express my satisfaction than regret at a circumstance, which demonstrates (upon experiment) your attachment to the former as well as approbation of the latter.

I rejoice that a spirit of liberality and philanthropy is much more prevalent than it formerly has

enfranchised us with all the privileges and immunities of free citizens, and initiated us into the grand mass of legislative mechanism."

Washington's reply states:

> Gentlemen:—I thank you with great sincerity for your congratulations on my appointment to the office which I have the honor to hold by the unanimous choice of my fellow-citizens, and especially the expressions you are pleased to use in testifying the confidence that is reposed in me by your congregation . . .
>
> I rejoice that a spirit of liberality and philanthropy is much more prevalent than it formerly was among the enlightened nations of the earth, and that your brethren will benefit thereby in proportion as it shall become still more extensive; happily

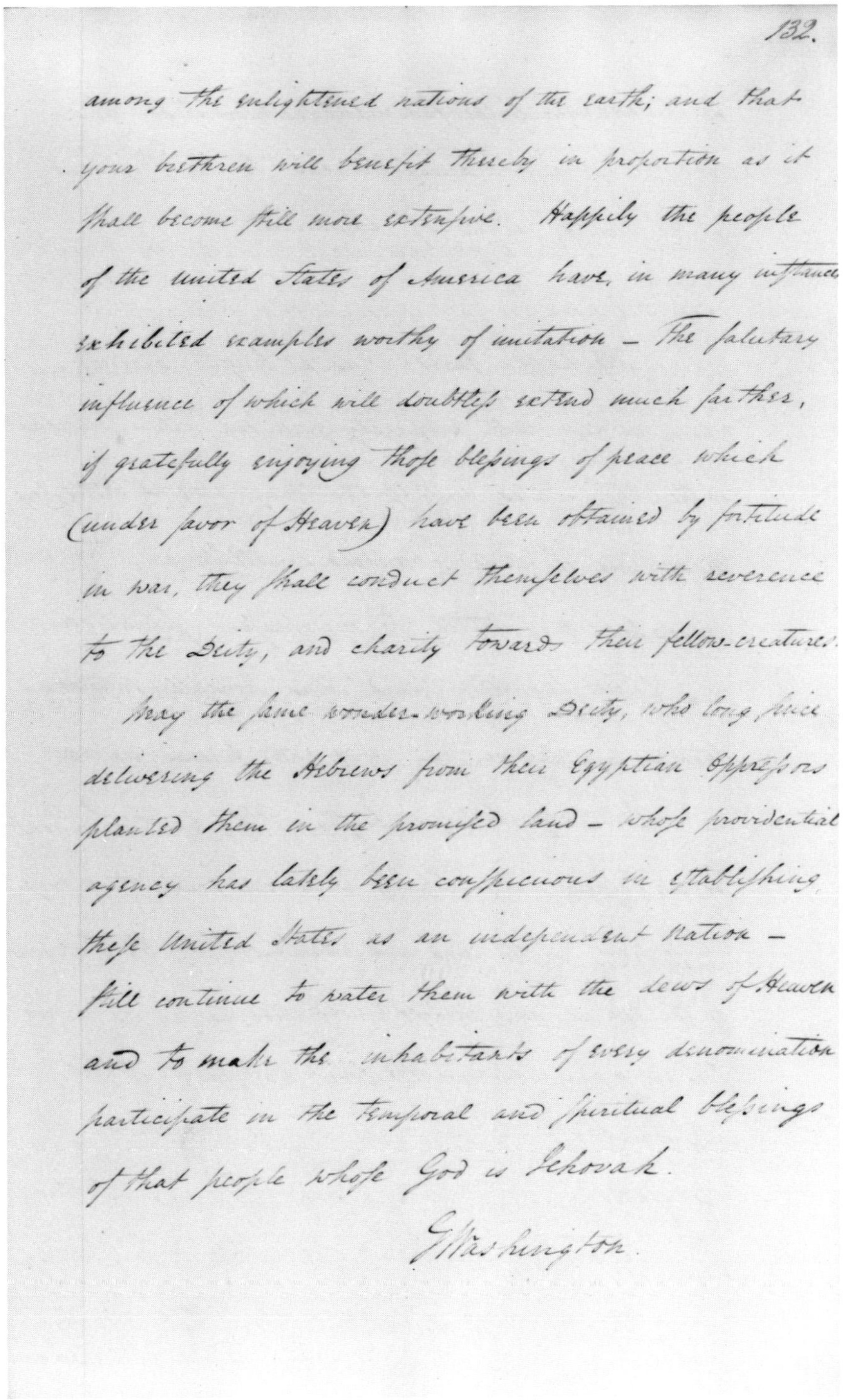

132.

among the enlightened nations of the earth; and that your brethren will benefit thereby in proportion as it shall become still more extensive. Happily the people of the united States of America have, in many instances exhibited examples worthy of imitation — The salutary influence of which will doubtless extend much farther, if gratefully enjoying those blessings of peace which (under favor of Heaven) have been obtained by fortitude in war, they shall conduct themselves with reverence to the Deity, and charity towards their fellow-creatures.

May the same wonder-working Deity, who long since delivering the Hebrews from their Egyptian Oppressors planted them in the promised land — whose providential agency has lately been conspicuous in establishing these United States as an independent Nation — still continue to water them with the dews of Heaven and to make the inhabitants of every denomination participate in the temporal and spiritual blessings of that people whose God is Jehovah.

G Washington.

Among the copies of President George Washington's correspondence with civic, fraternal and religious groups, in letterbook 38, series 2, April 16, 1789–August 17, 1790, is this text of a letter sent at the end of May 1789, to the Hebrew Congregation of the City of Savannah in response to theirs of May 6, written by Levi Sheftal, in which Washington expresses his pride that:

the people of the United States
have in many instances exhibited
examples worthy of imitation.

Manuscript Division, Papers of George Washington.

the people of the United States have in many instances exhibited examples worthy of imitation, the salutary influence of which will doubtless extend much farther if gratefully enjoying those blessings of peace which (under the favor of heaven) have been attained by fortitude in war, they shall conduct themselves with reverence to the Deity and charity toward their fellow-creatures.

May the same wonder-working Deity, who long since delivered the Hebrews from their Egyptian oppressors, planted them in a promised land, whose providential agency has lately been conspicuous in establishing these United States as an independent nation, still continue to water them with the dews of heaven and make the inhabitants of every denomination participate in the temporal and spiritual blessings of that people whose God is Jehovah.

G. Washington.

After seven months of planning, on December 13, 1790, Manuel Josephson, president of Philadelphia's Mikve Israel, wrote in behalf of the Hebrew Congregations of Philadelphia, New York, Charleston, and Richmond:

Sir:—It is reserved for you to unite in affection for your character and person every political and religious denomination of men; and in this will the Hebrew congregations aforesaid yield to no class of their fellow-citizens.

. . . The wonders which the Lord of Hosts hath worked in the days of our Forefathers, have taught us, to observe the greatness of His wisdom and His might throughout the events of the late glorious revolution; and while we humble ourselves at His footstool in thanksgiving and praise for the blessing of His deliverance; we acknowledge you, the Leader of American Armies, as his chosen and beloved servant; But not to your sword alone is present happiness to be ascribed; that, indeed, opened the way to the reign of Freedom, but never was it perfectly secure, till your hand gave birth to the Federal Constitution, and you renounced the joys of retirement to seal by your administration in Peace what you had achieved in war.

To the eternal God, who is thy refuge, we commit in our prayers the care of thy precious life; and when, full of years, thou shalt be gathered unto thy people, thy righteousness shall go before thee, and we shall remember, amidst our regret, "that the Lord hath set apart the godly for himself," whilst thy name and thy virtues will remain an indelible memorial on our minds.

Manuel Josephson.

To which Washington replied:

To the HEBREW CONGREGATIONS IN THE CITIES OF PHILADELPHIA, NEW YORK, CHARLESTON, AND RICHMOND.

Gentlemen:—The liberality of sentiment toward each other, which marks every political and religious denomination of men in this country, stands unparalleled in the history of nations.

The affection of such a people is a treasure beyond the reach of calculation, and the repeated proofs which my fellow-citizens have given of their attachment to me and approbation of my doings form the purest source of my temporal felicity.

The affectionate expressions of your address again excite my gratitude and receive my warmest acknowledgment.

The power and goodness of the Almighty, so strongly manifested in the events of our late glorious revolution, and His kind interposition in our behalf, have been no less visible in the establishment of our present equal government. In war He directed the sword, and in peace He has ruled in our councils. My agency in both has been guided by the best intentions and a sense of duty I owe to my country.

And as my exertions have hitherto been amply rewarded by the approbation of my fellow-citizens, I shall endeavor to deserve a continuance of it by my future conduct.

May the same temporal and eternal blessings which you implore for me, rest upon your congregations.

G. Washington.

On August 17, 1790, Washington honored Newport, Rhode Island, with a visit. The following morning, before his departure, deputations called upon the president to declare their affection and devotion. Moses Seixas, Warden of Kahal Kadosh Yeshuat Israel, the Hebrew congregation of Newport, presented to Washington a letter which opens with words of affection, esteem, and welcome. Seixas reminds him of the Jews' experience of liberation from foreign bondage and new nationhood in biblical days, and he states that no people has greater cause for loyalty to the new nation than the Jews. Seixas adds some of his own perceptions of what

Facing page:
President Washington received this congratulatory address from the Hebrew Congregations in Philadelphia, New York, Charleston, and Richmond, written by Philadelphian Manuel Josephson "on behalf and under the authority of the several congregations." This marked the first joint endeavor by a united American Jewry, comprising the leading communities of the North and the South.

Manuscript Division, Papers of George Washington.

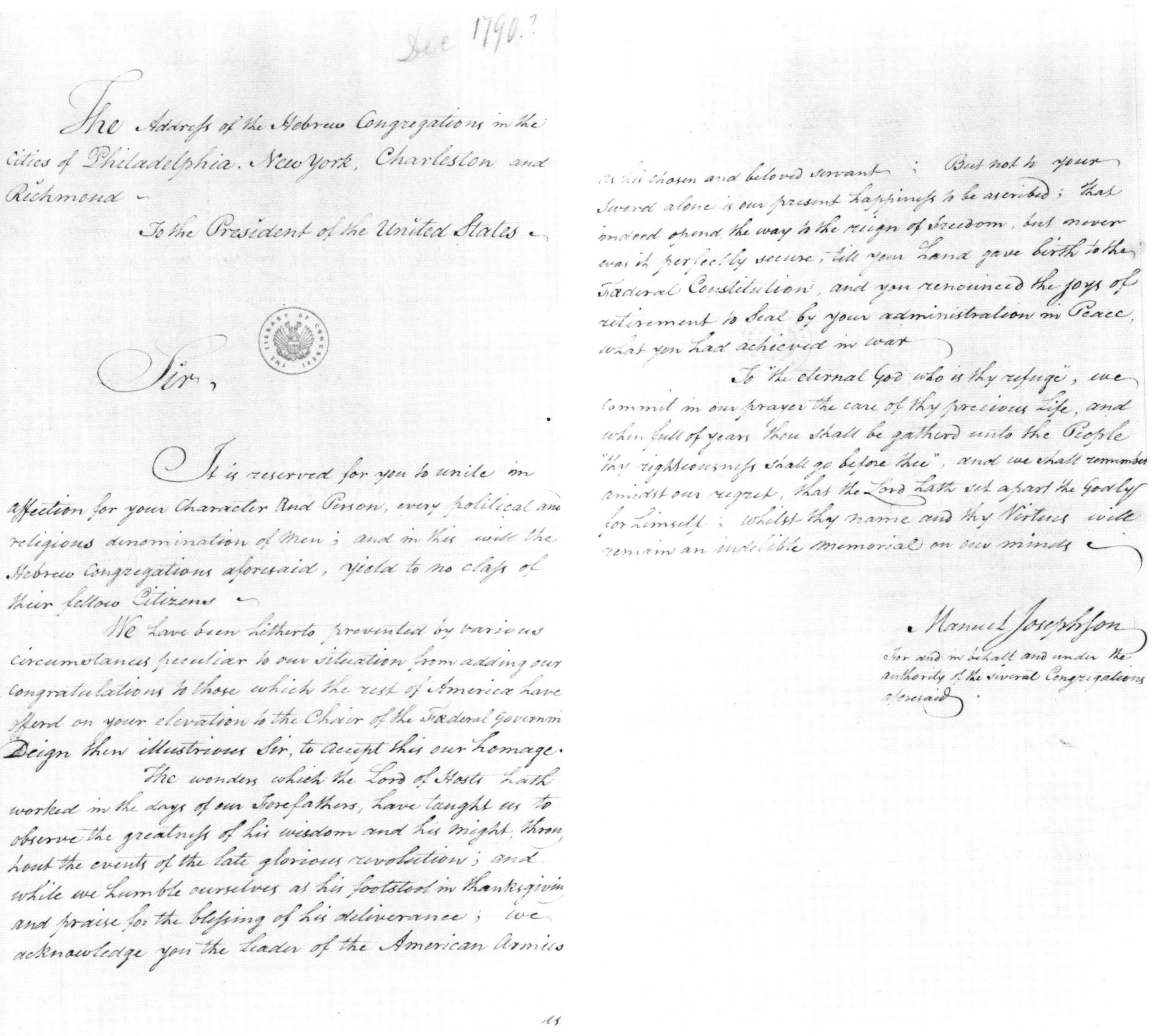
Dec 1790.?

The Address of the Hebrew Congregations in the cities of Philadelphia. New York, Charleston and Richmond —

To the President of the United States —

Sir,

It is reserved for you to unite in affection for your Character And Person, every political and religious denomination of Men; and in this will the Hebrew Congregations aforesaid, yield to no class of their fellow Citizens —

We have been hitherto prevented by various circumstances peculiar to our situation from adding our congratulations to those which the rest of America have offerd on your elevation to the Chair of the Federal governm[ent]

Deign then illustrious Sir, to accept this our homage.

The wonders which the Lord of Hosts hath worked in the days of our Forefathers, have taught us to observe the greatness of his wisdom and his might, throughout the events of the late glorious revolution; and while we humble ourselves at his footstool in thanksgivin[g] and praise for the blessing of his deliverance; we acknowledge you the Leader of the American Armies as his chosen and beloved servant; But not to your Sword alone is our present happiness to be ascribed; that indeed opend the way to the reign of Freedom, but never was it perfectly secure, till your hand gave birth to the Federal Constitution, and you renounced the joys of retirement to seal by your administration in Peace, what you had achieved in war.

To "the eternal God who is thy refuge", we commit in our prayers the care of thy precious Life, and when full of years thou shalt be gathered unto thy People "thy righteousness shall go before thee", and we shall remember amidst our regret, that the Lord hath set apart the Godly for himself; whilst thy name and thy Virtues will remain an indelible memorial on our minds —

Manuel Josephson

For and in behalf and under the authority of the several Congregations aforesaid.

makes this government unique and distinguished, meriting God's approval and his people's blessing, when he writes to Washington:

Sir:

Permit the children of the stock of Abraham to approach you with the most cordial affection and esteem for your person and merit, and to join with our fellow-citizens in welcoming you to Newport.

. . . Deprived as we hitherto have been of the invaluable rights of free citizens, we now—with a deep sense of gratitude to the Almighty Disposer of all events—behold a government erected by the majesty of the people—a government which to bigotry gives no sanction, to persecution no assistance, but generously affording to all liberty of conscience and immunities of citizenship, deeming every one of whatever nation, tongue, or language, equal parts of the great governmental machine.

This so ample and extensive Federal Union, whose base is philanthropy, mutual confidence and public virtue, we cannot but acknowledge to be the work of the great God, who rules in the armies of the heavens and among the inhabitants of the earth, doing whatever seemeth to Him good.

For all the blessings of civil and religious liberty which we enjoy under an equal and benign administration, we desire to send up our thanks to the Ancient of days, the great Preserver of men, beseeching Him that the angels who conducted our forefathers through the wilderness into the promised land may graciously conduct you through all the difficulties and dangers of this mortal life; and when, like Joshua, full of days and full of honors, you are gathered to your fathers, may you be admitted into the heavenly paradise to partake of the water of life and the tree of immortality.

Done and signed by order of the Hebrew Congregation in Newport, Rhode Island, August 17, 1790.

Moses Seixas, Warden

Washington's reply is characteristically large-minded and generous:

Gentlemen:

While I received with much satisfaction your address replete with expressions of esteem, I rejoice in the opportunity of assuring you that I shall always retain grateful remembrance of the cordial welcome I experienced on my visit to Newport from all classes of citizens.

The reflection on the days of difficulty and danger which are past is rendered the more sweet from a consciousness that they are succeeded by days of uncommon prosperity and security.

If we have wisdom to make the best use of the advantages with which we are now favored, we cannot fail, under the just administration of a good government, to become a great and happy people.

The citizens of the United States of America have a right to applaud themselves for having given to mankind examples of an enlarged and liberal policy—a policy worthy of imitation. All possess alike liberty of conscience and immunities of citizenship.

It is now no more that toleration is spoken of as if it were the indulgence of one class of people that another enjoyed the exercise of their inherent natural rights, for, happily, the government of the United States, which gives to bigotry no sanction, to persecution no assistance, requires only that they who live under its protection should demean themselves as good citizens in giving it on all occasions their effectual support.

It would be inconsistent with the frankness of my character not to avow that I am pleased with your favorable opinion of my administration and fervent wishes for my felicity.

May the children of the stock of Abraham who dwell in this land continue to merit and enjoy the good will of the other inhabitants; while every one shall sit in safety under his own vine and fig tree and there shall be none to make him afraid.

May the father of all mercies scatter light, and not darkness, upon our paths, and

Facing page: Presented by the Hebrew Congregation in Newport, Rhode Island, August 17, 1790, on behalf of "the children of the seed of Abraham" to the President of the United States of America and written by Moses Seixas, Warden of the Congregation, this address is the actual one received by America's first president. Note that the felicitous characterization of the government of the United States "which to bigotry gives no sanction, to persecution no assistance" that is found (two words transposed) in Washington's response was first used by Moses Seixas.

Manuscript Division, Papers of George Washington.

To the President of the United States of America.

Sir

Permit the children of the Stock of Abraham to approach you with the most cordial affection and esteem for your person & merits — And to join with our fellow Citizens in welcoming you to NewPort.

With pleasure we reflect on those days — those days of difficulty, & danger when the God of Israel, who delivered David from the peril of the sword, — shielded Your head in the day of battle: — And we rejoice to think, that the same Spirit, who rested in the Bosom of the greatly beloved Daniel enabling him to preside over the Provinces of the Babylonish Empire, rests and ever will rest upon you, enabling you to discharge the arduous duties of Chief Magistrate in these States.

Deprived as we heretofore have been of the invaluable rights of free Citizens, we now (with a deep sense of gratitude to the Almighty disposer of all events) behold a Government, erected by the Majesty of the People — a Government, which to bigotry gives no sanction, to persecution no assistance — but generously affording to All liberty of conscience, and immunities of Citizenship: — deeming every one, of whatever Nation, tongue, or language equal parts of the great governmental Machine: — This so ample and extensive Federal Union whose basis is Philanthropy, Mutual confidence and Publick Virtue, we cannot but acknowledge to be the work of the Great God, who ruleth in the Armies Of Heaven and among the Inhabitants of the Earth, doing whatsoever seemeth him good.

For all the Blessings of civil and religious liberty which we enjoy under an equal and benign administration, we desire to send up our thanks to the Antient of Days, the great preserver of Men — beseeching him, that the Angel who conducted our forefathers through the wilderness into the promised land, may graciously conduct you through all the difficulties and dangers of this mortal life: — And, when like Joshua full of days, and full of honour, you are gathered to your Fathers, may you be admitted into the Heavenly Paradise to partake of the water of life, and the tree of immortality.

Done and Signed by Order of the Hebrew Congregation in NewPort Rhode Island August 17th 1790.

Moses Seixas, Warden

that toleration is spoken of, as if it was by the indulgence of one class of people, that another enjoyed the exercise of their inherent natural rights. For happily the government of the United States, which gives to bigotry no sanction, to persecution no assistance, requires only that they who live under its protection should demean themselves as good citizens, in giving it on all occasions their effectual support.

It would be inconsistent with the frankness of my character not to avow that I am pleased with your favorable opinion of my administration, and fervent wishes for my felicity.

May the children of the Stock of Abraham, who dwell in this land, continue to merit and enjoy the good will of the other inhabitants, while every one shall sit in safety under his own vine and fig-tree, and there shall be none to make him afraid.

May the Father of all mercies scatter light and not darkness in our paths, and make us all in our several vocations useful here, and in his own due time and way everlastingly happy.

G Washington.

make us all in our several vocations useful here, and in His own due time and way everlastingly happy.

G. Washington

To bigotry no sanction, to persecution no assistance became, through its use by the country's first president, a revered phrase in America's national vocabulary.

The publication of the Hebrew Congregations/George Washington correspondence in a number of American newspapers in 1790 constituted a public declaration by the Father of his Country of the free and equal status of Jews in America, furthered by its inclusion in *A Collection of Speeches of the President of the United States* (Boston, 1796). The usefulness of the Washington pronouncements is illustrated by Governor Worthington employing them in 1824 in support of the "Jew Bill," which conferred upon Maryland Jews the full political rights heretofore denied them.

THE AUTHOR OF THE DECLARATION AND THE ARCHITECT OF THE CONSTITUTION

"By 1789, when the Constitution of the United States was adopted," Milton R. Konvitz, a foremost authority on First Amendment rights, in his *Fundamental Rights of a Free People* (Ithaca, 1957) states, "Virginia and Rhode Island were states in which complete religious freedom was enjoyed. Remnants of establishment or intolerance lingered in the other eleven states." That religious freedom was the law in Virginia, the largest and leading state of the union, was due in great measure to Thomas Jefferson's political leadership and even more so to James Madison's ideological arguments. His "Memorial and Remonstrance" made possible the enactment of Jefferson's Bill for Establishing Religious Freedom, which in 1786 became law in Virginia and which provides:

> that no man shall be compelled to frequent or support any religious worship, place or ministry . . . nor shall be enforced, restrained, molested . . . nor shall otherwise suffer on account of his religious opinions or belief; but that all men shall be free to profess, and by argument to maintain, their opinion in matters of religion.

Konvitz notes, "This was probably the first statutory enactment of complete religious freedom and equality in the world. In effect, when Virginia won religious freedom for herself, it won it also for the rest of the country."

Jefferson and Madison corresponded on the subject with two of America's leading Jews, Mordecai Manuel Noah and Dr. Jacob De La Motta. Each had delivered an address at the consecration of a synagogue—Noah in New York in 1818, De La Motta in Savannah in 1820. Each had sent published copies to the presidents, who responded with letters which remain important contributions in defining the meaning of freedom and equality in the United States, particularly for the Jews.

De La Motta's letter to James Madison and the retained responses of both presidents to both orators are now in the Library's Presidential Papers collection. In Jefferson's case, the copies are ones he actually inscribed by

Facing page:
President Washington sent gracious replies in 1790 to the Newport Hebrew Congregation and to the Philadelphia, New York, Charleston, and Richmond consortium, a portion of which we can read in this copy of his celebrated reply to Newport.

May the children of the stock of
Abraham who dwell in this land
continue to merit and enjoy the
good will of the other inhabitants.

Manuscript Division, Papers of George Washington.

his own hand, using a polygraph which he referred to as a "portable secretary." It was a writing machine which had two pens in tandem, so that the letters sent and the copies retained were identical.

It is not surprising that Mordecai M. Noah was chosen to deliver the discourse at the consecration of Shearith Israel's new synagogue on the 17th of April, 1818. Certainly the best known Jew in America, he had served as the U.S. Consul in Tunis, was now editor of the *National Advocate*, and a year earlier had been the chief orator at the forty-first anniversary celebration of American independence in which the Tammany Society had been joined by a half dozen kindred organizations. In addition, he was a faithful member of the congregation, which his great-grandfather, seventy years earlier, had served as hazzan. Noah's *Discourse* was published and widely disseminated. In his *Travels in England, France, Spain, and the Barbary States*, which appeared a year later, Noah published the letters he received about the *Discourse* from "three presidents of the United States, John Adams, Thomas Jefferson and James Madison."*

*For a more detailed account of Noah, see pp. 261–68.

Adams was a true son of Massachusetts, the only seaboard colony which did not have a Jewish community until well into the nineteenth century. The Federalist assumed a proper but patronizing posture. After acknowledging that "I know not when I have read a more liberal or more elegant composition," Adams allows:

> I have had occasion to be acquainted with several gentlemen of your nation, and to transact business with some of them, whom I found to be men of as liberal minds, as much honor, probity, generosity and good breeding, as any I have known in any sect of religion or philosophy.

Adams was a member of the committee which framed the Declaration of Independence, and having participated in the forging of the new nation, he was proud of its liberality.

> I wish your nation may be admitted to all the privileges of citizens in every country of the world. This country has done much. I wish it may do more; and annul every narrow idea in religion, government, and commerce.

The response Noah received from Madison was rather formal. Relations between the two were strained, because during the Madison administration Noah was recalled from his consulship, an action which Noah publicly attributed to bigotry.

> Montpelier, May 15
>
> Sir: I have received your letter of the sixth, with the eloquent discourse delivered at the consecration of the Synagogue. Having ever regarded the freedom of religious opinions and worship as equally belonging to every sect, and the secure enjoyment of it as the best human provision for bringing all, either into the same way of thinking, or into that mutual charity which is the only proper substitute, I observe with pleasure the view you give of the spirit in which your sect partake of the common blessings afforded by our Government and laws.

Jefferson's response must rank as one of his greatest statements of religious liberty and equality.*

*The Library's copy is the one Jefferson retained. The copy sent to Noah is in the Yeshiva University Museum.

> Monticello, May 28
>
> Sir:
>
> I thank you for the Discourse on the consecration of the Synagogue in your city, with which you have been pleased to favor me. I have read it with pleasure and

Facing page:
A statement of surpassing significance by philosopher-president Thomas Jefferson on the nature of democracy, the frailty of human character, the power of the free human spirit, and his faith in humankind. This copy in Jefferson's own hand of his letter on May 28, 1818, to America's most prominent Jew, Mordecai M. Noah, continues to remind us that:

More remains to be done,
for altho' we are free by
the law, we are not so in
practice.

Jefferson's letter was in response to Noah's published address which he had sent to Jefferson. Noah delivered the address at the consecration of New York congregation Shearith Israel's new synagogue building.

Thomas Jefferson to Mordecai M. Noah, May 28, 1818. Manuscript Division, Papers of Thomas Jefferson.

Sir Monticello May 28. 18.

I thank you for the Discourse on the consecration of the Synagogue in your city, with which you have been pleased to favor me. I have read it with pleasure and instruction, having learnt from it some valuable facts in Jewish history which I did not know before. your sect by it's sufferings has furnished a remarkable proof of the universal spirit of religious intolerance, inherent in every sect, disclaimed by all while feeble, and practised by all when in power. our laws have applied the only antidote to this vice, protecting our religious, as they do our civil rights by putting all on an equal footing. but more remains to be done. for altho' we are free by the law, we are not so in practice. public opinion erects itself into an Inquisition, and exercises it's office with as much fanaticism as fans the flames of an Auto da fé. the prejudice still scowling on your section of our religion, altho' the elder one, cannot be unfelt by yourselves. it is to be hoped that individual dispositions will at length mould themselves to the model of the law, and consider the moral basis on which all our religions rest, as the rallying point which unites them in a common interest; while the peculiar dogmas branching from it are the exclusive concern of the respective sects embracing them, and no rightful subject of notice to any other. public opinion needs reformation on this point, which would have the further happy effect of doing away the hypocritical maxim of 'intus ut lubet, foris ut moris.' nothing I think would be so likely to effect this as to your sect particularly as the more careful attention to education, which you recommend, and which placing it's members on the equal and commanding benches of science, will exhibit them as equal objects of respect and favor. — I should not do full justice to the merits of your discourse, were I not, in addition to that of it's matter, to express my consideration of it as a fine specimen of style & composition. I salute you with great respect and esteem.

Th: Jefferson

 Mr. Mordecai M. Noah.

instruction, having learnt from it some valuable facts in Jewish history which I did not know before. Your sect by its sufferings has furnished a remarkable proof of the universal spirit of religious intolerance inherent in every sect, disclaimed by all while feeble, and practiced by all when in power. Our laws have applied the only antidote to this vice, protecting our religious, as they do our civil rights, by putting all on an equal footing. But more remains to be done, for although we are free by the law, we are not so in practice. Public opinion erects itself into an inquisition, and exercises its office with as much fanaticism as fans the flames of an *Auto-da-fé*. The prejudice still scowling on your section of our religion altho' the elder one, cannot be unfelt by ourselves. It is to be hoped that individual dispositions will at length mould themselves to the model of the law, and consider the moral basis, on which all our religions rest, as the rallying point which unites them in a common interest; while the peculiar dogmas branching from it are the exclusive concern of the respective sects embracing them, and no rightful subject of notice to any other. Public opinion needs reformation on that point, which would have the further happy effect of doing away the hypocritical maxim of "*intus et lubet, foris ut moris*". Nothing, I think, would be so likely to effect this, as to your sect particularly, as the more careful attention to education, which you recommend, and which, placing its members on the equal and commanding benches of science, will exhibit them as equal objects of respect and favor. I should not do full justice to the merits of your Discourse, were I not, in addition to that of its matter, to express my consideration of it as a fine specimen of style and composition. I salute you with great respect and esteem.

Th. Jefferson.

Jacob De La Motta (1789–1845) was a native of Savannah who received his medical degree from the University of Pennsylvania at age twenty-one. Volunteering his services at the outbreak of the War of 1812, he was commissioned as a surgeon in the U.S. Army. Later he practiced medicine in New York, where he became a friend and disciple of Gershom Mendes Seixas, at whose funeral he delivered the eulogy. De La Motta then returned to Savannah, where he resumed his practice and soon became a leader both in his profession and in the Jewish community. It was natural that he be invited to deliver the consecration address at the dedication of the city's new synagogue on July 21, 1820. In appreciation, the congregation's Building Committee published the address, of which the Library has a copy. In a letter accompanying the pamphlet he sent to Madison, he writes:

Believing that you have ever been, and still continue to be, liberal in your views of a once oppressed people, and confident that you would cheerfully receive any information appertaining to the history of the Jews in this country, have induced me to solicit your acceptance of a Discourse pronounced on the occasion of the Consecration of the new Synagogue recently erected in our city.

We may assume that he sent a similar letter to Jefferson, whose reply to De La Motta is noteworthy for his felicitous inversion of "united we stand, divided we fall." Written in third person and dated September 1, 1820, it said:

Th. Jefferson returns his thanks to Dr. De La Motta for the eloquent discourse on the Consecration of the Synagogue of Savannah, which he has been so kind as to send him. It excites in him the gratifying reflection that his country has been the first to prove to the world two truths, the most salutary to human society, that man can govern himself, and that religious freedom is the most effectual anodyne against religious dissension: the maxim of civil government being reversed in that

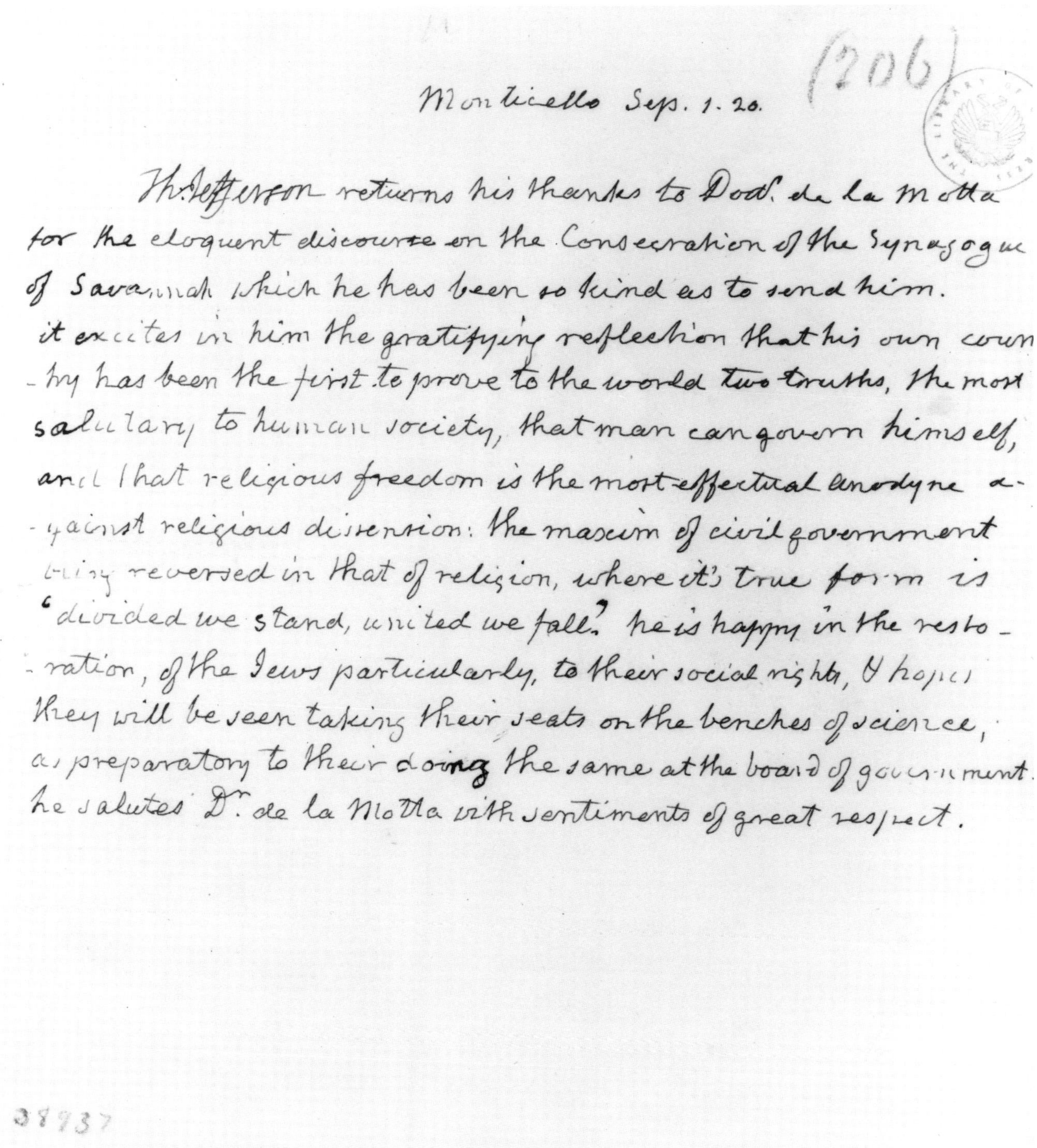

(206)

Monticello Sep. 1. 20.

Th: Jefferson returns his thanks to Doct. de la Motta
for the eloquent discourse on the Consecration of the Synagogue
of Savannah which he has been so kind as to send him.
it excites in him the gratifying reflection that his own coun
-try has been the first to prove to the world two truths, the most
salutary to human society, that man can govern himself,
and that religious freedom is the most effectual anodyne a-
-gainst religious dissension: the maxim of civil government
being reversed in that of religion, where it's true form is
'divided we stand, united we fall.' he is happy in the resto-
-ration, of the Jews particularly, to their social rights, & hopes
they will be seen taking their seats on the benches of science,
as preparatory to their doing the same at the board of government.
he salutes Dr. de la Motta with sentiments of great respect.

38937

In 1820, at the occasion of a synagogue consecration, a published address was sent by the orator Jacob De La Motta to Thomas Jefferson. In response, the sage of Monticello comments upon the true meaning of religious liberty in a pluralistic democracy:

the maxim of civil government
being reversed in that of
religion, where its true form
is, "divided we stand, united,
we fall."

Thomas Jefferson to Jacob De La Motta, September 1, 1820.
Manuscript Division, Papers of Thomas Jefferson.

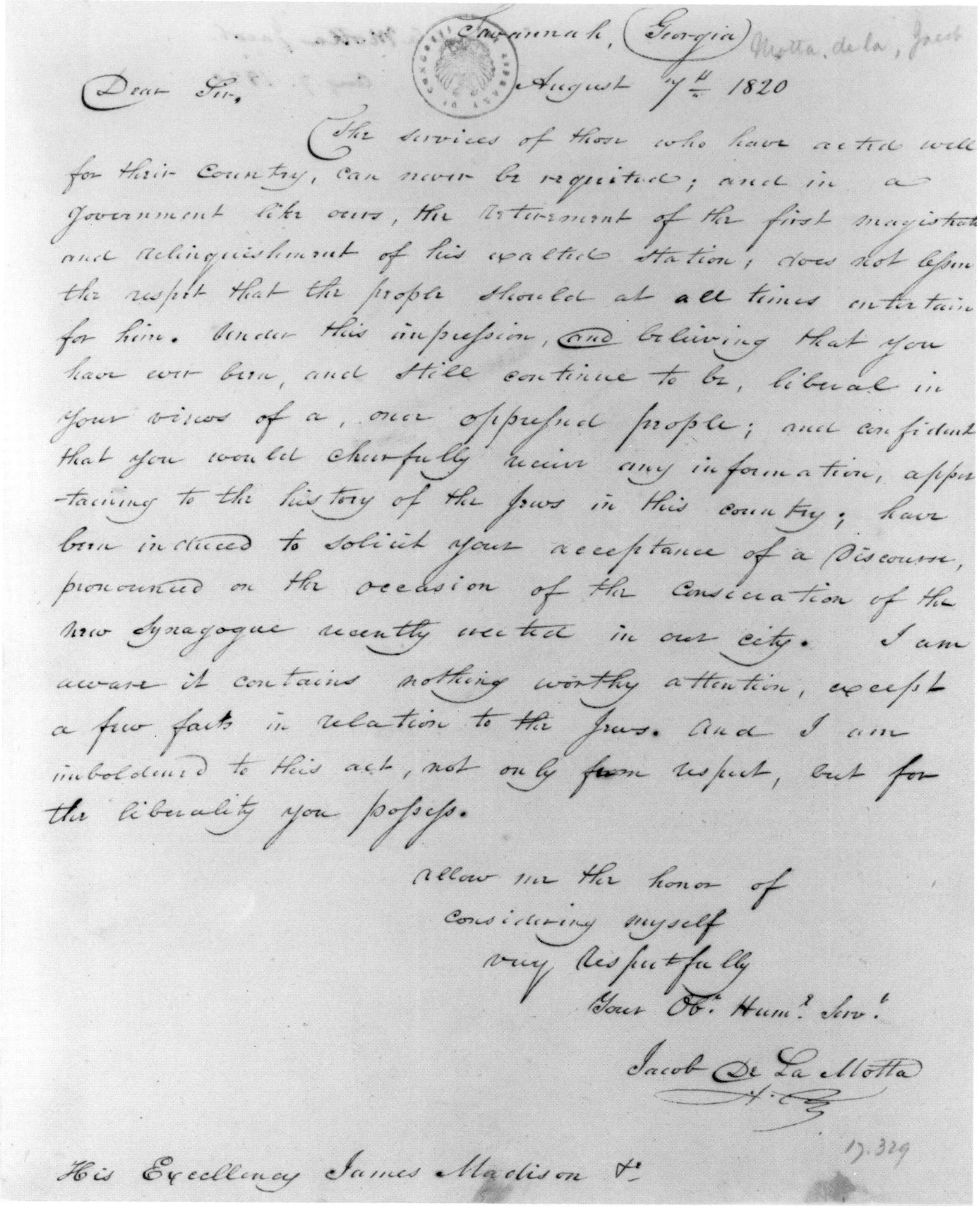

Savannah, (Georgia) Motta, de la, Jacob
August 7th 1820

Dear Sir,

The services of those who have acted well for their Country, can never be requited; and in a Government like ours, the Retirement of the first magistrate and Relinquishment of his exalted station; does not lessen the respect that the people should at all times entertain for him. Under this impression, and believing that you have ever been, and still continue to be, liberal in your views of a, once oppressed people; and confident that you would cheerfully receive any information, appertaining to the history of the Jews in this country; have been induced to solicit your acceptance of a Discourse, pronounced on the occasion of the Consecration of the new Synagogue recently erected in our city. I am aware it contains nothing worthy attention, except a few facts in relation to the Jews. And I am imboldened to this act, not only from respect, but for the liberality you possess.

Allow me the honor of
considering myself
very Respectfully
Your Obt. Huml. Servt.

Jacob De La Motta

17.329

His Excellency James Madison &c.

Jacob De La Motta sent a copy of his published address at the consecration of the new synagogue in Savannah, Georgia, to Madison as well as to Jefferson. With the address he sent this letter, in which he declares himself "confident that you would cheerfully receive any information appertaining to the history of the Jews in this country."

Jacob De La Motta to James Madison, August 7, 1820.
Manuscript Division, Papers of James Madison.

of religion, where its true form is "divided we stand, united, we fall." He is happy in the restoration of the Jews, particularly, to their social rights, and hopes they will be seen taking their seats on the benches of science as preparatory to their doing the same at the board of government. He salutes Dr. De La Motta with sentiments of great respect.

Madison's letter is more gracious and of greater relevance and utility to American Jews of the time who were striving to remove the disabilities which still remained in some state constitutions, particularly in Maryland, where Jews were in the midst of their struggle for adoption of the "Jew Bill."

To Doc[to]r de la Motta

Montpelier Aug: 1820

Sir
I have received your letter of the 7th inst. with the Discourse delivered at the consecration of the Hebrew Synagogue at Savannah, for which you will please to accept my thanks.
The history of the Jews must for ever be interesting. The modern part of it is at the same time so little generally known, that every ray of light on the subject has its value.
Among the features peculiar to the political system of the United States is the perfect equality of rights which it secures to every religious sect. And it is particularly pleasing to observe in the good citizenship of such as have been most distrusted and oppressed elsewhere, a happy illustration of the safety and success of this experiment of a just and benignant policy. Equal laws protecting equal rights, are found as they ought to be presumed, the best guarantee of loyalty, and love of country; as well as best calculated to cherish that mutual respect and good will among citizens of every religious denomination which are necessary to social harmony and most favorable to the advancement of truth. The account you give of the Jews of your Congregation brings them fully within the scope of these observations.

I tender you, Sir, my respects and good wishes.

James Madison

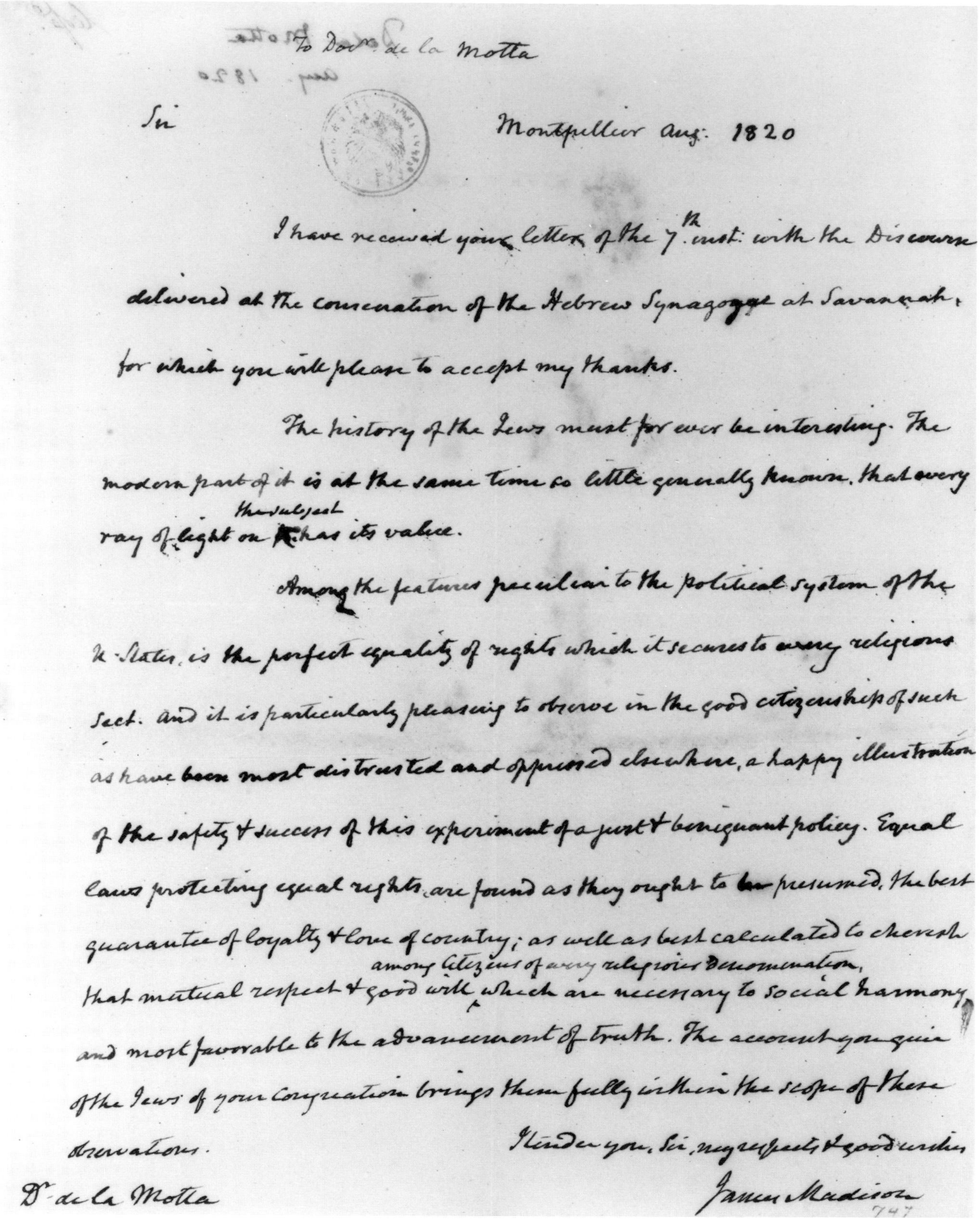

To Docr. de la Motta

Sir

Montpellier Aug: 1820

I have received your letter of the 7th. inst: with the Discourse delivered at the consecration of the Hebrew Synagogue at Savannah, for which you will please to accept my thanks.

The history of the Jews must for ever be interesting. The modern part of it is at the same time so little generally known, that every ray of light on the subject has its value.

Among the features peculiar to the political system of the U. States, is the perfect equality of rights which it secures to every religious Sect. And it is particularly pleasing to observe in the good citizenship of such as have been most distrusted and oppressed elsewhere, a happy illustration of the safety & success of this experiment of a just & benignant policy. Equal laws protecting equal rights, are found as they ought to be presumed, the best guarantee of loyalty & love of country; as well as best calculated to cherish that mutual respect & good will among Citizens of every religious denomination, which are necessary to social harmony and most favorable to the advancement of truth. The account you give of the Jews of your Congregation brings them fully within the scope of these observations.

I tender you, Sir, my respects & good wishes

James Madison

Dr. de la Motta

Madison replies to De La Motta's letter of August 7, 1820, observing that the history of the Jews,

must for ever be interesting. The modern part of it is . . . so little generally known, that every ray of light on the subject has its value.

James Madison to Jacob De La Motta, August 1820.
Manuscript Division, Papers of James Madison.

14

"FATHER ABRAHAM" AND THE CHILDREN OF ISRAEL

Lincoln: And so the Children of Israel were driven from the happy land of Canaan.
Kaskel: Yes, and that is why we have come to Father Abraham, to ask his protection.
Lincoln: And this protection they shall have at once.

Cesar J. Kaskel, apprising President Lincoln of
General Grant's Order Number 11

■ IN HIS SCHOLARLY STUDY OF *American Jewry and the Civil War* (Philadelphia, 1951), Bertram W. Korn writes that in the eulogy Rabbi Isaac M. Wise delivered after the assassination of President Abraham Lincoln, he claimed: "the lamented Abraham Lincoln believed himself to be bone from our bone and flesh from our flesh. He supposed himself to be a descendant of Hebrew parentage. He said so in my presence." There is no shred of evidence to substantiate Wise's assertion, Korn declares, and "Lincoln is not known to have said anything resembling this to any of his other Jewish acquantances." But, Korn asserts, Lincoln "could not have been any friendlier to individual Jews, or more sympathetic to Jewish causes, if he had stemmed from Jewish ancestry." He also points to the Robert Todd Lincoln Collection of Lincoln Papers in the Manuscript Division of the Library of Congress as a prime source "for the elucidation of Lincoln's contacts with various Jews . . . in particular . . . Abraham Jonas and Isachar Zacharie."

Some of the "elucidation" Korn mentions may be gathered from sixteen items, eight in manuscript and eight in print, garnered from the Library's rich lode of Lincolniana.

CORRESPONDENCE WITH THE PRESIDENT

In 1860, Lincoln wrote to Abraham Jonas (1801–1864) "you are one of my most valued friends." The friendship began soon after Jonas settled in Quincy, Illinois, in 1838. He came from Kentucky where he had lived for ten years, served in the State Legislature for four terms, and become the Grand Master of the Kentucky Masons. Before that he lived in Cincinnati; to which he came from England in 1819, to join his brother, Joseph, the first Jewish settler there. In Quincy, Jonas kept store and studied law, which became his lifelong calling. From 1849 to 1851, he served as postmaster and in 1861 was reappointed to that office by Lincoln. Two letters from the Jonas-Lincoln correspondence in the Library's collection are especially illuminating.

When Lincoln visited Quincy in 1854, he spent most of his time with Jonas, as we can see from his letter to Jonas on July 21, 1860. What occasioned Lincoln's letter was one from Jonas in which he told the presidential candidate: "I have just been creditably informed, that Isaac N. Morris is engaged in obtaining affidavits and certificates of certain Irishmen that they saw you in Quincy come out of a Know Nothing Lodge." Jonas feared that this purported association with a nativist antiforeigner political party would cost Lincoln many immigrant votes, so he alerted his friend in a "confidential" letter. Lincoln's lengthy reply states, in part:

> Yours of the 20th received. I suppose as good, or even better men than I may have been in American or Know-Nothing lodges; but in point of fact, I never was in one, at Quincy or elsewhere. I was never in Quincy but one day and two nights while Know-Nothing lodges were in existence, and you were with me that day and both those nights. I had never been there before in my life; and never afterwards, till the joint debate with Douglas in 1858. It was in 1854 when I spoke in some hall there, and after the speaking, you with others took me to an oyster saloon, passed an hour there, and you walked with me to, and parted with me at the Quincy House, quite late at night. I left by stage for Naples before day-light in the morning, having come in by the same route, after dark the evening previous to the speaking, when I found you waiting at the Quincy House to meet me . . .
>
> That I never was in a Knownothing lodge in Quincy, I should expect could be easily proved, by respectable men who were always in the lodges and never saw me there. An affidavit of one or two such would put the matter at rest.
>
> And now, a word of caution. Our adversaries think they can gain a point if they could force me to openly deny the charge, by which some degree of offence would be given to the Americans. For this reason it must not publicly appear that I am paying any attention to the charge.
>
> Yours Truly
> A. Lincoln

Whatever was done, or not done, by Jonas, must have been effective because the matter was never mentioned publicly during the campaign.

In a letter from Jonas to Lincoln on December 30, 1860, marked "Private," Jonas again alerts his friend:

> The purport of this communication must be my apology for troubling you—and my great anxiety in regard to your personal safety and the preservation of our National integrity will I think justify me on this occasion, when you have so much to think of and so many things to perplex you.
>
> You perhaps are aware, that I have a very large family connection in the South, and that in New Orleans I have six children and a host of other near relatives. I receive many letters from them, their language has to be very guarded, as fears are entertained that the sanctity of the mails, is not much regarded. On yesterday I received a letter from N.O. from one who is prudent, sound and careful of what he writes and among other things, he says "things are daily becoming worse here, God help us, what will be the result, it is dreadful to imagine. One thing I am satisfied of, that there is a perfect organization, fearful in numbers and contrauled by men of character and influence, whose object is to prevent the inauguration of Lincoln, large numbers of desperate characters, many of them from this city, will

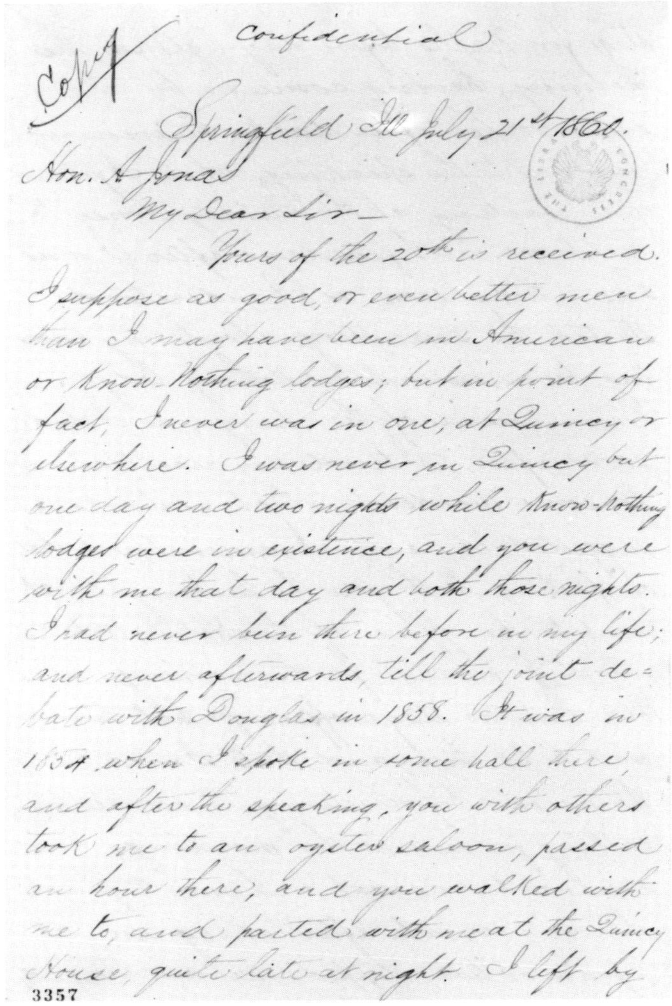

Copy

Confidential

Springfield Ill July 21st 1860.

Hon. A Jonas

My Dear Sir—

Yours of the 20th is received. I suppose as good, or even better men than I may have been in American or Know-Nothing lodges; but in point of fact, I never was in one; at Quincy or elsewhere. I was never in Quincy but one day and two nights while Know-Nothing lodges were in existence, and you were with me that day and both those nights. I had never been there before in my life; and never afterwards, till the joint debate with Douglas in 1858. It was in 1854, when I spoke in some hall there, and after the speaking, you with others took me to an oyster saloon, passed an hour there, and you walked with me to, and parted with me at the Quincy House, quite late at night. I left by

3357

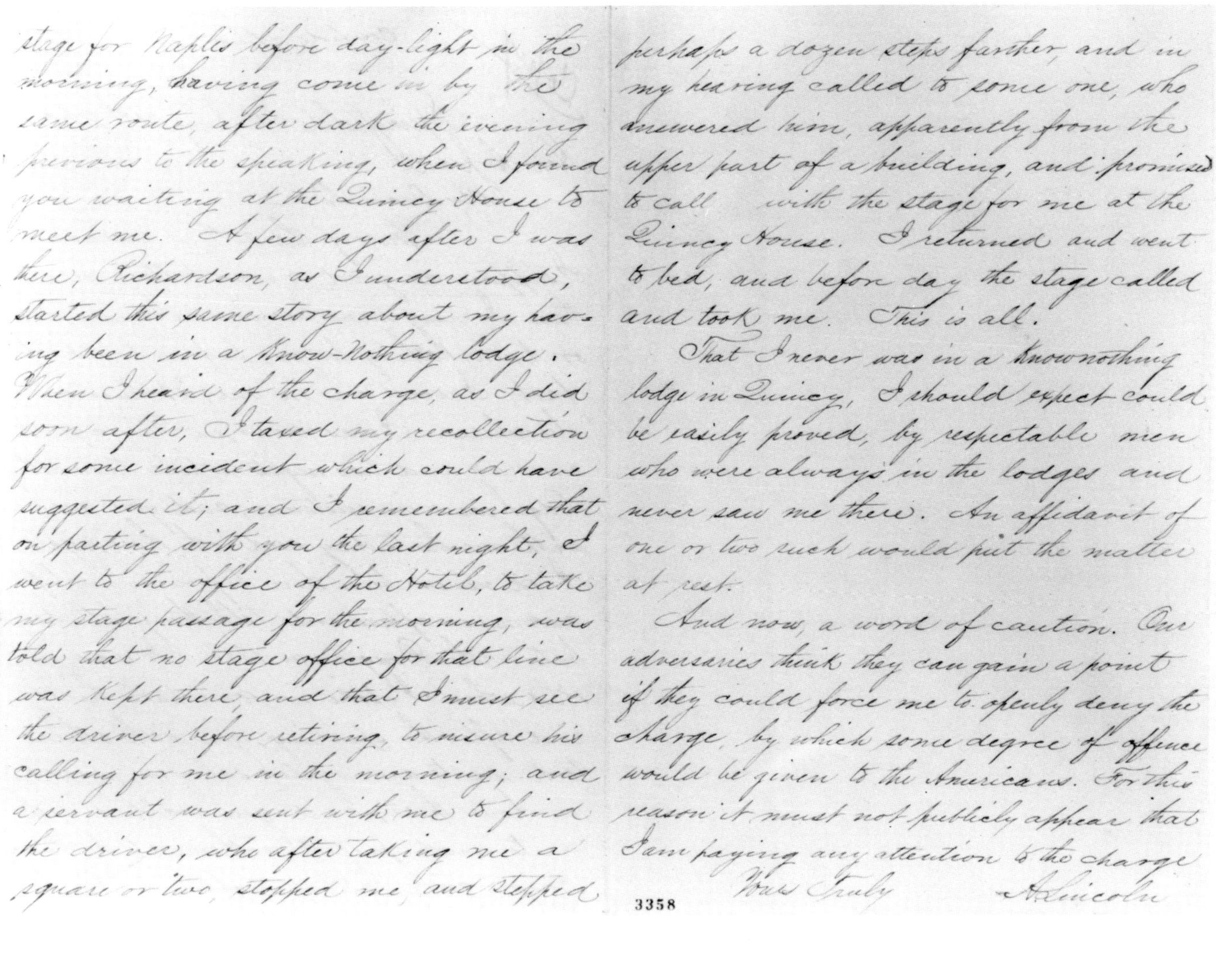

stage for Naples before day-light in the morning, having come in by the same route, after dark the evening previous to the speaking, when I found you waiting at the Quincy House to meet me. A few days after I was there, Richardson, as I understood, started this same story about my having been in a Know-Nothing lodge. When I heard of the charge, as I did soon after, I taxed my recollection for some incident which could have suggested it; and I remembered that on parting with you the last night, I went to the office of the Hotel, to take my stage passage for the morning, was told that no stage office for that line was kept there, and that I must see the driver, before retiring, to insure his calling for me in the morning; and a servant was sent with me to find the driver, who after taking me a square or two, stopped me, and stepped perhaps a dozen steps farther, and in my hearing called to some one, who answered him, apparently from the upper part of a building, and promised to call with the stage for me at the Quincy House. I returned and went to bed, and before day the stage called and took me. This is all.

That I never was in a Know-nothing lodge in Quincy, I should expect could be easily proved, by respectable men who were always in the lodges and never saw me there. An affidavit of one or two such would put the matter at rest.

And now, a word of caution. Our adversaries think they can gain a point if they could force me to openly deny the charge, by which some degree of offence would be given to the Americans. For this reason it must not publicly appear that I am paying any attention to the charge

Yours Truly A. Lincoln

3358

This letter marked "Confidential" discloses the intimate longtime friendship of Lincoln and Abraham Jonas, and Lincoln's political prudence as well as his political stance.

Abraham Lincoln to Abraham Jonas, July 21, 1860. Manuscript Division, Papers of Abraham Lincoln.

be in Washington on the 4th of March and it is their determination, to prevent the inauguration, and if by no other means, by using violence on the person of Lincoln. Men, engaged in this measure are known to be of the most violent character, capable of doing any act, necessary to carry out their vile measures." The writer of this, I know, would not say, what he does, did he not believe the statement above given to you. I cannot give you, his name, for were it known, that he communicated such matters to persons in the North, his life would be in danger—and I trust you will not communicate, having received any such information from me. I had seen rumors in the Newspapers to the like effect, but did not regard them much—this however alarms me, and I think is worthy of some notice. What ought to be done—you are more capable of judging, than any other person—but permit me to suggest—ought not the Governors of the free States, and your friends generally to adopt at once some precautionary measure—no protection can be expected from the damned old traitor at the head of the Government or his subordinates—something should be done in time and done effectually.

With great esteem and devotion
I am truly yrs—
A. Jonas

Jonas was one of the first to suggest Lincoln for the presidency. When Horace Greeley, the editor of the *New York Daily Tribune,* went to Quincy for a lecture in December 1858, he met with a number of leading Republicans to discuss the election of 1860. Abraham Jonas and his law partner Henry Asbury were among them. Asbury later recalled that when the discussion turned to who might be a strong candidate, he proposed a likely one:

Mr. Greeley and one or two others asked who I meant. I said gentlemen I mean Abraham Lincoln of Illinois. I am sorry to say that my suggestion fell flat, it was not even discussed, none of them seemed for Lincoln . . . Some one said Lincoln might do for Vice-President—at this point Mr. Jonas . . . said: Gentlemen there may be more to Asbury's suggestion than any of us now think.

Dr. Isachar Zacharie, an English-born chiropodist, first met Lincoln in September 1862 on a professional call. A satisfied patient, Lincoln gave the doctor a testimonial, "Dr. Zacharie has operated on my feet with great success, and considerable addition to my comfort." Within a few months Zacharie was in New Orleans on a mission for the president. Two years later, the *New York World* wrote that the chiropodist and special emissary "enjoyed Mr. Lincoln's confidence perhaps more than any other private individual." Zacharie also involved himself in politics, actively soliciting the "Jewish vote" for the president. When honored by Jews in 1864, he expressed what may well have been his ambition as Lincoln's friend and confidant:

Let us look at England, France, Russia, Holland, aye, almost every nation in the world, and where do we find the Israelite? We find them taken into the confidence of Kings and Emperors. And in this republican and enlightened country, where we know not how soon it may fall to the lot of any man to be elevated to a high position by this government, why may it not fall to the lot of an Israelite as well as any other?

In the Lincoln Papers at the Library there are thirteen letters from Zacharie to Lincoln, and one dated September 19, 1864, apparently as yet unpublished, from Lincoln to Zacharie:

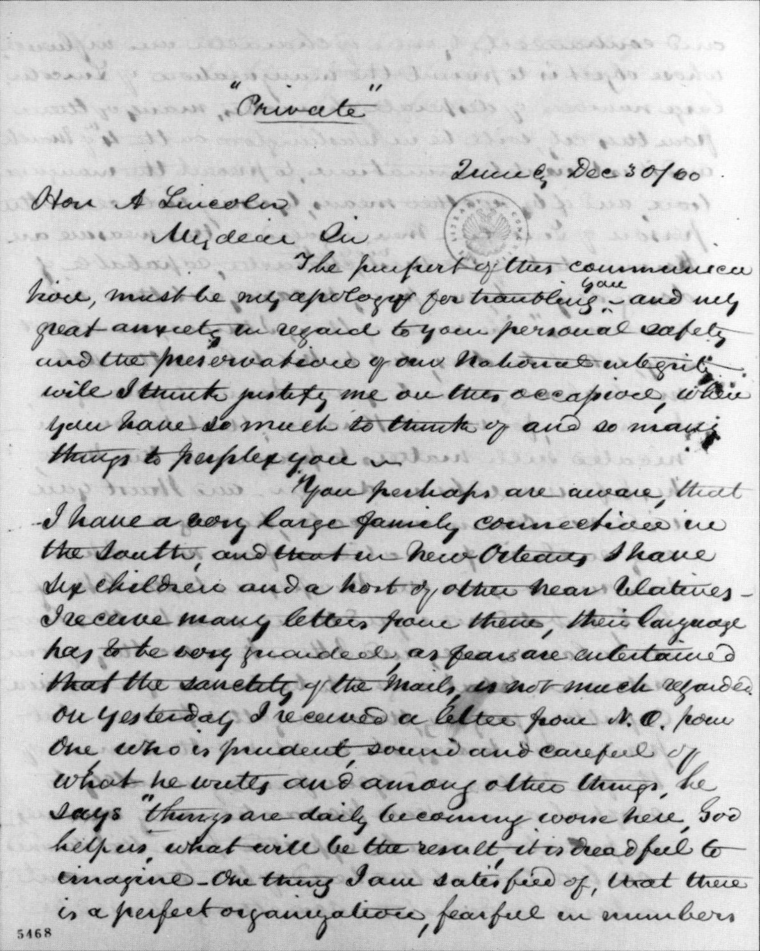

"Private"

Quincy, Dec 30/60

Hon A Lincoln

My dear Sir

The purport of this communication, must be my apology for troubling you — and my great anxiety in regard to your personal safety and the preservation of our National integrity will I think justify me on this occasion, when you have so much to think of and so many things to perplex you —

You perhaps are aware, that I have a very large family connection in the South, and that in New Orleans I have six children and a host of other near relatives — I receive many letters from there, their language has to be very guarded, as fears are entertained that the sanctity of the Mail, is not much regarded. On yesterday I received a letter from N.O. from one who is prudent, sound and careful of what he writes and among other things, he says "things are daily becoming worse here, God help us, what will be the result it is dreadful to imagine — One thing I am satisfied of, that there is a perfect organization, fearful in numbers

5468

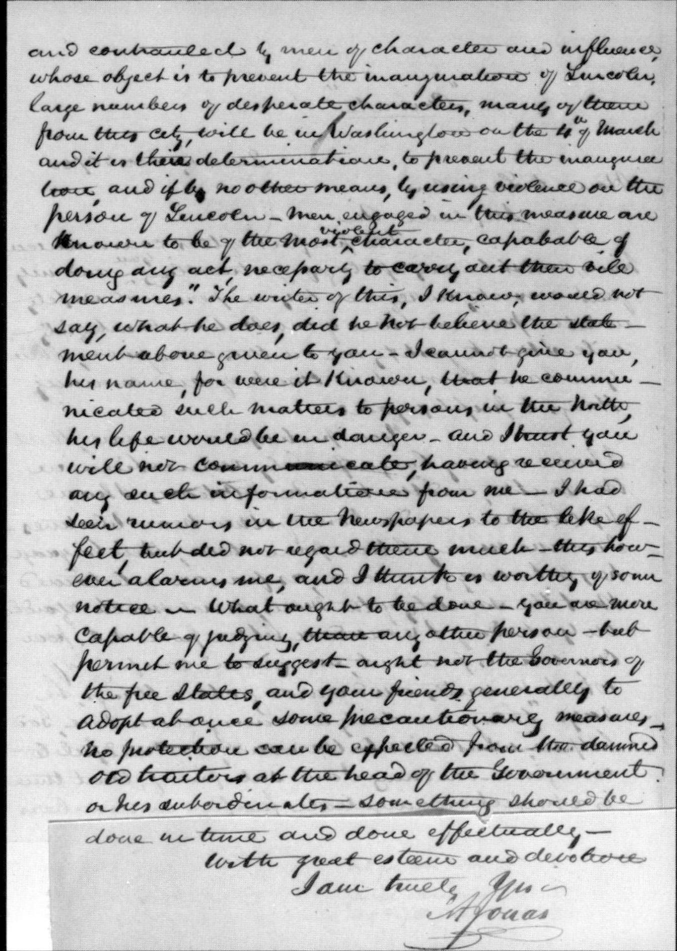

and controlled by men of character and influence whose object is to prevent the inauguration of Lincoln, large numbers of desperate characters, many of them from this city, will be in Washington on the 4th of March and it is their determination, to prevent the inauguration, and if by no other means, by using violence on the person of Lincoln — men engaged in this measure are known to be of the most violent character, capable of doing any act necessary to carry out their vile measures." The writer of this, I know, would not say, what he does, did he not believe the statement above given to you — I cannot give you his name, for were it known, that he communicated such matters to persons in the North, his life would be in danger — and I trust you will not communicate, having received any such information from me — I had seen rumors in the Newspapers to the like effect, but did not regard them much — this however alarms me, and I think is worthy of some notice — What ought to be done — you are more capable of judging, than any other person — but permit me to suggest — ought not the Governors of the free States, and your friends generally to adopt at once some precautionary measures, no protection can be expected from the damned old traitors at the head of the Government or his subordinates — something should be done in time and done effectually —

With great esteem and devotion

I am truly Yours

A Jonas

In this prescient letter marked "Private," friend Abraham Jonas warns Lincoln that he has been informed by a relative in New Orleans, that

> large numbers of desperate characters . . .
> will be in Washington on the 4th of March
> and it is their determination to prevent the
> inauguration, and if by no other means, by
> using violence on the person of Lincoln.

Abraham Jonas to Abraham Lincoln, December 30, 1860.
Manuscript Division, Papers of Abraham Lincoln.

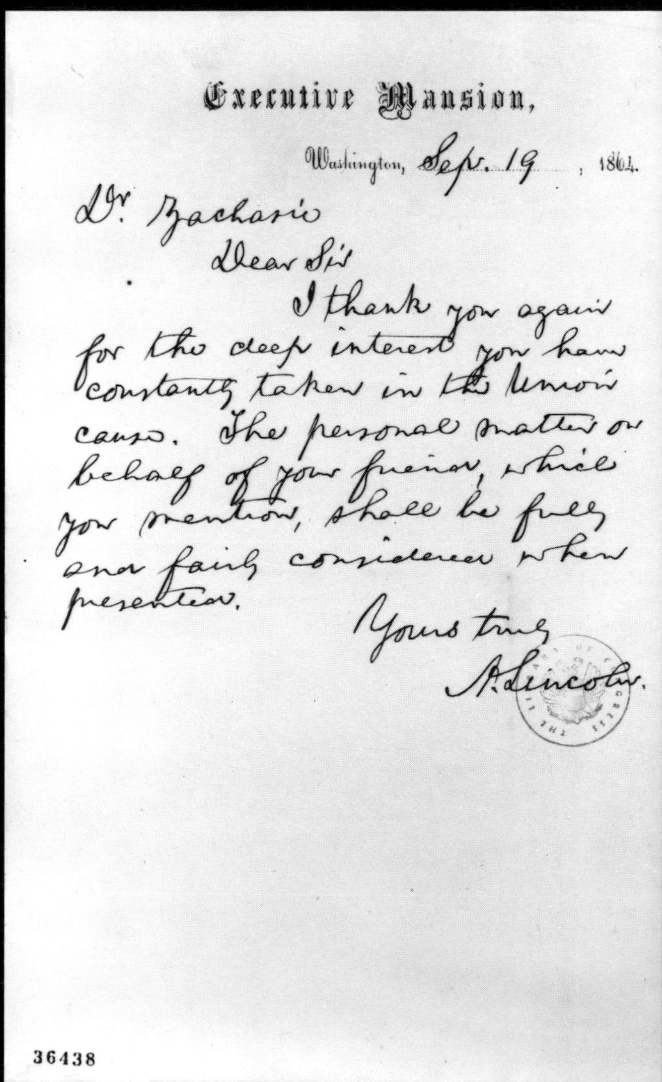

Executive Mansion,

Washington, Sep. 19, 1864.

Dr. Zacharie

Dear Sir

I thank you again for the deep interest you have constantly taken in the Union cause. The personal matter on behalf of your friend, which you mention, shall be fully and fairly considered when presented.

Yours truly

A. Lincoln

36438

This brief letter discloses that Isachar Zacharie served Lincoln as more than his chiropodist. It is known from other sources that Lincoln used him on occasion as a private agent, and that Zacharie was deeply involved in trying to secure for Lincoln, the "Jewish Vote."

Abraham Lincoln to Isachar Zacharie, September 19, 1864.
Manuscript Division, Papers of Abraham Lincoln.

Dear Sir
I thank you again for the deep interest you have taken in the Union Cause. The personal matter on behalf of your friend which you mentioned shall be fully and fairly considered when presented.

Yours truly
A. Lincoln

To which Zacharie replied:

Dear Friend,
Yours of the 19th came duly to hand, it has had the desired effect, with the friend of the Partie.

I leave tomorrow for the interior of Pennsylvania, may go as far as Ohio. One thing is to be done, and that is for you to impress on the minds of your friends for them not to be to[o] sure.

As rabbi of Congregation B'nai Jeshurun, the Rev. Dr. Morris J. Raphall (1798–1868), one of New York's more prominent clergymen, had gained renown as an orator, distinction as being the first rabbi to open the session of the House of Representatives with a prayer, and notoriety for his sermon *The Bible View of Slavery,* which was printed, reprinted, and widely distributed as a proslavery sermon by antiabolitionist forces. As Raphall told his congregation, when it assembled to mourn the martyred president, he knew Lincoln but slightly. He had met Lincoln only once, but on that single occasion the rabbi had asked a favor of the president and, as Raphall told his congregants, Lincoln had "granted it lovingly, because he knew the speaker to be a Jew—because he knew him to be a true servant of the Lord." The favor granted must have been the rabbi's request that his son be promoted from second lieutenant to first. Forty years later, in 1903, Adolphus S. Solomons of the book publishing firm of Philip and Solomons, in Washington, D. C., reminisced that he had helped Rabbi Raphall get an audience with the president, where that request was made and granted. Lincoln did even more for Raphall's son-in-law, Captain C. M. Levy.

Assigned to the Quartermaster Department in Washington, Captain Levy undertook as an added task to distribute special food and clothing to Jewish soldiers in the capital's hospitals. On October 9, 1863, a Captain C. M. Levy was court-martialed and dismissed from service for unspecified charges. Apparently appealed to, Lincoln must have responded with his fabled compassion, for on March 1, 1864, Raphall wrote him thanking him "for the generosity and justice with which you have treated my son-in-law Captain C. M. Levy."

My whole family unites with me in feeling that you are indeed his true benefactor. Happy shall we be that any thing you may at any time require of me or them, is thankfully obeyed by all of us.

I take the liberty of sending you a couple of my potographs [sic] and with sincere prayers for your continued health and prosperity I am Your obliged and respectful servant, M. J. Raphall.

The "potographs" may well have been the prints of a photograph of the rabbi, first published by P. Haas in New York, 1850, of which the Library has a fine copy.

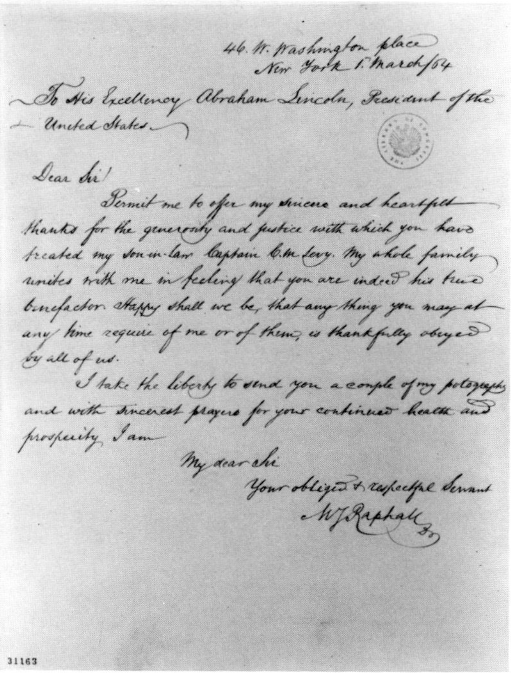

46. W. Washington place
New York 1. March /64

To His Excellency Abraham Lincoln, President of the United States

Dear Sir!
Permit me to offer my sincere and heartfelt thanks for the generosity and justice with which you have treated my son-in-law Captain C.M. Levy. My whole family unites with me in feeling that you are indeed his true benefactor. Happy shall we be, that any thing you may at any time require of me or of them, is thankfully obeyed by all of us.

I take the liberty to send you a couple of my potographs and with sincerest prayers for your continued health and prosperity I am

My dear Sir
Your obliged & respectful Servant
M J Raphall Dr

31163

New York's prominent rabbi, author, and orator, Morris J. Raphall, thanks Lincoln for "the generosity and justice with which you have treated my son-in-law Captain C. M. Levy . . . You are indeed his true benefactor." Levy, who had been with the Quartermaster Department, and had been distributing special food and clothing to Jewish soldiers in Washington's hospitals, was dismissed from service. Lincoln's fabled compassion, as this letter of gratitude indicates, apparently came to his rescue.

M. J. Raphall to Abraham Lincoln, March 1, 1864. Manuscript Division, Papers of Abraham Lincoln.

ORDER NO. 11

The *New York Times* called General Orders No. 11 issued by Major General U. S. Grant on December 17, 1862 "one of the deepest sensations of the war." Grant's order read:

The Jews, as a class violating every regulation of trade established by the Treasury Department and also department orders, are hereby expelled from the department within twenty-four hours from the receipt of this order.

Post commanders will see to it that all of this class of people be furnished passes and required to leave, and any one returning after such notification will be arrested and held in confinement until an opportunity occurs of sending them out as prisoners, unless furnished with permit from headquarters. No passes will be given these people to visit headquarters for the purpose of making personal application of trade permits.

Cesar J. Kaskel of Paducah, Kentucky, immediately set out for Washington to put the matter before President Lincoln. Ohio Congressman John A. Gurley escorted him to the White House, where Kaskel apprised the president of what Grant had done. Lincoln wrote a note to General-in-Chief H. W. Halleck, who sent a telegram to General Grant forthwith:

A paper *purporting* to be General Orders, No. 11, issued by you December 17, has been presented here. By its terms, it expells all Jews from your department. *If such an order has been issued,* it will be immediately revoked.

In the meantime the hue and cry had been raised, and delegations descended upon Washington. Editorials appeared in newspapers of the major cities, most of them attacking but some also defending Order No. 11. Jewish periodicals inveighed against the order, and two national Jewish organizations sent formal memoranda of protest. Both are in the Lincoln Papers and, hitherto not having been published, deserve quotation in toto.

United Order Bné B'rith Missouri Loge [sic] St. Louis, January 5, 1863:

To his Excellency
Abr. Lincoln
President U.S.

Sir:
An Order, Expelling and Ostracising all Jews as a class has been issued by Maj. Genl U. S. Grant and has been enforced at Holly Springs, Trenton, Corinth, Paducah, Jackson and other places.

In the name of the class of *loyal* citizens of these U.S. which we in part represent.

In the name of hundreds, who have been driven from their houses, deprived of their liberty and injured in their property *without* having violated any law or regulation.

In the name of the thousands of our Brethren and our children who have died and are now willingly sacrificing their lives and fortunes for the Union and the suppression of this rebellion.

In the name of religious liberty, of justice and humanity—we Enter our solemn Protest against this Order, and ask of you—the Defender and Protector of the Con-

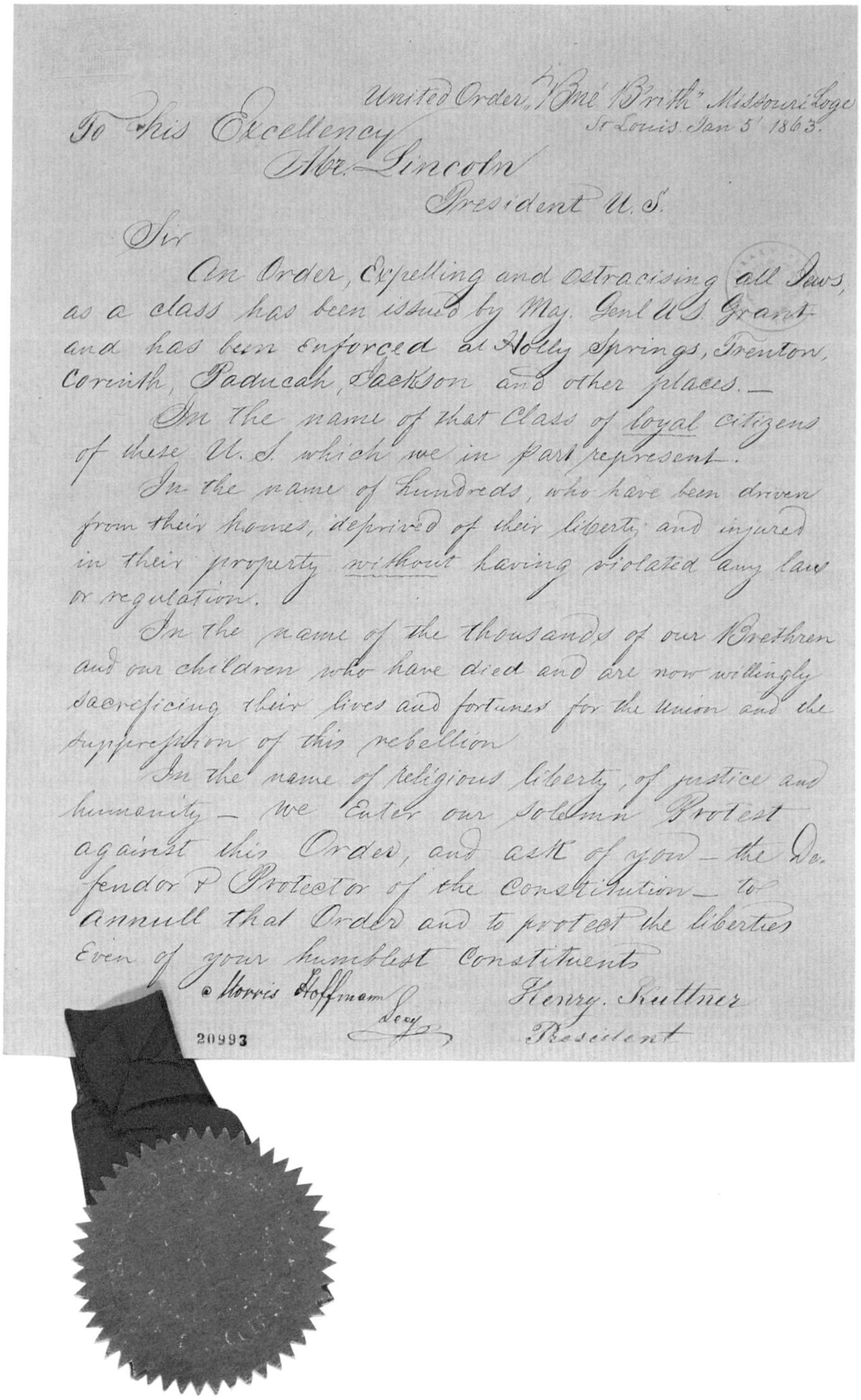

United Order, "Bné B'rith" Missouri Lodge
St Louis Jan 5' 1863.

To his Excellency
Abr. Lincoln
President U. S.

Sir

An Order, Expelling and ostracising all Jews, as a class has been issued by Maj. Genl U. S. Grant and has been enforced at Holly Springs, Trenton, Corinth, Paducah, Jackson and other places.—

In the name of that Class of loyal citizens of these U. S. which we in part represent.

In the name of hundreds, who have been driven from their homes, deprived of their liberty and injured in their property without having violated any law or regulation.

In the name of the thousands of our Brethren and our children who have died and are now willingly sacreficing their lives and fortunes for the Union and the suppression of this rebellion

In the name of religious liberty, of justice and humanity — we Enter our Solemn Protest against this Order, and ask of you — the Defender & Protector of the Constitution — to annull that Order and to protect the liberties Even of your humblest Constituents

Morris Hoffman
Secy

Henry Kuttner
President

20993

The first Jewish organization to formally protest against Order No. 11 "expelling and ostracizing all Jews, as a class . . . issued by Maj. GenL. U. S. Grant" was the United Order "Bné B'rith" Missouri Lodge. It protests,

In the name of hundreds who have been driven from their houses . . . of the thousands of our Brethren . . . who have died . . . for the Union . . . of religious liberty, of justice and humanity.

On the envelope in which the protest came, Lincoln writes "I have today, Jan. 5, 1863, written Gen. Curtis about this. A.L." The order was forthwith rescinded.

United Order "Bné B'rith" to Abraham Lincoln, January 5, 1863.
Manuscript Division, Papers of Abraham Lincoln.

stitution—to annull that Order and protect the liberties even of your humblest constituents.

Morris Hoffman
Secy

Henry Kuttner
President

The set of Resolutions adopted by the Board of Delegates of American Israelites at a special meeting of its Executive Committee in New York on January 8, 1863, Henry I. Hart, Esq., presiding, is longer and stronger.

Be it therefore *Resolved* that we have heard with surprise and indignation intelligence that in this present Century and in this land of freedom and equality an Officer of the United States should have promulgated an order worthy of despotic Europe in the dark ages of the World's history.

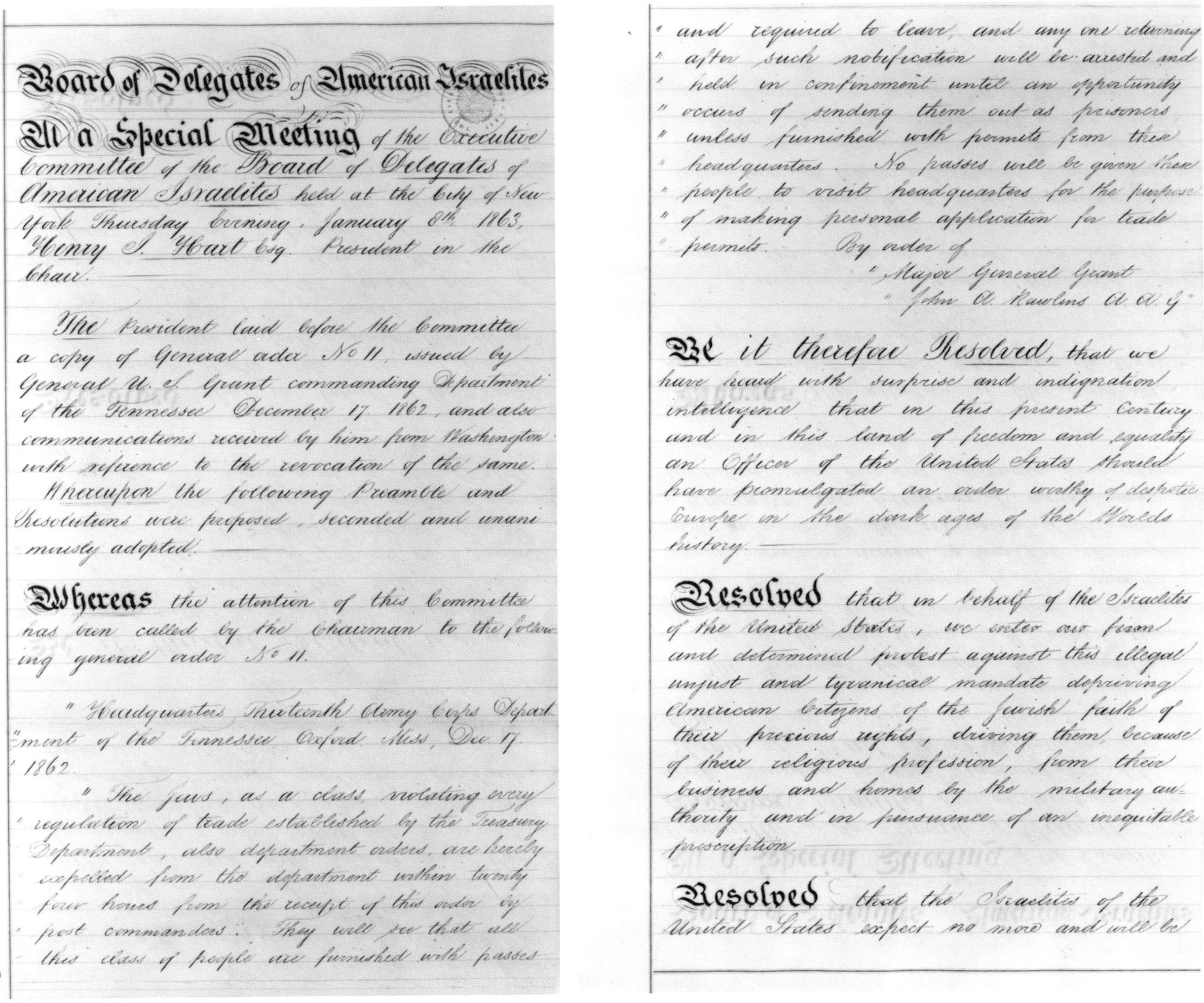
Board of Delegates of American Israelites

At a Special Meeting of the Executive Committee of the Board of Delegates of American Israelites held at the City of New York Thursday Evening, January 8th 1863, Henry I. Hart Esq. President in the Chair.

The President laid before the Committee a copy of General order No 11, issued by General U. S. Grant commanding Department of the Tennessee December 17. 1862, and also communications received by him from Washington with reference to the revocation of the same.

Whereupon the following Preamble and Resolutions were proposed, seconded and unanimously adopted.

Whereas the attention of this Committee has been called by the Chairman to the following general order No 11.

" Headquarters Thirteenth Army Corps Department of the Tennessee, Oxford, Miss, Dec 17 1862.

" The Jews, as a class, violating every regulation of trade established by the Treasury Department, also department orders, are hereby expelled from the department within twenty four hours from the receipt of this order by post commanders. They will see that all this class of people are furnished with passes and required to leave, and any one returning after such notification will be arrested and held in confinement until an opportunity occurs of sending them out as prisoners unless furnished with permits from these headquarters. No passes will be given these people to visit headquarters for the purpose of making personal application for trade permits. By order of

" Major General Grant

" John A. Rawlins A. A. G."

Be it therefore Resolved, that we have heard with surprise and indignation intelligence that in this present Century and in this land of freedom and equality an Officer of the United States should have promulgated an order worthy of despotic Europe in the dark ages of the Worlds history.

Resolved that in behalf of the Israelites of the United States, we enter our firm and determined protest against this illegal unjust and tyranical mandate depriving American Citizens of the Jewish faith of their precious rights, driving them, because of their religious profession, from their business and homes by the military authority and in pursuance of an inequitable prescription.

Resolved that the Israelites of the United States expect no more and will be

21089

Resolved that in behalf of the Israelites of the United States, we enter our firm and determined protest against this illegal unjust and tyrannical mandate depriving American Citizens of the Jewish faith of their precious rights, driving them because of their religious profession, from their business and homes by the military authority and in pursuance of an inequitable prescription.

Resolved that the Israelites of the United States expect no more and will be content with no less than equal privileges with their fellow Citizens, in the enjoyment of "life, liberty and the pursuit of happiness" as guaranteed by the Constitution of this Republic.

Resolved that it is peculiarly painful to the Israelites of the United States, who have freely tendered their blood and treasure in defence of the Union they love, to observe this uncalled for and inequitable discrimination against them. Claiming to be second to no class of Citizens in support of the Constitutional government, they regard with sadness and indignation this contumely upon the Jewish name, this insult to them as a community, on the ostensible ground that individuals supposed to be Jews have violated "regulations of trade established by the Treasury Department and Department Orders."

The outrage of American Jewry against General U. S. Grant's Order No. 11, which expels the "Jews as a class" from territories under the Thirteenth Army Corps, is conveyed to President Lincoln by this set of calligraphically inscribed Resolutions, adopted January 8, 1863.

Board of Delegates . . . to Abraham Lincoln, January 8, 1863.
Manuscript Division, Papers of Abraham Lincoln.

Resolved that it is in the highest degree obnoxious to them, as it must be to all fair minded American Citizens, for the general body to be made accountable for acts of particular persons supposed to belong to their denomination, but as has been frequently demonstrated, in many cases really professing other creeds. That if an individual be guilty of an infraction of discipline or offence against military law or treasury regulations, punishment should be visited upon him alone, and the religious community to which he is presumed to be attached, should not be subjected to insult, obloquy or disregard of its consitutional rights as a penalty for individual offences.

Resolved that the thanks of this Committee and of the Israelites of the United States be and they are hereby tendered to *Major General H. W. Halleck, General in Chief U. S. A.* for the promptness with which he revoked General Grant's unjust and outrageous order, as soon as it was brought to his attention.

Resolved that a copy of these resolutions duly attested, be transmitted to the *President of the United States, the Secretary of War, Major General Halleck and Major General Grant* and that the same be communicated to the press for publication.

Myer S. Isaacs
Secretary

DEAR MR. PRESIDENT . . . AGAIN

Myer S. Isaacs (1841–1904) was the precocious son of a noted father, the Reverend Samuel M. C. Isaacs, one of New York's earliest rabbis, and he was not quite twenty-two when he framed the resolutions. The father, born in Holland and educated in England, came to New York in 1839 to serve as the hazzan and preacher of Congregation B'nai Jeshurun, the city's first Ashkenazi synagogue. In 1857, he founded the *Jewish Messenger,* a weekly espousing the cause of traditional Judaism, and in 1859 he was the chief organizer of the Board of Delegates of American Israelites, designed to serve as the over-all organization of American Jewry. In both these efforts, he was assisted by his son.

The young Isaacs, in 1859, at age eighteen the top graduate of New York University, received his law degree two years later. He served as Secretary of the Board of Delegates of American Israelites from its organization until 1876, when he became its president. He was also coeditor of the *Jewish Messenger,* a practicing attorney, and a civic leader.

On October 26, 1864, Myer Isaacs sent a strongly worded letter to President Lincoln warning him against a deal that he allegedly made with a group of New York Jews who, presenting themselves as leaders of the community, had promised to deliver the "Jewish vote" for him. This letter is one of the germinal documents of early Jewish participation in the American political process.

Your Excellency,
As a firm and earnest Union man, I deem it my duty to add a word . . . with reference to a recent "visitation" on the part of persons claiming to represent the Israelites of New York or the United States and pledging the "Jewish vote" to your support, and, I am informed, succeeding in a deception that resulted to their pecuniary profit.

Having peculiar facilities for obtaining information as to the Israelites of the United States, from my eight years' connection with the Jewish paper of this city and my position as Secretary of their central organization, the "Board of Delegates" . . . I feel authorized to caution you, Sir, against any such representations as those understood to have been made.

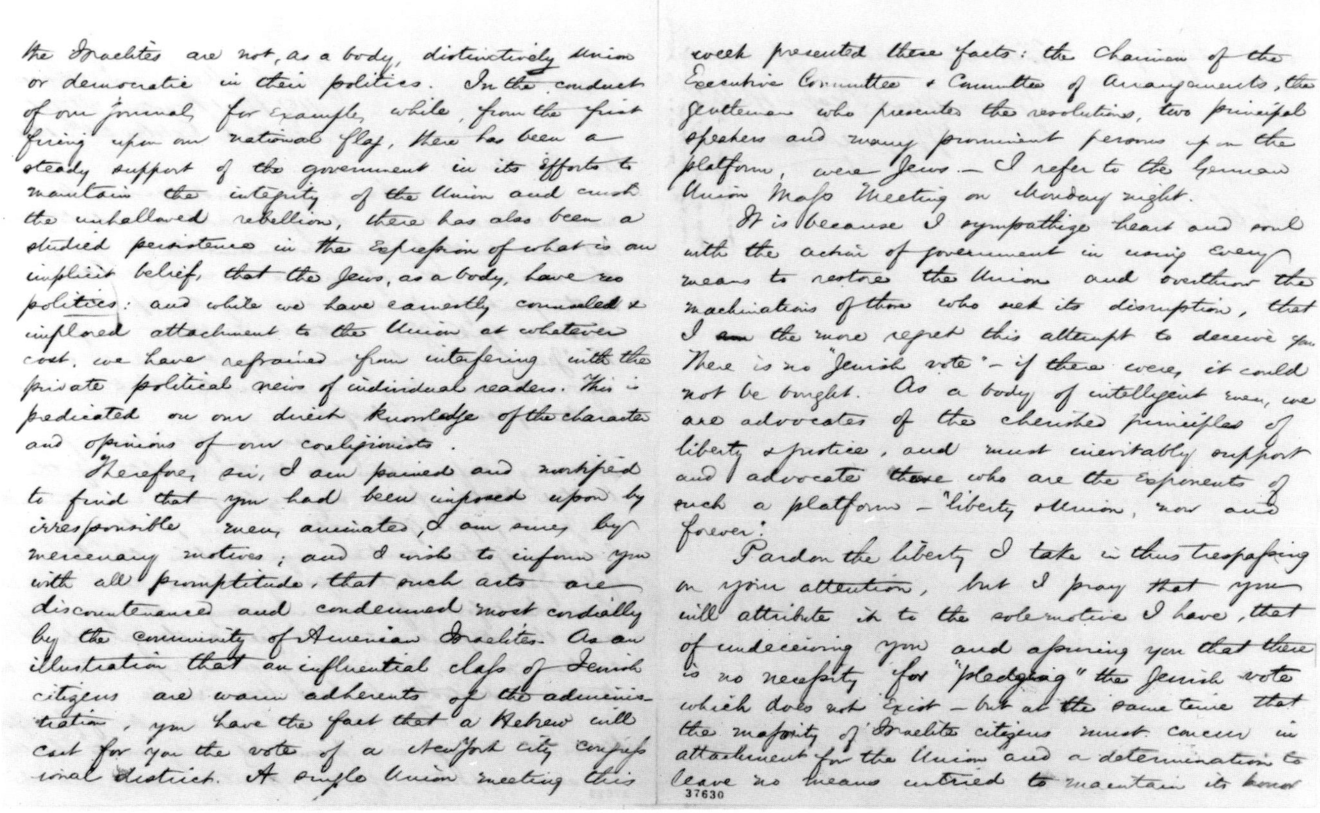

the Israelites are not, as a body, distinctively Union or democratic in their politics. In the conduct of our journal, for example, while, from the first firing upon our national flag, there has been a steady support of the government in its efforts to maintain the integrity of the Union and crush the unhallowed rebellion, there has also been a studied persistence in the expression of what is our implicit belief, that the Jews, as a body, have no politics: and while we have earnestly counseled & implored attachment to the Union at whatever cost, we have refrained from interfering with the private political views of individual readers. This is predicated on our direct knowledge of the character and opinions of our coreligionists.

Therefore, sir, I am pained and mortified to find that you had been imposed upon by irresponsible men, animated, I am sure by mercenary motives; and I wish to inform you with all promptitude, that such acts are discountenanced and condemned most cordially by the community of American Israelites. As an illustration that an influential class of Jewish citizens are warm adherents of the administration, you have the fact that a Hebrew will cast for you the vote of a New York city congressional district. A single Union meeting this week presented these facts: the Chairman of the Executive Committee & Committee of Arrangements, the gentleman who presented the resolutions, two principal speakers and many prominent persons upon the platform, were Jews. — I refer to the German Union Mass Meeting on Monday night.

It is because I sympathize heart and soul with the action of government in using every means to restore the Union and overthrow the machinations of those who seek its disruption, that I ~~am~~ the more regret this attempt to deceive you. There is no "Jewish vote" – if there were, it could not be bought. As a body of intelligent men, we are advocates of the cherished principles of liberty & justice, and must inevitably support and advocate those who are the exponents of such a platform – "liberty & union, now and forever."

Pardon the liberty I take in thus trespassing on your attention, but I pray that you will attribute it to the sole motive I have, that of undeceiving you and assuring you that there is no necessity for "pledging" the Jewish vote which does not exist — but at the same time that the majority of Israelite citizens must concur in attachment for the Union and a determination to leave no means untried to maintain its honor

37630

There are a large number of faithful Unionists among our prominent coreligionists—but there are also supporters of the opposition, and indeed the Israelites are not as a body, distinctly Union or democratic in their politics . . . the Jews as a body have no politics.

Therefore, Sir, I am pained and surprised to find that you had been imposed upon by irresponsible men . . . such acts are discountenanced and condemned most cordially by the community of American Israelites . . .

There is no "Jewish vote"—if there were, it could not be bought. As a body of intelligent men, we are advocates of the cherished principles of liberty and justice, and must inevitably support and advocate those who are the exponents of such a platform—"liberty and union, now and forever."

Pardon the liberty I take in thus trespassing on your attention, but I pray that you will attribute it to the sole motive I have, that of undeceiving you and assuring you that there is no necessity for "pledging" the Jewish vote which does not exist—but at the same time that the majority of Israelite citizens must concur in the attachment for the Union and a determination to leave no means untried to maintain its honor and integrity.

Yours most Respectfully,
Myer S. Isaacs

Secretary of the Board of Delegates of American Israelites, Myer S. Isaacs writes to Lincoln on the eve of the presidential election, October 26, 1864, that "the Jewish vote does not exist" but assures him that, "the majority of Israelite citizens must concur in the attachment for the Union and a determination to leave no means untried to maintain its honor."

Myer S. Isaacs to Abraham Lincoln, October 26, 1864. Manuscript Division, Papers of Abraham Lincoln.

Lincoln's private secretary, John Hay, responded at once, on November 1, 1864, assuring Isaacs concerning the "interview . . . between certain gentlemen of the Hebrew faith, and the President. No pledge of the Jewish vote was made by these gentlemen and no inducements or promises were extended to them by the President. They claimed no such authority and received no such response as you seem to suppose."

The letter that Philadelphia publisher and Jewish communal and congregational leader Abraham Hart, in his capacity as parnas (president) of the Mikveh Israel Congregation, wrote to Lincoln on April 23, 1862, enclosed a sermon and prayer that the Reverend Sabato Morais had delivered on the death of Lincoln's son, Willie. Both have been preserved in the Library's Lincoln papers.

Morais had a deep affection for Lincoln, and in his prayer were words, "which come forth from the heart":

> Bless the President of the United States; bless him for his sterling honesty, bless him for his firmness and moderation. Rekindle with joy his domestic hearth; pour on him the balm of divine consolation . . . Grant that the end of his career be the maintenance of this Government, unimpaired and unsullied as bequeathed by our illustrious ancestors.

Lincoln's reply to the "President of Congregation Hope of Israel," on May 13 is the only known letter Lincoln sent to a Jewish congregation. He acknowledges receipt of the "communication" and thanks Hart for his expressions of kindness and confidence. Three years later, Mikveh Israel and congregations throughout the United States joined in prayer and offered consolation to an again bereaved Lincoln family.

THE TRIBUTE OF THE SYNAGOGUE

A cluster of eight published eulogies and tributes to Abraham Lincoln delivered in synagogues in New York, Philadelphia, Baltimore, and New Orleans.

General Collection.

The American synagogue paid its tribute to the martyred president at special services on April 19, and again on the day designated for memorial services by President Andrew Johnson, June 1, 1865, which happened to be the second day of the Festival of Shavuot. Of the many memorial discourses heard in Jewish houses of worship, nine—five in German and four in English—were issued as special publications. The Library has eight of the nine. Listed below, these brief excerpts give some source of their mood and content.

1. *An Address on the Death of Abraham Lincoln, President of the United States, Delivered Before Congregation Mikve Israel of Philadelphia . . . by the Rev. S. Morais, Minister of the Congregation. On Wednesday, April 19, 1865, Philadelphia, 1865.*

The stillness of the grave reigns abroad. Where is the joyous throng that enlivened this city of loyalty? Seek it now, my friends, in the shrines of holiness. There, it lies prostrate; there, it tearfully bemoans an irretrievable loss, Oh! tell it not in the country of the Gauls; publish it not in the streets of Albion, lest the children of iniquity rejoice, lest the son of Belial triumph. For the heart which abhorred wickedness has ceased to throb; the hand which had stemmed a flood of unrighteousness, is withered in death.

2. *A Discourse Delivered Before the Congregation Mikve Israel . . . Thursday, June 1, 1865, the Day Appointed for Fasting, Humiliation, and Prayer, for the Untimely Death of the Late Lamented President of the United States, Abraham Lincoln by the Rev. S. Morais . . . Philadelphia, 1865*

If the essence of religion is what the great Hillel taught us, then I unhesitatingly say that the breast of our lamented President was ever kindled with that divine spark. "To forbear doing unto others what would displease us" . . . is the maxim he illustrated in the immortal document of emancipation that bears his honorable signature. It is that which he exemplified by his numerous acts of clemency . . .

We must bear his name with a blessing upon our lips.

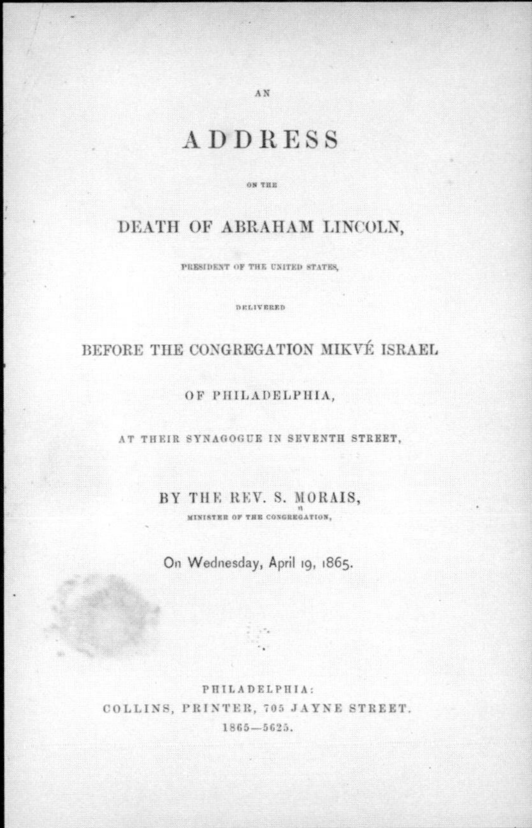

AN

ADDRESS

ON THE

DEATH OF ABRAHAM LINCOLN,

PRESIDENT OF THE UNITED STATES,

DELIVERED

BEFORE THE CONGREGATION MIKVÉ ISRAEL

OF PHILADELPHIA,

AT THEIR SYNAGOGUE IN SEVENTH STREET,

BY THE REV. S. MORAIS,

MINISTER OF THE CONGREGATION,

On Wednesday, April 19, 1865.

PHILADELPHIA:
COLLINS, PRINTER, 705 JAYNE STREET.
1865—5625.

The Rev. Sabato Morais, Congregation Mikve Israel, Philadelphia, April 19, 1865.

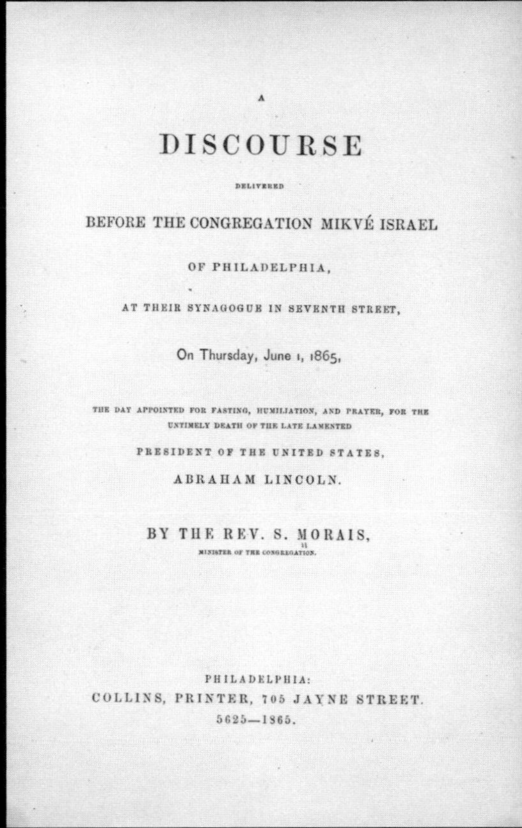

A

DISCOURSE

DELIVERED

BEFORE THE CONGREGATION MIKVÉ ISRAEL

OF PHILADELPHIA,

AT THEIR SYNAGOGUE IN SEVENTH STREET,

On Thursday, June 1, 1865,

THE DAY APPOINTED FOR FASTING, HUMILIATION, AND PRAYER, FOR THE UNTIMELY DEATH OF THE LATE LAMENTED

PRESIDENT OF THE UNITED STATES,

ABRAHAM LINCOLN.

BY THE REV. S. MORAIS,

MINISTER OF THE CONGREGATION.

PHILADELPHIA:
COLLINS, PRINTER, 705 JAYNE STREET.
5625—1865.

The Rev. Sabato Morais, Congregation Mikve Israel, Philadelphia, June 1, 1865.

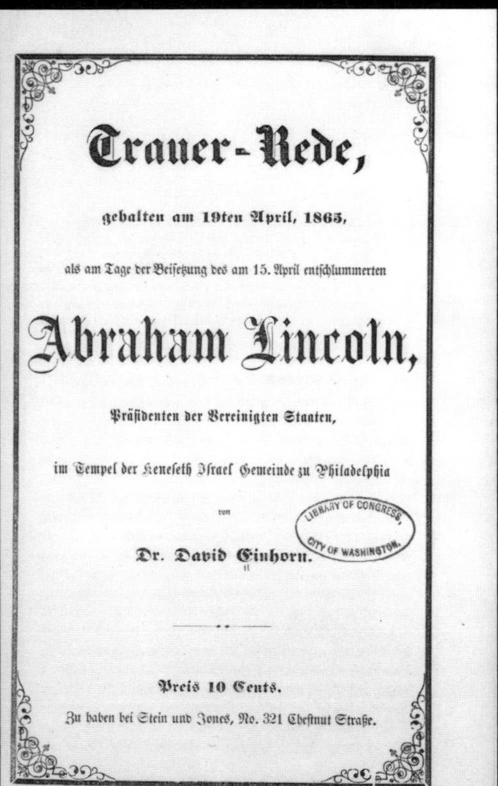

Trauer-Rede,

gehalten am 19ten April, 1865,

als am Tage der Beisetzung des am 15. April entschlummerten

Abraham Lincoln,

Präsidenten der Vereinigten Staaten,

im Tempel der Keneseth Israel Gemeinde zu Philadelphia

von

Dr. David Einhorn.

Preis 10 Cents.

Zu haben bei Stein und Jones, No. 321 Chestnut Straße.

The Rev. Dr. David Einhorn, Congregation Keneseth Israel, Philadelphia, April 19, 1865.

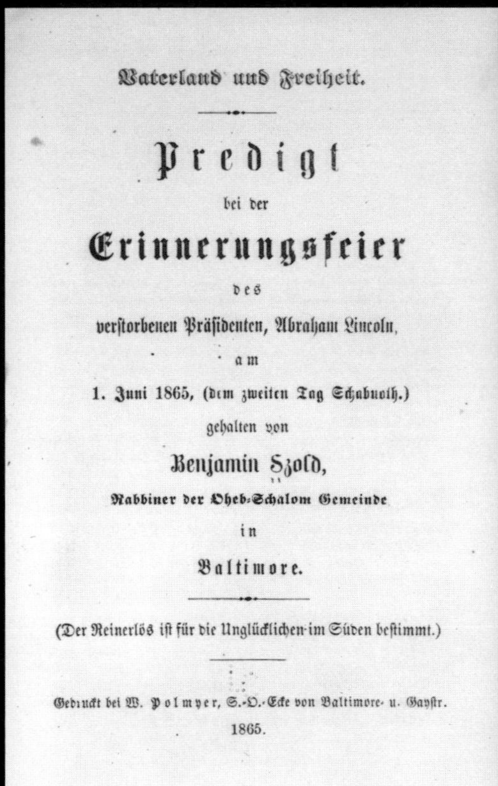

Vaterland und Freiheit.

Predigt

bei der

Erinnerungsfeier

des

verstorbenen Präsidenten, Abraham Lincoln,

am

1. Juni 1865, (dem zweiten Tag Schabuoth.)

gehalten von

Benjamin Szold,

Rabbiner der Oheb-Schalom Gemeinde

in

Baltimore.

(Der Reinerlös ist für die Unglücklichen im Süden bestimmt.)

Gedruckt bei W. Polmyer, S.-O.-Ecke von Baltimore- u. Gaystr.
1865.

The Rev. Benjamin Szold, Congregation Oheb Shalom, Baltimore, June 1, 1865.

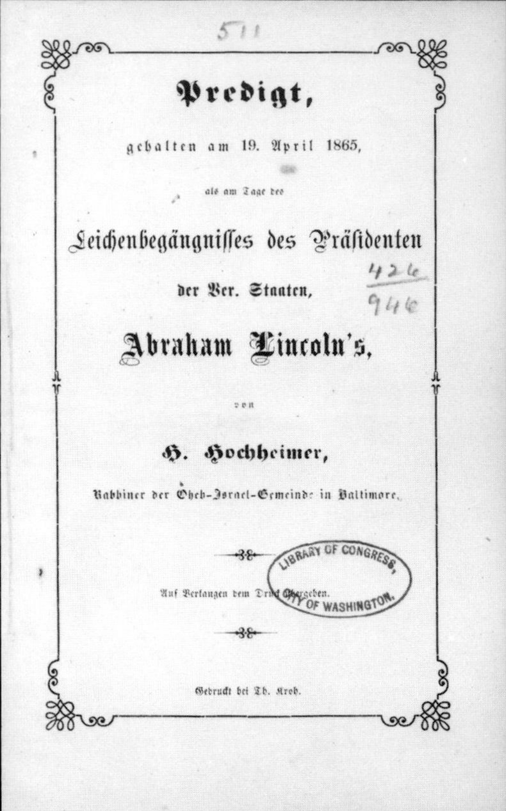

Predigt,

gehalten am 19. April 1865,

als am Tage des

Leichenbegängnisses des Präsidenten

der Ver. Staaten,

Abraham Lincoln's,

von

H. Hochheimer,

Rabbiner der Oheb-Israel-Gemeinde in Baltimore.

Auf Verlangen dem Druck übergeben.

Gedruckt bei Th. Kroh.

The Rev. Henry Hochheimer, Congregation Oheb Israel, Baltimore, April 19, 1865.

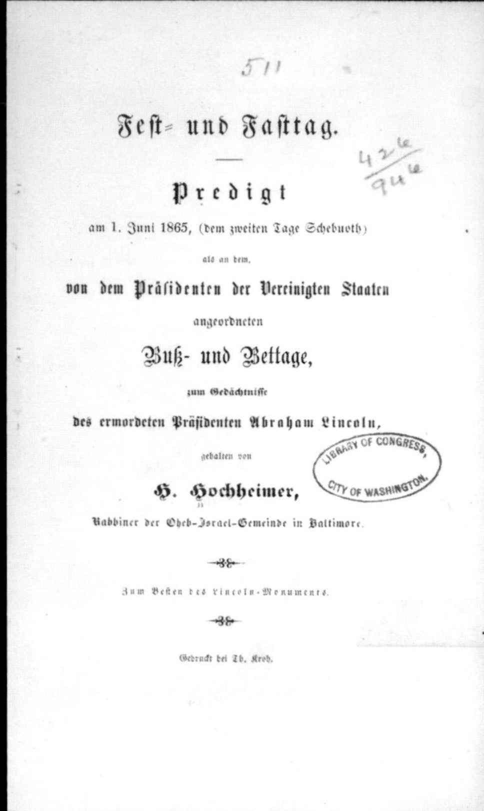

Fest- und Fasttag.

Predigt

am 1. Juni 1865, (dem zweiten Tage Schebuoth)

als an dem,

von dem Präsidenten der Vereinigten Staaten

angeordneten

Buß- und Bettage,

zum Gedächtnisse

des ermordeten Präsidenten Abraham Lincoln,

gehalten von

H. Hochheimer,

Rabbiner der Oheb-Israel-Gemeinde in Baltimore.

Zum Besten des Lincoln-Monuments.

Gedruckt bei Th. Kroh.

The Rev. Henry Hochheimer, Congregation Oheb Israel, Baltimore, June 1, 1865.

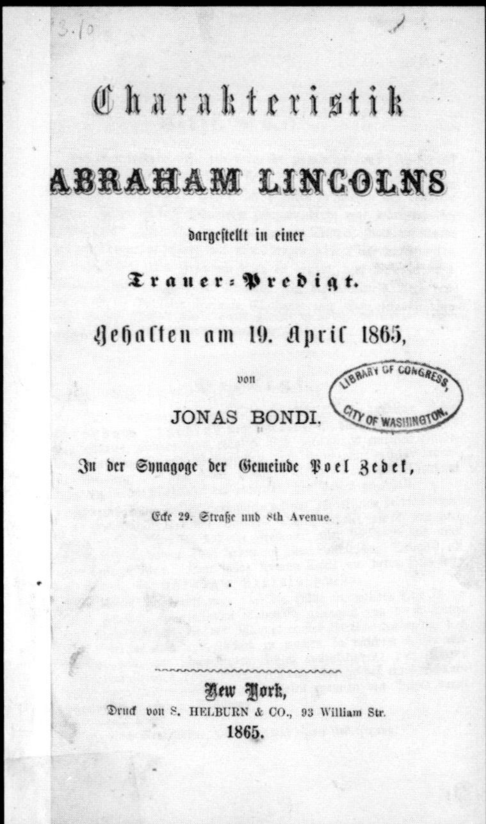

Charakteristik

ABRAHAM LINCOLNS

dargestellt in einer

Trauer-Predigt.

Gehalten am 19. April 1865,

von

JONAS BONDI.

In der Synagoge der Gemeinde Poel Zedek,

Ecke 29. Straße und 8th Avenue.

New York,

Druck von S. HELBURN & CO., 93 William Str.

1865.

The Rev. Jonas Bondi, Congregation Poel Zedek, New York, April 19, 1865.

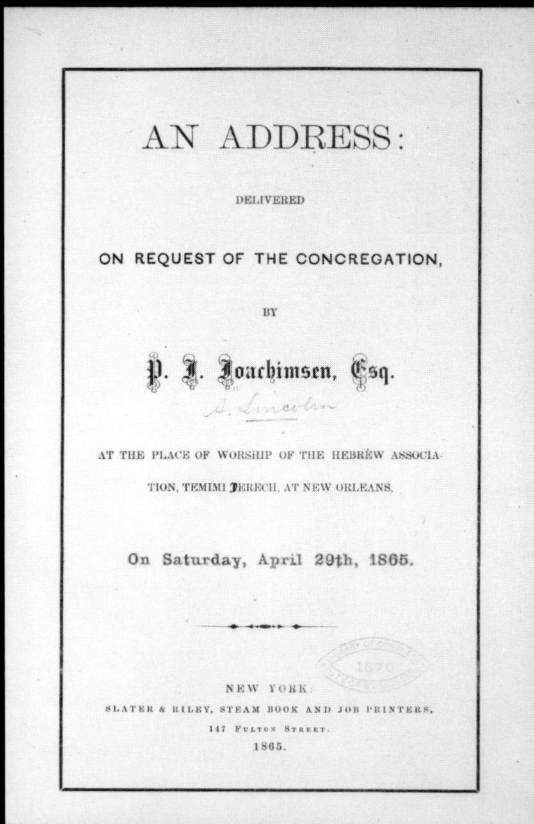

AN ADDRESS:

DELIVERED

ON REQUEST OF THE CONCREGATION,

BY

P. J. Joachimsen, Esq.

A. Lincoln

AT THE PLACE OF WORSHIP OF THE HEBREW ASSOCIATION, TEMIMI DERECH, AT NEW ORLEANS.

On Saturday, April 29th, 1865.

NEW YORK:

SLATER & RILEY, STEAM BOOK AND JOB PRINTERS,

147 FULTON STREET.

1865.

P. J. Joachimsen, Congregation Temimi Derech, New Orleans, April 29, 1865.

3. *Trauer-Rede (Mourning Discourse) gehalten em 19ten April 1865 . . . Abraham Lincoln Präsidenten der Vereinigten Staaten, in Tempel der Keneseth Israel Gemeinde zu Philadelphia von Dr. David Einhorn* (Philadelphia, 1865).

The murder of this high-priest of freedom must and will unite all who still have a spark of moral feeling into a brotherhood to preserve the union and crush that shameful institution [slavery]. All those who in former times misunderstood the deceased and denigrated his world-historic deed, must now learn to love and honor both. This would be the truly meaningful fulfilment of the saying of our Sages: "The death of the righteous atone for the age."

If Abraham Lincoln had one fault, it was his excessive generosity toward the rebels; he, whom the demagogues and the murderer himself called a tyrant!

4. *Vaterland und Freiheit (Fatherland and Freedom) Predigt bei der Erinnerungsfeier des verstorbenen Präsidenten Abraham Lincoln, am 1. Juni, 1865 . . . gehalten von Benjamin Szold, Rabbiner der Oheb-Schalom Gemeinde in Baltimore, Baltimore, 1865.*

Abraham Lincoln took the reins of government at a time when the Fatherland lay mortally ill, when there was little hope for its survival and revival . . . How Abraham Lincoln loved the suffering Fatherland. [In this day of Shavuot, this joyful holiday] we should feel joy that such a great moral figure lived among us, in our time, and that the history of this Republic became enriched through another great name, that by the side of Washington now stands Lincoln.

5. *Predigt . . . 19, April 1865 . . . Abraham Lincoln's von H. Hochheimer, Rabbiner der Oheb-Israel Gemeinde in Baltimore* (Baltimore, 1865).

6. *Fest-und Fasttag (Commemoration and Fast Day) . . . am 1. Juni 1865 . . . zum Gedachtnisse des ermordeten Präsidenten Abraham Lincoln . . . von H. Hochheimer . . .* (Baltimore, 1865).

When victory after victory were announced by his warriors, did he glory in the defeat of his enemies? No. He stretched forth his hand to the fallen. He spared them humiliation, offered them conditions honorable beyond their dreams, and as Abraham of old, he called out to them: "Let there not be strife between us, for we are brothers" [Genesis, 13:8].

7. *Charakteristik Abraham Lincolns . . . einer Trauer-Predigt . . . am 19. April 1865, von Jonas Bondi, in der Synagogue der Gemeinde Poel Zedek, New York 1865:*

Abraham Lincoln was a religious man, imbued with the fear of God, faithful to the religion of his ancestors, faithful also to the faith he absorbed with his mother's milk. That is not to say he was a fanatic, as some thought, that he would disdain one who in his eyes did not appear to be religious, Oh No! His conception of the faith into which he was born was his own private, personal conviction. He respected every true and ethical conception of Faith, respected every pious one, no matter what form that piety took. Who would question that Abraham Lincoln was a truly humane human being? His last act, the capitulation of Lee, proved that his was the mind of a noble victor, a person exemplifying the true biblical love—loving one's neighbor.

8. *An Address: Delivered on Request of the Congregation, by P. J. Joachimsen, At the Place of Worship of the Hebrew Association Temimi Derech, at New Orleans, On Saturday, April 29th, 1865, New York, 1865.*

Alas! that we should have occasion for an addition to our services to deplore the untimely loss, by violence, of the Chief Magistrate of the American people. Alas! that we should have to pray to God that in the history of the American people this may be forever the only time when national mourning shall be accompanied by national humiliation and national shame . . . Unaided by worldly fortune or powerful friends, he [Lincoln] attained to the fame of the most eminent patriots and statesmen—aye, even of Washington, the Father of his country. You can point him out to your children as one of the men worthy of emulation, as a pattern and as an example.

And we, as Jews, had a distinct ground to love, respect and esteem him . . . When an order was made to banish Jews as a class from a particular Department, and their immediate and indiscriminate departure was being carried out, our deceased President at once revoked the unauthorized command . . .

We can carry the memory of Abraham Lincoln with us as that of a triumphant martyr to humanity, and we can also carry into practice the lessons taught us by the short but eventful life of the great departed:

To be true and honest to ourselves and to our neighbors.

To stand bravely and fearlessly to the performance of our duties as citizens of this great Republic.

As we may have noticed, the eulogy was preached in New Orleans, but published in New York.

15

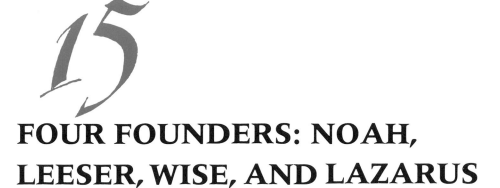

FOUR FOUNDERS: NOAH, LEESER, WISE, AND LAZARUS

AT THE BEGINNING OF THE nineteenth century there were fewer than two thousand Jews in the United States; at the century's end the number had risen to over a million. Synagogues increased in number from a half dozen to over eight hundred. In the course of the century, charitable and educational institutions were founded; cultural and fraternal organizations were established; and a periodical press in four languages was developed. During that time, too, American Jewry evolved from a tiny, hardly noticed presence in a few Eastern seaboard cities, to a visible factor in the social, economic, cultural, religious, and political life of the American nation. Many were the players in the drama of growth and unfolding, and the Library of Congress is a rich storehouse of books, pamphlets, broadsides, prints, and manuscripts which record and document those personalities and events. We choose four participants to represent the many.

MORDECAI MANUEL NOAH (1785–1851)

Mordecai Manuel Noah was born with America in the city of our nation's birth, Philadelphia, on July 19, 1785, halfway in time between the signing of the Treaty of Paris in 1783 and the adoption of the Constitution in 1787. In his person, Noah mirrored the new nation—willful, brash, adventurous, creative, combative, yet good-natured and generous. Similarly, his personal life reflected the Jewish community to which he belonged, patriotic and philanthropic, reverential of the religious tradition, respectful and supportive of its institutions yet growing ever more lax in religious observance, and desirous of changes in ritual and liturgy.

Mordecai was the first-born son of Manuel Noah, an immigrant from Mannheim, Germany, who had served in the Revolutionary War, and Zipporah Phillips, daughter of Jonas Phillips and Rebecca Machado, whose father had served as hazzan of the Shearith Israel Congregation of New

York. Though three of his grandparents were Ashkenazi, Noah stressed his Sefardi identity, for it gave him deeper roots in America and a more aristocratic status in the Jewish community. His association with the rapidly increasing Ashkenazi community grew closer through his marriage into one of that community's leading families and through his leadership, in the 1840s, of the Hebrew Benevolent Society, the united charity organization of a Jewish community now overwhelmingly Ashkenazi.

To Mordecai M. Noah, journalism and politics were one career. Journalism he practiced in the service of his political pursuits: political activity he was involved in to reinforce his journalistic enterprises. In the early Republic press and party were in symbiotic relationship. His consulship to the Kingdom of Tunis, his positions as sheriff of New York, surveyor of its port, and judge in its court of General Sessions, and his editorship of half a dozen newspapers were for him all of a piece—a career of public service. In the Jewish community, Noah served as its chief orator, delivering the major addresses at its important communal gatherings. As an accepted interpreter of Judaism to the general community, he informed his audience in newspaper articles and from the lecture platform about various aspects of Jewish religion and history, about Jewish concerns and aspirations. To Americans he was *the* representative Jew; to Jews, he was *the* quintessential American; Noah gained from both roles.

Noah believed that American and Jewish ideals and interests were congruent and that in his political endeavors his Jewishness was more an advantage than a handicap. From the time he petitioned for a consulship in 1811 to the time when he sent a letter to New York's Governor Seward in 1849, Noah relied on his Jewish identity to gain him political advantage, reminding the secretary of state and the governor that the Jewish community would appreciate and reward any favors shown to him, as a member and leader of the community. And as the Jewish community increased in numbers and affluence, so too did Noah's political influence and power. He fully believed that, because he was a Jew, his appointment to a governmental position of trust would be a powerful statement to the world both about the status of Jews in America and the nature of American democracy. As he wrote to Secretary of State James Monroe in 1811, his appointment to a consulship would "prove to foreign powers that our government is not regulated in the appointment of their officers by religious distinction." In a world darkened by bigotry, America was for him a beacon of freedom and equality, but his faith was soon tested.

Noah was appointed Consul to the Kingdom of Tunis, and in his *Travels in England, France, Spain and the Barbary States in the Years 1813–14 and 15,* New York, 1819, we read of his brief but eventful tenure. In it Noah explains the termination of his tenure by Secretary Monroe in the secretary of state's own words:

> At the time of your appointment, as Consul to Tunis, it was not known that the religion which you profess would form an obstacle to the exercise of your Consular functions.

Noah cried "Outrage!" as did others, Jews and gentiles alike. In his *Correspondence and Documents . . . ,* Washington, 1816, Noah complains not so much about the treatment he received, but about the injury to the young nation's freedoms:

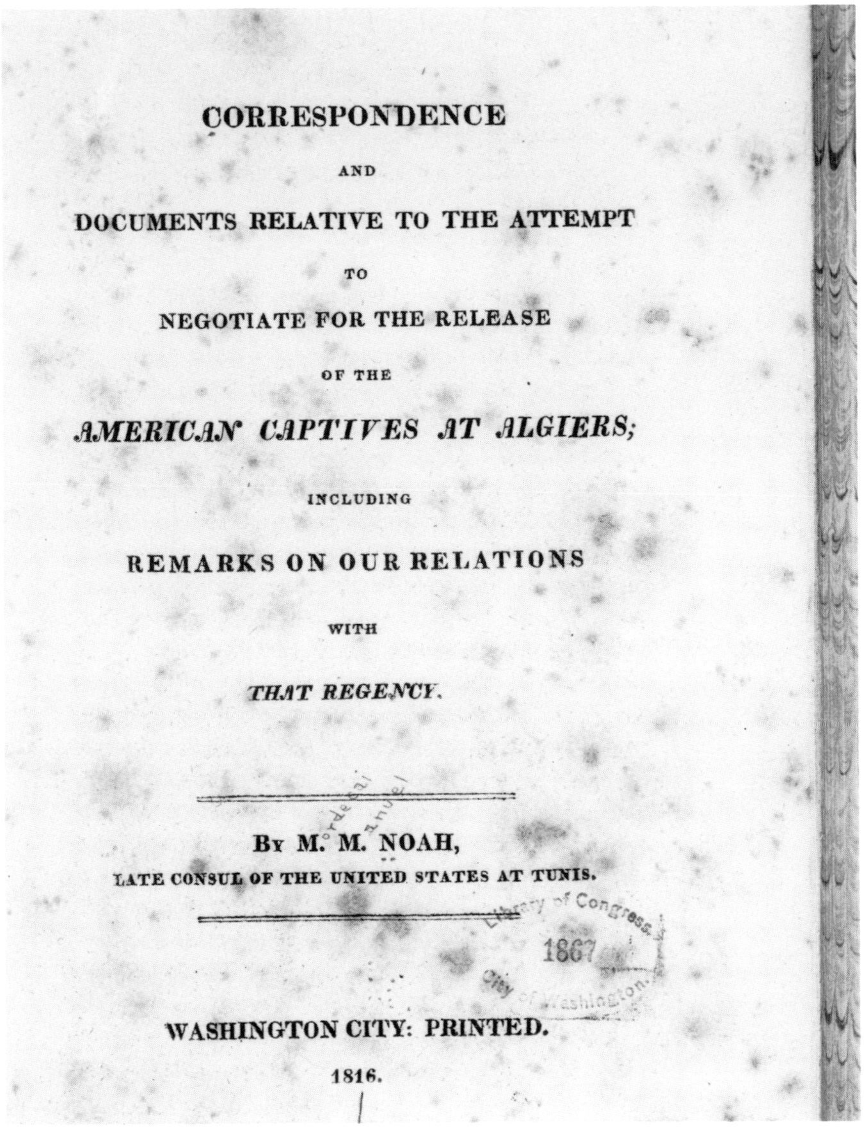
CORRESPONDENCE

AND

DOCUMENTS RELATIVE TO THE ATTEMPT

TO

NEGOTIATE FOR THE RELEASE

OF THE

AMERICAN CAPTIVES AT ALGIERS;

INCLUDING

REMARKS ON OUR RELATIONS

WITH

THAT REGENCY.

By M. M. NOAH,

LATE CONSUL OF THE UNITED STATES AT TUNIS.

WASHINGTON CITY: PRINTED.

1816.

His appointment as consul to the Barbary States terminated, Noah returns to America to plead his case, which he puts forth in this 128-page *Correspondence and Documents Relative to the Attempt to Negotiate for the Release of the American Captives at Algiers.* Its last paragraph is worthy of note:

> The institutions of the United States are the property of the nation. The faith of the people is pledged to their existence. The most distinguished feature in our compact . . . is religious liberty—is the emancipation of the soul from temporal authority—we cease to be free, when we cease to be liberal.

Mordecai M. Noah, *Correspondence and Documents . . . ,* Washington, 1816.
Rare Book and Special Collections Division.

> My dismissal from office in consequence of religion, has become a document on file in the department of State. This may hereafter produce the most injurious effects establishing a principle, which will go to annihilate the most sacred rights of the citizen.

The Library's holdings also contain the correspondence between Madison and Noah two years later concerning his dismissal. On May 6, 1818, accompanying the *Consecration Address,* Noah sent a letter to Madison which deserves a wider readership than the few scholars who may seek it out in the Manuscript Division.

> Dear Sir,
> I take the liberty to enclose to you a Discourse delivered at the consecration of the Jewish Synagogue in this city, under the fullest persuasion, that it cannot but be gratifying to you to perceive this portion of your fellow Citizens enjoying an equality of privileges in this country and affording a proof to the world that they fully merit the rights they possess. I ought not to conceal from you that it afforded me sincere pleasure, to have the opportunity of saying, that to your efforts, and those

Newspaper editor, playwright, diplomat, orator, and leader in the Jewish community, Mordecai M. Noah sent this letter on matters personal and civic to James Madison, with a copy of his address at the consecration of Shearith Israel's new synagogue building in New York. Madison's reply and those of Adams and Jefferson were published by Noah in his *Travels in England, France, Spain and the Barbary States* (New York, 1819).

The first page of Noah's letter reads in part:

I ought not to conceal from you that it afforded me sincere pleasure, to have the opportunity of saying, that to your efforts, and those of your illustrious colleagues in the Convention, the Jews in the United States owe many of the blessings which they now enjoy, and the benefit of this liberal and first example, has been felt very generally abroad and has created a sincere attachment toward this Country, on the part of foreign Jews.

Mordecai M. Noah to James Madison, May 6, 1818. Manuscript Division, Papers of James Madison.

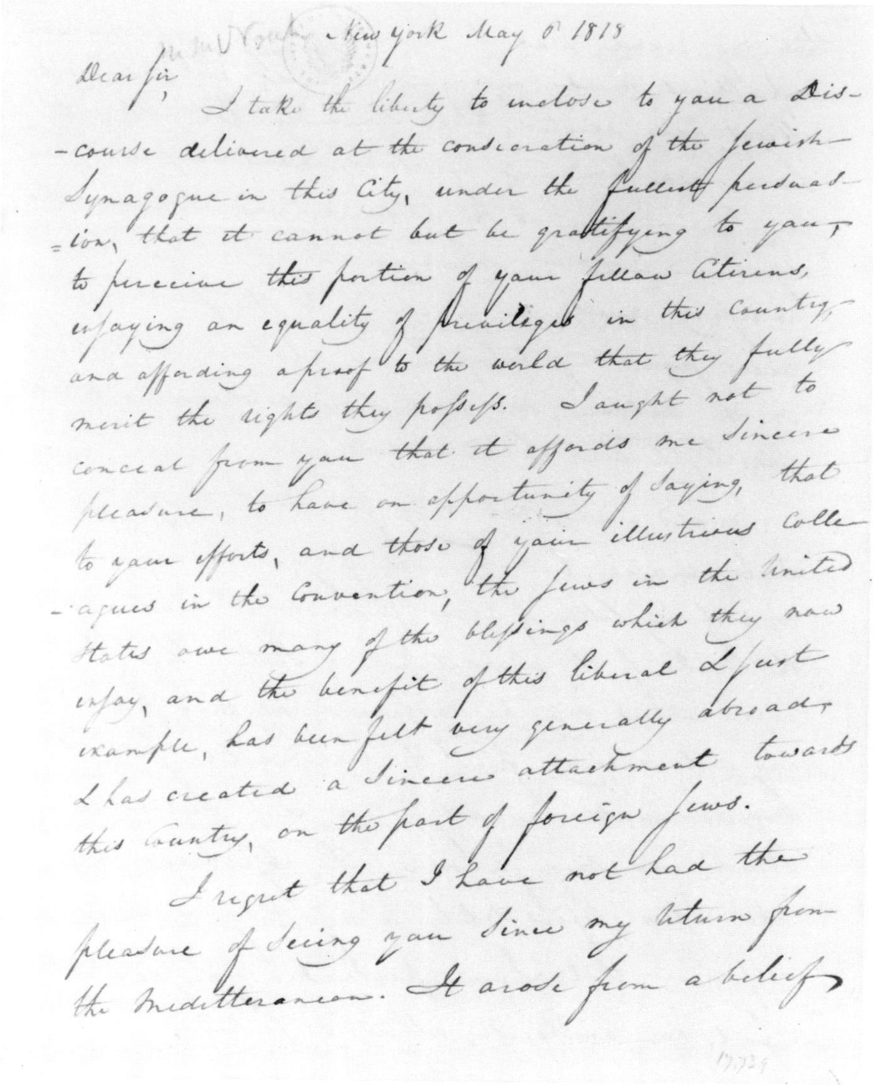

New York May 6 1818

Dear Sir,

I take the liberty to enclose to you a Dis-course delivered at the consecration of the Jewish Synagogue in this City, under the fullest persuasion, that it cannot but be gratifying to you, to perceive this portion of your fellow Citizens, enjoying an equality of Privileges in this Country, and affording a proof to the world that they fully merit the rights they possess. I ought not to conceal from you that it affords me sincere pleasure, to have an opportunity of saying, that to your efforts, and those of your illustrious Colleagues in the Convention, the Jews in the United States owe many of the blessings which they now enjoy, and the benefit of this liberal & first example, has been felt very generally abroad & has created a sincere attachment towards this Country, on the part of foreign Jews.

I regret that I have not had the pleasure of seeing you since my return from the Mediterranean. It arose from a belief

of your illustrious colleagues in the Convention, the Jews in the United States owe many of the blessings which they now enjoy, and the benefit of this liberal and first example, has been felt very generally abroad and has created a sincere attachment toward this Country, on the part of foreign Jews.

I regret that I have not had the pleasure of seeing you since my return from the Mediterranean. It arose from a belief that my recall was the result of very unfavorable impressions made on your mind; if these impressions have existed, I do sincerely hope that they have been removed by subsequent explanations, for I wish you to be assured, and I have no object in view in making the assertion, that no infamy arose in Barbary to the public service from my religion as relating to myself, on the contrary, my influence and standing abroad was highly creditable and flattering.

I could wish, not only for the sake of my coreligionaires, but for that of your administration, that if my letter of recall cannot be erased from the Books of the Department of State, that such explanations may be subjoined as may prevent any arising from the precedent;–for as my accounts are adjusted, and a balance struck in my favor, the objections in that letter, refers solely to my religion, an objection, that I am persuaded you cannot feel, nor authorise others to feel.

We can now better understand the second part of the previously cited letter from Madison to Noah as a response to the above:

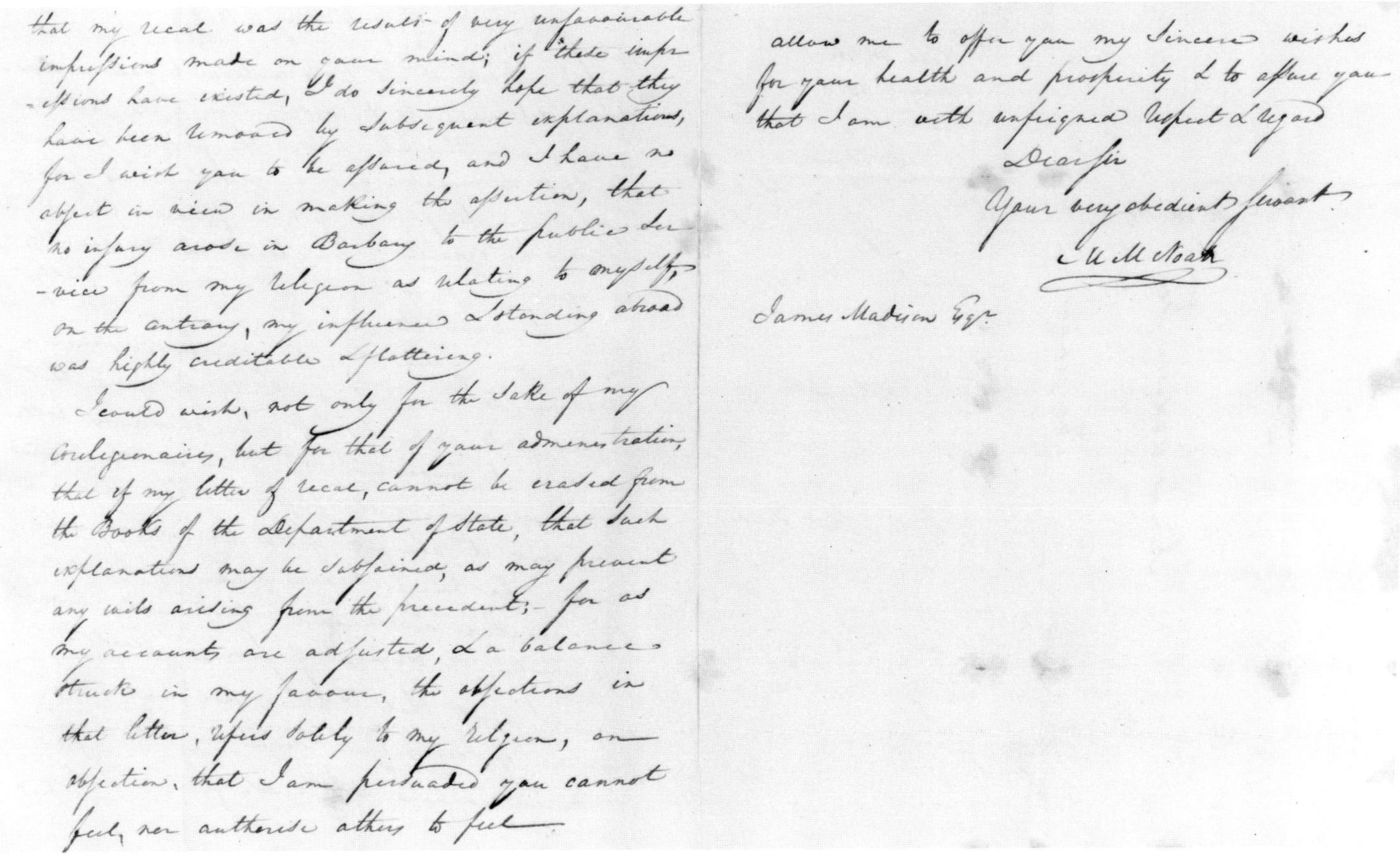

that my recal was the result of very unfavourable impressions made on your mind; if these impressions have existed, I do sincerely hope that they have been removed by subsequent explanations, for I wish you to be assured, and I have no object in view in making the assertion, that no injury arose in Barbary to the public service from my Religion as relating to myself, on the contrary, my influence & standing abroad was highly creditable & flattering.

I could wish, not only for the sake of my Coreligionaries, but for that of your administration, that if my letter of recal, cannot be erased from the Books of the Department of State, that such explanation may be subjoined, as may prevent any evils arising from the precedent;- for as my accounts are adjusted, & a balance struck in my favour, the objections in that letter, refers solely to my Religion, an objection, that I am persuaded you cannot feel, nor authorise others to feel.

allow me to offer you my sincere wishes for your health and prosperity & to assure you that I am with unfeigned respect & regard

Dear Sir

Your very obedient servant

M M Noah

James Madison Esqr.

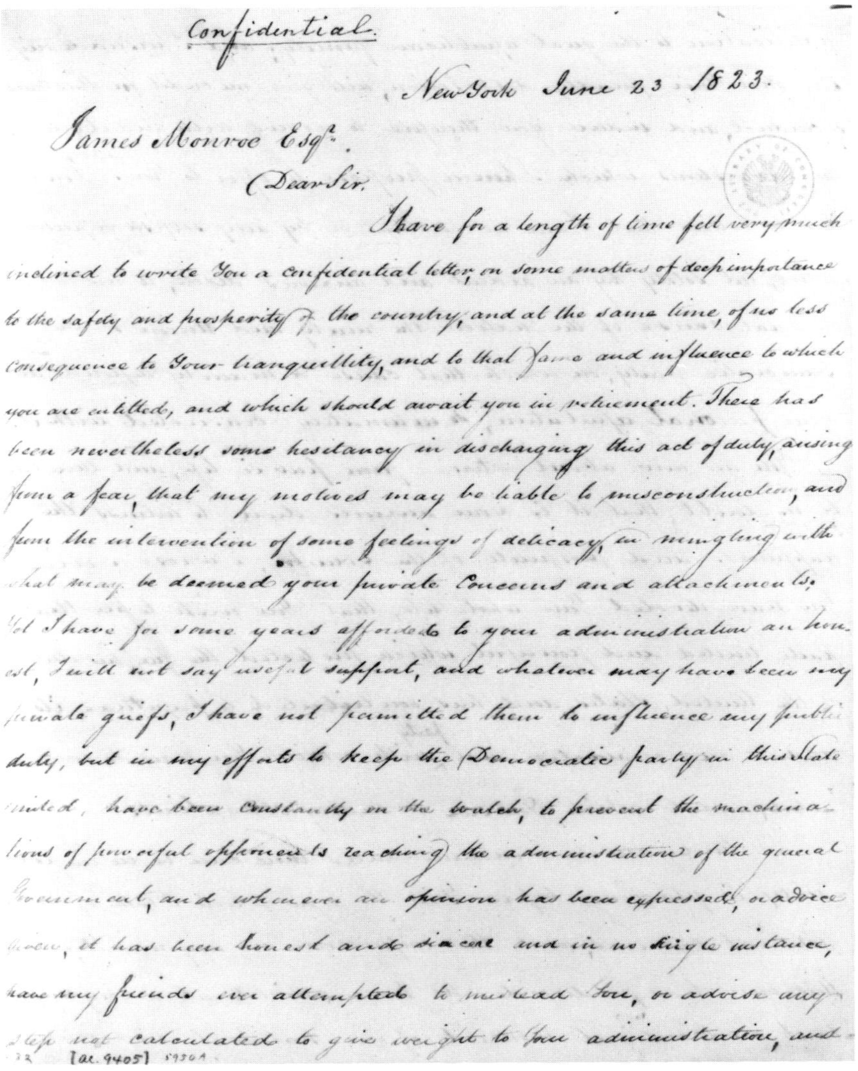

Confidential.

New York June 23 1823.

James Monroe Esqr.

Dear Sir.

I have for a length of time felt very much inclined to write You a confidential letter, on some matters of deep importance to the safety and prosperity of the country, and at the same time, of no less consequence to Your tranquillity, and to that fame and influence to which you are entitled, and which should await you in retirement. There has been nevertheless some hesitancy in discharging this act of duty, arising from a fear, that my motives may be liable to misconstruction, and from the intervention of some feelings of delicacy in mingling with what may be deemed your private Concerns and attachments. Yet I have for some years afforded to your administration an honest, I will not say useful support, and whatever may have been my private griefs, I have not permitted them to influence my public duty, but in my efforts to keep the Democratic party in this State united, have been constantly on the watch, to prevent the machinations of powerful opponents reaching the administration of the general Government, and whenever an opinion has been expressed, or advice given, it has been honest and sincere and in no single instance, have my friends ever attempted to mislead You, or advise any step not calculated to give weight to Your administration, and

[ac. 9405]

First page of a long political letter marked "Confidential" from Mordecai M. Noah to James Monroe, on "matters of deep importance to the safety and prosperity of the country, and at the same time, of no less consequence to your tranquility, and to that fame and influence to which you are entitled, and which should await you in retirement." He asks Monroe's support for the candidacy of William Crawford for the presidency, a bid which failed.

Mordecai M. Noah to James Monroe, June 23, 1823. Manuscript Division, Papers of James Monroe.

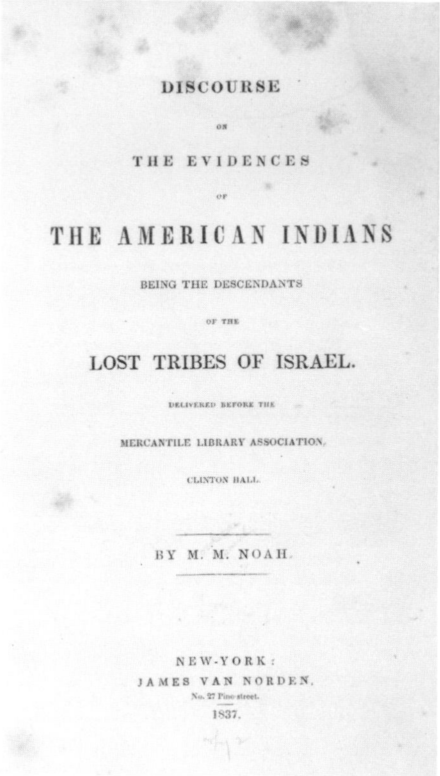

DISCOURSE

ON

THE EVIDENCES

OF

THE AMERICAN INDIANS

BEING THE DESCENDANTS

OF THE

LOST TRIBES OF ISRAEL.

DELIVERED BEFORE THE

MERCANTILE LIBRARY ASSOCIATION,

CLINTON HALL.

BY M. M. NOAH.

NEW-YORK:

JAMES VAN NORDEN,

No. 27 Pine-street.

1837.

Mordecai M. Noah was not alone in identifying the American Indians as descendants of the Ten Lost Tribes of Israel. The belief was widespread in early nineteenth-century America, a new nation steeped in the biblical heritage, seeking roots in antiquity. Noah took the opportunity in this address to assert his Jewish restorationist sentiments, predicting that "Syria [i.e., Palestine] will revert to the Jewish people."

Mordecai M. Noah, *Discourse on the Evidence of the American Indians Being the Descendants of the Lost Tribes of Israel*, New York, 1837.
General Collection.

Facing page:
Noah, the Jew, proclaimed his faith that the Jews will return to and rebuild their ancient homeland; Noah, the enterprising American, calls upon the American nation to take leadership in this endeavor, which will fulfill ancient promises and modern needs. In this proto-Zionist classic, Noah proposes a program which became a political movement a half-century later with the convening of the First Zionist Congress, and a reality a century later with the founding of the State of Israel.

Mordecai M. Noah, *Discourse on the Restoration of the Jews*, New York, 1845.
Rare Book and Special Collections Division.

As your foreign mission took place whilst I was in the administration it cannot be but agreeable to me to learn, that your accounts have been closed in a manner favorable to you. And I know too well the justice and candor of the present executive [Monroe] to doubt that an official preservation, will be readily allowed to explanations necessary to protect your character against the effect of any impressions whenever ascertained to be erroneous. It was certain, that your religious profession was well-known at the time you received your commission, and that in itself it could not be a motive in your recall.

Noah made peace with Monroe, for in the Monroe Papers we find a twenty-page letter from Noah, dated June 23, 1823, urging Monroe's support for William Crawford as candidate for the presidency. Crawford's bid failed, and with it Noah's political and editorial influence waned, but it gave Noah time to pursue a plan he had proposed some five years earlier, the establishment of a Jewish settlement on Grand Island on the Niagara River.

As an American and as a Jew, Noah was constantly looking for points where American and Jewish interests might intersect. In the early decades of the nineteenth century, America's greatest need was for immigrants. In his travels in Europe and Africa, Noah learned that Jews in the Old World desperately needed a haven for themselves and their children. To bring such Jews to a welcoming America would be a signal service to both.

The drama Noah staged in Buffalo on September 15, 1825, in dedicating Ararat as "A City of Refuge for the Jews," with men marching, band playing, and "Judge" Noah in regal vestments orating, was for both America and world Jewry. The pageant, the proclamation, and Noah's speech were intended to grab the attention of newspaper editors to whom description and text were sent. Accounts of the Ararat drama appeared in newspapers throughout the United States and in England, France, and Germany as well. The drama presented the Jews as the most desirable citizens a nation could want—able, ambitious, productive, and loyal; to the Jews of the Old World, it portrayed what kind of country America was for the Jews. Political dignitaries, leaders of society, and the general populace joined to celebrate the establishment of a city for Jews, while America's most prominent Jew proclaimed a Jewish state on American soil and welcomed his brethren to settle it.

One of the newspapers which published a full account of the proceedings was the *National Intelligencer*, Washington, D.C. In its September 29, 1825, issue it described the ceremonies attendant upon the laying of the cornerstone, with its Hebrew quotation and English inscription (the stone survives and is now in a museum on Grand Island) and Noah's address.

Noah linked American and Jewish interests in two discourses published eight years apart. His *Discourse on the Evidence of the American Indians Being the Descendants of the Lost Tribes of Israel*, New York, 1837, gives a hallowed antiquity to America—biblical origin to its first settlers. To Jews living in an America of rapidly growing nativist sentiments, it provided earlier antecedents than any descendants of the earliest European settlers could claim. Noah restates Jewish nationalist aspirations first sounded in his *Consecration* address of 1818, where he said:

Never were the prospects for the restoration of the Jewish nation to their ancient rights and dominion more brilliant than they are at present . . . They will march in triumphant numbers . . . and take their rank among the governments of the earth.

DISCOURSE

ON THE

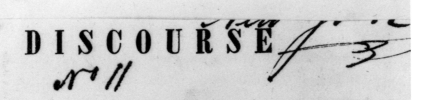

RESTORATION OF THE JEWS:

DELIVERED AT THE TABERNACLE, OCT. 28 AND DEC. 2, 1844.

BY M. M. NOAH.

With a Map of the Land of Israel.

NEW-YORK:
HARPER & BROTHERS, 82 CLIFF-STREET.

1845.

Now in 1837, he calls for action:

The Jewish people must now do something for themselves . . . Syria [i.e., Palestine] will revert to the Jewish nation by purchase . . . Under the co-operation and protection of England and France, this reoccupation of Syria . . . is at once reasonable and practicable.

Seven years later, the return to Zion became Noah's subject in a *Discourse on the Restoration of the Jews,* delivered twice in 1844 and published a year later. The role formerly allotted to England and France is now given to America. "I confidently believe in the restoration of the Jews . . . and believing that political events are daily assuming a shape which may finally lead to that great advent, I consider it my duty to call upon the free people of this country to aid us in any efforts which, in our present position, it may be prudent to adopt." He emphasizes the special affinity between America and Jewish national aspirations:

Where can we plead the cause of independence for the children of Israel with greater confidence than in the cradle of liberty? . . . Here we can unfurl the standard, and seventeen millions of people will say, "God is with you; we are with you; in his name and in the name of civil and religious liberty, go forth and repossess the land of your fathers. We have advocated the independence of the South American republics . . . we have combated for the independence of Greece . . . If these nations were entitled to our sympathies, how much more powerful and irrepressible are the claims of that beloved people, before whom the Almighty . . . swore they should be *his* people, and he would be their God; who for their protection and final restoration, dispersed them among the nations of the earth, without confounding them with any! . . .

The liberty and independence of the Jewish nation may grow out of a single effort which this country may make in their behalf . . . they want only protection, and the work will be accomplished.

In Noah's proposals we find classic Zionist assertions of future generations:

The Jews are in a most favorable position to repossess . . . the promised land, and organize a free and liberal government . . .

Every attempt to colonize Jews in other countries has failed . . .

The first step is to solicit from the Sultan of Turkey permission for the Jews to purchase and hold land . . .

Those who desire to reside in the Holy Land and have not the means, may be aided by . . . societies to reach their haven of repose . . .

Ports of the Mediterranean [will be] occupied by enterprising Jews. The valley of the Jordan will be filled by agriculturists from . . . Germany, Poland and Russia.

Noah wrote these words a half-century before Theodor Herzl wrote *Der Judenstaat,* and more than a century before the establishment of the State of Israel in 1948.

Newspapers Noah edited, patriotic plays he wrote, addresses he gave are preserved in the Library. Surely the most curious—and rarest—of Noachian items is a large illustrated folio broadside reading:

Mordecai M. Noah . . . duly sworn, deposeth and saith, that on the 20th day of June 1828 . . . he was most violently assaulted, by Elijah J. Roberts, who attacked him on the steps, and cow-skinned *HIM!!*

Roberts was a former business associate with whom Noah had a falling out.

BOSTON MUSEUM.

BY CHARLES A. V. PUTNAM & CO.

VOLUME 3. BOSTON, MASSACHUSETTS, SATURDAY, APRIL 26, 1851. NUMBER 46.

THE LATE M. M. NOAH.

The *Boston Museum* gave the entire front page of its April 26, 1851, issue to an obituary of Mordecai M. Noah, his bibliography, accomplishments, and contributions, and a two-column portrait.

Boston Museum, April 26, 1851.
General Collection.

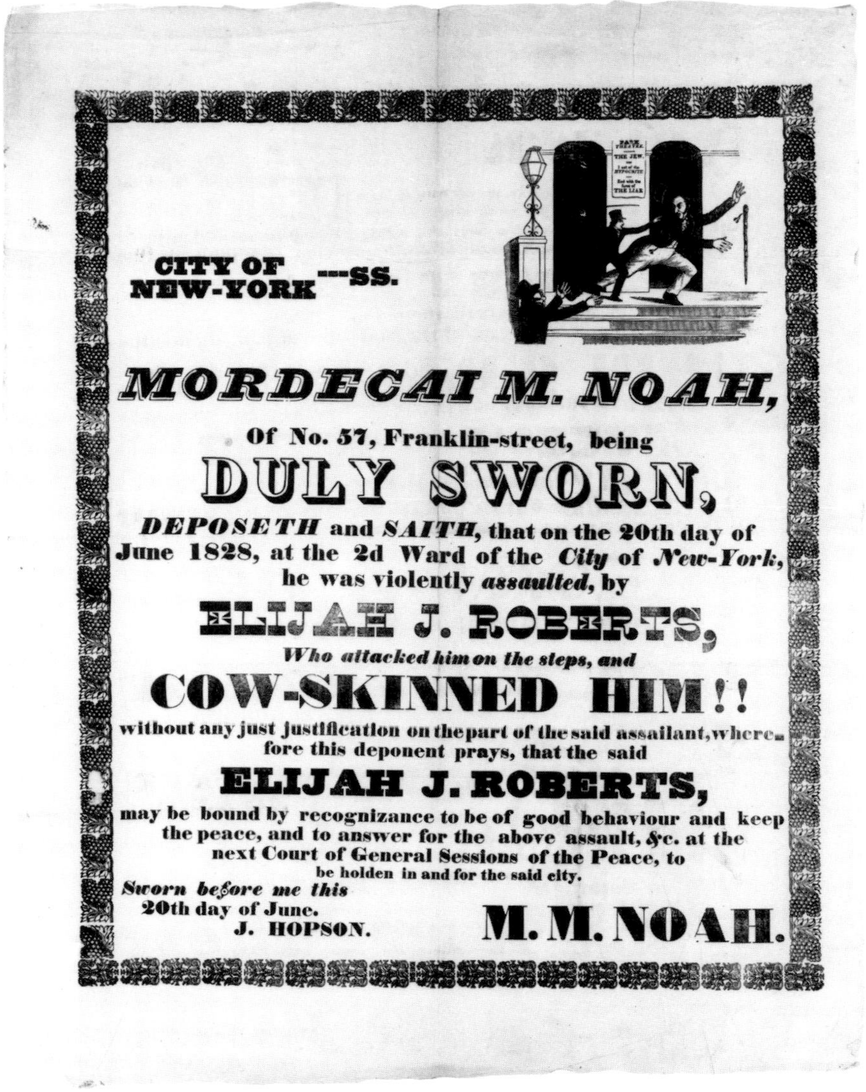
CITY OF NEW-YORK ---SS.

MORDECAI M. NOAH,

Of No. 57, Franklin-street, being

DULY SWORN,

DEPOSETH and *SAITH*, that on the 20th day of June 1828, at the 2d Ward of the *City* of *New-York*, he was violently *assaulted*, by

ELIJAH J. ROBERTS,

Who attacked him on the steps, and

COW-SKINNED HIM!!

without any just justification on the part of the said assailant, wherefore this deponent prays, that the said

ELIJAH J. ROBERTS,

may be bound by recognizance to be of good behaviour and keep the peace, and to answer for the above assault, &c. at the next Court of General Sessions of the Peace, to be holden in and for the said city.

Sworn before me this
20th day of June.
J. HOPSON.

M. M. NOAH.

Elijah J. Roberts, a former business associate, is accused by Mordecai M. Noah of having "attacked him on the steps." A close examination of the depiction of the attack on the upper right-hand corner of this broadside leaves one puzzled. The steps are of the Park Theater, whose playbill reads:

THE JEW
1 act of the HYPOCRITE
End with the farce of
THE LIAR

At the top of the steps, the purported victim, Noah, pronounced aquiline nose and large in body, has just dropped his formidable walking stick. His accused attacker looks half his size, his weapon, a small and thin walking stick. The entire depiction, especially the theater announcement, seems far more anti-Noah than critical of Roberts.

Rare Book and Special Collections Division.

More indicative of Noah is his obituary in the *Boston Weekly Museum*, where the entire front page of the April 26, 1851, issue is devoted to an account of his life and works and a two-column signed portrait of the deceased.

In his determined insistence on being part of America's political, social, and cultural life while at the same time participating in Jewish religious and communal life, Mordecal Manuel Noah demonstrated by example that in America a Jew could be both fully Jewish and fully American. As the first to do so publicly, dramatically, and successfully, Noah might well be called "The first *American* Jew."

A portrait of Isaac Leeser, published by I. Goldman in 1868, the year of Leeser's death.

Prints and Photographs Division.

ISAAC LEESER (1806–1868)

Born in Neunkirchen, Westphalia, Prussia, December 12, 1806, Isaac Leeser was orphaned at an early age. He received his secular education at a gymnasium in Münster, and his religious tutelage from Rabbis Benjamin

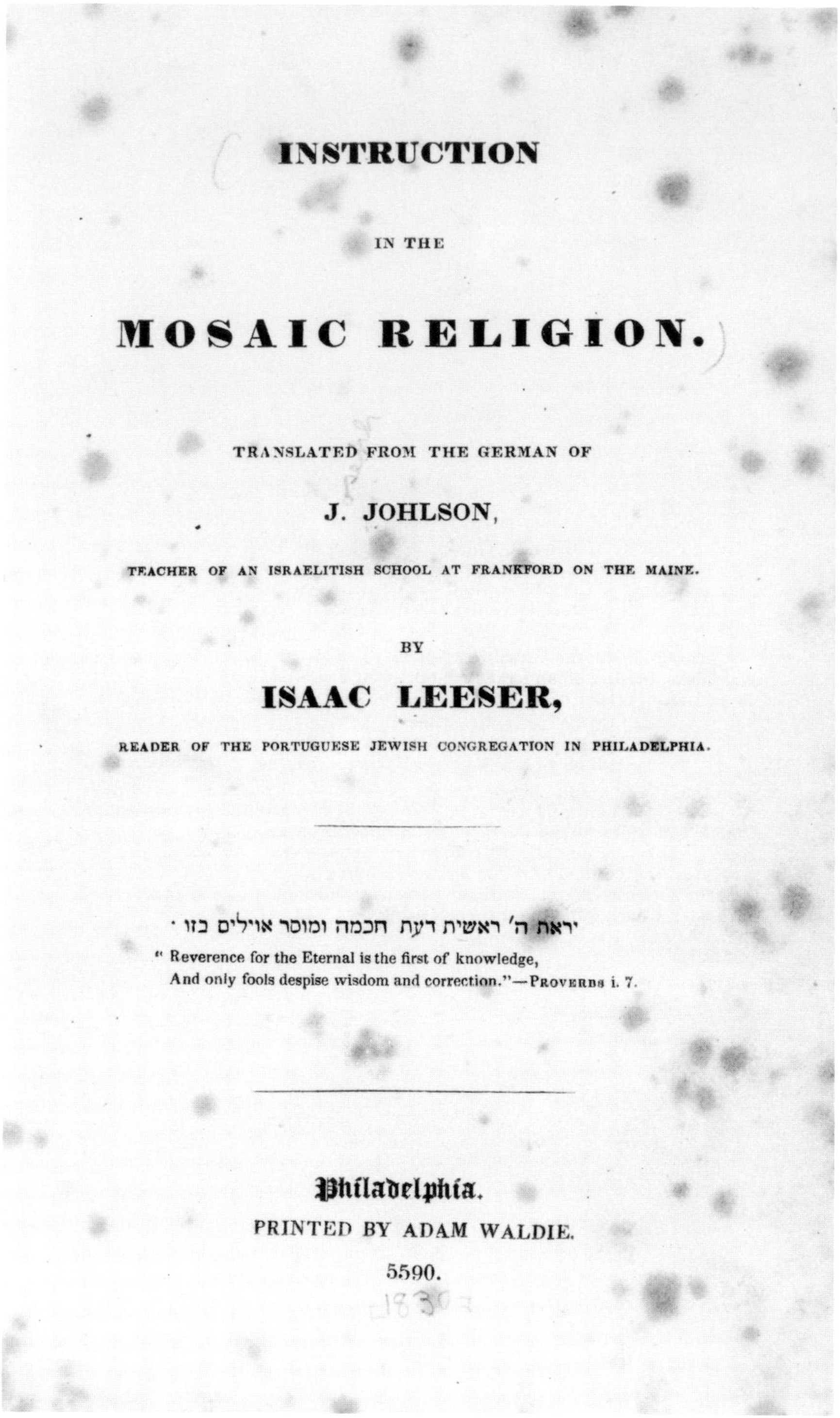
INSTRUCTION

IN THE

MOSAIC RELIGION.

TRANSLATED FROM THE GERMAN OF

J. JOHLSON,

TEACHER OF AN ISRAELITISH SCHOOL AT FRANKFORD ON THE MAINE.

BY

ISAAC LEESER,

READER OF THE PORTUGUESE JEWISH CONGREGATION IN PHILADELPHIA.

יראת ה' ראשית דעת חכמה ומוסר אוילים בזו ·

" Reverence for the Eternal is the first of knowledge,
And only fools despise wisdom and correction."—PROVERBS i. 7.

Philadelphia.

PRINTED BY ADAM WALDIE.

5590.

It is significant that this *Instruction in the Mosaic Religion*, Leeser's first issued work, is a textbook of religious instruction for the young (a translation and adaptation of a catechism by J. Johlson, a teacher in the school for Jewish children in Frankfurt-am-Main), for though Leeser attained distinction as an author, translator, editor, and a national leader of the American Jewish community, he considered himself, first and foremost, an educator.

Isaac Leeser (translator), *Instruction in the Mosaic Religion*, Philadelphia, 1830.
General Collection.

Cohen and Abraham Sutro. At age eighteen, Leeser joined his uncle Zalman Rehine in Richmond, Virginia, where he began to prepare for a business career while simultaneously assisting the local religious functionary, the Reverend Isaac B. Seixas. An article Leeser published in defense of Judaism brought him to public attention and also brought in 1829 an invitation to occupy the pulpit of Philadelphia's congregation Mikveh Israel. During the next forty years Isaac Leeser was the most prolific American Jewish writer and the most creative Jewish communal architect.

Leeser brought with him to Philadelphia his translation of J. Johlson's *Instruction in the Mosaic Religion.* He had it published there in 1830, appropriately dedicated to his uncle Zalman Rehine. The book is a catechism published in Germany and translated and adapted by Leeser for "the instruction of the younger . . . of Israelites of both sexes, who have previously acquired some knowledge of the fundamental part . . . of their religion." Leeser undertook its publication because there was a great scarcity of elementary textbooks for Jewish children. In 1838 he issued *The Hebrew Reader* and a year later, *Catechism for Younger Children.* The *Reader,* initially prepared for a newly established Sunday School in Philadelphia, was, in

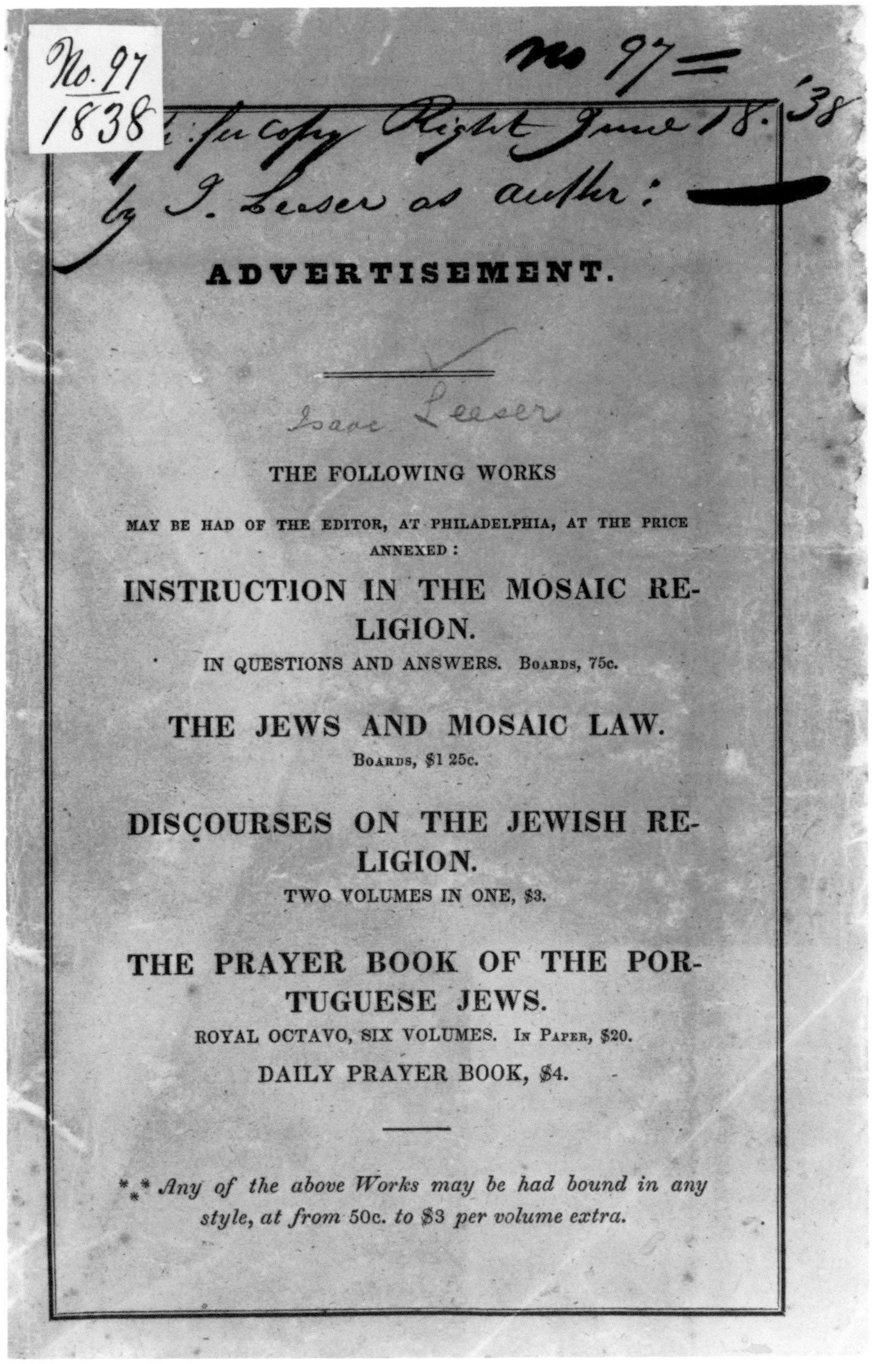

No. 97
1838

No 97=

for copy Right June 18. '38
by I. Leeser as author:

ADVERTISEMENT.

Isaac Leeser

THE FOLLOWING WORKS

MAY BE HAD OF THE EDITOR, AT PHILADELPHIA, AT THE PRICE ANNEXED:

INSTRUCTION IN THE MOSAIC RELIGION.

IN QUESTIONS AND ANSWERS. BOARDS, 75c.

THE JEWS AND MOSAIC LAW.

BOARDS, $1 25c.

DISCOURSES ON THE JEWISH RELIGION.

TWO VOLUMES IN ONE, $3.

THE PRAYER BOOK OF THE PORTUGUESE JEWS.

ROYAL OCTAVO, SIX VOLUMES. IN PAPER, $20.

DAILY PRAYER BOOK, $4.

*** *Any of the above Works may be had bound in any style, at from 50c. to $3 per volume extra.*

On the back page of the boards in which this copyright (June 18, 1838) copy of *The Hebrew Reader* is bound, we find an advertisement for some of Leeser's publications issued before 1838. The books are by no means inexpensive—a six-volume set of the Sefardi Prayer at $20, Daily Prayer at $4, and the volumes of his first published essays for $3.

Isaac Leeser, *The Hebrew Reader, No. l. The Spelling Book,* Philadelphia, 1838.
General Collection.

the words of Leeser, "used over a large surface as a first book of instruction in Hebrew," attaining a seventh edition in 1873. Of the *Catechism* Leeser wrote:

> If any event in my life can afford me some degree of satisfaction, it is the consciousness of having added one contribution . . . to satisfy the demand for information in the ways of the law of God. And it will be to me a far greater gratification than any public applause, could I be convinced that the thoughts offered in this guide to the young Israelites has led a few as sincere worshippers to the house of our God.

The Library has copies of both the *Reader* and the *Catechism* which Leeser himself had sent at the time of publication to establish his copyright. The *Catechism* is dedicated to "Miss Rebecca Gratz, Superintendent of the Sunday-School for Religious Instruction of Israelites in Philadelphia," whom Leeser credits with the founding of the school. But it was he himself who was the instigator of the school, for while still in Richmond he had, together with the Reverend Isaac B. Seixas, founded such a school, which met "with but partial success." As early as 1835, Leeser urged the establishment of a Jewish all-day school; and, in 1846, the Hebrew Education Society of Philadelphia was founded, chartered for "the establishment of a school or schools within . . . Philadelphia, in which are to be taught the elementary branches of education, together with the sciences, and modern and ancient languages, always in combination with instruction in Hebrew language, literature and religion."

Its charter also granted the right "to establish . . . a superior seminary of learning . . . the faculty of which . . . shall have power to furnish to graduates and others the usual degrees of Bachelor of Arts, Master of Arts and Doctor of Law and Divinity." In 1867, Leeser was instrumental in establishing the first rabbinical seminary in America, Maimonides College, which survived its founder by only four years, having to close its doors in 1873.

While still in Richmond, Leeser began his literary career with a defense of the Jews against an attack which first appeared in the *London Quarterly Review* and was reprinted in a New York newspaper. His works continued to involve him in polemics. In 1834, he published *The Jews and Mosaic Law*, a defense of the Revelation of the Pentateuch and of the Jews "for their adherence to same." The book's twenty-six chapters show wide reading in the contemporary religious literature. Leeser was aware that just as he was reading works on religion written by Christians, so too were many other young Jews. What was needed was a polemic arguing for loyalty to the ancestral faith and adherence to its ways.

Leeser's *Discourses, Argumentative and Devotional on the Subject of the Jewish Religion* (1837) were, as the title page reports, "delivered at the Synagogue Mikveh Israel, in Philadelphia, in the years 5590–5597" (1830–37). Its 590 pages are filled not only with sermons in the usual sense, but also with scholarly essays on such themes as God, the Holidays, and "The Messiah." An address on behalf of "The Female Hebrew Benevolent Society" of Philadelphia emphasizes his espousal of women's participation in Jewish communal enterprises. The copyright copies of both books may be consulted in the Library, as well as his liturgical and biblical publications. In 1845, he issued an edition of the Pentateuch in five volumes, entitled *The Law of God*, with Hebrew text, "edited and with former translations diligently compared and revised by Isaac Leeser." Eight years later, Leeser published a translation of the entire Bible, the first translation of the entire Bible into English by a Jew. His translation of the Sefardi prayer book into English was published in six volumes in 1837–38, and a decade later, in 1848, appeared *The Book of Daily Prayers for Every Day in the Year According to the Custom of the German and Polish Jews,* which he edited and translated.

Leeser founded and, for a quarter of a century from 1843–68, edited the first Jewish periodical, *The Occident.* (*The Jew,* which appeared in 1823–25, was merely a polemical response to a missionary publication.) He organized the first Jewish publication society and edited its publications. He inspired and helped to found a foster home for Jewish children, a Jewish hospital, and a union of charities. Nor can we ignore his contributions as an *American* clergyman, which may be glimpsed from two items in the Library's collection: a pamphlet, *Commemoration of the Life and Death of William Henry Harrison,* by Isaac Leeser, Philadelphia, 5601 (1841); and a letter from Leeser to President Lincoln, of August 21, 1862.

Leeser's funeral address is the first published eulogy for a president by a Jewish cleric. One brief section gives an idea of Leeser's democratic sentiments.

> In the brief sketch we have just furnished of the life and services of General Harrison, it will be perceived that he passed through every stage of promotion, and that he rose from a humble standard-bearer to the chief command of the army and navy, and the presidency of the councils of his native land; and he thus reached a station as high as human ambition can look for; because the voluntary suffrage of a free people raising one of their own fellow-citizens to the highest honour within their gift, is a far more enviable distinction than a throne inherited by a stripling from a royal ancestry, or acquired through violence by an adventurous military chieftain.

As Secretary of the Board of Ministers of the Hebrew Congregations of Philadelphia, Leeser wrote to Abraham Lincoln: "Many Israelites are serving in the army of the United States, and this city and vicinity being a locality where numerous hospitals for the sick and wounded soldiers have been established," he continues,

> it is to be expected that not a few persons of our persuasion will be brought hither in a condition to require spiritual no less than bodily care. In fact two at least of our persuasion have already died in the hospitals . . . It has at our last meeting been deemed highly expedient to have a Jewish chaplain appointed by the President of the United States.

On the back of that letter is written:

> Executive Mansion
> Aug. 23, 1862
>
> General
> The President directs me to refer the enclosed communication to you with the request that you will favor him with your opinion in regard to the legality and propriety of granting the request of the Board of Hebrew Ministers.
>
> John Hay
>
> The Surgeon General
> If possible the President would like this to be done.
>
> JH 4 Sept. 62

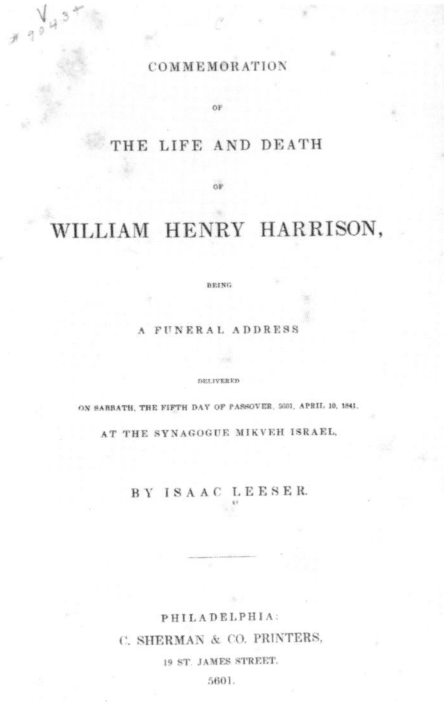

COMMEMORATION

OF

THE LIFE AND DEATH

OF

WILLIAM HENRY HARRISON,

BEING

A FUNERAL ADDRESS

DELIVERED

ON SABBATH, THE FIFTH DAY OF PASSOVER, 5601, APRIL 10, 1841,

AT THE SYNAGOGUE MIKVEH ISRAEL,

BY ISAAC LEESER.

PHILADELPHIA:
C. SHERMAN & CO. PRINTERS,
19 ST. JAMES STREET.
5601.

The first published eulogy for an American president by a Jewish clergyman is this pamphlet issued by Isaac Leeser in 1841. In it he argues that the American presidency is the highest station that human condition can look for, it being attained neither by the accident of birth nor wrested on the field of battle, but conferred "by a free people . . . [as] the highest honor within their gift."

Isaac Leeser, *Commemoration of the Life and Death of William Henry Harrison,* Philadelphia, 1841.
General Collection.

To the Hon. Abraham Lincoln

President of the United States of America

Sir

By order of the Board of Ministers of the Hebrew Congregations of Philadelphia, I take the liberty, as their secretary of addressing you briefly on a subject of great importance to us as a religious body.

Many Israelites are serving in the army of the United States, and this city and vicinity being the locality where numerous hospitals for the sick and wounded soldiers have been established, it is to be expected that not a few persons of our persuasion will be brought hither in a condition to require spiritual no less than bodily care. In fact two at least of our persuasion have already died in the hospitals, one of these had his religious affinities not made known to us till after he had been already buried without an Israelite being present. From the steps taken by us it is not probable that another Israelite will die under similar circumstances without some one of his fellow-believers being made cognizant of his case.

Nevertheless it has at our last meeting been deemed highly expedient to have a Jewish chaplain appointed by the President of the United States, to be invested with the privileges pertaining to ministers of other persuasions holding the same position. The act of the last session of Congress having

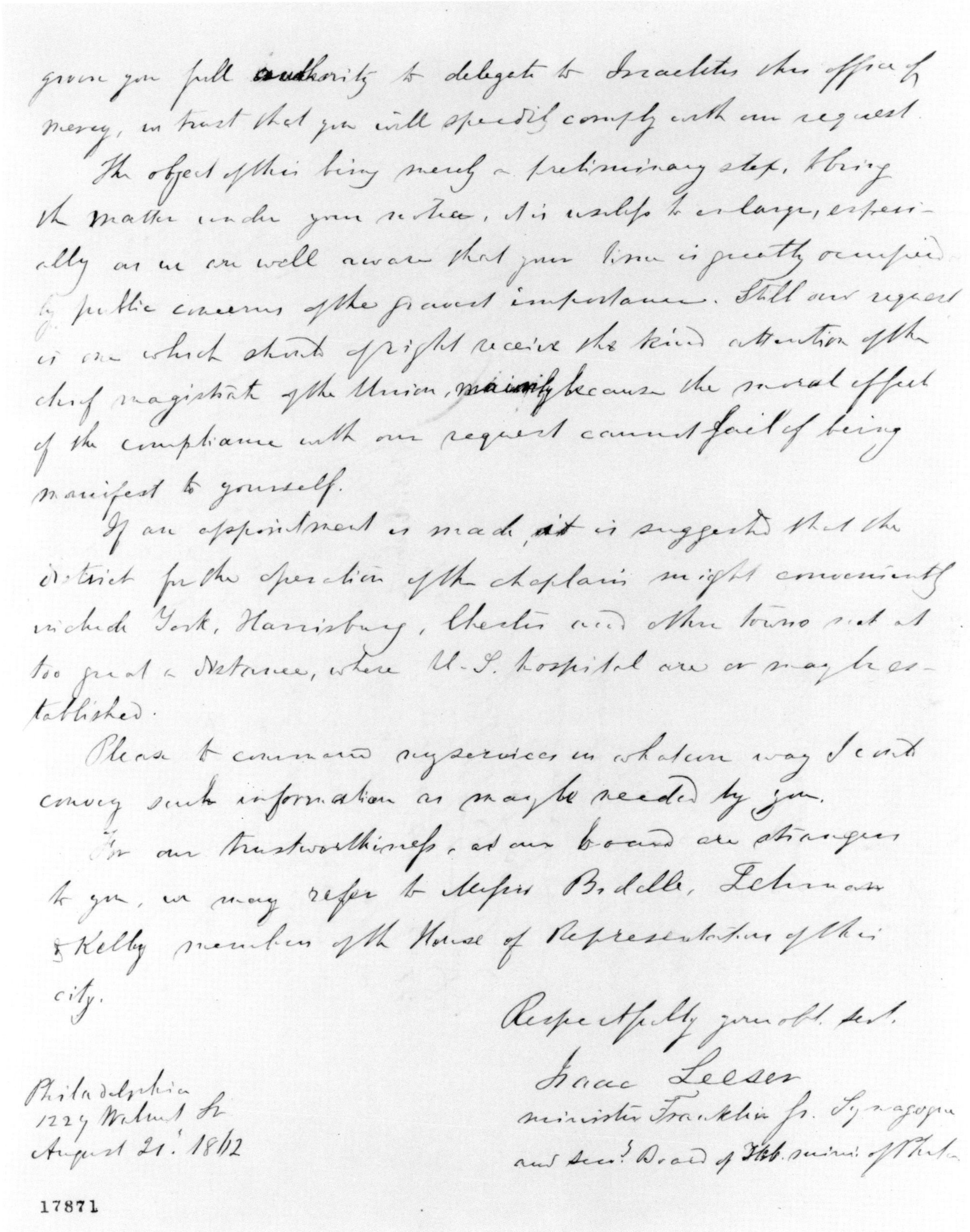
given you full authority to delegate to Israelites the office of mercy, we trust that you will speedily comply with our request.

The object of this being merely a preliminary step, to bring the matter under your notice, it is useless to enlarge, especially as we are well aware that your time is greatly occupied by public concerns of the gravest importance. Still our request is one which should of right receive the kind attention of the chief magistrate of the Union, mainly because the moral effect of the compliance with our request cannot fail of being manifest to yourself.

If an appointment is made, it is suggested that the district for the operation of the chaplain might conveniently include York, Harrisburg, Chester and other towns not at too great a distance, where U.S. hospital are or may be established.

Please to command my services in whatever way I can convey such information as may be needed by you.

For our trustworthiness, as our board are strangers to you, we may refer to Messrs Biddle, Lehman & Kelly members of the House of Representatives of this city.

Respectfully your obt. servt.
Isaac Leeser
minister Franklin St. Synagogue
and Secy Board of Heb. ministers of Phila

Philadelphia
1227 Walnut St
August 21st 1862

17871

In his capacity as Secretary of the Board of Ministers of the Hebrew Congregations of Philadelphia, Isaac Leeser wrote to President Lincoln on August 21, 1862, asking that a Jewish chaplain be appointed to minister to the spiritual needs of sick or wounded Jewish soldiers in military hospitals in Philadelphia and its vicinity.

Isaac Leeser to Abraham Lincoln, August 21, 1862.
Manuscript Division, Papers of Abraham Lincoln.

This frontispiece portrait faces the title page of Isaac Mayer Wise's *The Cosmic God* (Cincinnati, 1876). It portrays Wise at age fifty-six, the year he opened the rabbinical seminary he founded and headed till the end of his life, the Hebrew Union College in Cincinnati, Ohio.

Isaac Mayer Wise, *The Cosmic God,* Cincinnati, 1876.
General Collection.

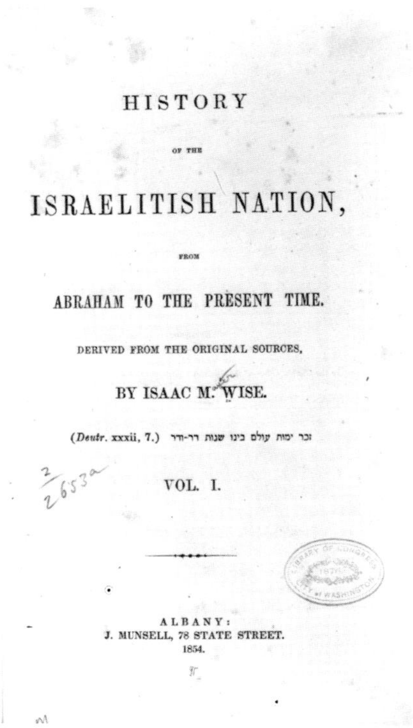

HISTORY

OF THE

ISRAELITISH NATION,

FROM

ABRAHAM TO THE PRESENT TIME.

DERIVED FROM THE ORIGINAL SOURCES,

BY ISAAC M. WISE.

(*Deutr.* xxxii, 7.) זכר ימות עולם בינו שנות דר-ודר

VOL. I.

ALBANY:
J. MUNSELL, 78 STATE STREET.
1854.

History of the Israelitish Nation, Isaac M. Wise's first published book, comprises the history of the Jewish people from Abraham to Solomon and is meant to be "a political history of the Israelitish nation." It was widely attacked by the Orthodox for having strayed from the traditional conception and depiction of the biblical period in Jewish history.

Isaac M. Wise, *History of the Israelitish Nation,* Albany, 1854.
General Collection.

The Surgeon General responds:

Respectfully returned to the President of the United States.
The Surgeon General considers it both legal and proper, that Chaplains of the Hebrew faith should be appointed in the Army.
Sept. 5, 62

The following day John Hay sent Leeser the good news, and on the president's behalf asked for the Board to "designate the proper person for the purpose." The Board chose the Reverend Jacob Frankel of Congregation Rodeph Sholom, who was commissioned on September 12, the first rabbi to serve as a military chaplain in the United States.

ISAAC MAYER WISE (1819–1900)

Bohemian born, Isaac Mayer Wise received a traditional Jewish education in Prague and Vienna, and absorbed Western culture as well. A job as teacher and rabbinic functionary in a small Bohemian town did not offer much of a future for this enormously energetic and gifted man, so he set out for the New World. After his arrival in New York in 1846, a rabbinic career in Albany, New York, and then for almost half a century in Cincinnati, Ohio, provided Wise with extraordinary opportunities. In 1854, the year he arrived in Cincinnati, he founded the weekly *The Israelite,* and for many years thereafter wrote most of its articles, as well as historical and polemical works and popular novels. In post-Civil War America, he was the best-known Jew and a well-regarded leader in American liberal religious circles. He believed that in time Judaism would become the religion of all enlightened men, but first it had to be modernized, democratized, and most important of all, Americanized. Wise was a leading exponent of a moderate, pragmatic Reform Judaism, responsive to the exigencies of contemporary American life. His signal contribution was the institutional structure he bequeathed to Reform Judaism by founding its Union of American Hebrew Congregations, Hebrew Union College, and the Central Conference of American Rabbis.

While Leeser still awaits a published biography, Wise has been the beneficiary of three, and a book of *Reminiscences* as well. One can, however, become acquainted with Wise through a few citations from works of his found on the Library's shelves.

History of the Israelitish Nation, Albany, 1854.

The nations of antiquity rolled away in the current of ages, Israel alone remained one indestructible edifice of gray antiquity, . . . preserved by an internal and marvelous power. It saw the barbarous nations pour their unnumbered hosts into the Roman empire, and made its home on the Thames, the Seine, the Ebro, the Po, and the Danube. It flourished with the Saracens, and suffered in the obscure and fanatical days of the Middle Ages. It saluted joyously the dawning light of science, art, civilization and justice, and cheered vehemently the birth of liberty and independence in America, and the resurrection of the European nations. The history of this nation is an important chapter of universal history, and as such alone it deserves careful examination.

History of the Hebrews Second Commonwealth, Cincinnati, 1880.

The book before you claims to be the first of this kind written from a democratic, free and purely scientific standpoint . . . It is the history of a people, and not of rulers and battles, the history of the life and growth in politics, religion, literature, culture, civilization, commerce, wealth and influence on other nations . . .

I have written this history with the proud feeling that man is better than his history, in which the onward march of enlightenment and humanization is so often interrupted by barbarous multitudes . . . Had the Hebrews not been disturbed in their progress a thousand and more years ago, they would have solved all the great problems of civilization which are being solved now under all the difficulties imposed by the spirit of the Middle Ages. The world is not yet redeemed.

Hymns, Psalms & Prayers, Cincinnati, 1868.

Dispersed as the house of Israel is in all lands, we must have a vehicle to understand each other in the house of God, so that no brother be a stranger therein; and this vehicle is the Hebrew [language] . . . the Hebrew sounds are sacred to the Israelite; they are holy reminiscences of his youth, which can as little be replaced to him in another language, as the Psalms of David can be fully reproduced in any other tongue.

The Origin of Christianity, Cincinnati, 1868.

Among the other sources which the author consulted, it is chiefly the Talmud and other rabbinical scriptures. He undertook the task of translating several hundred talmudical passages for this work, all rendered from the originals, and hopes to have expounded numerous passages in the New Testament, which are otherwise unintelligible. He hopes still more to have opened an entirely new avenue of research to Christian theology and criticism . . . without the Talmud, a perfect understanding of original Christianity is almost impossible, as the candid reader of this book will undoubtedly admit, after a careful perusal of it.

"On the Russo-Jewish Question," by D. I. M. Wise, in M. G. Landsberg, *History of the Persecution of the Jews in Russia,* Boston, 1892.

Russia contains one fourth of the inhabitants of all Europe, and one half of the entire number of Israelites. In the same proportion Russia is the misfortune of Europe and the Israelites. . . . The most admirable class of people in all Russia are the Jews, for most of them can read and write, and ninety per cent of the other Russians are analphabets . . . It is more than marvellous, it seems miraculous, that the Russian Jew preserved that intellectual and moral force which he possesses, surrounded as he was by rank demoralization, and down-trodden for centuries.

The Cosmic God, Cincinnati, 1876.

This book, conceived in sorrow, composed in grief, and constructed at the brink of despair, contains my mind's best thoughts, and my soul's triumph over the powers of darkness. My wife, my dearly beloved companion in this eventful life . . . was prostrated with an incurable disease . . . I prayed, I wept, I mourned, I despaired . . . I was drifting and whirling in a roaring current of lacerating contradictions, tormenting self-accusations bordering on self contempt.

Ruthless attacks upon my character, of restless assailants . . . embittered by joyless days. My energies failed. Insanity or suicide appeared inevitable . . . Once, at the midnight hour . . . I opened the Bible [and] read: "Unless thy law had been my delight, I should long since have been lost in my affiction" (Psalm 119:92).

It struck me forcibly. "There is the proper remedy for all afflictions." When those ancient Hebrews spoke of the law of God, they meant the whole of it revealed in God's words and works. Research, science, philosophy, deep and perplexing, problems most intricate and propositions most complicated, I thought, like the rabbis

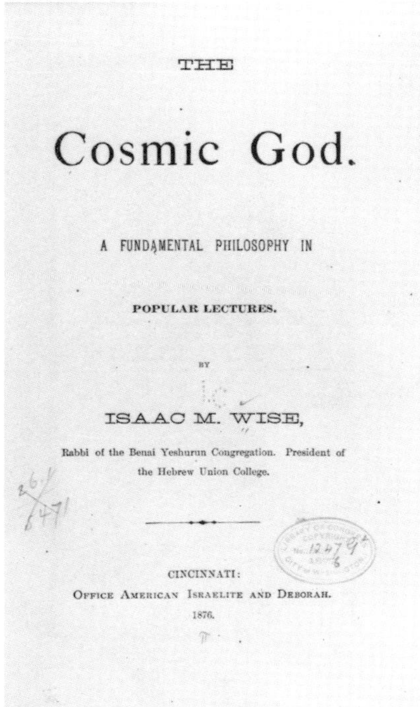

THE
Cosmic God.
A FUNDAMENTAL PHILOSOPHY IN
POPULAR LECTURES.
BY
ISAAC M. WISE,
Rabbi of the Benai Yeshurun Congregation. President of the Hebrew Union College.
CINCINNATI:
OFFICE AMERICAN ISRAELITE AND DEBORAH.
1876.

Isaac M. Wise called this book, *The Cosmic God,* "the first fruit of my independent research in science and philosophy." It had its origin in a series of lectures delivered in the fall and winter of 1874–75, at B'nai Yeshurun, Cincinnati, where he had served as rabbi since 1854. The book, "conceived in sorrow, composed in grief and constructed at the brink of despair," is dedicated to the memory of his wife Therese, who had died after a two-year illness in 1874.

Isaac M. Wise, *The Cosmic God,* Cincinnati, 1876. General Collection.

of the Talmud, must be the proper remedy for all maladies of the heart and reason. I plunged headlong into the whirlpool of philosophy, and, I believe, to have found many a gem in the fathomless deep. But the costliest of all gems I found is a calm and composed mind, a self-relying conviction. I found myself once more.

This 1887 portrait of Emma Lazarus, depicting the poet in the last year of her short life, was engraved by T. Johnson from a photograph by W. Kurtz.

Prints and Photographs Division.

EMMA LAZARUS (1849–1887)

Great-grandfather Samuel Lazarus had joined with Gershom Mendes Seixas in organizing *Kalfe Sedakah* a society for the relief of those stricken by yellow fever in the epidemic of 1798, and had himself fallen victim to it. His son, Eleazar S., American-born son of German Ashkenazic immigrants, became the leading authority on Sephardic liturgy in the first half of the nineteenth century. Eleazer also served as parnas (president) of the Shearith Israel Congregation, as did his eldest son, Samuel, who, like his father, would on occasion lead the service in the synagogue.

The second son, Moses, married Esther Nathan, the daughter of an aristocratic Sefardi family and made his fortune in the sugar refining business. They raised six daughters. Private tutorial schooling, stressing literature and languages, was provided for the Lazarus children; Hebrew education was not. Like others in their group, the Lazarus family relegated their Jewish religious life to the formal, occasional expression that good manners required.

Daughter Emma early displayed literary gifts, and in 1866 her proud father published "for private circulation," *Poems and Translations,* "written between the ages of fourteen and sixteen." This 207-page volume of thirty "original pieces" and translations from Heine, Dumas, and Victor Hugo, the dutiful daughter dedicated to her father. The poems betray no Jewish knowledge or interest. Twice she quotes biblical verses from Proverbs and Ecclesiastes, as epigraphs to poems, but the poems themselves lack Jewish content. "The Holy of Holies" is a young girl's lament of betrayal by a friend—nothing of religious sentiment, and no sensitivity to the special meaning of "Holy of Holies" in the Jewish religious tradition.

Ralph Waldo Emerson befriended her and became a guide and mentor, and Emma dedicated her *Admetus and Other Poems* to him. Of *Admetus, The Boston Transcript* wrote: "Emma Lazarus is a new name to us in American poetry, but 'Admetus' is not the work of a 'prentice-hand'; few recent volumes of verse compare favorably with the spirit and musical expression of these genuine effusions of Emma Lazarus." The great Russian novelist Turgenev wrote to her about her prose romance *Alide:* "An author who writes as you do is not a pupil in art anymore; he is not far from being himself a master."

For all the praise, spiritual unease troubled the young poet, an emptiness which the Judaism of her father and her uncle could not fill. The uncle, the Reverend Jacques Lyons, hazzan-minister of Shearith Israel, dispensed a proper, decorous, liturgy-centered religion which neither stirred her soul nor satisfied her heart.

When her friend Edmund C. Stedman, poet and critic, suggested that she turn to the Jewish tradition as a source of inspiration, she replied, as Stedman later remembered, that "although proud of her blood and lineage, the Hebrew ideals did not appeal to her." When Rabbi Gustav Gotth-

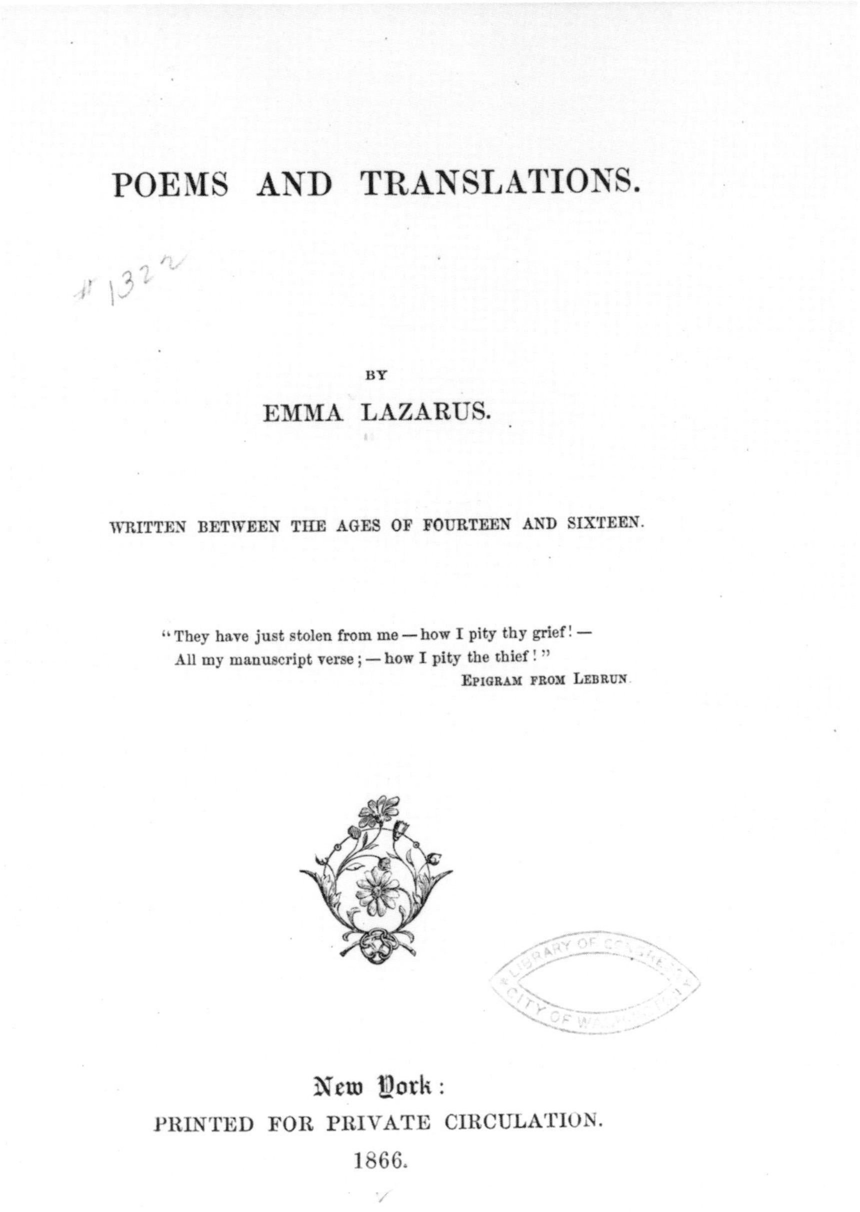

POEMS AND TRANSLATIONS.

BY

EMMA LAZARUS.

WRITTEN BETWEEN THE AGES OF FOURTEEN AND SIXTEEN.

"They have just stolen from me — how I pity thy grief! —
All my manuscript verse; — how I pity the thief!"
EPIGRAM FROM LEBRUN.

New York:
PRINTED FOR PRIVATE CIRCULATION.
1866.

Thirty original poems and forty-four translations from the German (Heinrich Heine) and the French (Alexander Dumas and Victor Hugo), seventy-four poetic pieces in all, written by Emma Lazarus between the ages of fourteen and sixteen, make up this book. Not one of them is of Jewish content or interest. Her "Jewish soul" as she termed it, was not awakened till later in life. The dedication is "To My Father," Moses Lazarus, who had the volume printed for private circulation in New York in 1866.

Emma Lazarus, *Poems and Translations,* New York, 1866. Rare Book and Special Collections Division.

eil invited her to contribute to a hymn book he was compiling, she replied: "I will gladly assist you as far as I am able; but that will not be much. I shall always be loyal to my race, but I feel no religious fervor in my soul."

What finally aroused her fervor was the plight of her people. The Russian pogroms of 1881, which followed on the assassination of Czar Alexander II, brought terror-stricken survivors to America. Emma Lazarus's first response was to go to Ward's Island to see what she might do for the hapless men, women, and children who crowded its facilities. The "loyalty to race" was not so much a kinship with preceding generations, but a bond with those of her generation who needed her and her gifts.

She began to read the literature of her people, to study the Hebrew language, and to associate more and more with Jews. When an article appeared in *The Century Magazine* justifying the pogroms, blaming the victims, and defending the czarist government, Lazarus responded with an impassioned defense of Judaism and the Russian Jew, entitled "Russian Christianity versus Modern Judaism," in the May 1882 issue of the magazine.

A half year later, *The Century* published her essay, "The Jewish Problem," which is particularly noteworthy for its Zionist stance. In a milieu in which Jewish national aspirations were denounced as contrary to the highest expression of Judaism and suppressed out of fear of accusations of dual loyalty, she hailed the Zionism espoused in George Eliot's novel *Daniel Deronda*. With high anticipation Lazarus greeted the colonies being planted in the Holy Land and took seriously English writer and traveler Laurence Oliphant's formulation of the Jewish problem as a choice for Jews of: "race-extinction by marriage in countries which are too civilized to attempt massacre, or of separation in a young nationality." She closed

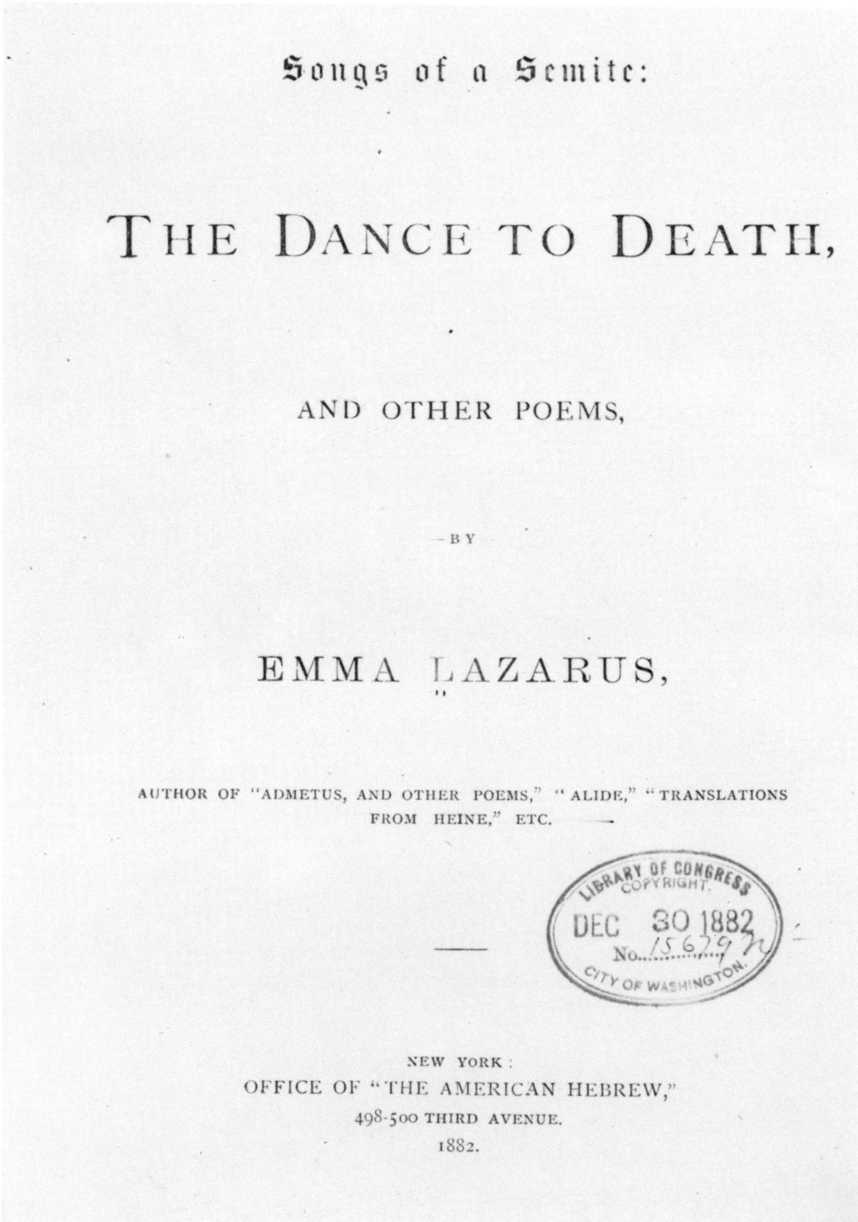
Songs of a Semite:

THE DANCE TO DEATH,

AND OTHER POEMS,

BY

EMMA LAZARUS,

AUTHOR OF "ADMETUS, AND OTHER POEMS," "ALIDE," "TRANSLATIONS FROM HEINE," ETC.

NEW YORK:
OFFICE OF "THE AMERICAN HEBREW,"
498-500 THIRD AVENUE.
1882.

Emma Lazarus's first book of poetry contained not one poem on a Jewish subject; her second was a reverential poem on the Jewish synagogue in Newport about a language and a way of life now dead. By 1882, her "national fervor" aroused, she published a volume of impassioned Jewish poetry and translations from the medieval Hebrew poets Solomon ibn Gabirol, Judah ha-Levi, and Moses Ibn Ezra, which she titled *Songs of a Semite.* Volume 2 of her posthumously published *The Poems of Emma Lazarus* offers poems on Jewish subjects on four-fifths of its pages.

Emma Lazarus, *Songs of a Semite . . .*, New York, 1882. General Collection.

her article by quoting the views of a young Russian Jew on this subject, "for they sum up the desires and ambitions of the nation":

> what they [the Jews] need is to be once more consolidated as a nation. . . . Let them organize with sufficient strength under a competent leader, and establish their central government. . . . In their present wretched condition the Jews have grown old. . . . But a new life will be instilled in them by such an achievement; and once more incorporated as a fresh and active nation, they will regain youthful vigor and power.

In 1883, celebrating America as the "Mother of Exiles" from whose beacon-hand glows worldwide welcome, Lazarus wrote "The New Colossus" to aid the Bartholdi Pedestal Fund. That sonnet, now inscribed on the pedestal of Bartholdi's Statue of Liberty in New York Harbor, has America proclaiming:

Give me your tired, your poor,
Your huddled masses yearning to breathe free,
The wretched refuse of your teeming shore.
Send these the homeless, tempest-tost to me,
I lift my lamp beside the golden door!

In devoting the rest of her brief life to Jewish causes, Emma Lazarus found new inspiration, writing such poems as "The Banner of the Jew," for *The American Hebrew:*

With Moses' law and David's lyre,
    Your ancient strength remains unbent.
Let but an Ezra rise anew
To lift the *Banner of the Jew!*

"The New Ezekiel" sang of dead bones which "twenty scorching centuries of wrong" produced, but:

The Spirit is not dead, proclaim the word,
    Where lay dead bones, a host of armed men stand!
I ope your graves, my people, saith the Lord,
    And I shall place you living in your land.

In 1882, *Songs of a Semite, The Dance to Death and Other Poems,* by Emma Lazarus, was published in New York by *The American Hebrew.* A five-act tragedy in verse, the "Dance to Death" is dedicated to the memory of George Eliot, "the illustrious writer, who did most among the artists of our day towards elevating and ennobling the spirit of Jewish nationality." The play is a passion-laden retelling of a fourteenth-century tale of Jewish martyrdom and heroism. In it, Susskind von Orb, a Jew, exhorts his coreligionists who have chosen martyrdom:

Fear ye we perish unavenged? Not so!
Today, no! to-morrow! but in God's time,
Our witnesses arise. Ours is the truth,
Ours is the power, the gift of Heaven. We hold
His Law, His lamp, His covenant, His pledge.
Wherever in the ages shall arise
Jew-priest, Jew-poet, Jew-singer or Jew-saint—
And everywhere I see them star the gloom—
In each of these the martyrs are avenged!

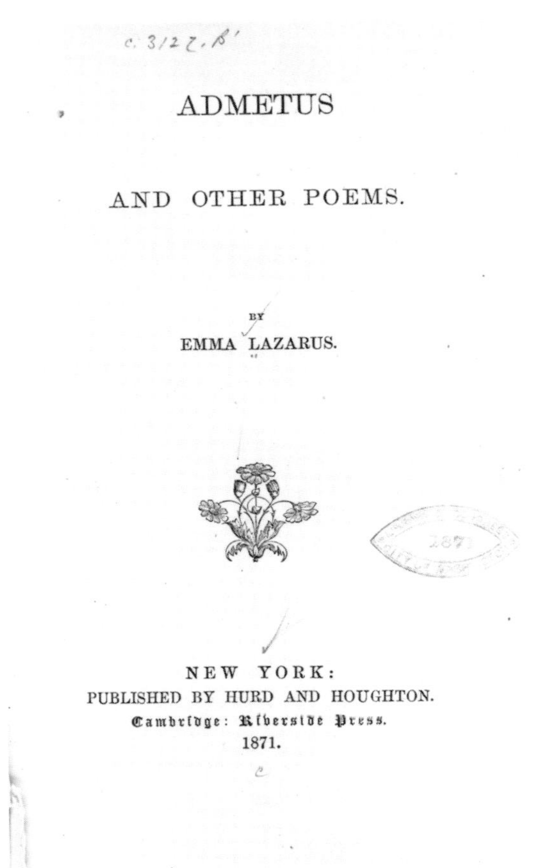
ADMETUS

AND OTHER POEMS.

BY

EMMA LAZARUS.

NEW YORK:
PUBLISHED BY HURD AND HOUGHTON.
Cambridge: Riverside Press.
1871.

Emma Lazarus dedicated *Admetus and Other Poems,* her second book of poems, which appeared in the twenty-second year of her life, "To my friend, Ralph Waldo Emerson," who had encouraged her poetic career. The volume contains perhaps her earliest poem on a Jewish subject, "In the Jewish Synagogue at Newport," written in July 1867, when she was not yet eighteen. The second of the eleven quatrains laments:

No signs of life are here: the very prayers
Inscribed around are in a language dead;
The light of the "perpetual lamp" is spent
That an undying radiance was to shed.

The last is reverential:

Nathless, the sacred shrine is holy yet,
With its lone floor where reverent feet once trod.
Take off your shoes as by the burning bush,
Before the mystery of death and God.

Emma Lazarus, *Admetus and Other Poems,* New York, 1871.
General Collection.

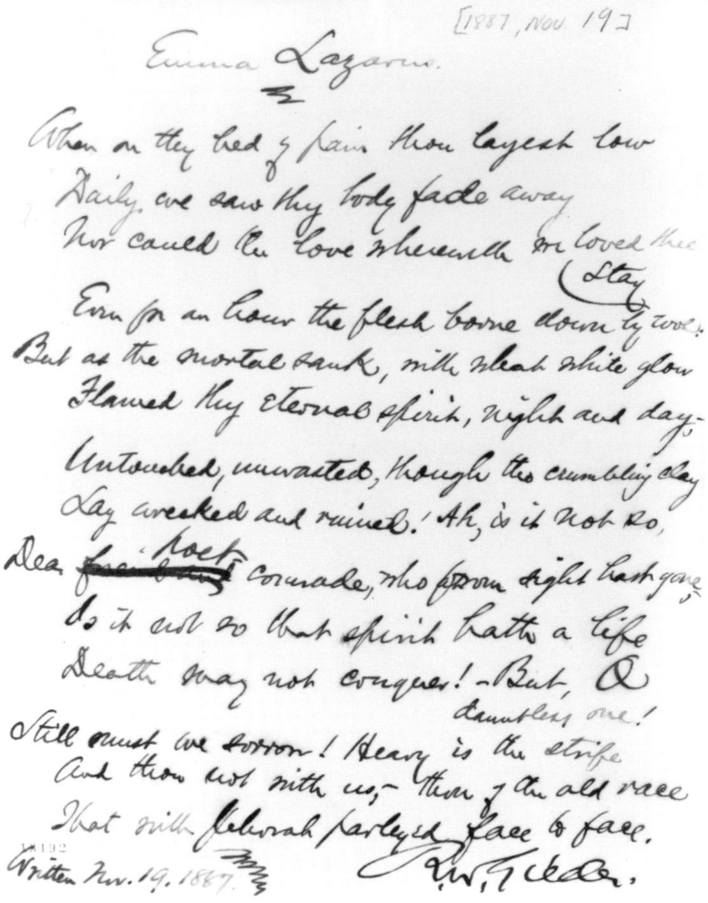
[1887, Nov. 19]

Emma Lazarus.

When on thy bed of pain thou layest low
Daily we saw thy body fade away
Nor could the love wherewith we loved thee stay
Even for an hour the flesh borne down by woe;
But as the mortal sank, with what white glow
Flamed thy eternal spirit, night and day,—
Untouched, unwasted, though the crumbling clay
Lay wrecked and ruined! Ah, is it not so,
Dear poet comrade, who from sight hast gone,
Is it not so that spirit hath a life
Death may not conquer! — But, O dauntless one!
Still must we sorrow! Heavy is the strife
And thou not with us,— thou of the old race
That with Jehovah parleyed face to face.

Written Nov. 19, 1887. R. W. Gilder.

The Grover Cleveland Papers contain this signed holograph sonnet, "Emma Lazarus," written on November 19, 1887, the day of her death, by Richard Watson Gilder, poet and editor of *The Century* magazine, which had published many of her poems and essays. It was sent by the author's wife to Mrs. Cleveland. Emma Lazarus apparently had a friend and admirer in the White House. The sonnet concludes:

Still must we sorrow! Heavy is the strife
And thou not with us; thou of the old race
That with Jehovah parleyed, face to face.

Richard Watson Gilder, "Emma Lazarus," November 19, 1887.
Manuscript Division, Papers of Grover Cleveland.

This eighty-page volume also contains poems on Jewish themes and translations from the medieval Hebrew poets Solomon ibn Gabirol, Judah HaLevi, Moses ben Ezra, and it brims with the author's religious fervor and national pride.

In a series of articles in *The American Hebrew,* which bore the title "An Epistle to the Hebrews," she makes her contribution "towards rousing that spirit of Jewish enthusiasm" and offers a program to the American Jews for the revival of that spirit:

> *First,* in a return to the varied pursuits and broad system of physical and intellectual education adopted by our ancestors; *Second,* in a more fraternal and practical movement towards alleviating the sufferings of oppressed Jews in countries less favored than our own; *Third,* in a closer and wider study of Hebrew literature and history; and finally in a truer recognition of the large principles of religion, liberty, and law upon which Judaism is founded, and which should draw into harmonious unity Jews of every shade and opinion.

Emma Lazarus did not complete her thirty-ninth year. Her sister Josephine, her senior by three years, and a gifted writer in her own right, lovingly gathered up her poems, to be published in two volumes as *The Poems of Emma Lazarus,* Boston and New York (1888). An appreciation (though unattributed, the work of Josephine) states:

> What Emma Lazarus might have accomplished, had she been spared, it is idle and even ungrateful to speculate. What she did accomplish has real and peculiar significance. It is the privilege of a favored few that every fact and circumstance of their individuality shall add lustre and value to what they achieve. To be born a Jewess was a distinction to Emma Lazarus, and she in turn conferred distinction upon her race.

16

HOLY TONGUE-HOLY LAND-HOLY WORDS

HOLY TONGUE

THE HEBREW LANGUAGE ARRIVED in the New World with the galleons of Columbus in 1492. Luis De Torres, the expedition's interpreter, was chosen for his knowledge of "Oriental tongues," Hebrew, Aramaic, and Arabic among them. Born a Jew and but recently converted, he chose to remain in the New World, settling in Cuba, where, in the words of Cecil Roth, "he soon set up his own small empire." If Torres's reason for not returning to Spain was a Marrano's fear of the Inquisition, the Holy Tongue not only arrived in the New World, but was pronounced there as well.

The Puritans brought to New England veneration for the Hebrew Bible and love for its language. Pilgrim father William Bradford, who arrived on the *Mayflower* and for some thirty years was governor of the Plymouth Colony, wrote a Hebrew grammar. Harvard College, established in 1636 to train a learned clergy, included Hebrew as a regular undergraduate subject, but then, as so often later, it did not prove to be popular. In 1653, Michael Wigglesworth (Harvard, 1651), a College tutor, complained:

> My pupills all came to me ysday to desire yy might ceas learning Hebrew: I wthstood it with all ye reason I could, yet all will not satisfy ym.

Miracle of miracles, a day later, he reports:

> God appear'd somewt inclining ye spt of my pupils to ye study of Hebrew as I had pray'd yet God would do.

Nonetheless, on leaving Harvard to take up his ministry in Malden, he complains again of the "pupills froward negligence in ye Hebrew." The lack of popularity of the subject may in part have been due to the personal and theological gloominess of the instructor. Wigglesworth was author of *The Day of Doom*, a frightening theological ballad, in which unbaptised infants are consigned, through God's infinite mercy, to the "easiest room in Hell."

A Hebrew Grammar

Seventy years later Harvard appointed a qualified instructor of Hebrew, Judah Monis. Born in the Barbary States or Italy in 1683, he received his education in Leghorn and Amsterdam, then apparently served in Jamaica and New York as a religious functionary. In 1715 he was a merchant in New York, and in 1720 he appeared in Boston. What caused him to come to the New World, and subsequently to leave a Jewish community in New York for Boston, which had but a few Jews duing all the eighteenth century, is not known. What is known is that Monis had a deep interest and some expertise in the Hebrew language, because in the year of his arrival in Boston he wrote to the authorities at Harvard asking their approval of his "Essay to facilitate the Instruction of Youth in the Hebrew Language, wch probably may be published if there may be a prospect of its being serviceable." Monis was apparently seeking an appointment to teach Hebrew at the College, and its aid in publishing his grammar. All Harvard College was ready to do at that time was to grant him a degree, an M.A., the only degree granted to a Jew until well into the next century, yet the Boston clergy were much taken with him as one "truly read and learned in the Jewish cabbals and Rabbins, a Master and Critic in the Hebrew." The "aged venerable Dr. Increase Mather" and his colleagues soon let Monis know that the price of an instructorship at Harvard was conversion to Christianity. This Monis did at a public ceremony held in College Hall on March 27, 1722. The Reverend Mr. Colman preached the baptismal sermon, and R. Judah Monis responded with the first part of a tripartite apology for his new faith. The sermon and the apology, *The Truth, The Whole Truth, and Nothing But the Truth,* were published the same year (Boston, 1722). Monis is aware that the sincerity of his conversion would be suspect and pleads that he embraced Christianity as "the only religion wherein I thought I could be saved, and not because I had self ends."

Now a convert, Monis received his appointment. Beyond the freshman year, all students had to attend his classes four days a week. By 1726, he had prepared a Hebrew grammar for use by his pupils, and in 1735, the College joined with Monis in publishing his manuscript in an edition of one thousand copies, which Monis could sell to his students.

The first Hebrew grammar to be published in the New World, for which a special font of Hebrew type was ordered from England, bears the title in Hebrew, transliterated Hebrew, and English: *Dickdook Leshon Gnebreet, A Grammar of the Hebrew Tongue, being an Essay to bring the Hebrew Grammar into English.* It was published "to Facilitate the Instruction of all those who are desirous of acquiring a clear Idea of this Primitive Tongue by their own studies . . . more especially for the Use of the students at Harvard-College at Cambridge, in New England." Because of the relatively large edition, and because students wrote not only their names but also notes in their copies, a fair number have survived. The Library has two. The one in the Rare Book and Special Collections Division contains a student's notes and comments; the copy in the Hebraic Section has notes, corrections, comments, and additions, and is of singular importance because it has a manuscript copy of an unpublished work by Judah Monis written on the recto and verso of a flyleaf:

An Alphabetical Catalogue of Nouns and verbs which consist of more than three Radicals called by the Grammarians Quadruples and Quintruples for the finding the Roots of which there is no Certain Rule; neither in the preceding or any other Grammar as I know of. Drawn for ease of those that are desirous of a clear understanding of this Tongue: (A work altogether new) Collected from [sic] Care and Diligence

pr. [?] Judah Monis A. M.

Facing page and overleaves:
Published in 1735 "to the . . . use of the students at Harvard-College at Cambridge, in New England," by the college's instructor in Hebrew, Judah Monis, with the approval and aid of the school, *Dickdook Leshon Gnebreet, A Grammar of the Hebrew Tongue* served a generation of Harvard students as their textbook for the study of Hebrew. One thousand copies were printed, a large edition for an early seventeenth-century American publication.

Appended to the Hebraic Section's copy of Monis's grammar is this two-page manuscript of his "Alphabetical Catalogue of Nouns and Verbs which consist of more than three radicals called by the Grammarians Quadruples and Quintruples . . ." This addendum, of an unpublished work by Monis, makes this copy of singular importance.

Judah Monis, *A Grammar of the Hebrew Tongue . . .*, Boston, 1735.
Hebraic Section.

דִּקְדּוּק
לְשׁוֹן עִבְרִית

DICKDOOK LESHON GNEBREET.

A

GRAMMAR

OF THE

Hebrew Tongue,

BEING

An ESSAY

To bring the **Hebrew Grammar** into **English**, to Facilitate the

INSTRUCTION

Of all those who are desirous of acquiring a clear Idea of this

Primitive Tongue

by their own Studies; In order to their more distinct Acquaintance with the SACRED ORACLES of the Old Testament, according to the Original. And Published more especially for the Use of the STUDENTS of *HARVARD-COLLEGE* at *Cambridge*, in NEW-ENGLAND.

נֶחְבַּר וְהוּגַּת בְּעִיּוּן נִמְרָץ עַל יְדֵי
יְהוּדָה מוֹנִישׁ

Composed and accurately Corrected,

By JUDAH MONIS, *M. A.*

BOSTON, N. E.
Printed by JONAS GREEN, and are to be Sold by the AUTHOR at his House in *Cambridge*. MDCCXXXV.

There follows an alphabetical listing of 118 words inscribed in Hebrew characters with English translations and notations where the word appears in the Bible, for example: *"Dardar* A Thistle, Genesis 3.18"; *"Kodkod* a Scull, Genesis 49.26." The handwriting of this Catalogue, different from the student's notes, might be Monis's own.

In 1760, Monis retired from Harvard and was succeeded by Stephen Sewall, who three years later issued *An Hebrew Grammar Collected Chiefly from those of Mr. Israel Lyons, Teacher of Hebrew in the University of Cambridge and the Reverend Richard Gray D. D., Rector of Hinton in Northamptonshire* (Boston, 1763), of which the Library has a fine copy. A year later, in his eighty-first year, Monis died. His tombstone in Westboro, Massachusetts, is inscribed:

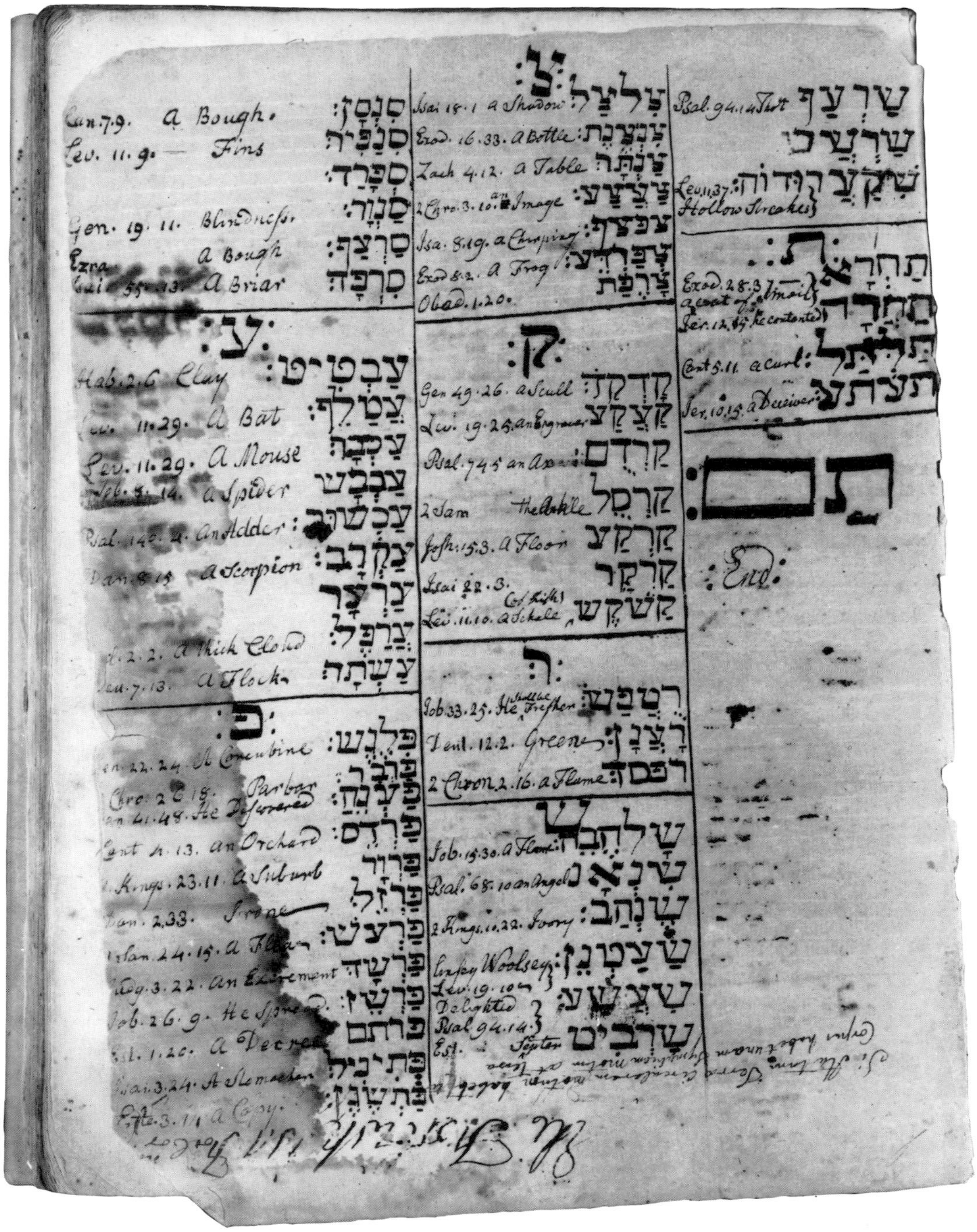

Here lie buried the remains of
RABBI JUDAH MONIS, M. A.
Late Hebrew Instructor
At Harvard College in Cambridge
In which office he continued forty years.

A Hebrew Psalter and Lexicon

The year 1809 saw the publication of the first Hebrew Psalter in America, indeed the first printing of any portion of the Hebrew Bible, *Sefer Tehilim, Liber Psalmorum Hebraice,* Cambridge, 1809; and of the two-volume *A Compendious Lexicon of the Hebrew Language,* by Clement C. Moore (1779–1863), printed in New York. Volume 1 contains "an explanation of every

בראשית

LIBER GENESIS.

CAPUT I. א

Deus creat cœlum et terram.

א בראשית ברא אלהים את השמים ואת הארץ : ב׳ רבתי
2 והארץ היתה תהו ובהו וחשך על־פני תהום ורוח
3 אלהים מרחפת על פני המים : ויאמר אלהים יהי
4 אור ויהי אור : וירא אלהים את האור כי טוב ויבדל
ה אלהים בין האור ובין החשך : ויקרא אלהים
לאור יום ולחשך קרא לילה ויהי ערב ויהי בקר יום
אחד : פ

3 Creat lucem, ac distinguit inter lucem et tenebras.

6 ויאמר אלהים יהי רקיע בתוך המים ויהי מבדיל בין
7 מים למים : ויעש אלהים את הרקיע ויבדל בין המים
אשר מתחת לרקיע ובין המים אשר מעל לרקיע ויהי
8 כן : ויקרא אלהים לרקיע שמים ויהי ערב ויהי בקר
יום שני : פ

6 Creat expansum, et separat aquas inferiores à superioribus.

9 ויאמר אלהים יקוו המים מתחת השמים אל מקום
י אחד ותראה היבשה ויהי כן : ויקרא אלהים ליבשה
ארץ ולמקוה המים קרא ימים וירא אלהים כי טוב :
11 ויאמר אלהים תדשא הארץ דשא עשב מזריע זרע עץ
פרי עשה פרי למינו אשר זרעו בו על הארץ ויהי כן :
12 ותוצא הארץ דשא עשב מזריע זרע למינהו ועץ עשה
13 פרי אשר זרעו בו למינהו וירא אלהים כי טוב : ויהי
ערב ויהי בקר יום שלישי : פ

9 Aquæ confluunt in unum locum. Terra apparet et producit fructus.

14 ויאמר אלהים יהי מארת ברקיע השמים להבדיל בין
היום ובין הלילה והיו לאתת ולמועדים ולימים ושנים :
טו והיו למאורת ברקיע השמים להאיר על הארץ ויהי
16 כן : ויעש אלהים את שני המארת הגדלים את
המאור הגדל לממשלת היום ואת המאור הקטן
17 לממשלת הלילה ואת הכוכבים : ויתן אתם אלהים
18 ברקיע השמים להאיר על הארץ : ולמשל ביום

14 Deus creat luminaria in expanso.

A ובלילה

word which occurs in the Psalms"; volume 2 is "a lexicon and grammar of the whole language." The Preface offers a modė of study which will enable "any person acquainted with the general principles of language, without the aid of a teacher, to read and understand the Holy Scriptures in the original Hebrew."

Moore hopes that "his young countrymen will find it of some service to them, as a sort of pioneer, in breaking down the impediments which present themselves at the entrance of the study of Hebrew." As Professor of Hebrew at General Theological Seminary in New York, Moore introduced two generations studying for the Episcopalian ministry to the Hebrew language. (He is best known as the author of the poem "A Visit from St. Nicholas," which opens with "Twas the night before Christmas.")

A Hebrew Bible

Five years later, the first Hebrew Bible in America, *Biblia Hebraica,* "editio prima Americana, sine punctis Masorethicis," was published in two volumes in Philadelphia in 1814. The title page indicates that it is a reprinting of the second edition of the Joseph Athias Bible, edited by Leusden with Latin notes by Everardo Van der Hought, and that the Hebrew is printed without vowels. In some of the first copies of the first volume off the press, an inserted page provides the history of its publication:

> In the year 1812, Mr. Horwitz had proposed the publication of an edition of the Hebrew Bible, being the first proposal of the kind ever offered in the United States. The undertaking was strongly recommended by many clergymen . . . and a considerable number of subscriptions for the work were obtained by him.
>
> Early in 1813, Mr. Horwitz transferred his right to the edition with his list of subscribers, to Thomas Dobson, the present publisher. . . . The first volume is now published. The printing of the second volume, which will complete the work, is considerably advanced; and the publisher hopes to have it completed in the course of a few months.

Mr. Horwitz's was not in fact the first proposal for printing a Hebrew Bible. In 1810, Mills Day of New Haven issued a proposal for "publishing by subscription an edition of the Hebrew Bible," and attached to the proposal a sample printing of the first chapter and a half of Genesis. The subscription price was $3.25 for each of the two volumes planned. Two years into the project, at age twenty-nine, Day died and the project died with him.

Jonathan Horwitz, recently arrived from Amsterdam with a font of Hebrew type, now made his proposal, but he was not alone. The New York publishing firm of Whiting and Watson announced its plan to publish a Hebrew Bible under the patronage of the Theological Seminary at Andover. Horwitz countered with an advertisement in the *New York Evening Post* (January 16, 1813), declaring not only that he had received the patronage of Harvard College and the Andover Theological Institution but also that both institutions had already subscribed for forty copies each. Horwitz had even more competition to contend with. Two leaders in missionary work, John M. Mason and James McFarlane, were ready to enter the field, and in 1812 the president of the London Society for Promoting Christianity Among Jews, the apostate Joseph Samuel Christian Frederick

Facing page: This first publication of the entire Bible in Hebrew in America appeared in Philadelphia in 1814. It was based on the second edition of the Athias Bible (see exhibit item 35) but, unlike that edition, it was printed without vowel marks. It was not till 1849 that a vocalized Hebrew Bible was published in America. Here we see the first page of *Bereshit,* Genesis.

Biblia Hebraica, 2 volumes, Philadelphia, 1814. Hebraic Section.

Frey, had already published the first volume of a vocalized Bible for the English-speaking countries. It was rumored that as soon as the project was completed, he would depart for the United States to see to its distribution there.

Faced with all this competition, what was a pious foreign Jew to do? Horwitz decided that discretion was the better part of valor. In 1813, he sold his type to the Philadelphia printer William Fry, and his subscription lists to the bookseller Thomas Dobson, and entered the medical department of the University of Pennsylvania from which he received his M.D. in 1815.

After the "lean years" which followed the Revolutionary War, in the early decades of the nineteenth century America was in the throes of a great religious revival. As part of its intellectual aspect, the study of the Hebrew language was renewed. Much of it revolved around Moses Stuart, Professor of Sacred Literature in the Theological Seminary at Andover, and his disciples. Grammars, lexicons, and chrestomathies were published, as well as books on the Bible and the Holy Land. The Jewish community was wary of these activities because the same scholars and divines were also involved in missionary activity. The appearance of a work on the Hebrew language which bore approbation from both leading Christian clergymen and leading Jews marked the beginning of friendlier intellectual discourse.

Hebrew Language

H. Henry's *Imrai Shaipher, A Hebrew Vocabulary* (New York, 1838), published by the Jewish printer M. Jackson, bore the recommendations, among others, of M. M. Noah and I. B. Seixas, Reader of K. K. Shearith Israel; as well as those of John Dowling, Pastor of the West Baptist Church; and the Reverend S. Luckey, Editor of the *Christian Advocate and Journal.* The author, who dedicates the volume to his father, P. Henry, Esquire, thanks Peter Westervelt for "revising the proof sheets," explaining "the English language not being my native tongue, I could not, myself . . . have undertaken to correct." Henry also laments his "want of proper assistance from books, which I was almost destitute of; for, a Bible, a Lexicon of but second rate quality, and a small Grammar, published in England in 1653, these were the only Heb. books, my library could boast of." He undertook nonetheless preparation of a handbook facilitating finding the roots of Hebrew words. (It is of interest to note that, in 1838, there was someone in America, as the author notes, who could inform him that the title he chose for his work had already been used in Europe by Naphtali Herz Wessely for a poetical work.)

During the nineteenth century, Hebrew grammars by Jews and non-Jews continued to appear. A few articles and letters in Hebrew appeared in the *Occident,* and in the 1860s two Hebrew volumes were published. In 1871 with the appearance of the Hebrew weekly *Ha-Zofeh ba'Arez ha-Hadashah* (The Watchman in the New Land), which began publication on June 11 and lasted for five years, the language became a living reality. Its editor, Zvi Hirsch Bernstein (1846–1907), was twenty-four years old when he arrived from Russia in 1870. Already a contributor to a number of Hebrew periodicals there, once in America he turned to publishing, founding *Die Post,* the first Yiddish periodical in America, which lasted but six months.

NO.2. HATSOFE B'EREZ HACHADOSHO שנה ראשונה.

הצופה
בארץ־החדשה

עומד על המצפה להגיד ולהשמיע קורות אחב"י בכל חלקי תבל בכלל ובאמעריקא בפרט וכל
תולדות העתים והזמנים אשר נחוץ ודרוש לדעת לכל אדם באשר הוא אדם·

מאתי

צבי הירש בערנשטיין·

צופה נתתיך לבית ישראל (יחזקאל ג')

התרל"א· נויארק ח תמוז NEW YROK· JUNE 27 1871

תוכן הענינים

מכתב תהלה.

נבחרי הקהלות באמעריקא·

The migration of Jews from Eastern Europe to the United States, which became a mighty wave at the end of the nineteenth century and the beginning of the twentieth, was not yet a trickle in June 1871, when Zvi Bernstein began the publication of the first Hebrew periodical in America, *Ha-Zofeh ba-'Arez ha-Hadashah* (The Watchman in the New World). The editor declared its mission to be:

To stand on the watchtower and report what was happening to our brethren in all parts of the world, especially in America, and the history of the times, which is needed to be known by every person.

Subscription: $4.20 annually; advertisements 10 cents a line; ads for the "public good" are free.

Ha-Zofeh ba-'Arez ha-Hadashah, New York, June 27, 1871.
Hebraic Section.

In his second year, he launched two periodicals, the four-language *Hebrew News* in Yiddish, Hebrew, German, and English, which soon folded, and *Ha-Zofeh*.

That paper's second issue contains a report on the annual meeting of the Board of Delegates of American Israelites; news items from Buffalo and Cincinnati as well as from Russia and Jerusalem; scholarly articles on the sources of Jewish surnames, the excommunication of Spinoza, and Jews in the East Indies; a report of new books; a letter from Vilna, and various announcements. Its front page carried praise from America's leading Hebraist, Rabbi H. Vidaver, of New York's Congregation B'nai Jeshurun, who wrote:

All who esteem and love will praise you; and everyone will hail you . . . for being the first to have the courage to plant this Hebrew shoot in the "Vineyard of Ben Shemen," when most of our people are interested only in the "fat of the land . . ."

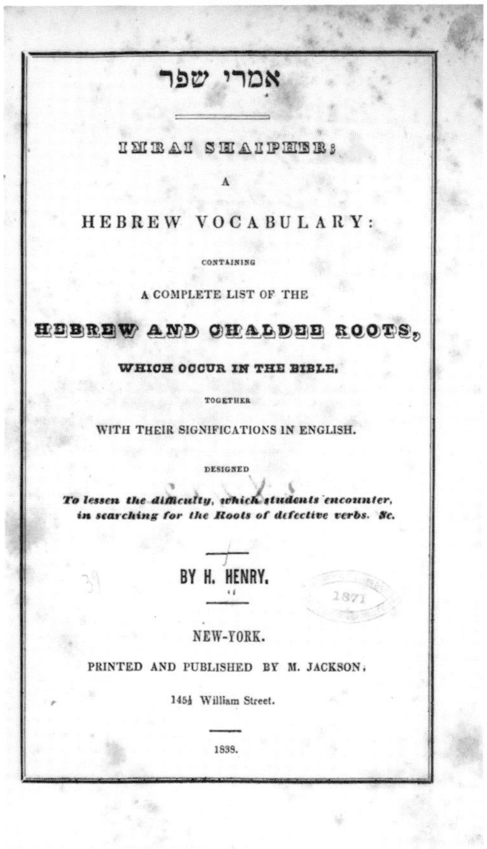
אמרי שפר

IMRAI SHAIPHER;

A

HEBREW VOCABULARY:

CONTAINING

A COMPLETE LIST OF THE

HEBREW AND CHALDEE ROOTS,

WHICH OCCUR IN THE BIBLE,

TOGETHER

WITH THEIR SIGNIFICATIONS IN ENGLISH.

DESIGNED

To lessen the difficulty, which students encounter, in searching for the Roots of defective verbs. &c.

BY H. HENRY.

NEW-YORK.

PRINTED AND PUBLISHED BY M. JACKSON,

145½ William Street.

1838.

The author, H. Henry, describes his work as "A Hebrew Vocabulary . . . designed to lessen the difficulty, which students encounter in searching for the roots of defective words etc." A recent immigrant, Henry acknowledges the help he received, "in revising the proof sheets . . . the English language not being my native tongue." The printer and publisher is Morris Jackson, son of New York's first Jewish printer and publisher, Solomon Henry Jackson.

H. Henry, *Imrai Shaipher, A Hebrew Vocabulary,* New York, 1838.
General Collection.

Be strong and of good courage, stretch forth the Hebrew pen and the blessings of those who honor the language will descend upon you—and among them am I.

HOLY LAND

Emissaries

On March 8, 1772, the Reverend Ezra Stiles, then Minister of the Second Congregational Church of Newport, Rhode Island (later, president of Yale University), attended a Purim service in the local synagogue. He recorded the occasion in his diary:

> There I saw Rabbi [Haim Isaac] Carigal I judge aet. 45. lately from the city of Hebron, the Cave of the Macpelah in the Holy Land. He was one of the two persons that stood by the Chusan at the Taubauh or Reading Desk while the Book of Esther was read. He was dressed in a red garment with the usual Phylacteries and habiliments, the white silk Surplice; he wore a high brown furr Cap, had a long Beard. He has the appearance of an ingenious & sensible Man.

The Holy Land visitor so colorfully described by Stiles was no stranger to the New World. A native of Hebron—he was born in 1733 and ordained as a rabbi twenty years later—Carigal had traveled widely in the Near East, Europe, and the Americas, acting on occasion as an itinerant rabbinic functionary. He had spent two years in Curaçao before returning to Hebron in 1764. In 1768, he once again resumed his travels. For two and a half years, he served as a teacher in London and then spent a year in Jamaica. In the summer of 1772 he made his way to Philadelphia, then New York, and arrived in Newport in 1773 in time to celebrate the Purim holiday and to make the acquaintance of Ezra Stiles.

The Reverend Mr. Stiles had great curiosity about Jews and Judaism, and from his voluminous diaries we learn that between 1759 and 1775 no less than six rabbis visited Newport. Stiles sought them out, conversed with them and described them and their conversations. Rabbi Carigal impressed him most, and they spent much time together. Carigal supplied information about the Jews in other lands, in particular the Holy Land, noting that "in all Judea or Holy Land A.D. 1773" there were about one thousand families of Jews and twelve synagogues. From him Stiles also learned that there were three rabbis "settled in America, one in Jamaica, one in Surinam and one in Curaçao," but "none on the Continent of North America."*

On May 28, the festival of Shavuot, Stiles was again in the synagogue, and this time he had the pleasure of hearing a sermon preached by Carigal in "Spanish" (Ladino?) which lasted for forty-seven minutes. Though few present were able to understand any part of the lengthy discourse, whose theme was "the Salvation of Israel," the occasion was auspicious for the twenty-five families who formed the Jewish community of Newport. Dignitaries from the community at large had been invited—Stiles noted Governor Wantan, Judge Oliver, and Judge Auchmuty—and all listened respectfully to the exotically garbed preacher speaking in a strange yet impressive tongue. "There was a Dignity and Authority about him, mixt with modesty," Stiles observed.

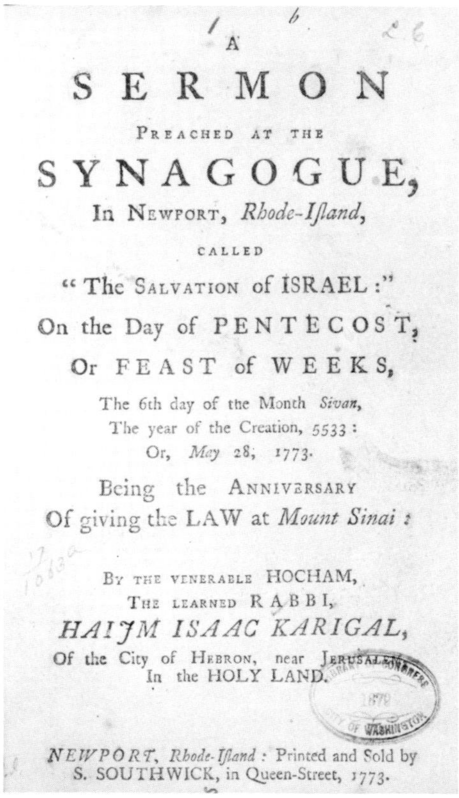

A
SERMON
PREACHED AT THE
SYNAGOGUE,
In NEWPORT, *Rhode-Island*,
CALLED
"The SALVATION of ISRAEL:"
On the Day of PENTECOST,
Or FEAST of WEEKS,
The 6th day of the Month *Sivan*,
The year of the Creation, 5533:
Or, *May* 28, 1773.
Being the ANNIVERSARY
Of giving the LAW at *Mount Sinai*:
BY THE VENERABLE HOCHAM,
THE LEARNED RABBI,
HAIJM ISAAC KARIGAL,
Of the City of HEBRON, near JERUSALEM,
In the HOLY LAND.
NEWPORT, *Rhode-Island*: Printed and Sold by
S. SOUTHWICK, in Queen-Street, 1773.

This, the first American Jewish sermon to be published, was preached by an emissary from the Holy Land, Haim Isaac Carigal—"the venerable hocham, the learned rabbi, of the city of Hebron, near Jerusalem, in the Holy Land," as he is described on the title page—on the festival of Shavuot, May 28, 1773, in Newport's beautiful synagogue, which is now a national shrine. The sermon, preached in Ladino (Judeo-Spanish), the language of Sefardi Jewry, was translated into English by Abraham Lopez and published contrary to Carigal's wishes.

Haim Isaac Carigal, *A Sermon Preached at the Synagogue, in Newport, Rhode Island*, 1773.
General Collection.

*There were Jewish religious functionaries in North America at that time, called hazzan or minister, but no ordained rabbis.

It was a moment that demanded preservation for posterity. Abraham Lopez, a native of Portugal and a former Marrano who had entered the Covenant of Abraham six years earlier, was entrusted with the task of translating the sermon into English. It was published later that year, the first Jewish sermon in America accorded that honor. Its title page reads: *A Sermon Preached at the Synagogue, in Newport, Rhode Island, Called "The Salvation of Israel," on the Day of Pentecost, or Feast of Weeks, the 6th Day of the Month of Sivan, the year of Creation 5533, or, May 28, 1773. Being the Anniversary of giving the Law at Mount Sinai: By the Venerable Hocham, the Learned Rabbi, Haijim Isaac Carigal, of the City of Hebron, near Jerusalem in the Holy Land.*

Sixty years later, another emissary, Rabbi Enoch Zundel of Jerusalem, went to America seeking aid for his impoverished brethren. With him he brought a letter to Mordecai M. Noah signed by a half dozen rabbis of the Holy Land beseeching aid. Translated by the Christian Hebraist William L. Roy, it reads in part:

> The voice of Zion speaks weeping and lamenting, for the wretched state of her children: For their faces are black with hunger . . . We are hungry, thirsty and naked. Our children ask for bread and we have none to give them.—And in addition to this, the Turks have laid us under a contribution of fifty thousand dollars, which if not paid will be the ruin of all the Jews here . . . and [we] have sent on the Rabbi Enoch Zindal [sic] . . . son of the great Rabbi Hersh, one of the most learned men in the world. He will fully explain to you our afflictions . . . Help him by any way and means in your power, by obtaining donations, and forming societies among all denominations. And we will pray for you in all the holy places . . . and we hope with all the scattered tribes and the Messiah at their head, to meet you soon in the Holy City, the desire of all nations.

The full text of the letter and an account of a meeting of Rabbi Zundel with the leading clergy of New York was published in the *New York Christian Intelligencer* and other newspapers.

> The evening was spent in hearing the Rabbi, who is a truly polite and accomplished man, detail many interesting things relative to Jerusalem, the holy city and the condition of the Jews there . . . He gave replies to many difficult questions proposed to him on various passages of the Hebrew Bible . . .
>
> He is fully in the belief of the Jews being recalled to their own land. And by the calculations he makes . . . it is to commence in the year 1841—only nine years hence.
>
> The Rabbi's people at Jerusalem had heard of the exceeding benevolence and charity of the Americans. These are his own words: *"You did much for the Greeks; and will you not admit, even as Christians, lovers of the Old Testament patriarchs and prophets, that you owe at least as much, nay, much more,* TO US THE JEWS?"
>
> And as this is the first appeal made to us as Christians, by the Jews, direct from Jerusalem, we should, by responding to the voice of suffering humanity, give them an evidence that we are, *as Christians,* their true and sincere friends.

Four ministers volunteered to receive any funds "which benevolent Christians may condescend to give."

Rabbi Enoch Zundel made such an impression that an engraving of him by A. A. Hoffay was published by N. M. Fried in 1833, showing the Rabbi wrapped in a prayer shawl and wearing a turbanlike head covering.

The first published American engraving of a contemporary Jew is this of an emissary from the Holy Land, Enoch Zundel. Arriving in New York in 1832, seeking aid for his impoverished countrymen, he met with Christian clergymen who pledged their help, as did Jewish congregations and individual Jews. His exotic figure made such an impression that an engraving by A. A. Hoffay of the rabbi in full regalia—turbanlike head covering, fringed prayer shawl, and open Hebrew book in hand—was published by N. M. Fried in 1833.

Portrait of the Rabbi Enoch Zundel, New York, 1833. Prints and Photographs Division.

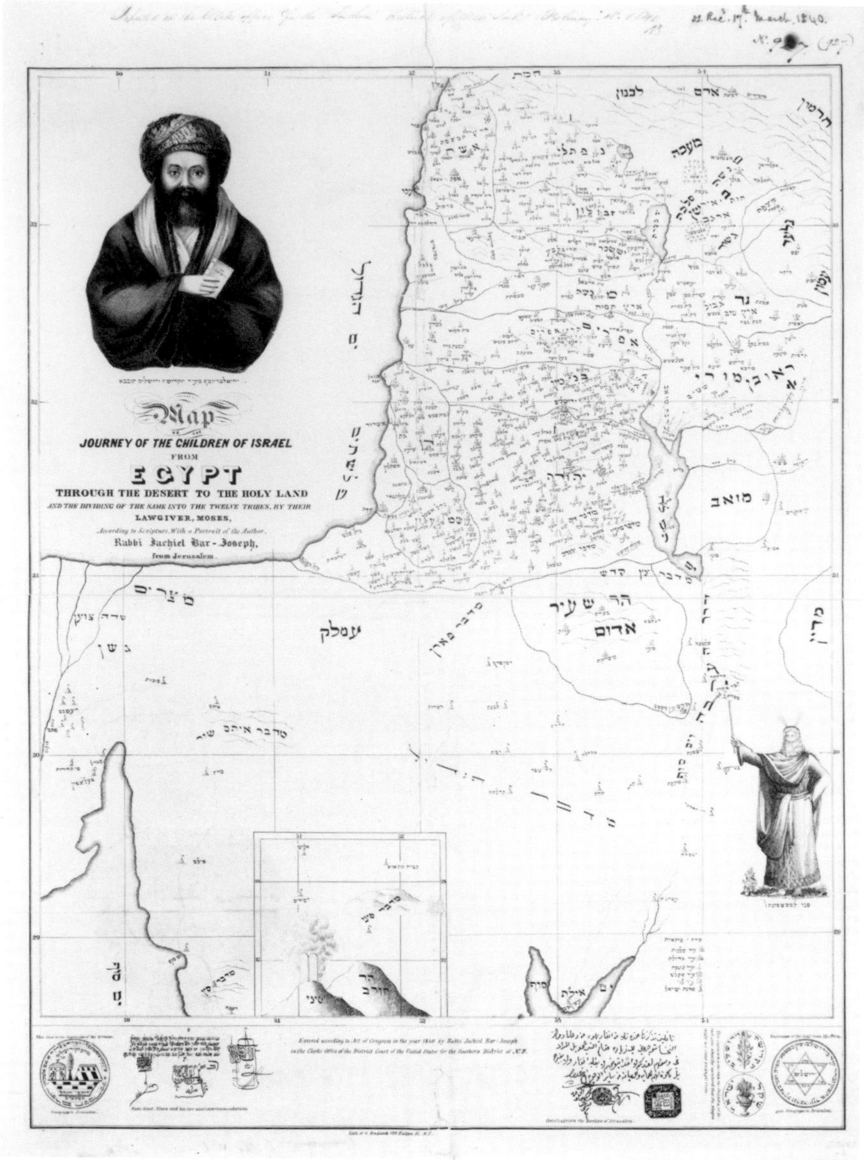

This exceedingly rare map of the Holy Land (the Library's may be a unique copy) bears the description:

Map of the journey of the Children of Israel from Egypt through the Desert to the Holy Land and the Dividing of the Same into Twelve Tribes, by their Lawgiver Moses, according to scriptures with a portrait of the author. Rabbi Jachiel Bar-Joseph, from Jerusalem.

The map, lithographed by G. Endicott, 152 Fulton Street, New York, may well have come to the Library as a copyright deposit, entered by the "author," an emissary from the Holy Land at the clerk's office of the District Court of the United States for the Southern District of New York.

Jachiel Bar-Joseph, *Map of the Journey of the Children of Israel. . .*, New York, 1840.
Geography and Map Division.

He holds an open book in his hands. The first published American engraving of a contemporary Jew, the Library's copy of this rare print is in pristine condition.

Maps

Rarer still is a map of the Holy Land published in New York seven years later, in 1840, by another Jerusalem emissary, Jachiel Bar-Joseph, *Map of the Journey of the Children of Israel from Egypt Through the Desert to the Holy Land and the Dividing of the Same into Twelve Tribes, by their Lawgiver, Moses.*

Lithographed by G. Endicott, 152 Fulton Street, New York, the map is all in Hebrew and shows the Holy Land dotted with cities, towns, and tiny historical vignettes. At the banks of the Jordan are the twelve stones placed there by the Children of Israel; above it is the altar erected by Joshua; and the tomb of Rachel is marked by a black monument. Cities are symbolized by buildings which identify them as royal, large, small, or city of refuge. The cartouche in the upper left-hand corner depicts a turbaned Rabbi Bar-Joseph, a tallit draped around his shoulder, holding a copy of *Hok L'Yisrael*, a biblical commentary beloved by the Sefardi Jews. At the lower right-hand side, Moses stands, rays of light shining from his head, his staff lifted toward the wanderers in the desert, with the biblical verse, "Turn ye northward" (Deuteronomy, 2:3).

The illustrations below the map give it special importance and impact. Beginning on the left, the seal of the Ashkenazi community of Jerusalem depicts the Wailing Wall and the mosques of Omar and Al-Aqsa, with the biblical verses, "Zion shall be redeemed through justice and those that return by righteousness" (Isaiah, 1:27) and "If I forget thee, O Jerusalem" (Psalm 137:8). An English description reads: "This seal is the impression of the German Sinagogue [sic] in Jerusalem." To the right, in Sefardi Hebrew script, is a receipt for payment of a debt, written in Alexandria, Egypt, in 1831, and signed in the customary florid style by three Sefardi rabbis, and Bar-Joseph's printed description reads: "Rabbi Jonoth Neron and his two associates recommendations." It is of course no such thing. Bar-Joseph had the document with him and used it for his own purposes, certain that no one would ever examine its contents. Further to the right is a document in Arabic dated 1833, extending protection to three Austrian Jewish pilgrims, and described as "Certificate from the Basham of Jerusalem." At furthest right are displayed two sides of a shekel coin, on one side imprinted "shekel of Israel," on the other "Of the holy Jerusalem," and to its right, "Impression of the Seal from the Portuguese Sinagogue [sic] in Jerusalem," a Star of David with the quotation from Isaiah, 1:27 repeated.

We may surmise that Bar-Joseph was not one of those many pious and selfless emissaries who travelled the world to seek aid for their impoverished Holy Land communities. Very likely, he represented only himself, and his reputation may have preceded him, for the Shearith Israel Congregation of New York refused him help on November 3, 1839, but on July 23, 1840, allotted him twenty dollars to assure his departure to Europe.

The poor of Jerusalem may not have benefitted from Bar-Joseph's stay in New York, but the Library of Congress did. It now holds one of the rarest items of Holy Land cartography, perhaps a unique copy, which came to it, as the map indicates, as a copyright deposit.

Entered according to Act of Congress in the year 1840 by Rabbi Jachiel Bar-Joseph in the Clerk's Office of the District Court of the United States for the Southern District of New York.

In the vault of the Library's Geography and Map Division is a unique map of a section of the Holy Land, an illuminated manuscript map, *Plan of the German American Colony near Haifa*, "surveyed and drawn by Jacob Schumacher citizen of the U.S. of N.A." In ink and watercolor, the map measures 74 by 105 cm. and is inscribed to the "Hon. Sh. Schurz, Senator." The reference is to Carl Schurz, Senator from Missouri, the first German American to enter the U.S. Senate. Jacob Schumacher, a resident of Zanesville, Ohio, was the first American "Tempelgesellschaft" (The Temple Society) adherent to settle in Palestine, arriving there in 1869, for the founding of its colony in Haifa. The Templers, a Lutheran pietistic, evangelical adventist group anticipating the imminent second coming of Jesus, established four colonies in the Holy Land during the nineteenth century

Jacob Schumacher, "citizen of the U.S. of N.A." (as he describes himself) and a Christian religious enthusiast, settled in the Holy Land, and produced this *Plan of the German American Colony near Haifa,* for the Templers, an adventist religious group which established four settlements of adherents in the Holy Land to await the imminent second coming of the Messiah. Note the ships *Uncle Sam* and *New York* flying the American flag.

Jacob Schumacher, *Plan of the German American Colony near Haifa,* 1873.
Geography and Map Division.

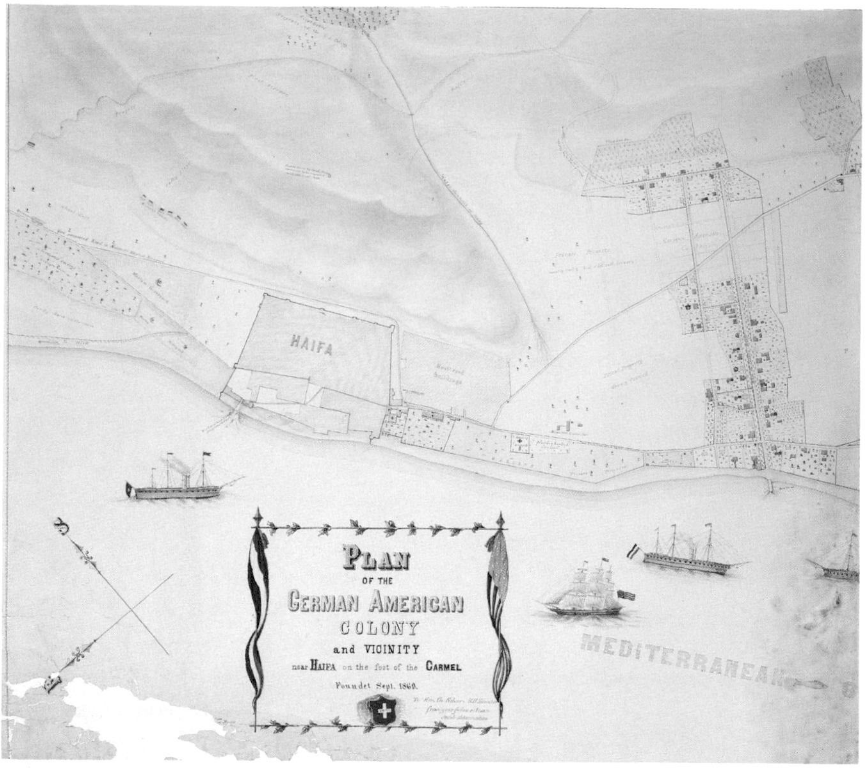

to await his arrival. Schumacher, serving as the architect of the Haifa settlement, was elected its head. The group had difficulty in getting residence rights from the Turkish govenment, and we may surmise that the *Plan* for a German American colony was sent to Senator Schurz, to solicit political support. To underscore the American nature of the enterprise, Schumacher drew two ships flying American flags off the Palestine coast, the *Uncle Sam* and the *New York.* He may well have been helped in the preparation of the plan and the drawing of the map by his sixteen-year-old son, Gottlieb, who later became a leading explorer, cartographer, architect, and archaeologist of the Holy Land.

Love of Zion

The love of Zion in the hearts of American Jews was given ideological and practical expression in the last decades of the nineteenth century when the *Hovevei Zion* (Lovers of Zion) movement took root in the Jewish immigrant community. Support for colonizing the ancient homeland was expressed through ideological pronouncement, philanthropic endeavor, and personal participation. From the rich store of early American Zionist material, we choose a manuscript and a pamphlet.

By vocation, Ralph B. Raphael was a manufacturer of fine hair jewelry; by avocation, he was a writer for the early American Hebrew periodical press. In such periodicals as Zev Schur's *Ha-Pisgah,* he addressed himself to contemporary issues confronting the East European Jewish immigrant community in America.

Raphael, a resident of Pittsburgh, was an early member of the American *Hovevei Zion* movement which, though small in number in the 1880s and 1890s, made a significant contribution to Hebrew culture in America and laid a foundation for the following century's Zionist activities. The American Lovers of Zion published periodicals and organized the first modern Hebrew schools in America, but the center of their devotion was the growing *yishuv* (the pre-State Jewish community of Palestine) of pioneers who were founding agricultural colonies in Palestine and who declared themselves the vanguard of a mass return to the soil of the ancient homeland.

In 1893, Raphael published *She-elat Hayehudim* (The Jewish Questions), an early Zionist tract, part polemic and part vision. It argued that the only place the Jewish nation could live in peace and security, in well-being, and dignity, the only place its spiritual life could be renewed and enhanced, was Zion. Only through life in the Holy Land reconstituted as an autonomous Jewish commonwealth, Raphael argued, can a solution be found to the endemic anti-Semitism which afflicts Jews even in the enlightened West, even in free democratic America.

Raphael is aware of the objections that have been raised to the Zionist dream, but he is confident that they can be overcome. He points to the already established agricultural colonies in Palestine, drawing an idealized picture of life on the soil, of entire families joined in an enterprise which straightens their backs, lifts their hearts, and transforms their very being. He hails the *halutzim* (pioneers) as the creators of the new Jew and a new society. For such an individual and such a society, no problem is too difficult, no challenge too great.

Let us imagine, he proposes, that the idea of resettling the land wins the majority of Jewish hearts and wins supporters among the nations; that Jews of America will buy land for those who wish to settle, and Jews in other countries will soon join in the enterprise. To the degree that Jews will settle on the land and make it flourish, the nations look with favor on the enterprise.

The nations of the world will appoint a commission of twelve judges to hear the claims of the various contenders for the Holy Land. Catholics, Greek Orthodox, Protestants, Moslems, and Jews make their presentations and pleas. After due deliberation the commission decides: *Palestine is for the Jewish people.* Above all other considerations, the enterprise and accomplishment of the new Jewish farm colonists "who have come to the land of their fathers . . . settling it to earn their livelihood by the sweat of their brow" will have persuaded the judges.

Raphael sets forth his political philosophy in seventeen points which constitute the commission's decision. Among them are:

The Turkish government is to be sovereign in all external matters;

Christian colonies may remain so long as they do not disturb the peace of the land;

Christian immigration is to be restricted, to be determined by Jews;

A Christian commission is to supervise the holy places;

A special Jewish agency is to be appointed by the nations to facilitate Jewish immigration;

The Jews may organize a militia to keep the peace;

For all internal matters, the Jews are to organize a republican form of government, which is to meet in Jerusalem;

The Jewish government may mint its own coinage, levy taxes, and elect a president who will serve for a five-year term;

The representative body, called the Sanhedria, is to be elected for a ten-year term and will be empowered to govern;

The president, vice-president and members of the Sanhedria must be Jews by birth.

Published at the Newark press of Ephraim Deinard, who retained the second half of Raphael's manuscript, the two-volume manuscript in the author's own hand came to the Library of Congress as part of one of the Deinard Collections acquired by the Library through the year 1920.

Deinard had a hand in an attempt by American Jews at the end of the nineteenth century to colonize Palestine. He was a founder of *Shavei Zion* No. 2 of New York, an organization to purchase land and establish a colony of American Jews in the Holy Land. The father of the *Shavei Zion* movement was Adam Rosenberg. Born in Baltimore in 1858 and raised in Germany, he returned at the age of twenty, studied law, and began to practice, but the cause of Zion rebuilt soon became his vocation as well as avocation.

Based on the Russian *Dorshe Zion* Society, its American counterpart proposed, according to its bylaws, published in Yiddish: a membership of 500, each member to contribute 200 dollars in annual payments of 40 dollars or weekly payments of a dollar to purchase land on which to establish themselves as an agricultural colony. Within three months, a second group was formed in New York, then others in Boston and Montreal. In fulfillment of the dream of life upon the land in a Zion rebuilt, immigrants in America were ready to relocate again. In June 1891, Rosenberg travelled with two colleagues to Palestine to buy land, and building began, but poor planning and inept relations with the Turkish authorities brought the project to an early end.

A memento of this first American enterprise at Zionism, with aliyah and settlement on the land, remains:

Constitution of the Shavei Zion Society No. 2, organized in New York, the first day of Sivan, 5651, June 7, 1891. "If I forget thee O, Jerusalem, may my right hand lose its strength."

This, too, came with the Deinard collections, and, as Deinard's rubber-stamped inscription attests, it was originally intended to become part of the Library in Jerusalem, but like the members of *Shavei Zion,* it never left the Land of Promise for the Promised Land.

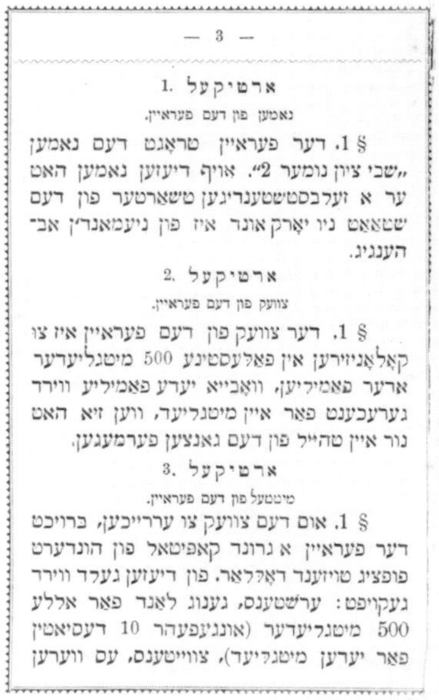
— 3 —

ארטיקעל 1.

נאמען פון דעם פעראיין.

§ 1. דער פעראיין טראָגט דעם נאמען „שבי ציון נומער 2“. אויף דיעזען נאמען האט ער א זעלבסטשטענדיגען טשארטער פון דעם שטאאט ניו יארק אונד איז פון ניעמאנד'ן אב־הענגיג.

ארטיקעל 2.

צוועק פון דעם פעראיין.

§ 1. דער צוועק פון דעם פעראיין איז צו קאלאָניזירען אין פאלעסטינע 500 מיטגליעדער אדער פאמיליען, וואָבייא יעדע פאמיליע ווירד גערעכענט פאר איין מיטגליעד, ווען זיא האט נור איין טהייל פון דעם גאנצען פערמעגען.

ארטיקעל 3.

מיטטעל פון דעם פעראיין.

§ 1. אום דעם צוועק צו עררייכען, ברויכט דער פעראיין א גרונד קאפיטאל פון הונדערט פופציג טויזענד דאָללאר. פון דיעזען געלד ווירד געקויפט: ערשטענס, גענוג לאנד פאר אללע 500 מיטגליעדער (אונגעפעהר 10 דעסיאטין פאר יעדען מיטגליעד), צווייטענס, עס ווערען

Among the many constitutions of religious, charitable, fraternal and cultural Jewish organizations in the United States held in the Hebraic Section is this of a society of Jews in New York, whose purpose was to establish and settle in a cooperative agricultural colony in the land of Israel. Articles 2 and 3 of its constitution, found on the page before us, state its purpose, "to colonize Palestine"; the number of its membership, 500 families; its capitalization, $150,000. The language of the constitution is Yiddish.

Constitution of the Shavei Zion Society No. 2, New York, 1891.
Hebraic Section.

HOLY WORDS

In 1766 there appeared in New York a prayer book entirely in English, *Prayers for Sabbath, Rosh-Hashanah, and Kippur, or The Sabbath, the Beginning of the Year, and the Day of Atonement . . . According to the Order of the Spanish and Portuguese Jews,* translated by Isaac Pinto, and "for him printed by John Holt in New York A.M. 5526." Excepting only a fifty-two-page

Evening Service of Roshashanah, and Kippur, published five years earlier in New York, it is the first published translation of the liturgy into English for synagogue use. The 1761 *Evening Service* lists neither translator, nor reason for the translation, but in this volume, Pinto, who was the translator of both, explains:

[Hebrew] being imperfectly understood by many, by some, not at all; it has been necessary to translate our Prayers, in the Language of the Country wherein it hath pleased the divine Providence to appoint our Lot. In Europe, the Spanish and Portuguese Jews have a Translation in Spanish, which as they generally understand, may be sufficient, but that not being the Case in the British Dominions in America, has induced me to attempt a Translation in English.

Not until 1770, four years later, was a prayer book with an English translation published in London, whose Jewish community was more than ten times the number of all American Jewry. Acculturation in the New World was swifter and more complete than in the Old.

Pinto, an English Jew, demonstrated his American loyalty as a signatory to resolutions favoring the Nonimportation Agreement, one of America's earliest acts of defiance against England. He was, as Ezra Stiles describes him, "a learned Jew at New York," who on his death in 1791, was extolled in this obituary in a New York newspaper:

Mr. Pinto was truly a moral and social friend. His conversation was instructive, and his knowledge of mankind was general. Though of the Hebrew nation, his liberality was not circumscribed by the limits of that church. He was well versed in several of the foreign languages. He was a staunch friend at the liberty of his country. His intimates in his death have lost an instructive and entertaining companion; his relations, a firm friend; and the literary world, an historian and philosopher.

In 1828, acculturation had made such progress in the New World that Abraham Israel Henriques Bernal, a religious functionary, teacher and scribe, found it necessary to translate into English the *Prayers said by the Spanish and Portuguese Jews during the Ceremony of Washing the Dead by Rabbi Hillel of Blessed Memory.* A small delicately written manuscript in Hebrew

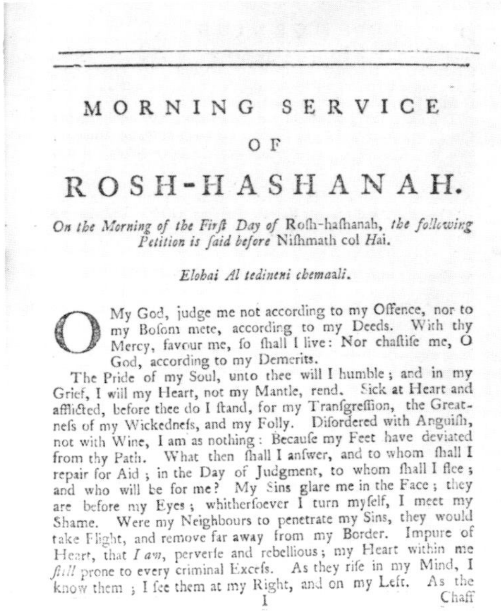

MORNING SERVICE

OF

ROSH-HASHANAH.

On the Morning of the First Day of Rosh-hashanah, *the following Petition is said before* Nishmath col Hai.

Elohai Al tedineni chemaali.

O My God, judge me not according to my Offence, nor to my Bosom mete, according to my Deeds. With thy Mercy, favour me, so shall I live: Nor chastise me, O God, according to my Demerits.

The Pride of my Soul, unto thee will I humble; and in my Grief, I will my Heart, not my Mantle, rend. Sick at Heart and afflicted, before thee do I stand, for my Transgression, the Greatness of my Wickedness, and my Folly. Disordered with Anguish, not with Wine, I am as nothing: Because my Feet have deviated from thy Path. What then shall I answer, and to whom shall I repair for Aid; in the Day of Judgment, to whom shall I flee; and who will be for me? My Sins glare me in the Face; they are before my Eyes; whithersoever I turn myself, I meet my Shame. Were my Neighbours to penetrate my Sins, they would take Flight, and remove far away from my Border. Impure of Heart, that *I am*, perverse and rebellious; my Heart within me *still* prone to every criminal Excess. As they rise in my Mind, I know them; I see them at my Right, and on my Left. As the

1 Chaff

The first Jewish liturgical publication in America was *Form of Prayer Performed at Jews Synagogue,* New York, 1760; the second, *Evening Service of Rosh-Hashanah and Kippur,* New York 1761; ours, the third, *Prayers for Sabbath, Rosh-Hashanah and Kippur,* is the most distinguished for it is a far more substantial work than the earlier, and because it credits the translator, Isaac Pinto, a teacher of languages and merchant of New York. It is virtually certain that he was the translator of the preceding volumes as well. All appeared before the first prayer book with an English translation was published in London in 1770. The Library purchased its copy in 1947 for 250 dollars. Forty years later a copy brought over one hundred times that amount at a public auction in New York.

Prayers for Sabbath, Rosh-Hashanah and Kippur, translated by Isaac Pinto, New York, 5526 (1766).
Rare Book and Special Collections Division.

This handbook is to be used by a member of a *Hevra Kadisha* (Holy Burial Society), which prepares the body of the deceased for burial. This manuscript manual written in Hebrew with an English translation contains both the pertinent instructions for the proper ritual preparation of the body and the prayers which accompany it. The scribe, Abraham de Jacob Israel Henriques Bernal, wrote it in Kingston, Jamaica, for D. K. Da Costa of that community, whose name appears on the cover. Bernal later served congregations in Philadelphia and Louisville, Kentucky. It is opened to the double title page, in Hebrew and English.

Rabbi Hillel, *Prayers said by the Spanish and Portuguese Jews during the Ceremony of Washing the Dead,* translated into English by A. I. H. Bernal (Scribe), Kingston, Jamaica, 5588 (1828).
Hebraic Section.

תפלות החולה

Kranken-Gebete.

Dieses Gebet soll nicht in Gegenwart von Frauen oder kleinen Kindern gebetet werden, indem es den Kranken zu sehr angreife und Nachtheil bringen könnte.

מודה אני לפניך יי אלהי ואלהי אבותי שרפואתי
ומיתתי בידך · יהי רצון מלפניך יי אלהי
ואלהי אבותי שתרפאני רפואה שלמה ויעלה
זכרוני ותפלתי לפניך כתפלות חזקיהו
בחליו ואם קרבה עת פקודתי למות תהא
מיתתי כפרה על כל חטאים ועונות ופשעים
שחטאתי ושעויתי ושפשעתי לפניך מיום
היותי על האדמה עד היום הזה ותן חלקי בגן
עדן וזכני לעולם הבא הצפון לצדיקים ותודיעני
אורח חיים שובע שמחות את פניך נעימות
בימינך נצח אמן:

A collection of prayers to be said by those seeking healing was published in New York (in Hebrew with instructions in German) by the *Hevra Ahim Rahamim* (Society of the Brothers of Mercy), organized in 1851. Open to a prayer asking God to "send full healing" or a place in paradise. The German instruction warns that this petition must not be said in the presence of women or small children for this could cause too great distress.

T'filat ha-Holeh, Kranken Gebete (Prayers for the Sick), New York, 1854.
Hebraic Section.

and English, it contains not only the prayers to be recited by the *Hevra Kadisha* (Holy Burial Society) but also instructions for the ritual preparation of the body for burial. Membership in this society was traditionally reserved for learned, pious, and respected members of the community, so that if a translation of the instructions and the liturgy was needed, it speaks of the poor state of Jewish knowledge in the Americas. The manual was written in Kingston, Jamaica, for D. K. Da Costa, a member of its most distinguished family. "Abr. of I. H. Bernal" is found among the subscribers of that city for Isaac Leeser's *Instruction in the Mosaic Religion* published in 1830. Bernal later went to the United States and in 1847 was the Hebrew teacher of Congregation Mikveh Israel in Philadelphia, and three years later was employed as a religious functionary of the Louisville, Kentucky, congregation.

A small pamphlet, *Kranken Gebete* (Prayers for the Sick), in Hebrew with instructions in German, issued by the Society of the Brothers of Mercy in New York in 1854, is among the rarest of American Jewish liturgical publications. A prayer, to be said by the sick person himself, carries with it the warning, "This prayer should not be pronounced in the presence of women or small children, for it may so upset the sick person as to cause him injury." It reads in part,

The prayer book prepared for and published by Temple Emanuel, New York, appropriately has the temple embossed in gold on its front cover.

Seder T'fillah, The Order of Prayer for Divine Service, revised by Dr. L. Merzbacher, Rabbi of the Temple Emanuel, 1855; second edition, revised by Dr. S. Adler, New York, 1863.
Hebraic Section.

I acknowledge before you, my God, and God of my fathers, that my healing and my death are in your hand. May it be thy will that you send me a full healing, and may my prayer rise before you as the prayer of King Hezekiah in his illness. But if my time has come, let my death serve as an atonement for all my sins and transgressions . . . from the time I was placed upon the earth to the present day. May my place be Paradise and make me worthy of the World to Come which is reserved for thy righteous . . . Amen

Three Reform prayer books appeared in the 1850s, each more radical than its predecessor. The first, *Order of Prayer for Divine Service, Revised by Dr. Leo Merzbacher* (1810–1856), "Rabbi at the Temple Emanu-el" of New York, was published in that city in 1855. Though prepared for one of the first and leading Reform congregations in America, it is an abridged form of the traditional prayer book, with Hebrew text and facing English translation, and it is paginated from right to left. The Kol Nidre prayer is omitted, but the five services for the Day of Atonement are retained, as is the prayer for restoration of the dead, "who revivest the dead . . . and killest and restorest to life." Because it departed from tradition, it could not be used in traditional congregations; and because its revisions were slight it was not adopted by Reform congregations either, so very few copies, especially of volume 1, have survived.

In 1846, Isaac Mayer Wise began to plan a new prayer book which was to be a liturgy appropriate to the American scene, for as he explained in the *Occident* (vol. 5, p. 109) "the strength of Israel is divided, because the emigrant brings his own *Minhag* [liturgical rite] from his home." He argued that "such a cause for dissension would be obviated by a *Minhag* America." Ten years later, the projected prayer book was published in Cincinnati in two versions, the Hebrew text plus an English or a German translation, the Hebrew paginated from right to left, the vernacular from left to right. The Hebrew title is *Minhag America, T'fillot B'nai Yeshurun* (the name of his congregation); the German, *Gebet-Buch fur den offentlichen Gottesdienst und die Privat-Andacht* (Prayer Book for Public and Private Worship); and the English, simply, *The Daily Prayers.* The form of the traditional prayer book was retained, but passages which did not conform to "the wants and demands of time" were freely deleted. Thus, where the Merzbacher prayer book has "send a redeemer to their children's children," Wise changes the Hebrew *goel* (redeemer) to *geulah* (redemption) and the translation to read "bringest redemption to their descendants." It came to be known as the Wise Prayer Book, as a fitting tribute to its architect and fashioner, who saw to its publication and promoted its distribution.

Dr. David Einhorn (1809–1879) was brought to Baltimore by the Har Sinai Congregation in 1855. A year later the first section of his *Gebetbuch für Israelitische Reform Gemeinden* (Prayer Book for Jewish Reform Congregations) was published in New York, a radical departure from the traditional prayer book. The Library's copy is as issued: paper wraps are preserved, and the cover states, "Copyright secured March 22, 1856, Publication Deposited April 15, 1856." Its main language is German, its pagination is from left to right, and its changes are both substantial and substantive. The traditional rubrics are dispensed with, and special prayers reflecting more the tenor of the age than the traditions of the faith are inserted. Two years later, in 1858, the completed work was published in Baltimore with *Olat Tamid* (Eternal Offering) added to its title. The tradi-

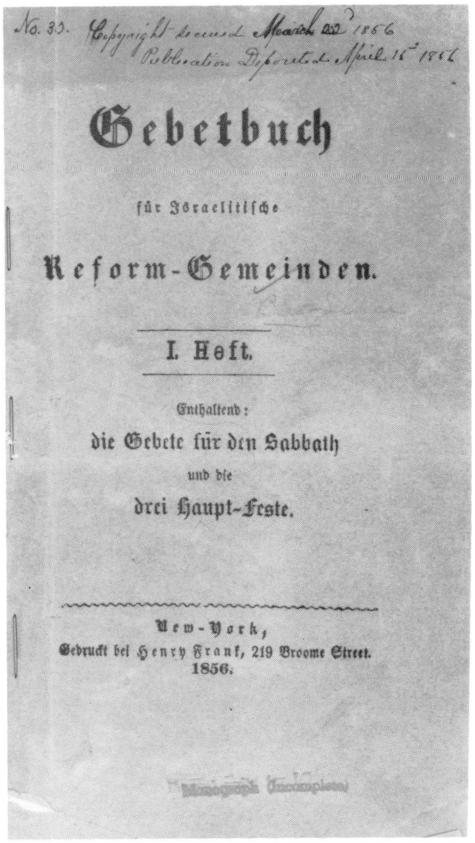
No. 83. Copyright secured March 22 1856
Publication Deposited April 15 1856

Gebetbuch

für Israelitische

Reform-Gemeinden.

I. Heft.

Enthaltend:

die Gebete für den Sabbath

und die

drei Haupt-Feste.

New-York,

Gedruckt bei Henry Frank, 219 Broome Street.

1856.

Monograph (Incomplete)

A pamphlet of prayers prepared by Rabbi David Einhorn for his Har Sinai Congregation, Baltimore. Unlike the prayer book which Merzbacher prepared for Temple Emanuel a year earlier, which is an abridgement and revision of the traditional Hebrew prayer book, the liturgy of Einhorn is a radical departure. Its language of worship is both German and Hebrew, and it is paginated from left to right. The complete text was published two years later in 1858, as *Olat Tamid.*

Gebethuch für Israelitische Reform Gemeinden, I. Heft, New York, 1856.
Hebraic Section.

סדר הגדה של פסח

מתורגם מלשון הקודש ללשון ענגליש

SERVICE FOR THE TWO FIRST NIGHTS

OF THE

PASSOVER.

IN HEBREW AND ENGLISH.

SECOND AMERICAN EDITION,

אשר הובארו לדפוס

על ידי יעקב בן שלמה : נוא־יארק :

בשנת לש.ה הבאה בירושלים רפ״ק

NEW-YORK.

PRINTED AND PUBLISHED BY J. M. JACKSON,

190 Houston St. and 203 Bowery.

5610.

The first American edition of the Passover Haggadah was published by Solomon Henry Jackson in New York in 1837. It is fitting that this second American edition be the publication of his son John M. Jackson, who succeeded his father as the Hebrew and English printer for New York's Jewish community. On the back cover Jackson announces that he can supply blank ketuboth (marriage contracts) printed to order "on parchment if required" and a family and pocket luach (calendar), and boasts that his prices are "as cheap as the cheapest!"

Seder Haggadah shel Pesah (*Service for the Two First Nights of the Passover*), second American edition, New York, 5610 (1850).
Hebraic Section.

tional day of mourning for the destruction of the Temple, Tisha b'Av, is turned into a day of commemoration and consecration:

> The one Temple in Jerusalem sank into the dust, in order that countless temples might arise to thy honor and glory all over the wide surface of the globe.

When Reform Judaism shaped its first official prayer book, *The Union Prayer Book,* the model chosen was Einhorn's *Olat Tamid.*

The Haggadah marked "Second American Edition" is, in a sense, the first. The first edition, so identified by its publisher S. H. Jackson, was printed in New York in 1837, and on both Hebrew and English title pages reads, "Translated into English by the late David Levy of London." No such attribution to a foreign source is found on his son's edition, which appeared in 1850, where the only credit noted is to the printer and publisher, J. M. Jackson, 190 Houston Street and 203 Bowery. The Hebrew chronogram on both reads "Next Year in Jerusalem."

A truly American note is found in a Haggadah published in New York in 1878. The text is traditional, the translation usual, but the seder table scene is new. It shows a turbaned father and a prim mother with the wise son, a *kippah* (skullcap) on his head and reading from a book, at their side. Across from them, the simple son sits bareheaded, as does the one "who knows not how to ask," while the wicked son, bareheaded, is leaning back on his chair, smoking a cigarette. Haggadah illustration is commentary.

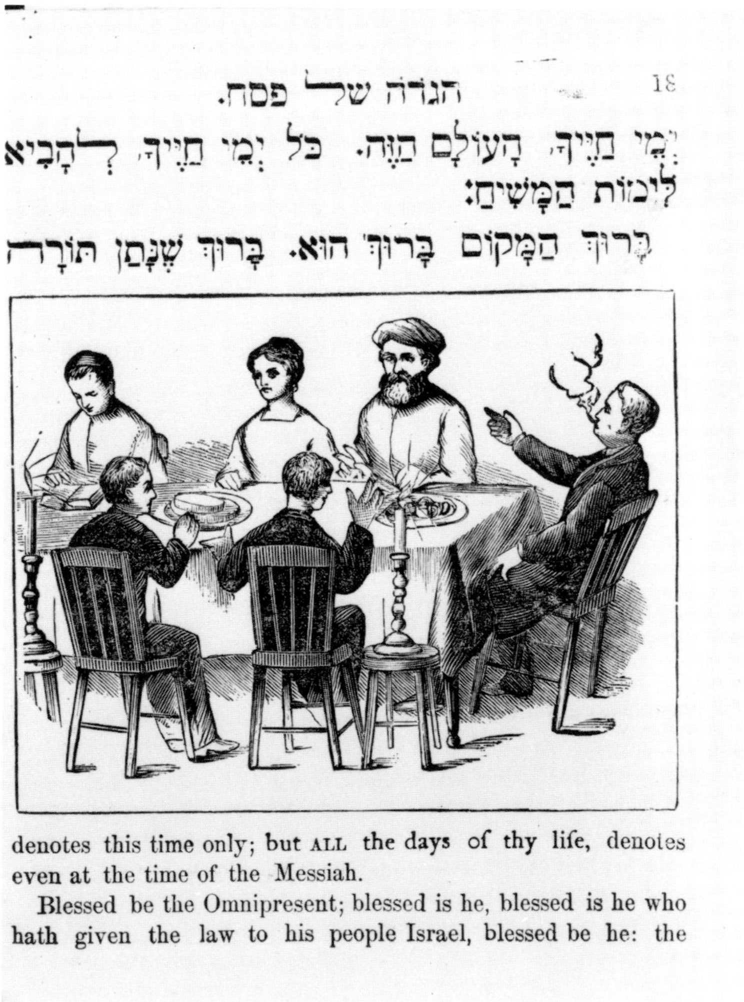

הגדה של פסח. 18

יְמֵי חַיֶּיךָ. הָעוֹלָם הַזֶּה. כָּל יְמֵי חַיֶּיךָ. לְהָבִיא לִימוֹת הַמָּשִׁיחַ:

בָּרוּךְ הַמָּקוֹם בָּרוּךְ הוּא. בָּרוּךְ שֶׁנָּתַן תּוֹרָה

denotes this time only; but ALL the days of thy life, denotes even at the time of the Messiah.

Blessed be the Omnipresent; blessed is he, blessed is he who hath given the law to his people Israel, blessed be he: the

Although the title page claims in large bold capital letters **WITH NEW ILLUSTRATIONS,** the only new one is the one shown here. An American family at the Seder table presents a new version of the depiction of the "four sons" described in the Haggadah. The wise son, kippah (skull cap) on head, is looking at the Haggadah before him; the simple son, or the backward one, is thumbing his nose and getting his finger burned by the candle; and the wicked son, bareheaded, his chair tilted back, is smoking a cigarette.

Seder Haggadah L'Pesah (Form and Relation of the Two First Nights of the Feast of Passover), New York, 1878.
Hebraic Section.

17

FROM SEA TO SHINING SEA

BY MIDNINETEENTH CENTURY the American Jewish community stretched clear across the continent from New York to San Francisco. More than one hundred congregations and an even larger number of charitable organizations served its needs. One monthly, *The Occident,* established by Isaac Leeser in 1843, and three weeklies, *The Asmonean* in New York, *The Israelite* in Cincinnati, and *The Gleaner* in San Francisco, reported its activities. News comprised only a small part of the reading matter, the greater

The masthead of the Jewish weekly, *The Asmonean,* of November 23, 1849. It was founded and published by English-born New York businessman Robert Lyon. It displays the American flag, on it a shield with the Star of David, in the star a lion, and above and below a wolf and ox, animals resident in the peaceable kingdom which Isaiah envisioned. The Hebrew legend is from Ecclesiastes: "Two are better than one, and a Threefold Cord is not quickly broken."

The Asmonean, New York, November 23, 1849. General Collection.

part being devoted to educational and polemical articles, and to occasional fiction and poetry.

In the first issue of *The Asmonean,* "For the Week ending Friday, October 26, 1849," publisher Robert Lyon, an English-born New York businessman, wrote to his subscribers:

> In the circular announcing our intention to publish the Journal, we set forth that the Asmonean would be devoted to the advocacy of a congregational Union of the Israelites of the United States, and the general dissemination of information relating to the people. That its columns would be open to all and every communication appertaining to our Societies, our Congregations, our Literature and Our Religion. That all Foreign and Domestic News would be collected up to the latest moment prior to going to press, and that all matters of public interest, would be temperately commented on.

Such turned out to be a true description of the journal's contents during its decade of publication, until the death of its publisher in 1858. From 1852 until his departure to Cincinnati in 1854, Isaac Mayer Wise, then in Albany, served as the journal's coeditor.

Not long after Wise arrived in the Queen City to serve as rabbi of Congregation B'nai Jeshurun, he decided to undertake the publication and editorship of a new weekly, which he called *The Israelite*. In his *Reminiscences,* he describes the tribulations of founding the journal:

As early as the month of May I began to take steps towards establishing a Jewish weekly. I wrote very many letters and received very glowing promises, which, however, were never kept. I began to look for some merciful individual who would . . . publish a weekly under my direction; but such a man was not to be found. . . . Finally I came across a visionary, Dr. Schmidt, the owner of the evening paper the *Republican* . . . [who] accepted my promise that I would make good all losses at the end of the first year. . . . I locked myself in my room from two o'clock in the afternoon till four in the morning, and wrote a prospectus . . .

I promised Judaism a sharp weapon. I promised progress, enlightenment, spiritual striving, a fearless organ. . . . I visited . . . M., where about ten Jewish families lived, to whom I gave the prospectus. Seven of them declared they could not read

THE ISRAELITE.

A weekly Periodical, devoted to the Religion, History and Literature of the Israelites,

PUBLISHED BY
CHAS. F. SCHMIDT,
OFFICE–NO. 21, EAST THIRD STREET.

SUBSCRIPTION TERMS.
Is published every Friday afternoon at the price of $3,00 per annum, payable invariably in advance.
Subscribers out of Cincinnati can receive the paper through the mail by sending in $3,00.

יְהִי אוֹר
"LET THERE BE LIGHT"

EDITED BY
ISAAC M. WISE,
DR. M. LILIENTHAL, CORRESP. EDITOR.

ADVERTISING TERMS;
One square, one time..$ 75 One square, one month $1 50
One square, two times. 1 00 One square, six months 4 00
One square, one year.....$6 00
Displayed advertisements half more than the above rates.

Vol. I. Cincinnati, O., October 27, 5615 A. M., 1854 A. C. No. 16.

(Continued from No. 15.)

THE CATASTROPHE AT EGER.

A NARRATIVE OF THE SIXTEENTH CENTURY.

Chapter V.

The proud mansion of Solomon Oppenheim contained this day sad looking inmates. The servants walked about upon their toes, so as not to cause the least noise. The countenance of old Hayim was pale, sad, and bewildered; his voice was low, and sounded more like weeping than speaking, his eyes were dim and red, evidencing want of rest and falling tears. The business apartments were equally still. The clerks wrote, read, or were otherwise occupied without being told what to do. Solomon Oppenheim silently sat in his room, occasionally looking anxiously in the street as if impatiently waiting for somebody. Finally the door opened and Rabbi Simon Ropha (the physician) stepped in. "You wish to see me, Mr. Oppenheim," said the doctor inquiringly. "Yes," was the reply, "I wish to know what you think of the disease of my son, and I am desirous to hear your candid opinion, not as physicians usually give to the relatives of their patients." After some hesitation the doctor replied, "Your son is dangerously sick; he suffers under the influence of a violent fever, the cause of which is yet a profound mystery to me, and therefore I have not yet succeeded in detecting the proper remedy. But," the doctor continued, "let us step up, and see, how the patient feels this morning." The two men went silently upstairs into the sick chamber of Hillel Oppenheim who glowing with fever, and apparently unconscious of his malady uttered unintelligible sentences and fragments.

While the physician observes his patient, we must cast a glance into the house of David Lœve. Jacob Lœve ignorant of the precarious state of health of Hillel, had gone up to the Baal Shem, asking him whether his last charm had the desired effect upon Esther's heart and affections. The Baal Shem instead of replying, took Jacob's hand, and led him directly to the room of Esther, which he entered without any farther ceremony. Esther welcomed her guests by offering them her right hand. The Baal Shem started back, and exclaimed, "God forbid, that I touch the hand of a woman." Esther well aware of this maxim of the pious, laughed and offered him her chair. The Baal Shem said again, "Heaven forbid, that I sit upon the chair of a woman, I do not like to bathe again to-day."—"Well then," said Esther, "what shall I do for you?"—"You shall become my wife," said the Baal Shem without ceremony, "because you love me."—"I can not be your wife," replied Esther with a smile, "because I do not love you."—"Where is the power of your secret art?" Jacob remarked ironically. The poor Baal Shem was not a little embarrassed, but was happily relieved by the appearance of a servant, who stated that an old man was outside who insisted upon seeing the Baal Shem instantly. Before a reply could be made Hayim, the old servant of Oppenheim, was in the room, and without paying the least attention to the surprise of Jacob, or waiting for permission to speak, he advanced towards the Baal Shem, and said, "Rabbi Laibish, I am the child of honest Jewish parents, and have been for twenty years an honest servant in the house of Oppenheim,"—Esther looked surprised at her brother—"but now," the old man continued, "Hillel, the son of my master, is dangerously sick." Esther sat down in her chair, and covered her face with her two hands. Jacob leaned over her whispering words unintelligible to the rest of the company. "You, Rabbi Laibish," the servant continued, "you are renowned as a mighty Baal Shem, you must know, whether the son of my master will recover or not; and I pray humbly, to tell me, if you know it." After having gone through the usual spell of disagreeable gestures, the Baal Shem replied in a grave and solemn tone, "Thus saith the Lord, 'Thou shalt not come down from that bed on which thou art gone up, but shalt surely die.'" (ii. Kings i. 4.) Hayim fell upon the chair standing close by him, almost fainting. Jacob gnashing his teeth, clenching his fists, and exclaiming most violently, "Believe him not, he is an impostor," he attempted to advance towards the Baal Shem; but Esther had clung her arms around his neck, and Jacob could not advance. The young man stood still, Hayim retired, but Esther did not release her brother, until her head and arms dropped down, and she laid unconscious in the arms of her brother. The terrified young man laid his fainting sister upon a sofa, and left the room to bring some medical assistance. Meanwhile the Baal Shem said seven times forward and again seven times backward, "I hope for thy salvation, O Lord;" and when Jacob came with water and restoratives, the Baal Shem told him, that he must stand still until he had repeated the verse said seven times more, forward and backward, then she would surely awake. Jacob casting a despicable look on the Baal Shem, applied the remedies, and Esther recovered her senses. When first opening her eyes, she asked, "Jacob, will he die?" Jacob, bidding the Baal Shem to leave the room who obeyed instantly, told his sister all the stories he knew of the Baal Shem, in order to relieve her mind, in which he did not succeed notwithstanding the influence he exercised on his sister and his proficiency in the art of persuasion. The poor girl trembled for the life of her lover, and would have done so, had the Baal Shem been silent.

Solomon Oppenheim and Rabbi Simon Ropha still sat at the bed side of Hillel, when Hayim came in, resembling more a corpse than a living creature. Death and despair were depicted in his troubled countenance. Unable to sustain himself any longer in an erect position he fell down at the feet of Solomon. Both men assisted him, and after some trouble they succeeded in placing him on a chair and restoring him so far, that he shortly spoke. The old man faithfully confessed what he had done on his own accord, and repeated literally the dreadful message of the Baal Shem. Solomon turned pale, the doctor looked carefully upon him; but it took him only a few moments to rise from his chair, and walking the room with his arms crossed over his breast, he said to the doctor, "My enemies are very mean and contemptible, and Hayim is an inconsiderate fool." This was as an electric shock upon the nervous system of Hayim; he looked round the room, and did not know what to say. Solomon turned to the doctor, told him, that he was obliged to attend some important business, and that he desired the doctor to inform him by this evening, whether he could leave for Prague by to-morrow; then he retired. The doctor took Hayim into another room, and gave him such a thorough scolding, that the poor old fellow forgot every word of the Baal Shem. After Hayim was thus cured of his cabalistic malady, the doctor inquired of him, if he knew whether Hillel was in love. "He did not tell me a word of it," said Hayim with a face as honest as ever was assumed by a stupid individual. "This is no reply to my question," the doctor remarked somewhat out of patience. "Did you not observe Hillel to have bestowed more attention upon one young woman than another?" Hayim considered for some time, then said, "Yes, I observed; he always speaks when attacked by the fever, of two lovers besides him, then he talks of duels, murder, soldiers, and other stupid things. Yes, yes doctor, he must be in love, I am not as stupid as you think." The doctor suppressing his impatience continued to question Hayim, if he could not remember, whether Hillel had any intimate acquaintance with a young woman, or that he was in love with one? "Of course do I know it," Hayim said with a self-satisfied mien. "Well, then tell me," the doctor urged. "I have a child," said Hayim with a stupid smile, "you have never seen the like; she can read and write as good as you, so help me Heaven, and she can sing and play the harp, as sure as I am the child of honest Jewish parents, and she is as beautiful as mother Sarah was"—"And has she two lovers?" the doctor interrupted him. "Two?" said Hayim, "Two lovers? What do you say? Ten, twenty, a hundred lovers she has, the whole congregation is in love with her; every young man wishes to have her for a wife."—"And do you know," the doctor asked hastily, "that Hillel is in love with her?"—"Of course do I," said Hayim. "But how do you know it," the doctor inquired. "Just listen," said Hayim, "and I will prove it to you, that Hillel must be in love with my child. When I was young I was a pupil of Rabbi Joseph, you knew Rabbi Joseph—he was an old man with a large cane in his hand, and used to wear a satin gown. Well then, Rabbi Joseph taught me an easy method to find out the unknown by what I know, he said he learned it of an old rabbi who was a Baal Shem, and now I always find the unknown by what is known to me in the self-same way. So I do know that Hillel is in love with my child, and Rabbi Joseph is my witness." The doctor had lost his patience, and lifting up his cane he threatened Hayim if he did not tell him directly, how he came to his knowledge of the alledged fact. Hayim started back a few steps, and continued in hasty words, "Just let me finish, and you will be convinced, it is sure that Hillel is in love with some girl; it is also sure that all young men in this city are in love with my child; then it must be sure, that Hillel is in love with my child."—"You are an old block-head," said the doctor leaving the room; on having reached the front gate he met with Dagobert Ernst whom the doctor invited to take a walk with him, and both went off arm in arm. Hayim supposing himself to be in possession of a costly and profound secret, said to himself that Hillel should not die, if the Baal Shem said so a thousand times, and as soon as possible he went to his family to tell his daughter, that she should love Hillel and none but Hillel. He had taken a sacred oath, that he would put the doctor and the Baal Shem to shame, and that Hillel must live to be his son-in-law.

In the afternoon the doctor returned to the house of Oppenheim, and was met in the hall by Solomon. "I believe," said the doctor in a confident tone, "that the disease of your son would not be half as invincible, had he the right kind of attendance and attention. Your servants faithful as they are, still are not the best kind of nurses for the sick bed. I have a woman in my employ especially suited for such precarious cases; she is at present employed with four patients of mine; still with your permission I will have her

Founded and edited by Isaac Mayer Wise, with his rabbinic colleague Max Lilienthal as corresponding editor, *The Israelite,* "A weekly periodical, devoted to the Religion, History and Literature of the Israelites," published in Cincinnati, was the longest running Jewish periodical in the history of American Jewish journalism. Its motto: "Let There Be Light." Here we see the masthead from its October 27, 1854, issue.

The Israelite, Cincinnati, October 27, 1854.
General Collection.

English; one said that a Jewish paper was a useless commodity, and two subscribed. . . . I visited Louisville. . . . I delivered two public addresses there. I was admired by the public. . . . My prospectus was received coldly, except by the few friends of reformed tendencies, who were very enthusiastic. At the end of June we had almost five hundred subscribers . . . and began to print and mail one thousand copies. The first number appeared on the sixth of July. It contained the beginning of a novel, "The Convert," a poem, news, leading articles, my Fourth of July oration, an opening article on the institutions of Cincinnati, and miscellanea.

Two years later, in 1856, Rabbi Julius Eckman (1805–1877) of San Francisco began to publish *The Gleaner* under even more trying circumstances. Ten years earlier, he had gone to Mobile, Alabama, to serve as rabbi, but his tenure there was brief, as it was subsequently in Richmond, Charleston, and New Orleans. In 1854, he accepted the pulpit of San Francisco's Temple Emanu-El, but at the end of one year was without a position. Temperamentally unsuited to the pulpit, Eckman devoted his life to his Heptsibah Hebrew School and his weekly newspaper. As late as March 1861, he had to plead with his subscribers:

We have a number of names in our book of subscribers who receive the "Gleaner" since the issue of the first number, without receiving any remittance, whatever, for subscription. . . .

Will our subscribers try to settle in some way. If not able to pay at all, or at present, a few lines to that effect will satisfy us. . . .

We shall be glad to assent to any mode of settling, as we, in a publication like the "Gleaner" cannot adopt strict mercantile rules. We wish the paper, as a religious messenger, with all its faults, to be received religiously.

In the Passover issue of that year, Rabbi Eckman wrote of the Festival in a brief sermonette ("Our Declaration of Dependence"), commented on "Dr. Raphael's Pro-slavery Sermon," reported on two letters of appeal for funds for the poor in Jerusalem, published a scholarly letter from Dr. Elkan Cohn (rabbi of Temple Emanu-El) on Sabbath observance, with citations in Hebrew from the *Mishneh Torah*, printed a reminiscence of "San Francisco in 1849," and reported on his Religious School.

In his *California Sketches* (Nashville, 1882), O. P. Fitzgerald remembered the rabbi.

Seated in his library, enveloped in a faded figured gown, a black velvet cap on his massive head . . . Power and gentleness, childlike simplicity, and scholarliness, were curiously mingled in this man. His library was a reflex of its owner. In it were books that the great public libraries of the world could not match—block-letter folios that were almost as old as the printing art, illuminated volumes that were once the pride and joy of men who had been in their graves many generations, rabbinical lore, theology, magic, and great volumes of Hebrew literature that looked, when placed beside a modern book, like an old ducal palace along-side a gingerbread cottage of to-day.

RIGHTS AT HOME AND ABROAD

These journals were established too late to report two battles waged by American Jews for rights at home and for the security of fellow Jews abroad. Source materials on both the struggle for the Jew Bill in Maryland

and the protest against the Blood Libel in Damascus are found in the Library's holdings.

In 1776, the year the Declaration of Independence proclaimed that "all men are created equal," Maryland adopted a constitution which provided that "all persons professing the Christian religion are equally entitled to protection in their religious liberty," and required that any person appointed or elected to a public office would have to take an "oath of support and fidelity to the state . . . and a declaration of belief in the Christian religion."

The new nation established, the Constitution adopted and the Bill of Rights enacted, Solomon Etting, head of a pioneer Jewish family of Baltimore, "and others" petitioned the Maryland Assembly in 1797 "to be placed on the same footing as other good citizens." The petition was termed "reasonable," but was not acted upon, a fate which annually befell subsequent petitions. In 1804, the struggle lapsed, not to be taken up again for fourteen years. In 1818, a champion arose in the person of Thomas Kennedy, a member of the Maryland House of Delegates who—together with Ebenezer S. Thomas, Colonel William G. D. Worthington, Judge Henry M. Brackenridge, and others—waged an eight-year, often acrimonious battle. In *Speeches on the Jew Bill* by H. M. Brackenridge, Philadelphia, 1829, the author adds a footnote to his speech of 1818:

> This speech was published in a pamphlet form by the Jews of Baltimore, and widely circulated. The bill had been lost, but public attention was awakened to the subject, both in Maryland and other states, and the matter was afterwards brought before the legislature, at each succeeding session. It gained strength, and after a struggle of six or seven years, prevailed. In Baltimore, it became a *sine qua non* of the election of the delegate, to avow himself in favour of it. The speeches of Mr. Worthington, and of Mr. Tyson . . . are published in this volume. I regret I have not the speech of Mr. Kennedy, . . . the first mover, and indefatigable supporter of the bill.

Fortunately, the Library does have a copy of the Kennedy speech in pamphlet form, *Civil and Religious Privileges* (Baltimore), 1823. We cite one passage:

> What does our test law say to the Hebrews: It tells them that they shall perform all the duties, and bear all the burthens of citizens without enjoying common privileges . . . We tell them your son may be all that is wise and good, he may take the first honors at school . . . let him be as wise and patriotic as Washington, he never can represent the people in the legislature, or command them in the militia. . . . This bill ought to pass even if it was only to do justice to the long oppressed Hebrew; but it is not for their benefit alone; it is establishing a general principle . . . sanctioned by reason, by religion and by common sense . . . approved by the patriots of the revolution, sanctioned by wisdom and virtue and tested by experience . . . Let us pass this bill . . . even on a dying pillow it will comfort us to think that we have done at least one good act in our lives . . . establishing religious freedom in Maryland . . .
>
> Lay old superstition low
> Let the oppressed people go,
> To the Bill none say no,
> Aye! unanimously.

An enfranchising bill was passed in 1825 and confirmed a year later. In that year, 1826, three decades after framing the original petition, Solo-

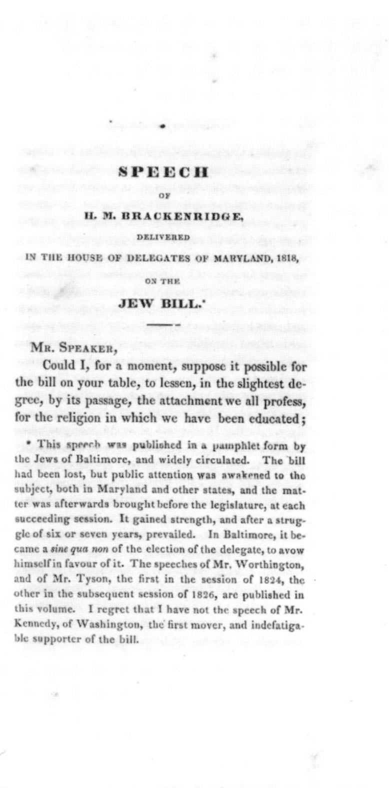

SPEECH

OF

H. M. BRACKENRIDGE,

DELIVERED

IN THE HOUSE OF DELEGATES OF MARYLAND, 1818,

ON THE

JEW BILL.*

Mr. Speaker,

Could I, for a moment, suppose it possible for the bill on your table, to lessen, in the slightest degree, by its passage, the attachment we all profess, for the religion in which we have been educated;

* This speech was published in a pamphlet form by the Jews of Baltimore, and widely circulated. The bill had been lost, but public attention was awakened to the subject, both in Maryland and other states, and the matter was afterwards brought before the legislature, at each succeeding session. It gained strength, and after a struggle of six or seven years, prevailed. In Baltimore, it became a *sine qua non* of the election of the delegate, to avow himself in favour of it. The speeches of Mr. Worthington, and of Mr. Tyson, the first in the session of 1824, the other in the subsequent session of 1826, are published in this volume. I regret that I have not the speech of Mr. Kennedy, of Washington, the first mover, and indefatigable supporter of the bill.

The pro-Jew Bill speeches of H. M. Brackenridge, W. G. D. Worthington, and John Tyson are included in this volume of Brackenridge speeches. The note by the author on his address states that it was at the time, in 1818, "published by the Jews of Baltimore, and widely circulated." This is the most direct statement we have of the involvement of the Maryland Jewish community in the promotion of the Jew Bill, which began in 1818 and was successfully concluded after eight years of persistent advocacy in 1826.

H. M. Brackenridge, *Speeches on the Jew Bill*, Philadelphia, 1829.
General Collection.

mon Etting was elected to the City Council and eventually rose to be its president.

In 1840, the head of a Franciscan monastery in Damascus disappeared. Thirteen Jews, including three rabbis, were accused of murdering the monk to use his blood for ritual purposes. Sixty-three Jewish children were taken hostage to force confessions, which were extracted under torture and later recanted by those tortured. Eventually, through the exertions of British and French Jewry, led by Sir Moses Montefiore and Adolphe Crémieux, the surviving accused—two had died under torture—were acquitted and released.

When news of this outrage reached American Jewry, it sprang into action. Meetings to protest the "Damascus Affair" were held in every Jewish community of size, and petitions were sent to the U.S. government urging the use of its good offices to effect the release of the accused undergoing torture. A full account of the meeting held at the Synagogue Mikveh Israel, Philadelphia, was published in a pamphlet, *Persecution of the Jews in the East,* Philadelphia, 1840. Reverend Isaac Leeser, the main speaker, proclaimed that "the Israelite is ever alive to the welfare of his distant brother, and sorrows with his sorrows." Abraham Hart, at thirty already a prominent publisher and communal leader, offered a resolution: "That we invite our brethren of Damascus to leave the land of persecution and torture and seek asylum in this free and happy land." Three leading Christian ministers in the City of Brotherly Love were present to express sympathy and pledge support.

The pamphlet concludes with copies of correspondence from the Jewish communities of Philadelphia and New York to President Martin Van Buren and the answering letters from the Secretary of State. The Jewish communities respectfully requested the president to instruct the American minister to Turkey and the consular officials accredited to the Pasha of Egypt "to co-operate with the Ambassadors and consuls of other powers, to procure for our accused brethren at Damascus and elsewhere an impartial trial . . . [and] to prohibit the use of torture." The State Department had already sent such instructions, and those of Secretary of State John Forsyth to David Porter, American Minister to Turkey, sent August 17, 1840, are significant:

> the President has directed me to instruct you to do everything in your power with . . . the Sultan . . . to prevent and mitigate these horrors. . . . The President is of the opinion that from no one can such generous endeavors proceed with so much propriety and effect, as from the Representative of a friendly power, whose institutions, political and civil, place on the same footing, the worshippers of God, of every faith and form, acknowledging no distinction between the Mahomedan, the Jew and the Christian.

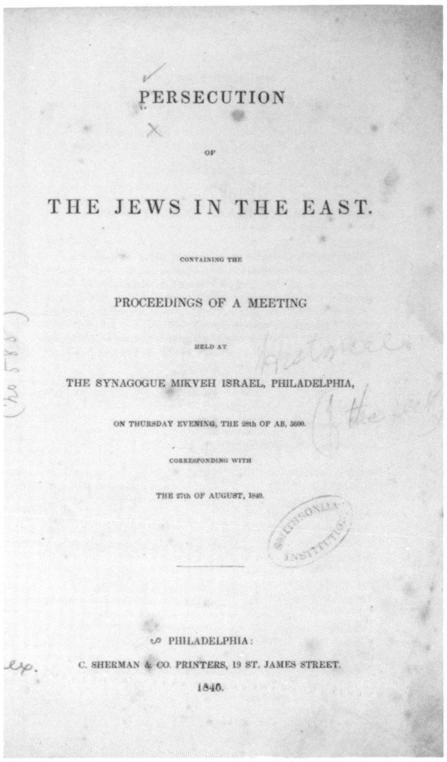
PERSECUTION

OF

THE JEWS IN THE EAST.

CONTAINING THE

PROCEEDINGS OF A MEETING

HELD AT

THE SYNAGOGUE MIKVEH ISRAEL, PHILADELPHIA,

ON THURSDAY EVENING, THE 28th OF AB, 5600.

CORRESPONDING WITH

THE 27th OF AUGUST, 1840.

PHILADELPHIA:

C. SHERMAN & CO. PRINTERS, 19 ST. JAMES STREET.

1840.

A reprint in pamphlet form of an account of a meeting held at the Mikveh Israel Congregation, Philadelphia, on August 27, 1840, to protest the persecution—imprisonment, torture, and execution—visited upon the Jewish community of Damascus, Syria, to which the *Pennsylvania Inquirer* and *Daily Courier* had devoted two-thirds of their news pages. The cause of the atrocities was the medieval blood libel accusation, which, after erupting over the centuries in England and Europe, now revived in the Near East. The intervention of the U.S. government marked one of its earliest involvements in the cause of human rights outside its borders.

Persecution of the Jews in the East, Philadelphia, 1840. General Collection.

WITHIN THE COMMUNITY

The internal communal life of Philadelphia and New York Jewry is revealed by the *Constitution and By-Laws of the Jewish Foster Home Society of the City of Philadelphia, 1855,* which was organized and run by the leading ladies of the community; and by the *Constitution and By-Laws of the Hebrew Benevolent Society of the City of New York, New York, 1865,* then in its forty-third year of service as the umbrella organization for Jewish charities.

We note with special satisfaction that the Library of Congress has a copy of *Substance of Address on Laying the Corner Stone of the Synagogue "Temime Dereck,"* New Orleans, 1866. The address was by Philip Phillips (1807–1884), who had served as a member of the House of Representatives from Alabama, 1854–55. His participation in a synagogue celebration is one of the first, if not the first, by a Jew who had served in the U.S. Congress.

Phillips's participation in Jewish life began early. At age eighteen, he was one of the founding members of the Reformed Society of Israelites in his native Charleston, South Carolina, and served as its secretary at age twenty-one. In 1856, as a resident of Washington, D.C., he contributed ten dollars to the city's Hebrew Congregation towards purchase of a Torah scroll. A year later he served as spokesman for a Baltimore delegation which had come to call upon President Buchanan to protest against a commercial treaty with Switzerland permitting Swiss cantons to discriminate against American Jews who might be visiting there.

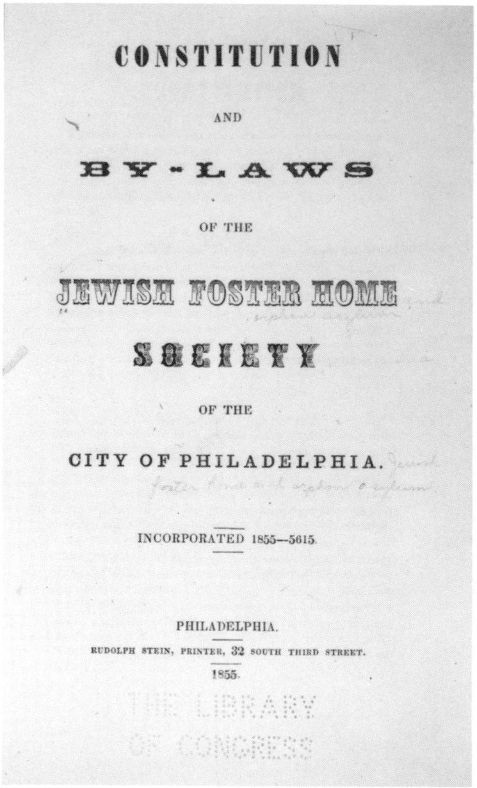

CONSTITUTION

AND

BY-LAWS

OF THE

JEWISH FOSTER HOME

SOCIETY

OF THE

CITY OF PHILADELPHIA.

INCORPORATED 1855—5615.

PHILADELPHIA.

RUDOLPH STEIN, PRINTER, 32 SOUTH THIRD STREET.

1855.

Founded as a home "for destitute and unprotected children of Jewish parentage" by Jewish ladies of Philadelphia. A leading spirit in this, as in all leading Jewish women's endeavors in Philadelphia, was its grande dame, Rebecca Gratz. The special Sabbath regulations which conclude the pamphlet provide:

On Friday previous to the Sabbath, the children shall be bathed, combed and dressed,—the children shall then be assembled, when the matron shall read to them the prayer for the eve of the Sabbath; after supper they shall sing, *Ain Kalohaynoo.*

Constitution and By-Laws of the Jewish Foster Home Society . . . , Philadelphia, 1855.
General Collection.

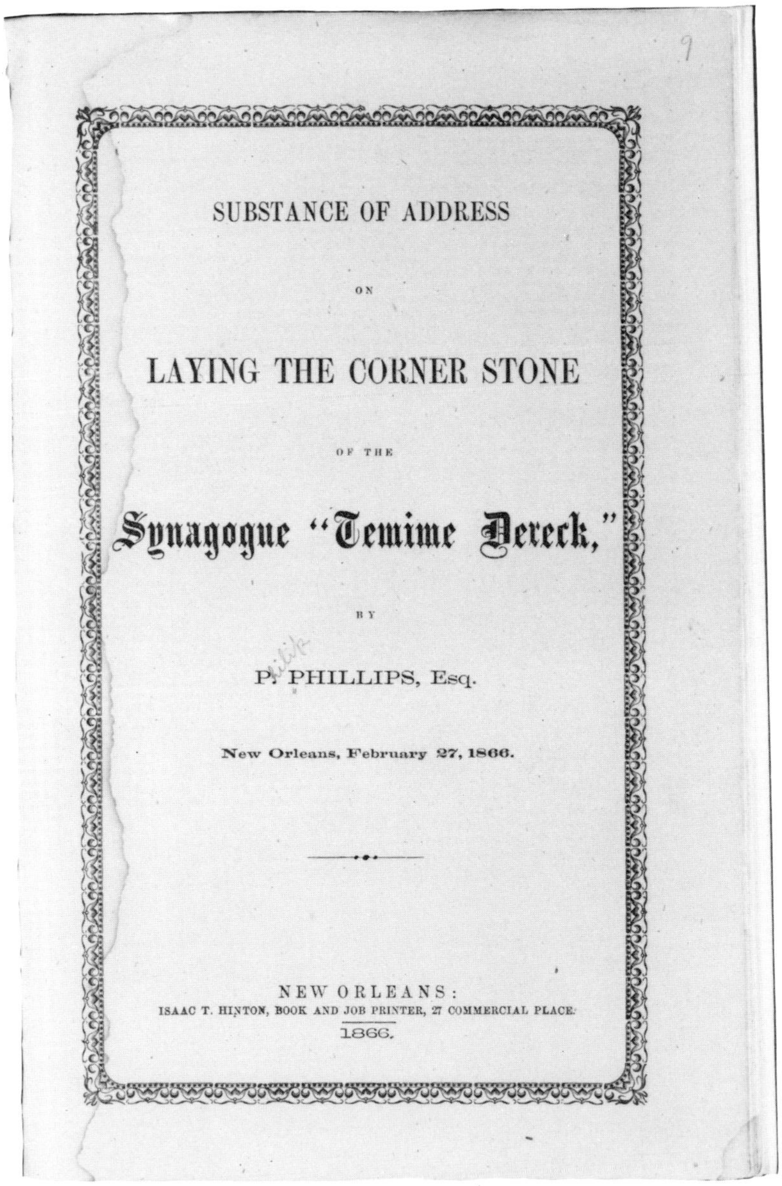

SUBSTANCE OF ADDRESS

ON

LAYING THE CORNER STONE

OF THE

Synagogue "Temime Dereck,"

BY

P. PHILLIPS, Esq.

New Orleans, February 27, 1866.

NEW ORLEANS:

ISAAC T. HINTON, BOOK AND JOB PRINTER, 27 COMMERCIAL PLACE.

1866.

The last in a group of nine published addresses of Philip Phillips, member of the House of Representatives from Alabama, 1854–55, is the *Substance of Address on Laying the Corner Stone of the Synagogue "Temime Dereck"* of New Orleans in 1866. It is one of the earliest—if not the first—participations in a synagogal function by a congressman. This copy was presented to John Selden, Esq. by W. H. Allen Phillips, Washington, February 14, 1884.

Philip Phillips, *Substance of Address . . . ,* New Orleans, 1866.
General Collection.

Phillips was admitted to the South Carolina bar in 1828, then moved to Mobile, Alabama, where, in 1834, he was elected to the state legislature and became a leading political figure. In 1853, he was elected to Congress, and when his term ended he remained in Washington to practice law before the Supreme Court.

Because of his wife's pronounced Southern sympathies (she was the former Eugenia Levy of Charleston), they had to leave the city during the Civil War and settled in New Orleans. In his consecration address, Phillips voiced the universalistic sentiments of his first Jewish affiliation, the Reformed Society of Israelites:

I look into the future . . . I see the coming day, radiant in glory . . . in which, though differing in creed and forms of worship, the voices of all shall unite in the grand anthem, "Hear, O, Israel, the Lord our God, the Lord is One!"

The Phillips Papers housed in the Library's Manuscript Division contain a brief autobiographical sketch, called "A Summary of the Principle Events of My Life," and two works by his wife. One is a diary entitled "Journal of Mrs. Eugenia Phillips," the other a memoir, "A Southern Woman's Story of Her Imprisonment During the War of 1861–62." Philip's writings are staid and proper, Eugenia's, fiery and dramatic. Because of his legal and oratorical skills, he sat in Congress; because of her intense Southern loyalties, she languished in "Beast" Butler's prison. After the war both returned to Washington, where Phillips resumed his law practice and became one of the capital's leading attorneys. He died in 1884 and was buried in the Levy family plot in the Jewish cemetery of Savannah, Georgia.

REFORM JUDAISM: ADVOCATES AND A CRITIC

The leading figure of the Reformed Society of Israelites was Isaac Harby (1788–1828), who led its secession from its mother congregation (Beth Elohim, Charleston, S.C.), prepared its prayer book, and gave voice to its philosophy and purpose in an address delivered before the Society on November 21, 1825. It can be found in *A Selection from the Miscellaneous Writings of the Late Isaac Harby Esq.*, Charleston, 1829.

What is it we seek? The establishment of a new sect? No; never . . . the abolition of the ancient language and form of Jewish worship? Far from it. . . . Every prayer, every ceremony, calculated to add dignity to external worship and warmth to true devotion was the ardent wish of members who compose your society. Our wish is to yield every thing to the feeling of the truly pious Israelite; but to take away everything that might excite the disgust of the well informed Israelite. To throw away rabbinical interpolations; to avoid useless repetitions; to read or chaunt with solemnity; to recite such portions of the Pentateuch and the prophets, as custom and practice have appointed to be read in the *original Hebrew;* but to follow such selections with a translation in English, and a lecture or discourse upon the law, explanatory of its meaning, edifying to the young, gratifying to the old, and instructive to every age and every class of society.

Be the promised land what it may . . . yet are we contented . . . to live in America; to share the blessings of liberty; to partake of and to add to her political happiness, her power and her glory; to educate our children liberally; to make them useful and enlightened and honest citizens; to look upon our countrymen and brethren of the same happy family worshipping the same God of the universe, though perhaps differing in forms and opinions.

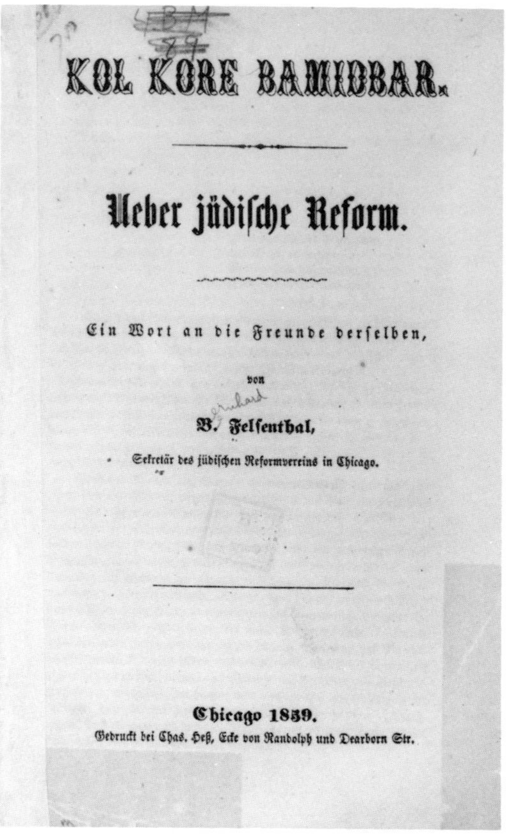
KOL KORE BAMIDBAR.

Ueber jüdische Reform.

Ein Wort an die Freunde derselben,

von

B. Felsenthal,

Sekretär des jüdischen Reformvereins in Chicago.

Chicago 1859.

Gedruckt bei Chas. Heß, Ecke von Randolph und Dearborn Str.

The subtitle of *Kol Kore Bamidbar* (A Voice Calling in the Wilderness) is "On Jewish Reform." Bernhard Felsenthal, then serving as secretary of Chicago's first Jewish Reform Society, called for religious reform in synagogue usage, liturgy, and ritual. He later became a leading Reform rabbi and one of America's early Zionist leaders.

B. Felsenthal, *Kol Kore Bamidbar* (A Voice Calling in the Wilderness), Chicago, 1859.
Hebraic Section.

We have here the earliest American expression of Reform Judaism—practical adaptation to the religious needs and sensibilities of the present and future generations of Jews who are at home in America. A generation later, when American Jewry was vastly increased and radically altered by the influx of Jews from Germany, Bernhard Felsenthal issued a call for the organization of a Reform Jewish congregation in Chicago, *Kol Kore Bamidbar* (A Voice Calling in the Wilderness), Chicago, 1859. Writing in German, and in a manner consonant with Jewish Reform in Germany, Felsenthal declared:

The sources of universal religious truths are: Nature *about* us—the universe; Nature *within* us—the life of the spirit and the history of mankind. The sources of specifically Jewish principles are the history of Judaism and its confessors. . . .

The only dogma which we consider binding upon all our members is: *Absolute freedom of faith and of conscience for all.* . . .

Every Israelite has the right and the duty to himself to search the sources of religious truth with the aid of his God-given intellect. For truth is not inculcated from without, but rather from within outward, shines the light of divine truth. . . .

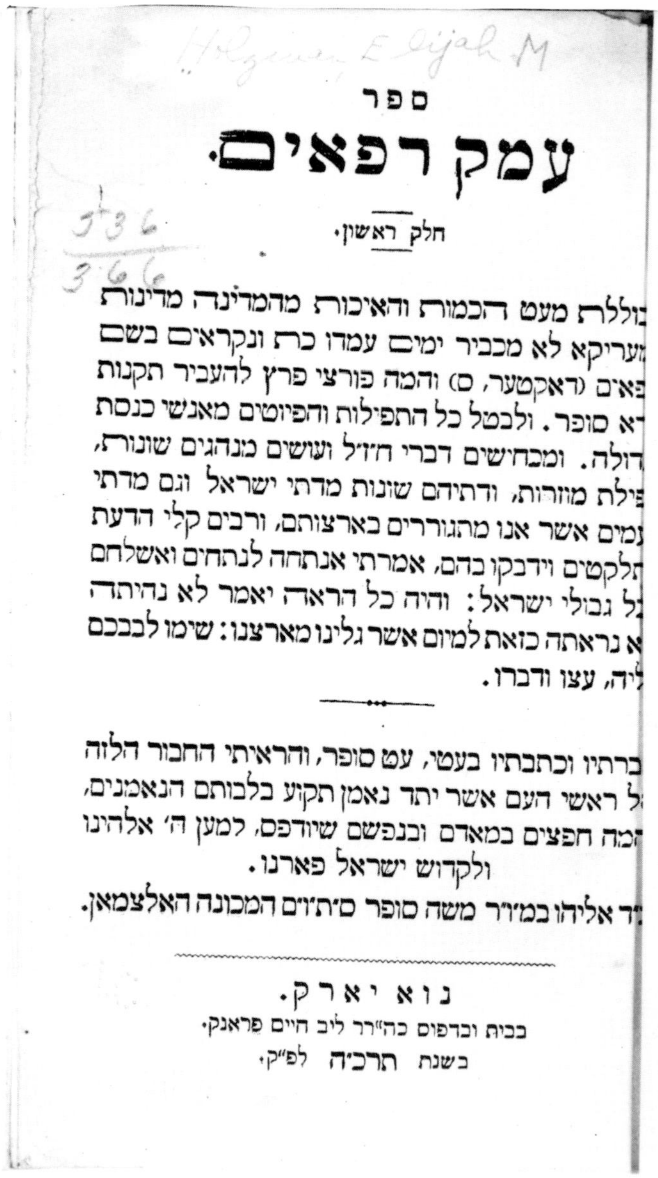
ספר

עמק רפאים.

חלק ראשון.

בוללת מעט הכמות והאיכות מהמדינה מדינות
מעריקא לא מכביר ימים עמדו כת ונקראים בשם
פאים (דאקטער, ס) והמה פורצי פרץ להעביר תקנות
רא סופר. ולבטל כל התפילות והפיוטים מאנשי כנסת
גדולה. ומכחישים דברי ח״ז״ל ועושים מנהגים שונות,
פילת מוזרות, ודתיהם שונות מדתי ישראל וגם מדתי
עמים אשר אנו מתגוררים בארצותם, ורבים קלי הדעת
תלקטים וידבקו בהם, אמרתי אנתחה לנתחים ואשלחם
בל גבולי ישראל: והיה כל הראה יאמר לא נהיתה
א נראתה כזאת למיום אשר גלינו מארצנו: שימו לבבכם
ליה, עצו ודברו.

ברתיו וכתבתיו בעטי, עט סופר, והראיתי החבור הלזה
ל ראשי העם אשר יתד נאמן תקוע בלבותם הנאמנים,
המה חפצים במאדם ובנפשם שיודפס, למען ה׳ אלהינו
ולקדוש ישראל פארנו.
ר אליהו במו״ר משה סופר ס״ת״ו״ם המכונה האלצמאן.

נ ו א י א ר ק.
בבית ובדפוס כה״רר ליב חיים פראנק.
בשנת תרכ״ה לפ״ק.

Anti-Reform polemics in nineteenth-century America took many forms: sermons, lectures, articles, editorials, debates—ideological and recriminatory. Surely one of the most interesting of weapons forged is this small volume of scholarly satire, utilizing biblical verses and Talmudic logic shaped and twisted for thrust and parry to attack and ridicule—all for "the sake of heaven." The author, a professional scribe with a penchant for waging "the battles of the Lord" is a skilled antagonist, his rapier thrusts now and again finding their marks. What gives this volume special bibliographic distinction is that it is the first Hebrew book published in America dealing with the contemporary scene.

Elijah M. Holzman, *Emek Refa ʿim* (Valley of the Dead), New York, 1865.
Hebraic Section.

A religious law which is not rooted either in the spiritual or physical nature of man is binding only so long as it continues to exert a sanctifying influence on head and heart, on character or conduct. . . .

Elijah M. Holzman, by trade a scribe, by avocation a satirical polemicist, makes Reform Judaism the target of his barbs in his twenty-eight-page pamphlet *Emek Refa'im* (Valley of the Dead), New York, 1865. It is the second Hebrew book, other than biblical or liturgical works, published in America. It may well be the first written here to be published, for the one that preceded it, a commentary on the Ethics of the Fathers, by an immigrant itinerant preacher, may well have been written in Europe. Not so this volume. Its theme is Reform Judaism in America; its villains are Rabbis Isaac Mayer Wise, Max Lilienthal, and Samuel Adler. The title is a play on the Hebrew words *refa im* which can also be read as *rofim*, doctors. He suggests that the rabbis who call themselves Doctors are the death of Judaism. In an English foreword, he synopsizes his argument:

A sect has arisen in Israel who attempt to form a new code for public worship, embracing instrumental and vocal music. Choristers composed of male and female voices, Israelites and non-Israelites, erasing the name Synagogue and substituting the word Temple. The whole of these changes emanating from men who call themselves Doctors, and who are in fact destroyers of all that is sacred; their lips move in sanctity, and deception is in their hearts.

The English synopsis does not begin to convey the rich scholarly satire of the Hebrew, which is full of biblical allusions, puns, irony, and word play. Though the author wrote that an English translation was "now in Press, and will shortly appear," no such edition appeared, for a successful translation would have been a tour de force of literary creativity.

THREE VIEWS ON SLAVERY AND SECESSION

Like American Jews themselves, America's rabbis were divided on the issues of slavery and secession. Rabbi George Jacobs of Richmond rented slaves for household work. His fellow townsman, the Reverend J. M. Michelbacher, believed slavery was ordained by God, sentiments shared by colleagues Simon Tuska of Memphis and James K. Gutheim of New Orleans. The rabbinic "hero" of the proslavery forces was Morris J. Raphall of New York who declared that though he himself did not favor slavery, the Bible did not prohibit it; indeed, biblical law guaranteed the right to own slaves. Rabbis Sabato Morais of Philadelphia, Bernhard Felsenthal of Chicago, and especially David Einhorn of Baltimore inveighed against slavery. Einhorn called it "a deed of Amalek, a rebellion against God"; Felsenthal hailed abolition, remarking, "should not the nation rejoice . . . The white people have become emancipated just as well as the black."

Three published sermons in the Library's holdings present some of the gamut of views.

Bible View of Slavery by the Reverend M. J. Raphall, New York, 1861:

The result to which the Bible view of slavery leads us is—1st, that slavery has existed since earliest times, 2d, that slaveholding is no sin, and that slave property

Rabbi of B'nai Jeshurun, New York's first Ashkenazi congregation, Morris J. Raphall had distinguished careers in England and America as rabbi, author, editor, and gifted orator. But he is most remembered for one sermon he preached on the eve of the Civil War, *Bible View of Slavery*, which was published and republished and widely distributed by the proslavery forces. Though he himself opposed slavery, he argued that the Bible permitted it—and became stamped as the proslavery rabbi. His portrait was published by P. Haas, long before, in 1850.

M. J. Raphall, Engraved Portrait, New York, 1850. Prints and Photographs Division.

is expressly placed under the protection of the Ten Commandments; 3d, that the slave is a person, and has rights not conflicting with the lawful exercise of the rights of his owner.

The Reverend Doctor M. J. Raphall's Bible View of Slavery, Reviewed by the Reverend D. Einhorn, New York, 1861:

A Jew, the offspring of a race which daily praises God for deliverance from the bondage of Egypt . . . undertakes to parade slavery as a perfectly sinless institution, sanctioned by God . . . ! A more extraordinary phenomenon could hardly be imagined. . . .

A religion which exhorts to spare the mother from the bird's nest, cannot consent to the heartrending spectacle of robbing a human mother of her child . . . Thus crumbles into a thousand fragments the rickety structure of Dr. Raphall . . . To proclaim in the name of Judaism, that God has consecrated the institution of slavery! Such a shame and reproach the Jewish religious press is in duty bound to disown and to disavow, if both are not to be stigmatized forever. If a Christian clergyman in Europe had delivered a sermon like that of Dr. Raphall, all the Jewish orthodox and reform pens would have immediately been set to work . . . to repel such a foul charge, and to inveigh against this desecration of God's holy name. Why should we, in America, keep silence when a Jewish preacher plays such pranks?

Dr. Einhorn preached this sermon and published it in his German-language periodical *Sinai* in pro-Confederate Baltimore.

A Sermon Delivered On the Day of Prayer, Recommended by the President of the C. [*onfederate*] *S.* [*tates*] *of A.* [*merica*], *the 27th of March 1863, at the Hebrew Synagogue "Bayth Ahabah,"* by the Reverend M. J. Michelbacher, Richmond 1863:

Prayer

Again we approach Thee, O God of Israel—not as a single meeting of a part, but as the whole congregation of all the people of the land. . . .

The man-servants and the maid-servants Thou has given unto us . . . the enemy are attempting to seduce, that they too may turn against us, whom Thou hast appointed over them as instructors in Thy wise dispensation!

We believe, O God, that piety cannot subsist apart from patriotism—we love our country, because Thou has given it unto us as a blessing and a heritage for our children . . . bring salvation to the Confederate States of America.

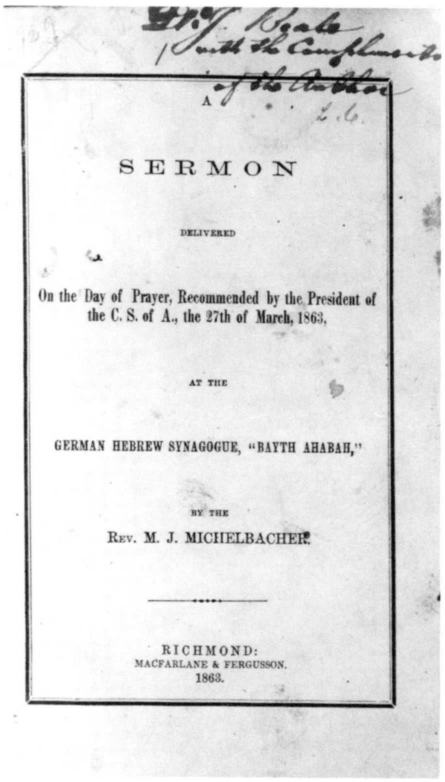
A

SERMON

DELIVERED

On the Day of Prayer, Recommended by the President of the C. S. of A., the 27th of March, 1863,

AT THE

GERMAN HEBREW SYNAGOGUE, "BAYTH AHABAH,"

BY THE

Rev. M. J. MICHELBACHER.

RICHMOND:
MACFARLANE & FERGUSSON.
1863.

On the Day of Prayer, recommended by the president of the C.S.A. March 27, 1863, the Rev. M. J. Michelbacher, of the German synagogue Bayth Ahabah, preached this sermon, "to which he added a prayer for the Confederate States of America "to crown our independence with lasting honor and prosperity," and for its president, Jefferson Davis, "grant speedy success to his endeavors to free our country from the presence of its foes."

Presentation copy to Dr. J(ames) Beale.

M. J. Michelbacher, *A Sermon Delivered . . . at . . . "Bayth Ahabah"* (House of Love), Richmond, 1863. Rare Book and Special Collections Division.

BACK TO THE SOIL

Nineteenth-century America looked upon the independent farmer as the quintessential American, the backbone of the nation. For Jewish immigrants to remain dwellers in self-created ghettos in the Northeast metropolises was not in the interest of America, the Jewish community, or the immigrant himself. In the middle of the century, back-to-the-soil movements were already stirring in Russia and being proposed for immigrant Jews in the United States.

In the Library's collection is a four-page circular in Hebrew and Polish issued by the Warsaw rabbinate at the end of 1841 in support of such endeavors in the Czarist empire. Little more than a compilation of Talmudic statements favoring agricultural pursuits, it was issued to counter widely disseminated assertions that the rabbis forbade Jews to "labor in fields and orchards outside the borders of the Holy Land." The rabbis feared that such views might be upsetting to the Czarist government, which was then favoring Jewish return to the soil. The tenor of their appeal can be gauged from the following excerpt from the compilation:

> Rabbi Eleazer said, "He who does not own land is not fully a person." . . . The rabbis of the Talmud were all persons of stature who could have chosen any vocation, yet they concluded that the best pursuit of man is to work the land. . . . this was never an undesirable occupation; we were forced to leave it. But now that God has privileged us to live under the sovereignty of a virtuous czar and his administrators who, solicitous for our welfare, are encouraging us to turn to agriculture, so that we may support our families in prosperity and honor, it is incumbent on those who are able to take advantage of the opportunity.

In the middle of the century plans were promulgated for Jewish agricultural colonies in America. In the first issue of *The Occident,* April 1843, Julius Stern of Philadelphia proposed the establishment of a Jewish colony in one of the Northwestern territories, where Jews might devote themselves to "agriculture and the breeding of cattle, which occupations are the best props of every state." Stern hoped the colony might eventually grow to become a Jewish state within the United States, "for never will [our holy religion] be able to appear in all its dignity, glory and greatness, so long as our people live dispersed among the followers of other creeds."

The most interesting and comprehensive proposal came from Simeon Berman (1818–1884) who, before he went to America in 1852, founded an agricultural settlement society in his native Cracow. In New York, Cincinnati and St. Louis he pursued his life's passion, the colonization of Jews on the soil. His infectious enthusiasm and vision won adherents to his cause, but he lacked the organizational skills to turn plans into reality. A dozen years after his first attempt to organize an agricultural society, he still had not succeeded. In 1865, in St. Louis, Berman published *Constitution und Plan zur Grundung eines Jüdischen Agrikultur-Vereins* (Constitution and Plan for the Founding of a Jewish Agricultural Society), in which he discusses how the Society is to be organized, how the settlers need to work together to provide for their present needs and plan their future well-being.

The purpose of the Society was to direct the Jews' attention toward farming and to provide the indigent among them with an opportunity to find independence on the land through cooperative efforts and with minimal expenses. "Ten thousand acres are to be bought in one of the states, fertile land in a good climate," he writes. "Cities are to be laid out, ten lots to an acre." Nor will the Jewish cultural and spiritual needs be neglected. "The staff of the colony's school should consist of two Hebrew, two German and two English teachers, with a rabbi as Superintendent."

What remains of the plan is an exceedingly rare German pamphlet recently acquired by the Rare Book and Special Collections Division.

Unsuccessful in the New World, in 1870 Berman left for Palestine, where he spent the last fourteen years of his life in colonization efforts. With the aid of the American consul, Berman persuaded the Ottoman government to grant his request to be allowed to purchase land. He settled in Tiberias and founded the Holy Land Settlement Society for the establishment of a cooperative colony on Lake Kinneret, and lived to see the establishment of the first Jewish settlements in the Galilee and in Judea.

Colonies were established in America as well. Members of the *Am Olam* (Eternal People) movement for cooperative living on the land went to the New World, and in spring 1882 thirty-two families founded a colony at Sicily Island, Louisiana, which a Mississippi flood wiped out. A dozen regrouped to found the colony Crimea in South Dakota in the fall of the same year, and Bethlehem of Judea was soon established nearby, but heavy debt and lack of farming experience took their toll. Both had to be liquidated three years later. The same fate overtook New Odessa, near Portland, Oregon. *Report of Mr. Julius Schwartz on the Colony of Russian Refugees at Cotopaxi, Colorado, established by The Hebrew Emigrant Aid Society of the United States*, New York, 1882, tells of the founding of an immigrant colony.

The tyrannical illiberality of the Russian Government overflowed the free shores of our country with suffering refugees. The desire to colonize these refugees, to make them farmers . . . to resave them from the . . . chains of poverty and desolation . . . speedily became a sentiment among our thinking co-religionists . . . It was decided that Government land be taken up in Colorado, and an experimental colony be founded . . . Proper persons, amongst them some trained farmers, were selected and on the third of May, the Colony consisting of thirteen families, left for Cotopaxi . . . the headquarters of a rich mining district . . . Opposite on the Arkansas River . . . land covered with fresh green grass forms the first link in the chain of farms that are under the cultivation of the expatriated Russian Jews.

The land proved arid, impossible to cultivate without irrigation, and the colony did not last three years.

Upper left: The typesetter, Naphtali ben Katriel Shmuel of Thorn, added a colophon to this commentary on the *Ethics of the Fathers, Avnei Yehoshua* by Joshua Falk, expressing his gratitude that it was his good fortune to set in type the first Hebrew book written and published in America. The author, an itinerant preacher, came to America in 1858, two years before its publication, and died in Keokuk, Iowa, in the year of its publication.

Joshua Falk, *Avnei Yehoshua* (The Stones of Joshua), New York, 1860.
Hebraic Section.

Right: Being the first book of Hebrew poems and the first Yiddish book published in America is the double distinction of this small volume of poems by Jacob Zevi Sobol, *Shir Zahav li-Khevod Yisrael ha-Zaken* (A Golden Song in Honor of Israel, the Ancient), New York, 1877. The poems in Hebrew and Yiddish are poems of praise of the Jewish people, the Hebrew language, and America. The Hebrew poems, though not distinguished, do convey the intended satire and irony; the Yiddish versions are in a stilted Germanic Yiddish, which the practitioner thought cultured, but which the great writers in Yiddish inveighed against as crude and artificial.

Jacob Zevi Sobol, *Shir Zahav li-Khevod Yisrael ha-Zaken*, New York, 1877.
Hebraic Section.

Lower left: Tractate *Bikkurim* (First Fruits) of the Palestinian Talmud, printed in Chicago in 1887 and again in 1890, is the first Talmudic tractate to be published in America. It is the distinction of Rabbi Abraham Eliezer Alperstein, the publisher and author of the commentaries which accompany the text, to be the first American Talmudic scholar to have his commentaries printed here.

Masekhet Bikkurim (Tractate First Fruits), with Commentaries by Abraham Eliezer Alperstein, Chicago, 1890.
Hebraic Section.

A TRIO OF FIRSTS

"Firsts" are dear to the hearts of bibliophiles and book collectors. Three such firsts are part of the Library's Hebraic collection: the first Hebrew book, the first Yiddish book, and the first Talmudic commentary by American authors published in the United States.

The colophon of *Avnei Yehoshua* by Joshua Falk, New York, 1860 reads:

I give thanks that it was my good fortune to be the typesetter of this scholarly book, the first of its kind in America. Blessed be the God of Israel who surely will not deny us the Redeemer.

This commentary on the *Ethics of the Fathers* is the first book written in Hebrew to be published in America other than the Bible and prayer books. Its author was born in Poland in 1799, arrived in America in 1858, served briefly as a rabbinic functionary in Newburgh and Poughkeepsie, New York, and became an itinerant preacher. He died in the year of the book's publication, while on a visit to a daughter in Keokuk, Iowa.

Jacob Zevi Sobel (1831–1913), born in Lithuania, received rabbinic ordination and taught at a yeshiva, but, turning away from orthodoxy, he went to America in 1876. A year later, he published a small volume of poems in Hebrew and Yiddish, *Shir Zahav li-Khevod Yisrael ha-Zaken* (A Golden Song in Honor of Israel, the Ancient), New York, 1877, which has the distinction of being both the first Yiddish book and the first book of

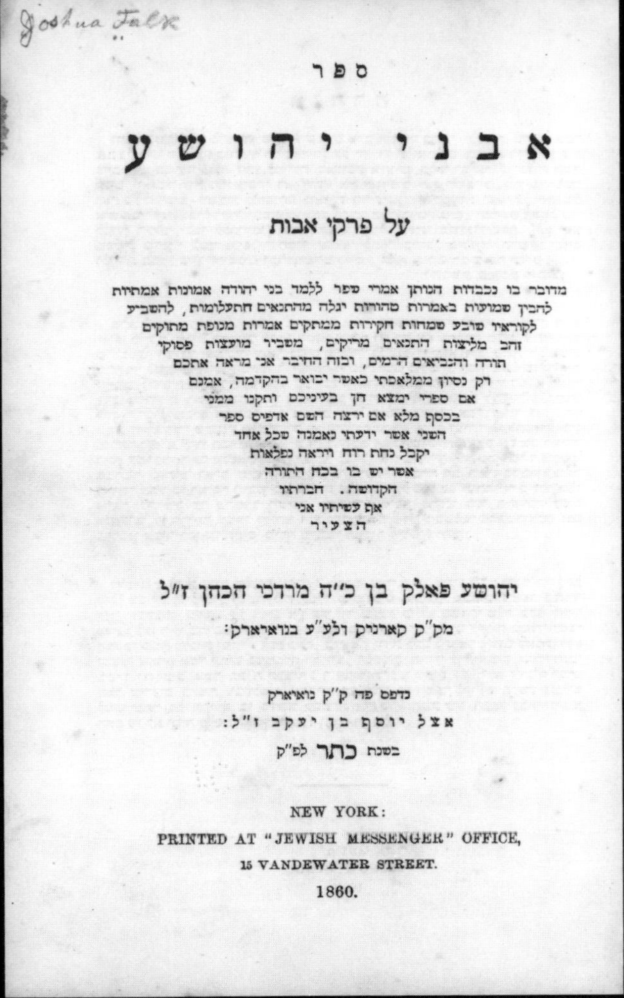

Joshua Falk

ספר

אבני יהושע

על פרקי אבות

מדובר בו נכבדות הנותן אמרי שפר ללמד בני יהודה אמונות אמתיות
להבין שמועות באמרות טהורות יגלה מהתנאים חתעלומות, להשביע
לקוראיו שובע שמחות חקירות ממתקים אמרות מנופת מתוקים
זהב מליצות התנאים מריקים, משביר מועצות פסוקי
תורה והנביאים הרמים, ובזה החיבור אני מראה אתכם
רק נסיון ממלאכתי כאשר יבואר בהקדמה, אמנם
אם ספרי ימצא חן בעיניכם ותקנו ממני
בכסף מלא אם ירצה השם אדפיס ספר
השני אשר ידעתי נאמנה שכל אחד
יקבל נחת רוח ויראה נפלאות
אשר יש בו בכח התורה
הקדושה. חברתיו
אף עשיתיו אני
הצעיר

יהושע פאלק בן כ"ה מרדכי הכהן ז"ל
מק"ק קארניק ולע"ע בנואוארק:

נדפס פה ק"ק נואיארק
אצל יוסף בן יעקב ז"ל:
בשנת כתר לפ"ק

NEW YORK:
PRINTED AT "JEWISH MESSENGER" OFFICE,
15 VANDEWATER STREET.
1860.

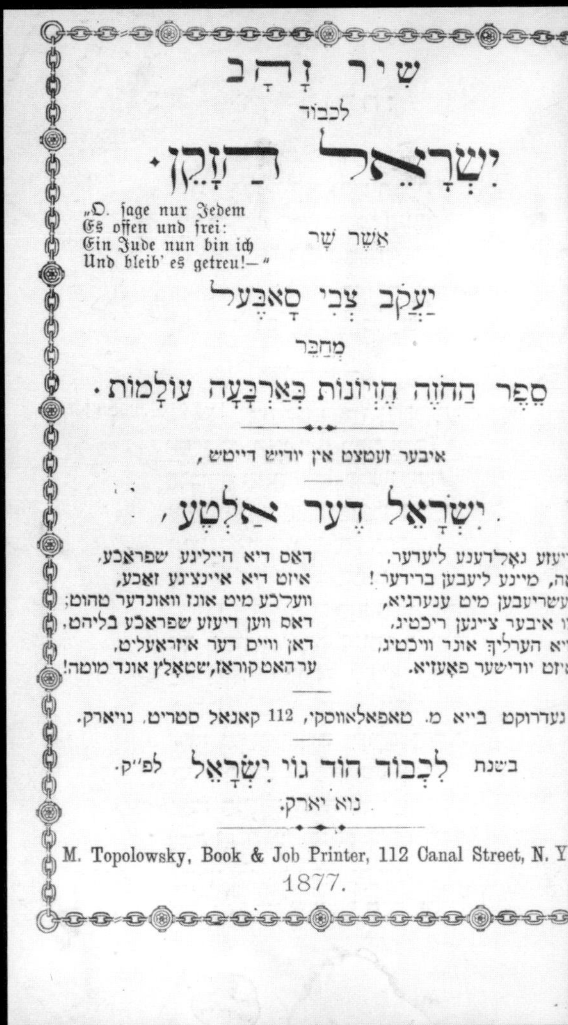

שיר זָהָב
לכבוד
יִשְׂרָאֵל הַזָּקֵן׃

„O. sage nur Jedem
Es offen und frei:
Ein Jude nun bin ich
Und bleib' es getreu!—"

אֲשֶׁר שָׁר

יַעֲקֹב צְבִי סָאבֶעל

מְחַבֵּר

סֵפֶר הַחֹזֶה הֶזְיוֹנוֹת בְּאַרְבָּעָה עוֹלָמוֹת׃

איבער זעטצט אין יודיש דייטש,

יִשְׂרָאֵל דֶער אַלְטֶע,

ריעזע גאלדענע ליערער,
אה, מיינע ליעבען ברידער!
געשריעבען מיט ענערגיא,
צו איבער ציינען ריכטיג,
ויא הערליך אונד וויכטיג,
איזט יודישער פאעזיא.

דאס דיא היילינע שפראכע,
איזט דיא איינציגע זאכע,
וועלכע מיט אונז וואונדער טהוט;
דאס וועז דיעזע שפראכע בליהט,
דאן וויים דער איזראעליט,
ער האט קוראז, שטאלץ אונד מוטה!

געדרוקט בייא מ. טאפאלאווסקי, 112 קאנאל סטריט, נויארק.

בשנת לְכְבוֹד הוֹד גּוֹי יִשְׂרָאֵל לפ"ק.
נוא יארק.

M. Topolowsky, Book & Job Printer, 112 Canal Street, N. Y.
1877.

Talmud Jerushalmi Bikkurim

מסכת בכורים
מן
תלמוד ירושלמי
עם פירוש
ספר הראל ופרי גנוסר

אשר חנן ה' אותי
בימי עני ומרודי לארץ הורידו בבודי
בארץ נודי חמסו הודי
בעיר אידי שדדו מאודי
ופידי. ומעודי.
היו לחם במחסור ביתי:

אברהם אליעזר אלפערשטיין
שנת דע ספר הראל לפק
פה
שיקאגא

LBO'13

Hebrew poems published in America. The poems, really not much more than doggerel, celebrate the Jewish people, America, and the Hebrew language. On the title page is a poem in German:

> Oh say it to all,
> Open and free;
> A Jew I am,
> And a Jew I will be!

and a poem in Yiddish (translated from the Hebrew):

> Israel, the Ancient
>
> These golden songs,
> I wrote, O brothers mine,
> To prove and demonstrate
> With energy and might:
> The poems our people write
> Are important, noble, great!
>
> Our holy tongue,
> For which we long,
> Blossoming in flower
> Uplifts the Jew,
> With power true,
> To courage, pride and power!

Sobel spent his last years in Chicago, teaching Hebrew and writing for the Hebrew and Yiddish press.

Masekhet Bikkurim min Talmud Yerushalmi (Tractate "First Fruits" of the Palestinian Talmud), Chicago, 1887 and 1890, is the first printing of a section of the Talmud in America. Published with three commentaries by Rabbi Abraham Eliezer Alperstein of Congregation Ohabei Shalom Mariapoler (Lovers of Peace of Mariapol) in Chicago, the title-page text is in an artistic frame of base and columns, topped by crowned lions supporting a majestic crown. The typography, in the classic style of Talmudic printing of text surrounded by commentary, compares favorably with the finest European typography. In the Introduction, Rabbi Alperstein commends friends in New York, Pittsburgh, Buffalo, and Montreal who made the book's publication possible, and also extols his congregation for its warmth and generosity.

In the second printing, the ninety-six pages remain the same, but the title page now has a brief Hebrew poetic dirge added:

> Favored was I by the Lord
> In days of wretched poverty,
> In the country of my wandering,
> In the city of my distress and disaster,
> My honor was cast to the ground,
> My glory violated.
> Robbed of my abundance and increase,
> My house lacked for food.

It was not God's doing, but the work of his formerly extolled congregants, whom he now calls, in a new Hebrew Introduction, "wild boars." There is also an errata list of no less than 258 typographical errors. Sad indeed were the scholarly rabbi's days in Chicago; his subsequent career in New York was more tranquil and prosperous.

ART FOR THE HOME

Arriving in ever increasing numbers during the last decades of the nineteenth century, Jewish immigrants to America did not find the Jewish ambience of the shtetl (small town) in the Jewish sections of the larger cities. To compensate, many made their homes as visibly Jewish as possible with religious prints and lithographs.

In 1874, the H. Schile company on New York's Lower East Side published three lithographs for the Jewish trade. A mizrach, an ornamental sacred picture placed on the east wall of a home for daily prayers directed toward Jerusalem, was preserved as issued, a black-on-white lithograph. Two lions which have human faces hold up a star of David in and about which is inscribed in Hebrew the verse most often found on a mizrach, "From the rising [East sun] unto the setting of the sun the Lord's name is to be praised!" (Psalms, 113:3). At the bottom as the title of the print, the verse is printed in English.

The other two lithographs are of Moses and Aaron. These have come down in their completed state, hand-colored in bright hues. Moses, in rich garb, a prayer shawl draped over his head and shoulders, holds the tablets on which the Ten Commandments are inscribed in Hebrew. Aaron, in ornate priestly vestments, holds a censer. Inscribed in Hebrew is the biblical verse, "And they shall make holy garments for Aaron thy brother, and for his sons" (Exodus, 28:4).

All prayer is oriented eastward, toward Jerusalem. To point the direction, a mizrach is hung on the eastern wall of the house. This one, published by H. Schile Company, is a lithograph, black on white, on which color could later be added by hand.

Mizrach, New York, 1874.
Prints and Photographs Division.

This *Gedenkblatt* or Memory Tablet "for dear and departed ones" in three languages, German, Hebrew, and English, leaves space on the pages of the open book to record the names and dates of death of the dear departed, so that their presence might remain in the home on whose walls this tablet would be hung, and their *Yahrzeit* observed. Published by A. M. Bleichrode.

Gedenkblatt (Memory Table[t]), New York, 1874.
Prints and Photographs Division.

Published as a black on white lithograph by the H. Schile Company of New York, the color added by hand, Moses, with a tallith (prayer shawl) on his shoulders, holding the Tablets of the Ten Commandments, would have been welcome in many a nineteenth-century American Jewish home.

Moses, New York, 1874.
Prints and Photographs Division.

The inscription in Hebrew makes this brightly colored lithograph of Aaron appropriate for the walls of a Jewish home. Produced by the H. Schile Company.

Aaron, New York, 1874.
Prints and Photographs Division.

First in B'nai B'rith's threefold mission is benevolence—brotherly love and harmony follow. A richly illustrated record of its fulfillment is *The Dying Ben B'rith: An Episode in the Yellow Fever Scourge of 1878.* We see a visit to the cemetery, drawn by Robert Schade, from a photo by Hugo Schroeder.

A. L. Baer, *The Dying Ben B'rith,* Milwaukee, 1883. General Collection.

Facing page: A member of B'nai B'rith, America's oldest and largest Jewish fraternal order, could proudly display his membership certificate, whose illustrations would remind all of the order's mission, and its threefold devotion: to country—the American eagle and shield; to faith—Abraham and Isaac, and Moses at Sinai; and to fraternal benevolence—visiting the sick, consoling the bereaved, caring for orphans.

Membership Certificate, B'nai B'rith, Milwaukee, 1876. Prints and Photographs Division.

In the same year A. M. Bleichrode, also of New York, published a *Memory Table* in three languages (Hebrew, German, and English), an open book, with lined blank pages awaiting the inscription of the family's vital statistics. Above is a depiction of the Cave of *Machpelah* in the city of Hebron, burial place of the patriarchs and matriarchs (a direct copy from S. Shuster's lithograph in *A Descriptive Geography . . . of Palestine* by Joseph Schwartz, Philadelphia, 1850). Flanking it are candelabra with burning candles, beneath which are inscribed, in Hebrew, "For the mitzvah is a lamp; and the Torah is light" (Proverbs, 6:23), and "the candle of the Lord is the soul of man" (Proverbs, 20:27). A man and a woman clasp hands above the verse, "The beloved and dear in their life were even in their death not divided" (Samuel II, 1:23). Above them, in Hebrew and German, is the rabbinic saying:

> *The Lord hath given:* Man comes out of the womb, his hands clasped, as if to say: All the world is mine, I will besiege fortified cities, amass the treasures of kings without measure.
>
> *The Lord hath taken away:* Man returns to his eternal home with hands spread open, as if to say: Naked I return there, nothing can I take with me. Neither possession nor great wealth will avail in the day of trouble and reckoning.

At the top, two putti angels aloft hold a banner which, in Hebrew with English and German translation, bears the legend, "A good name is better than good oil and the day of death than the day of birth" (Ecclesiastes, 7:1).

Two years later, in 1876, S. Eckstein published a beautifully illustrated Independent Order of B'nai B'rith membership certificate, lithographed by the American Oleograph Company of Milwaukee. B'nai B'rith, organized in New York in 1843, was the first Jewish fraternal order in the United States. By the end of the century it had lodges throughout the world, including Jerusalem. It not only served the needs of its members, but increasingly engaged in communal service endeavors. Its orphan asylum in Cleveland, for example, set standards rarely equalled. The Eckstein certificate depicts both the Order's Jewish heritage and its benevolence. At the top, under a crest of an eagle astride an American shield of stars and stripes, flanked by the ladies Liberty and Justice, is the motto: "Benevolence, Brotherly Love and Harmony." Beneath, angels on the altar, a seven-branched menorah (candelabrum), and crossed shepherds' crooks. Four panels depict Moses with the Tablets of the Commandments and Abraham and Isaac above, and below, a doctor visiting a sick brother, and lodge brothers calling upon a bereaved widow and orphans. At the bottom is the Cleveland Orphan Asylum and, in Hebrew, the priestly benediction: "The Lord bless thee, and keep thee; The Lord make his face to shine upon thee, and be gracious unto thee; The Lord lift up his countenance toward thee, and give thee peace" (Numbers, 26:24–26).

In Milwaukee, too, *The Dying Ben B'rith: An Episode in the Yellow Fever Scourge of 1878,* by A. L. Baer, was published in 1883, "Dedicated to the Asylums of the Independent Order of B'nai B'rith." In this account in verse of the Order's benevolence to the family of a brother smitten by the dread plague, what are particularly moving are Robert Schade's illustrations, none more so than a scene at the cemetery.

Origin of the Rites and Worship of the Hebrews, by M. Wolff, New York, 1859, is the most crowded with detail of Hebrew prints published in Amer-

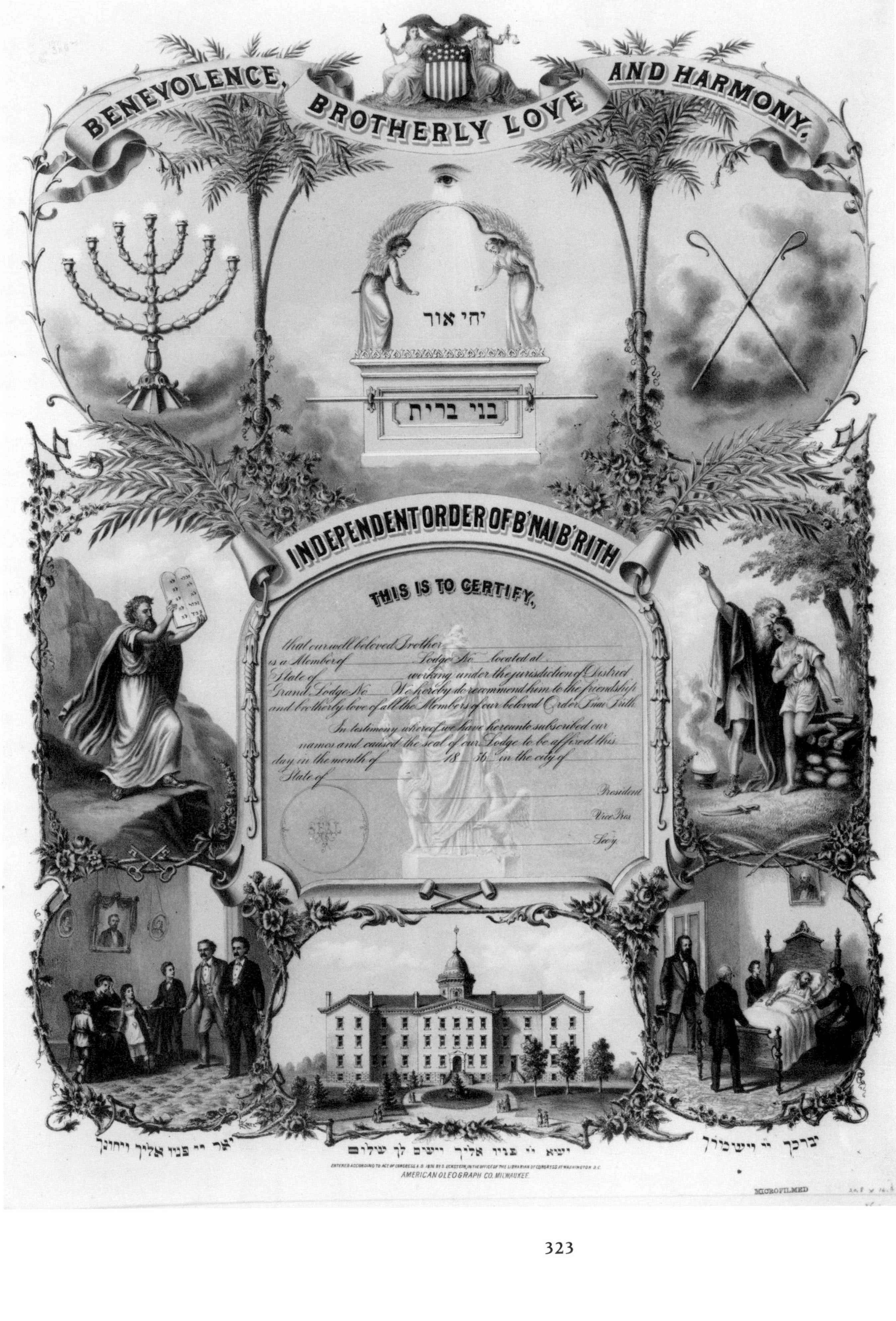
BENEVOLENCE, BROTHERLY LOVE AND HARMONY,
יהי אור
בני ברית
INDEPENDENT ORDER OF B'NAI B'RITH
THIS IS TO CERTIFY,
that our well beloved Brother
is a Member of Lodge No. located at
State of working under the jurisdiction of District
Grand Lodge No. We hereby do recommend him to the friendship
and brotherly love of all the Members of our beloved Order Bnai Brith
In testimony whereof we have hereunto subscribed our
names and caused the seal of our Lodge to be affixed this
day in the month of 18 56 in the city of
State of
President
Vice Pres
Secy
SEAL
יאר יי פניו אליך ויחנך
ישא יי פניו אליך וישם לך שלום
יברכך יי וישמרך
ENTERED ACCORDING TO ACT OF CONGRESS A.D. 1876 BY S. ECKSTEIN, IN THE OFFICE OF THE LIBRARIAN OF CONGRESS AT WASHINGTON D.C.
AMERICAN OLEOGRAPH CO. MILWAUKEE
MICROFILMED

ica. So complex is the medley of law and lore, literature and mysticism, that a special 112-page booklet, *Explication of An Engraving . . . ,* was published with it. The history of its publication, given in the words of its publisher, Max Wolff, "formerly Minister of the Congregation *'Ohabei Shalom,'* Boston, Massachusetts," is revealing:

> This pictorial representation was originally composed by the learned and accomplished Dr. Rosenberg, and by him published in Paris in the year 5611–1851. Some two years ago [1857] a copy . . . was presented to me. . . . Many called upon me to explain the plan; others, again desired to possess copies with an explication in the vernacular tongue, and urged me to undertake an Anglo-American edition from the French original; and when I reflected how little the spirit and profound character of the institutions of Israel are known among Gentiles, while even among Hebrews, here, in the United States, the study of the sacred language and literature . . . [and] the Talmud, is so greatly neglected . . . it struck me that I would be doing a good service . . . to edit and to publish.

A 112-page booklet went with this massively detailed engraving, which was so complex, filled with information, and replete with symbols of the Jewish tradition. Its publisher and author was Max Wolff, a religious functionary—a cantor in Boston and San Francisco.

Max Wolff, *Origin of the Rites and Worship of the Hebrews,* New York, 1859.
Hebraic Section.

18

FROM THE LANDS OF THE CZARS

■ NO EVENT HAD GREATER INFLUENCE on the course of American Jewish history than the assassination of Alexander II, "Czar of all the Russias," in St. Petersburg, in March 1881. Seeking a scapegoat, the government and people turned upon the Jews in pogroms in over a hundred towns and villages, wild excesses of violence, pillage, and plunder which continued well into the twentieth century. To "shield the Russian population against harmful Jewish activity," "Temporary Laws" were enacted on May 31, 1882, which limited Jewish residence to the Pale of Settlement, the eastern provinces of the czarist empire; expelled Jews from such cities as St. Petersburg, Moscow, and Kiev, and permitted all villages to expel theirs; limited the number of Jews in secondary schools and universities; and prohibited Jews from entering the legal profession and participating in local government.

The three-pronged solution to the "Jewish problem" proposed by the éminence grise of Russian politics, Konstantin Pobedonostsev, if not official government policy, seems to have become its goal: for one-third of the Jews, conversion; for another third, economic strangulation; for the rest, emigration. The Jews of Russia acted upon the third. Emigration, begun in the 1870s, brought two and one-half million Jews to America during the next half-century, doubling the Jewish population of the United States in each of the last two decades of the nineteenth century and the first of the twentieth.

Every division of the Library offers rich documentation of this extraordinary Exodus—departure, journey, and resettlement. We limit ourselves to a sampling of the graphic arts and to some literary creations that describe this great drama.

Among the immigrants was the thirteen-year-old Mary Antin who, with her mother, two sisters, and brother, joined her father in America in 1894. In her classic memoir, *The Promised Land* (Boston, 1912), she recalled:

> Hundreds of fugitives, preceded by a wail of distress, flocked into the open district [the Pale] bringing their trouble where trouble was never absent, mingling their tears with tears that never dried.

Passover was celebrated in tears that year. In the story of the Exodus we would have read a chapter of current history, only for us there was no deliverer and no promised land. But what said some of us at the end of the long service? Not "May we be next year in Jerusalem," but, "Next year—in America!" So there was our promised land, and many faces turned toward the West. And if the waters of the Atlantic did not part for them, the wanderers rode its bitter flood by a miracle as great as any the rod of Moses ever wrought.

The modern Moses is Uncle Sam cleaving the waters of the Atlantic to permit the Children of Israel to reach the shores not of the Promised Land but of the land of promise. The artists are "O&K," i.e., Frederick Burr Opper and Joseph Keppler. Their depiction of the Jews—hooked nosed, kinky haired—aroused vigorous criticism.

Frederick Burr Opper and Joseph Keppler, "The Modern Moses," in *Puck,* 1881.
General Collection.

This same historical metaphor was used in 1881 in a two-page cartoon in color in the magazine of humor and satire *Puck.* Its German edition captions the cartoon "Der Moderne Auszug aus Egypten" (The Modern Exodus from Egypt); in the English language edition it is called "The Modern Moses." Moses is Uncle Sam, his trousers the red and white stripes of the American flag, beams of light radiating from his white top hat. He stands on a Rock of Salvation and with his wand marked "Liberty" he cleaves the waters of the Atlantic. On the far horizon looms death in military helmet. A setting sun on the near shore emits its rays inscribed "Western Homes." Through the parted waters marked "Oppression" and "Intolerance" marches a long line of immigrants. Their depiction aroused an angry attack on the Austrian immigrant publisher and artist, Joseph Keppler. He was accused of perpetuating the German and Austrian anti-Semitic caricatures of the Jews: top-hatted men, bearded or whiskered, obese women and obstreperous children, all hook-nosed and kinky haired. The cartoon is signed "O & K," for Frederick Burr Opper—son of an Austrian Jewish immigrant and a New England (apparently not Jewish) mother—and Keppler, who neither apologized for nor changed his stereotype. Jews similarly depicted continued to appear in *Puck,* but these were no different in kind from equally coarse and offensive caricatures of Irish and Italian immigrants, venal politicians, or avaricious Robber Barons.

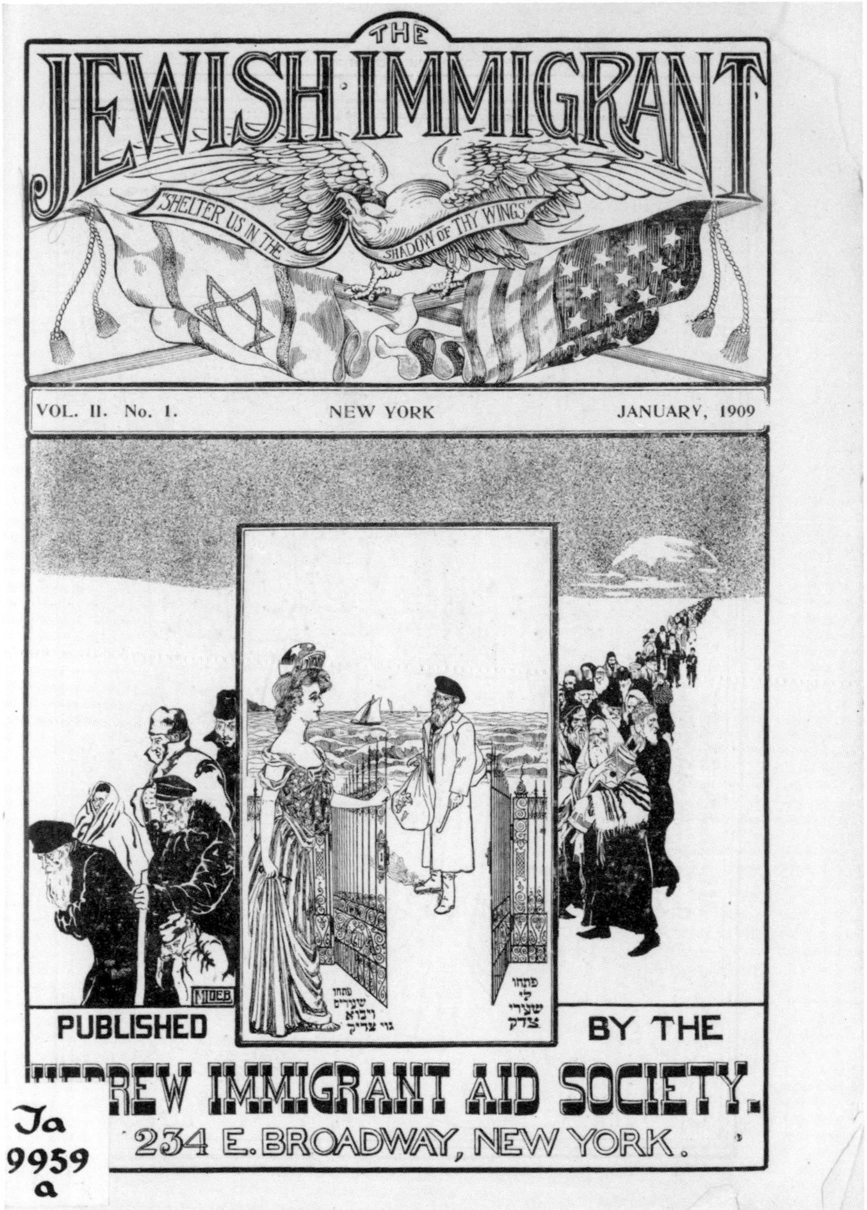

The front page of the Hebrew Immigrant Aid Society's journal, *The Jewish Immigrant*, shows a graphic presentation, lady "America" opening her gate to the wandering Jew seeking haven.

The Jewish Immigrant, New York, January 1909. Hebraic Section.

A benign portrayal of the same theme was on the cover page of the periodical, *The Jewish Immigrant*, published by the Hebrew Immigrant Aid Society beginning in 1908. The Atlantic, a welcoming America, and the long line of immigrants are also here, but in a center panel Lady Columbia, five-point star decorating her cap whose visor reads "America" in Yiddish, is opening her gates to a bearded Jew who has just stepped on her shores. On either side of the open gates are biblical verses. "Open for me the gates of righteousness" (Psalm 118:19), the immigrant asks; "Open ye gates, that the righteous nation may enter," America responds. The line of immigrants are Old World Jews in their customary dress; one, a white-bearded patriarch wrapped in a prayer shawl, carries a Scroll of the Law. The masthead bears American and Jewish flags intertwined, and above them, the American eagle holds a banner, inscribed "shelter us in the shadow of thy wings" (Psalm 17:8).

The shipboard experience is enshrined in a remarkable photograph, "The Steerage" (1907), by Hoboken-born Jewish photographer Alfred

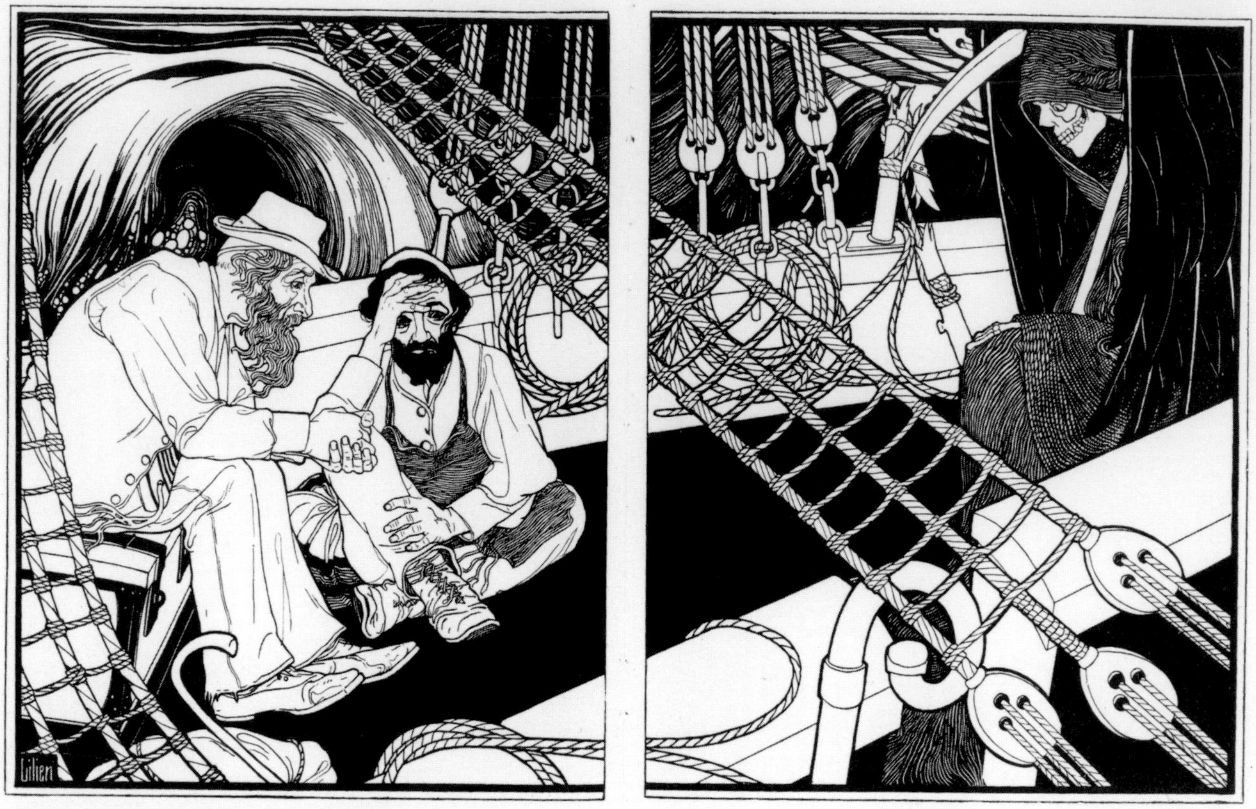

Austrian Jewish artist E. M. Lilien was the illustrator of the German edition of Morris Rosenfeld's *Songs of the Ghetto.* Two Jewish erstwhile immigrants have been sent back, being deemed "paupers." The poet writes:

America drives us back to Russia.
To Russia, because money we have not!

The artist captures the despair on their faces. And should the reader not plumb the depth of their despair, the skeletal face of death will evoke it.

Morris Rosenfeld, *Lieder des Ghetto,* translated by Berthold Feivel, illustrated by E. M. Lilien, Berlin, 1903. General Collection.

Facing page:
Original drawing by William Allen Rogers to illustrate, "Friday Night in the Jewish Quarter" in *Harper's Weekly,* April 19, 1890.

Prints and Photographs Division.

Stieglitz, the first of his craft to have his work accepted as art by American museums.

Many Jews came and were admitted to America, but a few were sent back. The "Poet of the Ghetto," Morris Rosenfeld, sang of their plight. Leo Wiener, Instructor in Slavic Languages at Harvard, translated the poem into prose in his *Songs of the Ghetto,* Boston, 1898, a collection of Rosenfeld's poems in transliteration and prose translation.

On the Bosom of the Ocean

The terrible wind, the dangerous storm, is wrestling with a ship on the ocean. . . .

Children weep, women wail; the people cry and confess their sins; souls flutter, bodies tremble in terror of the angry, destructive wind.

But below in the steerage, two men sit quietly; no pain assails them; they seek no salvation, they make no plans, just as if it were safe and calm about them.

"Who are you wretched ones . . . that you have no sighs and no tears even at the awful gates of Death?

Have you no fatherland, no country, no home . . . no friendly house. . . .
No one in heaven above to whom to cry when you are in trouble?"

"A mother has fondled us . . . a father . . . kissed us tenderly.
We have a house but it has been destroyed, and our holy things have been burned . . .

You know our country; it is easily recognized . . . by its cruel riots, its ruthless destruction, dealing death to the wretched Jew.

(4 1/2 in wide)

Yes we are Jews, miserable Jews, without friends or joys, without hopes of happiness . . . America drives us back to Russia. To Russia, because we have no money. . . .

. . . Earth is too mean to give us a resting place; we are voyaging, but, . . . no one waits for us.

The two Jews were turned back by the March 3, 1891, immigration law which barred entry to "paupers or persons likely to become a public charge." They are graphically depicted in the hold of the storm-tossed ship by E. M. Lilien in an illustrated German edition of the *Songs of the Ghetto, Lieder des Ghetto,* Berlin, 1903, translated from the Yiddish by Berthold Feivel and illustrated by Lilien. The two men are seated, one on a steamer trunk, the other on the floor, and in their eyes, staring into nothingness, is the despair of a two-millennial exile. Across the hold, black-winged skeletal death waits expectantly.

Morris Rosenfeld (1862–1923) went to New York in 1886 and became a pioneer of Yiddish poetry in America. "Poet Laureate of Labor," he sang of sweatshop and tenement, exploitation and poverty, a threnody of dashed hopes and thwarted expectations. His poems became folk songs, and his own life mirrored the poverty and sadness of his songs.

Ephraim Moses Lilien (1874–1925), an artist, illustrator, and printmaker, was the first artist to become an active Zionist. *Lieder des Ghetto* was one of his earliest important commissions, but the fullness of his talent is already evident. His drawings, done mainly in India ink, were a perfect medium for the somber themes of Rosenfeld's poetry.

Our two unfortunates had to leave, but as Rosenfeld saw it and Lilien depicted it, the plight of those permitted to remain was not much better: endless, unrewarding toil in the sweatshop. Illustrating "An der Nämaschine" (At the Sewing Machine), a pious clothing operator, bearded and in skullcap, his tsitsith (holy fringes) dangling, sits at his machine. Man and machine have become one. Behind him, his bejeweled employer literally sucks his lifeblood. Rose Pastor Stokes and Helena Frank catch the essence and tone of this poem in their volume of translations, *Songs of Labor* by Morris Rosenfeld, Boston, 1914:

The Pale Operator

If but with my pen, I could draw him,
    with terror you'd look in his face;
For he, since the first day I saw him,
    Has sat there and sewed in his place.

Years pass in procession unending,
    And ever the pale one is seen,
As over his work he sits bending
    And fights with the soul-less machine.

More subtle and powerful is Lilien's drawing for "Die Thräne auf dem Eisen" (A Tear on the Pressing Iron), where a presser is bending over his work table, heavy pressing iron in hand. He is completely enclosed in a spider web, in which flies have been caught, and lurking in the top corner of it is a malevolent black spider. Wiener's prose translation reads:

Oh, cold and dark is the shop. I hold the iron, stand and press;—my heart is weak, I groan and cough. . . . My eye grows damp, a tear falls, it seethes and seethes, and will not dry up.

"Are you perhaps the messenger . . . that other tears are coming? . . . when will the great woe be ended?"

I should have asked more of . . . the turbulent tear; but suddenly there began to flow more tears, tears without measure.

Long hours and drudgery were not limited to the sweatshop. The lot of the street peddlers was no better, and in foul weather, worse. Two original drawings by the illustrator William Allen Rogers, "The Fruit Vendor" and the "Candle Merchant," accompanying a brief sketch, "Friday Night in the Jewish Quarter," in *Harper's Weekly,* April 19, 1890, capture this perfectly. It is spring, but the vendor is dressed in winter hat, coat, and boots. Standing by his three-wheel pushcart, holding out two pieces of fruit in his right hand, he holds his left hand open in supplication, which matches the look on his wizened face.

To call the old woman selling candles a "merchant" is an act of compassion. The sad mute plea on a face wearied by the tribulations of life mark her a beggar as much as a vendor. Her clawlike fingers clutch her means of livelihood, a tray of Sabbath candles still unsold. One is reminded of one of Rosenfeld's most popular and lugubrious poems, "The Candle Seller" (translation by Stokes and Frank):

In Hester Street, hard by a telegraph post,
There sits a poor woman as wan as a ghost.
Her pale face is shrunk, like the face of the dead,
And yet you can tell that her cheeks once were red . . .
"Two cents, my good woman, three candles will buy,
As bright as their flame be my star in the sky!" . . .

She's there with her baby in wind and in rain,
In frost and in snow-fall, in weakness and pain. . . .
She asks for no alms, the poor Jewess, but still,
Altho' she is wretched, forsaken and ill,
She cries Sabbath candles, to those that come nigh,
And all that she pleads is, that people will buy.

But no one has listened, and no one has heard:
Her voice is so weak, that it fails at each word. . . .

I pray you, how long will she sit there and cry . . .
How long will it be, do you think, ere her breath
Gives out in the horrible struggle with Death?

In Hester Street stands on the pavement of stone
A small, orphaned basket, forsaken, alone.
Beside it is sitting a corpse, cold and stark:
The seller of candles—will nobody mark?
No, none of the passers have noted her yet . . .

Rogers also illustrated Sylvester Baxter's "Boston at the Century's End," in *Harper's Magazine,* November 1899, and among those illustrations is "The Jewish Quarter of Boston," of which the Library has the original. Mary Antin describes the "Quarter" in her *The Promised Land.*

Anybody who knows Boston knows that the West and North Ends are the wrong ends of the city. They form the tenement district, or, in the newer phrase, the slums of Boston . . . [it] is the quarter where poor immigrants foregather, to live, for the most part, as unkempt, half-washed, toiling unaspiring foreigners; pitiful in the eyes of social missionaries, the despair of boards of health, the hope of ward politicians, the touchstone of American democracy.

Original drawing by William Allen Rogers, illustrator of *Harper's Weekly*'s "Friday Night in the Jewish Quarter," for the April 19, 1890, issue.

Prints and Photographs Division.

Original drawing by Frederic Dorr Steele of Yetta, the heroine of Myra Kelly's "A Passport to Paradise," a moving story of children in the Lower East Side Jewish ghetto, which appeared in *McClure's*, November 1904.

Prints and Photographs Division.

William Allen Rogers's original drawing of "The Jewish Quarter of Boston," for Sylvester Baxter's article, "Boston at Century's End," which appeared in *Harper's Magazine*, November 1899.

Prints and Photographs Division.

Facing page:
In this fine original drawing, Frederic Dorr Steele captures the pathos in the life of the immigrant community described by Myra Kelly in her stories, which were favorites of the Theodore Roosevelt family.

Prints and Photographs Division.

On the other side of the coin is the tale of a Jewish immigrant girl, Yetta, the appealing sprite in Frederic Dorr Steele's original drawing to illustrate Myra Kelly's, "A Passport to Paradise," in *McClure's*, November 1904. Yetta is the heroine in one of Miss Kelly's touching tales about Jewish children of the Lower East Side. Born in Ireland, Myra Kelly lived most of her brief life—she died at thirty-five—in that section of New York, where she taught public school. Her stories appeared in leading magazines and were subsequently published in three collections. Theodore Roosevelt expressed the appreciation of many:

> Mrs. Roosevelt and I and most of the children know your very amusing and very pathetic accounts of East Side school children almost by heart, and I . . . thank you for them. While I was Police Commissioner I quite often went to the Houston Street public school and was immensely . . . impressed by what I saw there. I thought there were a good many Miss Bailies [the schoolteacher heroine of Miss Kelly's stories] there, and the work they were doing among their scholars (who were so largely of Russian-Jewish parentage, like the children you write of) was very much like what your Miss Bailey has done.

"A Passport to Paradise" is a bittersweet story of a little immigrant girl with a penchant for cleanliness, hard to achieve when water had to be brought up to the tenement apartment from the yard below; an ambition

FIRST CLASS
SHAVE
5
Steele July 04 N.Y.
"For Yetta was lost."
"A Passport to Paradise" Nov 04
24:61
Myra Kelly series McClures Nov '04

Immigrants in steerage wait as the first and second class passengers embark from New York harbor in Alfred Stieglitz's famed photograph taken in 1907, "The Steerage."

Alfred Stieglitz, "The Steerage," New York, 1907. Prints and Photographs Division.

to serve in the exalted position of monitor; and a longing for her country peddler father whom she sets out to find, arousing fears that she has become lost. Most of all it is a loving account of Jewish boys and girls and their relationship with their Irish teacher. Steele's drawing catches the pathos and wonder of the immigrant community in the Jewish neighborhoods of turn-of-the century American cities, where there was a natural community bound together by memory, empathy, and shared aspirations.

That community's interests and values were embodied in the Jewish immigrants' popular music, what Mark Slobin calls in *Tenement Songs*, Urbana, 1982, "the popular music of the Jewish immigrants." The title page illustrations of Yiddish sheet music, as well as the contents, are an as yet sparsely used prism through which to view the life of that community. Five of these popular songs, from the unmatched collection in the Library's Music Division, provide us a slice of that life.

Illustrations for *Leben Zol Amerika* (Long Live America) are the American icons that the Jews held dear: George Washington, Abraham Lincoln, and the Statue of Liberty. Washington represented the "Land of the Free and the Home of the Brave"; Lincoln symbolized opportunity, in going from "Log Cabin to the White House," so why not aspire to go from tenement to mansion, from public school to university? The Statue of Liberty

Left: Patriotic songs expressing the immigrants' love for America, loyalty to the "Land of the Free," intermingled with songs poking critical fun at the "Land of Columbus." Both were sung with equal fervor. This song opens with:

To express loyalty, with every
fibre of one's being, to
this Land of Freedom, is the
sacred duty of every Jew.

Solomon Smulewitz (Small) and J. M. Rumshisky, *Zei Gebensht Du Freie Land* (Long Live the Land of the Free), New York, 1911.
Music Division.

Below: Featured on the title page of the sheet music of *Leben Zol Amerika* (Long Live America) are the three favored icons of the American Jewish immigrant sensibility, George Washington, Abraham Lincoln, and the Statue of Liberty.

Leo Rosenberg and M. Rubinstein, *Leben Zol Amerika* (Long Live America), New York, n.d.
Hebraic Section.

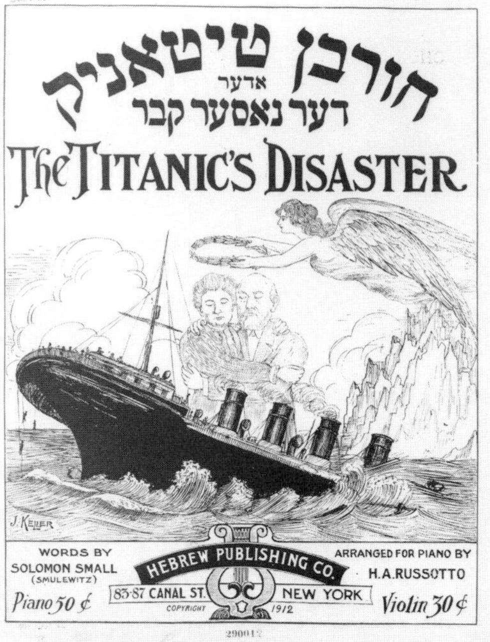

The sinking of the super trans-Atlantic liner, the *Titanic,* was a tragedy that engulfed all of America. The Jewish community was particularly touched by the drowning of Ida Straus, who refused a place on a lifeboat reserved for women and children, choosing to share the fate of her husband, the beloved philanthropist, Nathan Straus. The drawing by J. Keller portrays an angel placing the wreath of immortality on their heads.

Solomon Smulewitz (Small), *Hurban Titanic* (The *Titanic's* Disaster), New York, 1912.
Hebraic Section.

symbolized the welcome to all who had come and would yet come to America.

Zei Gebensht Du Freie Land, Long Live the Land of the Free, is doggerel, and pointedly patriotic:

Every Jew must express his loyalty to the Land of Freedom with all his being/Once settled he will surely appreciate a Land which gives him full and equal rights/ Yes! Yes!/ So become a citizen, take out the required papers/ Oy, Oy/ Become an in-law of Uncle Sam/ Cast your vote/ It gives you great power/ Then none can cause you hurt/ The world will esteem the Jew/ Defend the American Flag.

Refrain: Praised and blessed be this Land of Freedom/ Especially so the Jew/ It lifts its friendly hands to us . . .

Jewish bankers, doctors, engineers/ Business blossoms where Jews are present/ . . . Sculpture, music, journalism, the stage . . . Oy, Oy . . . / In this Land none will disturb you/what you will you can accomplish . . .

Refrain: Praised and blessed be this Land . . . etc.

Solomon Smulewitz's words are no better in Yiddish than in English, but J. M. Rumshisky's music is much better, and better still is the title-page illustration by Joseph Keller, where the American eagle glares at Lady Liberty whose name is on her patriotic bonnet, which like the gown is decorated with stars and bars. In her hand she holds a laurel wreath.

The sinking of the "unsinkable" *Titanic* in 1912 was mourned in some two hundred American songs. The Yiddish song *Hurban Titanic, oder der Nasser Kever* (The Wreck of the *Titanic*, or the Watery Grave) bears the English title *The Titanic's Disaster.* The words are by Solomon Small (Smulewitz), the cover drawing by J. Keller. The ship has struck an iceberg and as it goes down people are climbing down on ropes from the ship to the sea. Above the stricken ship float the spirits of Isadore and Ida Straus. Isadore was one of the three brothers who made Macy's one of America's leading department stores. Each of the brothers carved out a career of distinguished public service. As Secretary of Commerce and Labor, Oscar Straus was the first Jew to serve in the Cabinet; Nathan was one of America's most enlightened philanthropists with a lifelong interest in public health. (The Israeli city of Netanyah is named for him, in appreciation of his having given two-thirds of his fortune to communal projects in Jewish Palestine.) Isadore, the great merchant, served as a congressman. The folk favorite was Ida, and the final stanza of the song (in translation by Mark Slobin) tells why.

There stand, in woe/The thousands in need/And know that death/will dash them down/Then they cry, "Save yourselves/Into the boats quickly, women/No man dare/ Take a place there."/But listen to one woman-soul/who can say/"I won't stir from the spot/I'll die here with my husband."/Let small and great honor/the name of *Ida Straus!*

Translated by Mark Slobin, *Tenement Songs* (Urbana, 1982)

Keller has drawn an angel placing a wreath on the heads of the loving couple who are joined in an embrace.

What was more popular than a wedding, both on the stage and in life? Hardly a musical comedy or drama lacked a wedding scene. One of the best known songs in the immigrant repertoire was *Hoson Khalleh Mazel Tov* (Good Luck to the Bride and Groom), words and music by S. Mogulesco. Slobin offers an analysis of the title-page illustration:

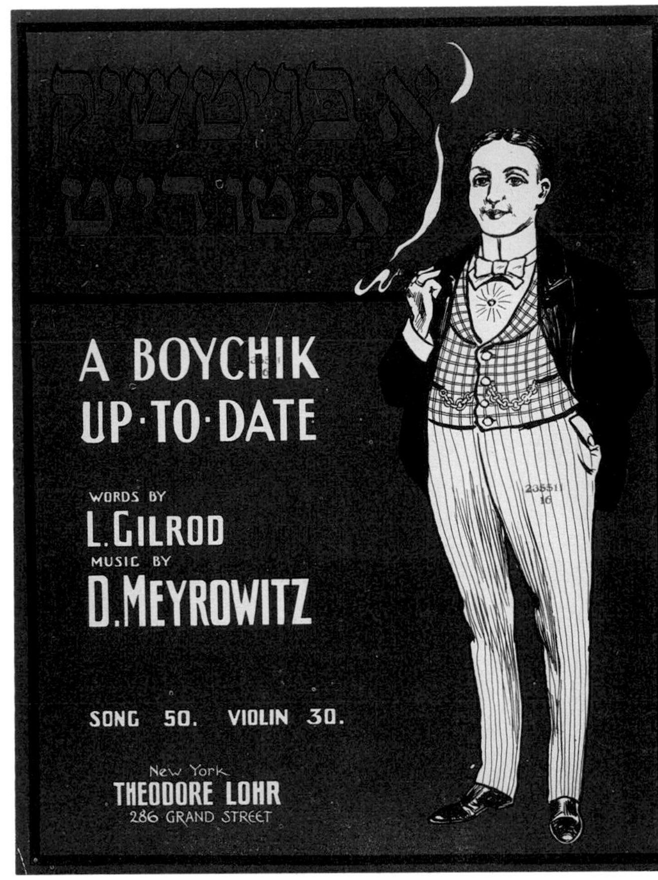

Left: Hardly a musical on the Yiddish stage was without a wedding scene. It made of the audience an extended family, joined in happy celebration, shedding shared tears of joy. Note the huppah (wedding canopy) held up by boys and girls, and the wedding garb of the celebrants and officiants, full dress and top hats.

S. Mogulesco, *Choson Kale Mazol Tov* (Good Luck to the Bride and Groom), New York, 1909.
Hebraic Section.

Right: The garish colors of this sheet music's title page match the pudgy, faddish, bejeweled "hero." The song is critical of this up-to-date dandy and, through him, the American scene which created him.

L. Gilrod and D. Meyrowitz, *A Boychik Up-To-Date* (An Up-to-Date Dandy), New York, n.d.
Hebraic Section.

The musical number dates back to the 1890s. The carefully drawn figures remain lifeless; perspective and anatomical details are weak. Yet there is a strong attempt to convey an ethnic scene in all its richness. The bored children, officious men, fearful bride, the self conscious matrons are all identifiable types, as if taken from the Yiddish stage.

The cover of *A Boychik Up-To-Date* (An Up-To-Date Dandy) is notable for its garish colors and its pudgy, faddishly clad, bejeweled "hero." The humor and satire make no pretense of subtlety. On the one hand is the knowledge by those who fashioned the song and issued the sheet music that many in the immigrant community would envy and take this modern American dandy as a model of someone "who has made it." On the other hand, it is not lost on them that there is much to decry in such tawdry Americanization, such vulgar acculturation. The "up-to-date dandy" is more a comical bumpkin than an elegant Edwardian gentleman.

The more intelligent purveyors of popular culture looked forward to a true Americanization, forecast by Henrietta Szold in her introductory article to Charles S. Bernheimer's *The Russian Jew in the United States*, New York, 1904:

> The time is not distant when the Russian Jew will have solved the elementary problems of American existence. . . . They will soon reach the point at which they will turn for guidance to the history of the Germans and their Sephardic predecessors. Eschewing the foolish pride of both, they will emulate the dignity and self-respect of the latter, and the sobriety and steadiness of purpose of the former. They will use the institutions created by them as the stock upon which to engraft their intenser fervor, their broader Jewish scholarship, a more enlightened conception of Jewish ideals, and a more inclusive interest in Jewish world questions.

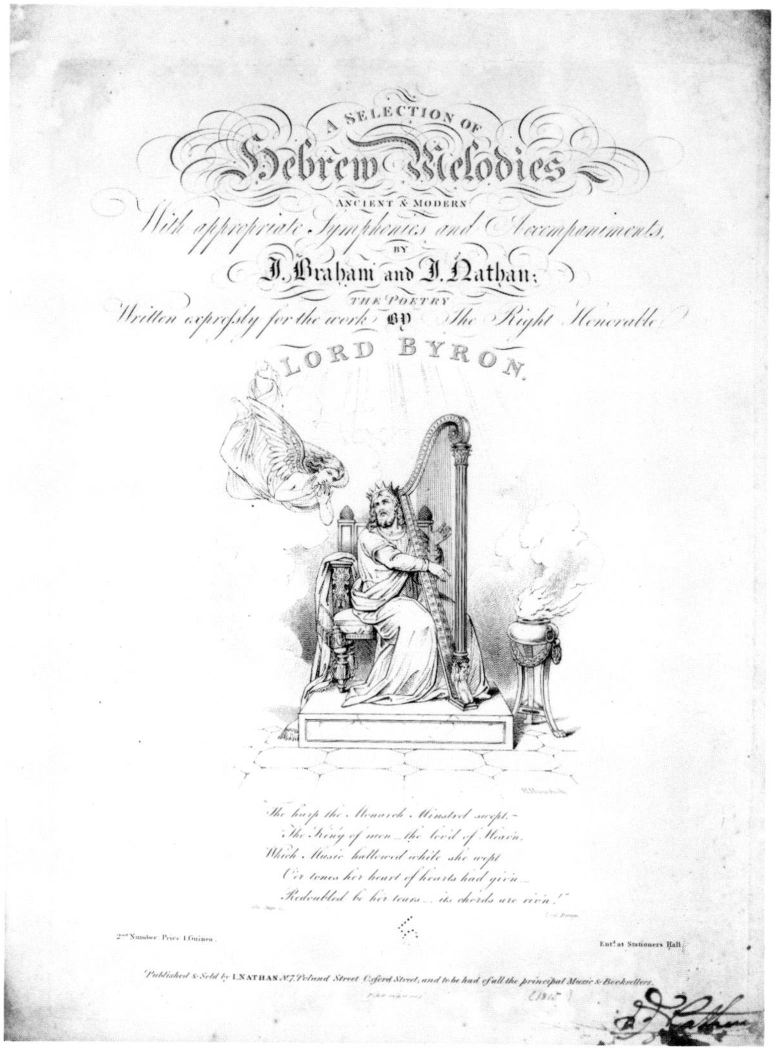

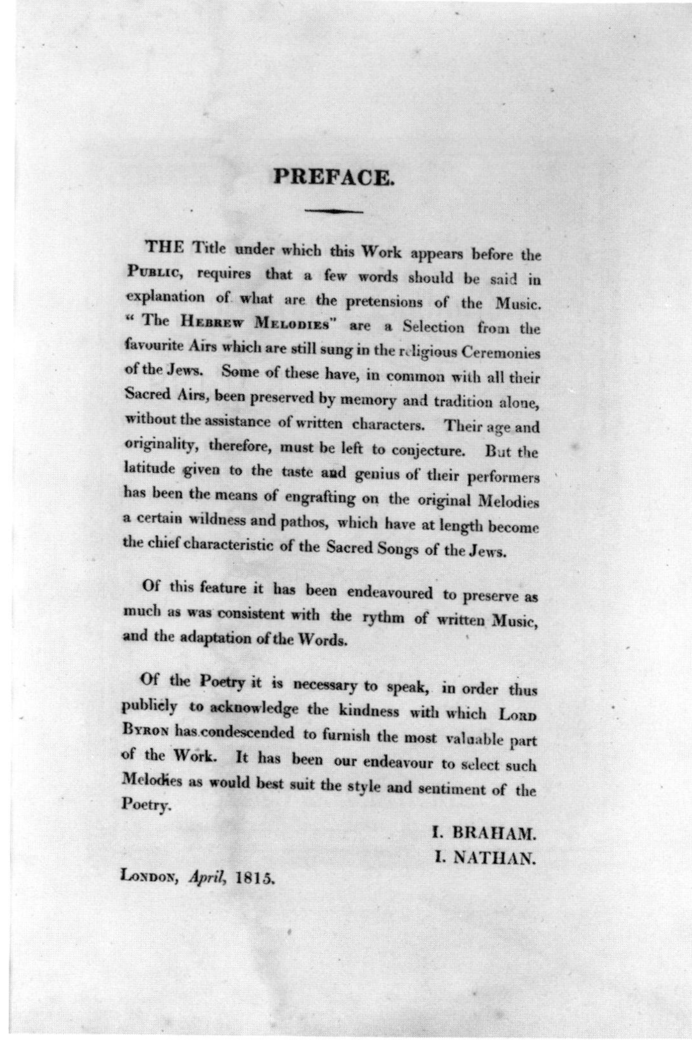

PREFACE.

THE Title under which this Work appears before the PUBLIC, requires that a few words should be said in explanation of what are the pretensions of the Music. "The HEBREW MELODIES" are a Selection from the favourite Airs which are still sung in the religious Ceremonies of the Jews. Some of these have, in common with all their Sacred Airs, been preserved by memory and tradition alone, without the assistance of written characters. Their age and originality, therefore, must be left to conjecture. But the latitude given to the taste and genius of their performers has been the means of engrafting on the original Melodies a certain wildness and pathos, which have at length become the chief characteristic of the Sacred Songs of the Jews.

Of this feature it has been endeavoured to preserve as much as was consistent with the rythm of written Music, and the adaptation of the Words.

Of the Poetry it is necessary to speak, in order thus publicly to acknowledge the kindness with which LORD BYRON has condescended to furnish the most valuable part of the Work. It has been our endeavour to select such Melodies as would best suit the style and sentiment of the Poetry.

I. BRAHAM.
I. NATHAN.

LONDON, *April*, 1815.

What gives special distinction to this two-volume copy of *A Selection of Hebrew Melodies, Ancient and Modern, with Appropriate Symphonies and Accompaniments by J. Braham and I. Nathan-The Poetry Written expressly for the work by the Right Honorable Lord Byron* is that the first title page bears the signatures of both Braham and Nathan, the second of Nathan himself who was truly the sole composer of the music. Braham, a popular soloist of the time, was "brought in" to give the publication the benefit of his popularity.

Lord Byron and I. Nathan, *A Selection of Hebrew Melodies . . . ,* 2 volumes, London, 1815.
Music Division.

19

"BREAK FORTH IN MELODY AND SONG"*

THE LIBRARY'S MUSIC DIVISION collection is remarkable in scope, quality, and beauty. From this rich lode, we cull a dozen nuggets: works by Jewish composers on Jewish themes. All but two are manuscripts in the authors' own hand.

The first great Jewish musical figure was the biblical King David, to whom Lord Byron paid tribute in one of his "Hebrew Melodies," a series of poems written at the request of the poet's friend, the Honorable D. Kinnaird, to be set to music by Isaac Nathan (1790?–1864).

THE HARP THE MONARCH MINSTREL SWEPT

The King of men, the loved of Heaven
Which Music hallowed while she wept. . . .
It softened men of iron mould,
    It gave them virtues not their own;
No ear so dull, no soul so cold,
    That felt not, fired not to the tone
    Till David's Lyre grew mightier than his throne!

It may well be that young Nathan himself initiated the project, and indeed in 1815 the poems were simultaneously published, with their musical edition, *A Selection of Hebrew Melodies, Ancient and Modern, with Appropriate Symphonies and Accompaniments, by J. Braham and I. Nathan; The Poetry Written expressly for the work by the Right Honorable Lord Byron.* The work was "published and sold by I. Nathan," to whom Byron had generously granted the copyright to his "Hebrew Melodies," of which he wrote to Nathan in January 1815:

> Murray being about to publish a complete edition of my *poetical effusions* has a wish to include the stanzas of the Hebrew Melodies—will you allow him that privilege without considering it an infringement on your copyright. I certainly wish to oblige the gentleman but you know Nathan it is against all good fashion to give and take back. I therefore cannot grant what is not at my disposal. . . .

The *Hebrew Melodies* was then Nathan's project, and a Jewish project he meant it to be. In the Preface to this two-volume work, Nathan wrote:

*Psalm 98:4

The Title under which this Work appears before the Public, requires that a few words should be said in explanation of what are the pretensions of the Music. "The Hebrew Melodies" are a Selection from the favorite airs which are still sung in the religious Ceremonies of the Jews. Some of these have . . . been preserved by memory and tradition alone, without the assistance of written characters. Their age and originality, therefore, must be left to conjecture. But the latitude given to the taste and genius of their performers has been the means of engrafting on the original Melodies a certain wildness and pathos, which have at length become the chief characteristic of the Sacred Songs of the Jews. . . .

What is described here in elegant Georgian English is what cantorial creativity does to melody. The signatories to the Preface, J. Braham and I. Nathan, were both sons of synagogue musicians. Braham, the son of the chorister of London's Great Synagogue, had prepared for the cantorate; Nathan, son of the cantor of the synagogue in Canterbury, studied for the rabbinate. Braham became one of the leading singers of his time, Nathan a respected musicologist. To the music of the "Hebrew Melodies," Braham contributed no more than his already well-known name. The work was all English-born Nathan's who, after a career as a music teacher in England, emigrated to Australia to become that continent's first resident professional composer. The Library's copy has the signatures of both Braham and Nathan on the engraved title page of volume 1, and that of Nathan in volume 2.

JACQUES HALÉVY

One of France's greatest composers, Jacques Fromenthal Halévy (1799–1862), was also the son of a cantor. His father, Elie Halfon Halévy, was the secretary of the Jewish community of Paris and a Hebrew teacher and writer as well. Musically gifted, Jacques was accepted as a student by the Paris Conservatory at age ten and subsequently became a member of its faculty, rising to the rank of professor in 1833. His lasting fame was assured by his grand opera *La Juive* (1835).

The work that gained Halévy early notice was a liturgical piece commissioned by the Consistoire Israélite du Départment de la Seine, for a public service in memory of the Duke de Berry, in the Jewish community's temple on March 24, 1820: *Marche Funèbre et De Profundis en Hébreu* for three voices and orchestra. On its engraved title page, Halévy was described as a member of the Royal Institute of Music and a recipient of the patronage of the King of France at the Academy of Rome.

Psalm 130, "Out of the depths have I cried unto thee, O Lord . . . Hear my voice; let thine ears be attentive to the voice of my supplications," was sung in Hebrew. Halévy's first biographer, his brother Leon, records that the *De Profundis*, "infused with religious fervor created a sensation, and attracted interest to the young laureate of the Institute." The Library's copy is bound in a volume of holograph manuscripts of works Halévy composed in 1822 in Vienna, among them another mournful psalm, "Psaume, Domine, ne in furore tuo arguas me" (Psalm, Lord, in thine anger, rebuke me not . . . (Psalm 6:2). It is possible that the Library copy of the *De Profundis* may have been the composer's own.

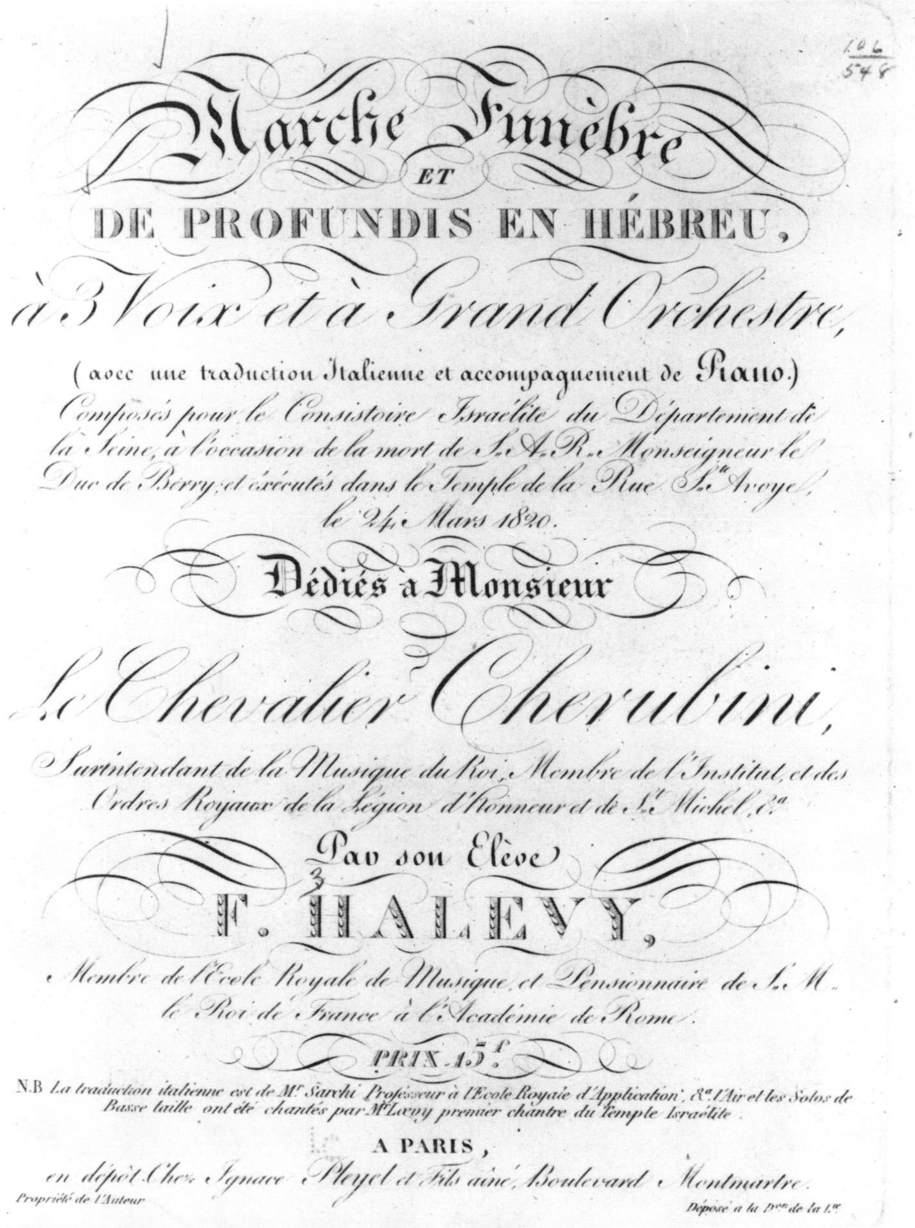
Marche Funèbre
ET
DE PROFUNDIS EN HÉBREU,
à 3 Voix et à Grand Orchestre,
(avec une traduction Italienne et accompagnement de Piano.)
Composés pour le Consistoire Israélite du Département de la Seine, à l'occasion de la mort de S.A.R. Monseigneur le Duc de Berry, et exécutés dans le Temple de la Rue Ste. Avoye, le 24. Mars 1820.
Dédiés a Monsieur
le Chevalier Cherubini,
Surintendant de la Musique du Roi, Membre de l'Institut, et des Ordres Royaux de la Légion d'Honneur et de St. Michel, &a.
Par son Elève
F. HALEVY,
Membre de l'Ecole Royale de Musique, et Pensionnaire de S.M. le Roi de France à l'Académie de Rome.
PRIX 15f.
N.B. La traduction italienne est de Mr. Sarchi Professeur à l'Ecole Royale d'Application; &a. l'Air et les Solos de Basse taille ont été chantés par Mr. Lovy premier chantre du temple Israélite.
A PARIS,
en dépôt Chez Ignace Pleyel et Fils ainé, Boulevard Montmartre.
Propriété de l'Auteur

Commissioned by the Consistoire Israélite du Départment de la Seine, for a synagogue service in memory of the Duke de Berry, March 24,1820.

Jacques Fromenthal Halévy, *Marche Funèbre et De Profundis en Hébreu,* Paris, 1820.
Music Division.

GIACOMO MEYERBEER

Few composers in the nineteenth century attained greater popular success than Giacomo Meyerbeer (1791–1864). Son of a banker, who was Berlin's wealthiest Jew, and a mother of culture and religious commitment, Jacob (as he was then called) showed musical genius early. Among the manuscripts in the Music Division is an early work of Meyerbeer in his own hand, *Hallelujah, Eine Cantatine für 4 Männerstimmen mit Begleitung einer Obligaten Orgel und der Chores ad libitum von J. Meyerbeer* (Hallelujah, A Cantatine for 4 Male Voices with Organ Accompaniment and by Choir ad libitum, by J. Meyerbeer). A note on the title page adds: "Original manuscript unpublished," and so it remains to the present day. An unpublished manuscript by the leading nineteenth-century Jewish composer is an important item of Judaica, as is a piece of his religious music. But is it also a Jewish composition in content?

A signed, unpublished, holograph musical manuscript by Giacomo Meyerbeer, *Hallelujah,* for four male voices with organ accompaniment, written to be sung at a service of the Berlin Jewish Reform Temple housed in the Meyerbeer home. The words are by Edward Kley, tutor of the Meyerbeer children and preacher at the temple.

E. Kley and G. Meyerbeer, *Hallelujah,* Berlin, 1815? Music Division.

No author is listed, but a reading of the text discovers neither christological words nor allusions. *The Grove Dictionary of Music* lists it among Meyerbeer's works as "autograph Us Wc," i.e., a manuscript at the Library of Congress, and provides us with some important information. It attributes the text to "E. Kley," who is, of course, Edward Kley, one of the earliest Reform Jewish preachers and a writer of hymns. The text is a series of doxologies:

> Holy, holy, holy
> Holy thou art—Thy name is Holy.
> Splendid and great in your works,
> All call upon you in awe
> Hallelujah!
>
> Oh thou who wast born of dust, a dove
> The Holy One who appears in myriads of suns!
> Stand silent in astonishment; Adore in prayer,
> Hallelujah!

It goes on for three more verses. The first two verses Kley used again in a hymn published in the *Allgemeines Israelitisches Gesangbuch,* Hamburg, 1833, where the last stanzas differ from those in the Library's manuscript.

Edward Kley (1789–1867), born in Silesia, educated in Breslau, served as a tutor in the Beer* household from 1807 to 1817, at the same

*Born Jakob Liebmann Beer, he changed his name to Meyerbeer to fulfill the condition set by his grandfather, Liebmann Meyer Wulf, that he add "Meyer" to his name to become his sole heir.

time acting as one of the preachers of the private Reform Temple in the home of early Reform leader Israel Jacobson. Meyerbeer, who was only two years younger, became his friend. For lack of space, the temple, with Kley as minister, was, in 1815, moved into the Beer home. By that time, Meyerbeer had already left Berlin to continue his musical studies in Darmstadt and in Paris. Among the letters from Kley to Meyerbeer, one dated October 31, 1815, reads in part, "Your Hallelujah, or better, our Hallelujah, has not been heard yet, for lack of a decent organ." The "Hallelujah" was probably prepared for use at the inaugural, or an early service of the temple in the Beer home. The manuscript is perhaps the earliest Reform liturgical composition extant, a work which throws important light on the beginnings of Reform Judaism's liturgical creativity.

ERNEST BLOCH

Ernest Bloch (1880–1959) recalled:

> For years I had a number of sketches for the Book of Ecclesiastes which I had wanted to set to music, but the French language was not adaptable to my rhythmic patterns. Nor was German or English, and I hadn't a good enough command of Hebrew. Thus the sketches accumulated and . . . lay dormant.

Eventually the sketches were turned into the *Schelomo:* Hebraic Rhapsody for Cello and Orchestra. The Library recently acquired the complete autograph score of the work, on whose title page is: "Schelomo Rhapsodie hébraïque pour Violincelle Solo et Grand Orchestre par Ernest Bloch Partition . . . Pour Alexandre et Catherine Barjansky." At the end of the sixty-three-page manuscript, with erasures, corrections, and alterations in pencil and blue, black, and brown crayon, the composer inscribed: "Ernest Bloch Janvier-Febrier 1916 Geneve."

Bloch was thirty-six years old when he completed his masterpiece in his native city. Later his work took him to the United States, to France, and back to America. A good portion of his oeuvre was on Jewish themes, among them *Trois Poemes Juifs* (1913), the *Israel Symphony* (1916), and *Avodath Hakodesh* ("Sacred Service") (1933).

Bloch recalled how he turned sketches which lay dormant into the *Schelomo:*

> One day I met the cellist Alexander Barjansky and his wife. . . . I played my manuscript scores for them, *Hebrew Poems, Israel* and the Psalms, all of them unpublished and about which nobody cared. The Barjanskys were profoundly moved . . . Finally in my terrible loneliness, I had found true and warm friends. My hopes were reborn, and also the desire to write a work for this marvellous cellist. Why shouldn't I use for my Ecclesiastes—instead of a singer limited in range, a voice vaster and deeper than any spoken language—his cello? . . . The Ecclesiastes was completed in a few weeks, and since legends attribute this book to King Solomon, I named it *Schelomo*.

MARIO CASTELNUOVO-TEDESCO

Son of an old Florentine Jewish family, Mario Castelnuovo-Tedesco (1895–1968) left Italy in 1939 to escape the recently enacted racial laws. One of the leading Italian composers of his day, he was drawn more and

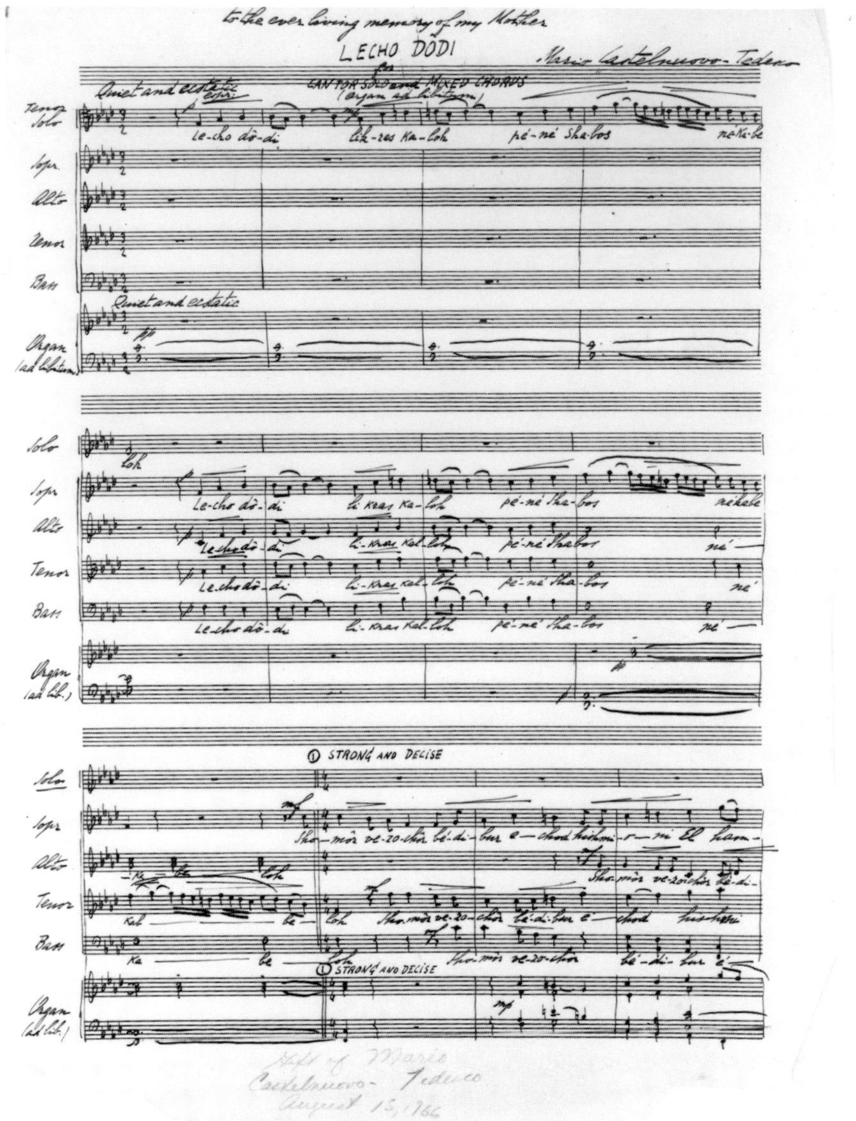

This music for *Lecho Dodi*, a song of welcome to "Bride Sabbath" at the Sabbath eve service, for cantor solo and mixed choir (organ ad libitum), was composed for the Amsterdam synagogue in 1937, and is dedicated by the composer "to the ever living memory of my Mother."

Mario Castelnuovo-Tedesco, *Lecho Dodi*, Amsterdam, 1937.
Music Division.

more to the music of his Jewish heritage, a spiritual and artistic journey begun in 1925, when he found in his grandfather's house a manuscript notebook of Jewish melodies. Like Ernest Bloch, he came to the United States and, among many other works on Jewish themes, composed a *Sacred Service* (1943). Among his manuscripts deposited in the Music Division are two liturgical works: *Lecho Dodi*, the opening hymn of the Sabbath eve service, a welcome to the Sabbath Bride, written in 1937 for the Amsterdam Synagogue and dedicated "To the everliving memory of my Mother," and a *Memorial Service for the Departed* (1960), "in memory of Lina Castelnuovo."

DARIUS MILHAUD

From our perspective, the life and career of Darius Milhaud (1892–1974) paralleled that of Castelnuovo-Tedesco to a remarkable degree. He, too, was the scion of an old Jewish family, one of the first to settle in southern France, and he also became one of his country's most distinguished composers. Milhaud was even more prolific and versatile, composing operas, symphonies, concerti, songs, and cantatas. With the fall of France in 1940, he fled to the United States, where he continued his fruitful career. Among his works on Jewish themes are *Poemes juifs* (1916), *Chants populaires hebraiques* (1925) and, like Bloch and Castelnuovo-Tedesco before him, a *Service Sacre* (Sacred Service) in 1947.

The Library's Koussevitsky Music Foundation Collection has the full manuscript of Milhaud's opera *David* (1952), which his biographer, Paul Collaer, calls "certainly one of his most important and accomplished works." Milhaud has written about its origins.

> Serge Koussevitsky . . . sent for me to tell me that he was arranging a great festival in Israel to commemorate the three-thousandth anniversary of King David [and of the city of Jerusalem, to be celebrated in 1954]. He had asked me to write a large work for that occasion. He told me I could choose my own collaborator. I thought immediately of Armand Lunel, for I find it very pleasant to work with him, as we can calmly discuss all problems without alienating him or risking the conflicts that spring from absurd touchiness.

Armand Lunel (1892-?), born in the same year and town, Aix-en-Provence, as Milhaud, also came of an old distinguished Jewish family and was his boyhood friend. A teacher of philosophy, Lunel achieved recognition with his prolific writing as one of the portrayers of life in Provence. The two friends had previously joined to produce *Esther de Carpentras* (1926), based on an old Provencal Purim play. The librettist and composer collaborated again to celebrate the ancient Jewish capital reborn and commemorate the great Jewish king, David. Their joint manuscript is one of the treasures of the Music Division.

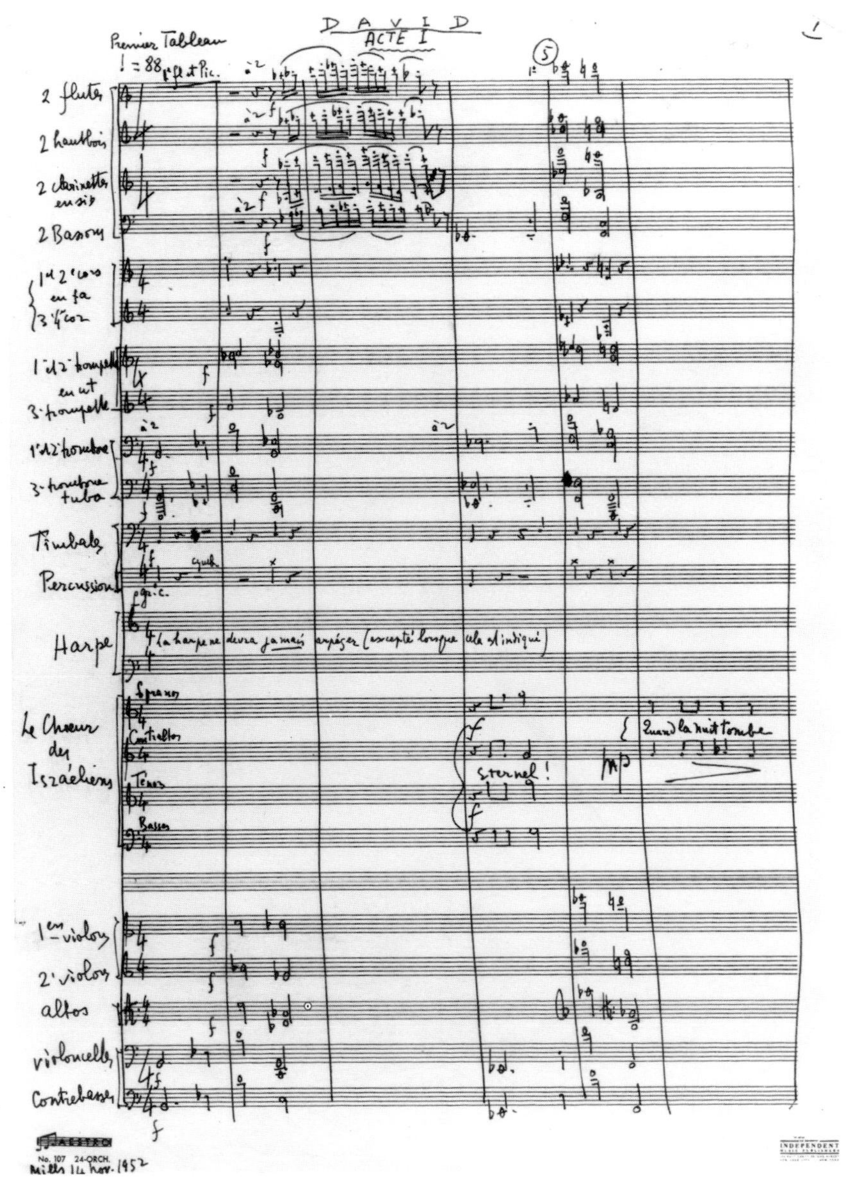

Just before his death in 1951, Serge Koussevitsky invited Darius Milhaud to compose a major work for a "great festival in Israel to commemorate the three-thousandth anniversary of King David." Milhaud responded with the opera *David* (1952), for which Armand Lunel, French novelist and lifelong friend wrote the libretto. The holograph manuscript of the opera is in the Koussevitsky Foundation Collection at the Library of Congress.

Darius Milhaud, *David,* 1952.
Music Division.

ARNOLD SCHOENBERG

The Koussevitsky Foundation also commissioned what turned out to be one of the first musical works on the Holocaust. The manuscript of the work, completed in 1947, in the composer's hand is in the Music Division: *A Survivor from Warsaw,* For Narrator and Men's Choir and Orchestra, opus 46 by Arnold Schoenberg (1874–1951). Schoenberg, who introduced the use of atonality and the twelve-note scale, was born in Vienna and grew up in that city during its era of manifest anti-Semitism. His radical musical innovation made him one of the most controversial and influential musical figures of the twentieth century. When the Nazis came to power in 1933, he was dismissed from his post as a director of a school for musical composition at the Prussian Academy of Arts in Berlin. His response was a formal, public return to the Jewish faith which he had left early in life. America offered a haven and became his home.

To the title page of the manuscript of *A Survivor from Warsaw,* Schoenberg added a note, "This text is based partly upon reports which I have received directly or indirectly," because he wrote the text as well as the music. His Narrator, describing a scene of heroic defiance in the Warsaw Ghetto, begins by saying:

> I cannot remember everything! I must have been unconscious much of the time. I remember only the grandiose moment when they all started to sing the old prayer they had neglected for so many years—the forgotten creed.

Text and music describe a roll call of doomed men on their way to the gas chamber.

> They started again first slowly one—two—three—became faster and faster: so fast it finally sounded like a stampede of wild horses and—quite of a sudden—in the middle of it they began singing the SCHEMA YISROEL.

The work concludes with the rhythmic singing of the Hebrew words of the traditional Jewish affirmation of faith:

> Hear, Oh Israel, the Lord our God, the Lord is One. And thou shalt love the Lord thy God with all thy heart, all thy soul, all thy might.

As he had done in 1933, Schoenberg responded in 1947 to the enemy who would destroy his people and its faith, with a dramatic outcry affirming his loyalty to both.

Schoenberg's *Kol Nidre* (1939), written five years after his arrival in the United States, and his three great works on biblical themes—*Die Jakobsleiter* (Jacob's Ladder), *Modern Psalms,* and his opera *Moses and Aaron*—all unfinished at the time of his death, show his continuing attraction to Jewish themes. He left his manuscripts and books to the National Library in Jerusalem. A portrait in oil of Schoenberg by George Gershwin hangs in the Library of Congress's Music Division.

Facing page:
"Dedicated to the Koussevitzky Music Foundation who commissioned it" by the composer, who adds a note on the title page of *A Survivor from Warsaw:*

This text is based partly upon reports which I have received directly or indirectly. A Sch

Schoenberg wrote the text as well as the music, whose theme is heroic defiance in the Warsaw Ghetto. Doomed men on the way to a gas chamber sing *Schema Yisrael.* Is the title Schoenberg chose of autobiographic import, the "Hear O, Israel" of one who defiantly returned to the faith of his fathers?

Arnold Schoenberg, *A Survivor from Warsaw,* n.p., n.d. Music Division.

AARON COPLAND

Brooklyn-born Aaron Copland (1900-1990), did more than any other composer to introduce the American musical idiom into classical music,

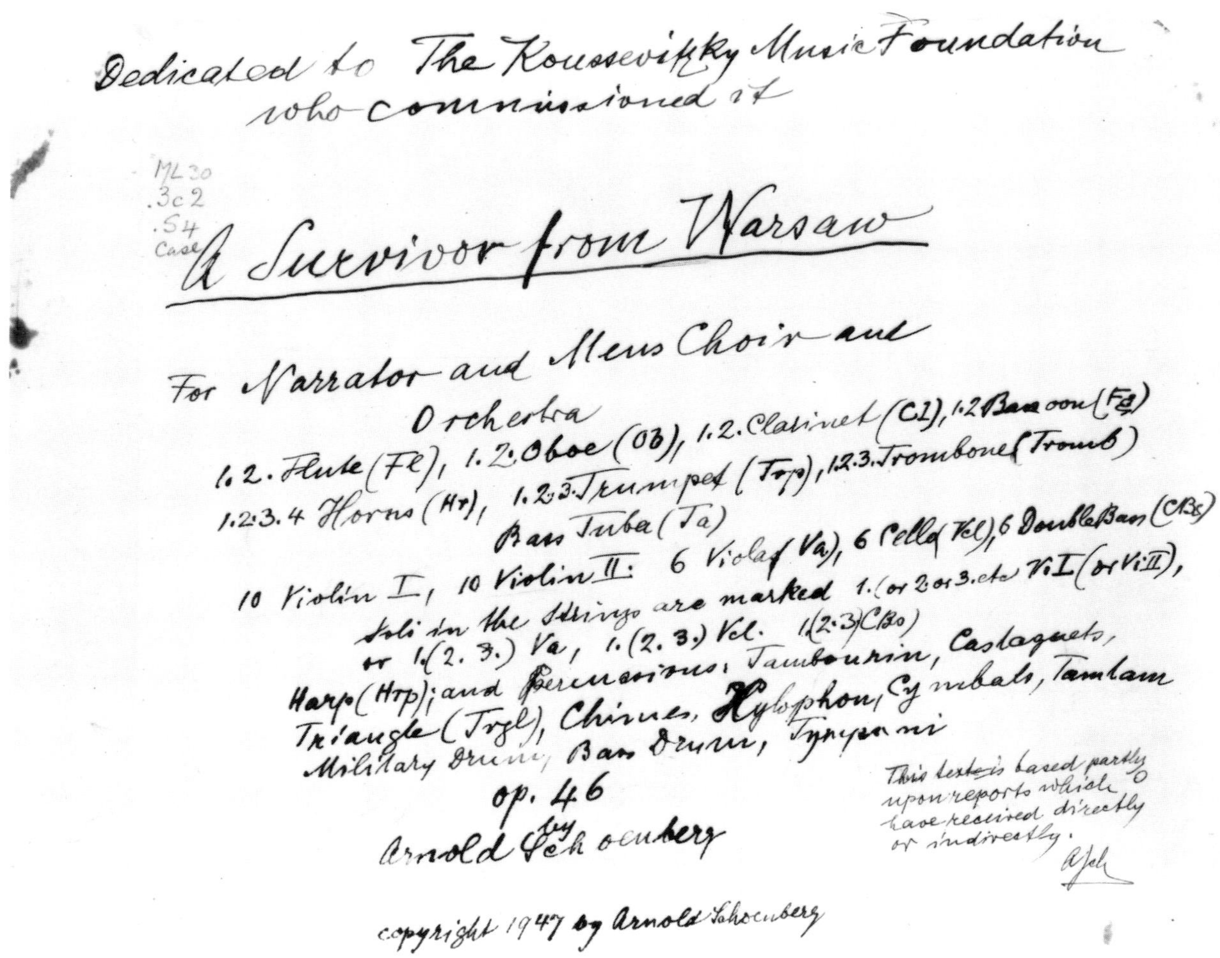

Dedicated to The Koussevitzky Music Foundation
who commissioned it

A Survivor from Warsaw

For Narrator and Mens Choir and
Orchestra
1.2. Flute (Fl), 1.2. Oboe (Ob), 1.2. Clarinet (Cl), 1.2 Bassoon (Fg)
1.2.3.4 Horns (Hr), 1.2.3. Trumpet (Trp), 1.2.3. Trombone (Tromb)
Bass Tuba (Ta)
10 Violin I, 10 Violin II, 6 Violas (Va), 6 Celli (Vcl), 6 DoubleBass (CBs)
Soli in the strings are marked 1. (or 2. or 3. etc ViI (or ViII),
or 1.(2.3.) Va, 1.(2.3.) Vcl. 1(2.3) CBs)
Harp (Hrp); and Percussions: Tambourin, Castagnets,
Triangle (Trgl), Chimes, Xylophon, Cymbals, Tamtam
Military Drum, Bass Drum, Tympani

op. 46
by Arnold Schoenberg

This text is based partly upon reports which I have received directly or indirectly.
ASch

jazz in *Piano Concerto* (1927), Western tunes in *Billy the Kid* (1938) and *Rodeo* (1942), folk airs in *Appalachian Spring* (1944), and Latin rhythms in *El Salon Mexico* (1937) and *Danzon Cubano* (1942). He did the same with a popular East European Jewish theme in his *Vitebsk* (1929).

On the first page of Copland's work sheets, he talks about using the tune "mipne ma" as it was sung in Vitebska, where the famous playwright Ansky was born, and which Ansky included as a melody in his play *The Dybbuk.* The play's Hebrew version (translated by the famous Hebrew poet, Hayyim Nahman Bialik) was performed in 1927 by the brilliant Habimah Theater of Moscow to audiences in New York, where Copland must have seen it. Its insistent melodic theme, "mipne ma?"—for what reason?—inquires,

Why? O why? / Has the soul descended from on high?

And states:

Descent from on high, / demands that man must ever try, / to rise upward!

In the course of the drama, the melody evinces many moods, yearning, compassion, command, the sigh of despair vying with the cry of exultation, but through it all that echoing question, "Why?"

LEONARD BERNSTEIN

Leonard Bernstein (1918-1990) burst upon the musical scene with meteoric brilliance. Charismatic conductor, wide-ranging composer, inspiring teacher, Bernstein has for almost four decades held center stage on the contemporary musical scene. Through it all, his Jewish artistic identity has always been visible. His oratoria *Kaddish,* sung in Hebrew, was first heard in Tel Aviv; his *Chichester Psalms* are sung in the language of their ancient authors.

The Bernstein Collection is one of the treasures of the Music Division. From it we have chosen two of his earliest works, both in the composer's own hand. The first, a liturgical work, commissioned by the Park Avenue Synagogue, *Hashkivenu,* for the Sabbath eve service, sings:

> Cause us, O Lord, to lie down in peace,
> And raise us up, O our King, unto life.
> Spread over us the tabernacle of Thy peace,
> And through Thy good counsel direct us.

The second, his first symphonic work, the *Jeremiah Symphony* (1944), opens with the movement, "Prophecy," which sounds the notes of the traditional cantillation with which the prophetic portion of the week is chanted in the synagogue at the Sabbath morning service. Its third movement, "Lamentation," calls for a soprano who sings, in the traditional melody, a portion of the biblical book of *Lamentations,* whose description of the destruction of Jerusalem and the suffering of its inhabitants is attributed to the Prophet Jeremiah.

On the occasion of Bernstein's seventieth birthday, a critic wrote in the *New York Times,* "It does seem reasonable that a former wonder boy should write incidental music for J. M. Barrie's *Peter Pan,* though not inevitable

Facing page: The composer describes this composition as: "Vitebsk, study on a Jewish melody for violin, cello and piano . . ." The playwright Ansky used this melody in *The Dybbuk,* transcribing it as it was sung in his native village Vitebsk.

Aaron Copland, *Vitebsk,* 1929.
Music Division.

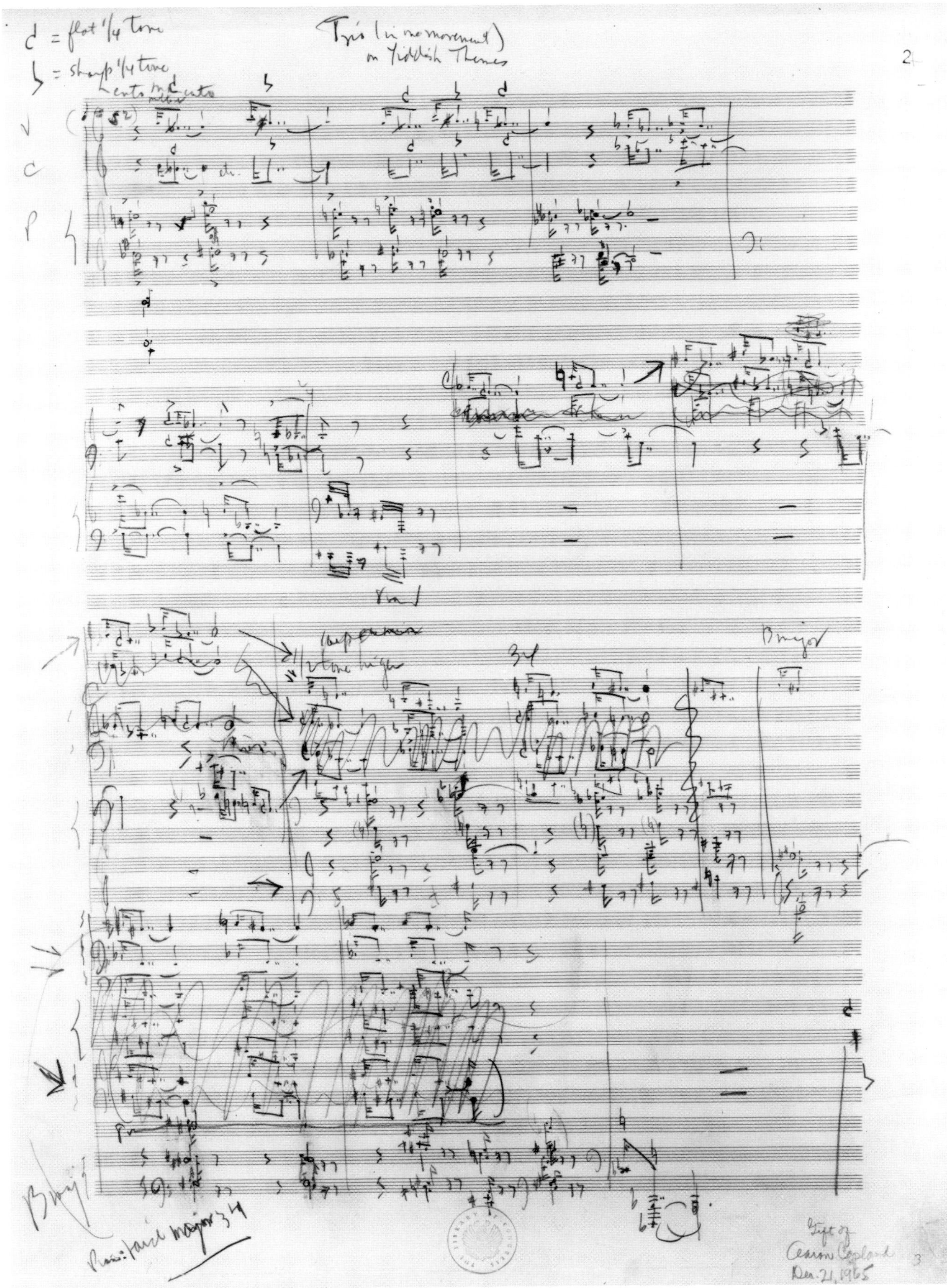
= flat 1/4 tone
= sharp 1/4 tone
B major
Gift of
Aaron Copland
Dec. 21, 1965

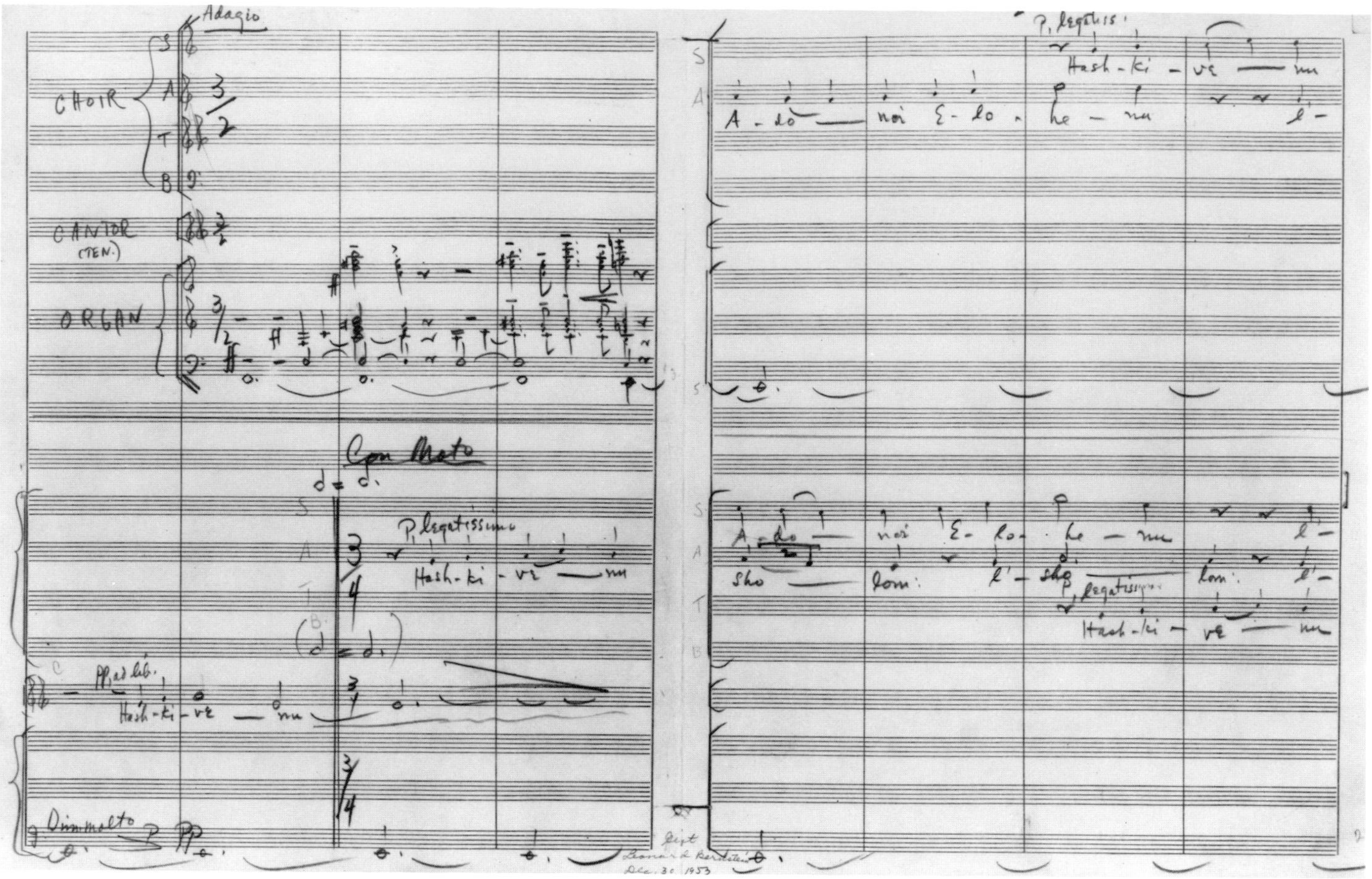

Hashkivenu, "Cause us, o Lord, to lie down in peace," was commissioned by the Park Avenue Synagogue from the twenty-seven-year-old composer, for use at its Sabbath eve service, April 4, 1945.

Leonard Bernstein, *Hashkivenu,* April 4, 1945. Music Division.

Leonard Bernstein's first symphonic work, the *Jeremiah Symphony,* written at age twenty-six, uses the traditional cantillations in which the prophetic portion of the week is chanted on the Sabbath in the synagogue. The soprano solo in the third movement, "Lamentation," is in the traditional melody used to chant the Book of Lamentations on the eve of *Tisha B'Av,* the fast commemorating the destruction of the Temple. According to an old tradition, the prophet Jeremiah was the author of *Lamentations.*

Leonard Bernstein, *Jeremiah Symphony,* 1944. Music Division.

that the same artist should be attracted to the Lamentations of Jeremiah as the basis for his Symphony No. 1." Not inevitable but certainly understandable, when we consider that whatever musical tradition the young Bernstein was entering, he was already in the spiritual tradition of Bloch, Milhaud, Castelnuovo-Tedesco and Schoenberg.

GEORGE GERSHWIN

Early in life, George Gershwin (1898–1937) frequented the Yiddish theaters on Second Avenue in New York's Lower East Side and was much taken with the music of Joseph Rumshisky. In 1915, Boris Thomashevsky, reigning star of the Yiddish Theater, invited Gershwin and Sholem Secunda to collaborate on a Yiddish operetta. Gershwin was willing, but Secunda refused to join with a young, musically untrained, publishing-house pianist. Later in life, when he was already a successful writer of popular songs, Gershwin signed a contract with the Metropolitan Opera to write an opera based on Ansky's *Dybbuk* and was ready to go to Europe to study Jewish music, but having learned that the rights to the play had already been given to Ludovico Rocca, he withdrew.

Gershwin's idiom was the American scene and its music. Beginning with jazz and popular songs, he broadened his talents thematically and musically, until they culminated in his greatest work, the opera *Porgy and Bess* (1935). In the vast Gershwin Collection in the Library, there is but one composition on a "Jewish theme," the sprightly ditty, *Mischa, Yascha, Toscha, Sascha,* of which Gershwin biographer Charles Schwartz tells:

> a humorous takeoff on the names of four famous Russian violinists: Mischa Elman, Jascha Heifetz, Toscha Seidel and Sascha Jacobsen. George and Ira [Gershwin] had originally written this tune around 1921. Gershwin frequently sang and played it at parties, particularly when any of the violinists who inspired the title was present.

The virtuoso violinists of this song title are Elman, Heifetz, Seidel, and Jacobsen, Russian Jewish violinists all, who made their way to America. The humorous lyrics of *Mischa, Yascha, Toscha, Sascha,* include "Dear Old Fritz"—Kreisler, that is, who was widely thought to be Jewish. Lyricist Ira Gershwin has the four proclaiming:

We're not high brows,
we're not low brows . . .
we're He-brows . . .

A signed photo of Kreisler accompanies the holograph manuscript of this humorous song now in the Gershwin Collection.

George and Ira Gershwin, *Mischa, Yascha, Toscha, Sascha.* n.d.
Music Division.

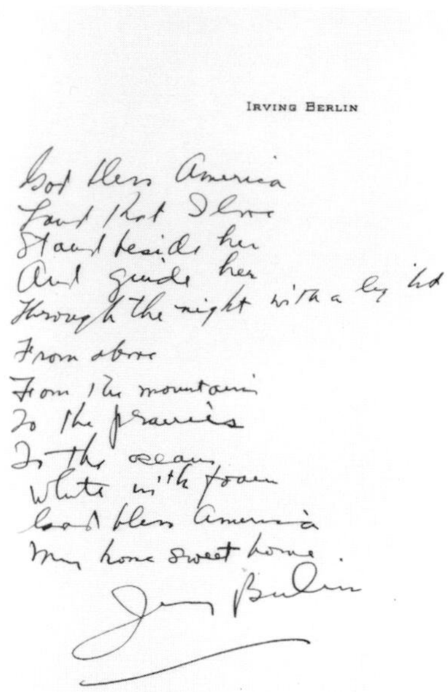
IRVING BERLIN

God bless America
Land that I love
Stand beside her
And guide her
Through the night with a light
From above
From the mountains
To the prairies
To the ocean
White with foam
God bless America
My home sweet home.
Irving Berlin

To express his gratitude to President Dwight D. Eisenhower for conferring upon him a special gold medal, Irving Berlin sent a signed holograph copy of the words of the song that has become a second national anthem, "God Bless America."

Irving Berlin, "God Bless America." n.d.
Music Division.

The lyrics add one more name to the four, "dear old Fritz," meaning Fritz Kreisler, who must have been at a party where it was sung. Among Gershwin's papers is a copy of part of the original manuscript of the song and on the page where Kreisler is mentioned, the violinist signed, "with kindest regards of Fritz Kreisler." Accompanying it is a signed photograph of the virtuoso with his famed violin. One refrain is:

We're not high-brows, we're not low brows,
    Any one can see,
You don't have to use a chart,
To see we're He-brows from the start. . . .
Mischa, Yascha, Toscha, Sascha.

The Gershwins refer, of course, to the unusual number of Jews among the world's greatest violin virtuosos, especially the Russian-born students of the great violin teacher, Leopold Auer, to whom due credit is given in the song.

One of George Gershwin's early jobs was transcribing the music of the songs Irving Berlin was composing, a craft that America's leading writer of popular songs never mastered. In 1917, Abraham Cahan already has his fictional immigrant millionaire cloak manufacturer speak in envy (the obvious reference is to Irving Berlin) of the "Russian Jew who holds the foremost place among songwriters and whose soulful compositions are sung in almost every English-speaking house." Of the 1,500 songs Berlin wrote, perhaps the best known is "God Bless America." When he received a special gold medal from President Eisenhower for composing it, Berlin wrote the words on his personal stationery and sent them to the Library of Congress.

God bless America
Land that I love
. . .
God bless America
My home sweet home.
    Irving Berlin.

For America it has become a second national anthem.

One of George Gershwin's early jobs was to transcribe Irving Berlin's songs to the musical page. The enormously prolific Berlin fashioned the words and music for some fifteen hundred songs, but never acquired the skill of actually setting down the musical notes on paper.

George Gershwin and Irving Berlin
Music Division.

AFTERWORD

■ WE HAVE NOW TRAVERSED four continents and four millennia in pursuit of landmarks of the civilization called Judaism. We have sought out historic markers on the highways and byways of Jewish life and creativity. Books, manuscripts, maps, and prints were encountered and persuaded to yield up their tales.

A journey that began with God's Creation continued through man's creativity. From the hills of the Holy Land, through the streets of Jerusalem, we wended our way to academies in Babylonia and printing houses in Italy, Turkey, and Amsterdam. We glimpsed Jewish life in the ghettos of Central Europe and the townlets of Eastern Europe. We entered the New World with the waves of Jewish immigrants seeking and finding political freedom and economic opportunity. We witnessed the German Jew's enterprise of community building and social integration, and beheld the Russian Jew's creativity in transforming oppressive slum into cultural enclave. And at journey's end, the sound of music, bringing to our mind's ear the drama of King David, the soul-searching of Solomon, the lamentations of Jeremiah; a mystic's melody from the Old World and a song of praise to the New.

Because the Library of Congress is so rich a repository of the treasures of the human spirit, we were able to accomplish this instructive journey within its confines and present the fruits thereof in one room and one book.

Ours has been but a small sampling of the cultural creativity of one people, one faith, one civilization. Yet, in a sense, we have encompassed far more. The languages of human discourse are many, the forms of cultural expression may be infinite, but the spirit of mankind is one. In the life and creativity of one civilization we glimpse the vitality and power of all humankind.

Many an early Hebrew book concludes with an apology by the author. It generally takes one of two forms: "so much more can be said on the subject but, alas, the allotted paper is already filled"; or "so that the allotted paper not be left blank, I add this thought . . . ," a final word, as it were. In that tradition, let me conclude.

We have run our course, so let us return to where we started, the Book of Books. In biblical Hebrew past and future intermingle: the same word can be used to express both. A single slim Hebrew letter, the *vov*, prefixed to a verb, works the magic of changing future into past and past into future. To the reader of English, the *vov* looks most like the letter I. A library works the same magic. It arrests time—stops it in its tracks, rolls it back—so that I, the reader, may live it again, reexperience its adventures of the spirit, ever mindful that in our yesterdays are the beginnings of our tomorrows.

FOR FURTHER READING

We provide here a brief list of books in English for those who would further pursue subjects suggested by *From the Ends of the Earth,* the exhibit and its companion volume.

The Library of Congress

Goodrum, Charles A., *Treasures of the Library of Congress,* N.Y., 1980.
Salamanca, Lucy, *Fortress of Freedom,* Philadelphia, N.Y., 1942.

Jewish History and Civilization

Roth, Cecil, *A Short History of the Jewish People,* London, 1970.
Grayzel, Solomon, *A History of the Jews,* Philadelphia, 1968.
Sachar, Howard L., *The Course of Modern Jewish History,* N.Y., 1963.
Wigoder, Geofrey, ed., *Jewish Art and Civilization,* 2 vols., Fribourg, 1972.
Metzger, Therese and Mendel, *Jewish Life in the Middle Ages,* N.Y., 1982.

The Hebrew Book

Posner, Raphael and Israel Ta-Shema, eds., *The Hebrew Book,* Jerusalem, 1975.
Gold, Leonard S., ed., *A Sign and a Witness: 2,000 Years of Hebrew Books and Illuminated Manuscripts,* N.Y., 1988.
Amram, David, *The Makers of Hebrew Books in Italy,* Philadelphia, 1909; London, 1963.
Bloch, Joshua, *Early Hebrew Printing in Spain and Portugal,* N.Y., 1938.
Hill, Brad Sabin, *Incunabula, Hebraica and Judaica,* Ottawa, 1981.
Marx, Moses, *Gershom Soncino's Wander-Years in Italy 1498–1527,* Cincinnati, 1969.
Roth, Cecil, *Studies in Books and Booklore,* Farnborough, England, 1972.

Hebrew Manuscripts

Narkiss, Bezalel, *Hebrew Illuminated Manuscripts,* Jerusalem, 1969.
Guttmann, Joseph, *Hebrew Manuscript Painting,* N.Y., 1978.
Sed-Rajna, Gabrielle, *The Hebrew Bible in Medieval Illuminated Manuscripts,* N.Y., 1987.

The Bible and Talmud

Berkowitz, David Sadler, *In Remembrance of Creation,* "Evolution of Art and

Scholarship in the Medieval and Renaissance Bible," Waltham, 1968.
Sandmel, Samuel, *The Hebrew Scriptures: An Introduction to Their Literature and Religious Ideas,* N.Y., 1963.
Bamberger, Bernard, *The Bible: A Modern Jewish Approach,* 1955.
Cohen, Abraham, *Everyman's Talmud,* London, 1949.
Adler, Morris, *World of the Talmud,* 1958.

Maimonides

Heschel, Abraham Joshua, *Maimonides,* N.Y., 1982.
Twersky, Isadore, ed., *A Maimonides Reader,* N.Y., 1972.
Goodman, Lenn Evan, ed., *Readings in the Philosophy of Moses Maimonides,* N.Y., 1977.
Mishneh Torah, The Code of Maimonides, Yale Judaica Series, New Haven, 1971, ff.
Guide of the Perplexed, ed. and trans., Shlomo Pines, Chicago, 1963.

Maps of the Holy Land

Nebenzahl, Kenneth, *Maps of the Holy Land,* N.Y., 1986.
Laor, Evan, *Maps of the Holy Land,* N.Y., 1986.

Jewish Life in the Old World

Abrahams, Israel, *Jewish Life in the Middle Ages,* Philadelphia, 1932.
Goiten, Shlomo D., *Jews and Arabs,* N.Y., 1955.
Roth, Cecil, *A History of the Marranos,* N.Y., 1959.
——— *The History of the Jews in Italy,* Philadelphia, 1946.
——— *A History of the Jews in England,* Oxford, 1964.
Lowenthal, Marvin, *The Jews of Germany,* Philadelphia, 1944.
Greenberg, Louis, *The Jews in Russia,* New Haven, 1965.
Dawidowicz, Lucy, ed., *The Golden Tradition,* N.Y., 1967.

. . . *and in the New*

Karp, Abraham J., *Haven and Home, A History of the Jews in America,* N.Y., 1985.
Marcus, Jacob R., *The Colonial American Jew, 1492–1776,* Detroit, 1970.
Blau, Joseph L. and Salo Baron, eds., *The Jews of the United States 1790–1840: A Documentary History,* 3 vols., N.Y., 1963.
Korn, Bertram, W., *American Jewry and the Civil War,* Philadelphia, 1951.
Cohen, Naomi, *Encounter with Emancipation: The German Jew in the United States 1880–1914,* Philadelphia, 1984.
Howe, Irving, *World of Our Fathers,* N.Y., 1976.

Music and Art

Idelsohn, A. Z., *Jewish Music,* N.Y., 1929.
Rothmuller, M., *Music of the Jews,* London, 1953.
Roth, Cecil, ed., *Jewish Art,* N.Y., 1961, 1971.

We especially call to the reader's attention the three multivolume Jewish encyclopedias which should be the first works consulted. The first listed is particularly strong in biographical presentations; the second, in its American material; the third, for its contemporary data.

The Jewish Encyclopedia, 12 vols., N.Y., 1901, ff.
The Universal Jewish Encyclopedia, 10 vols., N.Y., 1939, 1969.
Encyclopedia Judaica, 16 vols., Jerusalem, 1971.

EXHIBITION CHECKLIST

FROM THE ENDS OF THE EARTH

JUDAIC TREASURES OF THE LIBRARY OF CONGRESS

June 1991–August 1991
Madison Gallery
James Madison Memorial Building

An Exhibition Prepared by the
Interpretive Programs Office of the Library of Congress
Under the Direction of
Irene U. Burnham
Interpretive Programs Officer

■

Exhibition Coordinator
Jacqueline McGlade, Project Coordinator
Interpretive Programs Office

■

Exhibition Curator
Abraham J. Karp, Guest Curator

■

Exhibition Designer
Patricia Chester
Chester Design Associates, Inc.
Washington, D.C.

This checklist includes Judaic treasures displayed at the Library of Congress from June 1991 through August 1991 in the James Madison Memorial Building's Madison Gallery. Organized by chapter to facilitate use, the list contains a brief bibliographic citation for each item, the dimensions of the object (height by width in inches), and a page reference to an illustration accompanied by an explanatory caption. When the item referred to is a manuscript, information on the medium is provided as well.

CHAPTER 1

First Judaica and Judaic Firsts

Flavius Josephus
The Genuine Works of Flavius Josephus, the Jewish Historian
William Whiston, translator
London, 1737
$15\frac{3}{4} \times 11$ inches
Rare Book and Special Collections Division, Jefferson Library
[Illustrated on page 3]

Flavius Josephus
Flavii Josephi Antiquitatum Judaicarum
Oxford, 1700
$8\frac{1}{8} \times 5\frac{3}{8}$ inches
Rare Book and Special Collections Division, Jefferson Library
[Illustrated on page 4]

Talmud. *Baba Kamma*
Baba Kamma, Mi'masekhet Nezikin, De Legibus Ebraeorum . . .
Latin translation and commentary by Constantine L'Empereur
Leyden, 1637
$7\frac{3}{4} \times 6$ inches
Rare Book and Special Collections Division, Jefferson Library
[Illustrated on page 7]

B.D. Spinoza
Opera Posthuma Compendium Grammaticus Lingua Hebraeae
Amsterdam, 1677
$8\frac{1}{2} \times 6\frac{3}{4}$ inches
Rare Book and Special Collections Division, Jefferson Library
[Illustrated on page 8]

Joshua Montefiore
A Commercial Dictionary
Philadelphia, 1804
$8\frac{3}{4} \times 5\frac{3}{4}$ inches
Rare Book and Special Collections Division, Jefferson Library
[Illustrated on page 9]

Solomon ben Abraham Adret
Teshuvot She'elot ha-Rashba
Rome (?) 1469–72 (?)
$8\frac{1}{2} \times 6\frac{1}{8}$ inches
Hebraic Section
[Illustrated on pages 10–11]

Moses of Coucy
Sefer Mitzvot Gadol
Soncino, 1488
$12\frac{1}{2} \times 8\frac{3}{4}$ inches
Rare Book and Special Collections Division
[Illustrated on page 13]

Pentateuch with Targum Onkeles and Rashi
Bologna, 1482
$12\frac{3}{8} \times 8\frac{3}{4}$ inches
Rare Book and Special Collections Division
[Illustrated on page 14]

David ben Yosef Abudarham
Abudarham
Fez, Morocco, 1516
$10\frac{3}{4} \times 8\frac{1}{8}$ inches
Hebraic Section
[Illustrated on page 16]

Moses ben Nahman
Perush ha-Torah
Lisbon, 1489
$11\frac{3}{8} \times 8\frac{1}{4}$ inches
Hebraic Section
[Illustrated on page 16]

Yom Tov Zahalon
Lekah Tov
Safed, 1577
$7 \times 5\frac{1}{2}$ inches
Hebraic Section
[Illustrated on page 17]

Yaakov Yosef Katz
Sefer Toldot Yaakov Yosef
Korets, 1780
$12\frac{3}{4} \times 8$ inches
Hebraic Section
[Illustrated on page 19]

CHAPTER 2

The Book of the People of the Book

Sefer Torah
Eighteenth century (?)
Manuscript; ink on parchment/leather
$26\frac{1}{4}$ inches high
Hebraic Section
[Illustrated on page 20]

Megillat Esther
Fourteenth-fifteenth centuries (?)
Manuscript; ink on parchment
$30\frac{7}{8}$ inches high
Hebraic Section
[Illustrated on page 20]

Psalms
Commentary by David Kimhi
Bologna (?), August 29, 1477
$10\frac{3}{4} \times 8\frac{1}{4}$ inches
Hebraic Section
[Illustrated on page 24]

Psalms
Commentary by David Kimhi
Naples, 4th day in Nisan, 5247 (1487)
$10\frac{1}{8} \times 7\frac{5}{8}$ inches
Hebraic Section
[Illustrated on page 25]

Mikraot Gedolot
Venice, 1516–17
$15 \times 10\frac{1}{8}$ inches
Hebraic Section
[Illustrated on page 25]

Perush ha-Torah
Constantinople, 1522
$16\frac{1}{4} \times 11\frac{1}{4}$ inches
Hebraic Section
[Illustrated on page 26]

Torah, Nevi'im, Ketubim
Paris, 1539–44
$9\frac{3}{4} \times 6\frac{3}{4}$ inches
Rare Book and Special Collections Division, Rosenwald Collection
[Illustrated on page 26]

Biblia Hebraica
Amsterdam, 1667
$8\frac{3}{4} \times 5\frac{7}{8}$ inches
Hebraic Section
[Illustrated on page 29]

Hamishah Humshe Torah
Ortakoi, 1832–35
$10\frac{1}{4} \times 7\frac{1}{4}$ inches
Hebraic Section
[Illustrated on page 30]

Book of Leviticus
Safed, 1833
$8\frac{3}{8} \times 6\frac{1}{8}$ inches
Hebraic Section
[Illustrated on page 31]

Hamishah Humshe Torah
Berlin, 1933
$16\frac{3}{8} \times 11$ inches
Hebraic Section
[Illustrated on page 32]

Humash
Munich, 1947
$7 \times 5\frac{3}{4}$ inches
Hebraic Section
[Illustrated on page 34]

Biblia Italiana
Venice, 1494
$12\frac{1}{8} \times 8\frac{5}{8}$ inches
Rare Book and Special Collections Division, Rosenwald Collection
[Illustrated on page 37]

De Bibel Int Carte
Antwerp, 1516
9½ × 7½ inches
Rare Book and Special Collections Division, Rosenwald Collection
[Illustrated on page 39]

CHAPTER 3
The Sea of the Talmud and Some Shores It Has Touched

Talmud. *Yebamot*
Pesaro, 1508
12¾ × 9⅛ inches
Hebraic Section
[Illustrated on page 45]

Talmud. *Yebamot*
Venice, 1520
13½ × 9¾ inches
Hebraic Section
[Illustrated on page 45]

Talmud. *Nidah*
Frankfurt an der Oder, 1697
14⅛ × 10¼ inches
Hebraic Section
[Illustrated on page 49]

Johannes Coccejus
Duo Tituli Thalmudici Sanhedrin et Maccoth
Amsterdam, 1629
7⅝ × 6¼ inches
Hebraic Section
[Illustrated on page 50]

Talmud. *Middot*
Talmudis Babylonici Codex Middoth sive De Mensuris Templi
Translation and commentary by Constantine L'Empereur
Leyden, 1630
7⅞ × 6⅛ inches
Rare Book and Special Collections Division
[Illustrated on page 50]

Talmud. *Berakhot*
Edited by Dr. E. M. Pinner
Berlin, 1842
17⅝ × 11¼ inches
Hebraic Section
[Illustrated on page 51]

Talmud. *Berakhot*
Munich-Heidelberg, 1948
15¾ × 11 inches
Hebraic Section
[Illustrated on page 53]

CHAPTER 4
"From Moses to Moses, There Was None Like Moses"

Abraham Horowitz
Hesed Avraham
Lublin, 1577
10⅜ × 8 inches
Hebraic Section
[Illustrated on page 61]

Moses Maimonides
Moreh Nevukhim
Sabioneta, 1553
12 × 8⅝ inches
Hebraic Section
[Illustrated on page 62]

Moses Maimonides
Rabbi Mossei Aegypti, Dux seu Director Dubitatium aut Perplexorum
Paris, 1520
13 × 8¾ inches
Rare Book and Special Collections Division
[Illustrated on page 63]

Moses Maimonides
De Idolatria
Amsterdam, 1641
7⅞ × 6⅜ inches
Hebraic Section
[Illustrated on page 64]

Moses Maimonides
Igrot La-maor ha-Gadol
Venice, 1545
6⅛ × 4¼ inches
Hebraic Section
[Illustrated on page 65]

Moses Maimonides
Mishneh Torah
Venice, 1574
12½ × 8⅞ inches
Hebraic Section
[Illustrated on page 71]

Moses Maimonides
Mishneh Torah
Amsterdam, 1702
14½ × 9 inches
Hebraic Section
[Illustrated on page 72]

CHAPTER 5
Charting the Holy Land

Claudius Ptolemy
Map of the Holy Land
Cosmographica
Ulm, 1482
16⅞ × 11¾ inches
Geography and Map Division
[Illustrated on page 75]

Abraham Ortelius
Map of the Holy Land
Theatrum Orbis Terrarum
Antwerp, 1575
18½ × 12½ inches
Geography and Map Division
[Illustrated on page 76]

Willem Blaeu
Map of the Children of Israel in the Sinai Wilderness
Atlas Maior
Amsterdam, 1662–65
22 ½ × 13 ¾ inches
Geography and Map Division
[Illustrated on page 77]

George Braun and Franciscus Hogenberg
Map of Jerusalem
Civitates Orbis Terrarum
vol. 4, Cologne, 1612
16 ⅞ × 12 inches
Geography and Map Division
[Illustrated on page 79]

Nicholas Sanson
Map of the Holy Land
Judaea Seu Terra Sancta
Amsterdam, 1696
22½ × 33 inches
Geography and Map Division
[Illustrated on page 80]

Abraham bar Jacob
Map of the Holy Land
Haggadah shel Pesah
Amsterdam, 1781
10¼ × 19 inches
Hebraic Section
[Illustrated on pages 82–83]

"Holy Cities" Wall Plaque
Jerusalem (?), c. 1870
Manuscript; watercolor on paper
21⅝ × 31⅝ inches
Hebraic Section
[Illustrated on page 85]

Pullout Map of the Temple
Moses Gentili
Sefer Hanukat ha-Bayit
Venice, 1696
8¾ × 6⅜ inches
Hebraic Section
[Illustrated on page 88]

Moses Ivier
Architectural Map of the "Once and Future Temple"
Yom Tov Lipmann Heller
Zurat Beit ha-Mikdash
Grodno, 1789
8½ × 7⅜ inches
Hebraic Section
[Illustrated on page 88]

CHAPTER 6
Adding Beauty to Holiness

Megillat Esther. Benedictions
Italy (?), eighteenth century (?)
Manuscript; ink and gouache on parchment
13 × 16¾ inches
Hebraic Section
[Illustrated on page 91]

"The Washington Megillah"
Megillat Esther
Italy (?), eighteenth century (?)
Manuscript; ink and gouache on parchment
12⅜ inches high
Hebraic Section
[Illustrated on page 92]

"The Washington Haggadah"
Central Europe, January 29, 1478
Scribe: Joel ben Simeon
Illuminated manuscript; ink, gouache, and gold leaf on parchment
9⅛ × 5⅞ inches
Hebraic Section
[Illustrated on pages 94–97]

Seder Haggadah shel Pesah
Venice, 1629
13½ × 9⅝ inches
Hebraic Section
[Illustrated on page 98]

Seder Haggadah shel Pesah
Amsterdam, 1695
11¼ × 7⅝ inches
Hebraic Section
[Illustrated on page 100]

Haggadah shel Pesah
London, 1770
6¾ × 4⅜ inches
Hebraic Section
[Illustrated on page 102]

Haggadah shel Pesah
Basel, 1816
8¾ × 7 inches
Hebraic Section
[Illustrated on page 103]

Ma'ale Bet Horin
Vienna, 1823
12 × 9½ inches
Hebraic Section
[Illustrated on page 103]

Seder ha-Haggadah shel Pesah
Trieste, 1864
12⅜ × 9½ inches
Hebraic Section
[Illustrated on page 104]

Ketubah
Ancona, 1805
Manuscript; ink, gouache, and gold leaf on parchment
30½ × 22 inches
Hebraic Section
[Illustrated on page 107]

Ketubah
Maddalena on the Po, 1839
Manuscript; ink and gouache on parchment
28⅝ × 19⅜ inches
Hebraic Section
[Illustrated on page 108]

Ketubah
Corfu, 1812
Manuscript; ink and gouache on parchment
27⅜ × 18⅞ inches
Hebraic Section
[Illustrated on page 108]

Ketubah
Corfu, 1835
Manuscript; ink, watercolor, and gouache on parchment
28¾ × 19⅛ inches
Hebraic Section
[Illustrated on page 109]

Ketubah
Corfu, 1874
Manuscript; ink and gouache on parchment
22⅜ × 16⅛ inches
Hebraic Section
[Illustrated on page 109]

Ketubah
Galata, 1841
Manuscript; ink and gouache on paper
24½ × 18½ inches
Hebraic Section
[Illustrated on page 111]

Ketubah
Meshed, Persia, 1889
Manuscript; ink and watercolor on paper
27¼ × 22⅝ inches
Hebraic Section
[Illustrated on page 112]

Samaritan Ketubah
Shechem (Nablus), 1901
Manuscript; ink and watercolor on paper
28½ × 19¼ inches
Hebraic Section
[Illustrated on page 115]

Shivviti Plaque
Hebron (?), late nineteenth century (?)
Manuscript; ink and gouache on paper
15¾ × 11 inches
Hebraic Section
[Illustrated on page 116]

"The Ship of Jonah"
Micrography
1897
10 × 13 inches
Hebraic Section
[Illustrated on page 117]

"Portrait of Moise"
Micrography
Late nineteenth century
17½ × 14 inches
Hebraic Section
[Illustrated on page 118]

CHAPTER 7
Beauty Is in the Hands of Its Creator

Israel Fine
Nginash [Heb. Neginoth] Ben-Jehudah
Baltimore, 1907
9 × 5¾ inches
Hebraic Section
[Illustrated on page 120]

Siddur Tefillah
Mantua, 1557
6 × 4⅛ inches
Hebraic Section
[Illustrated on page 121]

Tefilat ha-Derekh
Isle of Djerba, 1917
2¾ × 2⅛ inches
Hebraic Section
[Illustrated on page 121]
Seder Tefilot L'Moadim Tovim
Amsterdam, 1739
2¼ × 1½ inches
Hebraic Section
[Illustrated on page 122]

Moses Zacut
Tikkun Hazot
Eighteenth century
Manuscript; ink on paper
7 × 5⅛ inches
Hebraic Section
[Illustrated on page 122]

Sefer Kol Bo
Rimini, 1526
12⅜ × 8¾ inches
Hebraic Section
[Illustrated on page 123]

Isaac ben Salomon Abi Sahula
Mashal ha-Kadmoni
Venice, 1546
7½ × 5⅝ inches
Hebraic Section
[Illustrated on page 125]

Isaac ben Salomon Abi Sahula
Mashal ha-Kadmoni
Frankfurt an der Oder, 1693
6⅛ × 3¾ inches
Hebraic Section
[Illustrated on page 126]

Isaac Leib Peretz
Gleichnisse
Lithographs by Jakob Steinhardt
Berlin, 1920
12⅝ × 10½ inches
Rare Book and Special Collections Division
[Illustrated on page 127]

Alef-Bet
Illustrations by Z. Raban, verses by L. Kipnis
Jerusalem-Berlin, 1923
9⅞ × 7 inches
Hebraic Section
[Illustrated on page 128]

Had Gadyo
Illustration by Menachem Birnbaum
Berlin, 1920
11½ × 9¼ inches
Hebraic Section
[Illustrated on page 130]

Abraham Sutzkever
Sibir
Illustrations by Marc Chagall
Jerusalem, 1958
13½ × 9¾ inches
Hebraic Section
[Illustrated on page 131]

Ben Shahn
Haggadah for Passover
Translation, introduction and historical notes by Cecil Roth
Boston, 1965
15¾ × 12 inches
Rare Book and Special Collections Division, Rosenwald Collection
[Illustrated on page 132]

David Moss
Song of David Haggadah
Rochester, New York, 1987
18¼ × 11¾ inches
Hebraic Section
[Illustrated on page 133]

Arthur Szyk
The Haggadah
Edited by Cecil Roth
London, 1940
11⅜ × 10 inches
Rare Book and Special Collections Division
[Illustrated on page 135]

CHAPTER 8
Witnesses to History

Shlomo Molcho
Derashot
Salonica, 1529
7¼ × 5½ inches
Hebraic Section
[Illustrated on page 141]

Tikkun K'riah
Amsterdam, 1666
4⅞ × 3 inches
Hebraic Section
[Illustrated on page 141]

Kundmachung
Lemberg, 1858
13⅛ × 16¾ inches
Hebraic Section
[Illustrated on page 144]

Hebrat G'milut Hasadim, Fraterna Della Misericordia
Degl' Ebrei Tedeschi di Venezia
Venice, 1794
16⅝ × 12 inches
Hebraic Section
[Illustrated on page 146]

Baale B'rith Avraham
Mantua, 1791
10⅛ × 7⅛ inches
Hebraic Section
[Illustrated on page 147]

Memorial Plaques
Mantua, 1818–1870
Various sizes
Hebraic Section
[Illustrated on pages 148–149]

Regolamento per L'Instituto Convitto Rabbinico
Padua, 1858
Broadside
23½ × 22 inches
Hebraic Section
[Illustrated on page 151]

Israel Ma'arabi
Hilhot Shehita
N.p., 1397
Scribe: Joseph ben Abraham ben Joseph
Manuscript; ink on paper
7½ × 5½ inches
Hebraic Section
[Illustrated on page 152]

Wall Calendar
Egypt, 1815
Manuscript; ink on paper
24¼ × 17⅞ inches
Hebraic Section
[Illustrated on page 153]

Koran. Hebrew
Cochin, 1757
Manuscript; ink on paper
7¼ × 5 inches
Hebraic Section
[Illustrated on page 154]

Sefer ha-Zohar
Mantua, 1558–60
7⅞ × 6 inches
Hebraic Section
[Illustrated on page 156]

Shefa Tal
Hanau, 1612
12 × 9⅛ inches
Hebraic Section
[Illustrated on page 157]

Minhagim
Amsterdam, 1707
7⅞ × 6⅜ inches
Hebraic Section
[Illustrated on pages 158–161]

Judah Horwitz
Sefer Amudei Bet Yehudah
Amsterdam, 1766
7½ × 4½ inches
Hebraic Section
[Illustrated on page 163]

Don Juan Lopez Cancelada
Decreto de Napoleon . . . Sobre Los Judios
Mexico, 1807
8¼ × 6¼ inches
Rare Book and Special Collections Divison
[Illustrated on page 164]

M. Altshuler
Hagodeh far Gloiber un Apikorsim
Moscow, 1927
7½ × 5½ inches
Hebraic Section
[Illustrated on page 165]

CHAPTER 9
"Let Her Works Praise Her"

Mitzvot Nashim
Padua, 1625
$7\frac{3}{8} \times 5\frac{1}{4}$ inches
Hebraic Section
[Illustrated on page 171]

Tehina Kol Bekhiya
N.p., n.d.
$7 \times 4\frac{1}{2}$ inches
Hebraic Section
[Illustrated on page 172]

Penina Moise
Fancy's Sketch Book
Charleston, South Carolina, 1833
$6\frac{3}{8} \times 4\frac{3}{8}$ inches
Rare Book and Special Collections Division
[Illustrated on page 175]

The Poems of Emma Lazarus
New York, (1889)
$7\frac{1}{8} \times 5$ inches
Rare Book and Special Collections Division
[Illustrated on page 179]

CHAPTER 10
"Enthroned on Praises"

Mahzor Minhag Roma
Casalmaggiore, 1486
$10\frac{1}{8} \times 7\frac{3}{4}$ inches
Rare Book and Special Collections Division
[Illustrated on page 183]

Mahzor Romi
Bologna, 1540
$12\frac{1}{2} \times 9$ inches
Hebraic Section
[Illustrated on page 186]

Mahzor, Sha'ar Bat Rabim
Venice, 1711
$13\frac{7}{8} \times 11$ inches
Hebraic Section
[Illustrated on page 187]

Orden de Las Oraciones de Ros-Ashanah y Kipur
London, 1740
$7\frac{3}{8} \times 5\frac{1}{8}$ inches
Hebraic Section
[Illustrated on page 188]

Orazioni Quotidiane
Basel, 1802
$7\frac{1}{4} \times 4\frac{5}{8}$ inches
Hebraic Section
[Illustrated on page 188]

Ordnung der Oeffentlichen Andacht . . .
Hamburg, 1819
$7\frac{7}{8} \times 4\frac{5}{8}$ inches
Hebraic Section
[Illustrated on page 189]

Rituel Des Prières Journaliènes
Metz, 1827
$8 \times 5\frac{1}{4}$ inches
Hebraic Section
[Illustrated on page 190]

Atirot Yeshurun
Posony (Pressburg, Bratislava), 1846
$7\frac{3}{4} \times 5$ inches
Hebraic Section
[Illustrated on page 190]

Tefilot Yisrael
Warsaw, 1869
$7\frac{1}{8} \times 5\frac{3}{8}$ inches
General Collection
[Illustrated on page 191]

Seder Tefilot ha-Falashim
Paris, 1876
$7\frac{5}{8} \times 5\frac{1}{4}$ inches
Hebraic Section
[Illustrated on page 192]

The Jewish Propitiatory Prayer
Bombay, 1859
$8\frac{3}{4} \times 5\frac{3}{4}$ inches
Hebraic Section
[Illustrated on page 192]

Simhat Mitzvah
Florence, 1793
$8 \times 5\frac{3}{4}$ inches
Hebraic Section
[Illustrated on page 193]

Hod Malchut
Livorno, 1808
$9 \times 7\frac{1}{8}$ inches
Hebraic Section
[Illustrated on page 194]

L'Elohei M'uzim Roni Todot
Mantua, 1789
$11 \times 7\frac{5}{8}$ inches
Hebraic Section
[Illustrated on page 194]

Order of Service and Prayer
London, 1830
$14\frac{1}{2} \times 9\frac{1}{2}$ inches
Hebraic Section
[Illustrated on page 195]

Bakashat ha-Hayim V'ha-Shalom L'Adoneno ha-Melech
Tunis, 1860
$8\frac{3}{8} \times 5\frac{1}{2}$ inches
Hebraic Section
[Illustrated on page 195]

CHAPTER 11
The Starry Skies in the Heavens Above—The Still Small Voice in the Heart of Man

Eliezer ben Jacob Belin
Sefer Ebronot
Offenbach, 1722
$8 \times 6\frac{3}{8}$ inches
Hebraic Section
[Illustrated on page 198]

David Gans
Nehmad Ve-Naim
Jesnitz, 1743
$8\frac{1}{8} \times 6\frac{1}{2}$ inches
Hebraic Section
[Illustrated on page 198]

Joseph Delmedigo
Sefer Elim
Amsterdam, 1629
$8\frac{1}{4} \times 6\frac{1}{4}$ inches
Hebraic Section
[Illustrated on page 199]

Tobias Cohen
Ma'aseh Tuviyyah
Venice, 1707
$9 \times 6\frac{1}{2}$ inches
Hebraic Section
[Illustrated on pages 200–201]

Solomon Almoli
Pitron Halomot
Cracow, 1580
$5\frac{7}{8} \times 3\frac{7}{8}$ inches
Hebraic Section
[Illustrated on page 202]

Hayyim Vital
Sefer ha-Gilgulim
Italy, eighteenth century
Manuscript; ink on paper
$9\frac{3}{4} \times 7\frac{1}{4}$ inches
Hebraic Section
[Illustrated on page 203]

Marpe La-Nefesh
1609
Manuscript; ink on paper
$7\frac{7}{8} \times 6$ inches
Hebraic Section
[Illustrated on page 204]

Sefer Sodot U'Segulot
Genoa, 1711
Manuscript; ink on paper
4 × 3¼ inches
Hebraic Section
[Illustrated on page 205]

Albert Einstein
"Einheitliche Feldtheorie"
July 6, 1938
Holograph; ink on paper
11 × 8½ inches
Manuscript Division, Albert Einstein Collection
[Illustrated on pages 208–209]

Albert Einstein
"Zur Electrodynamic Bewegter Körper"
November 1943
Holograph; ink on paper
11 × 8½ inches
Manuscript Division, Albert Einstein Collection
[Illustrated on page 210]

Albert Einstein
Letter to Sigmund Freud
April 29, 1931
Manuscript; ink on paper
11 × 8¾ inches
Manuscript Division, Sigmund Freud Collection
[Illustrated on page 212]

Sigmund Freud
"Ein Wort Zum Antisemitismus"
1938
Holograph; ink on paper
16 × 10 inches
Manuscript Division, Sigmund Freud Collection
[Illustrated on page 215]

Yahrzeit und Trauer-Andachtsbuch
Berlin, 1920
8⅞ × 6⅞ inches
Manuscript Division, Sigmund Freud Collection
[Illustrated on page 217]

Sigmund Freud
Der Mann Moses und die Monotheistische Religion
1937
Holograph; ink on paper
15⅝ × 9⅞ inches
Manuscript Division, Sigmund Freud Collection
[Illustrated on page 218]

CHAPTER 12
In the New World

Abraham Zacuto
Tabulae Astronomicae
Leiria, 1496
8½ × 6⅛ inches
Rare Book and Special Collections Division
[Illustrated on page 220]

Psalter
Genoa, 1516
12⅞ × 9¾ inches
Hebraic Section
[Illustrated on page 221]

Abraham Farissol
Iggeret Orhot Olam
Venice, 1586
5⅜ × 3¾ inches
Hebraic Section
[Illustrated on page 222]

Thomas Thorowgood
Jews in America
London, 1650
7½ × 5¾ inches
Rare Book and Special Collections Division
[Illustrated on page 223]

The Holy Bible . . . Translated into the Indian Language
Cambridge (New England), 1663
7⅞ × 6½ inches
Rare Book and Special Collections Division
[Illustrated on page 224]

Elyakim ben Avraham (Jacob Hart)
Ma'amar Binah L'Itim
London, 1795
8¼ × 5⅜ inches
Hebraic Section
[Illustrated on page 225]

Schreiben eines Deutschen Juden an den nordamerikanischen Präsidenten . . .
Frankfurt und Leipzig, 1787
6¼ × 3⅞ inches
Rare Book and Special Collections Division
[Illustrated on page 226]

The Holy Bible . . . Newly Translated out of the Original Tongues . . .
Philadelphia, 1782
6⅜ × 4 inches
Rare Book and Special Collections Division
[Illustrated on page 228]

Rev. G. Seixas
A Discourse . . .
New York, 1798
8 × 5⅛ inches
Rare Book and Special Collections Division
[Illustrated on page 229]

CHAPTER 13
"To Bigotry No Sanction"

George Washington
Letter to the Hebrew Congregation of the City of Savannah
May 1789
Manuscript; ink on paper
15¼ × 10 inches
Manuscript Division, Papers of George Washington
[Illustrated on pages 232–233]

Manuel Josephson
Congratulatory address to George Washington on behalf of Hebrew Congregations in Philadelphia, New York, Charleston and Richmond
December 13, 1790
Manuscript; ink on paper
13⅛ × 8 inches
Manuscript Division, Papers of George Washington
[Illustrated on page 235]

Moses Seixas
Congratulatory address to George Washington on behalf of the Hebrew Congregation of Newport, Rhode Island
August 17, 1790
Manuscript; ink on paper
14¾ × 9⅜ inches
Manuscript Division, Papers of George Washington
[Illustrated on page 237]

George Washington
Letter to Newport Hebrew Congregation
1790
Manuscript; ink on paper
15 × 10 inches
Manuscript Division, Papers of George Washington
[Illustrated on page 238]

Thomas Jefferson
Letter to Mordecai M. Noah
May 28, 1818
Manuscript; ink on paper
9⅞ × 7¾ inches
Manuscript Division, Papers of Thomas Jefferson
[Illustrated on page 241]

Thomas Jefferson
Letter to Jacob De La Motta
September 1, 1820
Manuscript; ink on paper
$8\frac{1}{4} \times 7\frac{5}{8}$ inches
Manuscript Division, Papers of Thomas Jefferson
[Illustrated on page 243]

Jacob De La Motta
Letter to James Madison
August 7, 1820
Manuscript; ink on paper
$9\frac{7}{8} \times 7\frac{7}{8}$ inches
Manuscript Division, Papers of James Madison
[Illustrated on page 244]

James Madison
Letter to Jacob De La Motta
August 1820
Manuscript; ink on paper
$9\frac{7}{8} \times 7\frac{7}{8}$ inches
Manuscript Division, Papers of James Madison
[Illustrated on page 246]

CHAPTER 14
"Father Abraham" and the Children of Israel

Abraham Lincoln
Letter to Abraham Jonas
July 21, 1860
Manuscript; ink on paper
$8 \times 16\frac{1}{4}$ inches
Manuscript Division, Papers of Abraham Lincoln
[Illustrated on page 249]

Abraham Jonas
Letter to Abraham Lincoln
December 30, 1860
Manuscript; ink on paper
$10 \times 22\frac{3}{4}$ inches
Manuscript Division, Papers of Abraham Lincoln
[Illustrated on page 251]

Abraham Lincoln
Letter to Isachar Zacharie
September 19, 1864
Manuscript; ink on paper
8×5 inches
Manuscript Division, Papers of Abraham Lincoln
[Illustrated on page 251]

United Order "Bné B'rith"
Letter to Abraham Lincoln
January 5, 1863
Manuscript; ink on paper
$9\frac{1}{2} \times 7\frac{3}{4}$ inches
Manuscript Division, Papers of Abraham Lincoln
[Illustrated on page 254]

Board of Delegates of American Israelites
Resolutions to Abraham Lincoln
January 8, 1863
Manuscript; ink on paper
$13\frac{3}{8} \times 8$ inches
Manuscript Division, Papers of Abraham Lincoln
[Illustrated on page 255]

Myer S. Isaacs
Letter to Abraham Lincoln
October 26, 1864
Manuscript; ink on paper
$9\frac{3}{4} \times 7\frac{7}{8}$ inches
Manuscript Division, Papers of Abraham Lincoln
[Illustrated on page 257]

Rev. Dr. David Einhorn
Congregation *Keneseth Israel*
Philadelphia, April 19, 1865
$8\frac{7}{8} \times 5\frac{7}{8}$ inches
General Collection
[Illustrated on page 259]

Rev. Sabato Morais
Congregation *Mikve Israel*
Philadelphia, April 19, 1865
$9\frac{1}{2} \times 6\frac{1}{4}$ inches
General Collection
[Illustrated on page 259]

Rev. Benjamin Szold
Congregation *Oheb Shalom*
Baltimore, June 1, 1865
$7\frac{1}{4} \times 4\frac{1}{2}$ inches
General Collection
[Illustrated on page 259]

Rev. Jonas Bondi
Congregation *Poel Zedek*
New York, April 19, 1865
$8 \times 5\frac{1}{8}$ inches
General Collection
[Illustrated on page 260]

Rev. Henry Hochheimer
Congregation *Oheb Israel*
Baltimore, April 19, 1865
$7\frac{1}{8} \times 4\frac{1}{4}$ inches
General Collection
[Illustrated on page 260]

CHAPTER 15
Four Founders: Noah, Leeser, Wise, and Lazarus

Mordecai M. Noah
Correspondence and Documents . . .
Washington, 1816
$9 \times 5\frac{1}{2}$ inches
Rare Book and Special Collections Division
[Illustrated on page 265]

Mordecai M. Noah
Letter to James Madison
New York, May 6, 1818
Manuscript; ink on paper
$9\frac{3}{4} \times 7\frac{7}{8}$ inches
Manuscript Division, Papers of James Madison
[Illustrated on page 266]

Mordecai M. Noah
Discourse on the Evidence of the American Indians Being the Descendants of the Ten Lost Tribes of Israel
New York, 1837
$8\frac{1}{4} \times 5\frac{1}{4}$ inches
General Collection
[Illustrated on page 268]

Mordecai M. Noah
Discourse on the Restoration of the Jews
New York, 1845
$8\frac{1}{2} \times 6$ inches
Rare Book and Special Collections Division
[Illustrated on page 269]

Portrait and Obituary of Mordecai M. Noah
Boston Weekly Museum
April 26, 1851
$21 \times 14\frac{1}{4}$ inches
General Collection
[Illustrated on page 270]

"Mordecai M. Noah, Of No. 57, Franklin-street . . ."
New York, June 20, 1828
Broadside
$25\frac{1}{2} \times 20\frac{1}{4}$ inches
Rare Book and Special Collections Division
[Illustrated on page 271]

Portrait of Isaac Leeser
Published by I. Goldman
1868
$13 \times 10\frac{1}{4}$ inches
Prints and Photographs Division
[Illustrated on page 271]

J. Johlson
Instruction in the Mosaic Religion
Translated by Isaac Leeser
Philadelphia, 1830
8 × 5⅛ inches
General Collection
[Illustrated on page 272]

Isaac Leeser
The Hebrew Reader, No. 1. The Spelling Book
Philadelphia, 1838
8⅝ × 5⅝ inches
General Collection
[Illustrated on page 273]

Issac Leeser
Commemoration of the Life and Death of William Henry Harrison
Philadelphia, 1841
9¼ × 6⅛ inches
General Collection
[Illustrated on page 275]

Isaac Leeser
Letter to Abraham Lincoln
August 21, 1862
Manuscript; ink on paper
9¾ × 7⅞ inches
Manuscript Division, Papers of Abraham Lincoln
[Illustrated on pages 276–277]

Isaac M. Wise
The Cosmic God
Cincinnati, 1876
8⅝ × 6 inches
General Collection
[Illustrated on pages 278–279]

Isaac M. Wise
History of the Israelitish Nation
Albany, 1854
8¾ × 5¾ inches
General Collection
[Illustrated on page 278]

Portrait of Emma Lazarus
Engraving by T. Johnson from a photograph by W. Kurtz
1887
7 × 5 inches
Prints and Photographs Division
[Illustrated on page 280]

Emma Lazarus
Poems and Translations
New York, 1866
7⅞ × 5½ inches
Rare Book and Special Collections Division
[Illustrated on page 281]

Emma Lazarus
Admetus and Other Poems
New York, 1871
7⅞ × 5½ inches
General Collection
[Illustrated on page 283]

Richard Watson Gilders
"Emma Lazarus"
November 19, 1887
Manuscript; ink on paper
8⅞ × 7 inches
Manuscript Division, Papers of Grover Cleveland
[Illustrated on page 284]

CHAPTER 16
Holy Tongue—Holy Land—Holy Words

Judah Monis
Dikdook Leshon Gnebreet, A Grammar of the Hebrew Tongue . . .
Boston, 1735
[Includes two-page manuscript; ink on paper]
9½ × 7⅜ inches
Hebraic Section
[Illustrated on pages 287–289]

Biblia Hebraica
Philadelphia, 1814
8⅞ × 5⅞ inches
Hebraic Section
[Illustrated on page 290]

H. Henry
Imrai Shaipher, A Hebrew Vocabulary
New York, 1838
9½ × 5¾ inches
General Collection
[Illustrated on page 293]

Ha-Zofeh ba-'Arez ha-Hadashah
New York, June 27, 1871
11¾ × 8½ inches
Hebraic Section
[Illustrated on page 293]

Haim Isaac Carigal
A Sermon Preached at the Synagogue, in Newport, Rhode Island
1773
7½ × 4¾ inches
General Collection
[Illustrated on page 294]

Portrait of the Rabbi Enoch Zundel
New York, 1833
9½ × 8⅛ inches
Prints and Photographs Division
[Illustrated on page 295]

Jachiel Bar-Joseph
Map of the Journey of the Children of Israel . . .
New York, 1840
34½ × 25¼ inches
Geography and Map Division
[Illustrated on page 296]

Prayers for Sabbath, Rosh-Hashanah and Kippur
Translation by Isaac Pinto
New York, 5526 (1766)
7⅜ × 6⅛ inches
Rare Book and Special Collections Division
[Illustrated on page 201]

Rabbi Hillel
Prayers said by the Spanish Portuguese Jews during the Ceremony of Washing the Dead
(Kingston, Jamaica), 5588 (1828)
Translation by A. I. H. Bernal, (Scribe)
Manuscript; ink on paper
5 × 3⅝ inches
Hebraic Section
[Illustrated on page 301]

Seder T'fillah, The Order of Prayer for Divine Service
Second edition, revised by Dr. S. Adler
New York, 1863
7⅛ × 4⅞ inches
Hebraic Section
[Illustrated on page 302]

Gebetbuch für Israelitische Reform Gemeinden
New York, 1856
8½ × 5¼ inches
Hebraic Section
[Illustrated on page 303]

Seder Haggadah shel Pesah
Second American edition
New York, 5610 (1850)
5⅞ × 4⅝ inches
Hebraic Section
[Illustrated on page 304]

Seder Haggadah L'Pesah
New York, 1878
7 × 5½ inches
Hebraic Section
[Illustrated on page 304]

CHAPTER 17
From Sea to Shining Sea

The Asmonean
New York, November 23, 1849
15½ × 11½ inches
General Collection
[Illustrated on page 305]

The Israelite
Cincinnati, October 27, 1854
15½ × 10½ inches
General Collection
[Illustrated on page 306]

H. M. Brackenridge
Speeches on the Jew Bill
Philadelphia, 1829
9⅛ × 5⅞ inches
General Collection
[Illustrated on page 308]

Persecution of the Jews in the East
Philadelphia, 1840
9¼ × 5¾ inches
General Collection
[Illustrated on page 309]

Constitution and By-Laws of the Jewish Foster Home Society
Philadelphia, 1855
8⅝ × 5½ inches
Hebraic Section
[Illustrated on page 310]

Philip Philips
Substance of Address
New Orleans, 1866
9¼ × 6 inches
General Collection
[Illustrated on page 310]

M. J. Michelbacher
A Sermon Delivered on the Day of Prayer Recommended by the President of the C.S. of A., the 27th of March, 1863 at the German Hebrew Synagogue, "Bayth Ahabah"
Richmond, 1863
9 × 5¾ inches
Rare Book and Special Collections Division
[Illustrated on page 314]

Joshua Falk
Avnei Yehoshua
New York, 1860
7⅞ × 5⅛ inches
Hebraic Section
[Illustrated on page 317]

Jacob Zevi Sobol
Shir Zahav li-Khevod Yisrael ha-Zaken
New York, 1877
6¾ × 4½ inches
Hebraic Section
[Illustrated on page 317]

Talmud Yerushalmi. *Bikkurim*
With commentaries by Abraham Eliezer Alperstein
Chicago, 1890
13¼ × 8½ inches
Hebraic Section
[Illustrated on page 317]

Mizrach
New York, 1874
28 × 21¾ inches
Prints and Photographs Division
[Illustrated on page 319]

Gedenkblatt Memory Table[t]
New York, 1874
21 × 16¼ inches
Prints and Photographs Division
[Illustrated on page 319]

Moses
New York, 1874
28¼ × 21⅞ inches
Prints and Photographs Division
[Illustrated on page 320]

Aron
New York, 1874
27 × 21⅜ inches
Prints and Photographs Division
[Illustrated on page 321]

A. L. Baer
The Dying Ben B'rith
Milwaukee, 1883
10⅜ × 7¼ inches
General Collection
[Illustrated on page 322]

Membership Certificate, B'nai B'rith
Milwaukee, 1876
23¾ × 19 inches
Prints and Photographs Division
[Illustrated on page 323]

Max Wolff
Origin of the Rites and Worship of the Hebrews
New York, 1859
39 × 26¾ inches
Hebraic Section
[Illustrated on page 324]

CHAPTER 18
From the Lands of the Czars

Morris Rosenfeld
Lieder des Ghetto
Translated by Berthold Feivel, illustrated by E. M. Lilien
Berlin, 1903
10⅛ × 8⅛ inches
General Collection
[Illustrated on page 328]

William Allen Rogers
"The Peddler"
Harper's Weekly, April 19, 1890
20⅞ × 13¼ inches
Prints and Photographs Division
[Illustrated on page 329]

William Allen Rogers
"The Candle Seller"
Harper's Weekly, April 19, 1890
10¼ × 5 inches
Prints and Photographs Division
[Illustrated on page 331]

William Allen Rogers
"The Jewish Quarter in Boston"
Harper's Magazine, November 1899
12 × 9¾ inches
Prints and Photographs Division
[Illustrated on page 332]

Frederick Dorr Steele
"Yetta"
McClure's, November 1904
14 × 10¾ inches
Prints and Photographs Division
[Illustrated on page 332]

Leo Rosenberg and M. Rubenstein
Leben Zol Amerika
New York, n.d.
13½ × 10½ inches
Hebraic Section
[Illustrated on page 335]

Solomon Smulewitz (Small) and J. M. Rumshisky
Zei Gebensht Du Freie Land
New York, 1911
13⅞ × 10⅝ inches
Hebraic Section
[Illustrated on page 335]

Solomon Smulewitz (Small)
Hurban Titanic
New York, 1912
13½ × 10⅝ inches
Hebraic Section
[Illustrated on page 336]

L. Gilrod and D. Meyrowitz
A Boychick Up-to-Date
New York, n.d.
13¾ × 10⅝ inches
Hebraic Section
[Illustrated on page 337]

S. Mogulesco
Choson Kale Mazol Tov
New York, 1909
13½ × 10½ inches
Hebraic Section
[Illustrated on page 337]

CHAPTER 19

"Break Forth in Melody and Song"

Isaac Nathan
A Selection of Hebrew Melodies . . .
London, 1815
14⅝ × 11 inches
Music Division
[Illustrated on page 338]

Jacques Fromenthal Halévy
Marche Funèbre et De Profundis en Hébreu
Paris, 1820
13¼ × 10½ inches
Music Division
[Illustrated on page 341]

Giacomo Meyerbeer
Hallelujah
Berlin, 1815 (?)
Holograph; ink on paper
9¾ × 13⅛ inches
Music Division
[Illustrated on page 342]

Mario Castelnuovo-Tedesco
Lecho Dodi
Amsterdam, 1937
Holograph; ink on paper
15 × 11 inches
Music Division
[Illustrated on page 344]

Darius Milhaud
David
1952
Holograph; ink on paper
15 × 11 inches
Music Division
[Illustrated on page 345]

Arnold Schoenberg
A Survivor from Warsaw
N.p., n.d.
Holograph; ink on paper
11 × 17½ inches
Music Division
[Illustrated on page 347]

Aaron Copland
Vitebsk
1929
Holograph; ink on paper
15¾ × 11¾ inches
Music Division
[Illustrated on page 349]

Leonard Bernstein
Hashkivenu
April 4, 1945
Holograph; ink on paper
12 × 9⅝ inches
Music Division
[Illustrated on page 350]

Leonard Bernstein
Jeremiah Symphony
1944
Holograph; ink on paper
13½ × 10¾ inches
Music Division
[Illustrated on page 350]

George and Ira Gershwin
Mischa, Yascha, Toscha, Sascha
n.d.
Holograph; ink on paper
6¼ × 4¼ inches
Music Division
[Illustrated on page 351]

Irving Berlin
"God Bless America"
195(?)
Holograph; ink on paper
11 × 7¼ inches
Music Division
[Illustrated on page 352]

INDEX

Page numbers for illustrations appear in boldface. Titles of works are alphabetized according to the first word following the initial articles in all languages. In addition, the Hebrew word Sefer (Book) has been treated as an article when not considered an essential part of the title.

Aaron, lithograph of, 319, **321**
De Abbreviaturis Hebraicis (Buxtorf), 41
Aboab, Isaac, 162
Abrabanel, Isaac, 99, 203
Abraham bar Jacob, 78, 80, 82–84, 99–100, 103
Abraham Hayyim de Tintori, 14
Abudarham (commentary on the prayers), 15, **16**
Abudarham, David ben Yosef, 15
Adams, John, 240
Adelkind, Cornelius, 60, 63
Adelkind, Israel, 44
Adler, Samuel, 313
Admetus and Other Poems (Lazarus), 280, **283**
Adret, Solomon ben Abraham, 10–12
Ahad Ha-am, 55–56
Aitken, Robert, 228
Alantansi, Eliezer ben Abraham, 68
Aldabi, Meir Ibn, 162
Alef-Bet (Alphabet) (Kipnis), **128**
Alexander, Alexander, 99, 102
Alkabez, Solomon ibn, 15
Almohads (Islamic sect), 56
Almoli, Solomon, 202
Almosino, Moses, 200
Alperstein, Abraham Eliezer, 316, 318
Alsheikh, Moses, 168, 204
Das Alte Testament deutsch (Luther translation), 38, **40**
Altshuler, M., 165
Am Olam (Eternal People), 316
American Jewry
  agricultural colonies, 314–316
  Civil War years, 247–262
  Colonial period, 228
  emissaries from the Holy Land, 294–296
  in the nineteenth century, 263–284
  Indians descendants of the Lost Tribes, 222–224, 268
American Jewry and the Civil War (Korn), 247
The American Traders Compendium, 9
Americans No Jewes, 224
Amram (ninth-century gaon), 182
Amram, David W., 167, 183
[Sefer] Amudei Bet Yehudah (The Pillars of the House of Judah) (Judah Hurwitz), 162, **163**
Ancona Jewish community, 105–106
Andover, Theological Seminary, 291–292
Andrichom, Christian von, 79, 84
Anspach, Joel, 190
Anti-Semitism
  in America, 299
  in Colonial America, 228
  in Vienna, 214
Antin, Mary, 325, 331
Antiquitatum Judaicarum (The Antiquities of the Jews) (Josephus), **4**, 5
Arba-ah Turim (Code of Jewish Law) (Jacob ben Asher), **68**
Asbury, Henry, 250
Ashkenazi, Abraham ben Isaac, 17
Ashkenazi, Eliezer, 197
Ashkenazi, Feibush. *See* Joel ben Simeon
Ashkenazi, Jacob ben Isaac, 172
Ashkenazi, Shamma ben Yisrael, 110–111
Ashkenazi Jewish community, 22, 68, 143
  custom of ketuboth, 105, 110
  in America, 264
  of London, 150
  of Venice, 146
The Asmonean (periodical), **305**, 306
Astronomy, importance in religion of, 197–198, 219
Athias, Abraham, 72
Athias, Immanuel, 72
Athias, Joseph, 26, 28, 72, 291
Atirot Yeshurun, Israel Fomaszai (Prayer of Israel), **190**
Atlas Major (Blaeu), **77**, 78
Auerbach, B. H., 49
Avnei Yehoshua (The Stones of Joshua) (Falk), **316**
Avodah Zara (tractate), 47
Azulai, Hayim Joseph David, 31, 155

Baale B'rith Abraham (Members of the Covenant of Abraham), 145, **147**
Baba Kamma Mi'masekhet Nezikin (Mishnah of the Tractate Baba Kamma), 5, 7
Baba Meziah (tractate), 42
Baer, A. L., 322
Bahya ben Joseph ibn Pakuda, 170
Bak, Israel, 18, 31
Bakashat ha-Hayim V'ha-Shalom L'Adoneno ha-Melech (Entreaty for Life and Peace of Our Master, the King), **195**
Battier, Friedrich, 102
Bay Psalm Book. *See Whole Book of Psalmes Faithfully Translated into English Metre*
Beckman, John Christopher, 47
Bedersi, Jedaiah ben Abraham, 55–56
Beer, Jakob Liebmann. *See* Meyerbeer, Giacomo
Behinat Olam (Examination of the World), 55
Behmer, Marcus, 33
Belini, Eliezer ben Jacob, 197–198
Belleli family, 110
Bene-Israel Improvement Society, 191
Benjamin of Tudela, 106, 113
Benveniste, Immanuel, 47
Berakhot (tractate), 44, 52, **53**, 54, 202
Berlin, Irving, 352
Berman, Simeon, 315
Bernal, Abraham Israel Henriques, 301–302
Bernheimer, Charles S., 337
Bernstein, Leonard, 348, 350–351
Bernstein, Philip S., 52
Bernstein, Zvi Hirsch, 292
De Bibel Int Carte, 38, **39**, 40
Bible. *See Biblia; Holy Bible*
Bible View of Slavery (Raphall), 252, 313–314

Biblia Ebraea (1667), 28, **29**
Biblia Ebraea (Hutter—1587, 1603), 26, **28**
Biblia Hebraica (Philadelphia—1814), **290**, 291
Biblia Italiana (1494), 36, **37**
Biblia Latina (1476), **36**
Bikkurim (tractate, Palestinian Talmud), 316, **317**
Birnbaum, Menachem, 128–130
Blaeu, William, 77–78
Bleichrode, A. M., 322
Bloch, Ernest, 343
Bloch, Moses, 170
Blumenfeld, Kurt, 211
B'nai B'rith, 213
membership certificate, 322, **323**
United Order of, 253–254
B'nai Mikra (Children of Scripture), 28. *See also* Karaite community
B'nai Soncino (Sons of Soncino), 182
B'nai Zion, 145. *See also* Lemberg Jewish community
Board of Delegates of American Israelites, 254–256, 293
Bomberg, Daniel, 23–25, 44, 184
Bondi, Jonas, 260–261
The Book of Daily Prayers for Every Day in the Year According to the Custom of the German and Polish Jews (Leeser), 275
Book of Esther. *See* Esther, Book of
Book of Judges. *See* Judges, Book of
Book of Leviticus (Rashi and Azulai commentaries), **31**
Book of the Religion, Ceremonies and Prayers of the Jews, 189
Book of Ruth, *See Iggeret Shmuel*
Boston, Jewish Quarter, 331, **332**
A Boychik Up-To-Date (An Up-To-Date Dandy) (song), **337**
Brackenridge, Henry M., 308
Bradford, William, 285
Bragadini, Alvise, 46, 69–71
Bragadini Press, 99
Braham, J., 338–340
Brahe, Tycho, 198
Braun, George, 79, 84
Brauner, Ida, 128–129
Braverman, Hillel, 117
Bresslau, I. M., 190
Breydenbach, Bernard von, 74–75
Brill, Joel, 103
Brit Milah (Circumcision), 145, 147, **161**
British Army, first Jewish commissioned officer, 8
Budko, Joseph, 127
Bunting, Heinrich, 73
Buxtorf, Johannes, 41, 64

California Sketches (Fitzgerald), 307
Cancelada, Don Juan Lopez, 162–163
"The Candle Seller," poem by Morris Rosenfeld, 331
Caravita, Joseph ben Abraham, 14
Carigal, Haim Isaac, 294
Caro, Joseph, 17, 69, 71
Casimir the Great (King of Poland), 162
Castelnuovo-Tedesco, Mario, 343–344
Catechism for Younger Children (Leeser), 273–274
Celsius, Olaf, 49
Censorship, 23–24, 46, 70, 183–184
Cesana family, 106–107
Chagal, Marc, 130–131, 134
Charleston (South Carolina) Jewish community, 173–174, 310–311
Child, Sir Josiah, 9–10
Choson Kale Mazol Tov (Good Luck to the Bride and Groom), **337**
Circumcision. *See Brit Milah*
Civil and Religious Privileges (Kennedy), 308
Civitates Orbis Terrarum (Braun and Hogenberg), **79**, **84**
Coen, Colombo (Joshua Cohen), 102
Cohen, Benjamin, 272
Cohen, Johan, 38
Cohen, Joseph and Jacob Hai, 185
Cohn, Tobias, 200–201
Cologna, Abraham, 193
Colonization of Jews, 314–316
Columbus, Christopher, 219–222
Commemoration of the Life and Death of William Henry Harrison (Leeser), **275**
Commentary on the Pentateuch. See Perush ha-Torah
A Commercial Dictionary (Montefiore), **8–9**
A Compendious Lexicon of the Hebrew Language (Moore), 289, 291
Compendium Grammaticus Lingua Hebraeae (Spinoza), 6, **8**
Conat, Abraham and Estellina, 167
Confederate States of America, Jewish support for, 314
Consolacam as tribulacoems des Israel (Consolation for the Tribulations of Israel) (Usque), 138
Constitution and By-Laws of the Hebrew Benevolent Society of the City of New York, New York, 1865, 310
Constitution and By-Laws of the Jewish Foster Home Society of . . . Philadelphia, 1855, 309, **310**
Constitution of the Shavei Zion Society, No. 2, **300**
Constitution und Plan zur Grundung eines Jüdischen Agrikultur-Vereins (Constitution and Plan for the Founding of a Jewish Agricultural Society), 315
Copland, Aaron, 346, 348–349
Cordovera, Moses, 204
Corfu Jewish community, 106, 108–110
Correspondence and Documents . . . (Noah), 264, **265**
Coschelberg, Solomon, 100
The Cosmic God (Wise), **278**, **279**, 280
Cosmographica (Ptolemy), **75**
Crawford, William, 268
Crescas, Asher ibn, 64
Cremieux, Adolphe, 309
Die Cronica van der hilliger stat van Coellen, 35
Cursory Remarks on Men and Measures in Georgia, 228

The Daily Prayers. See Gebet-Buch für den offentlichen Gottesdienst und die Privat-Andacht; Minhag America
Dalalat al-Ha'rin (Guide for the Perplexed) (Maimonides), 58–59
"Damascus Affair," 309
David (Milhaud), 344, **345**
Davidovitch, David, 105, 113
Day of Atonement, 184
Ele-Ezkara (These Things Do I Remember), 196
The Day of Doom (Wigglesworth), 285
Day, Mills, 291
De La Motta, Jacob, 239, 242–243, 245–246
letter to James Madison, **244**
De Lyra, Nicholas. *See* Nicholas De Lyra
De Mordo family, 108–110
De Osmo family, 108–110
Decreto de Napoleon . . . Sobre Los Judios, 162, **163**
Deinard Collection. *See* Library of Congress
Delmedigo, Joseph, 199–200; portrait of, **199**
Derashot. See Sefer ha-Mefo'ar
Dickdook Leshon Gnebreet, A Grammar of the Hebrew Tongue, being an Essay to bring the Hebrew Grammar into English (Monis), 286, **287**
A Discourse Delivered in the Synagogue . . . (Seixas), 228, **229**, 230
Discourse on the Evidence of the American Indians Being Descendants of the Lost Tribes of Israel (Noah), **268**, 270
Discourse on the Restoration of the Jews (Noah), 268, **269**, 270
Discourses, Argumentative and Devotional on the Subject of the Jewish Religion (Leeser), 274
Dobson, Thomas, 291–292
D'Ortas, Samuel, 220
Dowling, John, 292
Drach, David, 164–165, 190
Dreams, interpretation of, 202–203, 211, 213
Dresner, Samuel H., 18
Duo Tituli Thalmudici Sanhedrin, et Maccoth, 49, **50**
Duran, Profiat, 64
The Dying Ben B'rith: an Episode in the Yellow Fever Scourge of 1878 (Baer), **322**

[*Sefer*] *Ebronot* (Book of Intercalations) (Belin), 197, **198**
Ecclesiastical Council of Rimini, 184
Eckman, Julius, 307
Egyptian Jewry, 152–153
"Ein Wort Zum Antisemitismus" (Freud), 214, **215**
Eine neue Bestimmung der Molekuldimensi-

onen (A New Determination of Molecular Dimensions) (Einstein), 206–207
"Einheitliche Feldtheorie" (Unified Field Theory) (Einstein), 207, **208–209**
Einhorn, David, 259, 261, 303–304, 313–314
Einstein, Albert, 205–211
letter to Freud, 211, **212**
portrait by Robert Kastor, **206**
Eliasoff family, 110
Eliezer ben Isaac Ashkenazi, 17, 20
Elijah ben Solomon Zalman (Vilna Gaon), 155
[*Sefer*] *Elim* (The Book of Elim) (Delmedigo), **199,** 200
Eliot, George, 282–283
Eliot, John, 224
L'Elohei M'uzim Roni Todot (To the Lord of Might Sing Gratitude), 193, **194**
Elyakim ben Avraham. *See* Hart, Jacob
Emek Refa'im (Valley of the Dead), **312,** 313
Emerson, Ralph Waldo, 280
"Emma Lazarus" (Gilder), **284**
Endicott, G., 296
English Jewry, 150
naturalization of Jews, 9–10
[*Sefer*] *Eshet Hayil* (Book for the Woman of Valor), 172
Esther, Book of (scrolls), **17, 20,** 89–90, **91–92**
Estienne, Robert, 26–27
Ethics of the Fathers. See Pirke Avot
Etting, Solomon, 308–309
Etz Hayyim (Tree of Life) (Vital), 163, 203–204
Even Sapir (Saphir), 143
Evening Service of Roshashanah, and Kippur, 189, 301
Exodus from Egypt
maps of, 77–80

Fable of the Ancient. *See Mashal ha-Kadmoni*
Falashas, of Ethiopia, 191
Falk, Joshua, 316
Fancy's Sketch Book (Moise), 174, **175**
Farrisol, Abraham, 222
Fekete, Herman, 190
Felsenthal, Bernhard, 312–313
Fievel, Berthold, 330
Fine, Israel, 119–120
Fiorentino, Solomone, 189
Firkowitz, Abraham, 30–31
Fitzgerald, O. P., 307
Flavii Josephi Antiquitatum Judaicarum, 4, 5
Foa family, 64
Foa, Tobias, 44, 63
Fonseca, Daniel da, 162
Former Prophets (Kimhi), 23
Frankel, Jacob, 278
Frankel, S. I., 190
Franklin, Benjamin, 225
Frauen-Machzor (Holiday Prayer Book for Women), **172**
Freedom of religion
in Maryland, 307–309
in Virginia, 239–240
Freud, Sigmund, 205, 211–218
portrait by Robert Kastor, **213**
Frey, Joseph Samuel Christian Frederick, 291–292
"Friday Night in the Jewish Quarter," drawings by William Allen Rogers, 328, **329, 331**
Fuller, Thomas, 81, 84
Fundamental Rights of a Free People (Konvitz), 239
Fürst, Julius, 64

Gabirol, Solomon Ibn, 282, 284
Galata (Constantinople) Jewish community, 110–111
Gans, David, 35, 198–199, 200
Gebeden der Nederlandsche Israeliten (Prayer Book for the Israelites of the Netherlands), **190**
Gebet-Buch für den offentlichen Gottesdienst und die Privat-Andacht (Prayer Book for Public and Private Worship), 303
Gebetbuch für Israelitische Reform Gemeinden (Prayer Book for Jewish Reform Congregations), **303,** 304
Gedenkblatt (Memory Tablet), **319**
Gedichte (Kleeberg), 177, **178**
Gentili, Moses, 88
The Genuine Works of Flavius Josephus, the Jewish Historian, 2, **3**
Geographica sacra, 81
George IV (King of Great Britain), death of, 193, 195
German Jewry, 49, 227
Germanus, Benedictine Donnus Nicholaus, 75
Gershwin, George, 351–352
Gersonides (Levi ben Gershom), 23, 167–168
Gilder, Richard Watson, 284
Gilrod, L., 337
Giustiniani, Agostino, 220, 222
Giustiniani, Marco Antonio, 44, 46, 60, 64–65, 69–71
The Gleaner (periodical), 305, 307
Gleichnisse (Peretz), **127**
Go Out and See. *See Ze'enah U-re'enah*
"God Bless America" (Berlin), **352**
Godines, Benjamin, Senior, 162
Die Goldene Kayt (The Golden Chain) (periodical), 130
Goldstein, Moses Elijah, 117
Goodrum, Charles A., 1–2, 74
Gottheil, Gustav, 280–281
Gottschalk, Michael, 47
A Grammar of the Hebrew Tongue . . . See Dickdook Leshon Gnebreet
Grant, Ulysses S., General Order No. 11, 253–256
Gratz, Rebecca, 310
Graziano, Abraham Joseph (*Ish Ger*), 155–157
Greeley, Horace, 250
Gufo shel Pesah (Essence of Passover or a Haggadah for Jewish Tots), 165
Guide for the Perplexed. *See Dalalat al-Ha'rin; Moreh Nevukhim; Rabbi Mossei Aegypti Dux seu Director Dubitatium aut Perplexorum*
Gunzenhauser, Joseph ben Jacob, 25
Gurley, John A., 253
Gutenberg Bible, 34–35
Gutheim, James K., 313
Gutmacher, Elijah, 120

H. Schile Company, 319–321
Haas, William, 100
Had Gadyah (Birnbaum), 128–129, **130**
closing song of Passover Seder, 129–130
Haggadah/Haggadot, illustrated editions, 98–104, 134–136. *See also* Moss Haggadah; Shahn Haggadah; Szyk Haggadah; Washington Haggadah
(Amsterdam—1695), **100**
(Basel—1816), 100, 102, **103**
(London—1770), **102**
(Munich—1947), 166
(New York—1850), **304**
(New York—1878), **304**
(Venice—1629), **98,** 99
(Venice—1740), **101**
(Vienna—1823), **103**
Haggadah shel Pesah. *See* Haggadah/Haggadot
Hagodeh far Gloiber un Apikiorism (Haggadah for Believers and Atheists) (Altshuler), **165,** 166
Halévy, Jacques Fromenthal, 340, **341**
Halevy, Joseph, 191
Halleck, H. W., 253
Hallelujah . . . (Meyerbeer), 341, **342**
Hamishah Humshe Torah (Five Books of the Torah)
(1832–35), 28, **30,** 31
(1933), 31, **32,** 33–34
[*Sefer*] *Hanukat Ha-Bayit* (Gentili), **88**
Harby, Isaac, 311
Harrison, William Henry, eulogy, 275
Hart, Abraham, 176, 257–258, 309
Hart, Jacob, 225–226
Hasan-Rock, Galit, 125
Hashkivenu (Bernstein), 348, **350**
Hasidism (Jewish religious movement), 18–19
Hay, John, 257, 275, 278
Hayim, Raphael, 103
Healing for the Soul. *See Marpe La-Nefesh*
Hebrat G'milut Hasadim, Fraterna Della Misericordia Degl'Ebrei Tedeschi de Venezia (Brotherhood of Charity of the Ashkenazi Jewish Community of Venice), **146**
Hebrew Benevolent Society, 264
Hebrew Bible, in America, 291–292. *See also Biblia Hebraica;* [*Sefer*] *Tehilim, Liber Psalmorum Hebraice*
Hebrew Education Society of Philadelphia, 274

Hebrew grammar, 285–288
An Hebrew Grammar Collected Chiefly from those of Mr. Israel Lyons . . . (Sewall), 288
Hebrew Illuminated Manuscripts (Narkiss), 89, 93
Hebrew Immigrant Aid Society, 327
Hebrew language, 292–294
Hebrew lexicon, 289, 291
Hebrew Melodies. See A Selection of Hebrew Melodies . . .
Hebrew News, 293
Hebrew Psalter. *See Sefer Tehilim, Liber Psalmorum Hebraice*
The Hebrew Reader (Leeser), **273**
Hebrew University (Jerusalem), 207, 214
Hebron, 84–85
Heller, Yom Tov Lipmann, 47, 88
Henry, H., 292–293
Herzl, Theodor, 270
Hesed Avraham (Compassion of Abraham) (Horowitz), 60, **61**
Ha-Hibur ha-Gadol (Zacuto), 219
Hilhot Shehita (Laws of Ritual Slaughtering) (Ma'arabi), **152**
Hirsch, Zvi, 165
Hirschenson, Hayyim, 120
History of the Hebrews Second Commonwealth (Wise), 279
History of the Israelitsch Nation (Wise), **278**
History of the Jews in the Duchy of Mantua (Simonsohn), 167
History of the Jews in Modern Times (Mahler), 225
History of the Printing of the Talmud. See Ma'amar Al Hadpasat Ha-Talmud
Hochheimer, Henry, 260–261
Hod Malchut (Glory of Sovereignty), 193, **194**
Hoffay, A. A., engraving of Enoch Zundel by, **295**
Hoffman, Morris, 254
Hogenberg, Franciscus, 79, 84
Holt, John, 300
The Holy Bible . . . Newly Translated Out of the Original Tongues, 228
The Holy Bible . . . Translated into the Indian Language, **224**, 225
Holy Land
  charting of, 73–88
  emissaries to America, 294–296
  holy cities of, 84, **85**
  maps of, 296–298
  Temple of Jerusalem, 87–88
Holy Land Settlement Society, 315
Holzman, Elijah M., **312**, 313
Horowitz, Abraham, 60–61
Horowitz, Shabbetai Sheftel, 155
Horwitz, Jonathan, 291
Houting, Henrico, 49
Hovevei Zion (Lovers of Zion), 298–299
Hovot ha-Levavot (Duties of the Heart) (Bahya ben Joseph ibn Pakuda), **170**
Hulin (tractate), 46
Humash. See Hamishah Humshe Torah
Hurban Titanic (The Titanic's Disaster) (song), **336**
Hurwitz, Joseph, 191
Hurwitz, Judah ben Mordecai ha-Levi, 162–163
Hutter, Elias, 26, **28**
Hymns, Psalms and Prayers, In English and German (Wise), 177–178, 279
Hyneman, Rebekah, 174, 176–177

Ibn Ezra, Abraham, 23, 90, 200
Ibn Ezra, Moses, 282
Ibn Gabir, Joseph, 67
Ibn Shem-Tov, Joseph, 64
De Idolatria (On Idolatry) (Maimonides),**64**
Iggeret ha-Nehamah (Epistle of Consolation) (Maimonides), 56
Iggeret ha-Shemad (Epistle on Apostasy) (Maimonides), 57
Iggeret Orhot Olam (A Tract on the Paths of the World) (Farissol), **222**
Iggeret Shmuel (Epistle of Samuel) (Uzeda), **168**, 169
Igrot L'Ha-maor Ha-Gadol . . . Rabeinu Moshe Hamaymoni (Epistles to the Great Luminary Our Master Moses Maimonides), 64, **65**, 67
Illustrated books, 125–134
Imrai Shaipher, A Hebrew Vocabulary (Henry), 292, **293**
Instruction in the Mosaic Religion (Leeser translation), 272, 302
The Interpretation of Dreams
  (Almoli), 202
  (Freud), 211, 213
Isaacs, Myer S., 256–257
Isaacs, Samuel M. C., 256
Israel Baal Shem Tov, 18–19
Israel ben Shmuel, 170
The Israelite (periodical), 278, 305, **306**, 307
Isserles, Moses, 198
Italia, Raphael Hayim, 38
Italian Jewish community, 150–151
Itinerarium Sacrae Scripturae (Bunting), 73

Jabez, Solomon and Joseph, 46
Jachiel Bar-Joseph (nineteenth-century emissary), 296–297
Jackson, John M., 304
Jackson, M., 292
Jackson, Solomon Henry, 304
Jacob ben Asher, 68–69
Jacob ben Naphtali ha-Kohen, 119
Jacobs, George, 313
Jaffe, Abraham, 47
Jaffe, Kalonymus ben Mordecai, 60
Jaffe, Sarah, 47
Jaffe, Solomon Zalman, 47
Das Jahre des Juden (The Jewish Year) (Nadel), 127
Jefferson, Thomas
  library of, 1–2, 6, 8–9
  on religious freedom, 239–240, **241**, 242, **243**
Jenson, Nicolaus, 36
Jeremiah Symphony (Bernstein), 348, **350**, 351
Jerusalem
  description of, 74
  first Hebrew Press, 31
  map of, 73
  temple of, 87–88
Jerusalem (Mendelssohn), 227
Jewes in America (Thorowgood), 222, **223**, 224
Jewish calendar, 152, **153**, 154, 197
The Jewish Immigrant (periodical), **327**
Jewish life and customs (seventeenth century), 158–161
Jewish Origins of the Psychoanalytic Movement (Klein), 214
"The Jewish Problem" (Lazarus), 282–283
Jewish Propitiatory Prayers: Or A Prayer for the Forgiveness of Sins, 191, **192**
The Jewish War (Josephus), 5
The Jews and Mosaic Law (Leeser), 274
The Jews and the Renaissance (Roth), 91
Joachimsen, P. J., 260–261
Joel ben Simeon, 93–94
Johlson, J., 272–273
Johnson, Andrew, 258
Jonas, Abraham, friendship with Abraham Lincoln, 247–251
Jones, Ernest, 214
Joseph ben Abraham ben Joseph, 152
Joseph II (Emperor of Austria), 192–193
Josephson, Manuel, letter to George Washington, 234, **235**
Josephus Flavius, 2–5
Judaea Seu Terra Sancta (Sanson), **80**, 81
Judah ben Sholom (Shukr Kuhayl), 143
Judah ha-Levi, 282
Judah ha-Nasi, 42
Judah Loew ben Bezalel, 198
Der Judenstaat (Herzl), 270
Judges, Book of (Targum Jonathan), 23

Kabbalah (Jewish mysticism), 138, 140, 155–157, 200, 202–205
Kalfe Sedakah, 280
Karaite community, 28, 30–31, 152, 200
Kaskel, Cesar J., 247, 253
Kastor, Robert, portraits of
  Albert Einstein, **207**
  Sigmund Freud, **213**
Katz, Isaac ben Judah Leib, 170
Katz, Jacob Joseph. *See* Yaakov Yosef ben Zevi ha-Kohen Katz
Katz, Naftali ben Yitzhak, 49
Katz, Rachel, 170
Keller, J., 336
Kelly, Myra, 332, 334
Kennedy, Thomas, 308
Kepler, Johannes, 198
Keppler, Joseph, 326
Kesef Mishneh (Caro), 71
The Ketubah (Davidovitch), 105, 113
Ketuboth (marriage contracts), 50, 89, 104–114, 168

Kiddushin (tractate), 53
Kimhi, David, 23–25
Kipnis, Levin, 128
Kirchmayer, K., 103–104
Kitab Jami al-Salawot wa al-Tasebih (Collection of All Prayers and Praises), 188
Kleeberg, Minna, 177–178
Klein, Dennis B., 214
Kley, Edward, 342–343
Koch, Johannes, 50
[Sefer] Kol Bo, 121–122, **123**
Kol Kore Bamidbar (A Voice Calling in the Wilderness) (Felsenthal), **312**, 313
Konvitz, Milton R., 239
Kopel family, 110–111
Koran (Hebrew translation), **154**, 155
Korn, Bertram W., 247
Kranken Gebete (Prayers for the Sick), **302**, 303
Kuttner, Henry, 254

Lamentation on the Dread Decrees of 1648 (Heller), 47
Latter Prophets. *See Nevi'im Ahronim*
The Law of God (Leeser), 274–275
Laws of the Congregation of the Great Synagogue, Duke Palace, London, 150
Lazarus, Emma, 179–180, 219, 280–284; portrait of, **280**
Leben Zol Amerika (Long Live America) (song), 334, **335**
Lecho Dodi (Castelnuovo-Tedesco), **344**
Leeser, Isaac, 271–278, 302, 305, 309
  letter to Abraham Lincoln, 275, **276–277**
  portrait of, **271**
Leghorn Jewish community. *See* Livorno Jewish community
De Legibus Ebraeorum, 5, **7**
Lehmann, Behrend, 47, 49
Leib, Ya'akov ben Yehudah, 99
Lekah Tov (Zahalon), **17**
Lemans, Moses, 190
Lemberg Jewish community, 144–145
Leo X, Pope, 184, 192
The Leper and Other Poems (Hyneman), **176**
L'Estrange, Roger, 224
Leusden, Johannes, 26, 28
Levi, Azriel Isaac, 193
Levi, Raphael, 225
Levita, Elijah, 184
Levy, Capt. C. M., 252
Library of Congress
  Deinard Collection, 300
  history of, 1–2
  Rosenwald (Lessing J.) Collection, 26, 35–37, 74, 132–133
Lieder des Ghetto (Songs of the Ghetto) (Rosenfeld), **328**, 330
Lilien, Ephraim Moses, 328, 330
Lilienthal, Max, 52, 313
Lincoln, Abraham
  eulogies in synagogues for, 247, 258, **259–260**, 261–262
  friendship with
    Abraham Jonas, 247–251
    Isachar Zacharie, 250–252
  letter from Isaac Leeser, 275, **276–277**
  letter from Morris J. Raphall, **252**
  on Grant's General Order No. 11, 253–255
Liturgical collections, 192–196
Livorno Jewish community, 193–194
London Society for Promoting Christianity Among Jews, 291
Lopez, Abraham, 295
Lovers of Zion. *See Hovevei Zion*
Luckey, S., 292
Lunel, Armand, 345
Luria, Isaac, 17, 31, 202–205
Luther, Martin, 38, 40
Lyon, Robert, 305

Ma-amar ha-Ibbur (Maimonides), 56
Ma'amar Al Hadpasat ha-Talmud (Rabbinovicz), 41
Ma'amar Binah L'Itim (An Essay on the Understanding of the Times) (Hart), **225**
Ma'arabi, Israel, 152
Ma'aseh Tuviyyah (The Work of Tobias) (Cohn), 200, **201**
Madison, James, 239–240, 244
  letter to De La Motta, 245, **246**
  letters from Mordecai M. Noah, 265, **266–267**, 268
Mahler, Raphael, 225
Mahzor, defined, 182–183
Mahzor L'Nusach Barcelona Minhag Catalonia (Festival Prayer Book . . . Custom of Barcelona of the Catalonian Rite), 138, **139**
Mahzor Minhag Roma (Prayer Book of the Roman Rite—1486), 182, **183**
Mahzor Romi (Roman Rite Festival Prayer Book—1540), **186**
Mahzor, Shar'ar Bat Rabim, **187**
Mahzor (Soncino), 184, **185**
Maimonides (Moses ben Maimon), 46, 51, 55–72, 104, 182, 197
Mainz Bible, 34–35
The Makers of Hebrew Books in Italy (Amram), 167, 183
Malermi, Niccolo, 36
Der Mann Moses, Ein Historischer Roman (The Man Moses, A Historical Novel)(Freud), 216
Der Mann Moses und die Monotheistische Religion (Moses and Monotheism) (Freud), 214, **218**
Mantino, Jacob, 64
Mantua Jewish community, 145, 193–194
  printing, 167
  synagogue memorial plaques, 147, **148–149**
Map of the Journey of the Children of Israel . . . (Bar-Joseph), **296**, 297
Maps and Mapmakers (Tooley), 75
Maps of the Holy Land (Nebenzahl), 75
Marche Funebre et De Profundis en Hebreu (Halévy), 340, **341**
Marpe La-Nefesh (Healing for the Soul) (Zahalon), **204**, 205
Marranos, 138, 162
Marriage contracts. *See* Ketuboth
Marshall, Gen. George C., 34
Marx, Moses, 12
Maryland
  "Jew Bill," 239, 307–308
  Jewish community, 307–309
Mashal ha-Kadmoni (Fable of the Ancient) (Sahula)
  (Frankfurt an der Oder—1693), **126**, 127
  (Venice—1546), **125**, 126
Masius, Andreas, 46
Mason, John M., 291
Mather, Increase, 286
May, Gustave, 118
McFarlane, James, 291
McNarney, Gen. Joseph, 52, 54
Mears, Abraham, 189
Mefasher Halmin, 202
Megillah scrolls, **20**, 22, 90, **91–92**
Megillat Esther. *See* Esther, Book of
Meir ben Baruch of Rothenburg, 41–42
Melekhet Mahashevet (Gentili), 88
Memory Tablet, **319**, 322
Menasseh ben Israel, 162, 200, 222
Mendelowitz, Shneur Zalman, 114, 116–117
Mendelssohn, Moses, 60, 162, 226–227
Mendes, Grazia, 167
Menorah, 114–118
Merian, Mattaeus, 99
Merzbacher, Leo, 302–303
Meshed Jewish community, custom of ketuboth, 112–113
Messiahs, 137–143
Meyerbeer, Giacomo, 341–343
Meyrowitz, D., 337
Michelbacher, J. M., 313–314
Micrography, 114–118
Mikraot Gedolot (Rabbinic Bible), 24, **25**
Milhaud, Darius, 344–345
Millot ha-Higayon (Terms of Logic) (Maimonides), 56
Minhag America. T'fillot B'nai Yeshurun, 303
Minhagim (Customs), **158–161**
Minhat Shai, 38
Mischa, Yascha, Toscha, Sascha (Gershwin) (song), **351**, 352
Mishnah, definition of, 42
Mishneh Torah (Maimonides commentary), 46, 51, 56–59, **66**, 67–72, 182, 197
Mitzvot Nashim (Laws for Women), **171**
Mizrach, **319**
Modena, Leone, 98–99, 203
"The Modern Moses," cartoon by Opper and Keppler, **326**
Mogulesco, S., 337
Moise, Penina, 173–175
Molcho, Shlomo (Diego Pires), 138–140
Monis, Judah, 285–289
Monroe, James, 268

Montefiore, Joshua, 8–9
Montefiore, Lady Judith, 74
Montefiore, Sir Moses, 8, 74, 309
Monterinos, Antoine, 222–224
Moore, Clement C., 289, 291
Morais, Sabato, 258–259, 313
Moreh Nevukhim (Guide for the Perplexed) (Maimonides), **62,** 63–64
Morpurgo, Abraham Hayyim, 38, 102–104
Moses, Five Books of. *See* Pentateuch
Moses, lithograph of, 319, **320**
Moses and Monotheism (Freud), 214, 216
Moses of Coucy, 13
Moss, David, 133, 136
Moss Haggadah, **133,** 136
Muhammad al-Sadiq (Bey of Tunis), 195–196
Music, 338–354
Music of Jewish immigrants, 334–337
Musikalische Novellen (Peretz), 127
Mysticism, Jewish. *See* Kabbalah

Nachmanides (Moses ben Nahman), 12, 15–16, 23, 26
Nadel, Arno, 127
Nahalat Shiv'ah, **142**
Nahmias, David and Samuel, 70
Napoleon I (Emperor of France), 193–194
Narkiss, Bezalel, 89, 93
Nasi, Reyna, 50, 167–169
Nathan, Isaac, 338–340
Nazir (tractate), 49
Nazism, 32–34, 52, 130, 207
Nebenzahl, Kenneth, 75
Nedarim (tractate), 52
Nedivot, Samuel ben Isaac, 15–16
Nehmad ve Naim (Delightful and Pleasant) (Gans), **198**
Nekcsei-Lipocz Bible, 35
Nevi'im Ahronim (Latter Prophets, with Kimhi commentary), 23, **24**
"The New Colossus" (Lazarus), 283
A New Determination of Molecular Dimensions (Einstein), 206–207
A New Discourse of Trade (Child), 9–10
New World, Jews in the, 219–230
New York Jewish community, 309–310, 332–334
Newport (Rhode Island), Jewish community, 234–239, 294–295
Nginash Ben-Jehudah (Fine), 119, **120**
Nicholas De Lyra, 38
Nidah (tractate), 49, 170–171
Nieto, Isaac, 188
Noah, Mordecai Manuel, 230, 239–240, 263–271, 292, 295
  letters to James Madison, 265, **266–267,** 268
  obituary, **270,** 271
  portrait of, **270**
Norsa, Solomon, 193
Norzi, Yedidiah Shlomo, 38

The Occident (periodical), 275, 303, 305, 315
Oif Watkatjen Krajzende Fal Ich (In Circular Distances I Fall) (Zitman), 128, **129**
Olat Tamid (Eternal Offering), 303–304
Opera Omnia Graeca et Latina (Judaeus), 6
Opera Posthuma (Spinoza), 6, **8**
Opper, Frederick Burr, 326
Orazioni Quotidiane per uso degli Ebrei Spagnoli e Portoghesi, **188,** 189
Orden de Benedictiones, 162
Orden de Las Oraciones de Ros-Ashanah y Kipur, **188**
Order of Prayer for Divine Service. See Seder T'fillah
Ordnung der Oeffentlichen Andacht . . . nach dem Gebraunche des Neuen Tempel-Vereins (Order of Service . . . According to the Rite of the New Temple Congregation), **189,** 190
The Origin of Christianity (Wise), 279
Origin of the Rites and Worship of the Hebrews, print by Max Wolff, 322, **324**
Ortelius, Abraham, 76
Ovadia family, 106–107
Oxford University, first Jewish undergraduate, 8

Padua, rabbinical seminary, 150–151
"Palestinae sine Totius Terrae Promissionis Nova Descriptio" (map), 77
Parenzo, Moses ben Gershon, 99
Passover Haggadah. *See* Haggadah/Haggadot
Passover Seder, closing song of. *See Had Gadyah*
Peirush ha-Ralbag 'al ha-Torah (Gersonides commentary), **168**
Pelah ha-Rimon, 47
Pentateuch. *See also Hamishah Humshe Torah;* Torah
  (Alsheikh commentary), 168
  (Gentili commentary), 88
  (Gersonides commentary), 23, 167, **168**
  (Leeser—*The Law of God*), 274–275
  (Nachmanides commentary), 12, **15–16,** 23, **26**
Pentateuch with Targum Onkeles
  (Porteiro translation), 15
  (Rashi commentary), **14,** 15, 23
Peregrinatio in Terram Sanctam (Journey to the Holy Land) (Breydenbach), 74, **75**
Peretz, Isaac Leib, 127
Persecution of the Jews in the East, **309**
Perush ha-Torah (Nachmanides—1489), 12, 15-**16**
Perush ha-Torah le-Rabi Moshe bar Nachman (Nachmanides—1522), **26**
Philadelphia Jewish community, 174, 234, 272–273, 309–310
Phillips, Eugenia (Levy), 311
Phillips, Philip, 310–311
Philo Judaeus, 6
Philonis Iudaei Opera Omnia Graeca et Latina, 6
Picart, Bernard, 122, 125
Pilgrimages
  guide book, 85–87
  to the Holy Land, 74–75
Pinner, E. M., 51
Pinto, Isaac, 189, 300–301
Pires, Diogo. *See* Molcho, Shlomo
Pirke Avot (Ethics of the Fathers), 313, 316
  Maimonides commentary, 60, 61
Ha-Pisgah (periodical), 298
A Pisgah-Sight of Palestine (Fuller), **81,** 87
Pitron Halomot (Interpretation of Dreams) (Almoli), **202**
Pius VI, Pope, 192
Plan of the German American Colony near Haifa (map), 297, **298**
Poems and Translations (Lazarus), 280, **281**
The Poems of Emma Lazarus, **178,** 284
Polish Jewry, 46–47, 49, 60
Polygot Psalter, 220, **221**
Porteiro, Samuel, 15
"Portrait of Moise" (micrography), 117, **118**
Die Post (Yiddish periodical), 292
Pratensis, Felix, 24–25
Prayer books, 181–196
  in America, 300–304
Prayers for Sabbath, Rosh-Hashanah, and Kippur . . . According to the Order of the Spanish and Portuguese Jews (1766), 189, 300, **301**
Prayers Said by the Spanish and Portuguese Jews during the Ceremony of Washing the Dead (Hillel), **301,** 302
Prayers for Shabbath, 189
Principles of Faith, 57
The Promised Land (Antin), 325, 331
Proops, Solomon ben Joseph, 158–161
Prosnitz, Isaac, 47
Psalms (Kimhi commentary), 23, **24–25**
Ptolemy, Claudius, 75
Purim Festival, 89–90, **160.** *See also* Esther, Book of

Raban, Zev, 128
Rabbi Mossei Aegypti Dux seu Director Dubitatium aut Perplexorum (Guide for the Perplexed) (Maimonides), **63,** 64
Rabbinic Bible. *See Mikraot Gedolot*
Rabbinical Committee of Rescue. *See Vaad ha-Hatzalah*
Rabbinovicz, Raphael, 41
Rajpurker, Joseph Ezekiel, 191
Ralbag. *See* Gersonides
Rambam. *See* Maimonides
Ramban. *See* Nachmanides
Raphael, Ralph B., 298–299
Raphall, Morris J., 252, 307, 313–314
  portrait of, **313**
Rashba. *See* Adret, Solomon ben Abraham
Rashi (Bible commentator), 14–15, 23, 31
[*Sefer*] *Raziel,* 155, **157**
Reform Judaism, 303–304, 311–313, 342–343
Reformed Society of Israelites, 311
Reggio, I. S., 150
Regolamento per l'Instituto Convitto Rabbinico (Regulations of the Rabbinical Institute), 150, **151**

Rehine, Zalman, 272–273
Religious freedom. *See* Freedom of religion
Remembrance of Jerusalem. *See Zikaron Birushalyim*
Reminiscences (Wise), 306
Responsa of Adret. *See Teshuvot She-elot ha-Rashba*
Reuveni, David, 138, 140
Revwich, Erhardus, 74
Rituel Des Prières Journalienes (Ritual for Daily Worship), **190**
Roberts, Elijah J., 270–271
Rogers, William Allen, drawings by, 328, **329, 330, 332**
Roosevelt, Theodore, 120
Rosenberg, Adam, 300
Rosenberg, Alfred, 52
Rosenberg, Leo, 335
Rosenfeld, Morris, 328, 330
Rosenwald Collection. *See* Library of Congress
Rosh Hashanah (tractate) (Houting commentary), 49
Rossi, Giovanni Bernardo De, 14–15
Roth, Cecil, 91, 184, 285
Roy, William L., 295
Rubinstein, M., 335
Rumshisky, J. M., 335–336
Russia
  emigration to U.S., 316, 325
  Jewish community, 279
  Jewish history, 51–52, 191
  Karaite community, 30–31
  pogroms of 1881, 281–282, 325
"Russian Christianity versus Modern Judaism" (Lazarus), 282
The Russian Jew in the United States (Bernheimer), 337
Ruth, Book of. *See Iggeret Shmuel*

Saadiah Gaon, 188, 200
Sabbioneta, printing in, 63
Safed, 84–85
  Hebrew printing in, 17–18
Sahula, Isaac ben Salomon Abi, 125
Salonica Jewish community, 46, 138–139
Samaritans, 113–115
Samuel ben Nahman (Palestinian Amora), 204
Sanchez, Gabriel, 219
Sanson, Nicholas, 80
Santangel, Luis de, 219
Saphir, Jacob, 143
Sassoon, David, 191
Sassoon family, 117
Savannah Jewish community, 242–245
Schiff, Mortimer J., 26
Schoenberg, Arnold, 346–347
Scholem, Gershom, 140, 202
*Schreiben eines Deutschen Juden an den nordamerikanischen Präsidenten O*** (A Letter of a German Jew to the American President O..), **226,** 227
Schumacher, Jacob, 297–298
Schurz, Carl, 297
Schwarz, Arthur Z., 13
Science and religion, 197–218
Scrolls, 20–22, 90, 91–92
Seder B'rachot (Order of Benedictions), 162
Seder ha-Avodah . . . Minhag Kehal Bayit Hadash (Order of Service . . . According to the Rite of the New Temple Congregation), 189
Seder Haggadah shel Pesah. See Haggadah/Haggadot
Seder Rav Amram, 182
Seder Tefillah (Order of Prayer), 189
Seder Tefilot ha-Falashim (Order of Prayers of the Falashas), 191, **192**
Seder Tefilot L'Moadim Tovim (Order of Prayer for the Holidays), 120, **122**
Seder T'fillah, The Order of Prayer for Divine Service, **302,** 303
Seder T'filoth K'Minhag K. K. Sefarad, 162
Sefardi Jewish community, 22, 31
  custom of ketuboth, 105, 110
Sefer. For titles beginning with the word Sefer see also under the second word in the title
Sefer ha-Gilgulim (Book of Transmigration) (Vital), **203**
Sefer ha-Hezyonot (Vital), 202
Sefer ha-Mefo'ar (Molcho), 139–140, **141**
Sefer ha-Mitzvot (Maimonides), 104
Sefer Hatakanot (Book of Ordinances and Enactments and Customs . . . of the Holy City, Jerusalem), 31
Sefer Mitzvot Gadol (Moses of Coucy), **13**
Segal, Issakar Berman. *See* Lehmann, Behrend
Seixas, Gershom Mendes, 228–231, 242, 280
  letter to George Washington, 234–236, **237**
Seixas, Isaac B., 272, 274, 292
A Selection from the Miscellaneous Writings of the Late Isaac Harby Esq., 311–312
A Selection of Hebrew Melodies, Ancient and Modern, **338,** 339–340
A Sermon Preached at the Synagogue, in Newport, Rhode Island (Carigal), **294,** 295
Sewall, Stephen, 288
Shabbetai Zvi, 140–143
Shahn, Ben, 136
Shahn Haggadah, **132,** 136
Shavei Zion Society, 300
Shavuot Festival, 294
She-elat Hayehudim (The Jewish Questions) (Raphael), 299–300
Shefa Tal (Horowitz), 155, **157**
Sheftal, Levi, letter to George Washington, 231, **232–233**
Shekalim (tractate), **169**
Shemona Perakim (Eight Chapters) (Maimonides), 60, **61**
Shilton HaSechel (Supremacy of Reason), 55
Shimoni, Eliezer, 138
"Ship of Jonah" (micrography), **117,** 118
Shir Zahav li'Khevod Yisrael ha-Zaken (A Golden Song in Honor of Israel, the Ancient) (Sobol), 316, **317,** 318
Shivviti plaques, 114, **116**
[Sefer] Shorashim, Book of Roots, 121
Shukr Kuhayl. *See* Judah ben Sholom
Shulhan Aruch (Caro), 17, 69, **71, 72**
  Azulai commentary, 155
[Sefer] Shvilei Emunah (Paths of Faith) (Aldabi), 162
Sibir (Siberia) (Sutzkever), 130, **131,** 134
Siddur Tefillah (Order of Prayer—Roman Rite), 119, **121**
Sifra di-Zeni'uta (Book of Concealment), 155
Simhat Mitzvah (Joy of the Commandment), 192, **193**
Simonsen, David, 12
Simonsohn, Shlomo, 167
Slavery
  in tropical colonies, 9
  proslavery sermon, 252, 307, 313–314
Slobin, Mark, 334, 336
Smulewitz, Solomon, 335–336
Sobel, Jacob Zevi, 316, **317,** 318
[Sefer] Sodot U'Segulot . . . (A Collection of Secret Formulas), **205**
Solomon ben Isaac. *See* Rashi
Solomons, Adolphus S., 252
Soncino family, 182–183
Soncino, Gershom, 12–13, 44, 67–68, 121, 125, 184–185
Soncino Gesellschaft der Freunde des jüdischen Buches, 31–34
Soncino, Joshua Solomon, 24, 44, 121, 183
Soncino, Moses, 138–139
Song of David Haggadah (Moss), **133,** 136
Songs of the Ghetto (Rosenfeld), 328, 330
Songs of Labor (Rosenfeld), 330
Songs of a Semite, The Dance to Death and Other Poems (Lazarus), **282,** 283
Sound of Weeping. *See Tehina Kol Bekhiya*
Spanish Jewry, 56
  history of Hebrew printing, 15
Speeches on the Jew Bill (Brackenridge), **308**
Spinoza, Baruch, 6, 8
Statue of Liberty, 179, 283
Stedman, Edmund C., 280
Steele, Frederic Dorr, drawings by, **332–333**
"The Steerage," photograph by Alfred Stieglitz, 327–328, **334**
Steinhardt, Jakob, 93, 127
Steinschneider, Moritz, 26
Stella, Tilemanno, 77
Stern, Julius, 315
Stieglitz, Alfred, 327–328, 334
Stiles, Ezra, 294, 301
Straus, Ida, 336
Stuart, Moses, 292
Substance of Address . . . Synagogue "Temime Dereck" (Phillips), **310,** 311
Suleyman I (the Magnificent), 138, 142
A Survivor from Warsaw (Schoenberg), 346, **347**
Susmans, Yehudah Leib, 162

Sutro, Abraham, 272
Sutzkever, Abraham, 130–131, 134
Szold, Benjamin, 259, 261
Szold, Henrietta, 337
Szyk, Arthur, 134–136
Szyk Haggadah, 134, **135**, 136

Tabulae astronomicae (Zacuto), **220**
Talmud. *See also under specific names of individual tractates*
  (Amsterdam—1644), **45**
  censorship of, 46
  (Cracow—1605), **45**
  definition of, 42
  (Frankfurt an der Oder—1697), 47, **48**, 49
  (Lublin—1619), **45**
  (Munich-Heidelberg—1948), 52, **53**, 54
  (Pesaro—1508), 44, **45**
  (Venice—1520), **45**
Talmud Babli, Babylonischer Talmud, Tractat Berachoth, Segensprüche, **51**
Talmudis Babylonici Codex Middoth sive De Mensuris Templi, 49, **50**
Tefilat ha-Derekh (Prayers for a Journey), 120, **121**
[*Sefer*] *Tefilot Sukkot* (The Tabernacles Service), 189
Tefilot U-Vakashot (Prayers and Petitions), **196**
Tefilot Yisrael (Prayers of Israel), **191**
[*Sefer*] *Tehilim, Liber Psalmorum Hebraice* (Hebrew Psalter), 289
Tehina Kol Bekhiya (A Penitential Prayer: Sound of Weeping), **172**
Tenement Songs, 334, 336
"Terra Sancta quae in Sacris Terra Promissionis olim Palestina" (map), **77**
Teshuvot She-elot ha-Rashba, **10–11**, 12
T'filat ha-Holeh, Kranken Gebete (Prayers for the Sick), **302**, 303
Thalmut. Objectiones in dicta Talmud, 43
Theatrum Orbis Terrarum (Ortelius), **76**
Theobaldus, 43
Thomas, Ebenezer S., 308
Thorowgood, Thomas, 222–223
"Die Thrane auf dem Eisen" (A Tear on the Pressing Iron), drawing by Lilien, 330–331
Tibbon, Moses ibn, 60
Tibbon, Samuel ibn, 59, 63
Tiberias, 84–85
Tiffenbach, E. W., 33
Tikkun Hazot (Order of Service for Midnight Devotions) (Zacut), 120–121, **122**
Tikkun K'riah (Penitential Prayers for Night and Day), **141**
Tikkun Soferim (Pentateuch), 122, **124**, 125
[*Sefer*] *Toldot Yaakov Yosef* (Yaakov Yosef ben Zevi), 18-19
Toledano, Eliezer, 15, 16
Toleranzpatent, 192
Tooley, R. V., 75, 84
Torah. *See also* Pentateuch
  description of, 21–22
  Sefardi scroll, **20**, 22
Torah, Nevi'im, Ketubim, 26, **27**
Torat Moshe, 168
Torres, Luis de, 219, 285
Tosaphists, 44
Tractus Itinerum Mundi (Tract on the Paths of the World) (Farissol), 222
Transmigration of souls, 202–203
Die Traumdeutung (Interpretation of Dreams) (Freud), 211, 213
Travels in England, France, Spain and the Barbary States in the Years 1813–14 and 15 (Noah), 264
Treasures of the Library of Congress (Goodrum), 1, 74
Treves, Johanan, 184–185
Tribes of Israel, maps, 81, 84
Truman, Harry S, 34
The Truth, The Whole Truth, and Nothing But the Truth (Monis), 286
Tseli Esh (Roasted in Fire) (Modena), **98**, 99
T'shuvot Sh'elot V'Igrot (Responsa, Queries, and Epistles), 64
Tunis Jewish community, 195–196
Tur Yoreh Deah (Jacob ben Asher), 15, 69
Turim. See Arba-ah Turim
Tuska, Simon, 313
Twersky, Isadore, 58

"Unified Field Theory" (Einstein), 207, **208–209**
Union Prayer Book, 304
Unmoral im Talmud (Immorality in the Talmud), 52
Usque, Samuel, 138
Uzeda, Samuel di, 168–169

Vaad ha-Hatzalah (Rabbinical Committee of Rescue), 34
Valley of the Dead. *See Emek Refa'im*
Van Buren, Martin, 309
Vecinho, Joseph, 219–220
Venture, Marduchee, 190
Vidas, Elijah de, 204
Vidaver, H., 293–294
Vilna Gaon. *See* Elijah ben Solomon Zalman
Virginia, Bill for Establishing Religious Freedom, 239
Vital, Hayim, 163, 202–204
Vitebsk (Copland), 348, **349**
A Voice Calling in the Wilderness. *See Kol Kore Bamidbar*
Voss, Dionysius, 64

Washington, George
  letter to Hebrew Congregation of City of Savannah, 231, **232–233**
  letter to Hebrew Congregation of Newport, Rhode Island, 234–237, **238**, 239
  letter to Hebrew Congregations, 234
  visit to Jewish community of Newport, Rhode Island, 234–235
Washington Haggadah, 92–93, **94–97**, 98
Washington Megillah, 90, **91–92**
The Watchman in the New Land. *See Ha-Zofeh ba-'Arez ha-Hadashah*
Weinstein, Myron M., 154–155
Weizmann, Chaim, 207, 211
Whiston, William (translator), 2
Whole Book of Psalmes Faithfully Translated into English Metre, 225
Wigglesworth, Michael, 285
Wise, Isaac Mayer, 177–178, 247, **278**, 279–280, 303, 306, 313
Wolff, Max, 322, 324
Wolfson, Harry A., 5–6
Woman's Strength (Hyneman), 176
Women
  as poets, 173–180
  as printers, 167, 170–171
Worthington, William G. D., 308

Yaakov Yosef ben Zevi ha-Kohen Katz, 18–19
Yahrzeit (anniversary of death) memorial plaques, 147–149
Yahrzeit und Trauer-Andachtsbuch, 216, **217**, 218
Yebamot (tractate), 44
Yemenite Jewish community, 143
Yerushalmi, Yosef Hayim, 216
[*Sefer*] *ha-Yuhasin* (Zacuto), 220

Zacharie, Isachar, friendship with Abraham Lincoln, 250–252
Zacut, Moses, 121–122
Zacuto, Abraham, 219–220
Zahalon, Abraham ben Isaac, 204–205
Zahalon, Yom Tov, 17
Zebah Pesah (Passover Sacrifice) (Abravanel), 98–99
Ze'enah U-re'enah (Go Out and See), 172, **173**
Zei Gebensht Du Freie Land (Long Live the Land of the Free) (song), **335**, 336
Zemah David (Offspring of David) (Gans), 35, 198
Ziegler, Jacob, 77
Zifroni, Israel ben David, 98
Zikaron Birushalyim (Remembrance of Jerusalem), 85, **86**
Zionism, 211, 268, 270, 282, 298–300
Zitman, David, 128–129
Ha-Zofeh ba-'Arez ha-Hadashah (The Watchman in the New Land), 292, **293**, 294
Zohar, 155, **156–157**, 202
Zundel, Enoch, 295–296
  portrait of, **295**
"Zur Electrodynamic Bewegter Körper" (Einstein), **210**, 211
Zurat Beit Ha-Mikdash (The Form of the Holy Temple) (Heller), **88**